Letters of H. P. Lovecraft

VOLUME XII

LETTERS TO MAURICE W. MOE AND OTHERS

Maurice W. Moe

H. P. Lovecraft

Letters to Maurice W. Moe and Others

Edited by David E. Schultz and S. T. Joshi

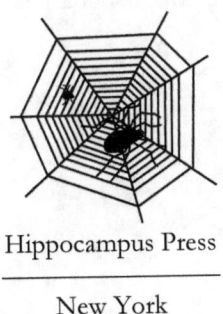

Hippocampus Press
New York

Copyright © 2018 by Hippocampus Press
Introduction and editorial matter copyright © 2018
by David E. Schultz and S. T. Joshi

Owl illustration by Bernard Austin Dwyer on page 566 from *O-Wash-Ta-Nong* 3, No. 2 (Spring 1938).
Vincent Starrett letter to Samuel Loveman on page 583 courtesy of Ray Betzner, *Studies in Starrett* blog. www.vincentstarrett.com/blog/2017/2/11/one-letter

The letters of H. P. Lovecraft are published with the permission of Lovecraft Holdings, Ltd., The Estate of H. P. Lovecraft, Robert C. Harrall, Administrator, and John Hay Library, Brown University.

Published by Hippocampus Press
P.O. Box 641, New York, NY 10156.
http://www.hippocampuspress.com

All rights reserved.
No part of this work may be reproduced in any form or by any means without the written permission of the publisher.

Cover design and Hippocampus Press logo by Anastasia Damianakos.
Cover production by Barbara Briggs Silbert.

First Edition
1 3 5 7 9 8 6 4 2

ISBN 978-1-61498-218-0

Contents

Introduction 7
Letters 37
   To Maurice W. Moe 37
   To Robert E. Moe 393
   To Bernard Austin Dwyer 423
   To Samuel Loveman 487
   To Vincent Starrett 521
Appendix 533
   Maurice W. Moe 533
     Why I Am Not a Freethinker 533
     The Church and the World 538
     Life for God's Sake 541
     Looking Backward 542
     "Once an Amateur, Always an Amateur" 544
     First Steps in the Appreciation of Poetry 544
     Maurice W. Moe on Amateur Criticism 546
     Through the Eyes of the Poet 547
     Imagism 551
     Literary Appreciation 552
     From *Poem Comments* 553
     From *Imagery Aids* 555
     Introduction to Poetry 556
     In a Sequestered Churchyard Where Once Poe Walked 559
     Edwin and the Red Knight 560
     Seven O'Clock 564
   Bernard Austin Dwyer 565
     Ol' Black Sarah 565
     Beautiful Night 566
     Fairies 566
     The Snake-God 567
     Letters to *Weird Tales* 571
        Quinn's Masterpiece 574
        A de Grandin Movie 575
        Who Is This Gal? 575
     Letter to Strange Tales 576
        "Oy! Oy! Oy!" 576
   Samuel Loveman 577
     Collecting Curious Books 577
     A Conversation with Ambrose Bierce 578
     A Holiday Post-Card 580
     The Coast of Bohemia 580

> A Whittier Discovery.. 581
> [Untitled] 583
> *Vincent Starrett.. 583*

Glossary of Frequently Mentioned Names.. **585**
Bibliography.. **591**
Index **615**

Introduction

When the first volume of H. P. Lovecraft's *Selected Letters* appeared in 1965—more than twenty-five years after the undertaking was first announced—most patrons of Arkham House were well familiar with the names of such correspondents as the writers Frank Belknap Long and Clark Ashton Smith, but not many others. The second volume (1968) added a few more recognizable names: Vincent Starrett, Farnsworth Wright, August Derleth, and Donald Wandrei. Most readers probably obtained *Selected Letters* because of interest in Lovecraft's fiction, published mostly in *Weird Tales*, other pulp magazines, and Arkham House's editions of Lovecraft's work. Imagine the bewilderment among such patrons for the first time encountering such unfamiliar names as Rheinhart Kleiner,[1] Alfred Galpin, James F. Morton, and perhaps most baffling of all, Maurice W. Moe, whose name appears on the first page of the published letters, following a letter to Lovecraft's mother. These lesser known individuals (known well these days only because of their association with Lovecraft) invariably were colleagues in what was then a mostly little-known aspect of Lovecraft's existence—his enthusiastic involvement in amateur journalism.

When Lovecraft was a youth he himself was an amateur journalist. For seven years, he produced the *Scientific Gazette* and the *Rhode Island Journal of Astronomy*, which ceased publication more or less in 1904 and 1907, respectively, when Lovecraft was in high school. He once observed that "high-school was a mistake. I liked it, but the strain was too keen for my health, and I suffered a nervous collapse in 1908 immediately after graduating, which prevented altogether my attending college."[2] Not only did Lovecraft not attend college, he also did not graduate from high school. From 1908 to 1914, he found himself adrift. He tried unsuccessfully to revive his journals in 1909, but he must have recognized that as a young man of college age, his boyhood pastime could not be sustained. He also ceased writing his astronomy column for the Providence *Tribune* in 1908 and subsisted as something of a hermit until around January 1914, when he commenced writing a new column for the Providence *Evening News*.

At the very same time, Lovecraft became engaged in a mock literary battle with John Russell in the letter column of the *Argosy*, a popular fiction magazine published by the Frank A. Munsey Company. The exchange lasted for the better part of 1914, and it did not go unnoticed. In April, after reading the lively exchange of letters, written in verse, Edward F. Daas of Milwaukee, Official

---

1. Kleiner's first name was in fact misspelled throughout the series as "Reinhardt."
2. HPL to Bernard Austin Dwyer, 3 March 1927, p. 432.

Editor of the United Amateur Press Association, asked Lovecraft if he would join the organization. Lovecraft did so with alacrity; his name is first seen on the membership list in the *United Amateur* for May 1914. Lovecraft later recruited Russell. Recruiters such as Daas sought members for UAPA by combing through the letter columns of popular magazines and employing other means seeking prospective members. Lovecraft's letters to the *Argosy* towered over the largely semi-literate fan mail published there. He suddenly became a big fish in a very small pond, a feat soon repeated in the somewhat larger UAPA, and yet again as a writer publishing in *Weird Tales*.

When he joined the UAPA, Lovecraft was only twenty-three years old. After more than five years of floundering following his failure to graduate from high school, he now had something to give his life purpose. His revived astronomy column allowed him to continue to explore a subject that long interested him, and amateur journalism allowed him to interact with like-minded individuals all around the country. Lovecraft soon was corresponding with various amateurs and writing reams of verse and other material for their little publications. The following year, he became First Vice-President of the UAPA (August 1915–July 1916) and in time served in various other administrative capacities, including the presidency. After scouring the publications of others, Lovecraft began to publish his own journal, the *Conservative*, the title boldly giving notice to what readers could expect from its editor. Amateur journalism, a hobby to most people, became Lovecraft's career. As he avers in his famous essay "What Amateurdom and I Have Done for Each Other" (1921): "What I have given Amateur Journalism is regrettably little; what Amateur Journalism has given me is—life itself" (*CE* 1.273)

By December, Lovecraft was corresponding with Maurice W. Moe, primarily about matters pertaining to amateur journalism, but also branching into myriad other subjects. Lovecraft's earliest letters to amateurs following his enrollment into the UAPA, as he emerged from the cocoon he had spun around himself, were filled with autobiographical insights into his life, and his letters to Moe are no exception.

Maurice Winter Moe (1882–1940) was born in Milwaukee, Wisconsin, an only child, in a small frame house at 8th Street and Wisconsin Avenue where the Milwaukee Public Library now stands. His father, James G. Moe, was a Civil War veteran. Maurice attended school in Milwaukee and then the University of Wisconsin at Madison, earning his B.A. in 1904. He undertook three years of graduate work on a teaching scholarship, with courses in Hebrew, Greek, and Biblical Literature, but he did not earn his M.A. Lovecraft told a correspondent: "He specialised in Semitics at the U. of Wis., & can even read Assyrian cuneiform a bit."[3] The *North American Review* for 1 October 1907 listed

---

3. HPL to Adolphe de Castro (14 October 1934).

Moe as a member of the Esperanto Society. Moe did not become a teacher following his course work, nor apparently did he pursue the subjects of his study in his future career. He was appointed assistant custodian of the Milwaukee government building by postmaster D. C. Owen, and he worked as a clerk at the Milwaukee Post Office until he married Laura Ellis of Milwaukee in 1911. He then took a teaching position at the Appleton (Wisconsin) High School. Moe's two sons, Robert Ellis (1912–1992) and Donald James (1914–1994), were born there. Lovecraft regaled correspondents with an anecdote Moe told him of Robert's lisping recitation at the age of three of lines from Macbeth's soliloquy.

In the years following his schooling in Madison, Moe became involved in amateur journalism with others in the Milwaukee area, such as Daas, William C. Ahlhauser, Harry Lehmkuhl, E. C. Dietzler, and Margaret Ragsdale. He contributed articles on English for Ahlhauser's *Cynosure* as early as 1909 and also wrote for various other amateur journals. In Appleton, Moe organized the Appleton High School Press Club, which included a student who became one of Lovecraft's "protégés"—Alfred Galpin, Jr. Lovecraft's play *Alfredo* (1918) includes Moe as a character under the guise of Cardinal Maurizio and Alfred Galpin as Alfredo, along with other characters based on other of his fellow amateur journalists. Moe's students issued their own amateur journal, the *Pippin*. Lovecraft wrote two poems, unpublished in his lifetime, honoring the group and its paper. He served as critic in the Department of Private Criticism for the *Credential: An Occasional Magazine Representing the New Member*. Moe also issued his own paper, the *Apprentice*. Following his days as an amateur, he wrote numerous articles for the *English Journal* and other professional journals.

Moe, eight years Lovecraft's senior, enjoyed physical exertion; he rowed, swam, roller skated, and played volleyball with avidity, despite suffering from ankylosing spondylitis, a type of arthritis in which there is long-term inflammation of the joints of the spine.[4] Lovecraft once reported that "Maurice W. Moe [. . .] is trying a novel experiment this summer for the sake of his health. He has undertaken a labourer's work on one of the new buildings of Lawrence College [in Appleton], lifting planks, shovelling mud, and wheeling bags of cement like a seasoned workingman. While painful at first, the regimen is proving actually beneficial, and Mr. Moe is proud of the physical prowess he is beginning to exhibit."[5]

In the *United Official Quarterly* for January 1916, "Mr. Maurice W. Moe, the distinguished Private Critic," offered a keen observation of Lovecraft's

---

4. MWM told HPL how his wife would "iron" his back twice a day to bring him relief.
5. "News Notes" (*United Amateur*, July 1917; *CE* 1.170). In recognition of this feat, HPL penned the poem "To M. W. M.": "Behold the labourer, who builds the walls / That soon shall shine as Learning's sacred halls; / A man so apt at ev'ry art and trade, / He well might govern what his hands have made!" (ibid.)

verse, which was filling the pages of the amateur papers. As quoted by Lovecraft, Moe wrote as follows:

> "You are," he writes, "steeped in the poetry of a certain age; an age, by the way, which cut and fit its thought with greater attention to one model than any other age before or since; and the result is that when you turn to verse as a medium of expression, it is just as if you were pressing a button liberating a perfect flood of these perfectly good but stereotyped formulae of expression. The result is very ingenious, but just because it is such a skillful mosaic of Georgian 'rubber-stamp' phrases, it must ever fall short of true art."

Lovecraft responded (in his "Department of Public Criticism" column of April 1916), "Mr. Moe is correct. We have, in fact, heard this very criticism reiterated by various authorities ever since those prehistoric days when we began to lisp in numbers. Yet somehow we perversely continue to 'mosaic' along in the same old way! But then, we have never claimed to possess 'true art'; we are merely a metrical mechanic."[6]

In 1918 the Moes moved to Madison, and Maurice worked for the Biblical Alliance, selling religious literature and traveling around the state. Lovecraft informed one correspondent: "For years he [Moe] was associated with the late William Jennings Bryan (supplying the brains, perhaps, while poor old Bill supplied the wind & braying!) in some sort of scheme called the 'Biblical Alliance', for giving bible courses to students in state universities where such teaching is barred."[7]

Moe returned to Milwaukee in 1920. HPL wrote in "News Notes" (*United Amateur*, November 1920): "Maurice Winter Moe is receiving felicitations on his return to the teaching profession, for which he is so conspicuously well fitted. He now fills a post at the West Division High School, Milwaukee, Wis., where his success is already notable, and in addition conducts much valuable work in connexion with boys' clubs and the Y. M. C. A." (*CE* 1.264). Lovecraft wrote the lengthy poem "On the Return of Maurice Winter Moe, Esq., to the Pedagogical Profession" (*Wolverine*, June 1921), to commemorate the event. At that time, Moe lived at 2303 Prairie Street (later renamed Highland Avenue, and still later Highland Boulevard)[8] until 1931, when he then took up residence at 1034 N. 23rd Street. Both locations were a few short blocks from the high school. Moe also maintained a "study" at 1043 North

---

6. *CE* 1.108. Just as HPL was chairman of the "Department of Public Criticism," Moe served as chairman of the *Credential*. The first issue—1, No. 1 (April 1920)—lists him as on the board in that capacity. Presumably Moe's criticisms for those who approached him were not published but provided privately.
7. HPL to Adolphe de Castro (14 October 1934), *Crypt of Cthulhu* No. 46 (Eastertide 1987): 42.
8. HPL alludes to this in "Ibid": "In the roseal dawn the burghers of Milwaukee rose to find a former prairie turned to a highland!" (*CF* 2.416).

MOE BOOK TESTS

Still going strong in 48 states. Still the shortest, surest device for testing outside reading. Over 700 tests, 500 in print. 5 cents each; great reduction for sets. Sample for stamp.

MOE WORD HUNTS

Latest Moe invention! Pupils clamor for them, then search the dictionary for hours. Greatest scientific vocabulary-builder. Send stamp for circular.

MAURICE W. MOE
West Division High School   Milwaukee, Wis.

MOE BOOK TESTS

Still going strong in 48 states. Still the shortest, surest device for testing outside reading. Over 700 tests, 500 in print. 5 cents each; great reduction for sets. Sample for stamp.

IMAGERY AIDS

Latest Moe invention! Nothing like them anywhere! Teach poetry-readers to see or sense in every figure the poet's addition to reality. Ask for circular.

MAURICE W. MOE
West Division High School   Milwaukee, Wis.

MOE'S TESTS AND DRILLS

1. A & B Essentials Test
(See El. Eng. Review, Jan., 1927)

Reveals class rate on eight flagrant errors like period, capital, and apostrophe, and shows where to direct attack.

$1.00 per 100 postpaid

2. Comma Usage Drills
(See Eng. Jrnl., Feb., 1927)

Reduces all comma usage to three teachable rules. Four forms.

$1.00 per 100 postpaid

3. Home Reading Tests
(See Eng. Jrnl., June, 1926)

Quick, sure test of pupil's reading without spoiling the book for him.

5 cents each. Send for title list

MAURICE W. MOE
2303 Prairie St.   Milwaukee, Wis.

22nd Street, also nearby. In his later years, he moved to an apartment at 1810 W. Wisconsin Avenue, which was farther from the school but still within walking distance. Walking to and from work likely suited Moe well.

A diligent pedagogue, Moe continually strove to interest students in a subject that was no elective. One magazine noted that "Maurice W. Moe, head of the English department of the Appleton schools, uses classic phonographic selections by great actors in the teaching of literary appreciation in his English work."[9] Moe's approach to teaching English seems to have employed a good deal of gimmickry to stimulate interest, and even actual appreciation, in his pupils. He surely was effective, for as he wrote Lovecraft, "my past pupils say, not one here and there but almost without exception, they get a grip on good literature that lasts them all their life."[10] Moe wrote and sold numerous tests for English teachers to use in their classes. He published articles full of ideas for attempting to make English class more interesting to bored high school students. He had his students assist in preparing the tests for printing—at first by

---

9. *School Education* 36, No. 5 (January 1917): 42
10. MWM to HPL, 28 June 1930; TLS, JHL.

hectograph, then later by a professional printer. In his letters to Lovecraft, Moe regularly engaged in word play of various kinds—just as his correspondent often did. And if he did not himself introduce the "word ladder" game[11] to Lovecraft, he discussed it with avidity. Lovecraft, who usually had no use for games of any kind, solved the puzzles with gusto and bragged when he solved them with fewer steps achieved by others.

Moe's playfulness with words was manifested in other ways. The early readers of Lovecraft's *Selected Letters* surely were baffled by very early letters addressed to such unusually named entities as the Kleicomolo, the Gallomo, and others. They came to realize that these were round-robin letters. The letters were Moe's brainchild. Lovecraft describes the genesis of the letters in a letter to Rheinhart Kleiner, one of the participants:

> Mr. Moe has recently outlined a plan for a rather unique sort of rotating correspondence between four congenial United members. He proposes to have a letter constantly going around in definite order, each member of the chosen circle addressing the *three* others as he writes; & when the letter comes around to him again, taking out what he wrote before and substituting a fresh epistle. He proposed Ira A. Cole for membership, & asked me to name the fourth party. I named you, & shall, if you care to participate, start off the enterprise by sending you a letter written to you, Cole, & Moe. You will then add to this a letter addressed to Cole, Moe, & me, sending same to Cole. Cole will add a letter for Moe, myself, & you, & Moe one to me, you, & Cole; which, when I receive it, I shall deprive of my former letter, adding a fresh one to you, Cole, & Moe. Of course, when you receive it again, you will take out your old letter, adding another to Cole, Moe & me. And so on, till death breaks the continuity of the circle, or quadrangle. Moe has named this band after its members, thus! Klei(ner) Co(le) Mo(e) Lo(vecraft)—or "The Kleicomoloes"; When I write, I shall address my letter: "Dear Kleicomo", omitting my own part of the name. You will say "Dear Comolo"; Cole, "Dear Kleimolo"; & Moe, "Dear Kleicolo"! What a nomenclature! As Moe said to me, if you deem this idea too childish, you need not feel at all obliged to bother with it; but it has its interesting side, & Moe seems to have expended no little thought in devising it. He says that a similar sort of letter goes on its perpetual round through the hands of various separated members of his family; in fact, it was from this family letter that he derived his "Kleicomolo" inspiration.[12]

---

11. The game was invented in 1877 by Lewis Carroll, who called them "doublets." Word ladders or laddergrams were appearing regularly in the newspapers at around the time HPL and MWM were playing the game, having been introduced in "A Line o' Type or Two," a popular column in the *Chicago Tribune* edited by Bert Leston Taylor. J. E. Surrick and L. M. Conant published a book of such puzzles called *Laddergrams* in 1927.

12. HPL to Rheinhart Kleiner, 14 June 1916, *Letters to Rheinhart Kleiner* 36.

Moe relished the round-robin letters. He put his students to work typing them, and he shared bound "volumes" of the letters with his associates. The letters lasted only until 1920 but had a brief resurgence in 1934 in a "Neo-Kleicomolo" group (ultimately known as the Coryciani).

As Lovecraft noted, and as will be evident (albeit one-sidedly) in the letters herein, their postal exchanges sometimes were heated in discussion of religion. He once described Moe as his "old Presbyterian friend and adversary."[13] In the Gallomo exchange, Lovecraft's and Galpin's attacks resulted in Moe dropping out of the round-robin, but Moe continued to write to Lovecraft, and he was not averse to apprising Lovecraft of his continued adult Bible study or to defending his religious viewpoints. As Lovecraft noted, his own exchanges with Moe remained amicable, despite their difference of opinion, and they remained friends for life.

Lovecraft first met Moe in person in 1923, nine years after they became acquainted through the mails. He describes the occasion thus:

> Maurice Winter Moe, Esq., arriv'd in Providence by boat on the early morning of August 10, 1923. Going to the Tavern of the Y. M. C. A., he sent me a message which brought him to meet me at ten a.m. Imagine the dramatick pleasure of that occasion—the first personal meeting, of those who had for nine long years fought by mail in the most amiable and diverting fashion conceivable! Our recognition was mutually instantaneous, and despite our different theological views we found each other extremely agreeable. Small Alfredus is a naughty boy to be rude to Ol' Mocrates, for the Milwaukee sage possesses that warmth of heart and natural good feeling which form, in a cosmos devoid of absolute values or fixt purpose, the highest and most considerable things we may justly reckon as values. I am ever partial to the man of kindness and virtue, and such I found honest Mocrates to be. Wou'd that my Alfredus-child were less deterr'd by those little narrownesses which are, after all, but trivial excrescences upon a character both noble and amiable in its essence.[14]

The next day Lovecraft took Moe, Albert A. Sandusky, and Edward H. Cole on a walking trip to Marblehead. After trudging for hours, the latter three protested and refused to go any farther, and Lovecraft grudgingly relented.

Lovecraft painfully recounted a decade later that Moe's only memory of meeting him was when his weight had ballooned to 200 pounds, some sixty pounds over his usual weight, which at 140 was exceedingly low. (Moe, shorter in stature than Lovecraft, came to weigh 150.) Moe had come with his family, and Lovecraft met them as well. Moe met Lovecraft in person again on 18–19 July 1936, by which time Lovecraft had long ago shed his excess

---

13. HPL to Woodburn Harris, 19 May 1935, AHT.
14. HPL to FBL, 4 September 1923, *SL* 1.247.

weight and also had grayed considerably.

In September 1923, Lovecraft wrote "The Unnamable." The character Joel Manton, principal of "East High School," is based on Moe. Like Moe, he is a religious believer, in contrast to Carter's (and Lovecraft's) skepticism.

Moe dropped out of amateurdom in 1925 as the result of a feud with Noah F. Whitaker, editor of *Pegasus*. Whitaker wrote to extraordinary length (some forty-one pages, one of the four pieces being twenty pages long, published in three issues of the *Plain Speaker,* a journal published specifically to extend the tempest in a teapot), relentlessly excoriating Moe for what appear to be innocuous comments about Whitaker's verse—certainly no worse than the comments Moe had once made about Lovecraft's. Whitaker's vitriol, and the lengths to which he carried it, are embarrassingly juvenile:

> Maurie accuses us of dealing in "stock terms well worn with use, stock situations and themes[,] and stock appeals to emotions." In speaking of our poetry he says—"the amount he presents in two issues would be a good two years output for the average poet." [. . .]
>
> Maurie tells us that poetry, to be good, must be written on new themes with new situations, new appeals to the emotions and with a new form of expression—brand new! Maurie seems to think that words and apt phrases are like postage stamps—made to be used once and kissed goodbye forever. A new Noah Webster would have to be born daily to supply a poet with the vocabulary and metaphorical material Maurie prescribes. We do not believe Maurie is right in his views. We believe it is the senseless scramble for uncommon forms of expression that has given to modern verse a stilted and unnatural soul appeal, or rather robbed it of all appeal—crushed the life out of it. But we will presently prove that Maurie doesn't practice the things he preaches to us. After we had shuffled over and looked through a bundle of amateur papers—a bundle almost as big as a bale of hay, we did, at last, find one solitary little poem with Maurie's name to it. It is the kind of poem that Maurie himself so bitterly condemns, and we are amazed at his flagrant inconsistency. When we get through with Maurie's mud-shower which he has substituted for criticism we will turn our spot-light on Maurie's poem [i.e., "A Clean Page"]—unravel it maybe. Be patient, Maurie, boy, be patient; we'll speak of your poem, yep, give it "favorable mention".——15

Whitaker's sneeringly condescending tirade continues ad nauseam. Needless to say, Moe's criticism was hardly mud-slinging, and Noah F. Whitaker, author of *Love and Lunacy and Other Poems,* is not remembered these days as a great poet.

In the aftermath, Lovecraft wrote to fellow amateur Paul J. Campbell: "I wish you could get him [Moe] to rejoin amateurdom, but just now he is holding off because of remaining bitterness over the Whitaker feud of 1925—when the Warren group then controlling the National took sides against him for intricate

---

15. Noah Whitaker, "Moe-ing Time," *Pegasus* (October 1924): 23.

political reasons.[16] I think such grudge-harbouring rather childish—indeed, I think the original feud rather silly on both sides—but one has to forgive the touch of naive self-esteem which gives a certain type of person that easily ruffled & amusingly humourless sort of austere dignity. Whitaker himself is out of amateurdom—but what a comic figure he was in his heyday!"[17] Helm C. Spink, official editor of the National Amateur Press Association, also wrote Moe urging him to rejoin, but Moe remained resolute in staying out of amateur journalism, saying he was through with it for good—this despite his early article "'Once an Amateur, Always an Amateur.'" In the mid-1930s, however, his work began to appear again in various amateur journals.

Maurice Moe, like Samuel Loveman, was the inspiration for or instigator of a number of Lovecraft's memorable writings. When Moe reported to Lovecraft that "A girl cobbled me up a pretty fair theme on 'Friendship' evidently with Bartlett close at hand, and during the course of it she slipped me this: 'As Ibid remarks in his "Lives of the Poets,"'"[18] Lovecraft responded within the body of his letter with a satirical biography of Ibid. Moe thought of submitting the piece to the *American Mercury* or the *Atlantic*, but decided that the piece was too specialized for a general readership, and it remained unpublished in Lovecraft's lifetime.

Many of Lovecraft's surviving essays were written for Moe's delectation: "Observations on Several Parts of America" (1928; from which Moe extracted and published "Sleepy Hollow To-day" for a textbook for students), "Travels in the Provinces of America" (1929), and "Some Causes of Self-Immolation" (1931), "which sprang from a suggestion of my own in which I outlined several possible causes which I thought covered the field of human motivation; but the maestro, as usual, proceeded to show me what a child I was by doing this piece of solid thinking on the subject."[19] It is quite likely that Lovecraft wrote *A De-*

---

16. See HPL to Hyman Bradofsky, 12 January 1936 (ms., JHL): "Human psychology is such that one who complains against an offender is always placed in an oddly disadvantageous light—as M. W. Moe discovered a decade ago when he asked for official redress after the undeniably insulting attacks of one Noah F. Whitaker. Whitaker was inexcusable—but Moe ought to have fought him independently instead of requesting his expulsion. If he had done so, all sympathy would have been with him. Instead, he made an appeal & succeeded in having Whitaker voted out at the next convention—but his victory proved a hollow one. As soon as the official screws were put on Whitaker, popular sympathy turned in his favour; & at the next convention the expulsion & punishment were rescinded. This displeased Moe so much that he was amateurically inactive for years."
17. HPL to Paul J. Campbell, 27 September 1930, ALS, JHL. HPL apparently was unaware that Campbell took Whitaker's side.
18. MWM to HPL, 17 December 1927; TLS, JHL.
19. MWM to August Derleth, 22 March 1939; TLS, WHS.

scription of the Town of Quebeck . . . and "Charleston" with Moe in mind, for although he does not mention sending the essays to Moe in his surviving letters, Moe knew of them and probably read them. Moe was enthralled with all Lovecraft's travelogues, and he continually urged his friend to submit them to magazines for publication. Lovecraft, however, always demurred.

Moe may have inadvertently inspired Lovecraft to undertake his most ambitious poem—the sonnet sequence *Fungi from Yuggoth*. In 1927, Moe conceived the idea of a textbook that could be used to teach appreciation of poetry to be called *Doorways to Poetry*. Work on the book proceeded slowly:

> [. . .] "Doorway [*sic*] to Poetry" creeps on this petty pace from day to day when it should be striding toward the publisher right now. But I prefer to test every step and every drill and exercise in classes before letting it get into print. Inclosed are two tissue copies from master copies I made this morning for tests to be used Monday in class. This was easy compilation, as I had merely to elect the form and imagery mutilations from my various objective literature tests turned out last summer. I suppose that this will seem ludicrously juvenile to you as a real test of form and imagery, but I think you still fail to fathom the abysmal shallowness (I just had to perpetuate that mixed metaphor; it was so delicious) of the average high school junior or senior.[20]

The fact that Moe mentions "drills and exercises" and that he live-tested in the classroom leads one to think that the booklet *Imagery Aids* (1931), published years later by the Kenyon Press, of Wauwatosa, a city adjoining Milwaukee, might have been a much shortened version of or extract from *Doorways to Poetry*. Moe had told Lovecraft he might be able to get him work through the press,[21] but that also did not come to pass. A brief biography of Moe characterized *Doorways* as "a short work," which *Imagery Aids* surely is, but surely a major publisher would not have handled a small booklet. Regarding Moe's plans, Lovecraft wrote:

> Macmillan sure would prove a brainless dolt
> Did he not vie in eagerness with Holt—

---

20. MWM to HPL, 17 December 1929; TLS, JHL.
21. See HPL to Elizabeth Toldridge, early August 1930: "Kenyon Press [. . .] is about to undertake this business [vanity publishing]—with some sort of easy-payment plan annexed. This [. . .] is the outfit for which I shall probably do more or less regular revision if it ever gets its programme started" (155). The plan fell through: "The Kenyon Press has so overloaded itself with job work that Sweet's projected editorial service for would-be authors seems to have been indefinitely postponed. I am sorry for your sake as well as my own, for I am convinced that there are considerable kudos to be had from this form of service, probably with less agony than your present revision entails." (MWM to HPL, 7 March 1930; TLS, JHL).

> But be their sense of judgment more or less,
> You need not care—for you've the Kenyon Press[.][22]

It is not clear just what sort of book Moe had written. To be sure, Moe's and Lovecraft's comments on the book indicate it was meant to be a textbook. Moe's *Imagery Aids* and various other materials he prepared for use in his English classes, such as *Poem Comments* (1934) and *First Steps in the Appreciation of Poetry* (1935), typically offer short poems, or only a few lines, with explanation as to what the struggling student should look for.

Moe eventually enlisted Lovecraft's assistance in the venture. Lovecraft received the manuscript on 29 April 1929, at a time when he himself was rarely writing verse, after writing reams of it over the previous fifteen years. This was not, however, Lovecraft's usual revision job for paying clients. Moe was capable enough to write his books. What he needed was various examples of meter and rhyme, for Lovecraft was more knowledgable of the rules of prosody than Moe, as Moe acknowledged:

> In spite of your anticipations my book is going to give you in many cases a chance to chuckle sleevewards, for as I get into this subject I realize more and more that I have only the merest smattering of technical knowledge of poetry, and my empirical methods are the antithesis of your scientific ones. If I grow opulent enough from the sale of my book tests and other material before this is ready for publication, I am going to send you the ms. for paid revision, for, believe me, it will need it.[23]

Although Moe declared he would pay Lovecraft for his work, Lovecraft told another correspondent "I'm not going to take pay from Moe, even though he insists. It goes against the grain for a gentleman to charge money for a favour extended a friend. But the job does take time, confound it!"[24] Lovecraft's letters to Moe contain much highly technical terminology as to scansion and types of metrical feet. This information may have been provided only for Moe's edification, not intended to be included in the actual book. Regardless, Lovecraft invested a lot of time on the book, even if he may not have done much in the way of editing or rewriting.

Lovecraft had been musing about his old poetical methods for much of 1928. Donald Wandrei's *Sonnets of the Midnight Hours* (1927) opened Lovecraft's eyes to a more natural, less stilted manner of self-expression, and Lovecraft

---

22. It is only in this poem/letter that there is mention of possibly submitting the book to Henry Holt & Co. In a letter to Donald Wandrei of 12 September, HPL said that if Macmillan rejected the book, it was next to go to American Book Company, and if rejected again, then to the Kenyon Publishing Co.
23. MWM to HPL, 9 August 1927 (ms., JHL).
24. HPL to James F. Morton, 30 July 1929 (*Letters to James F. Morton* 174).

worked out the possibilities of such in his letters to the poet Elizabeth Toldridge. When Moe's manuscript landed on Lovecraft's desk, his poetical dry spell ended. His letter to Moe of 25 July 1929, as preserved in the Arkham House transcripts, is written entirely in verse (not unlike those written to John Russell fifteen years before). The title "An Epistle to the Rt. Honble Maurice Winter-Moe, Esq., of Zythopolis, in the Northwest-Territory of His Majesty's American Dominions" bears a striking resemblance to the titles of Lovecraft's travelogues. The letter is full of reminiscences of 1904 (the year of Moe's graduation), similar to his prose reminiscences of 1900 in letters 30, 32, 39, and 64. Moe relished the letter and did something unexpected with it.

> By the way—some recent heroicks of mine, on the departed glories of 1904, are about to be seen by every member of the U. of Wis. class of '04! How come? This way. Moe told me he was going to prepare a festive booklet to give each member of the class—commemorating the twenty-fifth anniversary—& the idea of '04 memories mov'd me to write him a reminiscent letter about old days & ways. It happen'd to be composed entirely in heroicks, & Moe liked it—so he took all the impersonal couplets & put 'em in his booklet![25]

With his "Epistle" Lovecraft (apparently) also wrote two sonnets at Moe's request demonstrating in form while discussing in subject matter the difference between the Shakespearean and the Petrarchan sonnets. Moe was delighted: "O Weaver of Dreams, how fortunate I am to know thee! My Slave of the Lamp, I have but to rub and say, 'Two sonnets, an Italian and an Elizabethan,' and they trickle in by return mail. Don't talk of mediocrity to me. You never do anything that is mediocre. They are perfect!"[26]

Lovecraft's letters to Moe show he clearly relished the job at hand.

> Have been working like hell lately, helping our fellow-amateur Maurice W. Moe prepare his manual of poetick appreciation—"Doorways to Poetry"—for publication. It's going to be a great book—the best & most explicit guide to the art of knowing good verse from bad that I've ever seen in the course of a long & not unobservant life. Moe knows how to put his finger on the difference betwixt poesy & hokum, knows how to make the reader see what he has his finger on, & knows how to test the reader's knowledge in a truly illuminative way. The book ought to be a tremendously useful & popular high-school text, besides having some vogue as a guide for private readers. This is the first truly enjoyable revision job I have ever tackled![27]

Lovecraft regarded it the most enjoyable bit of revision work he had ever done. He found the work, if it can be called that, so pleasurable that he was

---

25. HPL to James F. Morton, 30 July 1929 (*Letters to James F. Morton* 175).
26. MWM to HPL, [c. 1 August 1929]; TL, JHL.
27. HPL to Wilfred B. Talman [September 9, 1929]; ALS, JHL.

inspired to resume writing poetry. He wrote forty-five poems between July 1929 and January 1930, forty-two of those in seven weeks' time between November 1929 and January 1930.

Lovecraft's work on Moe's book did not constitute "revision"—that is, the usual copy editing and text preparation he did for clients. He may have done some of that, but it appears that what he mostly did was to provide metrical examples from the works of other poets to illustrate specific points Moe wished addressed. Moe observed, "I have noted all the detailed comments with the ms. before me, and I only wish you had found more to criticize [. . .] I am delighted with the hand-made specimens of feet and meter that never existed [. . .]"[28]

> I hear frequently from good old Moe, & am daily expecting to hear of the acceptance of his poetry-appreciation textbook by some standard firm. This book—whose MS. I looked over last year, & for which I furnished many metrical exercises—is really a marvellously fine thing, & ought to do more than any other influence to teach mediocre minds to distinguish betwixt real poetry & hackneyed sentimentalism.[29]

Lovecraft wrote Paul J. Campbell: "Glad his book was accepted. I read it in MS., made some suggestions, & contributed some specimen verses & exercises. The whole thing seems to me great stuff—the best, & practically the only, attempt I've seen to get at the real differences between authentic poetry & Eddieguest hokum & make them so plain that any kid or layman can see them. I'm really tremendously enthusiastic about it, & am giving it advance recommendations among all the amateurs & among the various pseudo-poetic attempters for whom I do revision."[30] Lovecraft even praised the unpublished book to the critic and editor William Stanley Braithwaite, perhaps thinking that Braithwaite, because of his position at the *Boston Transcript*, could endorse the book. But Campbell's mention of acceptance was premature; Moe's book never saw print. Despite initially expressing interest, Macmillan returned the book. Moe was later informed by his colleague Sterling A. Leonard, who spoke to Dr. H. L. Knowlton of Macmillan about the book's rejection, that "the whole staff liked it immensely but felt that it would never be a seller in any income-producing quantity and decided to reject it and not disappoint me with little driblets of royalty for a really excellent piece of work."[31] Moe then tried the American Book Company, a textbook publisher, but it, too, rejected the book. Moe sought for the next ten years, though perhaps not very hard, to get the book published. Lovecraft informed a correspondent, "There is a

---

28. MWM to HPL, [c. 1 August 1929]; TL, JHL.
29. HPL to Alfred Galpin, c. September 1930 . . . (*Letters to Alfred Galpin* 159).
30. HPL to Paul J. Campbell, 31 October 1930; ALS, JHL.
31. MWM to HPL, 31 August 1930; TLS, JHL.

possibility that 'Doorways' may get published within a year—albeit in somewhat humble form. [. . .] it is a vastly better & fuller treatise than the Teter one; though the latter is the best cheap aid now available."f[32]

R. H. Barlow informed August Derleth late in 1937 that "Moe's Doorway to Poetry will be included" in the next issue of his magazine, *Leaves*.[33] Chester P. Bradley offered to publish the work in his *Perspective Review*.[34] though it is difficult to imagine how two would-be publishers of magazines would pull off such a feat. Bradley published an article by Moe, "Introduction to Poetry" (1935), that seems as though it could have been lifted from his unpublished book, for its theme is that poetry should be something that can by appreciated by all. Another blow to the book's publication was the appearance of a book by Louis Untermeyer called *Doorways to Poetry* (1938). Moe was so fond of the name of his own book that he was reluctant to change it, but he recognized that Untermeyer's book would not allow him to keep his preferred title. In July 1938, Moe was still hopeful that his book could be published, even in a format so humble as a mimeographed booklet printed by Barlow. He considered Barlow's suggested *Gateways to Verse* and *Portals to Poesy*.

> My reference to a title-page and a following flyleaf lead up to the next item I had listed for discussion. If you are planning LEAVES to continue the format of the last issue, it has occurred to me that possibly here is an opportunity to get the book out myself in a cheap experimental form, sell it in the limited manner that my personal advertising of my Moe Word Hunts and Moe Book Tests has been able to move those products, and then, after a year or two, approach some publishing house with the results of this retail campaign to show that the text does meet a certain demand. There are one or two considerations which such a project would force upon us. One is that as a book for which good coin of the realm is to be exacted the typography in the stencil-work would have to be a shade neater than the last issue of LEAVES in some of its pages. As an amateur magazine, that was so admirable in its quality and in the scope of its subject matter that one easily overlooked slovenly page appearances; but my experience with stencil-cutting this summer has taught me that with time and care one can achieve a degree of neatness

---

32. HPL to Duane W. Rimel, 23 July 1934; *Letters to F. Lee Baldwin, Duane W. Rimel, and Nils Frome* 198. HPL refers to George E. Teter's *An Introduction to Some Elements of Poetry*, a booklet (46 pp.) only slightly longer than Moe's *Imagery Aids* (34 pp.).

33. R. H. Barlow to August Derleth, 7 November 1937; TLS, WHS. The second and final issue of *Leaves* appeared in the summer of 1937.

34. See Chester P. Bradley to HPL, 15 July 1935 (TLS, JHL), in which he informs HPL that he wrote Moe for permission to use all or part of Moe's book in his little magazine on the basis of HPL's suggestion in "Lovecraft Offers Verse Criticism" that the NAPA "make some effort toward securing the issuance, serially or otherwise, of 'Doorways to Poetry'" (*CE* 1.391).

that pleases the eye practically as fully as a type-set page. If my teaching program were not so overloaded, I would like to take over the job of cutting these stencils for you myself, but I know I should go down a physical wreck some time in the fall if I tried it, and I have planned to do too many things with the precious margin of health I know retain to endanger that.[35]

In the end, Moe's pet project was never published, and the disposition of the manuscript is unknown. This is to be regretted, for it probably would shed considerable light not only on Lovecraft's work on the book, but also on its influence on his poetical reawakening.

In late 1934 Moe asked Lovecraft to contribute an article of his choice for an amateur magazine being produced by his students. Lovecraft wrote an essay on traces of Roman architecture in America and sent it to Moe. It is not known if the magazine, or Lovecraft's essay, ever appeared, and Lovecraft believed his work had been lost. This presumably was one of several items that Moe sheepishly admitted to August Derleth he had failed to return to the author. It survives only in the Arkham House transcripts. Lovecraft's essay "Heritage or Modernism: Common Sense in Art Forms" (*Californian*, Summer 1935) served as an introduction to the Roman architecture piece. At around this time, when Moe was unable to secure a summer teaching position, Lovecraft offloaded revision work that he did not have time to do (or did not want to do) on Moe.

As mentioned, Moe visited Lovecraft for the second and final time on 18–19 July 1936, as he and his son Robert (who was working in Bridgeport, Connecticut) came to Providence. Lovecraft had been corresponding regularly with Robert since 1934. Since they had a car, they managed to visit several of the surrounding towns—Pawtuxet, Warren, and Bristol. At that time Moe and Lovecraft were participating in the Coryciani correspondence group. After Lovecraft, R. H. Barlow, and Adolphe de Castro wrote their acrostic poems on Poe on 8 August 1936, Moe himself wrote one of his own and then hectographed all four as *Four Acrostic Sonnets on Edgar Allan Poe* (1936), perhaps the rarest of all Lovecraft publications. August Derleth reprinted Moe's poem in his anthology, *Poetry out of Wisconsin* (1937). Shortly after Lovecraft's death, Moe wrote the brief but poignant memoir, "Howard Phillips Lovecraft: The Sage of Providence."

Within days of Lovecraft's death on 15 March 1937, August Derleth began assembling anything he could find written by Lovecraft for the purpose of preservation in print. He wrote to friends and associates across the country, but in the case of those living in Wisconsin, he and Donald Wandrei visited them in person. He wrote in his journal:

---

35. MWM to R. H. Barlow, 18 July 1938 (TLS, George Smisor's posthumous microfilm of Barlow's papers).

13 April, 1937: [. . .] To Milwaukee today. Don driving cautiously. . . . Three hours to Milwaukee, where we saw Bloch at once: a tall, unnaturally thin youth with thick glasses, who had all his Lovecraft material ready for us to take along. [. . .] Talked with him for an hour before the three of us went out to West Division High School to see Maurice Moe. Went directly to his class room, where he worked with his students. He did not see us enter; so we sat down and watched him for a while, not liking to disturb his energetic conversation with his students, whom he seems to hold to him very welll. [sic] Not a large man, but full of life, full of appreciation for many things. He spotted us at last, and having introduced ourselves, we were shown his unique word-finding tests, an elaborate but excellent system designed to increase the vocabularies of his students. [. . .] Moe congenially led us to his study, where he revealed to us the almost invaluable trove of Lovecraft material he had collected in the 25 years of correspondence with HPL. Piled our arms high with it, and so presently we left him, went down town, and were off on the way home again.[36]

Moe later sent additional material that he unearthed after Derleth left. He wrote, "My search for that elusive one-paragraph dream masterpiece failed to turn it up, but it did unearth two more caches of Lo material, and I am this day sending them to you by express. I don't know what your editorial policy will decide about the travelogs, but it seems to me that no omnibus volume on Lo would be complete without at least a judicious selection from his descriptions of Quebec and Southern cities like Charleston, Annapolis, et al. I am ashamed to find 'Please Return' on many of my inclosures, a mute testimony to my imperfections as a correspondent."[37] His mention of a "one-paragraph dream masterpiece" is intriguing. Was it contained within the body of a letter? Was it a separate, titled piece? Or was it simply Lovecraft's early account of a dream that he eventually wrote and published as "Polaris" or "The Statement of Randolph Carter"? It is not known what became of Moe's Lovecraft items. Some—such as "Ibid" and an early cycle of satirical poetry collectively titled "Perverted Poesie or Modern Metre"—were published in the late 1930s in George W. Macauley's amateur journal *O-Wash-Ta-Nong*, where memoirs by Moe and his son Donald also appeared. A few items have found their way to the Lovecraft collection at the John Hay Library, but much else has been lost or continues to be held privately. Edward F. Daas mentioned in a letter to Hyman Bradofsky dated 23 April 1948 that upon Moe's death, Moe's "widow turned over his personal and a.j. things to me."[38] What these items may have been is unknown.

Maurice Moe died of subacute bacterial endocarditis in 1940. As a writer

---

36. August Derleth, "Sac Prairie Journal" (TMS, WHS).
37. MWM to August Derleth, 17 April 1937; TLS, WHS.
38. Kenneth W. Faig's, *Moshassuck Review* (November 1997): 1.

he is forgotten, and few if any of his students survive today, but Moe is remembered as one of H. P. Lovecraft's staunchest friends and admirers, and his personal collection of Lovecraftiana has yielded some of Lovecraft's most memorable writings.

Of Maurice Moe's two sons, Robert Ellis Moe (1912–1992) was the more scholarly. He graduated from his father's alma mater in 1933 and became an electrical engineer specializing in television and radio, becoming employed in May 1934 by General Electric Co., in Bridgeport, Connecticut, moving later to Owensboro, Kentucky. He met Lovecraft once when he was ten years old. Lovecraft's first surviving letter to him, replying to Moe's announcement that he had moved to Connecticut, dates to 13 February 1935. Less than a month later, Moe drove to Providence to meet Lovecraft again (2–3 March 1935), when they visited Warren, Bristol, East Greenwich, and Wickford, Rhode Island), on 27–28 April (when they visited Newport, Rhode Island, and New Bedford, Massachusetts), and again on 19 September 1936 (in the company of Eunice French). On 18–19 July 1936, he met Lovecraft again, this time in the company of his father. He later was in charge of design of radar receivers and indicators for the government division of the Electronics Department at Syracuse, New York.

The name Bernard Austin Dwyer (1897–1943) appears often in Lovecraft's letters from December 1926 onward. Dwyer must have contacted Lovecraft in the usual way—by writing him in care of *Weird Tales*. In time Dwyer was sending Lovecraft various of his creative efforts—poems, fiction, drawings—and Lovecraft was soon encouraging Dwyer to write to his other correspondents for advice and criticism. Lovecraft praised his work highly, but often apologized to others for its crudeness. He tended to overpraise when he recognized sincerity. It was not long before Lovecraft went to visit Dwyer, who lived in Kingston/West Shokan, along the Hudson River in upstate New York. They met in person only twice—once in 1928 and again in 1929—at Dwyer's home.

Lovecraft considered Dwyer to be a "true mystic," a man with a cosmic outlook not unlike his own, and only one of a rare few in Lovecraft's circle. It is worth noting that Dwyer was one of three to whom Lovecraft related at length his Roman dream, the others being Frank Belknap Long and Donald Wandrei.[39] Lovecraft did not often take advice from others as to what or how he should write, mostly because the commentators completely missed the point of a story; but he rewrote "The Whisperer in Darkness" when Dwyer

---

39. Long incorporated the long discourse in his short novel *The Horror from the Hills*. Wandrei posthumously published the version sent him as "The Very Old Folk."

pointed out its flaws.[40]

Dwyer had submitted some of his work to *Weird Tales*, but it was rejected. The story he had sent to Lovecraft, Smith, Derleth, E. Hoffmann Price, and Donald Wandrei—"Flash"—was never published. His name does not show in databases of magazine publications, except for a few minor items, including letters published in *Weird Tales* and *Strange Tales*. Only one poem by him appeared there. At Lovecraft's urging, Dwyer wrote to several of Lovecraft's own correspondents. In fact, he corresponded fairly heavily with August Derleth, even well after Lovecraft's death.

This text of a "story" attributed to H. P. Lovecraft—"The Evil Clergyman"—derives from a letter to Dwyer, probably written in the summer or fall of 1933.[41] At August Derleth's urging, Dwyer submitted the text to *Weird Tales*, where it was published as "The Wicked Clergyman," and he had payment for the story ($15) sent directly to Lovecraft's surviving aunt, Annie E. P. Gamwell. The original letter has not surfaced, and it does not survive even among the Arkham House transcripts. Derleth reprinted the text under its present title in several editions. Lovecraft immortalized Dwyer, a man of large stature (six feet three inches and carrying "excess" weight according to Lovecraft), in "The Battle that Ended the Century" as "Knockout Bernie, the Wild Wolf of West Shokan," the only foe formidable enough to spar with "Two-Gun Bob, the Terror of the Plains"—that is, Robert E. Howard.

Ultimately, Dwyer did not pursue a writing career. In the 1930s he entered the CCC and became the editor of the camp paper in Peekskill, New York, *Blue Mountain Survey*, in which he published his story, "The Old Dark House."

Samuel Loveman (1887–1976), a native of Cleveland, was a poet, playwright, amateur journalist, and bookseller. He joined amateur journalism around 1905 and published much of his verse—most of it of a classicist, *fin-de-siècle* cast—in the amateur press and, later, in little magazines. Loveman is remembered today less for his own writing than for his association with Hart Crane, Ambrose Bierce, H. P. Lovecraft, and other writers. He corresponded with Bierce, Clark Ashton Smith, Vincent Starrett, and other writers of note.

Loveman wrote to Ambrose Bierce in 1908, thinking that Bierce was an editor at *Cosmopolitan*, submitting his poem "In Pierrot's Garden" for publica-

---

40. See Steven J. Mariconda, "Tightening the Coil: The Revision of 'The Whisperer in Darkness,'" in Mariconda's *H. P. Lovecraft: Art, Artifact, and Reality* (New York: Hippocampus Press, 2013), 190–200.

41. HPL remarks in a letter to Clark Ashton Smith (22 October 1933) that "Some months ago I had a dream of an evil clergyman in a garret full of forbidden books, & of how he changed his personality with a visitor. Fra Bernardus of West Shokan is urging me to make a story of it" (*Dawnward Spire* 466–67).

tion. Bierce, who was not on the editorial staff, said he would include the poem in his column "The Passing Show," but he ceased working for *Cosmopolitan* before the poem could be published. Bierce tried the poem on other publications, but none took the poem. Loveman sent Bierce his first book, the slim self-published volume *Poems* (1911). He published Bierce's letters to him as *Twenty-one Letters of Ambrose Bierce* (Cleveland: George Kirk, 1922), with a preface that Lovecraft quoted extensively in "Supernatural Horror in Literature." It was Bierce who put Loveman in touch with George Sterling, and in time Sterling connected Loveman with his protégé Clark Ashton Smith.

Loveman's writings were printed in a great variety of little publications from 1905 to 1910. After his *Poems* appeared, he dropped out of the NAPA and seemed to go entirely silent. Lovecraft joined the UAPA in April 1914; he not only started to appear in many amateur journals, but also began to serve the organization in various offices. It is not known precisely how Lovecraft stumbled on Loveman. Indeed, the publications in which Loveman's work appeared were outside of the circle in which Lovecraft's appeared. Presumably, Lovecraft obtained copies of journals antedating his own advent into amateur journalism, and it was in those publications that he came across Loveman's work. He had been reading Loveman's poetry in old amateur papers since at least 1915, apparently provided to him by Paul J. Campbell and probably others as well. Lovecraft's admiration was so great that he published the poem, "To Samuel Loveman, Esq., on His Poetry and Drama, Writ in the Elizabethan Style," in a journal published by an amateur in Cleveland, but apparently not seen by Loveman. But it was two years before Lovecraft could find a way to write to the poet whose work he treasured because of its fantastic leanings: "it certainly is hard work finding anyone interested in the weird. I never encountered one till 1917, when I stumbled simultaneously on Cook & Loveman."[42]

A correspondent must have informed Lovecraft of how to reach Loveman. And so in 1917, Lovecraft wrote to him expressing admiration for his verse. Lovecraft himself did not relate what transpired, but Loveman did:

> It is now nearly thirty years ago that I received a letter, fantastically worded and written in an obsolete style that simulated the early 1700's, with meticulously-rounded sentences that made me hover (as I read) between sheer envy and downright laughter. I remember the inscription at the close: "I remain, dear Sir, your Most Humble, Obedient Servant, Howard Phillips Lovecraft, Esquire." The gist of the letter was this: the writer had long been an ardent admirer of my poetry, and its appearance had, from time to time, excited his admiration to such a degree that he had made bold to institute in-

---

42. HPL to Donald Wandrei, 27 March 1927 (*Mysteries of Time and Spirit* 67). Since HPL had read SL's work for several years, by "1917" he meant the time when he first wrote SL.

quiries as to my whereabouts. He had, he asserted, practically given up any hope of finding me, when a clue to my location was indicated. Hence, his letter of inquiry: was I alive or dead? Would I write to him if I were still in the land of the living? I had always been a legend to him—could I, or rather would I, remove his doubts?[43]

Loveman obliged, and it appears Lovecraft acted quickly to urge Loveman back into amateur journalism. Lovecraft wrote: "Loveman has become reinstated in the United through me. Jew or not, I am rather proud to be his sponsor for the second advent to the Association. His poetical gifts are of the highest order, & I doubt if the amateur world can boast his superior."[44]

It was not long before their correspondence and Loveman's amateur activity were somewhat disrupted. Loveman was drafted into the Army in June 1918, serving as a corporal in the Headquarters Detachment, 4th Regiment Casuals (White), at Camp Gordon, Georgia. He was swiftly promoted to corporal, then sergeant. Nevertheless, his poor health prevented him from serving overseas. When Loveman's military service ended in January 1919, Lovecraft began to urge him to join the UAPA. Lovecraft may not have been happy that Loveman also became a member of the National Amateur Press Association. No matter. He was awarded a UAPA poetry laureateship in September 1920, for which Lord Dunsany was the judge. Loveman began contributing again to the amateur press and even published three issues of his own little magazine, the *Saturnian* (June–July 1921, August–September 1921, March 1922), containing his own poems as well as his translations from Heine, Baudelaire, and Verlaine.

Lovecraft first met Loveman in April 1922 in New York, when Sonia H. Greene (Lovecraft's future wife) invited both to visit her, with the express intention of getting the two poets to meet. (She later stated that she also wished to help overcome Lovecraft's anti-Semitism through personal contact with a sensitive Jewish man.) In August of that year, Lovecraft visited Loveman and Alfred Galpin in Cleveland. Loveman had become a close friend of the young poet Hart Crane after meeting him in 1921, and he introduced Lovecraft to Crane's friends, including William Sommer, William Lescaze, Edward Lazare, and Gordon Hatfield. At this time, Loveman showed to Lovecraft the artwork and poetry of Clark Ashton Smith, which whom Loveman had been corresponding since 1913. Lovecraft was so smitten with Smith's work that he immediately typed a gushing letter to Smith expressing his admiration. Lovecraft did not know that several years previous, Loveman had lent Smith the typescript of his story "Beyond the Wall of Sleep." Thus, Smith actually knew of Lovecraft well before Lovecraft knew of Smith.

---

43. "Howard Phillips Lovecraft," *Out of the Immortal Night* 219.
44. HPL to Rheinhart Kleiner, 8 November 1917; *Letters to Rheinhart Kleiner* 119.

Loveman was no mere correspondent. He and Lovecraft became close friends, and Loveman had great influence on Lovecraft in many ways, even if unintentionally. In December 1919 Lovecraft had a dream involving himself and Loveman, which he wrote almost verbatim into the story "The Statement of Randolph Carter" (1919), the Harley Warren character representing Loveman. About a year later Loveman figured in another dream, which Lovecraft wrote as the prose-poem "Nyarlathotep" (1920). In March 1923, Lovecraft wrote "Hypnos." The manuscript bears the dedication "To S. L.," and the references to Greek antiquity therein are a nod to similar images Loveman used in his poetry.

In 1922–23 Loveman assisted Lovecraft in editing *The Poetical Works of Jonathan E. Hoag*. Loveman appeared occasionally in later issues of Lovecraft's *Conservative*, notably with the controversial poem "To Satan," printed on the front page of the July 1923 issue. Lovecraft had anonymously praised Loveman's poetry effusively in the "Bureau of Critics" column of the *National Amateur* (March 1922); this review served as the springboard for an attack on Loveman himself by the amateur critic Michael Oscar White in an installment of his series "Poets of Amateur Journalism" (*Oracle*, December 1922). In turn, White was attacked and Loveman defended by Frank Belknap Long ("An Amateur Humorist," *Conservative*, March 1923) and Alfred Galpin ("A Critic of Poetry," *Oracle*, August 1923). Lovecraft himself responded to White in the "In the Editor's Study" column of the *Conservative* for July 1923.

Loveman was apathetic about the preservation of his own work. Lovecraft insisted that Loveman get his work on paper, but Loveman did not often take pains to do so. Indeed, many of Loveman's poems, preserved in Lovecraft's handwriting among his papers, were dictated by Loveman to Lovecraft and otherwise might have been lost. Some fifty manuscripts of Loveman's poetry, many in Lovecraft's hand, and many of which were unpublished before Loveman's work was gathered in *Out of the Immortal Night*, are held among the Lovecraft papers at the John Hay Library. Lovecraft made gifts of the manuscripts of "Hypnos" and "The Shunned House"[45] and a duplicate typescript of *Fungi from Yuggoth* to Loveman as well. When Loveman published a collection of his verse in 1936, Lovecraft encouraged all his correspondents to purchase it and slipped notices of the book in his letters.

In September 1924 Loveman came to New York, following Hart Crane and settling at 78 Columbia Heights in Brooklyn Heights. (When Crane was writing *The Bridge*, he lived at the Roebling House at 110 Columbia Heights. Roebling oversaw construction of the Brooklyn Bridge from the very room

---

45. SL surely cherished the manuscript of the story. HPL informed his aunt: "Loveman veritably throws fits over this bit of cheerful morbidity, & vows he'll bring it to the attention of a publisher's reader" (HPL to Lillian D. Clark, 29 November 1924; ms, JHL) *Letters to Family and Family Friends* 234.

where Crane was staying.) Lovecraft had arrived in March, when he eloped with Sonia Greene, taking up residence at Sonia's place at 259 Parkside Avenue in Flatbush, but eventually setting up quarters (for himself) at 169 Clinton in Brooklyn Heights around 31 December 1924. Loveman resided at Clinton Street for two weeks in May 1925 in a room on the first floor across from Lovecraft. Another Kalem, George W. Kirk, also lived in the building in the room above Lovecraft's from February to June 1925. For the next year and a half Lovecraft and Loveman were closely in touch as members of the Kalem Club, although Loveman did briefly return to Cleveland in 1925, having preemptively quit a job from which he was going to be released. The two met Hart Crane on several occasions in late 1924. By September 1925 Loveman had secured a job at Dauber & Pine bookshop (Fifth Avenue and 12th Street) and worked there for the next several years. In March 1926 he arranged for Lovecraft to be paid to address envelopes for a stint lasting less than three weeks, the only remunerative work (aside from sales of his stories and poems and sporadic revision work) that Lovecraft secured during his New York stay. In 1926 W. Paul Cook published Loveman's long neo-Grecian poem, *The Hermaphrodite*, which Lovecraft had read and admired years earlier. The July 1926 *United Amateur* included a poem by Loveman about Lovecraft, "To Mr. Theobald."

Loveman claimed (with no evidence) that Lovecraft was so depressed during the latter stages of his New York stay that he carried poison on his person so that he could commit suicide if he felt unduly depressed.[46] After Lovecraft returned to Providence, he and Loveman communicated chiefly by mail. Loveman advised Adolphe de Castro and Zealia Bishop to approach Lovecraft for revision work. Loveman also made efforts to interest publishers in Lovecraft's work. He showed Lovecraft's stories to Vincent Starrett and suggested to Allan Ullman of Alfred A. Knopf that he consider Lovecraft's tales for book publication. These efforts came to naught, but Loveman remained undaunted. Loveman came to Providence in January 1929, and the two visited Boston, Salem, and Marblehead for a few days.

Lovecraft was instrumental in getting nineteen poems by Loveman from his personal file into the Summer 1935 issue of the *Californian*. In January 1936 the Caxton Press issued Loveman's *The Hermaphrodite and Other Poems*, the only substantial volume of his poetry published in his lifetime. In 1944 W. Paul Cook published Loveman's play *The Sphinx*, which Lovecraft had long admired.

Around 1948, Sonia H. Davis revealed to Loveman the depth of Lovecraft's anti-Semitism. This information does not appear in his two memoirs of Lovecraft, "Howard Phillips Lovecraft" (in *Something about Cats*) and "Lovecraft as a Conversationalist" (*Fresco*, Spring 1958). These articles generally are genial,

---

46. Joshi, *I Am Providence* 2.621.

and Loveman seems not to have been moved by Mrs. Davis's revelation. In fact, Loveman wrote to August Derleth on 1 December 1949, "I look forward to the publication of the letters [of Lovecraft] with a great deal of eagerness. I have practically nothing at all, or I would have tend[er]ed them to you. All my material was either destroyed or confiscated when I left Cleveland for New York."[47]

This statement poses the question: what actually happened to Loveman's "material"? Many manuscripts of stories and poems given to Loveman have been offered for sale. And this book contains eight letters of Lovecraft. So not "all" material of one kind or another was "destroyed or confiscated." Who "destroyed" Lovecraft's papers? Who "confiscated" them? Loveman claimed that it was *he* who destroyed his letters from Lovecraft, but when, or if, this occurred is not known. In "Lovecraft as a Conversationalist," he claimed to possess 500 pages of Lovecraft's letters, but it appears that he is referring to letters to Frank Belknap Long, which Loveman bought in the early 1940s when Long needed money. Lovecraft's letters to Walter J. Coates also passed through Loveman's hands.

In later years, Loveman turned against Lovecraft. In the brief article "Of Gold and Sawdust," Loveman viciously denounced Lovecraft as a racist and a hypocrite for concealing his "smouldering hatred" of Loveman. It is profoundly disappointing that following Lovecraft's death, upon learning of Lovecraft's feeling about Jews in the abstract, Loveman renounced Lovecraft entirely. Loveman believed Lovecraft was not being honest with him. But one would have to ask: If Lovecraft did not like or respect Loveman as an individual, why would he have spent so much time with him and corresponding with him? Why would he make trips to Cleveland and New York for the express purpose of meeting him? Why would he champion Loveman's verse and tirelessly promote his book? When W. Paul Cook published Loveman's *The Hermaphrodite* (1926), Lovecraft proofread it *five times* to ensure perfection—a heroic feat, given that it was not even his own book.[48] Lovecraft ba-

---

47. SL to August Derleth, 1 December 1949; TLS, WHS.
48. The book, alas, was imperfect. See HPL to James F. Morton, 17 November 1926: "The Herm book is all right—but god damn James Joseph Moloney of the Culinary type force for working his ancestral brogue into the word *blasphemies* on page 23. Get this, 'bo—
Bow pale-checked to their blashphemies
Sink me, Sir, does he want me to get a light check'd suit to perform my genuflections in, or does he refer to the anaemic nature of the remittances secured by my toil? And to think I read them ——— ——— proofs *five* ——— ——— times! That line was O.K. in the last set except that the compound epithet was given in the good old-fashion'd way—with elision—which Samuelus went back on at the last moment. I mark'd this one thing for alteration—& see what they done to the whole ——— ——— line!" (*Letters to James F. Morton* 122–23.)

ses characters in his fiction on Loveman. His letters to others offer no evidence of "smouldering hatred"—quite the opposite, in fact. Lovecraft wrote with nothing less than keen admiration for Loveman. He recognized Loveman's moodiness and strove to rally him when his spirits flagged: "As to cynicism . . . It's damn good stuff, too—honestly, it's unbelievably cheering as compared with the lugubrious teleology & febrile ethics of such hapless neurotics as Cook & Loveman. Poor Loveman is in a frightful state of melancholy—I have to cheer him up with twenty-page sermons in favour of nonchalant cynicism."[49] Even Hart Crane called Loveman "the eternal martyr," for he complained constantly about his lot. It is known that Loveman made gifts to Lovecraft of various items from his collection of various rare artifacts, but Lovecraft also made similar gestures to Loveman. Either on or before 14 January 1925, the date when Lovecraft and others of the Kalem Club presented various gifts for Loveman (including a bookcase) and decorated his room as a surprise on his thirty-eighth birthday, Lovecraft wrote the poem "To Samuel Loveman, Esq., upon Adorning His Room for His Birthday." Not long thereafter, he wrote "To Saml Loveman Esq.," having suggested that the Kalems give Loveman some *writing materials,* which the poet sadly lacked."[50]

Lovecraft definitely had strong opinions about Jews, generally believing that the ideals and culture of New England and the United States needed to be kept separate from those of what he regarded as an unanchored culture of a nomadic peoples. (In this regard, Lovecraft felt that Germany, or any country, should try to remain free of Jewish mores and culture.) Be that as it may, it is an abstract concept. The reality is that Lovecraft had friends, indeed even a wife, who were Jewish. Granted, all probably would have been offended by, or at least disappointed in, some of Lovecraft's beliefs. But Kenneth Sterling, who likely knew that Lovecraft made disparaging comments about Jews in general, said Lovecraft never made such comments to him and always treated him with respect, always offered him assistance with his own writing. Lovecraft's stands on race and bloodlines may be difficult to comprehend when counterposed against his very real friendships with Jews. They may be signs of cognitive dissonance, perhaps, but not of hypocrisy. It is evident that Lovecraft thought highly of Loveman and his work and truly enjoyed and relished his company. Loveman seemed to have forgotten an earlier opinion he had expressed of Lovecraft:

> I have never known him to hold the slightest resentment against any one; I have never known a human being to secrete less envy, malice, morbidity and intolerance, than did Howard. Toward the worst of rascals or scoundrels, there was not a single line of remonstrance. "Only another arrangement of

---

49. HPL to James F. Morton, 24 June 1923; *Letters to James F. Morton* 49.
50. HPL to Lillian D. Clark, 22 January 1925; *Letters to Family and Family Friends* 1.238.

chemical molecules," he was wont to ascribe to any persons malingering in the long and particularly fine range of his lifelong friendships or acquaintances.[51]

Charles Vincent Starrett (1886–1974), American poet, fiction writer, journalist, and critic, was known to Lovecraft before the two corresponded. Lovecraft recognized Starrett as the man "who introduced the work of Machen to America."[52] Starrett had published *Arthur Machen: A Novelist of Ecstasy and Sin* (1918) and *Buried Caesars: Essays in Literary Appreciation* (1923), with pieces on Machen and Ambrose Bierce. He also edited *The Shining Pyramid* (1923), a collection of stories by Machen. Starrett, a newspaper reporter, also wrote fiction for such magazines as *Saucy Stories, Black Cat, Smart Set, Snappy Stories, Short Stories,* and *Saturday Evening Post,* which Lovecraft did not read (although he looked at the *Post* when at the barbershop), and also *Weird Tales.* His first story in *Weird Tales* was "Penelope" (May 1923), and he published two other stories there that same year. *Weird Tales* published Lovecraft's first story, "Dagon," in October of that year, after the last of Starrett's stories to be published there until 1932, along with his letter to the editor expressing disdain of "Penelope": "'Penelope' is clever—but Holy Pete! If the illustrious Starrett's ignorance of astronomy is an artfully conceived attribute of his character's whimsical narrative, I'll say he's right there with the verisimilitude!"[53] Lovecraft had written the editor in confidence and was embarrassed to see his offhand comment in print. Lovecraft wrote to C. M. Eddy, Jr. with relief, "he [Edwin Baird, editor of *Weird Tales*] says I haven't offended Vincent Starrett, whom he knows well, and denominates a thorough good fellow."[54] He surely was surprised that "Penelope," with its scientific error, was included in a book issued by the publisher of *Weird Tales, The Moon Terror* (1927), especially since a book of Lovecraft's own stories tentatively considered by the same publisher never appeared. In any case, even if Starrett did not notice Lovecraft's letter, he should have noticed "Dagon" in the same issue. Either Starrett did not remember "Dagon" or never read it at all—nor any of Lovecraft's other works over the next three years.

Starrett met members of "the gang"—the Kalem Club—in 1927, the year after Lovecraft left New York to return to Providence. The circumstances of such a meeting are unknown, although Lovecraft mentioned once that Armitage Trail (pseudonym of Maurice Cooms) claimed to be friends with Farnsworth Wright and J. C. Henneberger (former owner of *Weird Tales*) and

---

51. "Howard Phillips Lovecraft," *Out of the Immortal Night* 220.
52. HPL to Donald Wandrei, 12 April 1927; *Mysteries of Time and Spirit* 76.
53. HPL to Edwin Baird, c. June 1923, *WT* 2, No. 3 (October 1923): 82; in *H. P. Lovecraft: Uncollected Letters,* ed. S. T. Joshi, West Warwick, RI: Necronomicon Press, 6.
54. HPL to C. M. Eddy, 20 October 1923; transcript, Place of Hawks.

also Starrett. Trail may have arranged the meeting among Starrett and "the gang" in early April 1929. Frank Belknap Long and Samuel Loveman showed Starrett two of Lovecraft's stories, of which Long reported he spoke favorably. Lovecraft received a letter from Starrett shortly thereafter on 11 April. Lovecraft's letter in reply of 14 April suggests that Loveman may have shown him "The Shunned House," the manuscript of which Loveman possessed and in which Loveman hoped to interest prospective publishers. The other story may have been "Hypnos," for Loveman owned that as well. Starrett wrote Lovecraft inquiring if Lovecraft could lend him stories to read.

By way of reply, Lovecraft sent Starrett "a dozen tales illustrating different phases of my writing."[55] It would seem that Starrett himself had requested that Lovecraft send a representative sampling of his work, for while he awaited a response from Starrett, Lovecraft wrote: "I don't imagine Starrett will ever try to publish a book of my tales! Anyway, I shall be interested to hear what he has to say—I told him to take his time about reading the dozen specimens I sent."[56] Starrett held on to the stories for roughly four months. Lovecraft was faintly hopeful that Starrett could exert some influence on prospective publishers of his work, but it seems that Starrett was not in any position to do this himself. Lovecraft's letters to Starrett are polite, even a bit stiff, and the two never launched into a lengthy, vital correspondence, and they ceased communication in less than a year.

Among Lovecraft's papers is a letter from one Arthur E. Scott (19 December 1927), formerly a prolific pulp writer but at the time a literary agent, who had written to Lovecraft at the suggestion of Starrett sending his advertising circulars: "If you think that I could be of any service to you in your work I shall be glad to hear from you."[57] Clearly, nothing came of this. Lovecraft's final letter to Starrett, in which he makes no mention of hearing from Scott, is a lengthy discourse on the artist John Martin, about whom Starrett had inquired. The reason the correspondence was so short-lived is unknown, although Lovecraft's lengthy comment on Martin (much of it copied or paraphrased from the *Encyclopaedia Britannica*) may have been a bit much for Starrett. Nevertheless, Lovecraft remained familiar with Starrett's work. Following Lovecraft's death, Starrett wrote several brief memoirs and appreciations (as part of reviews in the *Chicago Tribune* of various Lovecraft books published by Arkham House), and even a poem.

Starrett found much merit in Lovecraft's "Supernatural Horror in Literature" as published in the *Recluse* in the summer of 1927. He suggested some other minor writers of weird fiction not mentioned in the essay, but Love-

---

55. HPL to Donald Wandrei, 12 April 1927; *Mysteries of Time and Spirit* 76.
56. HPL to Donald Wandrei, 21 April 1927; *Mysteries of Time and Spirit* 85.
57. Ms., JHL, on verso of a ms. page of "The Dreams in the Witch House."

craft never felt compelled to mention them in a future reprint of the piece.

Starrett may have been the most prestigious author with whom Lovecraft corresponded. Over the years he wrote a few more weird tales and verse, some for *Weird Tales*, others for the *Arkham Sampler*. Some of his weird fiction is gathered in *The Quick and the Dead* (1965), and August Derleth's anthologies of weird verse *Dark of the Moon* (1947) and *Fire and Sleet and Candlelight* (1961) include some of his poems. After Lovecraft's death Starrett took note of several of Lovecraft's volumes in his column in the *Chicago Tribune*, reviewing *Beyond the Wall of Sleep* (2 January 1944), *Marginalia* (4 March 1945), *Something about Cats* (18 December 1949), and *The Shuttered Room* (10 January 1960); the first two of these are reprinted in his *Books and Bipeds* (1947). In the first of these reviews he made the memorable, if not entirely accurate, comment: "he was his own most fantastic creation—a Roderick Usher or C. Auguste Dupin born a century too late."[58] These reviews, generally favorable and appearing in a widely read and prestigious venue, contributed more than their share to the augmentation of Lovecraft's reputation in the 1940s, counteracting to some degree Edmund Wilson's hostile review-article "Tales of the Marvellous and the Ridiculous" (*New Yorker*, 24 November 1945).

A Note on the Text
As with some other volumes in the *Collected Letters* series, this one depends heavily on the Arkham House transcripts. Only thirteen manuscript letters or postcards by Lovecraft to Maurice W. Moe are known to exist; in fact, more missives to Robert Moe exist than missives to Maurice. These are held by the John Hay Library, except for letter 50, a photograph of which was published in *Marginalia*. The balance—some sixty letters—are from the transcripts. It is clear that we lack not only letters to Moe but also other round-robin letters, to say nothing of the portions that Arkham House chose not to transcribe. The fifteen letters and cards to Robert E. Moe are held by the John Hay Library.

No manuscript letters to Bernard Austin Dwyer are known to exist. The texts herein are entirely from the Arkham House transcripts. The letter in which Lovecraft described his dream of an "evil clergyman" does not exist, although following Lovecraft's death Dwyer, at August Derleth's suggestion, submitted that brief vignette to *Weird Tales*, which published it as a story. Conversely, the letters to Loveman, few as they are, derive entirely from manuscripts, most held privately. Only one letter to Loveman is represented in the Arkham House transcripts; the typed letter survives among August Derleth's papers at the Wisconsin Historical Society. It appears Loveman never submitted his letters for the transcription project. The letters to Vin-

---

58. "Books Alive," *Chicago Sunday Tribune* (2 January 1944): Sec. 6, p. 12. Rpt. as "Lovecraft" in *LR* 427.

cent Starrett are all held at the Lilly Library of the University of Indiana–Bloomington.

As noted, Lovecraft and Moe participated in various "round-robin letters," to which they and various others contributed content for circulation among the respective groups. A single Molo letter (no. 17) is contained herein. Three fragmentary Kleicomolo letters are contained in *Letters to Rheinhart Kleiner* (see letters 17, 20, and 24 therein). Seven fragmentary Gallomo letters are contained in *Letters to Alfred Galpin* (see letters 6–12 therein). These, as well as letters to the Coryciani (Neo-Kleicomolo), will appear in a subsequent volume.

Acknowledgments

The editors would like to think the following for their assistance in preparation of this volume: Stefan Dziemianowicz, Kenneth W. Faig, Jr., Derrick Hussey, Donovan K. Loucks, Christopher O'Brien, J.-M. Rajala. Jordan Douglas Smith, John H. Stanley and Christopher Geissler of the John Hay Library, Brown University, Providence, RI, Lee Grady of the Wisconsin Historical Society, and the staff of the Special Collections department of the University Wisconsin–Madison, where the Library of Amateur Journalism is housed. Letters to Vincent Starrett are printed courtesy of the Lilly Library, Indiana University, Bloomington, Indiana.

Abbreviations

AT	*The Ancient Track* (2nd ed. 2013)
CE	*Collected Essays* (2004–06; 5 vols.)
CF	*Collected Fiction* (2015–17; 4 vols.)
LL	Joshi, *Lovecraft's Library* (2017 edition)
LR	Cannon, *Lovecraft Remembered* (1998)
SHL	*The Annotated Supernatural Horror in Literature* (2nd ed. 2012)
SL	*Selected Letters* (1965–76; 5 vols.)
WW	Joshi, *A Weird Writer in Our Midst* (2010)

FBL	Frank Belknap Long, Jr.
HPL	H. P. Lovecraft
MWM	Maurice W. Moe
SL	Samuel Loveman

ALS	autograph letter, signed
AMS	autograph manuscript
ANS	autograph note, signed
JHL	John Hay Library, Brown University
TLS	typed letter, signed
TMS	typed manuscript
WHS	Wisconsin Historical Society

*H. P. Lovecraft and Maurice W. Moe
in Providence, 18 or 19 July 1936*

Letters to Maurice W. Moe

[1]   [AHT]
598 Angell St.,
Providence, R.I.,
December 8, 1914

Mr. Maurice W. Moe,

Dear Sir:—

Through Mr. Daas, I learn that you would 'like to see me get away from the heroic couplet, and see what I could do in other forms'. I fear that it is quite beyond me thus to leave a form of expression on which I seized almost by instinct, and in which nearly all my rhythmical efforts are cast. As the strength of Antaeus depended on his contact with Mother Earth, so does any possible merit in my verses depend on their execution in this regular and time-honoured measure. Take the form away, and nothing remains. I have no real poetic ability, and all that saves my verse from utter worthlessness is the care which I bestow on its metrical construction.

I am really a relic left over from Queen Anne's age. I do not know how it came about, but from the time of my earliest recollection, I have seemed to fall into the mental habits of two centuries ago. My constitutional feebleness kept me from regular attendance at school, so that I acquired what little knowledge I possess from a rather indiscriminate perusal of the volumes of the family library. Curiously enough, I never felt at home save with the writers of the late seventeenth and early eighteenth centuries. Longfellow, Tennyson, and Browning were aliens; Dryden, Addison, and Pope were intimate friends. My classical knowledge was confined to Latin, a fact which still further bound me to a period whose inspiration was in everything more Latin than Greek. In this manner my style was formed; not as conscious archaism, but as though I had actually been born in 1690 instead of 1890. Every image, every turn of expression, every word, which I acquired, was of the artificial, regular, definite, Queen Anne type, so you can readily perceive how vague, over-familiar, abrupt, and amorphous, modern poetry must appear to me. My literary appreciation begins with Dryden, and ends with Goldsmith and Dr. Johnson.

Now I am perfectly aware that this is no more than downright perverted taste. I know as well as any man that the beauties of poetry lie not in the tinsel of flowing metre, or the veneer of epigrammatical couplets; but in the real richness of images, delicacy of imagination, and keenness of perception, which are independent of outward form or superficial brilliancy; yet I were false and hypocritical, should I not admit my actual preference for the old resounding decasyllabics. Verily, I ought to be wearing a powdered wig and knee-breeches. I have written in iambic octosyllabics like those of Swift, in decasyllabic quatrains, as in Gray's *Elegy,* in the old ballad metre of Chevy-Chase, in blank verse like Young's and Thomson's, and even in anapaests like those in Beattie's "Hermit",[1] but only in the formal couplet of Dryden and Pope can I really express myself. Once I privately tried imitations of modern poets, but turned away in distaste. Their vocabulary and technic alike seem utterly strange to an ancient like myself.

    I wonder if you care for the science of Astronomy? This has been a source of fascination to me for twelve years—just half my life. For the past eight years, ever since I was sixteen, I have contributed to the local press a series of monthly astronomical articles, the two latest of which, from *The Providence Evening News,* I herewith enclose. Recently a quack named Hartmann, a devotee of the pseudo-science of Astrology, commenced to disseminate the usual pernicious fallacies of that occult art through the columns of *The News,* so that in the interests of true Astronomy I was forced into a campaign of invective and satire. I began seriously, with "Science versus Charlatanry", which I followed up with "The Falsity of Astrology", but eventually the stupid persistence of the modern Nostradamus forced me to adopt ridicule as my weapon. I thereupon went back to my beloved age of Queen Anne for a precedent, and decided to emulate Dean Swift's famous attacks on the astrologer Partridge, conducted under the nom de plume of Isaac Bickerstaffe (or Bickerstaff—I have seen it spelled both ways).[2] Accordingly I published a satirical article wherein I gave with an air of solemn gravity the most nonsensical collection of wild prophecies that my brain could conceive; the whole entitled "Astrology and the Future", and signed "Isaac Bickerstaffe, Jr." I there "predicted" the end of the world by an explosion of internal gases in the year 4954. Hartmann scarce knew whether or not to take me seriously, and kept up his mountebank performances, so I prepared another Bickerstaffe paper whose ridicule should become more open toward the end. In this final effort, "Delavan's Comet and Astrology", I explained how the human race shall be preserved after the destruction of the earth, by transportation to the planet Venus! Even the obtuse intellect of the charlatan must have now discovered the sarcastic nature of the ponderous prophecy, for he has now quietly ceased to inflict his false notions on a gullible public.

    Very truly yours,
        H. P. Lovecraft.

[Enclosure: "The Power of Wine: A Satire."]

Notes

1. Scottish poet James Beattie (1735–1803), a precursor of the Romantic movement.

2. Jonathan Swift, under the pseudonym Isaac Bickerstaff Esq, predicted the death of then famous Almanac-maker and astrologer John Partridge (1644–1714?) as part of a hoax. The astrologer J[oachim] F[riedrich] Hartmann (1848–1930) had published an article, "Astrology and the European War," in the *Evening News* (4 September 1914). HPL's various responses to Hartmann are gathered in *CE* 3 under "Science versus Charlatanry"; Hartman's pieces appear there in the Appendix.

[2]   [AHT]

598 Angell St.,
Providence, R.I.,
December 17, 1914

Mr. M. W. Moe,
Appleton, Wis.,

Dear Mr. Moe:—

I read with the keenest interest your opinions on the heroic couplet, especially your belief that it contains in itself a suggestion of satire. As a matter of fact, I am not prepared entirely to contradict this conclusion of yours, for I can readily feel the strong epigrammatical or antithetical tendency of the metre. However, I must continue to maintain that in the proper hands it can take on a noble epic fire impossible to any other measure, and at the same time keeping free from any trace of the ludicrous. I may not myself be able to employ it to such advantage, but feel sure that no one could take "Pope Alexander's" translation of *The Iliad* as a burlesque. "Quinsnicket Park" (one hundred twelve lines) which I wrote for a co-öperative paper to be issued by the *United's* recruiting committee, is an attempt at non-satirical heroic verse.[1] If the publishing enterprise meets with disaster, I shall send you a manuscript of this piece, since I am very anxious for your opinion of it. My "Teuton's Battle-Song" really demanded a more rugged and Saxon structure, but I knew better than to attempt to work in any such unaccustomed medium. I wonder how it would have sounded in the style of Macpherson's Ossian![2] "On his high throne in the golden palace laughs the Father of Gods. As in the time of old calls he to his children in Midgard. Loud in the thunders of Gormal resounds the voice of the lofty son of Woden. Swift as the rain-clouds before the storm ride through the high heaven the Dysae". etc. etc. I think I had better remain astride of my "rocking horse". I recently tried the "Hiawatha" type of blank verse in translating a curious bit of primitive Teutonic martial poetry which Dr. Blair quotes in his "Critical Dissertation on the Poems of Ossian". This fragment is a funeral song composed in Runes by the old Danish monarch Regner Lodbrok (eighth century A.D.). In the Middle Ages Olaus Wormius made the rather incoherent Latin version which Blair uses.[3] It is in stanzas, each headed by the words "Pugnavimus ensibus". In translating, I end each stanza with a rhyming couplet. I give a sample, together with my unusual version.

>Pugnavimus ensibus,
>Alte tulimus tunc lanceas
>Quando viginti annos numeravimus
>Et celebrem laudem comparavimus passim
>Vicimus octo barones
>In oriente ante Dimini portum
>Aquilae impetravimus tunc sufficientem
>Hospitii sumptum in illa strage
>Sudor decidit in vulnerum
>Oceano perdidit exercitus aetatem.

>Tr. by H. P. L.
>
>With our swords have we contended.
>Ere two score of years we counted
>High we bore our glist'ning lances.
>Wide we heard our fame and praises.
>Barons eight with ease we conquer'd
>In the east before the harbour
>Of Diminium. In that carnage
>We the rav'ning eagle glutted.
>Dripping wounds fill'd up the ocean.
>Weary of the hopeless fray,
>All the host dissolv'd away.

When I told you I had silenced my astrological antagonist, I spoke prematurely. Last Monday he "came back" with a long, rambling, and belated reply. I am preparing a serious answer and another Bickerstaffe paper, both of which I will send you if they are accepted by *The News*. This time the "Professor" is very amusing. In the course of his vapourings he traces the word "superstition" back to two *Greek* words: "super", *the supernatural,* and "stitio", *to fear,* the whole meaning *"the fear of God"!!!!!* This fearful and wonderful etymological feat must interest the author of "Word Curiosities" (*The Cynosure*, January, 1909).[4] In my satire I am going to touch particularly on this point. I enclose "Science versus Charlatanry", my opening gun in the campaign, which I had mislaid when I wrote you before. I hope that you can, as you say, make some use of my anti-astrological efforts.

I beg to remain
>Your obedient servant,
>H. P. Lovecraft.

Notes

1. In fact, the poem was written in 1913, a year before HPL's entry into amateur journalism. The cooperative paper appears to be the *Badger*, edited by George S. Schilling.
2. The Scottish poet James Macpherson (1736–1796) attempted to pass off poetry he had written as translations of the fragments of the ancient Scottish poet Ossian. The chief works he produced were *Fingal* (1762) and *Temora* (1763). The hoax, initially criticized by Samuel Johnson, was definitively exploded in the early 19th century. There is, however, some evidence that some of the poems were based on old Scottish folktales.
3. HPL refers to a critical work by Hugh Blair. HPL misread a passage in Blair and came to think of the Danish scholar Olaus Wormius (Ole Wurm, 1588–1654) as living in the medieval era. HPL later made Wormius the Latin translator of the *Necronomicon*. See S. T. Joshi, "Lovecraft, Regner Lodbrog, and Olaus Wormius," in *Lovecraft and a World in Transition* (New York: Hippocampus Press, 2014), 465–72.
4. An article by MWM in *Cynosure*, edited by William C. Ahlhauser (1879–1941), of Milwaukee.

[3]   [AHT]

598 Angell Street, Providence, R.I.,
January 1, 1915.

My Dear Mr. Moe:—

As before, I was delighted to receive your interesting and instructive letter; and I cannot begin the New Year better than by replying.

The suggestions which you offer for club programmes are welcome indeed, and I shall try very soon to adapt some of them to the individual requirements of the local organisation. I have not seen "The Weakly Squawk",[1] though it is mentioned very favourably in some of the older papers which Mr. Daas sent me. If you feel that you can trust your single, solitary copy to the mercy of the mails, I should much appreciate a brief glance at it. I wonder if it resembles the enclosed "Gotham Weekly Gazette", which is published in the N. Y. Sunday Tribune? Until very recently, comic supplements were terrae incognitae to me. For over fifty years our family paper has been the N. Y. Tribune, which most conservatively declined to print such frivolous innovations. Lately, however, The Tribune has lost some of its primitive simplicity, and about a month ago surprised its subscribers with a crude, glaring, multicoloured leaflet of alleged humour. I have each week discarded this supplement without perusal, but shall henceforth search it for hidden gems of facetiousness. Probably most of the local club members are used to this sort of thing, and would welcome a "literary" programme based upon it. I shall look for "Johnny Tissadirl"[2] in the amateur papers, though I have not seen the "Smatter Pop"?[3] series of pictures from which it is derived.

I fear that the "Mary-had-a-little-lamb" idea could not yet be applied successfully in the Providence club, for not one of the local members seems to possess even the faintest idea of what metre or versification is. I never before saw such an aggregation of rhythm-deaf individuals. A rhyming contest, however, might be the very best method of introducing to them the first principles of prosody.

Your "Thriller programme" strikes me very favourably. Undoubtedly these local amateurs are highly erudite in literature of the "Nick Carter" or "Diamond Dick" school,[4] and would hail with delight the chance to produce tales of rapid action. The keener minds of Dunn and perhaps Basinet would perceive the element of the ridiculous in overstrained melodrama, and might be able to turn out rather good burlesques of thrilling but trite situations. I should like very much to see some of the opening sentences you have used.

I can well understand from your letters and the amateur journals how popular and efficient a teacher you must be; The Pippin[5] alone shows how great an interest you are able to inspire in your classes. I think that in the person of Mr. Schilling,[6] the "lurking, dark-brow'd villain", you have produced a real lover of literature. In his plans for a co-operative paper he exhibits much taste and discrimination. Your profession is one in which a capable man can exercise a vast influence for good, and Appleton is fortunate in having your services.

Amateur journalism certainly ought to be a powerful weapon in the hands of the instructor of English. A scholar must undoubtedly take more real interest in his compositions if he can look forward to their appearance in print. I remember how in my own fragmentary school days I used to love to insert my work in a rural paper called The Pawtuxet Valley Gleaner.[7] Once I gave to my English teacher (she was an elderly, good-natured lady named Mrs. Blake) an essay entitled "Is there Life in the Moon"? Not knowing of my astronomical recreations, she imagined from my rather stiff and polysyllabic style that it was not perfectly original, but perhaps paraphrased from some magazine article. Accordingly, she detained me after school and inquired if I had not drawn upon some published article for my information. Rather to her surprise, I declared unhesitatingly that I had copied my essay word for word, title and all, from a country paper; and that if she desired, I would show her the clipping. I then handed her a clipping of the article from The Gleaner, with the heading in bold type: "IS THERE LIFE IN THE MOON? BY H. P. LOVECRAFT." She was quite satisfied, and never again questioned the originality of my work.[8]

Your recent success in bringing amateur journalism to the notice of your fellow-instructors is highly remarkable. I truly believe that you will be hailed as a second founder of the U.A.P.A. As a member of the Recruiting Committee I have just received the names of five educators, including two Wisconsin high-school Principals, who have joined within a month. One of them at Athens, Wis., has formed a club obviously modelled after your own.

I am immensely gratified to see the associations breaking away from the domination of petty, immature politicians, and joining themselves more closely to the older and more conventional forms of instruction. Your Chicago address may have opened a new epoch in the history both of English teaching and of amateur journalism.

So confusing is the mixture of ignorance and erudition found in my work, that I do not wonder you desire an autobiography. I suppose I am rather a problem in psychology—the result of literary and artistic environment and heredity, as contrasted with mediocre native capacity and the imperfect education made necessary by ill health and a sensitive, nervous temperament.

THE AUTOBIOGRAPHY OF H. LOVECRAFT, ESQ.

Since all well-regulated autobiographers begin at least two generations back, I suppose I must do the same in my reminiscences. The Lovecrafts were a family of small country gentry in Devonshire, and though they furnished many clergymen to the Church of England, I have not heard of any member who rose to eminence or distinction. I dare say that they were much the same as other petty rural 'squires. My paternal grandfather, George by name, (whom I never saw) emigrated to Rochester, N.Y., in the first half of the nineteenth century, and engaged in a remunerative occupation. He later removed to Mount Vernon, N.Y., and married Helen, daughter to Lancelot Allgood, Esq., another English emigrant, of a family whose ancestral seat is the manor of Nunwick, near Hexham, in Northumberland. This union was blessed with three children: Emma, now wife of Mr. Isaac Hill, Principal of the Pelham, N.Y. High School; Mary; and Winfield, father of the present writer. My father was educated both privately, and at a military school, making modern languages his specialty.

Turning to my maternal ancestors, from whom my middle name is derived, we find a typical line of New-England Yankees. The first Phillips of this branch came to Rhode Island from Lincolnshire in the latter part of the seventeenth century, and established himself in the western part of the colony, afterward the town of Foster. My great-grandfather, Jeremiah Phillips, owned one of the first mills in Foster; and, tragically enough, was killed in its machinery when still a young man, leaving Whipple, my grandfather, a lad of thirteen. My grandfather was educated at the East Greenwich Academy (then call The Providence Conference Seminary) and after a brief career as a teacher in the country schools married his own cousin, Miss Rhoby Place, later building a mill and settling at Greene, R.I.[9] (He himself named the village, since he owned all the land it covered. It was formerly "Coffin's Corner") The children of Whipple and Rhoby Phillips are Lillian D., now wife of Dr. Franklin C. Clark of Providence; Sarah S., mother of the autobiographer; Edwin E.; and Anna, now wife of Mr. Edward Gamwell, Associate Editor of The Boston Budget and Beacon. My mother and Aunt Lillian were both educated at the Wheaton Seminary in Norton, Massachusetts, and are both accomplished landscape painters in oil. My Aunt Lillian also attended the State Normal School, and was for some time a teacher. In 1873 my grandfather disposed of his estate and interests at Greene, and removed to Providence, where he entered into the real estate business. At the time of his death in 1904 he was President of The Owyhee Land and Irrigation Co., an Idaho corporation.

Sarah S. Phillips and Winfield Lovecraft were married on June 12, 1889, and on August 20, 1890, the only child, Howard Phillips Lovecraft, was born at the Phillips home, No. 454 Angell Street, Providence. The Lovecrafts soon afterward took up their residence in Auburndale, Massachusetts, where they lived with the family of the well-known poetess, Miss Louise Imogen Guiney, a friend of my mother's, until their permanent home should be built.

It is around the life in Auburndale that my earliest recollections centre. The Guiney house, with its tower chamber, and the huge St. Bernard dogs which the authoress used to keep about the place, are distinct memories of a two-year-old. We there met the aged Dr. Oliver Wendell Holmes shortly before his death, though I admit having no independent remembrance of seeing him. Miss Guiney used to make me recite the jingles of Mother Goose, and whenever she would inquire of me: "Whom do you love"?, my infantile treble would pipe up "Louise Imogen Guiney"!

In 1893 my father was seized with a complete paralytic stroke, due to insomnia and an overstrained nervous system, which took him to the hospital for the remaining five years of his life. He was never afterward conscious, and my image of him is but vague. This of course disrupted all plans for the future, caused the sale of the home site in Auburndale, and the return of my mother and myself to the Phillips home in Providence. Here I spent all the best years of my childhood. The house was a beautiful and spacious edifice, with stable and grounds, the latter approaching a park in the beauty of the walks and trees.

As a child I was very peculiar and sensitive, always preferring the society of grown persons to that of other children. I could not keep away from printed matter. I had learned the alphabet at two, and at four could read with ease, though making most absurd errors in the pronunciation of the long words I loved so well. At five I added penmanship to the list of my accomplishments. Amongst my few playmates I was very unpopular, since I would insist on playing out events in history, or acting according to consistent plots. Thus repelled by humans, I sought refuge and companionship in books, and here was I doubly blessed. The library was stocked with the best volumes accumulated both by the Phillipses and the Lovecrafts, including a good many tomes over a century old, and bearing on the fly-leaves such inscriptions as "Tho. Lovecraft, Gent. His Book, 1787", or "Stephen Place's Book, bought by Him in Boston, May 1805". My maternal grandmother, who died when I was six, was a devoted lover of astronomy, having made that subject a specialty at Lapham Seminary, where she was educated; and though she never personally showed me the beauties of the skies, it is to her excellent but somewhat obsolete collection of astronomical books that I owe my affection for celestial science. Her copy of Burritt's "Geography of the Heavens" is today the most prized volume in my library.

Grimm's Fairy Tales were my delight until at the age of seven I chanced upon Hawthorne's "Wonder Book" and "Tanglewood Tales". Then and there began an undying passion for classical mythology, which was soon increased by Bulfinch's "Age of Fable". All the world became ancient Greece to me; I looked for Naiades in the fountain on the lawn, and forebore to break the shrubbery for fear of harming the Dryades. My attempts at versification, of which I made the first at the age of six, now took on a crude, internally rhyming ballad metre, and I sang of the exploits of Gods and Heroes. (I enclose a specimen entitled "The New Odyssey", written in 1897 (age 7) which my mother has preserved, and which I must ask you to return)[10] About this time I tried attendance at school, but was unable to endure the routine.

Naturally, the quotations in Bulfinch led me to a perusal of the classics in translation, and in particular of that marvellous literary mosaic known as "Garth's Ovid".[11] This is of course wholly in heroic couplets, Dryden and Addison contributing the best parts. The even decasyllabic rhythm seemed to strike some responsive chord in my brain, and I forthwith became wedded to that measure in which most of my subsequent poetical efforts were cast. I now sought everything within my reach that pertained to the age of the classical translators. The books which I used were not modern reprints, but musty old volumes written with "long ſ's". By some freak of childish perversity, I began to use long ſ's myself and to date everything two centuries back. I would sign myself "H. Lovecraft, Gent., 1698", etc. Latin came quite naturally to me, and in other studies my mother, aunts, and grandfather helped me greatly. To my grandfather I owe much. He had travelled extensively in Europe, and was forever delighting me with accounts of London, Paris, and Rome. His graphic description of the ruins of Pompeii produced a particularly strong impression on me, since I was always fond of musing over past grandeur.

When I was ten I set to work to delete every modern word from my vocabulary, and to this end adopted an old Walker's Dictionary (1804) which was for some time my sole authority. All the Queen Anne authors combined to form my literary diet. About this period I developed an interest in the science of Chemistry, and established a laboratory in the cellar. Later on I became fairly proficient in elementary chemical analysis. At the age of twelve my style both in prose and verse was so far formed, that I think you could recognise my workmanship after reading my present efforts.

In 1902 I tried school again, this time with greater success, for I succeeded in graduating from the grammar grades. In January, 1903, astronomy began to engross me completely. I procured a small telescope, and surveyed the heavens constantly. Not one clear night passed without long observation on my part, and the practical, first-hand knowledge thus acquired has ever since been of the highest utility to me in my astronomical writing. In August 1903 (though I knew nothing of the press associations) I commenced to publish an amateur paper called "The R.I. Journal of Astronomy", writing it by hand, and duplicating it on a hectograph. This I continued for four years, first as a weekly, later as a monthly. I was now under the instruction of a private tutor.

My two uncles-in-law, Dr. Clark and Mr. Gamwell, both Brown University men, stimulated my intellectual activities immensely. Dr. Clark is a physician and student of the highest type, whose articles have had a wide circulation in medical journals, whilst Mr. Gamwell is an editor and all-around literary man of very thorough scholarship.

In 1904 the death of my beloved maternal grandfather broke up the home at 454 Angell St., and caused my mother and myself to take our present smaller quarters at No. 598 on the same thoroughfare. Here I was brought into closer contact with the Rev. James Pyke and his aged mother, both poets, whom we had always known, but who were now our next-door neighbors.[12] Mr. Pyke could scarcely approve my old-fashioned style in writing, yet admitted that I could only with difficulty leave a mode of expression so spontaneous and natural to me.

In the same year I entered the Hope Street High School, where I found an admirable staff of teachers, each one of keenest sympathy and understanding for an awkward, nervous and retiring youth. For a year and a half I followed the full curriculum, but during the remainder of my attendance was forced by ill health to absent myself for long periods, and to piece out as good a special course as pedagogical ingenuity might devise. I was particularly devoted to Latin, Ancient History, Physics, and Chemistry.

Meanwhile (1906) I had "broken into print". My first printed piece was a brief attack on astrology, quite like my present work in that direction, published in The Providence Sunday Journal.[13] In August, 1906, I commenced a series of monthly astronomical articles in The Providence Tribune, and began to contribute miscellany to The Pawtuxet Valley Gleaner, a country paper which my mother's family had taken years before when they lived at Greene. Later I changed my monthly articles from The Tribune to The News (where I obtained more favourable space) and was deprived of my other medium through its failure and discontinuance.

In 1908 I should have entered Brown University, but the broken state of my health rendered the idea absurd. I was and am prey to intense headaches, insomnia, and general nervous weakness which prevents my continuous application to any thing. For a time I tried a correspondence course in chemistry, but soon realised that regular duties were not for me.

Thus does the chronicle grow less and less promising. From 1909 onward my efforts have been toward supplying those defects in liberal education which irregular instruction has caused, and I sometimes flatter myself that my style is daily shewing an increase in maturity, depth, and polish. Yet I know that my knowledge is really very limited and fragmentary, and that I have no right to the proud title of "educated man". It is almost with envy that I view the steady and regular progress of a healthy and vigorous youth like my cousin Phillips Gamwell. He will ere many years surpass me;[14] a thought that gives me the feeling of an old man who sees the younger generation take his place. I have merely learnt what I have ardently desired to know, and what has come easily to me. Whilst I shew great erudition in one subject, I may be in total ignorance of another equally important. Though I love to hear music, I have no true musical taste; I studied the violin for two years, but could not bear the monotony of practice. In pictorial art I am utterly unversed. Of Greek I have only the barest rudiments, and but little more of French. German repelled me so much that I know nothing of it. The few words of Spanish which I know are of little more consequence, though I love the stately Castilian pronunciation. Mathematics I detest, and only a supreme effort of the will gained for me the highest marks in Algebra and Geometry at school. In everything I am behind the times. Contemporary literature and drama are a mere blank to me, whilst modern political and social ideals are equally alien. I cannot even now excuse the revolution of America from England, and through the influence of heredity am at heart an Englishman despite my American birth. My knowledge of the world is no more than could be expected from one reared in seclusion; I have never been outside the three states of Rhode Island, Massachusetts, and Connecticut! The dry and disagreeable nature of my conversation has excluded me from social popularity; and the hermit-like existence which I lead has made me so introspective that I have unconsciously become a supreme egotist. I suppose that retirement has warped my judgment, and led me to consider everything merely in its relation to myself. I welcome amateur journalism as a possible means of obtaining a greater breadth of mind. Until I took the local club in hand I had never come into personal contact with the real masses, the "mobile vulgus",[15] and I find much food for reflection in their condition.

Such is the life of a peculiar and incompletely instructed character. After reading it, you may well marvel at the temerity which permits me to seek a place amongst amateurs of brilliant attainments and solid education.

I do not suppose I can offer any apology which will justify the foregoing reams of dulness. You asked for "a few autobiographical details" and have received a volume. I sincerely hope that you will tell me something of your own career, for I detect a certain similarity in our tastes, and feel that perhaps you are what I might have been, had not my ill health and nervous temperament made me the eccentric that I am.

I enclose a satirical piece introducing the Providence amateurs to the United at large, modelled after your own "A. J. Bird" verses.[16] I shall let the local club publish it in the first number of the paper which they expect to issue some time in January. If there is any possible form of flattery which I have neglected to use in these lines, please let me know. I have added a few notes to explain personal allusions. Since I am wholly unacquainted with the club-ites, this is really the best I can do. Basinet tells me that two of the members, Reilly and Byland,[17] may drop out in the near future; but I thought that even so, I might as well immortalise them in numbers.

 I wish I might organise a club amongst my own few acquaintances, but most of them are now dispersed beyond the radius of easy communication. One of my earliest friends, Chester P. Munroe, son of State Senator A. P. Munroe, is now in Asheville, N.C.,[18] and may come into the United soon. He has not yet written much for publication, but has a love of narrative and descriptive prose, and is capable of development.

 But here I really must stop. I ought to know better than to scribble on to such an unconscionable extent.

 With best wishes, and hoping to hear from you again,
  I remain,
   as ever,
    Your obt. servt.
     H. P. LOVECRAFT

P.S. I found the November BOOKMAN at the public library, and enjoyed Goldsmith's newly discovered verses very keenly.[19]
     H. P. L.

[Enclosure: "To the Members of the U. A. P. A. from the Providence Amateur Press Club" (as by "A. J. Bird, Jun."); with explanatory notes.]

Notes

1. Published by Merritt Roblee of "Skateville" (near Hales Corners), WI.
2. So transcribed in AHT, possibly in error. It has not been found. Note that Gertrude L. Merkel published in *Badger* (January 1915) a story called "'Kithadurl'" about one Willie Kithadurl," meaning Willie Kiss-a-Girl. Possibly HPL's Johnny Tissadirl was meant to be Willie Kithadurl, or something similar.
3. "S'Matter, Pop?" (initially "Nippy's Pop" [1910]) by Charles M. Payne (1873–1964) was a comic strip that ran from 1911 to 1940.
4. Nick Carter was a fictional character, first appearing as a dime novel private detective in 1886 and then in various other formats, such as the *Nick Carter Detective Magazine*. Diamond Dick was a character created by William B. Schwartz, first appearing in 1878; he was inspired by herbal-medicine promoter and showman George B. McClellan (1858?–1911), who himself went by the nickname Diamond Dick.
5. The *Pippin* was an amateur journal produced by the Appleton High School Press Club in Appleton, WI, where MWM was a teacher at the time. HPL wrote two poems in appreciation of receipt of the *Pippin*.
6. George S. Schilling replaced Edward F. Daas as Official Editor of the UAPA for

the 1914–15 term. He was the editor of the *Badger*, for which HPL was an assistant editor of the June 1915 issue.

7. In the summer of 1906, HPL began writing a series of astronomy articles for the *Pawtuxet Valley Gleaner*, a rural weekly published in Phenix, RI. HPL stated that he wrote for the paper in 1906–08, but no copies of the *Gleaner* beyond 1906 have come to light.

8. In a much later letter, to Robert E. Howard (25[–29] March 1933), HPL claims that the article he presented to Ms. Blake was "Can the Moon Be Reached by Man?," appearing in the *Pawtuxet Valley Gleaner* for 12 October 1906. See *A Means to Freedom: The Letters of H. P. Lovecraft and Robert E. Howard* (New York: Hippocampus Press, 2009), 583.

9. Whipple V. Phillips (1833–1904) and Robie Alzada Place (1827–1896) were first cousins through common descent from John Rathbun (1750–1810) and his wife Sarah Casey (1755–1813).

10. The title of the poem on the cover of the surviving manuscript is "The Poem of Ulysses, or The Odyssey," although elsewhere in the text the title "The New Odyssey or Ulyssiad for the Young" (among other titles) can be found. This version, called a "Second Edition," dates to 8 November 1897; the first edition appears to have been written prior to HPL's seventh birthday (20 August 1897).

11. Sir Samuel Garth (1661–1719) was a British poet who assembled a celebrated translation of Ovid's *Metamorphoses* (1717), with contributions by John Dryden, Alexander Pope, and many other distinguished poets of the day. HPL owned the Garth translation in the Harper & Brothers ed. of *Ovid* (1837).

12. James Tobey Pyke (1858–1935) was for a time HPL's neighbor, residing at 237 Butler Avenue, around the corner from HPL's home at 598 Angell Street. By January 1916, Pyke had moved to East Providence (see "Introducing Mr. James Pyke," *Conservative*, January 1916; *CE* 1.97). HPL wrote the poem "To the Rev. James Pyke" and published some of Pyke's poetry in his *Conservative*.

13. HPL refers to a letter to the editor published as "No Transit of Mars."

14. Phillips Gamwell (b. 1898), son of Annie E. P. and Edward F. Gamwell, died of tuberculosis on 31 December 1916.

15. "The fickle mob."

16. "To the Members of the United Amateur Press Association . . ." "A. J. Bird" means *ajay bird*, or an amateur journalist.

17. Reilly is unidentified. The other is Frederick Aloysius Byland (1894–1967).

18. Presumably Munroe facilitated the appearance of HPL's late astronomy column, "Mysteries of the Heavens Revealed by Astronomy," in the *Asheville Gazette-News* (February–May 1915).

19. Walter Jerrold, "A New Found Poem by Oliver Goldsmith's." *Bookman* (New York) 40, No. 3 (November 1914): 253–54.

[4]   [AHT]

598 Angell St., Providence, R.I.,
January 16, 1915

My dear Mr. Moe:—

I perceive that you are not inclined to concur in my belief

that the Teutonic is the highest of all racial stocks, but while I may have spoken too dogmatically, my opinion is none the less very firm. In treating of this matter I must first define the term "Teuton" exactly as I understand it, in order that no misconception may arise. The pure Teutons are the "Xanthochroi" or light-haired, blue-eyed, pale-skinned dolichocephali as described by Huxley,[1] amongst whom the class of languages we call "Teutonic" arose, and who today constitute the majority of the Teutonic-speaking population of the world. In ancient history, they played a minor part, retaining their primitive, unspoiled, savage condition as though held in reserve by Fate to await the downfall of the Graeco-Roman peoples. It is possible, though not perfectly established, that the Achaean or Homeric Greeks were Teutons, but these had given place to the aboriginal Ionian and invading Dorian stocks before the opening of Greek history. Considering the place of the Teuton in mediaeval and modern history, however, I see no possible way of denying him an actual biological superiority over the rest of mankind. In widely separated localities and under widely diverse conditions his innate racial qualities alone have raised him to pre-eminence. There is not a branch of modern civilisation that is not of his making. As the power of the Roman Empire declined, the Teuton sent down into northern Italy, Gaul, and Spain the re-vivifying elements which saved those countries for posterity. Though now largely lost in the mixed population, the Teutons are the true founders of all the so-called Latin races. The mediaeval aristocracy of Spain and Italy was Gothic, just as that of Gaul was Frankish. All the life had fled from the old population; the Teuton only was creative and dominant. Is it not true, that as the native elements have absorbed the Teutonic invaders, the civilisations of the various Latin states have declined? Do not the France, Spain, and Italy of to-day bear every mark of national degeneracy?

Turning to the lands whose population is mainly Teutonic, we behold a striking proof of the qualities of the race. England and Germany are the supreme empires of the world, whilst the virile virtues of the Belgians have lately been demonstrated in a manner which will live forever in song and story. The Swiss and Dutch need no encomium from me; history sings their praises more loudly than can I. The Scandinavians are immortalised by the exploits of the Vikings and Normans, whose conquests over man and Nature extended from the sun-baked isles of Sicily to the ice-bound shores of Greenland, even attaining our own distant Vineland across the sea. The Teutonic mind is masterful, temperate, and just. Is it necessary to say that no other race is equally capable of self-government, or to recall the fact that not one square inch of Teutonic territory is governed save by its own inhabitants? An illustration of the superiority of the Teuton may be found in the condition of the British Isles. Wherever the Saxon or Scandinavian invaders have swept the native Celts aside, or largely mixed with them, civilisation has followed, whilst the remaining purely Celtic areas are manifestly in a very crude state. England, most of Scotland, and eastern Ireland are the seat of a brilliant civilisation, whilst the people of the extreme northern Scottish highlands and the west or central Irish bogs are little above barbarism. Whether the ancient Greeks and Romans were the equals or superiors of the Teutons we need not consider. Both of these races had declined and become vitiated with the vilest strains before our own ancestors appeared on the stage of history. Our contemporaries require even less attention. The mercurial southern Frenchman, the indolent Spaniard, the excitable, vindictive Italian and the semi-barbarous Slav all stand out in sharp contrast to the vigorous and dominant Teuton. We cannot attribute the inferior characteristics of the various non-Teutonic nationalities to non-racial conditions; a race makes its own conditions. Where can you find a decadent or vicious Teutonic state? Austria-Hungary, of course, is too cosmopolitan to serve as a criterion. In New-England the replacement of the original English stock by mixed races has been attended with a disgusting deterioration of the whole tone of the community. The mongrel intruders, unfitted to participate in the blessings of a democracy, form a repulsive lower class without mind or morality. In the Middle West, where the immigration is mostly Teutonic, newcomers are easily assimilated, and the population never loses approximate homogeneity. Here, however, the very thought of assimilation is absurd. In the better districts of our cities every doorplate bears an old Yankee name, whilst the slums are merely bits of Ireland, Italy, Judaea, or the like, as the case may be. Non-Teutonic races have created an unsound, unnatural, and ominous social order. Is it any wonder, then, that I burst into indignant verse against such conditions?[2] Dogmatic I may be, but methinks I have much evidence on my side.

My theological beliefs are likely to startle one who has imagined me an orthodox adherent of the Anglican Church. My father was of that faith, and was married by its rites, yet, having been educated in my mother's distinctively Yankee family, I was early placed in the Baptist Sunday school. There, however, I soon became exasperated by the literal, Puritanical doctrines, and constantly shocked my preceptors by expressing scepticism of much that was taught me. It became evident that my young mind was not of a religious cast, for the much exhorted "simple faith" in miracles and the like came not to me. I was not long forced to attend the Sunday school, but read much in the Bible from sheer interest. The more I read the Scriptures, the more foreign they seemed to me. I was infinitely fonder of the Graeco-Roman mythology, and when I was eight astounded the family by declaring myself a Roman pagan. Religion struck me so vague a thing at best, that I could perceive no advantage of any one system over any other. I had really adopted a sort of Pantheism, with the Roman gods as personified attributes of deity. When I was eleven, I summed up my feelings in a poem supposed to be the utterances of a Roman pagan in the time of the Imperator Constantinus. I give it entire:

TO THE OLD PAGAN RELIGION

Olympian Gods! How can I let ye go,
And pin my faith to this new Christian creed?
Can I resign the deities I know
For him who on a cross for man did bleed?

How in my weakness can my hopes depend
On one lone God, though mighty be his power?
Why can Jove's host no more assistance lend,
To sooth my pains, and cheer my troubled hour?

Are there no Dryads on these wooded mounts,
O'er which I oft in desolation roam?
Are there no Naiads in these crystal founts,
Nor Nereids upon the ocean foam?

Fast spreads the new; the older faith declines;
The name of Christ resounds upon the air;
But my wrack'd soul in solitude repines,
And gives the Gods their last-received prayer.

My present opinions waver betwixt Pantheism and rationalism. I am a sort of agnostic, neither affirming nor denying anything. I recognise the profound and beneficial moral influence of Christianity, and have a sincere and appreciative respect for all regular Protestant denominations. I could not, however, tolerate Papists, Adventists, Christian Scientists, or Mormons. Their absurdities exceed all bounds of human credulity. I can scarcely wait for your essay, "Why I Am Not a Freethinker". I understand that Mr. Morton is a man of liberal education, so that your controversy must have been a veritable Gigantomachia.[3] Did you read Ira A. Cole's article, "The Gods of our Fathers" in *The United Official Quarterly*? His theology seemed so much like mine, that I wrote him a letter, whereupon he gave further details of his Nature-worship. Reared in the open, he has without the aid of a classical education acquired a truly Graeco-Roman cast of mind.

I remain
  Very sincerely yours
    H. P. Lovecraft.

Notes

1. HPL refers to two essays by British biologist Thomas Henry Huxley (1825–1895), "On the Methods and Results of Ethnology" (1865) and "On the Aryan Question" (1890). Huxley defines the term "Xanthochroi" as denoting those races that "are 'yel-

low' haired and 'pale' in complexion." See *Man's Place in Nature and Other Anthropological Essays* 231.

2. HPL refers to such poems as "Providence in 2000 A.D." (1912) and "New-England Fallen" (1912), which feature attacks on non-Teutonic immigrants in New England.

3. In Greek mythology, the battle between the Gigantes and the Olympian gods for supremacy of the cosmos.

[5]   [AHT]

598 Angell St.,
Providence, R.I.,
February 7, 1915

My dear Mr. Moe:— Nowhere have I seen the essentials of Christianity better defended than in your essay "Why I am not a Freethinker". Your appeal to Semitic history on the one hand, and to the facts of Nature on the other, form an argument well calculated to offset anything Mr. Morton could have written. Yet I do not believe that any human agency could give me any real faith in any one religion as distinguished from any other. That one particular tribe of Semites happened to develop a religion superior to those of the adjoining tribes, and that its influence kept them above the general level of their kind, seems not enough to establish the supremacy of that individual religion. Rather the superiority of the tribe of Israel caused its members to interpret the common Semitic religion in a purer manner than the others. In other words it was not their religion that made the Jews the purest of Semites; it was the purity of the Jews that made their religion what it was.

The vastly superior Aryan stock likewise had a single primitive Nature-religion. As the tribes separated, their religions became separate. The Romans acquired a set of stern abstract gods with whom they attempted to bargain, and whom they sometimes tried to cheat; the Greeks formed the idea of a very human set of deities, with the grossest vices as well as the virtues of mortals; whilst our own ancestors, the Teutons, looked up to a pantheon of hardy, virtuous gods, who kept their race in a state of virile purity long after the Greeks and Romans had sunk to the depths. Shall we then say that the religion of Asgard, the faith of Thor, Woden, and Valhalla is the only true religion, because it kept the Teutons high above their effeminate southern neighbours, and has brought to them the supremacy of the earth today? I could fall down in prayer before the altar of a Woden far more readily than before one of the Hebrew Jehovah, for I am a Teuton, and I might recognise that it is Woden who has kept my race above all others.

In considering the effect of religion on the Semitic mind, we must recognise that this branch of the white race is above all others prone to fanaticism, and to the unreasoning following of some deity or another. In later years did not the Arabs carry everything before them under the influence of their Allah and his only true prophet Mahomet?

As to the natural craving of primitive man for some sort of religion, is this not merely the intermediate stage between the beast who lacks all curiosity and the educated man who understands the workings of Nature? Is it not simply mankind's first vague gropings after an explanation of things; the hazy dawn of his intellectual activity and unrest?

So much for orthodox religion. As to the existence of some vague deity, who can say? Are not the natural forces of the universe in themselves some sort of god? Are not the immutable laws of Creation in themselves some sort of vast, omnipotent intelligence? Deity needs not personality nor human form to be truly divine; that which is supremely great, incomprehensible, and unalterable may be called "God" as well as by any other name. But under this assumption, God is everywhere and in everything; this is true Pantheism. If we desire more intimate and more easily understood forms of Deity, we must personify the more common attributes of Deity, creating a system of Gods and Heroes, and adopting Polytheism.

Is it not true that all races distinguished for their mental power, the logical Greeks, the judicial Romans, and the dominant Teutons of today, arose from Polytheistic stock? I cannot understand how we Teutons, descendants of hardy Pagan men of the North, and heirs to the manly virtues bequeathed by the worship of Alfadur, Woden, and Thor, should so tenaciously adhere to an alien Asiatic, Semitic, Southern form of religion.

You may think it strange that an ignoramus like myself should fail to be converted by such a truly wonderful argument as you offer in your essay, but you must remember that I am one who feels the influence of biological *race* above all else. I am first of all a Teuton and an Aryan. My hair and eyes are too light brown, my nose too straight, my skin too white, and my stature too tall for me to contain a Semitic or Jewish mind. I am atavistic; I belong in the forests of central Germany where my ancestors dwelt before they ever heard of the strange religion which came to them second hand from Judea through Rome; before they ever conquered the isle of Britannia where they laid the foundations of the world's present centre of civilisation. Yes, I fear that I am indeed a hopeless Pagan, and if I ever see a future life it will be in Asgard or the regions beyond the Styx rather than the Semitic heaven or h———.

Hoping to hear from you at your convenience, and trusting that my frank Paganism has not shocked you too much,
I remain
      Your obt. humble servant,
      H. P. Lovecraft.

[6]   [AHT]
598 Angell St.,
Providence, R.I.,
February 8, 1915

My dear Mr. Moe:—
      The illness from which I have suffered recently is well calculated to sustain my mother's contention, that I have never grown up. It was chicken-pox! My maladies certainly have a decidedly juvenile cast. At the age of nineteen I was nearly killed by the measles, and now, at twenty-four, I must undergo the ignominy of another equally childish ailment. This, however, was not severe. The News article which I sent you yesterday was composed and typewritten whilst the disease was at its worst.[1]
      Best regards from
H. P. Lovecraft.

Notes

1. Presumably a clipping of HPL's "The February Skies," [Providence] *Evening News* 46, No. 61 (30 January 1915): 8.

[7]   [AHT]
598 Angell St.,
Providence, R.I.
September 17, 1915

My dear Mr. Moe:—
      I am prepared to defend against all opponents and for an indefinite period the suppression of the "r" sound in the places where I suppress it. "Born" and "dawn" make a perfect rhyme. The vowel sound is settled by Webster, who gives it the "ô" mark, as in "fôr", which stands at the bottom of the page as a sample. This distinguishes it from "borne". Now for the "r". I have investigated this matter at some length, and am not willing to acknowledge its permissibility at the places where the New-Yorkers and perhaps some Westerners roll or trill it. That is, "far" is not "färrr......" but "fäh", or simply "fä". There is something repulsive to me in the pronunciation "bôrrrr....n" instead of "bôrn" or "bawn". I recognise trillings and rollings in other tongues, Spanish, for instance, with its "Santa Marrrr...ea" for "Santa Maria", but I deem such no part of classic English. Mrs. Louise H. Collins of Mississippi, one of Mrs. Renshaw's latest recruits, has taken up this question in a long essay lately submitted to me for criticism. Mrs. Collins is a lady of sixty years, and has studied the subject considerably, seeking now to uphold the Southern (as well as New-England) suppression of the redundantly rolled "r". Her arguments are all good, and will soon, I trust, appear in the amateur press. I believe that the suppressed roll is characteristic of the best London speech, which is of course the

standard. What matter if the majority do roll the "r"? The speech of the centre of culture is the standard. We call the language of Dante "Italian", yet how many persons outside of Tuscany ever spoke it in his day? The lower classes in England mumble and mouth the language in every conceivable manner, but gentlemen throughout the realm seek to emulate the tones of the capital. The native accent of Boston, America's literary capital, ought to be sought after if one desires a pure American standard, and it is needless to say that no good Bostonian or New-Englander ever rolled an "r" except through affectation. I can assure you that the rolled "r" is but seldom heard in the best Rhode Island circles, though of course some New Yorkers have imported it. Yet their children will probably abandon it to deserved oblivion. And since the splendid old original stock of the Virginia and New-England colonies reject it, I believe that "rrrr......." is doomed to annihilation. The *Encyclopaedia Britannica* calls it a North-of-England provincialism, and John Walker's *Rhetorical Grammar* (Boston Edition, 1814), whilst advocating a *slightly sounded* "r", admits without reserve that:

"In England, and particularly in London, the 'r' in 'bard', 'card', 'regard', etc. is pronounced so much in the throat that it is little more than the middle or Italian 'a', heard in 'father', as in 'baad', 'caad', 'regaad', etc."

I said that Walker recommended a slightly stronger "r", but you may see from another passage *how little rolling* he wished:

"Thus, 'Rome', 'river', 'rage' may have the 'r' as forcible as in Ireland; but 'bar', 'bard', 'card', 'regard', etc. must have it nearly as soft as in London."

I think that the consensus of British, New-England, and Southern opinion robs our language of the unpleasant "rrrr....", hence as a New-Englander of British blood I should not alter the usage I have followed ever since my childish lips first began to pronounce words.

I remain
    As ever,
        Your ob^t humble serv^t,
            H. P. Lovecraft.

[8]   [AHT]

            598 Angell St.,
              Providence, R.I.,
                May 18, 1916

My dear Mr. Moe:—

    As to the final "rrr...", I readily admit that classic poets seem to regard it in their choice of rhymes, since it undoubtedly was prevalent before the Augustan Age of letters. Tradition heeded it as such things as walked or unconfined were heeded. The poets felt it necessary to discriminate between "born" and "dawn", just as they found it necessary to omit the letter "e" in walk'd, unconfin'd, etc. In an age when every one pronounced "walked" as a monosyllable, it was deemed proper by the poets to *write* it "walk'd". From a like attention to precedent and etymology, they refrained from recognising the extinction of "rrrr....". Indeed, as I quoted from Walker, the *previous* existence of "rrr..." was well known, and its complete omission very mildly censured; even as Addison lamented the dropping of the final syllable of "walked", or the substitution of "walks" for "walketh".

But my standard is eighteenth century London—the civilisation of Dr. Johnson and his club. I am sure Mr. Garrick never "rrolled rrr's" on the stage of Drury-Lane Theatre![1] And indeed, 'tis hard for me to think of former great actors and orators doing this thing. If I may make a much-despis'd heroick couplet—

> Kind Heav'n! Is't thus great BETTERTON[2] did rage,
> And with arrtistic Rrr...s adorrn the stage?

(If you wish to retaliate, you may write *my* pronunciation of the last line as follows—

"And with ah-tistic ah's adawn the Stage")

My use of rhymes like "born"—"dawn" was wholly unconscious. Since the sounds were to me identical, I neglected to investigate etymological principles. However, I believe that our controversy has resulted in a victory for you, since out of respect to tradition I shall probably abandon my former practice, just as I always drop the elided vowel in verbs like "adorn'd" or "view'd". You have shewn me another good old-fashion'd practice to follow! Of course, I shall not change my *pronunciation;* I shall merely discard such opportunities for rhyme as are afforded by "war" and "law", and the like. One of the pieces I enclose has an instance of the objectionable method you censure, but my latest piece, one hundred sixteen lines,[3] follows your precept. I can reply in one sentence to two of your paragraphs; that containing your observations on the progress of language, and that containing strictures on my use of well-worn expressions in verse. My answer is, that the chief aim of my writing is to achieve the Georgian atmosphere with as much fidelity as is possible to one living in this degenerate age.

I care not how much English may decay; what was good enough for Sam Johnson is good enough for me! A perpetually changing language is a mark of barbarism; 'tis said that some savage dialects change beyond recognition in four or five generations; yet classick Latin endur'd unchang'd for centuries, save in a few unscholarly particularities of immaterial nature. 'Twas only amongst the vulgar, that the sonorous lines of Virgil, and the polish'd periods of Cicero, failed to serve as models till the fall of the Empire. I deem the Golden Age of our language a just pattern for posterity, and will have naught of the new-fangled tricks of the passing hour. I own with readiness, that I am a complete "crank"; yet if being old-fashioned amuse me, I vow, no one is the worse thereby!

As to my "poetry", pray do not imagine for a moment that I am deluded concerning its quality. No one knows better than I, that there is *absolutely nothing to it*. It is merely a succession of sounds balanced to please *my* ears alone; and its verbiage is selected wholly with the desire to mirror the atmosphere of the age I admire so much. I employ those expressions which I find most frequently in Georgian authors, especially pairs of words—a noun with its accustomed adjective, as copied from one bard by another throughout the classic age, till the two have become virtually welded into one word, or stock phrase. I revel in such reminiscent lines as

>The humble swain, in verdant copse at ease,
>Enjoys the shade, and thanks th' o'erhanging trees.

Each phrase and image is to me laden with literary associations. Every penny-a-line hack in Grub Street from 1680 to 1810 has probably used these very words; if not in this exact order, at least, in a manner not far different. Such words and expressions are *scenery*, as it were, to set the stage for the reënactment of the past. What a quaintly idyllic little world those artificial writers made for themselves and their publick! I would fain dwell therein forever—blest with sights that have never been seen, and happiness that has never existed!

>Benignant spirits bless th' adjacent mead,
>And swains their flocks through fertile pastures lead;
>The friendly Fauns the neighb'ring grove protect,
>Whilst crystal founts a Naiad train reflect.
>At eventide sweet Orpheus tunes his lay
>To lull the hills, and speed the fading day;
>Nor sings alone, for o'er th' expansive wold
>Fair Philomela chants from throat of gold.
>Such joys as these no others can excel;
>In this sweet country ever would I dwell!
>No sordid sight or tainted thought intrudes,
>But all is shap'd to suit my changing moods:
>All churls are honest, and all squires are kind,
>And King and boor enjoy th' untarnish'd mind.
>'Tis ever sunshine when I wish it so,
>But at my will the gentle torrents flow.
>The bard is here supreme in ev'ry joy,
>No cares oppress, or cruel truths annoy:
>When all the world my weary spirit pains,
>May I not flee where Pan, idyllic, reigns?
>Seize on my pencil, and in rhyme depart
>For regions where fond mem'ry warms the heart?
>Stay! vandal critick, ere thy ruthless line
>Destroy the only solace that is mine![4]

(The above is impromptu, though its nature robs the statement of all imputation of vanity!)

I am enclosing two of my metrical crimes. "An American to Mother England" was published in Herdman's *Poesy* last January,[5] but will be reprinted in *The United Official Quarterly* in order that I may enter it for laureateship (of course, I have no hope of first honours).[6] The other one, to General Lee,[7] was designed for his birthday, and will not be timely until Jan. 19 rolls around again. Be not too harrsh with them! They need not be return'd or even sav'd. But I cannot come to believe that "Charrley of the Comics" is my masterpiece! I would hesitate before affixing my name publicly to that! As to my freakish odd metrical work, let me shew you something in a very unusual form. This "catchy" dactyl was used by Miss Grace I. Gish of Roanoke, Va., whose verse "What Are the Apple-Trees Whispering" I corrected lately. I added the following observation in the same metre:

> List to the dactyls a-ripping,
> Blithesomely, carelessly, rippling,
> Metre is haunting,
> Accents a-flaunting,
> Clever the rune,
> Vibrant the tune.
> Syllables proper, and not a word wanting.
> Perfect the rhyme,
> Rhythmic the time,
> Images lofty, and subject sublime!

Possibly I shall adopt this metre for the Dept. of Publick Criticism!
I am ever sincerely yours,
H. P. Lovecraft.

Notes

1. David Garrick (1717–1779), celebrated British actor and a member of Samuel Johnson's literary circle.
2. Thomas Betterton (1635?–1710), the leading British actor during the later 17th century.
3. HPL's "latest" was "The Smile."
4. Now published as ["The Solace of Georgian Poetry"], *AT* 426–27.
5. Edward F. Herdman, editor of *Poesy*.
6. The poem was not so reprinted.
7. "Lines on Gen. Robert Edward Lee."

[9] [AHT]

598 Angell St.,
Providence, R.I.
June 1, 1916

My dear Mr. Moe:—

First of all, I wish to disavow completely the idea in your letter, that I had said *your* pronunciation of the final "rrr..." would be considered as affected here. If I conveyed that impression through careless writing, let me here apologise. What I really meant to say was exactly in line with your own idea—I merely stated that some *Rhode-Islanders* copy the rolled "r" *deliberately* from New-Yorkers. This is what I meant by *affectation*. No child born and bred here pronounces the word "father", as other than "fä´-thä˝", hence when he begins, in later life, to depart from general custom and say "faththirrrrrr........", it is only natural to attribute the change to affectation. Personally I can say that I scarcely knew of such a thing as a rolled "rrr..." until I was in school, and heard it from a boy whose parents were from New York. I will admit that we used to plague this youthful scion of the Empire State rather cruelly—out-rolling him in our mimicry. One fellow, I remember well, used to mock him by crying: "Oh, dearrrr....! Look who's herrrr......e!" every time he met him. Later on, however, I heard the rolled "rrr.." from others, mostly New-Yorkers, and I had come to look upon it as a New York localism—such as "woild" for "world", or "momunt" for "moment". Your letter of criticism regarding my "born–dawn" rhyme was my first clear impression that the usage was common in the West as well as in New York. As you see—I have paid very little attention to modern affairs and practices. But an article by a new United member, Mrs. Collins of Mississippi, received about the same time as your criticism, lent additional interest. She takes a position *exactly opposite* to yours, holding that the rolled "rrrr...." is *totally inadmissible*. She erroneously believed that the "r" is rolled *throughout the North,* and I had much difficulty in convincing her that in New-England it is heard no more than in her native South. But as I said before—*copying* may alter the state of affairs. Edward H. Cole, whom you once designated as your *ideal* amateur, *does* roll his "rrrr....'s", though he is, so far as I know, a native New-Englander. He must do so deliberately, for philological reasons best known to himself, since it is *certainly not natural* in this part of the country. So here we stand—I *do not* consider your pronunciation affected, since it is that of your locality, and I claim for myself an equal lack of affectation, since I adhere to the sounds amongst which I grew up.

Speaking of authority in these matters, I cannot regard anything as really authentic if it departs from good London usage. London is the centre of our culture, and if we do not attend its precepts we shall have nothing but chaos and eventual Babel. I never opened a copy of the Standard Dictionary in my life, though it used to lie about on various tables at high school. It is too modern and liberal for a Conservative. I use Stormonth's Dictionary, which my father (not fah-thirrr....) used before me! That is a genuine London product, compiled and published in Great Britain. The old book I cited on "rrrr..." was Walker's Rhetorical Grammar, 1814.

Your "family letter" plan[1] is very good, and I should like to nominate *myself* as one of your circle. Another desirable participant is Rheinhart Kleiner, whose correspondence is delightfully literary and interesting. Ira A. Cole is certainly well fitted for such a thing, even though you object to the sentiment of his "Pantheist" in the recent *Trail*. I approved this piece, and advised him to let Hutchinson print it—wherein our opinions differ. I like Cole's refreshing primitiveness—he is positively primordial.

As to my "pomes" in various metres, I can only say that they make *me* laugh. I am going to perpetrate a hoax with "The Bride of the Sea", publishing it under the name of *"Lewis Theobald, Jr.",* to confuse the critics. Theobald, of course, was the original hero of the Dunciad.[2] I wonder if any self-constituted reviewers will "fall for it"!

Sincerely,
H P Lovecraft.

Notes

1. HPL writes of the advent of the Kleicomolo, one of several round-robin letter exchanges conceived by MWM, where each syllable represented the name of a given correspondent (Klei = Rheinhart Kleiner; Co = Ira A. Cole; Mo = MWM; Lo = HPL). Others to suggested by HPL were the Gallomo, Gremolo [including Sonia Greene], and Lologallo [including FBL and SL]. *Coryciani* derives its name not from its members but from the Corycian Cave on the slopes of Mount Parnassus (the home of the Muses), named after the nymph Corycia.

2. Lewis Theobald (1688–1744), British editor and author, irked Alexander Pope by criticizing his edition of Shakespeare in the treatise *Shakespeare Restored* (1726). In response, Pope made Theobald the antihero of the first version of his mock-epic poem *The Dunciad* (1728). HPL dedicated "Unda, or the Bride of the Sea" to MWM.

[10]   [AHT]

598 Angell St.,
Providence, R.I.,
August 29, '16

My dear Mo:—
    I was the other day perusing a volume of Mr. Lowell's verse at random, when I came upon a note in the introduction of the "Bigelow [*sic*] Papers" which recalled to my mind our old "rrrr..." controversy. Mr. Lowell seems to be on your side, since he recognises the suppression of the burr or roll as a New England peculiarity. He adds, 'that the Yankee shows considerable ingenuity in evading the pronunciation of the letter, even before a vow-

el'.¹ However, I am govern'd by London standards, and have no intention of acquiring a roll or brogue of any sort.

EPITAPH ON Y^E LETTERR RRR........

Dearr readerr, pause—and shed a tearr,
Forr one that ly'th interred herrre.
Poorr Masterr Rrr scant welcome found
On sterrn New-England's rocky ground;
Sorre spurrn'd on Earrth, and torrn with woes,
In burial soon he gain'd repose:
Today we hearr the roll no morre,
Save that of ocean on the shorre!

Lvdovicvs.Theobaldvs.Ivnior.

But I must not further borre a busy man. Only too soon will you be subjected to the ordeal of perusing my part of the Kleicomolo letter.
Wherefore, Sir,
    I have ye honour to subscribe myself
        Yr most oblig'd humble Servt.
           H. P. Lovecraft.

Notes

1. The passage quoted is found in the introduction to the long poem *The Biglow Papers* (1848) by James Russell Lowell (1819–1891).

[11] [ALS, JHL]

598 Angell St.,
Providence, R.I.,
May 30, 1917.

My dear Mo:—

    I received your welcome note of 27th inst., and will endeavour to forward suitable U.A.P.A. literature to your possible recruit as soon as I can—probably this afternoon. It both pleases & surprises me to learn that amateur journalism has at last received recognition in a real *book*—even though only in a footnote, and under the doubtfully correct name of "National Association of Amateur Journalists".¹ I shall inform the Lincoln High School that genuine amateur journalism is to be found exclusively in the *United*—Rev. Graeme Davis to the contrary notwithstanding!² I trust that you may soon find the missing Kansas City request for information.
    Your new college connexion is indeed interesting and unusual—and will, I trust, prove beneficial to your purse & physique. Such laborious exercise,

coupled with a wholesome & primitive diet, should do much toward restoring the strength which mental overtaxation & sedentary life tend to exhaust. In the matter of *grey hair*, I may overtake you ere long; for at the age of 26 I possess an appreciable number of silvery strands, scattered impartially over a thick thatch of brown. I doubt not but that five years more will find me quite perceptibly iron-grey in my hirsute [*sic*] colour-scheme.

Realising the utter inconsequentiality of one man more or less in this insignificant world, I lately endeavoured to justify my hitherto useless existence by ending it in the army. Specifically, I attempted despite my frail & nervous physique to enlist in the R.I. National Guard; trusting to the sheer force of psychological stimulus to keep me alive and on my feet until a Hunnish missile might gracefully dispose of me. Since I have no actual *disease* or abnormal organs, I nearly passed the physical tests by judicious restraint in answering questions; but my mother & family physicians were finally able to frustrate my belligerent ambitions and bring about my rejection for physical disability. I presume they will do the same thing when the draft occurs; though for mine own part I think I could do much worse than greatly extinguish (if not distinguish) myself in a more or less effulgent blaze of martial glory. I am told that a week of camp life & its hardships would probably wreck my constitution forever; but who can tell until it is attempted? And besides, what is the life or health of one weakling, when thousands of sturdy and useful young men are to be killed, crippled, and disfigured in a few months? Verily, 'tis amusing to make so great a stir about a little matter like this, when in the interminable recesses of ethereal space all mankind is but a superfluous atom! My despised theories of ultimate & absolute truth are (or ought to be) quite comforting in this hour of stress & trial! And speaking of eccentric theories, my sense of humour impels me to enclose for your perusal & amusement a *negro* advertisement which appears each day in the *Providence News*. Behold! from the humblest of races springs the greatest of prophets—Justus J. Evans, D.G., The Founder, Constructor, and Archbishop of the Only & Original "Almighty Church"—modestly described by himself as "the WISEST TEACHER that there is now in creation, so far as man is concerned."[3] Yea, verily, the African is a peculiar animal! I suppose Evans is a typical black "exhorter" who has saved up enough money to break into print—and he has certainly "broken in" with commendable vigour! The negro mind is a singular thing—a centre of grotesquely distorted ideas & extravagant conceptions that would brand any Caucasian brain as idiotic or insane. I wonder how even so plebeian a paper as the *News* can bring itself to accept such ludicrous advertising. Rev. W. Sunday[4] must look to his laurels, now that this ebony victim of megalomania & exaggerated ego hath dawned above the theological horizon!

I trust that Klei, or Co, (whichever the offender may be) will set aside his indolence or business for a sufficient time to permit the early return of the Kleicomolo to its source. A delay until autumn would be lamentable indeed;

though of course a *real* classic is immortal, and loses nothing by the passage of the ages. I enclose a couple of my recent offences in the domain of versification, both of bellicose type. You will observe that I make no attempt at creating truly artistic poesie, but merely scribble to suit myself.

> Let others seek th' Aonian spark divine—
> For me, the accent and the measur'd line!

Regarding Campbell's second sacrifice upon the cruel altar of Hymen, I must say that he has my complete sympathy—though it seems as if previous experience might have forewarned him. According to my view, the best thing which a man may have betwixt himself and the fair, is *distance*. As P.J.C. related the catastrophe to me, his second venture was a "spite marriage"; due to the injured feelings which resulted from his heartless & summary jilting by a fair, frivolous & flirtatious amateuress of Piqua, Ohio. This calculating and fickle damsel, to whom he was engaged in the spring of 1915, decided to relocate her affections after Campbell underwent his hospital ordeal—and the Sage of Georgetown, smarting under the slight, thought his engagement ring too good to be wasted; so placed it upon the finger of one whom he now lovingly describes as a "crass red nurse". (P.J.C.'s lack of chivalrous sentiment is quaintly refreshing. His ethical code spurns such mediaevalism!) The nurse, an illiterate coal-miner's daughter, proved uncongenial as a life partner; so has been allowed to drift away into the dim corridors of unpleasant memories. But lest you grow fatigued, I will close my epistle with this page.
  With best wishes,
    Sincerely,
      H. P. Lovecraft

P.S. I received & appreciated *The Pippin*. Your scholars are bright & enterprising, giving ample justification to my estimate of you as a pedagogue—an estimate which you modestly protest is overdrawn! H.P.L.

Notes

1. Unidentified.
2. Rev. Francis Graeme Davis (1881–1938) was Official Editor (1917–18) and President (1918–19) of the NAPA. At that time he wrote harshly of the rival UAPA in his amateur journal, the *Lingerer*, leading to HPL's essay "A Reply to *The Lingerer*," *Tryout* 3, No. 7 (June 1917): [9–12] (*CE* 1.157–58).
3. Evangelist Justus J. Evans (1860–1925), founder of the Almighty Church of God, held camp meetings and traveled throughout the Eastern and Midwestern states to raise funds for the Almighty Church Training Colony in Vienna, OH.
4. Billy Sunday (1862–1935), the histrionic evangelist who began touring the country, holding outdoor revival meetings, in 1896. In 1916 he was conducting a particularly popular series of meetings on the East Coast.

[12]   [AHT]
                            598 Angell St.,
                               Providence, R.I.,
                                  Dec. 27, 1917

Rev. Maurice Winter Moe, D.D.,
Westminster Presbyterian Church,
Milwaukee, Wis.,[1]

My dear Dr. Mo:—
            And now for another bit of testimony in the courtmartial of the letterr... rrr.....! At the last sitting of the court, the prosecution summoned Mr. John Keats as a witness. Our next is Mr. Edgar A. Poe, late of Baltimore, Richmond, and other places. Mr. Poe offers as evidence the opening quatrain of his "Valentine" to Mrs. Frances Sargent Osgood:

> "For her this rhyme is penn'd, whose lum'nous eyes,
>   Brightly expressive as the turns of *Leda*,
> Shall find her own sweet name, that, nestling lies
>   Upon the page, enwrapp'd from ev'ry *reader*.['] !!!!

However—we have one point to concede to the defence. In our edition of Holmes there is given a copy of the Doctor's first verses, writ at college; and the rhyme in the following couplet is particularly marked, as if to call the reader's attention to something youthful and incorrect: (This is a translated passage from the *Aeneid*).

> "Thus by the pow'r of his impartial *arm*
> The boiling ocean trembled into *calm*."[2]

But though Holmes disapproved this rhyme in later days, it none the less illustrates what must have been his *ordinary manner of speech*—and incidentally the speech of cultivated Boston.
    I am, Sir,
        Ever yr. most oblig'd, obedient, humble Servt
            H. Lovecraft.

Notes

1. On Milwaukee's East Side at 2308 E. Belleview Place (now closed).
2. "Translation from *The Æneid*, Book I," in *The Poetical Works of Oliver Wendell Holmes* 2.384.

[13] [AHT]

Providence, R.I.
Feby. 3, 1918

My dear Mo:—

Your evangelical career is one which I can follow with more admiration than comprehension. I can appreciate the moral value of religion—but how are you going to make anyone believe it? It is becoming increasingly difficult, and in another generation will be virtually impossible. So while I agree with you that the church should be kept alive as long as possible, I do *not* agree with you that the line between churchgoer and worldling should be drawn with greater sharpness. I even believe it should be further erased. My reason is not abstruse. Since it is probably impossible to draw many more persons into the church, why put a stigma upon those outside? Why expect more honour and virtue from a church member than from any other man of morals? If you expect less from a worldling, you will receive less. If you deny the heights of virtue to the worldling, he will drift away to a lower level. What incentive will the average man have to excel in character, if you tell him he *cannot* be good without accepting a system of thought impossible of belief? The "I am holier than thou" attitude cannot but do more harm than good in the end. As to an auto-amusement programme—I fear that is rather a step back to 17th century Massachusetts and Connecticut! Carried to extremes, this principle would obliterate culture and learning again, just as it did after the fall of the Roman Empire—when the classics were forgotten and the monk-ridden masses believed Virgil was a great magician and semi-Christian prophet. Amusement is a vital and logical necessity to mankind, and no church or government can ever legislate the need of amusement out of human nature. Good sense teaches when pleasure is normal and when it is excessive, but Puritanism carries more evils than boons in its train. Hear the heathen rage![1] But never mind—the Holy Ghost is with you, whilst he will not even speak to me! I must rest content as a hardened worldling, and suffer the scorn of the godly—though I honestly believe, without undue conceit, that my moral code in no way falls below the strictest ideals of the psalm-singer and pulpit-pounder. I am no great success in this world, and doubtless will not be in the next, but when it comes to a catalogue of crimes and evils I really cannot think of any worse offence than writing bad verse and not rolling my "rrr...s". I suppose, though, that a true theologian would say I have no positive virtue, since I am not tempted to evil. I just glide along in my uneventful loquacious way, doing what seems to me right and logical. I have no inclination to do anything else. But if I had liquorish, homicidal, and thieving tendencies, and called in the Holy Ghost to conquer them, I should doubtless be one of the Lord's Anointed! I fear I am scheduled for a trip to Purgatory some day—that middle region of immorality devoted to the sinners and unbelievers not good enough for Paradise but not bad enough for the utterly torrid zone. I am destined to perpetual obscurity, since Fate will allow me to see neither the Lord nor the central character of Milton's "Paradise Lost".

  I am, Sir, ever your most oblig'd obedient Servt
         Lo.

Notes

1. Ps 2.1: "Why do the heathen rage, and the people imagine a vain thing?"

[14] [AHT]
          598 Angell St.,
          Providence, R.I.,
          May 15, 1918

My dear Mo:—

  I am interested in your experiences as a phonograph star. Something over a decade ago I conceived the idea of displacing Sig. Caruso as the world's greatest lyric vocalist, and accordingly inflicted some weird and wondrous ululations upon a perfectly innocent Edison blank. My mother actually liked the results—mothers are not always unbiased critics—but I saw to it that an accident soon removed the incriminating evidence. Later I tried something less ambitious; a simple, touching, plaintive, ballad sort of thing a la John McCormack.[1] This was a better success, but reminded me so much of the wail of a dying fox-terrier that I very carelessly happened to drop it soon after it was made. I have since confined my artistic talents to literature. My vocalism is of too *recherché* an excellence to please an unappreciative public. If you send a record of your voice, I am sure I can find some local store or business school where it can be played. It will gratify me immensely to listen to the Attic accents of the honoured Chief Kleicomolo. As you suggested once before, the record can be sent around our circle; though perhaps Co will lack facilities for its use. Perhaps, however, some veteran ranchman of the plains may possess an archaic talking machine which will handle cylinder records.

  Your plans for the future are indeed radical! So great has seemed your adaptation to progressive pedagogy, that your choice of another field appears surprising to one not familiar with the earlier ideals and training you received at the University. However, if this Biblical Alliance really matures as its founders hope—and from the facts you give I judge it is very likely to do so—there is no question but that it offers a better opportunity for you. The success encountered by the promotors of the Alliance is indeed remarkable. Apparently there is still so much popular interest in the Hebrew Scriptures—possibly there will be still more during the emotional war-time period. That the work will be more or less permanent, I cannot doubt. Just as Graeco-Roman classicism and mythology lived long after the abandonment of the old religion, so must

Biblical culture endure as a branch of study, on account of the vast influence it has exerted on history since the age of Augustus, and on literature since the beginning of the mediaeval period. Your new duties will, I judge, be very pleasing; even though they may involve a bit more travelling than a man of domestic tastes might relish. In general, you seem admirably well fitted for the new position. Your tastes and mode of thought seem to be increasingly theological; and in this age theologians of your mental calibre are rare indeed! You will be a veritable prize for the Alliance officials. A man of keen, forceful, logical mind, and thorough education, who is yet thoroughly enthusiastic over the value of religion, and able to take the religious point of view without doing violence to intellectual convictions and personal ideals of logic.

I will not, as you fear, dispute the worthiness of your choice in this matter. It is the duty of every person to act according to his most honest individual convictions; and believing as you do, I may agree without reservation that you have pursued the most sensible and commendable course possible. All I hope is, that the Alliance will not seek to create a little moral oligarchy of the devout; condemning everyone, no matter how virtuous and honourable, who cannot accept the extravagant mythology of the Jews and their successors. Your paternal lecture to me on the subject of "VICIOUS abstractions of philosophy" etc. is interesting. I, also, wish that I could have reached the trenches; though my wish is based on less holy and academic reasons. Instead of studying the rudiments of piety, I fear I should have been busy keeping up with the requirements of warfare, quite forgetting the allegorical embellishments. In other words, my wish was to kill Huns, and spread Anglo-Saxon supremacy. Practical and primitive! Your implication that trench life awakes the religious instinct is a theory quite prevalent, though not altogether unchallenged. Of course, the life destroys all power of real thought, and brings the beast near the surface—hence it would not be remarkable if grovelling superstition should appear along with the rest. (See next Kleicomolo—with enclosed clipping from *N.Y. Tribune*). But a large number of observers challenge this theory, and state that religious harangues bore and exasperate the men. One French soldier in particular wrote many letters to the *North American Review* about a year ago, denying that Frenchmen as a class had ceased to be rationalists, even amidst the most mind-wrecking stress. Far from inculcating ideas of the supernatural, the war has made French soldiers very materialistic. Life is short—life is cheap—life is to be lived while one may—then—pouf! It is all over—but *France*, the glorious and eternal, still lives and will always live! I am afraid you injure your side of the argument when you state that in the hellish, maddening turmoil of trench warfare one may "come to realise how instinctive is communion with the supernatural; how perverted and perverting is the civilisation that can 'refine' that instinct out of a man's nature." Do you think that the trenches afford the best atmosphere for calm thought; that their inhabitants are liable to be most free from mental stress, psychopathic disorders, and excited hallucinations? Possibly in a state of shell-shock a man may be exceedingly religious—but before you give this as evidence of the reality of the supernatural, you must prove that shell-shock affords its victims better opportunities for accurate thinking than the normal atmosphere of home, school, or college.

Your wonderment 'what I have against religion' reminds me of your recent *Vagrant* essay[2]—which I had the honour of perusing in manuscript some three years ago. To my mind, that essay *misses one point altogether*. Your "agnostic" has neglected to mention the very crux of all agnosticism—namely that the Judaeo-Christian mythology is NOT TRUE. I can see that in your philosophy *truth per se* has so small a place, that you can scarcely realise what it is that Galpin and I are insisting upon. In your mind, MAN is the centre of everything, and his exact conformation to certain regulations of conduct HOWEVER EFFECTED, the only problem in the universe. Your world (if you will pardon my saying so) is *contracted*. All the mental vigour and erudition of the ages fail to disturb your complacent endorsement of empirical doctrines and purely pragmatical notions, because you voluntarily limit your horizon—*excluding certain facts, and certain undeniable mental tendencies of mankind*. In your eyes, man is torn between *only two* influences; the degrading instincts of the savage, and the temperate impulses of the philanthropist. To you, men are of but two classes—lovers of self and lovers of the race. To you, men have but two types of emotion—self-gratification, to be combated; and altruism, to be fostered. But you, consciously or unconsciously, are leaving out a vast and potent *tertium quid*—making an omission which cannot but interfere with the validity of your philosophical conceptions. You are forgetting a human impulse which, despite its restriction to a relatively small number of men, has all through history proved itself as real and as vital as hunger—as potent as thirst or greed. I need not say that I refer to that simplest yet most exalted attribute of our species—the acute, persistent, unquenchable craving TO KNOW. Do you realise that to many men it makes a vast and profound difference whether or not the things about them are as they appear? Let me use an analogy, since you love concreteness. You recognise a difference between mere pleasure and true happiness. As a consistent theologian, you must chaw this distinction. You point to two men; one a merely frivolous creature, amusing himself by drowning his cares in wine or gaiety; the other a conscientious worker of good, who takes satisfaction in knowing that he is properly adjusted to society and his fellowmen. Both are equally contented, but you will undoubtedly say that only the second man is truly happy. You will say, and rightly, that the joy of the first man is merely mental apathy; and that if ever he should be forced to think about himself and his relation to others around him, he would be acutely dissatisfied—would seek to find his place in life and thereby satisfy the new misgivings which thought aroused in him. But at this point you and other orthodox thinkers find it expedient to "draw a herring across the trail" and turn to other lines of investigation. For the very distinction you draw between empty pleasure and true happiness would by one more step of ratiocination force you to acknowledge the element of the *absolute* whose existence you are so anxious to deny or conceal. In differentiating between pleasure and happiness, you concede that the reality of the source of contentment is a very important thing. Otherwise the serenity of the sensualist and of the saint stand on a level. If effect is all we are to consider, the drunken loafer or the madman who fancies himself a King may be deemed just as blessed as the person whose happiness is founded on actual things. If there be not some virtue in plain TRUTH; then our fair dreams, delusions, and follies, are as much to be esteemed as our sober waking hours and the comforts they bring. If TRUTH amounts to nothing, then we must regard the phantasma of our slumbers just as seriously as the events of our daily lives. Several nights ago I had a strange dream of a strange city—a city of many palaces and gilded domes, lying in a hollow betwixt ranges of grey, horrible hills.[3] There was not a soul in this vast region of stone-paved streets and marble walls and columns, and the numerous statues in the public places were of strange bearded men in robes the like whereof I have never seen before or since. I was, as I said, aware of this city visually. I was in it and around it. But certainly I had no corporeal existence. I saw, it seemed, everything at once; without the limitations of direction. I did not move, but transferred my perception from point to point at will. I occupied no space and had no form. I was only a consciousness, a perceptive presence. I recall a lively curiosity at the scene, and a tormenting struggle to recall its identity; for I felt that I had once known it well, and that if I could remember, I should be carried back to a very remote period—many thousand years, when something vaguely horrible had happened. Once I was almost on the verge of realisation, and was frantic with fear at the prospect, though I did not know what it was that I should recall. But here I awaked—in a very cramped posture and with too much bedclothing for the steadily increasing temperature. I have related this in detail because it impressed me very vividly. This is not a Co romance of reincarnation—you will see that it has no climax or point—but it was very real. I am now trying to recall if I felt any sensation or had any notion of *heat* in the dream. The excessive covering would account for that, if I did. But as a matter of fact, I cannot remember such an impression.

At this point you will ask me whence these stories! I answer—according to your pragmatism that dream was as real as my presence at this table, pen in hand! If the truth or falsity of our beliefs and impressions be immaterial, then I am, or was, actually and indisputably an unbodied spirit hovering over a very singular, very silent, and very ancient city somewhere between grey, dead hills. I thought I was at the time—so what else matters? Do you think that I was just as truly that spirit as I am now H. P. Lovecraft? I do not. "'And there ye ar-re', as Mr. Dooley says."[4]

I recognise a distinction between dream life and real life, between appearances and actualities. I confess to an overpowering desire to know whether I am asleep or awake—whether the environment and laws which affect me are external and permanent, or the transitory products of my own brain. I admit that I am very much interested in the relation I bear to the things about me—the time relation, the space relation, and the causative relation. I desire to know approximately what my life is in terms of history—human, terrestrial, solar, and cosmical; what my magnitude may be in terms of extension,—terrestrial, solar, and cosmical; and above all, what may be my manner of linkage to the general system—in what way, through what agency, and to what extent, the obvious guiding forces of creation act upon me and govern my existence. And if there be any less obvious forces, I desire to know them and their relation to me as well. Foolish, do I hear you say? Undoubtedly! I had better be a consistent pragmatist: get drunk, and confine myself to a happy, swinish, contented little world—the gutter—till some policeman's No. 13 boot intrudes upon my philosophic repose. But I *cannot*. Why? Because some well-defined human impulse prompts me to discard the relative for the absolute. You would encourage me as far as the moral stage. You would agree with me that I had better see the world as it is than to forget my woes in the flowing bowl. But because I have a certain *momentum*, and am carried a step further from the merely relative, you frown upon me and declare me to be a queer, unaccountable creature, "immersed . . . . . in the VICIOUS abstractions of philosophy!"

Here, then, is the beginning of my religious or philosophical thought. I have not begun talking about *morality* yet, because I have not reached that point in the argument. *Entity* precedes morality. It is a prerequisite. What am I? What is the nature of the energy about me, and how does it affect me? So far I have seen nothing which could possibly give me the notion that cosmic force is the manifestation of a mind and will like my own infinitely magnified; a potent and purposeful consciousness which deals individually and directly with the miserable denizens of a wretched little flyspeck on the back door of a microscopic universe, and which singles this putrid excrescence out as the one spot whereto to send an onlie-begotten Son, whose mission is to redeem those accursed flyspeck-inhabiting lice which we call human beings—bah!! Pardon the "bah!" I feel several "bahs!", but out of courtesy I only say one. But it is all so very childish. I cannot help taking exception to a philosophy which would force this rubbish down my throat. 'What have I against religion?' That is what I have against it! (Do not mistake me—I have a great deal *for* it as well. I do *not* 'deny it a place in the life of the world'. I am coming to this about twenty or thirty pages farther on!!)

Now let us view *morality*—which despite your preconceived classification and identification has nothing to do with any particular form of religion. Morality is the adjustment of matter to its environment—the natural arrangement of molecules. More especially it may be considered as dealing with organic molecules. Conventionally it is the science of reconciling the animal *homo* (more or less) *sapiens* to the forces and conditions with which he is surrounded. It is linked with religion only so far as the natural elements it deals with are deified and personified. Morality antedated the Christian religion, and has many times risen superior to co-existent religions. It has powerful support from very non-religious human impulses. Personally, I am intensely moral and intensely irreligious. My morality can be traced to two distinct sources, scientific and aesthetic. My love of truth is outraged by the flagrant disturbance of sociological relations involved in so-called "wrong"; whilst my aesthetic sense is outraged and disgusted with the violations of taste and harmony thereupon attendant. But to me the question presents no ground for connexion with the grovelling instinct of religion. However—you may exclude me from the argument, if you will. I *am* unduly secluded though unavoidably so. We will deal only with materials which may presumably lie within my feeble reach. Only one more touch of ego. I am *not* at all passive or indifferent in my zeal for a high morality. But I cannot consider morality the essence of religion as you seem to. In discussing religion, the whole fabric must bear examination before the uses or purposes are considered. We must investigate the cause as well as alleged effects if we are to define the relation between the two, and the reality of the former. And more, granting that the phenomenon of faith is indeed the true cause of the observed moral effects; the absolute basis of that phenomenon remains to be examined. The issue between theists and atheists is certainly not, as you seem to think, the mere question of whether religion is useful or detrimental. In your intensely pragmatical mind, this question stands paramount—to such an extent that you presented no other subject of discussion in your very clever *Vagrant* article. But the "agnostic" of your essay must have been a very utilitarian agnostic (that such "utilitarian Agnostics" do exist, I will not deny. *Vide* any issue of *The Truthseeker!* But are they typical?)!5 What the honest thinker wishes to know, has nothing to do with complex human conduct. He simply demands a scientific *explanation* of the things he sees. His only animus toward the church concerns its deliberate inculcation of demonstrable untruths in the community. This is human nature. No matter how white a lie may be—no matter how much good it may do—we are always more or less disgusted by its diffusion. The honest agnostic regards the church with respect for what it has done in the direction of virtue. He even supports it if he is magnanimous, and he certainly does nothing to impair whatever public usefulness it may possess. But in private, he would be more than a mere mortal if he were able to suppress a certain abstract resentment, or to curb the feeling of humour and so-called irreverence which inevitably arises from the contemplation of pious fraud, howsoever high-minded and benevolent.

The good effects of Christianity are neither to be denied, nor lightly esteemed, though candidly I will admit that I think them overrated. For example, the insignia of the Red Cross is practically the only religious thing about it. It is purely humanitarian and philanthropic, and has received just as much of its vitality from agnostic—or Jewish—sources, as from Christian sources. I once heard of a foot powder called "White Cross". Was it by divine healing that it relieved (or claimed to relieve) tired feet? Likewise the Y. M. C. A. There is some cant and psalm-singing in this organisation, but I have read from many reliable sources (including *The Outlook*)[6] that its work in France is more social than religious. In its campaign for support it has proclaimed its social purpose, nor has any of my tainted agnostic money, contributed for moral and ethical reasons, been contemptuously returned! These nominally Christian societies usurp the lion's share of social service merely because they are on the ground first. Free and rational thought is relatively new, and rationalists find it just as practicable to support these existing Christian charities as to organise new ones which might create a division of energy and therefore decrease the efficiency of organised charity as a whole. And by the way—was not Belgian relief work largely non-religious? I may be mistaken—but all this is aside from my main argument anyway. I am not protesting against the recognition of Christianity's accomplishments. This has nothing to do with absolute bases of faith.

But I have one more fling to take—this one at religion vs. common sense in the world wide battle against rum. Roughly, we may group the principal nations as follows regarding intensity of religion. Germany must in the mass be accounted religious, since the scepticism of the literati does not reach the masses. The latter still believe in the blood-thirsty Pentateuch of Moses, and in Gott's beloved partner, Wilhelm II, Rex et Imperator.

1. Russia
2. Germany
3. England
4. United States
5. France

How do these nations stand regarding Rum? We find "Holy Russia"—save during the last days of the monarchy—sodden with vodka—a bestial spectacle. Germany, with some restraint from sceptical upper classes, is bloated with bad beer. England's workmen are incurably addicted to ale and gin—and the omnipresent clergy smile at them, using wine in their own sacraments. Coming to the States, we find infinitely less religion but infinitely less drunkenness. In France there is no religion, and despite the prevalence of weak wine, little drunkenness. Now has religion been the dominant force against Rum? Emphatically no! For years the preachers wore out their lungs shouting temperance at true believers who prayed and drank with equal gusto. The modern "dry" movement is entirely and absolutely practical; based on the superfluous, crime-inciting, efficiency-impairing nature of liquor. Liquor is an anomaly—it is unscientific, and detrimental to the social order. Until hardheaded men of "the world" realised this and began to work for prohibition, the temperance movement was a farce. Today, with agnostic support, watch the National Amendment sweep on to victory! About the "Story of Bob and Orry"—who doubts the power of emotional appeal to reach a few cultured persons? I am perfectly willing to give evangelism credit for anything like this. We know that thousands of brilliant and cultivated men are able to limit their horizons sufficiently to accept religion; and religion being once accepted, evangelism must of course have a potent influence. Judge Dean was probably religious from the first. You must realise that the average non-scientific man of affairs, however worldly in thought and shady in morals, generally has some ill-defined supernatural cobwebs in the back of his brain. He is not at all sure there is not a Lord, a Jesus, and all the rest—he recognises a sort of Kingdom of Heaven, but considers himself out of it. He believes in the vague divinity of Jesus, but has not actively "accepted" him—whatever that means. Shew me a typical drunkard or dissolute character, and I will lay a heavy wager that he believes in the existence of the supernatural. The very weakness which fails to carry him beyond the gross in life, also fails to carry him beyond the allegorical, concrete, and primitive in philosophy (I should be glad to see any such person become a devout consistent Christian). I place prime faith in the honour of an agnostic. Any man who has enough regard for natural order and natural truth to search beyond the blazed trail of orthodoxy, may be relied upon to uphold to the last those precepts of scientific adjustment on which morality is based. The agnostic is a thinker—therefore a prohibitionist and moralist. The very mental impulse which creates agnosticism, is a philosophical yearning toward something better and more perfect. The world is safe in the hands of rational agnostics.

But lest you think I have wandered far from my previously expressed respect for religion as a lever to move the masses, let me reaffirm that respect. I recognise the power of the primal—which amongst the illiterate, semi-literate, and a few of the literate, is a force capable of much good if skillfully wielded. Conversely, I recognise the dangerous potentialities of an ignorantly atheistical mob—a mob whose atheism comes not from thought, but from copying others. All rationalism tends to minimise the value and importance of life, and to decrease the sum total of human happiness. In many cases the truth may cause suicidal or nearly suicidal depression. Therefore, I concede that the church deserves support as long as it can exist, and that agnosticism ought never to be diffused artificially. Yea, more. I will concede that men of religion are justified in hindering the spread of agnosticism among those whose opinions are not particularly settled, and who might easily be swayed either way. But ordinary sense tells us that faith cannot hang on forever. After the war chaos there will be an inevitable reaction toward hard facts. The time is coming when the old formulae will cease to enchant, for nothing can last eternally which is not founded on demonstrable truth. And for that future we must provide while there is time. Without attacking religion in any way, let us admit that virtue and honour are possible outside its charmed circle. Let us cultivate morality as an independent principle. Let us cultivate philanthropy for its own sake. True, religion has hitherto done marvels for these things—but religion will some day perish, and these things must never perish. If you, as I infer, like artistic Victorian media through which to receive ideas; let me recommend to you the recent verse of Thomas Hardy.[7] Hardy is a Victorian who has survived his age—and in his transition from prose to verse he has burst forth with renewed philosophic splendour. He recognises with regret the passing of Christianity. He loves it as he loves classic mythology, but he cannot believe it. A few years ago he wrote a poem on the *death* or *funeral* of God—a poem which doubtless caused many a pair of devout hands to rise in a gesture of holy horror.[8] But Hardy thinks.

I hope this page can end my pagan harangue! I have no wish to persecute thee, (pardon some light remarks in prose and verse in coming Kleicomolo) but I do wish you could understand the compelling power and grim reality of man's quest for TRUTH. I fancy I can go as far as Porcius Festus, Esq. in the direction of concession. In fact, I believe I should never think of using such brutal language as that which P. F. used in Acts XXVI-24.[9]

Your most Oblig'd Ob[t.] Humble Servt,
Lo.

Notes

1. John McCormack (1884–1945), immensely popular Irish tenor.
2. "The Church and the World."
3. This dream was the basis for the story "Polaris" (1918), presumably written around this time.
4. Mr. Dooley was a character created in essays by the journalist and humorist Finley Peter Dunne (1867–1936). The expression was used as the last line of MWM's article.
5. The *Truth Seeker* (1873–2003) was one of the leading freethought journals of the later 19th and early 20th centuries.
6. The *Outlook* (New York; 1870–1935) was a weekly magazine, published initially as the *Christian Union* (1870–1893).
7. HPL refers to the poetry and verse dramas that Thomas Hardy (1840–1925) wrote after he abandoned the novel following the hostile reception of *Jude the Obscure* (1895).
8. I.e., "God's Funeral."
9. Porcius Festus was procurator of Judea from about 59 to 62 CE. HPL alludes to this verse: "And as he thus spake for himself, Festus said with a loud voice, Paul, thou art beside thyself; much learning doth make thee mad."

[15]   [AHT]

The Vatican, 5/9/19:

Ambrosius Origenus Lactantius Hieronymus Chrysostomos, Esq.,[1]
Reverend Sire:

   Continuing de re Theologica, your dissertation on spontaneous Righteousness will surely be welcomed by Editor Samples—whom, by the way, I will bid send you an half dozen copies of your incotinian homily when it appears.[2] Concerning the substance of the recent article, let me make but one comment. The more the Holy Church tries to separate itself from some imaginary entity called "The World", the less influence it will have. It was the now defunct Puritan sect that denounced bear-baiting not because it hurt the bear but because it amused the spectators. There is no such thing as a wicked antichristian entity called "The World". The world, as it is, has much good and much evil; much pleasure and much pain. That which is good is not *necessarily* pleasant, but that which is pleasant is not necessarily not good. We have too much pain; too little pleasure. Pleasure, *per se*, is not to be discouraged except when it is demonstrably detrimental according to the proven standards of natural morality. Life is too little colourful to make it right for any black-robed apostle of melancholy to run amuck and blast the gaiety of nations. It is not hard to see what pleasures are innocent and what are otherwise. Let us make war on *evil*, not on *pleasure;* for the two are far from synonymous. Perhaps that is, in truth, the object of the more liberal theologians; but the narrower fanatics need restraint.

   Su Seguro Servidor:[3] Luis Teobaldo.

Notes

1. HPL alludes to the early Christian writers St. Ambrose, Origen, Lactantius, St. Jerome, and St. John Chyrsostom.
2. John Milton Samples (1887–?) of Macon, GA, editor of the *Silver Clarion,* an amateur paper that HPL characterized as "an able and consistent exponent of that literary mildness and wholesomeness which in the professional world are exemplified by *The Youth's Companion* and the better grade of religious papers." "Comment" (1918; *CE* 1.198). MWM's piece was "Spontaneous Righteousness." The reading "incotinian" in AHT appears to be a mistranscription.
3. Spanish for HPL's customary "Yr obt./faithful servt."

[16] [AHT]

L. Theobald, Jun.
   General Secretary
Edward Softly
   Gen. Financial Secretary

THE AUGUSTAN ALLIANCE
Pan-Saxon and Agnostic
"The Preeminence of Pope in Literature"

Tel. Will's 1719[1]

Grave Building
Providence, R.I.
[May 1919][2]

Venerated Apostle:—Since I do not feel like doing anything else today, I will treat your two recent cards as a letter and make them an excuse for this reply. How can mortal flesh (unless sustain'd by a divine pow'r!) endure such strenuous travel and excitement? I am sure I shall feel a sympathetick exhaustion upon perusing your diurnal diary cards! And to think that 19,180 people have endured Bryanine oratory![3] I hope casualties were slight. By the way, I hope that you carefully suppressed the *text* when shewing my geographical opus to the "Braying Jackass of the Platte" (to use an expression of A. Galpin Senior's). If memory informeth me aright, my allusions to the silver-tongued ex-cabinet minister were painfully frank.[4] Since W. J. B. is really a well-meaning, good-hearted soul, I should hate to offend him. (On the other hand, I should relish wickedly a chance to tell W. W. to his face what I think of him and his egotistical weltpolitik!) In renaming the features of Nova Germania, I followed the dual system of my fellow-Romans of an earlier aera in the original provinces of Gallia and Germania Inferior. In most cases I Latinised the native names, but in a few instances (like that of Colonia Agrippina) superseded the original designations by new ones. It is a fact, for example, that the trading post now called Galpinium (after the celebrated proconsul and man of letters A. Galpinius Secundus) was formerly a native village peopled by the Suevi and Celtae, and known as Appleodunum. It is said that an effort is being made in the senatus to recognise the great deeds of Cn. Mauritius Pius Mo by altering the name of Madisonium (the capital of the province) to Augusta Mauritii or Forum Monis. Other towns named from heroes are Raasinium (originally Millovacum), whose title comes from the prince Raasiovistus of the Allemanni; and Hutchinsonium—(an ancient seat of learning once called Veiovegus*), named from Hutchinsonium Anareōn, a celebrated Grecian philosopher, political economist, and gallant.[5] I am glad you are enjoying the twin municipalities of Minneapolis and Paullopolis. The latter, 'tis said, was named from the illustrious L. Aemilius Paullus Macedonicus, conqueror of the monarch Perseus and father of Scipio the younger. The etymology of Minneapolis is more obscure, but pious Christians declare that it is traceable to M. Minucius

---

*Pedantick antiquarians affect to trace this venerable city to a prehistorick colony of refugees from VEII, after the taking of that town by siege.

Felix (fl. 2nd cent. A.D.), author of the Christian dialogue "Octavius", and founder of the Foedus Biblicum[6] whereof Cn. Mauritius Pius Mo is the present head. From the picture I can well imagine that the Taberna Paulina is aliquanta caupona.[7] I trust that all your tour was as successful financially as that part which antedated your card of the 11th. Surely the Foedus Biblicum is getting to be aliquantum foedus! I lately perused an article in a new British periodical, which causes one to look a bit more tolerantly at religion. The author—Arthur Machen—believes that the superstitious instinct of man is still primitively strong enough to demand organised expression; and says that without Christianity the rabble turn to *spiritualism,* just as drunkards without good liquor turn to wood-alcohol and other destructive stimulants.[8]

Speaking of the ignorant rabble—James Laurence Crowley[9] hath just inundated me with some of his "poetry" for revision. The task is repugnant, but I hate to disappoint the poor devil. In order to transform part of the task from drudgery to amusement, I am going to choose the least absurd gem and revise it before your eyes as a part of this molo—an entertaining example of Boeotian paraphrase. First we will see what poor James has went an' did!

Autumn*

Capricious Autumn—the time of harvest!
˘ — ˘ — ˘ — ˘ ˘ — ˘ —

To you / fair Sum/mer gives / her fare/well kiss / and seeks her rest.
Dawn's nectar no longer refreshes, but leaves a stain
On leaf and flower, ere they flee to shelter before wind and rain.
˘ — ˘ — ˘ ˘ — ˘ — ˘ —

Thy gor/geous beau/ty is / beyond / compare / and though it lives for a day,
It gives a hint of bleak tomorrows (another Heroick!)—and decay.

—James Laurence Crowley.
(Fac-simile signature)

First—to see what metre James wants to use. Search *me!!* When in doubt, ever ye h. c.!! Let's begin—

Capricious autumn, time of harvest bliss!

I put in that *bliss* as a possible rhyme for *kiss* in the next line. It is always wise to be foresighted! Now for l. 2—

On the bright (gay) Summer prints her parting kiss;
　　　　　　　　　　　　　　＼alliteration

---

*(he made an heroick and didn't know it!!)

Not so bad—so long as I don't have to sign my own name to the thing. But now, how the ____ am I going to dispose of that residue—"and seeks her rest?" Obviously I must drag in a few more r. s. phrases. How's this?

> The genial season, in fair verdure drest,
> Lingers a while, then turns to seek her rest.
>
> (*could* be worse!)

Now comes a mess which needs liberal entangling:

> Dawn's potent wine, its fresh'ning virtue fled,
> To leaf and flow'r imparts a stain of red

I know it *doesn't* turn *flowers* red—but this is "Po'try", so who gives a hang for the facts so long as it sounds interesting? Oh, well—one *can* take a little more pains—so how's this for the last line?

> Stains the green leaf and bows the blossom's head?
>   bends

What's that you say—mixed metaphor? Not at all—dawn's wine stains the green leaf—that's clear enough—and causes the blossom (being *drunk*) to bow or bend its head in alcoholic stupor! All very obvious! But possibly a better passage may be devised—

> Dawn's nectar, robb'd of all its fresh'ning power,
> Stains the green leaf, and drugs the languid flower;

That's better! Now another residue to get rid of—

> Whilst falling herbage skims along the plain,
> In flight before the winter wind and rain.

Too many participles—a plethora of *-ings*—what shall be did? Well, for one thing, get rid of the second *ing* by changing *with'ring* to *languid* as above. And to make the job fairly complete—for *threat'ning* read *chilly*. Oh, the deuce! That spoils the idea of the pome! What we want is *present* fulness of beauty, but *future* chill and death. Let's stick in *winter* instead of chilly—that gives the *idee!* Now to proceed—dead easy!

> Gay glows thy beauty, Autumn, for a day,
> Yet hints of bleak tomorrows—and decay!

Done? Thank the Lawd!

Now to see how the dark thing looks when assembled:

Autumn
by J. Crowley, Gent.

Capricious Autumn, time of Harvest Bliss!
On thee gay Summer prints her parting Kiss;
The genial Season, in fair Verdure drest,
Lingers a while, then turns to seek her Rest.
Dawn's Nectar, robb'd of all its fresh'ning Pow'r,
Stains the green Leaf, and drugs the languid Flow'r,
Whilst falling Herbage skims along the Plain
In flight before the Winter Wind and Rain.
Bright glows thy Beauty, Autumn, for a Day,
Yet hints of bleak Tomorrows—and Decay!

The other night I suddenly woke to find myself out of bed and seated at a table, with pen and paper beside me. The gas was not lighted, yet a singular radiance seemed to pervade the apartment. As I searched for the source I chanced to glance in a neighbouring mirror, and there beheld to my amazement a tongue of mysterious flame playing in the air above my forehead! When I lit the gas, the flame disappeared. I then turned to the table to view what I had written, and found that all the writing was in absolutely unknown characters. The next day I took the sheets of paper to the Linguistic department of Brown University and begged Prof. B. to translate the strange text; but he could not even identify the alphabet employed! However—he passed it around amongst his colleagues, and Prof. D. of Semitic languages and literature discovered that it was cursive Hebrew. Upon reading the text, Prof. D. found that what I had written consisted solely of ecstatic praises of the lord Jehovah and his Holy Ghost, all couched in antique Hebrew of the purest quality!! What do I hear you say? You are *slightly* sceptical? How *can* you be, when you were not shocked at Co's recent recital? Am I suddenly demented? Nay, O Sage, I am merely a d——d liar!! But what is Co? Echo respondit, "Qualis est Co?" Ah, me!

But I must desist ere thy patience be gone.

Yrs. in ye Bowells of Xt (as Rev. Cotton Mather used to sign himself): T. Lucretius Carus.

P.S. I will enclose a quaint bit of vers-libre burlesque by our local *Journal* "Colyumnist."

Notes

1. HPL refers to Will's Coffee House in London, a favorite meeting-place for the literati of the early 18th century.
2. AHT provides the date "5/20," but the letter must date to May 1919 (see n. 3).

3. William Jennings Bryan (1860–1925) was giving a series of lectures advocating Prohibition in mid-May 1919, beginning in New York City and proceeding at least as far west as Columbus, Ohio.

4. HPL apparently alludes to his comments on Bryan when he was secretary of state under Woodrow Wilson (1913–15), during which he banned the serving of alcohol in the White House. ("W. W." in the following sentence refers to Wilson.) Although praising Bryan's temperance efforts, HPL stated that Bryan "was a bungler in politics and a stranger to dignity" ("Liquor and Its Friends" [1915], *CE* 5.16).

5. HPL has devised Latin coinages for individuals and place-names in Wisconsin: A. Galpinius Secundus (Alfred Galpin); Appleodunum (Appleton, home of Lawrence College, where Galpin was enrolled); Cn. Mauritius Pius Mo (MWM); Madisonium (Madison, the state capital); Raasinium (Racine); Hutchinsonium and Veiovegus (Weyauwega, home of amateur journalist Alfred L. Hutchinson [1859–1930], editor of the *Trail*). In his footnote, HPL claims that Veiovegus was settled by refugees from Veii, an Etruscan city northwest of Rome that was conquered by the Romans in 396 B.C.E.

6. HPL's coined Latin for Biblical Alliance (see MWM 14).

7. Latin for "some tavern."

8. See Arthur Machen, "Has Spiritualism Come to Stay?" *John O'London's Weekly* 1 (18 April 1919): 4.

9. Crowley (1885–1962) was an amateur poet whose work HPL repeatedly criticized as "saccharine and sentimental" (*CE* 1.105). HPL's pseudonym Ames Dorrance Rowley is a parody of Crowley's name.

[17] [AHT, as a letter to the Molo]

Thursday, May 18, 1722

Simplicity; a Poem

By L. Theobald, Jun.

Whilst the town-Muse with fever'd accents bays,
Chok'd by the time, and mov'd to hectick lays;
Whilst learn'd Confusion, weighing on the mind,
Turn ev'ry head to thoughts of jumbled kind;
Whilst weary'd singers hide in sapient fear
The thrill of joy at what the past held dear.
See o'er the rural mead, serene and bright,
A radiant god who puts the clouds to flight!
Simplicity! blest Nature's first ally;
Child of the balmy groves and lucent sky;
Friend of the breezes and the vernal rain,
And of each early flow'r that decks the plain;
Spirit benign, that gleams in ev'ry glade,
And smiles assuring from the leafy shade;
Kin of the Oreads on the craggy mounts;

Kin of the nymphs that haunt the grotto founts;
God of the vale, the thicket, and the slope,
And last kind guardian of declining Hope!

Thus sings the bard whose gaze in wisdom leaves
The scene where sad Sophistication grieves;
Who scans the truth that shows at calm content,
And hoards the wonder worldlier men have spent;
Laughs at the poison letter'd sorc'rers brew,
Nor pants for pleasures that he never knew.
For him the gay reviving spring unfolds
Perennial beauties o'er the fragrant moulds;
His ear alone the feather'd wand'rers please
With tales of faery world beyond the seas;
His favour'd eye in ev'ry wind may trace
Ethereal spirits of celestial grace;
And he, unspoil'd, may childlike bask again
Beneath the beams of Saturn's golden reign.
Mark yonder rise, o'er whose smooth em'rald crest
Trips sprightly Maia, in white blossoms drest;
Her verdant wand the air with perfume fills,
Tips the warm boughs, and paints the conscious hills;
Lights up the matin fields with crystal dew,
And gilds the sunset's airy cliffs anew;
Her sportive train to ev'ry scene impart
Unwonted spells, and cheer the languid heart;
Dancing and song enchant the world around,
Till Pan makes joyous at the pleasing sound.
In noontide stillness, when no urban eye
May chill the bliss or mar the revelry,
Simplicity descries on ev'ry hand
The prancing presence of the antique band:
Here laurell'd Muse all their arts rehearse,
And ivy'd Bacchus waves his budding thyrse;
Here myrtled Venus spreads her genial fire,
Whilst aureate Phoebus sounds the festive lyre;
Here, here alone, those lavish gifts are flung
To those whose fancy stays for ever young.
Behold yon hamlet, blest with mellow years,
That bosom'd in the oaky vale appears;

Here urban eyes* a stupid life discern;
And urban minds† unwholesome secrets learn;
But wise *Simplicity*, with fresher gaze,
Refines the whole, and sifts the brighter rays;
Spurns the dull thoughts that darkly flit between,
And as a picture‡ glories in the scene:
Spires mixt with verdure; walls with ivy fair;
Calm leafy ways—a prospect rich and rare.
Simplicity! Chief boon of suff'ring man!
First of the blessings in th' eternal plan!
May thy glad mantle ever shield my form
From the dread terrors of the circling storm.
With thee beside me, may I tranquil rest
Close to benignant Nature's soothing breast;
Nor ever spy, too keen of wit or soul,
The lurking hemlock in the flow'r-wreath'd bowl!

                                        May 1722

As to my chronicle of social activities since November—it includes the big trip whereof thou hast heard, but does not depart much from the usual monotony. Events do not excite me as they did a coupla years ago, when I first emerged from my decade and more of total hibernation. All life is a bally bore, and I am getting more and more yawningly conscious of it. Here—there—what the deuce does it matter? As our wise little friend says—Bah!

Jan. 3–4 I took a Newton-Centre trip—to the Maison Middleton-McMullen.[1] The prime features of interest were the kids—Kenneth (eleven) and Robin (eight). They are absolutely the most captivating, brilliant, and well-bred infants I have ever seen since the infancy of my late cousin Phil; and Robin is an exquisite elf fit to inspire an artist. They are mischievous and irrepressible—and they transported me back to my own youth when I was with them . . . . . a quarter of a century through the dim corridors of the monster Time! Your Robert and Donald are undoubtedly very like them. On that trip I picked up some amazing old book bargains in Cornhill, Boston—including a Cooke's Hesiod (1740) and a volume of the old *Gentleman's Magazine* so dear to Mr. Pope and Dr. Johnson.

From then till April I vegetated without an intermission—feeling like hell, for the most part. March 25 I had a call from the old-timer Leonard E. Tilden, the Fossil who is trying to get "paound pustage" for amateur jour-

---

*Sinclair Lewis, Esq.
†Sherwood Anderson, Esq.
‡Schopenhauer hath observ'd, that the world is beautiful as an object.

nals.² April 1 Mrs. Greene was here during the course of an Eastern trip. Then on April 4 a long-distance call opened the big affair.

On April 1, in response to Mrs. Greene's repeated inducements, Loveman had hit N.Y. in quest of a commercial situation. Finding his hostess absent, he was so depressed that he almost went home immediately; but a local friend persuaded him to wait at an hotel. April 3 Mrs. Greene reached home and found the disconsolate one on her doorstep, as it were. She succeeded in slightly cheering him up, but not in getting him a job; and by the next evening he was about to depart in tenebrous discouragement. Mrs. Greene had turned her entire flat over to him, stopping at a neighbour's herself, but not even that super-hospitality seemed likely to hold him. Then, since the bard had done me the undeserv'd honour of wishing I were there, Mrs. Greene called me up on the long-distance as an expedient for cheering her guest. You can imagine my ecstatic delight at hearing at last the actual voice of the poet I had admired for seven years—and to whom I had written commendatory verses before I knew whether he was living or dead!³ It was a great conversation, but I never expected to *see* the celebrity at the other end. He was resolved to go home at once! But Morton and Kleiner, with whom he was in touch, added their voices; and he decided to tarry "one more day". On the evening of the 5th I was called up by the assembled Loveman–Greene–Morton–Kleiner forces and invited to join them. The later presence of my kid protege Frank Belknap Long Jr. was promised, and Loveman said he would stay in N.Y. only on condition that I came. It was the suddenness and unexpectedness which finally turned the trick. I accepted, packed a valise, and on the following sunny morning caught the ten-six for New York.

I spent the five-hour journey reading Dunsany and peering at waystations. New-London is a dingy little burg—a Victorian relic. New-Haven seems alert and metropolitan from the station angle. Ditto for Bridgeport. Shortly before three p.m., the train reached the lofty and colossal Harlem River viaduct (Only by chance did I secure the unique panorama—because the train was a Washington, D.C. express. Ordinary N.Y. trains go by a tamer route and into the Grand Central Station), and I saw for the first time the Cyclopean outlines of New-York. It was a mystical sight in the gold sun of late afternoon; a dream-thing of faint grey, outlined against a sky of faint grey smoke. City and sky were so alike that one could hardly be sure that there was a city—that the fancied towers and pinnacles were not the merest illusions. It was ten miles away, approximately—that is, the skyscraper region was. Actually, the train had crossed to Long Island, there to move south till a tunnel should take it under the East River and the streets of Manhattan to the Pennsylvania Station.

The station was reached on time, and I was supposed to be met by Loveman and Mrs. Greene; but by some mishap in calculation the reception committee had become lost in the mazes of the vast terminal. I waited a while, then made a scientific search which finally unearthed Mrs. Greene. Loveman had returned to Brooklyn is discouragement! By means of subway and taxi, we beat Loveman to 259 Parkside—meeting him just as he ascended the steps. Some meeting! Loveman is all right and then some! Absurdly as Mrs. Greene overpraises most persons, I doubt if there is any vital inaccuracy in even the wildest of her Lovemanic rhapsodies and dithyrambs. A great boy, Samuel!

Loveman is of good size, and gracefully proportioned; dark, spectacled, and blessed with a distinguished baldness. His aspect is of the greatest refinement—his voice is soft and mellow, and his hands and feet exceptionally small. Refined, cultivated, and aesthetic, he seeks to conceal the artist beneath the outwardly assumed dress and manners of commonplace good-fellowship. Agonisingly sensitive and retiring, he affects as much as possible the aggressive and almost jaunty attitudes of the modern business-man; producing a net result captivatingly boyish. To describe his kindness, delicacy, thoughtfulness, and innumerable kindred virtues, would take volumes. His modesty is incredibly extreme—he has not even kept track of his own work, so that many magnificent early pieces are probably lost beyond recovery. I made him recall some, and set one down. It was exquisite—I must induce Cook to publish a book of collected Loveman poetry. The sensitiveness of Loveman is painful—his nerves and emotions are highly organised. A kind word is balm to him, and a cruel word crushes him wholly. Incidentally, you will gasp at learning that he is an intimate friend of our old *Chitrib* pal P. D. S.!! I learned of it wholly by accident. In the course of a conversation about Klei, I happened to speak of our passage through *Pawtucket* in July 1920. The name attracted Loveman, and he mentioned it as the home of 'his friend Sherman'. Just then my unconscious mind went back to other days and registered something at the unexpected combination Pawtucket—Sherman. Amazedly I asked if he meant Philip Darrell Sherman, the only and immortal P. D. S., and he gave a surprised affirmative. Microscopic are the dimensions of this obscure planet! By the way—does P. D. S. still grace the colyum which presumably survives the late B. L. T.?[4]

Loveman read me his unfinished masterpieces, "The Hermaphrodite" and "The Sphinx", and I forthwith relegated the once supreme Ernest A. Edkins to second place amongst amateurs, once and for all! Loveman makes language a thing of music, line, colour—"The Hermaphrodite" is a frieze, and "The Sphinx" is a poisonous flower grown in Syrian marshes where the Orontes winds down to the sea from Antioch.

To resume the history of the voyage—after a long Lovemanico-Theobaldian session, during which I read my latest hell-beater "Hypnos" and received the flattering verdict that it's the best thing I ever wrote; Mrs. Greene returned from town, whither she had gone unnoticed during the two-Love introductory whirl of words, and took both guests to dinner at a neighbouring refectory. Nothing as sensational as the Pfister orgy[5]—just broiled chicken with modest concomitants which I cannot recall in Mocratic detail—but a neat and quietly tasteful meal in surroundings of the same description. Upon our return to 259 we were soon privileged to hail the well-beloved Klei, emancipated from diurnal toil and vespertine nourishment. Then followed another whirl of words, which lasted till one a.m.—long after Mrs. Greene had been turned out of her own house and home for the night. The *Lokleilo* trio wrote a joint epistle to our kidlet friend in Madison, chinned some more, and then dispersed. Klei hit the trail, and Lolo hit the hay—Samuelus, good ol' scout, insisted that the less hardy and less easily somnolent Theobald take the only available bedchamber whilst he dumped down on the parlour couch—which is convertible into a bed or bedlet of a sort. I couldn't make him alternate—damn generous cuss—and I hadn't the heart to tell him I didn't sleep much anyway!

Friday dawned successfully, and all hands proceeded to the Manhattan section. Loveman and I took an omnibus up 5th Ave. to the Metropolitan Museum of Art, where we spent the entire day. Some day! For us were the sinister wonders of Ægyptus—we entered the nighted tomb of antique Perneb, transferred stone by stone from its age-long habitat beside the cryptical Nilus (in another place we saw the actual mummy of a priest of 2700 B.C.—the actual uncovered face, brown and withered, and the actual clawlike hands of a holy man who lived 4600 years ago!). For us were likewise the glories of fulgent Hellas—we found a young athlete's head (original—fifth century B.C.) so beautiful that the poetic Lovemanos went quite wild, purchased a half dozen postcard pictures of it, and chose it as the illustration for his "Hermaphrodite". Nor were the obscure secrets of dark Etruria absent—we saw a chariot, sixth century B.C., which might well have borne some warlike Lucume, Arnus, or Lars Porsenna. Paintings there were in abundance—by old masters and new—and many of these afforded us the keenest aesthetick gratification. But for me the supreme thrill—not only of the museums but of all New-York—came from the majestick memorials of mine own classical spirit-home—S.P.Q.R. Roma. I felt Rome the moment I entered the Musaeum—the main hall is like a gigantick atrium, with the effect enhanced by an heroick (Roman original) statue of the Imperatur Gallienus silhouetted against the archway leading to the southerly wing. How different is a Greek like Lovemanos from a Roman like Theobaldus! He worshipped every statue of Hellenick beauty, whilst I tingled with exaltation at every eagle-nosed, gesturing effigy of a Roman consul or imperator! The summit of all grandeur was the great model of the Pantheon, built by M. Vipsanius Agrippa, three times consul, during the principate of our divine lord Octavianus Augustus. *Ave, Marce, bene fecisti!*[6] The present model, restored by Charles Chipiez,[7] shows the magnificent edifice at the height of its glory; with the exquisite frieze and statuary which once adorned and surmounted it. The exterior is awe-inspiring—but when one stoops and enters!!! The head of the spectator of the interior comes well above the floor level, in a large circular aperture provided for such rubbernecking. The effect is that of being in the temple itself, for the smallness of the walls and dome seems but natural to an eye in the centre of a floor so vast. I raised my hand to shut off the disillusioning aperture and wooden rim—raised my hand and gazed at tier on tier of mounting Corinthian columns; niche on niche of heroic statues of gods and deified Augusti; vistas of marble beauty and sublimity, and a gold-inlaid dome that is the wonder and glory of the world, and whispered of even by the remote Parthians beyond the Euphrates, and the Germans and Sarmatians beyond the Rhine and Danube. I gazed, intoxicated with the mounting pride of a civis Romanus—a patrician of the Lolii Pagani and the Valerii Messalae—gazed at the supernal grandeur and loveliness which was Rome's might and proud splendour expressed and crystallised in lines of titanic sweep and more than martial grace. And as I gazed I sneered at the trifling arts and pleasures of the Greeks, and spat upon the grey dream of dim centuries of cursed superstition and effeminacy to come after our Roman world should die of weariness and barbarian blood;—superstition and effeminacy bred of some of the Syrian cults which infest the slums of the Suburra and trans-Tiber regions. And in the arrogance of a Roman I turned to my companion, the Syrian Greek ΛΟΒΜΑΝΟΣ, and chanted unto him the lines of our Roman Bard, who is Homer and Hesiod in one, and with twice their elegance—the one, the immortal Publius Maro, for whom Mantua is proud:

EXCVDENT.ALII.SPIRANTIA.MOLLIVS.AERA.
CREDO.EQVIDEM.VIVOS.DVCENT.DE.MARMORE.VVLTVS.
ORABVNT.CAVSAS.MELIVS.COELIQVE.MEATVS.
DESCRIBENT.RADIO.ET.SVRGENTIA.SIDERA.DICENT.
TV.REGERE.IMPERIO.POPVLOS.ROMANE.MEMENTO.
HAE.TIBI.ERVNT.ARTES.PACISQUE.IMPONERE.MOREM.
PARCERE.SVBIECTIS.ET.DEBELLARE.SVPERBOS.[8]

After the Museum we went down to Madison Square on omnibus—as far as it went—and feet, and took a surface car (a common ornery closed car of the vintage of about 1895, just like a small town car except that its trolley was on the bottom instead of on top, running in a slot to the Avernian caves much like the gripper of an antique cable-car) down Broadway to the tall building section. The cloud-piercers certainly present a sight fairly unique, but that was not what we went for. We were bound for 206 and George Julian Houtain. His office is a cramped dump on the ninth floor of a building which the neighbouring Woolworth tower quite dwarfs, but there was nothing cramped about G. Julian's laugh! Same old side-shaker! (Vide your files—and my epistle describing Epgephian convention of July 3–5, 1920!) Loveman was a bit embarrassed, because Mrs. Greene now hates Houtain and rather resents the fact that everyone else doesn't—but Old Theobald wasted no time in worries, since a true cynic gives not a damn what anyone else thinks. If Mrs. Greene objected, she had my permission to go to hell and complain to the devil! Houtain would receive me as a guest at 1128 Bedford even if Mrs.

Greene should kick me out of 259 Parkside! No damn human being, however worthy and generous, can dictate to the Old Gent whom he shall associate with!! Houtain may be a rascal in a sort of Nietzschean way, but I should worry. As an unmoralist too languid and indolent to be unmoral myself, I have to have an unmoral friend to sustain my reputation for cynical viciousness—and Houtain is the most friendly bird out of gaol! Loveman, already depressed by the snappish remark of an old fool museum attendant, (who simply made an infernal ass of himself, and at whom Loveman should mere have laughed tolerantly!) was still further depressed by the atmosphere of feudism radiating from Houtain's accounts of his clashes with various amateurs; so after a time I took him out and cheered him up at a Childs beanery. We got back to Parkside safely, and Loveman heaved a sigh of relief when he found that Mrs. Greene could amicably survive the shock of learning that we had not only been to Houtain's, but had made a dinner engagement at his house for the next evening.

> Now sound the clarions and awake the drums,
> For matchless MORTON in his chariot comes!⁹

Just as we were about 0.75 through an excellent dinner prepared by Mme. Greenevsky, good ol' woollybean blew in to bear us off to a stupid musicale on which his honest heart was set. It was at the home of an ex-member of the United—one Adeline E. Leiser—and most of the local amateurs, including our benign hostess, were none too enthusiastic about it because they had not been invited. It didn't sound very inviting (pardon paronomasia) to Loveman and me, but we'd do damn near anything for good old Jim. Morton is, in a sense, a pathetic figure. Always animated by a futile and quixotic idealism and determination to be true to his own convictions, he has wasted a magnificent brain on radical nonsense, squandered a vigorous life in espousal of unsound causes, and alienated most of those whose respect he really deserves through his conscientious advocacy of repellent ideas. His one paramount aesthetic desire—to express himself poetically—is frustrated by lack of the natural gift; and with his critical skill he tragically realises it. For him is none of the fatuous complacency of a Bush or a Baldwin.¹⁰ Now the years are creeping up on him, and he is not taken as seriously as he used to be. He is spoofed instead of combated—because he has become good-natured instead of fiery. His eccentricity, manifested in antique rubber collars, round-domed felt hats, and pouches and pockets full of handy paraphernalia, has become of that gentle, elderly sort which bespeaks the lovable "character". He is poor and lonely, and is beginning to realise how the world has passed him by—he, James Ferdinand Morton, Jr., Harvard A.B., A.M., grandson of S. F. Smith¹¹ and descendant of those Mortons who were the greatest landed proprietors on the New-Towne of the Massachusetts-Bay Colonie; and for whom Morton-Street in Newton Centre was named. Blessed old duffer! he has become of late a believer in matrimony, and proposes once a week to the ornate Mme. Greene—but alas, the fair are fickle, and now that he is getting stout and elderly he does not make much impression. After giving Mme. Greene what is probably the greatest intellectual training she ever received, he is now regarded by her with an increasing impatience which she threatens to amplify to direct vanishment. I regret such cavalier treatment of a pure Anglo-Saxon by a foreigner; but it is only the common way of all mankind—bah! Thus did an Hibernian Delia treat our precious little Anglo-Saxon Damon back in Appletonium![12] But Old Theobald is all for Mortonius—we hope to have a session in Rhode Island this summer, ascending Durfee Hill, (805 feet) the highest altitude in the State. James Ferd wants the record of having ascended the highest elevation in every New England State—he will always be a true Yankee of the old stock for all his wild notions and alien residences! At present Morton's only income is from the Bush work of which he so nobly relieves me. If he would ask for the requisite pull from influential friends, he could easily land a highly-paid lecturing job in the N.Y. schools, but this his pride will not let him do. Work of confining kind repels him, anyway—last January Mrs. Miniter told of his career in Boston thirty years ago. He was just out of Harvard with a master's degree; but lived in one damp cellar room in the Irish slums of South Boston, refusing both worldly employments and cash assistance from his family. He ate only one meal a day—beans at a dingy lunch room—but pieced it out with broken crackers which some grocers sold him and some grocers gave him. He never had car fare, and used to walk miles to the Hub Club[13] meetings; where his hunger (always proudly *denied*) made him cross and almost combative until he could be tactfully offered refreshments. His clothes, always scrupulously clean, were invariably in disorder, and almost falling off his back; and his barbering was generally quite impossible. Independence and intellectual integrity were the only values he recognised—and he won the ardent admiration even of those who were reluctant to be seen walking beside so tattered and nondescript a figure. There is much of the heroic in James Ferdinand Morton, Jr., and I would give anything to see his worth recognised and rewarded as it should be. Justice, however, is the most flimsy of illusions; and honesty and goodness bring rewards only when chance weaves extraordinary circumstances about their possessor. Of the three radicals and lovers of mankind, Christus, Debs, and Mortonius, one became the nucleus of a world-wide cult, another became a popular idol of the discontented, whilst the third—is not taken seriously any more. Like the young men in Oscar Wilde's prose-poem "The Master", Mortonius must say—"All things that this man has done I have done also. And yet they have not crucified me."

But gawdamighty—I've clean branched offen the thing my Hero wanted Loveman and me to attend! We went—and kept awake through the whole programme of bourgeois Victorianism at the lyre. One of the singers could almost have sung if provided with a real song, whilst a yellow-haired young man resembling a truck-driver did noble service with a French horn in warding off the ever-present peril of obvious nodding. The best thing came from Mortonius—a pair of dramatic recitations of which the second was the famed mad scene by "Monk" Lewis—the "I-am-not-mad-but-soon-shall-be" thing.[14] James F. reeled it off splendidly, ending in a shriek and a fall to the floor. He has a great reputation for this performance in B. P. C.[15] circles—it is the inevitable Morton encore. The triangular walk back to Parkside—Lovemanus–Mortonius–Theobaldus—was the best part of the evening; a literary symposium with the Elizabethan dramatists as chief ingredient. Morton left us at the door, and when we got in we found a note from Mme. Greene saying she would not be there next morning and telling us to get our own breakfast. (N. B. Loveman got the breakfast.)

Saturday was sightseeing day—and who could ask for a better guide than ours—good ol' Klei? We met—Loveman–Theobald, Mortonius, and Klei, in front of the Woolworth Building, after the two Loves had indulged in a tour of old bookstalls in Vesey-Street. (I picked up some good Poe-iana) The assembled clan's first move was up—clean up to the top of N.Y.! It costs half a ducat per rube, and is worth it. Loveman was dizzy, but your grandpa wasn't—gawd knows how hard I worked when I was ten years old to conquer my native tendency to dizziness from altitudes! I walked on high railway trestles, and hell knows what not! But I digress. All Manhattan, Brooklyn, and Jersey City lay below, outspread like a map—in fact, I told Mortonius that the city-planners had done an excellent job in making the place almost as good as the map in my Hammond Atlas at home.

At length descending, we set out for the studio of Louis Keila,[16] where rest in imperishable marble (plaster) the sculptured (modelled) features of our James Ferdinand. We took the 9th Ave. elevated—which is just the same as when built, save that steam has yielded to electricity. Klei says that it was opened in 1879, but to look at the cars yuh'd think that date incredibly recent. I can't believe that Poe didn't take those rattletraps up to Fordham in '45—or that he didn't kick about their unpleasant obsoleteness. I am sure that the one we were in must have been the re-modelled stage coach which ran from Fraunce's [*sic*] Tavern to Kingsbridge in the reign of George II. But anyhow, the damn thing didn't fall to pieces before it got to 14th St., and there lay the Keila hangout. 14th St. is a poor imitation of Westminster St. in Providence—in fact, N.Y. is more like Providence than Boston. It didn't impress me much except when seen at a distance and from certain angles—then it can be utterly unique and occasionally almost sublime. Somebody said that Old Man Daedalus' architectural masterpiece was in Crete—but that guy was a liar. It's in 14th St.—and Louis Keila is the original Minotaur. How in Pete's name he ever finds his way from the street to his office, I can't tell yuh! The building is apparently of the Petrus Stuyvesant period—maybe it was the Old Boy's gubernatorial mansion before His Britannick Majesty's fleet relieved the Netherland States-General of colonial responsibility—and is composed of a thousand corridors and one or two rooms. There would have been light in the halls if I had carried an electric torch. And there was an anaemic lift. Keila is a tough guy from the slums—half Greek and half Jew. He has no manners or refinement, but is unmistakably gifted in sculptural art. He has done Pres. Harding's bust, and sports a framed acknowledgement and autographed portrait from His Normalcy. Morton likes the fellow immensely, and is trying to civilise him. The Morton bust is very good indeed—shewing Jim in a characteristic and quizzically smiling mood. Keila was going to make some small replicas for sale, but gave up the idea. It was interesting to see statue and model side by side—both bore the test very well. But at this point came parting's sweet sorrow—Jacobus had to skip for a lecture he was scheduled to deliver, leaving Klei as sole guide for the out-of-town buyers. He was some little guide, at that—we'll tell de woild! After Keila, bookstalls. Everybody right tew hum, even if it was in bustling and remote Novum-Eboracum. Then a d. store and some post—1919 hootch, (coca-colas for Klei and Sam, orange phosphate for Theobaldus) and the subway for the financial district. In the sub. we saw Houtain's *Home Brew* on sale, and I picked up a copy with sophisticated nonchalance and pointed out my name and work[17] ..... Reg'lar author'n' ever'thin' ..... Then we came to the surface on Old New-York—the financial district and heart of the town in Dutch and early British days. Wall St. was the old North boundary—it enclosed a village beside which Appleton would be a metropolis and even Elroy a great city.[18] Trinity Church represents the Britannic period at its best—I saluted it—not the ecclesiastical mockery but the symbol of Royal dominion. Here we got some skyscraper vistas which enabled me to echo very faintly Klei's worship of his native burg. Now came the subway again—to Brooklyn. A stranger can tell when he is under the river (it's really a *strait*, not a "river") by the pressure on his ear-drums—the tube is very deep. When we came up for air we were in the City of Churches, (oh, what a place for you, Old Thing!) and proceeded to a hash joint to satisfy Klei's gastric pangs. My gawd, the belly in that boy! It was just the same in Providence in '18–'19–'20. Yuh have to keep him filled to the neck or he languishes by the wayside. Some ethereal bard, we'll broadcast it to the blue! Loveman and I could only sip coffee and admire the way *The Piper* punished his pork an'. Next we hit the old residential district, which is the world's only replica of Boston's Back Bay. For a cent I'd have taken oath I was in Beacon-Street with the Charles peeping betwixt the brick mansions. At Montague St. we found an abandoned garden and broken flight of steps which set both the poets off mooning—you may hear the echoes in some amateur journal. But the big thing was Manhattan Bridge and the view of the New-York skyline there obtained. Right there I surrendered to Klei about the beauties of his home town. Out of the waters it rose at twilight; cold, proud, and beautiful; an Eastern city of wonder whose brothers the mountains are. It was not like any city of earth, for above purple mists rose towers, spires, and pyramids which one may only dream of in opiate lands beyond the Oxus; towers, spires and pyramids that no man could fashion, but that bloomed flower-like and delicate; the bridges up which fairies walk to the sky; the visions of giants that play with the clouds. Only Dunsany could fashion its equal, and he in dreams only. And as I gazed upon this gorgeous phantom sight I said to the wise men about me, "Behold the beauty of earth, which is mineral, titanic, and frore; even as a palace of ice by the ultimate boreal pole, which hath nothing of man it. For this was the world born, and the contemplative moon. And as insects unseen and unsung have reared in warm seas the loveliness that is coral, branching and glorious; so have insects called men, a little seen and a little sung, reared to the sky these pinnacles of breathing stone. Let us be patient. Not long will insects swarm upon earth, but long will stand the beauty whose creation was their task. And when the world is ice and the heavens are dim, and the jest called life long-forgotten; then will rubescent stars drink from these unvocal flowers of stone the joy and loveliness that were made for the delight of stars."[19]

Then the gang crossed the bridge and hit some filthy Jew slums in Manhattan. At the Bowery we got a subway train back to Brooklyn, and at seven we breezed into the palatial apartment of the Houtains—an archaic dump over a shop. Georgius was the same old noise-factory, and his wife the same faint and colourless echo. He has an old maid sister who is a good cook. Conversation was trivial—what t'hell else could ya expect?—but exceedingly animated. Wine was produced—and everybody but Grandpa drank. And yet it was Grandpa who made the most noise! In discussing Morton's "I-am-not-mad" recitation, I chanced to mention my boyhood dramatics—I was a thunderous "heavy" in them days. Nothing would satisfy the gang but a demonstration, so I let 'em have my favourite—from what is normally the last end of W. S.'s "Henry VI", but what my old pal Colley Cibber stuck into "Richard III"—the tower stuff—

> "What, shall th' aspiring blood of Lancaster
> Sink i' the ground? I thought it would have mounted!
> See how my sword weeps for the poor King's death!
> Oh, may such purple tears be always shed
> From those that wish the downfall of our house!
> If any spark of life be yet remaining,
> Down, down, to Hell; and say I sent thee thither!"[20]
>
>   (stabs him again)
> etc. etc. etc.

Seventeen years ago I used to spout this by the yard, but only last month did I receive the flattery which would once have pleased me so, but which now strikes indifferent cynick-ears! To my vast astonishment, my audience took the damn thing seriously; and Loveman himself couldn't let the subject alone during the residue of the visit! He said it was truly fiendish and artistic, and that it had a sinister convincingness which Morton's performance lacked!! He solemnly asseverated that I ought to cultivate dramatic expression as something capable of development beside literary expression—advice which I promptly forgot with polite satisfaction that it should have been so flatteringly given. I had rather see drama than erupt it—it's too damn hard work, and gets one's hair mussed up. Nor is it as interesting as writing. By the way—this heavy stuff marked the first full restoration of my voice—which had given out during the Loveman–Kleiner discourse of Thursday night as it did four years ago when Klei's first Providence trip marked my resumed contact with the world of men.

Houtain saw us to the nearest elevated, and in due time we reached Parkside and the hay.

Sunday morning Loveman and I explored Prospect Park, fed the squirrels, and talked literature. At noon I did some kodak shooting, during which process there dawned upon us the new infant celebrity who was to form our principal focus of interest during the entire residue of the sojourn—

FRANK BELKNAP LONG, JR.

Long, whose phantasies you have doubtless read (I believe you once mistook one for Theobaldian stuff!) is an exquisite boy of twenty who hardly looks fifteen. He is dark and slight, with a busy wealth of almost black hair and a delicate, beautiful face still a stranger to the gillette. I think he likes the tiny collection of lip-hairs—about six on one side and five on the other—which may with assiduous care some day help to enhance his genuine resemblance to his chief idol—Edgar Allan Poe. Long is a sartorial triumph from spats to Fedora—he will undoubtedly carry a cane some day—and affects a mode subtly suggesting the Poe and the poet. But dost fancy I am describing a vapid dude? Fergit it, 'bo! The kid's a baby wonder—a secondary Galpinius—all wool and a yard wide! A scholar; a fantaisiste; a prose-poet; a sincere and intelligent disciple of Poe, Baudelaire, and the French decadents. He is as modest as Loveman himself, and the years seem likely to develop amazing gifts in him. I may be partial, because he flattered me by informing me that he always carries my picture in his pocket book (!!), but I don't think so. Loveman shares my view, and even our lofty little Galba person is beginning to take notice of him. Long is a cynic and a deist of the Voltaire type—he will be a materialist before he is through college. He attends N. Y. University, but is now out because of his convalescence from last winter's appendicitis operations. His life was despaired of, and he is still in bandages. He cannot walk swiftly yet, and has to retire each night at nine p.m.

At dinner—about one-thirty—were Loveman, Theobald, Long, Mme. Greene, and the latter's flapper offspring, yclept Florence—a pert, spoiled, and ultra-independent infant rather more hard-boiled of visage than her benignant mater.[21] Trough-exercise was no sooner completed than a sizeable gang began to assemble—for this Sabbath had been appointed as the proper season for a fairly representative Blue Pencil conclave to do honor to the divine Lovemanus. Combatants in the H. H. war were barred, as was the arrogant Isaacsonius; but there was quite a bunch at that, including my United recruit Paul Livingston Keil, a very nice 'rah-'rah boy with a penchant for things Indian.[22] Among this august assemblage was a severe and angular palaeoparthenoid personage whose name awaked dim memories in my aged brain. She was introduced as Miss "Vel-shert"—and a second's reflection convinced me that this must be the pronunciation of the Hun patronymic spelled VOELCHERT. My gawd—the person who introduced to amateur journalism the one and only ΜΟΚΡΑΤΕΣ. On ascertaining that such was indeed the case, I expressed with enthusiasm my admiration of Mocratic excellence, and my appreciation of the genius which secured for the United an exemplar so illustrious! One hilarious interlude occurred. Loveman had established telephonic communication with a little Jew whom he had known in the army—a bird whose name is pronounced Lashinsky—Yahveh knows how it's spelt. At Camp Gordon this specimen had been a timid, shrinking, even tearful object—the typical Yiddisher in man's-size surroundings—and Loveman had been sort of kindly foster-father to him through racial and humanitarian sympathy. In the midst of the meeting, Lashinsky shewed up—oh, boy! What had Yahveh—plus three years of civilian clothes—wrought!! Oi, oi! Coarse, strident, voluble, and gesticulant, the creature began boasting of his success in life as a moichant in der cloding pizness and a vaudeville singer, dancer, and jazz-composer in odd moments. He vent on de piano and drummed out his latest composition, an' den he began to dance in der jazzyvay all der room aroundt, den he sat it himself down, and began to tell Loveman and everybody else what fools they were to waste time on highbrow art and literature. "I tell you," said he, "I'm a lowbrow, an' in six days I get more out of life than you do in six years. I get the money, get good clothes, have a good time and a goil for every day in her week—vot more could you vant?" By the time he could be got rid of, Loveman was in a fit of depression which lasted all the rest of the day. It mattered not that everybody laughed and obviously enjoyed the escape from boredom, or that they clearly understood how little Loveman could have suspected the disconcerting metamorphosis of his one-time pathetic protege. Loveman's sensitiveness was outraged, and for him were only pain and humiliation!

The gathering, from which Mortonius had to be absent on account of a lecture, dispersed at twilight; whereupon Mme. Greene, who cannot keep still for two consecutive seconds, piloted Loveman and me through Prospect Park, which we had already explored. Upon returning to 259, Mortonius was discovered on the doorstep; and his amiability met with so haughty a reception that my Anglo-Saxon pride rebelled! I took him under my own thoroughly British wing, and let the foreigners shift for themselves during the residue of the evening; which included supper (how these birds do *eat!*) and a trip down to see the famed "White Way" and some of its denizens all lit up. The illumination is unique and extensive, but neither superlatively impressive nor in any sense truly artistic. At the elevated station at 6th Ave. and 42nd St. I lost my fellow Anglo-Saxon, whose home is far to the north in the semi-African jungles of Harlem; and the depleted party was haled to a swell eatery where the waiters hardly speak English and have no spots on their immaculate shirt-fronts. Eating again—my gawd! What are their stomachs made of! Our hostess ordered a strawberry concoction probably closely akin to what she handed you at the Ppffister—and of which I was able to partake only because I had made the preceding meal a matter of urbane evasion.

Thereafter once again to Parkside via subway—then more or less oblivion. It was hard work persuading Loveman to remain in N.Y. all this time, but perfect team-work did it. He saw that he could get no position, though Mme. Greene tried with frantic generosity to secure one for him—even unto the last moment.

Monday was Long–Poe day. Dinner at Long's, then as large an expedition as possible to the Poe cottage at Fordham—on the mainland north of Manhattan, but within the present limits of the vast municipality. Loveman and I started out early and went to the Public Library, later taking a Riverside Drive omnibus and reaching the Long apartment at eleven-thirty. The Greene flat is of much elegance on a small scale, but the Long menage *really* "belongs". It is a sumptuous place at the corner of 100th St. and West End Ave.—one alights from the 'bus at a picturesque landing stage at 100th and Riv. Drive a point embellished by a firemen's memorial having the most beautifully tasteless and anachronistic bas-reliefs. Loveman and I are agreed on one thing—that all really great sculptural art died utterly with the Hellenic period. Long's pater is a dentist—a genial fellow of fifty-three who looks as though the numerals ought to be read the other way around. It is from him that Frank Jr.—called "Belknap" by his doting parents—gets his youthfulness. Long Sr. has a thick shock of black hair without a touch of grey, and on his boyish face is not a solitary line. During the war they used to hold him up for his draft registration card! Mrs. Long is very cultivated, and takes vast interest in her lone chick's achievements. She sometimes calls him "dear" and "darling" right afore comp'ny—and he bears it bravely though without noticeable pleasure. He's some boy! Young Belknap, by the way, loathes and abhors his native New-York—he says it is sordid and oppressive, and that he only really lives when up in Maine for the summer. Even Atlantic City, whither they frequently go, is not agrestic enough for this delicious little Melibeus!

Dinner at the Long's is a very formal institution—all the approved courses in rigidly proper order from fruit down through soup, meat, salad, etc. etc. to an appropriately proper dessert. Woe to the maid who mixes the menu or transposes the courses—one such blunder did occur on this occasion, and Mrs. Long was careful to inform us that the services of the culpable ancilla would terminate with the week! The delights of the Long household are enhanced by two parrots and an exquisite "coon" cat from Maine—a sumptuous creature with silky mane who answers to the simple title of "Felis", bestowed by his affectionate young master. My coming *Conservative* will contain a prose-poem by Kid Belknap, inspired by "Felis". About dessert time good old James F. blew in—and Samuelus had to blow out, summoned by a last fruitless business call on the telephone. This delayed the Fordham party—we waited till Loveman called up from the city to tell us whether he could come or not. He couldn't, so Jim, Belknap, and Grandpa started off alone—the first one hundred percent Aryan, Anglo-Saxon gang to get together during the entire "convention"! GOD SAVE THE KING. We, the dominant British stock who founded this system of colonies, started north to pick up young Keil, who lives at the top of a young Woolworth building in Fordham—a baby Bunker Hill Monument without an elevator, whose interminable stairs were too much for our little Longlet. Finally we got up, but found Paul Livingston out. His ma and kid sister brought forth some weak lemonade and stale cookies, (*eating* again, after that Long orgy!) and finally the missing youth appeared. Thereupon the quartette, still one hundred per-cent Aryan, sallied forth for a Bronx omnibus—and Poe.

We arrived at the cottage just too late to get in, but the exterior was an eyeful. Prior to 1913 it was a disgrace—rented to any old tenant and altered beyond recognition. In the above year it was purchased by a memorial association, moved out of the path of the ever-encroaching apartment-house wave to a safe spot in a park, and restored to its 1844–49 aspect. Even the *grounds*, as shewn in prints of the Poe period, were re-created—walks and trees. Today it is a thing to stir the pulses. Fordham is now hopelessly fused into the solid mass of elevateds, apartment-house cliffs, busses, and boulevards which is New-York. But in Poe's day it was a village of magical charm, with verdant arcades, purling brooks, and fragrant sylvan lanes leading to quaint and antique Highbridge—a favourite haunt of the great one. You will realise what beauty has been destroyed by the fiendishly gnawing city when you reflect that the sketch "Landor's Cottage" was partially inspired by the author's own humble, rented home.

We had a date to meet Klei on the Pub. Libe steps at six-thirty, so soon bade adieu to the place of beautiful memories. Keil had to go home, and Long's health would not allow him to be in on the evening jaunt, but the latter kid was so anxious to see Loveman again that he rode down town with us on the elevated, only to ride back again after he had paid his respects to the Divine Syrian—to say naught of the ever-genial Klei. It was not certain that Loveman could be held another day—I could not get him to promise till late that night! After Long's departure—more *eating!* An automatic beanery in a basement—gorge and guzzle—bah! But after a while we pried Klei loose from his trough and set him at the head of a guiding party. We walked in pairs—Klei–Lo ahead, Loveman–Morton behind—so that my detachment reminded me of the good old Kleiner visits in Providence. Mme. Greene may have told you that Klei has rather retrograded through intimacy with Houtain—but that is only superficially true. If I had him in Providence for a week I could bring back the old Kleiner . . . . . he admitted to Loveman and me that he sometimes wishes he had never left his old dream-world. A good old boy, Klei! Our course lay down 5th Ave. to Washington-Square—once the centre of fashionable society under George III, but now very decadent. The "Greenwich Village" nuts have been there and departed—and there is a slight prospect of at least a partial rehabilitation to ancient glory. There is a Roman arch there, under which I walked with pride of a patrician triumphator. We sat on a bench in this clearing for nearly an hour, discussing all manner of learned things. Then the hour of a Writers' Club meeting drew near. Klei and Jim both belong, but the former funked. J. Ferd had to go because he had a speech to deliver. Some orator! This was our final adieu, for Loveman had intimated that if he stayed another day he wanted the company only of Long and myself—why the especial choice, only de lawd knows.

Klei, now at the head of a triangular expedition with the same personnel as Saturday's, proceeded to lead us into the slums; with "Chinatown" as an ulterior objective. My gawd—what a filthy dump! I thought Providence had slums, and antique Bostonium as well; but damn me if I ever saw anything like the sprawling sty-atmosphere of N.Y.'s lower East Side. We walked—at my suggestion—in the middle of the street, for contact with the heterogeneous sidewalk denizens, spilled out of their bulging brick kennels as if by a spawning beyond the capacity of the places, was not by any means to be sought. At times, though, we struck peculiarly deserted areas—these swine have instinctive swarming movements, no doubt, which no ordinary biologist can fathom. Gawd knows what they are—Jew, Italian, separate or mixed, with possible touches of residual aboriginal Irish and exotic hints of the Far East—a bastard mess of stewing mongrel flesh without intellect, repellent to eye, nose, and imagination—would to heaven a kindly gust of cyanogen could asphyxiate the whole gigantic abortion, end the misery, and clean out the place. The streets, even in the centre, are filthy with old papers and vegetable debris—probably the street-cleaners dislike to soil their white uniforms by visiting such infernos.

And then Chinatown appeared. Here cleanliness reigned, for certain enterprising rubberneck-wagon owners use it as a sort of seat of local colour—they have fake opium joints which they point out as the real thing. Doyers St., the main thoroughfare, is narrow and crooked. It is fascinatingly Oriental, and Loveman rhapsodised on the evil faces of the natives. Probably it was only the usual low-caste physiognomy of the coolie type which so thrilled him—but bless me! let the poets find thrills where they can!

We emerged on the Bowery, and proceeded to cross Manhattan Bridge to Brooklyn. Here we saw the city skyline electrically illumined, but it did not equal that flower-like, fairly-like vision in the twilight, when softly golden pinnacles reached up to consort with the first stars of evening. Loveman and I were damn near dead with tramping, but I refused to show it. Morton had called me the most nonchalant and imperturbable person he had ever seen, whose cynical poise could not be shaken even by a River Beach rollercoasting thunderbolt, so I resolved to justify his flattery or die standing and jesting. How Klei stands such tramping about, only the local small gods of the city can reveal. By the time we reached a homeward subway I was ready to write a joint two-Love elegy.

Tuesday morning—last full day—found me a pretty drowsy customer. I went out and purchased a much-needed new collar, and returned to rest in the deserted flat whilst Loveman and Mme. Greene went about their respective Metropolitan affairs. I had arranged to meet Loveman at the Pub. Libe at noon—but eheu! I got to sleep and was nearly an hour late! We went to Long's again for dinner, and found an entire change of dietetic programme just as elaborate as the first spread. They do that sort of thing right along—we would we all, no doubt, if we had the dough! I can recall traces of it in mine own household in extreme youth, ere chill penury had got in his most repressive work. After the ordeal we fared northward again to the shrine of the only vital force which America has yet contributed to the general current of world-literature. The day, like all the others of the trip, was delightfully and unseasonably hot—which sustained my tropic-loving bulk wonderfully.

At Fordham—thank Pegāna—we found the Poe cottage open, and forthwith entered a small world of magic. Poor Poe, a creature of poverty driven from pillar to post in hired houses and with no stable, ancestral furniture, left very little with which to embellish the interior; but his own desk is there, and the chair in which he wrote "Annabel Lee", and the bed on which his wife died. The rest of the furniture was chosen from among the semi-antiques in strict accordance with the known styles of the period and the various accounts in letters of, to, and about Poe and his home. It is believed to represent with fair accuracy the actual furniture of the cottage during Poe's occupancy. Our friend Burton Rascoe,[23] late of the *Chitrib* and now of the *N.Y. Tribune*, recently made a bonehead play in writing up the cottage—he spoke of 'Poe's taste in furniture', as though the stuff were really his. There are several Poe busts, a couple of awkward stuffed ravens, and some good Poe portraits. There are specimens of his handwriting and a lock of his hair. The atmosphere grows on one and finally grips one—it is so terribly vivid—the 'forties recalled in every sombre detail. The pitiful poverty shows—something sombre broods over the place. I seemed to feel unseen bat-wings brush my cheek as I passed through a bare, cramped corridor . . . . . the house is so pathetically small . . . . . and such hideous things have been written there. Such was the home of the man to whom I probably owe every genuine artistic impulse and method I possess. My master—the great original whose titanic powers I can so feebly seek to copy . . . . . Edgar Allan Poe.

It was deuced hard to break away, but it hadda be did. We hit the elevated in an effort to get to the Museum of Natural History, but lo! Our little native N.Y. guide Belknap got the wrong train and landed us on the east instead of the west side of Central Park! Damn! Having arranged to meet Mme. Greene at 57th St., we had no time to cross over, but consoled ourselves by strolling slowly down town beside the delectable *rus in urbe*.[24] It was early spring—and some early flowers were in bloom. Magnolias were white, and there were other flowering shrubs as delicate as a Japanese print. A shower sprang up, and we sought the shelter of the porch of a magnificent mansion. Then it cleared in the west—the sun shone golden, and a rainbow appeared in the east. (Loveman looked for it in the WEST—haw! Poetic soul doesn't give scientific accuracy!)

We met Mme. Greene in front of her lid shop, and after a ceremonious farewell kid Long hiked for the northbound elevated. Too bad he wasn't able to keep with us—but he has to be careful of his convalescent anatomy. When he is better, he and Mortonius will be great pals—Jim Ferd has a vast paternal admiration for his unusual qualities. Meanwhile he is getting more closely in touch with the United—Loveman, Galba, and Theobald. Great Kid, we'll say! After the adieu the residual triad hiked to a Dago Cafe of semi-subterranean altitude on 49th St., where the lavish Mme. Greene made what appeared to be a sturdy effort to buy the place out. Actually, I suppose it was what they call their regular dinner, Italian-style,—but I'd like to see the human being who could eat it all! I wonder what they do with the inevitable residuum? Chicken, spaghetti, and other things were included—damn me if I can remember. The order of courses had no relation to Anglo-Saxon dining customs, and gawd knows I didn't try to tackle half of 'em. When we broke away it was to attend a performance, in the 49th St. Theatre, of that rather well known Muscovite melange of cleverly dippy vaudeville called the "Chauve Souris" and managed by a comical fattish cuss of long speeches and short English named НIКIТА БАЛIЕВ (since the limit of your linguistick attainment is Assyrian cuneiform, I'll translate it—Nikita Balieff.)[25] It was a balmy sort of mess in spots, but pretty damn good at that. The star act was a company of ginks dressed up with inimitable cleverness as *wooden soldiers*. Their musical drill was sure some knockout—it brought down the house. Take it from me—in a couple years ham companies'll be tryin' to put over that act in every tank town on the small-time circuit! It's a bird, and no mistake! When the show let out, darn the luck, it was raining again, but not all the aqueous wrath of the sky could dampen the spirits of the irrepressible Mme. Greene—so she led the docile guests to a

Russian restaurant (*eats* again—bah!) on thirty-something street. We trifled lightly with cake and coffee, and finally hit the Parkside trail. After Mme. Greene's departure Loveman and I finished valise-packing and prepared to snatch a bit of rest before our simultaneous embarkation for opposite points on the morrow. He gave me some books to remember him by—good boy!

Wednesday we were up betimes, and guided by Mme. Greene to the Grand Central Station via the underground. It's quite a dee-po, but not so artistic as the Pennsylvania—or, for that matter, as the Union Station in Worcester. But it beats by a mile anything in Boston or Providence. My train left for the East at eight-thirty-three a.m.; Loveman's for the West at eight-forty-five. Mine was N.Y.N.H.&H.; his was N.Y.C.&H.R. Mme. Greene bade the twain a joint farewell when the time arrived for her to hit 57th St. and work; and thereafter Lovemanus and I discoursed in the manner of a Greek and a Roman about to part in brotherly amity. Then train time approached. I got a good seat and slept all the way home, so that the next sight I recall was our own marble-domed R.I. State House, the habitat of an equally marble-domed legislature. Loveman had a trying trip—noisy fellow-passengers, wakefulness, and ennui generally. His trip was also over twice as long as mine. At one-twenty, I was on Providence soil, whilst he didn't hit Cleveland till midnight. I'll say it was some trip. Whilst it lasted I kept up very well, though not sleeping much. Afterward I did very little but sleep—I'm hardly over it yet! But it was worth it.

Loveman, Kleiner, and I agreed to write some verses on the event, and I said I would use them as jewels in a prose travelogue setting of my own. I didn't want to bother; but I knew those birds would never keep their promises, so made mine with the cynical assurance that I'd never have to keep it. And so it turned out—this epistle is the only travelogue I've perpetrated, and it is very strictly for an audience of exactly one. Little Belknap has evolved the only really literary echo of the event—he has written a prose-poem entitled "At the Home of Poe", and has dedicated it to his old Grandpa Theobald. Good kid.

Pictures were taken by Long, Keil, and Theobald. I haven't seen Keil's,[26] but will enclose Long's and mine. Please return all—only ones I have left. You will note the horrible fact that Old Theobald is getting fat. I have jumped from a 15¼ to a 15¾ collar, and gawd only knows where I'll end. I refuse absolutely to mount a pair of scales—or to diet or exercise.

> "O, that this too, too solid flesh wou'd melt,
> Thaw, and resolve itself into a dew!"[27]

If you have read this damn thing through, you sure have my sympathy! Let's hear from you, Old Top!

CVRA. VT. VALEAS.

M. LOLLIVS. PAGANVS.

Notes

1. HPL refers to the home of the amateur poet S. Lilian McMullen, who generally wrote under the pseudonym "Lilian Middleton." See HPL's essay "The Poetry of Lilian Middleton" (1922; *CE* 2.51–56).
2. Leonard E. Tilden (1861–1937), a veteran amateur journalist of New Hampshire, and later Washington, DC, was attempting to secure second-class postage rates for amateur journals.
3. "To Samuel Loveman, Esquire, on His Poetry and Drama . . ." In his memoir of HPL, SL summarized the first letter he received from HPL: "the writer had long been an ardent admirer of my poetry . . . He had . . . practically given up any hope of finding me, when a clue to my location was indicated. Hence, his letter of inquiry: was I alive or dead?" ("Howard Phillips Lovecraft" [1948], *LR* 204).
4. Bert Leston Taylor (1866–1921), American journalist and author of the "A Line o' Type or Two" column in the *Chicago Tribune* (1909–21). Sherman (1881–1957) of Pawtucket, RI, contributed to Taylor's column.
5. The Pfister is a fine hotel in downtown Milwaukee.
6. "Hail, Marcus, have you done well."
7. Charles Chipiez (1835–1901), French architect and Egyptologist. Among his books is *A History of Art in Ancient Egypt* (1883).
8. A celebrated passage in Virgil's *Aeneid* (6.847–53) in which the shade of Anchises (father of Aeneas) prophesies the future greatness of Rome: "Others will forge breathing bronzes more smoothly / (I believe it at any rate), and draw forth living features from marble / They will plead lawsuits better and trace the movements / Of the sky with a rod and describe the rising stars. / You, O Roman, govern the nations with your power—remember this! / These will be your arts: to impose the ways of peace, / To show mercy to the conquered and to subdue the proud" (tr. Jane Mason).
9. "The Isaacsonio-Mortoniad," ll. 93–94. For line 93, read "Sound now the trumpets, and awake the drums,".
10. John Osman Baldwin (1871–1942), an amateur poet whom HPL frequently took to task for various deficiencies. "We will merely urge Mr. Baldwin to exercise a greater care in composition, since his theme deserves better presentation. He is, as we have before remarked in these columns, a genuine poet of more than usual endowments." "Department of Public Criticism" (November 1918; *CE* 1.211).
11. Samuel Francis Smith (1808–1895), author of "My Country, 'Tis of Thee."
12. HPL refers to various love affairs in which Alfred Galpin was involved during his years at Appleton High School. HPL wrote many poems about "Damon" (Galpin) and "Delia" (possibly Margaret Abraham).
13. An amateur group in Boston associated with the NAPA.
14. HPL refers to a short verse play, *The Captive* (1803), by Gothic novelist and playwright Matthew Gregory Lewis (1775–1818), that features a soliloquy by a female captive consigned to a dungeon in which the line "I am not mad, but soon shall be" appears.
15. The Blue Pencil Club, an amateur group in Brooklyn associated with the NAPA.
16. Louis Keila (1883–1954), an artist and sculptor living in New York.

17. At this time, the third installment of "Grewsome Tales" (i.e., "Herbert West—Reanimator") had appeared in the April 1922 issue of *Home Brew*.

18. Elroy, a small town in central Wisconsin, was the home of E. E. Ericson, who frequently served as Official Printer of the UAPA.

19. The above is a pastiche of Dunsany's "A City of Wonder" (in *Tales of Three Hemispheres*), a prose-poem that records Dunsany's impressions of the New York skyline.

20. Shakespeare, *Henry VI* 5.6.61–67. The passage does not appear in Colley Cibber's adaptation of *Richard III* (1699).

21. Florence Greene (later Florence Weld, 1902–1979) later became a journalist and was the first reporter to cover the romance of Edward VIII and Mrs. Wallis Simpson. She had already been estranged from her mother previous to Sonia's marriage to HPL and never again spoke to her mother after the ceremony.

22. Charles D. Isaacson took HPL to task for comments HPL had made in the first issue of the *Conservative*, especially regarding racial matters and Walt Whitman. See Isaccson's "Concerning the Conservative," *In a Minor Key* 2 [1915]: [10–11]. In response HPL wrote the essay "In a Major Key" and the poems "Gems from 'In a Minor Key'" and "The Isaacsonio-Mortoniad," although the latter remained unpublished in HPL's lifetime. The amateur journalist and printer Paul Livingston Keil (1900–1953), author of *Arrowheads and Such: What You Want to Know about Them*, wrote a memoir of HPL, "I Met Lovecraft," *Phoenix* 3, No. 6 (July 1944): 149, telling of his accompanying HPL and others to the Poe cottage in the Bronx (see below).

23. Burton Rascoe (1892–1957), American journalist, editor, and literary critic for the *New York Herald Tribune*.

24. Literally, "the country in the city," or a section of a city that presents the illusion of being a rural area.

25. *La Chauve-Souris* (*The Bat*), a touring revue during the early 1900s originating in Moscow and then Paris, directed by Nikita F. Balieff (1877–1936), a Jewish-Russian-Armenian-born vaudevillian, stage performer, writer, and impresario.

26. Paul Livingston Keil's photograph of HPL, FBL, and Morton at the Poe cottage has been frequently reproduced.

27. *Hamlet* 1.2.129–30.

[18] [AHT]

Providence, R.I.,
June 21, 1922

My dear Mo:—

Your new friend Mme. Greenevsky is livening up the social programme hereabouts. She is representing her firm at Magnolia, Mass., an ultra-fashionable watering-place on the coast near Gloucester, an hour's ride northeast from Boston; and Sunday she blew into Providentia for the afternoon and evening. For friendliness and generosity she sure beats hell—she is so stuck on my younger aunt Mrs. Gamwell, that she's trying to get her to come to N.Y. and permanently share her abode! And strange to say, my aunt likes her immensely despite a racial and social chasm which she doesn't often bridge. Gawd! Even the dowagers are getting democratic in these decadent days! But damme if Mme. Greenevsky ain't a good sort, after all. She is trying to get the whole bally family to visit her in Magnolia, and failing to do that, is insisting that the old gent accept an invitation for a week or two beginning July 1st. An absolutely free trip, mind ya—like that one your friend Bob in Detroit give ya a couple years or so ago. Lawd knows it's a helluva imposition—I declined as many times as courtesy permitted—but if she is determined to blow de coin, it ain't no business of mine to stop her! I gave ample warning, too, what an infernal bore the old man's senile prattle would get to be after a few days! So unless sumpun new toins up, I'll soon have Magnolian material for another forty paged *Molo*. From wot I 'ears, de scenery had orta be good for about twenty pages—cliffs, chasms, 'n' ever'thin'. Last Sunday Mme. Greene hit Providence at one-forty-five. My younger aunt and I were at the dee-po to meet her, but she missed us and went on a wild-goose-chase in a taxi up to the house and back! When she finally did heave in sight, my aunt took her to the Crown Hotel for eats (they're as bad as Kleiner!) and put one over on her by paying the check herself! Thereafter occurred a triangular walk to the house, a five-hour session of quadrangular discussion in which the three females got so far away from literature that Grandpa dropped out now and then for an old-gentlemanly nap, more *eats* (gawdelpus!) around nine p.m., and finally a walk back to the deep-o with Grandpa as the sole local guide. This jaunt terminated in a watery grave. The day was dubious, and Mme. Greenevsky had borrowed an umbrella. About half way down town the overhead sprinklers started, and sail was hoisted. I had no sunshade of me own, for I hate such devices like the devil. All would have been well had the one existing contraption been of sturdy timber—but! Just at the foot of the hill—some five squares from the dee-po—the celestial nimbi began to unload their aqueous cargo in earnest, and the damn portable Pantheon-dome dissolved into its constituent molecules like Ol' Doc Holmes' uni-equine vehicle;[1] the umbrellian debris was cast into the nearest convenient gutter! Without being totally dissolved, the navigators finally reached port ten or fifteen minutes before train-time; and the only way I could stop Mme. Greenevsky from hiring a taxi to cart my remains home for identification was to point out that not all the streams of Pater Oceanus could make me wetter than I was! My 1921 straw hat and 1918 summer suit sure were objects which Triton would have delighted to drape with fraternal seaweed. Mme. Greenevsky had a wonderfully opportune cloak—but as for her hat—it's damn lucky she's in the millinery business! That lid'll never unfold its flowers to the summer sun again. And as I left the station on me 'omeward way—behold! The bally rain, having done its worst, had stopped! Mme. Greenevsky sure had some visit—beginning with a false-alarm taxi ride and ending with a flood. I apologised on behalf of the Providence which had brought such calamities. But at that 'twas less of a blow than her Galpin visit. The kid fairly withered her with devastating and chilly superiority, and finished the job with a scornfully critical letter little short of barbaric! It took a hades of a lot of reassuring to make her refrain from renouncing all the world in mortification at so unworthy a personality as Galba represented her as possessing. Some boy!

Let's hear from ya, kid!
      Yr obt THEOBALDVS.

Notes

1. HPL refers to Oliver Wendell Holmes's celebrated poem "The Deacon's Masterpiece; or, The Wonderful 'One-Hoss Shay'" (included in *The Autocrat of the Breakfast Table*, which HPL owned), in which it is said of the vehicle: "You see, of course, if you're not a dunce, / How it went to pieces all at once."

[19]   [AHT]

Prof. Dr. Moritz Vinter Moli,
    University of Viskonsin,
        Milwaukee, Nova Germania.

[c. late September 1922]

Hey, Mowruss, ol' Sport!
    I must look rural in this great and awesome city—the other day a slick young fellow sold me the Woolworth Building and the Statue of Liberty! However—*I* wasn't sold, since the goods were really delivered. I paid a quarter for the W. and a dime for the S. of L., and carried 'em away in my pocket. . . . I shall use 'em for paperweights or mantelpiece ornaments. If I can't stay in N.Y., I'll at least carry some of it back to Providence. And oh, boy! the book shops!!! There are three main centres—59th St., 4th Ave., and Vesey St.—and I've done 'em all. I'll keep the express companies busy betwixt N.Y. and Prov. . . . . and by the time I'm through I'll be broke and N.Y. will be bookless and illiterate. Some shops! Last Monday I copped an Ovid in *black-letter*, printed in *1567*, when Bill S. was a squalling brat in his father's dooryard at Stratford, aged 3. Believe muh, some archaick lingo in the latest Henry VIII style! Get this—for a sample—

        The Argument of the
          ix Epistle, entituled
            Deianeira to Hercules

The heauie stepdame iuno by hir fraude
And friende Eurystheus purposde to destroy
Alcides: for the Prince of Mycene lande
Stirde him to conquer Monsters. But with laude
And life he scapt away, nor had annoye

> By any beast the Champion tooke in hande:
> Bulles, Dragones, Dogges, and Semitaurs he slewe,
> And aye more greane his gotten glorie grewe.

—I purposely chose an "argument" in Roman type, because it's a damn sight harder to imitate the black-letter of the text proper. However—here's a line—or two—

> Beholde the world by thee that liues at quiet ease,
> As wyde as watrie Nereus girdes the ground with Frothie Seas.

This is the oldest book I ever owned—not quite a real incunabula, but not exactly modern at that! Only Loveman, among the amateurs, can beat that date—*1567!*

As for most of my acquisitions—here's a few. Pater—Marius the Epicurean, De Maupassant—Works—6 vol. Gautier—Mlle. de Maupin. Flaubert—Salammbo, Tempt. St. Anth. Bloomfield—Farmer's Boy. Lucian—Dialogues of Dead, Trip to Moon, etc.[1] Thucydides, Plautus, Terence. Wilde—Pomes, Voyages of Mandeville, Hakluyt's Voyages, Old English Baron—eighteenth century horror tale by Clara Reeve, Fantastics by La Motte Fouque,[2] Pepys' Diary complete, Ingram's Life of Poe, *1st Edition,* Nat. History of Selborne,[3] Poe's Eureka, Spenser's Shepherd's Calendar, Swift's and Cowley's Essays,—and more yet besides! Some of this stuff was abysmally cheap—like abstracting sweetmeats from an infant! And reading—oh, boy! Everybody's lending me everything! In Cleveland I ate up Remy de Gourmont and Edgar Saltus, and here I'm finishing Wilde, beginning George Moore and the decadents, and going strong on other assorted matter. Kleiner has lent me a strange thing—"The Hasheesh-Eater", by Fitzhugh Ludlow, a kind of improved De Quincey. I am also *beginning* to appreciate musical and pictorial art—though Gawd knows I may never make much progress in 'em.

Had to cut short there and hasten up to Belknap's house—he and Morton and I had dinner together and explored the one remaining *rural* section of Manhattan Island. You'd be surprised at the dense forests and country roads one can find north and west of Broadway and Dyckman St. We stopped first at the old Dyckman farmhouse—B'way and 204th St.—the only remaining Dutch farm on the island. It is the property of an historical society, and is maintain'd with assiduous care; furnish'd as befits the 18th century Netherland manner, and adorn'd with a variety of quaint and curious objects peculiar to its period. Compar'd with the Morris–Jumel Mansion, Gen. Washington's hdqts. during the revolt of 1775–83, it is very small and crude; the Dyckmans having belong'd only to the yeoman or small-gentry class. It is, however, mark'd with a singular neatness characteristic of the Hollanders; and its low winding stairways, divided doors, "winter kitchen", and other typical features, contribute not a little to that quaintness which delights the contemplative visitor. Whilst in this agrestic cot, I discover'd a comely and animated black cat, which I doubt not is directly descended from the mousers of Amsterdam, Haarlem, and The Hague. I held him in my arms during the majority of my sojourn, and bade him adieu with sincere cordiality and unaffected regret. Thence we proceeded to the forest of Inwood; which so closely resembles the wilds of New England, that I could not believe myself but twelve miles from the 60-story Woolworth building. There is here a tulip tree 250 years old, planted by one of the original Dutch colonists. At a future date Belknap and I purpose to visit Van Cortlandt Park, on the mainland but within the corporate limits of the city, where stands the Van Cortlandt Mansion; erected in the reign of His Majesty George the Second, but having much of the old Dutch architecture about it. Speaking of the Netherlandish past—this section containing Parkside Ave. was originally the old Dutch village of Flatbush. Down the street one may see the only remnant which has not been wiped out by the spreading of the city with its mechanical cliffs of apartments and its stereotyped rows of mediocre shops—the Georgian spire of the Dutch Reformed Church (founded 1654) built in 1796.

In the circumjacent churchyard are interments dating back to 1747, with most of the inscriptions and epitaphs in the Dutch language. The nature of this necropolis was, so far as the amateur world is concern'd, discover'd solely by myself; for none of the local members had the least idea that such a thing as a Dutch cemetery existed in New York. Last week I visited the place by moonlight, and chipped a piece off one of the crumbling stones of 150 years ago. A flock of birds descended from the sky and pecked queerly at the ancient turf, as if seeking some strange kind of nourishment in that hoary and sepulchral place . . . . . I carry the gravestone fragment with me, and wonder at night whether anyone or any *thing* will come out of the darkness to claim it and exact vengeance . . . . . good story stuff!

De re anthologica—nigger Braithwaite sure has put the old *Conservative* on the map[4] . . . . and the ironic thing is that the particular issue containing the Jacksoniana never was published! Ericson held it up indefinitely, though he was paid, and now I am out of amateur journalism without having published it! Braithwaite has seen some Middletoniana, but I fancy it's too conventional as yet to take his eye. Even the "Irish Weather" imagery is obvious and sugar-and-watery as compared with the stark imagery and flashes of genius in Jackson poetry at its best. And yet, it would not surprise me if after all Mrs. McM. were the greater poet in the end, for she has a conscious and intelligent mastery of her medium—which W. V. J. lacks totally. Mrs. McM. is studying desperately under several instructors, and is making titanic efforts to secure the ecstatic expression which is real art. She now tends toward the cynical rather than the optimistic—a good sign if she can keep it up without sinking chronically into free verse. Loveman is greater than L. M. and W. V. J. combined—someday I shall get that Loveman Issue out, and then Braithwaite will have a juicy watermelon to roll his eyes over! I plan to send copies to all the representative critics . . . which reminds me that I guess I'll send you MSS. of "Sphinx" and "Hermaphrodite" when Klei returns 'em to me.—Sorry, but I ain't got no more U.A.'s with "Tender Irish Weather."[5] Tough luck. However, I'll shoot you a lotta other amachoor choinals as soon as I hit 598. The Kid didn't send me his collection—and I will now tell him to return it to you.

Kidlet and I have discovered a poet as great as Loveman—indeed, Alfredus says he's greater, and calls him the greatest living poet of America. I allude to Loveman's California friend Clark Ashton Smith, about whose hideous sketches and water-colours I think we wrote you from Cleveland. Smith is an American Baudelaire—a master of ghoulish worlds no other foot ever trod. I own both his published books, and shall purchase his third this fall when it appears. Kid Belknap has copied the entire text of one of the books on his typewriter—a stupefying task, and a sincere tribute. Here's a typical Ashtonsmithic sonnet—

           THE REFUGE OF BEAUTY
            by Clark Ashton Smith

> From regions of the sun's half-dreamt decay,
> All day the cruel rain strikes darkly down;
> And from the night thy fatal stars shall frown—
> Beauty, wilt thou abide this night and day?
> Roofless, at portals dark and desperate,
> Wilt thou a shelter unrefus'd implore,
> And, past the tomb's too-hospitable door,
> Evade thy lover in eluding Hate?
> Alas, for what have I to offer thee?
> Chill halls of mind, dank rooms of memory,
> Where thou shalt dwell with woes and thoughts infirm;
> This rumour-throng'd citadel of sense,
> Trembling before some nameless Imminence:
> And fellow-guestship with the glutless worm.[6]

If that ain't supreme poesy, I'm a damned liar! Galpinius and I now correspond with Smith—who, by the way, says he likes my yarns immensely. Loveman is busy publishing the letters Ambrose Bierce wrote him—and when he is through with that task he intends to write and publish a critical brochure on the late Edgar Saltus.[7]

Just now Belknap, Alfredus, and I are amusing ourselves with a series of mutual hoaxes—which we do not take too seriously. Last month Belknap and I concocted an account of an 125-year-old hermit from Maine, who had in his possession an undiscover'd poem of Poe's. I wrote the "poem"; and although Kidlet didn't swallow the Poe yarn, he praised the verses to the skies in an analytical critique, assuming that we had cribbed it from some standard bard!!!! When we put him wise to the fact that it was written at Long's house, amidst gusts of merriment, by the very old Theobald whose verse he so cordially despises, he began to see defects! And yet he had spoken so eloquently of its "sincerity"!!! One on Galba this time. And here's the spasm:

TO ZARA
By Edgar Allan Poe (?)
Inscribed to Miss Sarah Longhurst—June 1829.

I look'd upon thee yesternight
Beneath the drops of yellow light
That fell from out a poppy moon
Like notes of some far opiate tune.
I look'd and sigh'd, I knew not why,
As when a condor flutters by,
And thought the moonbeams on thy face
Timid to seek thy resting-place.
O sacred spot! Memorial bow'r!
Unsuited to the mocking hour
When winds of myrrh from Tempë's lake
Stir soft, yet stir thee not awake!
Thy clear brow, Zara, rests so fair
I cannot think death lingers there;
Thy lip as from thy blood is red,
Nor hints of ichors of the dead:
Canst thou, whom love so late consum'd,
Lie prey to worms—dissolv'd, entomb'd?
And he, whose name suffus'd thy cheek
With ecstasies thou couldst not speak;
Will he in fancy hold thee ever
Fair as thou art, decaying never,
And dreaming, on thine eyelids press
A tribute to thy loveliness?
Or will his fancy rove beneath
The carven urn and chisell'd wreath,
Where still—so still—the shroud shall drape
Grotesque, liquescent turns of shape?
No, Zara, no! Such beauty reigns
Immortal in immortal fanes;
Radiant for ever, ever laden
With beams of uncorrupted Aidenn,

And naught that slumbers here tonight
Can perish from a lover's sight.
Where'er thy soul, where'er thy clay
May rise to hail another day,
Thy second soul, thy beauty's flame,
The songs of passionate lutes shall claim;
Pale, lovely ghost—so young, so fair,
To flutter in sepulchral air—
To flutter where the taper dies
Amidst a mourner's choking sighs!

Ho, hum! 'Twas kinda fun writin' it, with young Belknap peering over me shoulder. But I gotta quit. Write soon.
    With every good wish, believe me, Sir,
        Yr most obt. Servt.
            Theobaldus

Pardon me a moment—I feel a sort of epileptic or metric fit coming on. Please excuse anything I do to the now attractive expanse of white paper below:

THE GREATEST LAW
By C. Raymond[8] and Ludwig von Theobald

Arise, ye swains! for fair Aurora's light
Shews the wild geese in scurrying matin flight;
In shifting ranks their silent course they take,
And for the valley marshlands quit the lake:
Tho' loose they fly, in various modes arrang'd,
Their eyes are steady, and their goal unchang'd.
Thus in brute instinct Nature shews her law;
Excites our wonder, and compels our awe.
But hark! from yonder grove the pleasing peal
Of redbreasts, winging to their morning meal;
In softer tones the lusty bluejay chants,
While maple shades the bobbing grackle haunts:
From neighb'ring wall the bluebird's carol rings,
And in the mead the lark rejoicing sings.
Forests and fields attend the welcome strain,
And hail the advent of the feather'd train;
Swift pour the airy legions from the shores
Where Mexique's Bay its genial currents pours:
In waves unnotic'd throng the tuneful band,
To glad the soul, and cheer the Northern strand,

Obedient to the sway of Jove's all-pow'rful hand.
Alive with song the gentle bluebird floats;
The hermit thrush disdains melodious notes;
None marks their solid course, but as they come,
Each gains a greeting to his Northern home.
Now drip the maples with their vernal juice,
While growing thorns their swelling buds unloose;
On grassy slopes the furry coils untwine,
Where soon hepatica's white blooms will shine.
Almighty Pan! whose vast unchanging will
Clothes the green wildwood and enrobes the hill,
How calm the workings of thy great decrees!
How still thy magic o'er the flow'ry leas!
No march of feet, or sound of timbrel shakes
The sylvan scene, or stirs the drowsy brakes:
In songful peace the law resistless moves,
And pleases while it rules the meadows and the groves.

PART II. WHY TREES ARE TALL—*by Ward Phillips*

Attend! Attend! ye dreaming Dryad throng!
Bend your green boughs, and mark the rising song!
Awake, ye Naiads, feel the vernal thrill,
And from each fount increase the crystal rill!
O'er rolling plains let rural Fauns disport,
While Pan, their King, holds universal court:
All Nature's choir, with ever-youthful voice,
Proclaims the spring, and bids the world rejoice.
'Twas at this joyful time that o'er the wold
Roam'd a sad swain, oppress'd with grief untold;
Damon his name, who found his Delia cold.
Six feet and one the slender stripling tow'rs,
Bends o'er the trees, and stoops to glimpse the bow'rs;
A comely youth, in wit and learning great,
Skill'd in each art, and master of debate—
Yet pensive now, since Eros' cruel dart
Had pierc'd his own, but not his Delia's, heart.
Th' unhappy youth his burning misery
In sonnets carv'd on many a hoary tree;
Till ev'ry bird, and ev'ry rustling wind
Could read the tale—"My Delia is unkind!"
It chanc'd one noon, that on a woodland steep
The heavy-lidded shepherd dropt to sleep;

Worn out with weeping, he in dreams implor'd
His cruel Delia for a gentle word;
Till mov'd beyond his wont, he spake aloud
The fruitless plaint, while still in slumber bow'd.
Now at this sound the pitying trees are mov'd,
Carv'd on their bark the woeful truth appears,
And their deep roots are damp with Damon's tears.
From out each trunk the patron Dryad starts,
And all behold the youth who touch'd their hearts;
Around his slumbrous form in throngs they press,
To mark his grief, and praise his loveliness.
"Sisters, behold!" the grave Ptelea cry'd,
"The lovely victim of a Delia's pride!
"So fair a stripling should not pine alone—
"I vow, I'll make the tender boy mine own!"
Scarce had she spoke, when winsome Phegia's voice
Oppos'd the speaker, and denounc'd the choice;
"It is not meet," the rival nymph declar'd,
"That with thy age his tender youth be pair'd;
"I, I alone, deserve a wife's estate;
"A bright companion, and a fitting mate!"
But as they quarrel, other nymphs exclaim
In rising tones, and utter Damon's name:
The blooming Drusa owns a loving fire,
And sad Aegeira swells the amorous choir;
Sphendamnia with Oesua now contends,
And female strife the forest quiet rends.
"He's mine!" each screams, and seeks to clutch the prize,
Yet fails to clasp the idol of her eyes;
"He's mine!" Aloft the echoing cry proceeds,
And frets the Fauns that roam the upland meads.
The youth, awaked, the beauteous train beholds,
Whilst ev'ry nymph her arms about him folds.
He sees—he screams—ungentle to the fair
When he perceives his Delia is not there—
But all too late; for in a frenzy'd mood
The Dryads hold him in their native wood.
Each swears to keep him, and as lawful pelf
Labours in vain to draw him to herself;
Till the mad band, their strength diversely bent,
Grasp but sad fragments, by the tussle rent.
Thus Thracia's savage matrons wildly tore
The pensive Orpheus on swift Hebrus' shore.

Ptelea gains his head, so lately deck'd
With twining myrtle, and vast intellect;
Young Phegia wins an arm, whose pendent hand
The magic quill of genius could command.
All mourn alike, throughout the sighing grove,
The hapless object of their common love;—
When lo! on high supernal rays diffuse,
And shew Apollo with each wrathful Muse:
Down from Parnassus swoop the angry train
T' avenge their fav'rite—but they swoop in vain.
For the quick Dryads, as they view the sky,
Back to their shelt'ring trees in terror fly.
The mangled swain they with themselves enclose,
And where he roam'd, an empty forest grows.
In genuine tears stand Phoebus and the Nine;
Like mortals in their grief, but in their wrath divine.

Meanwhile young Damon's friends, in lonely quest,
Search for the tender lad they lov'd the best.
"Damon!" In vain the aged Theobald cries!
"Damon!" Oft wipes wise Mocrates his eyes.
No sign, no word, the vanish'd youth conveys,
Tho' each sad comrade for a letter prays;
And anguish'd poets sing their grief in Dorick lays.

But one bright day, within the heart of spring,
The sorrowing Theobald went a-wandering;
With eyes intent upon the heav'ns above,
In grief he trod each w. k. mead and grove,
Till suddenly his elevated glance
Observ'd a most unusual circumstance!
What may this mean—that ev'ry tree in sight
Shou'd rise to more than twice its wonted height?
What novel influence sways the Dryad throng
That trees shou'd grow so lanky and so long?
Thus mus'd the bard, till thro' the tow'ring trees
Spread a low sound, as of a passing breeze;
Old Theobald pauses, and with straining ears
A tale of wonder from the branches hears.
"In this tall grove," low sigh'd the leafy train,
"Behold the Damon thou hast sought in vain!

"By Dryads captur'd, and by Dryads torn,
"In hoary trees my spirit is reborn;
"My body, lost, has yet this pow'r alone—
"To give the trees dimensions like its own:
"So mark thou well; henceforth shall woods arise
"Whose verdant branches touch the airy skies.
"My soul survives, altho' my frame be dead,
"And turn'd to wood—so like my Delia's head!"
Thus paus'd the prison'd youth, and nevermore
His accents bless'd the Appletonian shore.
E'er must his spirit own the Dryad thrall,
And trees grow graceful, Galpinesque, and tall!!

(The End—Thank Gawd!)

Now thou knowest, O Mokrates, what a d—— fool a poet can become when he cuts loose on spring poetry! But really—the sad silence of #779 Kimball deserved metrical celebration—or rather lamentation! But enough of nonsense!! (P.S. Before I seal this missive I *may* copy the Raymond paraphrase to send *Tryout*. He is short of copy!)[9]

Notes

1. Unidentified.
2. Unidentified.
3. By Gilbert White.
4. William Stanley Braithwaite (1878–1962), editor of *Anthology of Magazine Verse,* book reviewer for the *Boston Transcript,* and one of the leading African-American literary figures of his time. HPL corresponded with him briefly in 1930. Braithwaite's anthology for 1921 published Jackson's poems "The Cobbler in the Moon" (85–88), "Finality" (88–89), "The Tricksy Tune" (89–91), "Eyes" (92), "Deafness" (92–95), "Hoofin' It" (95–97), and "The Purchase" (97) as "reprinted" from HPL's *Conservative,* but he did not in fact publish the poems as he had planned to.
5. Lilian Middleton, "In the Tender Irish Weather," *New York Times* (15 October 1921): 12. Rpt. *Literary Digest* 71, No. 6 (5 November 1921): 30.
6. In *Ebony and Crystal* 81.
7. SL had written a critical study of the work of the American novelist Edgar Saltus (1855–1921) in 1924, but the publisher abandoned plans to publish the book after the manuscript had already been accepted.
8. Clifford S. Raymond (1875–1950), reporter and later chief editorial writer at the *Chicago Tribune*. HPL had paraphrased Raymond's prose from the *Tribune* for his poem "Spring."
9. The poem did not appear in *Tryout* or anywhere else in HPL's lifetime.

[20]   [AHT]

Our Customary Habitation—
10 July, 1923

Reverend Sir:—

Since my last epistle to you, I have twice been in the Province of the Massachusetts-Bay. June 14 I went to Boston in the evening, dined at Shepard's Colonial with Cole and Sandy,[1] and thereafter proceeded to aid the two gentlemen mention'd in putting over a political victory at a beastly dull Hub meeting. I stayed the night at Cole's—which is a delightful tho' microscopick hangout in Wollaston, and a fine place for you to stop—and on the following day did Concord with him and Sandy in a benzine bus which the latter little bimbo had borrowed. We saw everything worth seeing—North Bridge, graveyards, and old dumps—and dined at the Wright Tavern, built in 1747, and unchanged since 1775, when Major Pitcairn made it the headquarters of His Majesty's troops. I saluted as I leant on the very bar where the good Major used to sip his toddy, and listen'd to the ticking of the same clock that he used to hear. The past . . . . . the past . . . . . God Save the King! Later Sandy dumped me in Cambridge, and I beat it for Maplewood, where I bummed a night's lodging off the Parker–Miniter outfit.[2] The next day I did my beloved *Marblehead* in a solitary tour, and discover'd a whole new section I had not before seen.[3] Oh, boy! How can I describe it without becoming incoherently lyrical? The past lives—lives, I tell you!! Really, that *Globe* article (which *Tryout* Smithy had sent me a month before) cannot do the place justice, because it is conceived in a spirit of rational prose rather than in one of sheer ecstasy. You *must* see Marblehead for yourself! The section which was new to me last month was really the best of all—between the hideous Victorian bulk of Abbott Hall and the harbour. It comprised the principal hill, with its incredible network of streets without sidewalks, and its ancient houses set at all possible angles on moss-grown rock foundations and weird terraces. Marblehead is a garland of unending delights—one could live there rapturously for ever, discovering new wonders each day . . . . . little corners where graceful vines creep, curious bits of sunken garden where vivid flowers bloom and where exotic stone images lurk amidst the grass, marvellous doorways carved two hundred years ago by beauty-loving sailors and having rough stone steps flanked by conch-shells brought from the far Hesperides . . . . . the past . . . . . the past . . . . . Verily, here alone survives the maritime New-England of yesterday, with the glamour of ships and the salt winds of eighteenth-century voyages. On this occasion I stayed in Marblehead till nine-thirty p.m., when candles shone thro' small-pan'd windows, revealing old-world panelled interiors and ancient fireplaces and mantels. Then I went directly home, reaching 598 at two a.m., after a trip I hardly remember . . . . . a trip I hardly remember, so full was it of antique dreams and pictures of narrow lanes and gables and chimneys in old and glamorous seaports.

From that time till July 3 I dreamed of old Marblehead. On that date I set out for the Boston near-convention—with Marblehead as an ultimate destination. The day was rottenly rainy, so I cut the Concord–Lexington trip and arrived at the Parker–Miniter joint in time for the evening's festivities. I guess it was pretty festive; crowds, and a professional character-reader, and everything . . . . . but it was rather a bore except for the famous old-time amateur W. R. Murphy, who had come from Philadelphia specially for the event, but who was too ill to do any heavy talking or fighting. W. R. Murphy—now literary editor of the *Philadelphia Publick Ledger,*—is a curious fellow—frail in health, and with a physique and size exactly like Sandusky's. He left the next morning without taking further part in the proceedings.

July 4 the gang dined at a real eighteenth century coffee-house in Joy St. (formerly Belknap St.) on Beacon Hill. The scene was delightful—narrow hilly street, quiet Georgian courtyard, and a tiny gambrel-roof'd house antedating 1750, with ancient panell'd interior, brick fireplace untouch'd by the years, and round wooden tables exactly like those at Will's and Button's.[4] I looked about for Mr. Addison's group, but cou'd find no members of it; yet was consol'd by the shade of Mr. Dryden, which I am certain inhabited a far shadowy corner beyond the massive chimney with the carven mantel and row of pewter plates. After this the delegates repair'd to the wharves and boarded a vessel for the trip around the harbour. I was as bored on board as during the similar trip of 1921, though my head-ache was not quite so acute. Subsequently, after landing and loafing around the U.S. Hotel—a curious decayed joint whose heyday was the Civil War period—we went to Boston Common to hear the July 4 municipal celebration and see the fireworks. Lynch, who has a pull with the crooked Irish Mayor Curley,[5] got us a reserved front bench; but the show was bum. The fireworks were excellent, however, and amply worth waiting for. The next day—Thursday—just one week ago—I took a solitary jaunt to Salem and Marblehead, where I saw all manner of wonders, and looked up a boarding-place for my aunt Mrs. Gamwell, who wished to spend a week in the marvellous Marblehead about whose glories her eccentrick nephew had been so vociferously raving since last December. I found her a good room in an ancient house perched half-way up a precipice facing Front St.—a house inhabited by an ancient grandam named Bixbee; widow of the artist who design'd the Town Seal of Marblehead, and (*qualis parva est terra!*)[6] well acquainted with many Providence artists known to our family.

The next day—Friday—I dined with Cole, his wife, and Mrs. Miniter, at the Cambridge home of Mr. and Mrs. Denys P. Myers—goodly folk, though distressingly given to platitudinous points of view. I thought I had shaken them—but not so . . . . . ho, hum! The food was piquant, anyway . . . . . .

And the next day—Saturday—I set out with Cole and Mrs. Miniter for the inevitable Marblehead again. We did the Lee Mansion (you will be ecstatic over the mahogany carving and wainscotting on the lower floor—brought back from Old England) finely, but Cole had to beat it before we tackled the Hooper Mansion—which, by the way, is the most fascinating thing on earth . . . . . a gentleman's residence—period 1750—furnished with such homelike detail that you expect to see him descending the artistic staircase in periwig and small-clothes. The antiques composing this dream are for sale . . . . . and the reason they are still there is that I was dead broke! About seven-thirty p.m., as Mrs. Miniter and I were exploring Circle St., where Capt. Ireson dwelt, I saw a familiar figure in the distance. A second look convinced me, and I overtook and hail'd it. It was my aunt, who had responded with lightning avidity to a card I had sent her Thursday, and who was duly ensconced in the cliff-balanced Bixbee residence! Some chance meeting! She and Mrs. Miniter were exceedingly glad to meet, and conversed most congenially. We visited Fort Sewell, Old Burying Hill, and the Azor Orne house, where Mrs. Miniter bought a fine old teapot to supplement [her] excellent collection of inherited antiques. Dusk now fell, and I left my aunt with a warning to watch for me the next day—when I should return to act as a super-guide and induct her into the remotest arcana of the Georgian and Queen-Anne past.

The next morning—Sunday—I bade the Parker–Miniter household farewell, and proceeded to Marblehead to show my aunt the sights. It was a great day—easily the best of the trip—for without boasting I can say that my family has a certain degree of intelligence and cultivation which makes them better and more alertly appreciative companions than any of the Boston amateurs save possibly Cole. I made my aunt admit that I had not overrated Marblehead, and she appeared to share my lavish enthusiasm for the wondrous houses and byways. The charm of Marblehead is impossible to isolate . . . . it is not in any one thing, but in the collocation of various things . . . . . and in the perspective of the beholder. The Lee and Hooper mansions were closed because of the holiday, (NOTE—you must arrange to see Marblehead on a *week-day*) but I made my aunt promise to visit them later in the week. I hope she has done so—she's still there—hell, how I envy her! We crossed in the ferry to Marblehead Neck, (where, b. t. w., I had lost my 1906 Waterman the Thursday before) and later returning, set out to explore *behind* Old Burying Hill.

Now I had never been behind Old Burying Hill before—chiefly because I thought there was nothing there except open country. Fancy, then, my delirious astonishment upon rounding the curve where the road drops from the crest, and espying in a deep valley far below and ahead of me the ancient roofs and sagging walls of humble *Barnegat*,[7] where the lowly sailors dwelt in the eighteenth century, and which I had thought to be long pulverised by the relentless march of time. But it was there still—for Time exists not in Marblehead! We descended, and properly observ'd the idyllic vale and antient shipyard, then follow'd the road northwest around Burying Hill.

What wonders now engag'd my ravisht sight,
Mellow and magick in the golden light?
Behold on ev'ry hand the rocky steeps
O'er which the vivid verdure splendid creeps:
Ahead rise bold a train of spectral trees
Whose branches whisper in the evening breeze,
Whilst to the east, o'er crags of sombre dye,
A purple ocean joins th' aethereal sky.
Here flit the myriad sails, a snowy band,
And here the stately stone-built beacons stand;
Close to the shoar, and pleasing to the gaze,
Fair verdant islands strew the wat'ry ways.
But lo! new marvels gild the ancient air
As o'er the road our eager footsteps fare;
See yonder meadow fring'd with hoary oaks
Whose guardian shade a Druid spell invokes,
And where at night a firefly throng recall
Forgotten years, and witchcraft's ghoulish pall.
Here at the bend, where, salt and shallow, reach
A cove's dim waters on a mossy beach,
Behold that gloomy mansion, set about
By titan tree-trunks in daemoniac rout,
Smother'd with shocking ivy, still it rears
Uncanny walls, and counts two hundred years.
Stranger to sun, immers'd in humid shade,
With willows like vast octopi array'd,
It leers perpetual from the deeps of time,
And mirrors gulphs down which no man may climb.
Upward and on—thus runs our pleasing course,
Each novel turning lovelier than its source;
Meads, groves, and steeps successive charm the soul,
And hint at ev'ry bend a brighter goal.
Ecce! Eureka! What is this that dawns
From the still crest, across the sloping lawns?
What faery glimmer of celestial seas,
And crystal spires that rise from distant leas?
Can a meer earth such beauteous sights contain;
Such marvels deck the dull terrestrial main?
'Tis sunset's magick, 'neath whose kindly spell
All things are true, and all high wonders dwell:
Thus Salem Harbour greets congenial skies,
While Salem's towers and steeples distant rise.
Entrancing sight! The eye can scarce withdraw

> From such a prospect of irradiate awe!
> Dim fall the vesper shades, and far behind
> The lights of Marblehead of home remind.
> Now for the vale, where shadows eldritch wait
> To mock the trav'ler with their hints of fate;
> The dark'ning skies a thousand stars disclose,
> While the lone cotters seek their calm repose.
> Again the narrow streets and terrac'd hills,
> Where Georgian mem'ry each keen spirit fills:
> Black are the winding ways, save for yon gleam
> Of fanlight, or yon chequer'd window's beam—
> O'er all the town the past unchanging broods,
> And Time trips lightly in his mildest moods![8]

Oh, well,—anyhow it was a great walk, and M'head is a great place. I accompany'd my aunt to her stopping place, and afterward threaded the dark old streets for a full hour alone, fancying myself in the eighteenth century. Then I hopped on a tram-car for Lynn, and was home by two a.m. Some trip, I'll say! And now you must come hither yourself, and drink of the past at its very fountain head. Believe me or not, I can actually lead you through the streets of a Georgian town, and shew you my own eighteenth century as a living reality. Come East, young man; come East!

Ho, hum! Well, that's that. Slip me a line and tell me what you think of the Big Town, and don't for your life fail to arrange for a peppy New-England week-end!

   Yr expectant and obt Servt
        Lo.

Notes

1. Albert A. ("Sandy") Sandusky.
2. HPL refers to a house in Maplewood (a district in the Boston suburb of Malden) shared by Edith Miniter and the printer/publisher Charles A. A. Parker, who published some of the later issues of HPL's *Conservative* and later published the poetry magazine *L'Alouette*.
3. HPL first visited Marblehead on 17 December 1922.
4. Button's was another coffee house where the London literati liked to gather.
5. James Michael Curley (1874–1958), mayor of Boston (1914–18, 1922–26, 1930–34, 1946–50); also U.S. representative (1911–13, 1943–47) and governor of Massachusetts (1935–37).
6. "What a small world!"
7. The Barnegat section of Marblehead was the roughest neighborhood in town.
8. Now published with the title "[On Marblehead]."

[21]   [ALS, JHL]
            [HOTEL KIMBALL . . . / Springfield, Massachusetts]
                                                                    Button's
                                                              31 July[, 1923]

Mocrates, My Son:—
                I am sensible of an extream Pleasure, at learning of the definite Time of your Journey to New-England; & shall on Aug. 10 await the Coach from New-York with a most singular Expectancy. I have, as I lately appris'd you, made so bold as to ask my Son Samuel to accompany us, if he carries out his Design of a Tour of the Eastern Provinces; & can aſsure you, that if he does, our Convocation will be distinguisht by so great a Brilliancy as to sink into Confusion the absurd Pretensions of the Boston Provincial Little-Wits, Scholiasts, & Petits-Maitres. But whether or no he can come, our Gathering can want nothing of Lustre with a Mocrates forming part of it! 'Tis hard to say with Justice, how acutely I am awaiting a Sight of that Face, whose Outlines I am now learning with Care, from the Miniature you so kindly sent, & from the Portraiture of the late Convention! I shall examine with Attention, every slender spectacled Gentleman on the Coach; & tho' you may miſs recognizing me, (for I am more ugly than any Miniature ever painted of me) I am confident I shall not fail to select that Scholar, whose keen Intellectuals must needs shine thro' the heaviest Disguises of the Spectacle-Maker. I return the Portraiture you sent, congratulating you alike upon your well-preserv'd Figure, & upon that pleasing Family which is a Prop of your declining years. Lud, Sir, but young Donald hath a Tallness surprizing in one so youthful! He is like to catch up in highth with Robert, & perhaps to shoot above him, just as the phantastical Conceptions of Literature, or the Imagination, can in a single Day overtop the most laborious Discoveries of Science, or the most ingenious Inventions of Mechanicks. Well, Sir, I have ever a partial Eye for Youth, tho' all my little Grandboys are grown up & long at Oxford.

    I trust that the Inclemency of the Weather was no Bar to a pleasing Seſsion of the Blue-Pencil Club, & that you all met at some convenient Coffee-House & deliver'd your Eſsays without any Hinderance. 'Zounds! But I shou'd be hard put to it, to chuse any Novel as my favourite; for tho' I know the Fictions of Mr. Fielding, & Mons. de Balzac, to be the greatest ever writ, I have scarce any Relish for them; but am for ever craving something of a wild Gothick Cast, like the Volumes of Mrs. Radcliffe, Mr. Lewis, & Mr. Maturin. I believe, altogether, that I like no Fiction better than the "Melmoth" of the Rev. Mr. Maturin, tho' I have beheld only Extracts from it, included in a Book my small child Belknap gave his old Grandpa last Christmas.[1] They have not the whole of "Melmoth" in the Libraries at Providence and New-York, & tho' I saw it in Cleaveland, 'twas forbidden to be taken from the Building, so that I had no Chance to peruse it. In this Book are many ingenious Incidents of a Horror not surpafs'd by Mr. Poe himself, whilst the Ending is as pleasingly ghoulish & awful as anything in the whole Expanse of our Literature.

I am now perusing "The Lock & Key Library", which I first saw in Cleaveland, & bought at a Bargain for a guinea & a half in New-York. 'Tis a collection of the Choicest Horrors & Mysteries in the Writings of all Nations, drawn from all over our terraqueous Globe, from the Kingdoms of the Tartary Cham & the Grand Turk, to the Provinces of New-Spain & the South Seas. I am most partial to the Work of our English Authors, both British & Provincial, & have just read with much Satisfaction the shocking Tale of Mrs. Mary E. Wilkins-Freeman, intitul'd "The Shadows on the Wall." I have also re-read something I knew in youth, the "Wolfert Webber" of Mr. Irving, whose easie agreeable Stile ought to be copy'd by the harsher Prose-Writers of this degenerate Aera. Now that you are in the Town of New-York, I shou'd advise you to make a Search for that Pirate Gold to which Mr. Irving alludes; & wou'd recommend your going to the Dutch Tavern north of the Town, at Corlear's Hook, to listen to the Legends there told. There is a little humoursome Fellow there, much along in Years, who knows every spot in the Province where Kidd or Blackbeard set Foot; to say nothing of one silent swarthy Man with Ear-Rings & a slit Lip, who they do say was with Bradish's Crew in the old Days. But for your most authentical Information, you must go down to the old Fort, at the point of the Battery, where you will find the cabin of an old blackamoor Fisherman nam'd Sam, who can take you to a Spot where he saw six Men bury a Chest. Shou'd you wish to find that Spot alone, I can only say, that 'tis four miles north of New-York, on a plateau overlooking the Sound a little above Blackwell's Island; to be reach'd from the nearest Village (Bloomen-Dael, where my Grandson Belknap lives) by a long wooded Lane pafsing by a burnt Dutch Farmhouse, the only Building nigh the Sound at that Point. I will not mention the Supernatural guardians suppos'd by the Dutchmen to be sett about the Treasure, for I am a Man of Sense with no Credence in these silly Legends & Cock-Lane Spectres. These Dutch, Sir, as you have no doubt found out, are an odd superstitious Race; tho' very pleasing & worthie, & much more affable than the sour Country-Folk in New-England.

'Fore Gad! But your scholasticall Atchievements are like to sett a new Model for Learning at King's College! I vow, Sir, they never before saw a Student of such Bright & Solid Parts; & wou'd wager they would give you a Post as Preceptor there if you were but to ask them. Why not try, & settle in the Eastern civiliz'd Provinces? Sink me if any College cou'd ask a better Tutor! At any rate, let me urge you to accept literally the Conjecture of your fellow-student, & publish your collegiate Compositions in the best pedagogical Periodicals. To be widely known as an Authority upon Education, is an Advantage no Man may justly belittle.

I rejoice that you have been seeing the Town with the gay young Mohocks & Maccaronies,[2] & trust you enjoy'd the Covent-Garden Follies; which

I ever recommend, but which I did not my self see, so great was the Charge & so compleat was my Preoccupation with the Antiquities of the Region. That you are not ardent in your Liking for antient Sights, I regret to learn; but trust I shall so instruct your Taste, that you cannot thenceforward live apart from them. For mine own Part, I do not see how any Man of acute Sensibilities can dwell in a new Town where there is nothing mellow & traditionally Beautiful. The West, Sir, is abominably crude & garish; because it rose up too quickly to poſseſs any slow natural Growth, & because its Rise was in an Aera when nothing beautiful was created. Moreover, even its recent Adornments are of a blowsy mechanical kind, design'd at wholesale by some weary Hack who hath made plans for countless other Places, & who never expects to live in Sight of his Work. This, Sir, is Death to all true Beauty. Nothing is beautiful that is not unique; that did not, as it were, evolve naturally out of the Race & Landskip, so that it cou'd not have evolv'd among any other People or in any other Place. Your Western towns, Sir, are as alike as Peas; so that any two of 'em cou'd be exchang'd without their Inhabitants being sensible of the Fact. They are like tradesmen & small Citizens, so wanting in Distinctiveness & Personality, that they can not gratifie the Imagination, or ease the aesthetick Sense. In the several Countries of Europe, & in the Eastern Provinces of America, the Buildings were wrought lovingly & carefully by hand Craftsmen who were full of the Dreams of our ancestral Past, & of the loveliness of the scenery in which they labour'd. They work'd simply & slowly, & with a genuine Fire whose Effulgence came from the Circumstance that they were truly expressing themselves, & fashioning forms of Beauty which they meant to have around them, & around their descendants for ever. The hideous American Vice of dull Monotony & Duplication had no part in the Labours of our Colonial artificers. They built Beauty in an Individual Way, as we may see by noting the local Peculiarities of every Town & Colonie, & the grand Divisions of Architecture distinguishing the North, the Middle Provinces, & the South. I have only to go to Marblehead to see lines & Arrangements which we have not in Providence, whilst in New-Hampshire are Stiles foreign to all of Southern New-England. I have even obſerv'd a Kind of Rosette on the Pilasters of Colonial Doorways in the Warwick country of Rhode-Island, which nowhere else finds any Exemplar, & which is undoubtedly the Invention of some local Craftsman of that Territory. In New-York we discover that delightful Contrast, which arose from the Juxtaposition of two Nations. The tasteful Simplicity of the Low-Dutch, united with the Claſsick Beauty of our own English, Schools of Architecture; so that out of the Combination we have both Cottages & Mansions of the pleasantest Sort conceivable. If you are Wise, Sir, you will this week seize a Pleasure which I miss'd thro' sheer Ignorance; & make a Trip to see *the oldest edifice within the Corporate Limits of New-York*, & so far as I know, the only surviving House in the Province *built actually during the Sovereignty of the Holland States-General & the Governorship of*

Petrus Stuyvesant. It is the Schenck house, built in 1656 on the outskirts of Flatbush, & to be reached by taking a Flatbush-Ave Chaise to the End of the Line, connecting with a Bergen Beach Chaise, alighting at Mill Basin Road, & walking to the right a quarter of a Mile; the structure appearing to the left, & having an Aspect not unlike the accompanying Design, which is copy'd from the article where (too late to avail my self of it) I learnt of the Place. No, Sir, I defy you to shew, that any modern Constructure (unlefs fashion'd in a reverent antiquarian Spirit) can have a tenth as much Lovelinefs as a true Colonial House, whose advantages are so numberlefs. Reflect, if you will, that the Colonial Edifices were put up in a clafsick age, when the Graeco-Roman aesthetick had just joyn'd with the native English manor-house Stile; & when that composite Pattern was so new & fresh, & so finely develop'd by men of Genius like Sir Ch: Wren & Mr. Gibbs,[3] that it had all the Vitality of a Renaissance Product. This pure Type, homogeneously representative of our British nation, & infinitely adaptable to agreeable local Variations, was introduc'd at just the proper Time; when correctness of Taste had fully emerg'd from Puritan Darkness & Chaos, & before it had sunk into Victorian corruption. Thus nobly born, & inheriting all the instinctive Traditions of the past, it hath ever since remain'd with us; picking up all those little Dreams & Memories which come like Ivy from long endurance in one spot, & which alone are capable of imparting that Mellowness which pleases the delicate Sensibilities. It is full of the elemental Substance of Beauty; an unaffected simplicity proceeding both from its clafsical Heritage, & from its Construction by Simple People in a Simple Age free from tawdry Notions. It can never be surpass'd, because our Nation & Civilization are both sunk into their final Decline; this being an Aera of improving critical Taste, but not of strong creative Genius. Henceforward we may only restore & copy, as I am much gratify'd to see we are doing.

The ugliness of Western towns may be mitigated by judicious Imitation of more approv'd Models, but they can not soon atchieve the subtler atmosphere of Mellowness. This is because they were conceiv'd in the Victorian Age, that disgusting debauch or aesthetick coma & paralysis of the human Spirit, & because they have grown up too swiftly among a Race of belated Pioneers who though mechanically advanced by virtue of their Time, are intellectually still in that Aera of Simplicity & Struggle for material Wealth, which the East outgrew about the Decade 1740–50—the period of Gov. W: Shirley in the Massachusetts-Bay, who with his Retinue & Household introduc'd to the Provinces the Aristocratic Thought & gentle Manners of Great-Britain. The West can not yet be beautiful because it has not developed the imaginative Sensitiveness of a settled Region. It is yet adolescent—full of crude & vain Hopes, & callow

Flatbuſh, A. D. 1656

Designs for practical Comfort & Improvement—& attaches to wealth, conventionality, locomotives, & bathtubs, that Importance which an old Nation attaches only to Beauty & to Truth. Not until it throws aside exaggerated Practicality, Optimism, & Common-Sense, in Disgust & Weariness; not until it subordinates civic & economic preoccupations from a just Conception of their fundamental Insolvableness; can the west be truly civiliz'd enough to love & create real Beauty. That is why I shou'd die, faint, or scream aloud in dawning Madness, if I had to dwell long in a Western town. That is probably why my Son Samuel hates his native city of Cleveland so violently, & why my little grandson Alfredus is so nervously overwrought. I know how transported with Delight I was, when, upon returning from Cleveland, I first beheld near Albany the pleasing Diversity of the Eastern Landskip, with a quaint Village embosom'd betwixt green Hills, & a white Georgian steeple rising over ancient Roofs & above a verdant sea of foliage. O Antiquity most venerable, & Tradition most Immemorial! O Beauty, Ravishing in a Thousand Forms! And are ye not all One, like that Aphrodite of Old who was both Uranian & Dionaean, both the Anadyomene of the dreaming Grecians, & the Mother & Battle-Spirit, thro' Aeneas & Iulus, of the ROMAN Line? Thou, thou alone art deserving of the Love & Worship of a truly civiliz'd Mankind; thou, whose Fanes & Altars a small Band must preserve till Death, against the Ignorance & Insensitiveness of the forward-looking Goth, & the phrensy'd Pafsion of the iconoclastick Vandal.

Well, Sir, I will have done before I drown you in a Cataract of Rhetorick. But I hope I have shewn you why I love antient Scenes, & why I believe you can not but be transported at the Georgian Wonders of Marblehead.

Hoping to hear from you soon, & in truth to behold you in 10 Days, I am ever, Sir, yr moft humble,

moft obt Servt

Lo.

P.S. You might return that Miniature of Sandufky & me, fince I pofsefs no other.

Notes

1. In Saintsbury, *Tales of Mystery*. Further extracts are in Julian Hawthorne's *Lock and Key Library*, vol. 7.
2. The Mohocks were a gang of violent, well-born criminals that terrorized London in the early 18th century, taking their name from the Mohawk Indians. Maccaronies were English dandies of the 18th century who affected Continental mannerisms and clothes (as in the song "Yankee Doodle").
3. Sir Christopher Wren (1632–1723); James Gibbs (1682–1754).

[22] [AHT]

5 August [1923]

Mocrates, My Son:—

    I am confident, Sir, that I can convert you to the beauties of architecture, and of the eighteenth century, by one brief sight of Marblehead. What you say of the beginnings of New-England architecture is very true. Not only were the first dwellings made directly from the best feasible British plans, but many of them, including the oldest surviving house in the English part of these Colonies (The Fayerbanks or Fairbanks house in Dedham, Mass., built 1636. I have never seen this house, but mean to do so soon.),[1] had their frame and timbers cut and shap'd in Old England, and transported on shipboard to be put together here. By 1670 or 1680 all the towns on the coast were very well built up in an architecture like that of European towns of the time; stout, peaked, many-gabled houses with a second story overhanging on the side toward the street (This feature, wrongly ascrib'd by the ignorant to principles of fortification, was in truth characteristick of all European towns, and can be trac'd back to the MAENIANVM of the Romans.), and with the facade often cover'd with stucco, whilst carv'd ornamental brackets seem'd to support the overhang. The windows open'd outward on hinges, and had small diamond-shap'd panes of bluish leaded glass, whilst the doorways were extremely plain, with dull iron knockers. Furniture was in most cases sparse and sadly plain, tho' the better sort of men had some fine Elizabethan heirlooms, dark, massive, and finely carv'd. The china and pewterware were simple, yet far from ugly. Of these antient gabled town houses of New-England's first wave of building, only four specimens survive in original form, of which I have any knowledge. These, moreover, have all been at one time very much defac'd and alter'd, and lately restor'd at a great expense. They are the Paul Revere house in Boston, (1676) and the Seven-Gable house (1668), the John Ward house (1685—a belated specimen), and the Hooper bakery (1683—also belated) in Salem. Farmhouses of that time are quite numerous, but they have no distinctive features. What swept off these old landmarks was fire and alteration. Before the general use of fire-engines, (circa 1720) all the towns were frequently devastated by extensive conflagrations, whilst the houses that remain'd were pretty generally alter'd by their owners to conform to later stiles. There is in these old houses a quaint kind of European picturesqueness nowhere else visible in America, but their plainness and want of original taste is painful. It is perhaps aesthetically well, that they were superseded by a more pleasing sort of edifice.

    The change of form, which gave birth to what we today know as "Colonial" architecture, sprang without any doubt from the great fire in London, and the subsequent rise of an architectural renaissance led by Christopher Wren, the designer of buildings, and Grinling Gibbons, the master of woodcarving. It must be remark'd, that at this period architecture and decoration had sunk to their very nadir; so that although neither Wren nor Gibbons ever equall'd the divine artisans of Greece and Rome in their atchievements, they deserve almost as much credit for what they brought out of a state of nearly total Gothick disorder.

The distinctive feature of this renaissance, was the flexible adaptation of the Greek and Roman designs to our English sort of building. In London, the full Roman design took root, as far as it cou'd, in publick structures like St. Paul's; whilst an happy combination of the classical and the Gothick patterns, gave birth to what we carelessly call the "Georgian" steeple. When James Gibbs, a pupil of Wren, submitted competing designs for the spire of St. Martin's-in-the-Fields, the rejected one was sent to the Colonies, where it was adopted unchanged by the First Baptist Church[2] of Providence, which my ancestors attended. (1775) This is the only purely London-design'd steeple in the colonies, and is pronounc'd by experts the finest of all. But this is merely one incident in the architectural revolution. It was the felicity of the new school, to have an infinite degree of flexibility; so that individual designers might bend it to their taste, and employ it for the expression of their own personality and the adornment of their own particular landscape. Such a designer was John H. Greene, Esq.,[3] of Providence, who plann'd many of our finest mansions, and conceiv'd the steeple of the Unitarian Church, whose bell was cast by Paul Revere, Esq. The growth of the renaissance was slow. First of all changes was one hardly related to it, but coming in as a sort of revulsion against peaked gables; I refer to the rise of the hipp'd or gambrel (the use of the word gambrel in this connexion, is by some adjudg'd of American colonial origin) roof, whose extensive use in dwellings is quite peculiar to Colonial America. This first appear'd about 1685 or 1690, and was follow'd by a growth of classical ornamentation about doorways—an ornamentation springing out of a conventional arrangement of lights which had gradually develop'd; one large light above, and two narrow lights flanking, the door. Sometimes these narrow lights were dispens'd with, but they may be reckon'd a characteristick feature. I do not think there is any authentick instance of a true "colonial doorway" before 1710 or 1715. Thereafter, the employment of classical scrolls and pilasters, and other pleasing devices, became very common; and afforded infinite opportunities for clever artistical creation on the part of the ship-carpenters who were the only carvers in the colonies. The earlier colonial doorways are relatively crude, and have certain distinctive qualities which any observer may identify; though in a few cases the importation of genuine English carving or the employment of genuine English artizans brought finer results. The same is true of interiors—mantels, wainscotting, and cornices. Early American work has certain roughnesses, and can be told from the imported work such as that of the Lee Mansion in Marblehead. A few houses have imported work by Grinling Gibbons himself. About 1750 ridge-poles went out, and the gambrel roof began to disappear. Chimneys mov'd from the centre to the ends of houses, and flat or modified mansard roofs are seen. At the same time a monstrous improvement in the quality of American carving and designing is observ'd; so that many surviving mansions and publick buildings of the age are of extreme beauty. The lamentable rebellion of ambitious upstarts sensibly retarded the growth of fine work; but about 1785, when peace had return'd and wealth was returning, a marvellous advance occurr'd. The carvers and architects of this aera, amongst whom Samuel McIntire of Salem takes a very great place, were artists of the truest sort; and introduc'd a fineness of workmanship and delicacy of detail never before known this side of London. The new century did not interrupt this growth, which proceeded uncheck'd till near 1825. Then, however, American architecture tottered upon its pinnacle, push'd by the contagion of the romantick movement, preparatory to its plunge into the nauseous and nameless abominations of Victorianism, whose hideous culmination occurr'd betwixt 1870 and 1880. The departure from architectural Colonialism came disguis'd as wholesome progress—a vaunted return to *purely Grecian* patterns. Alas! *Timeo Danaos et dona ferentes!* [4] Betwixt 1820 and 1840 the Parthenon facade (in debas'd form) reign'd supreme; its chief Providence examples being the arcade, (1826) the Historical Society Building, Manning-Hall in Brown University, and several other publick structures, all still standing. (This tradition has just been reviv'd by the new home of the People's Bank, which was founded in the neo-Hellenic age of the twenties.) In Boston it is observable in St. Paul's Cathedral, where my father and mother were marry'd. But the idea of change and romantick antiquarianism having been introduc'd, excess and incongruity were impossible to check Wearying of the classical models, and (note dawn of nineteenth century vulgar obtuseness to taste and beauty) insensible of the need of excluding forms alien to the new-classical designs now firmly seated as the keynote of all the towns, a sudden rage for the *Gothick* now began (1835–40) to develop. At first this was fairly inoffensive, since a *pure* Gothick stile was follow'd (a foretaste—and a singular one—of the Gothick craze, is found in certain earlier churches like St. John's (1810) in Providence);[5] giving to some extent the atmospherical impression of some old English town where Georgian houses have grown up about an antient Gothick abbey. In the pure Gothick stile are several churches of Salem, Grace Church in Providence,[6] and Gore Hall (now demolish'd to make way for the pure Georgian (by order of Pres. Emeritus Eliot, an enthusiast for Colonial architecture) Widener Library) at Harvard College.[7]

 But the pure Gothick departed as swiftly as did the classical; this crepuscular lesser evil giving way at length to the shocking blackness of bastard Victorianism. Of the nightmares of this hybrid architectural aera I have no need to tell you; since your own West arose in that age, and has ever since insulted you with that age's barbarism. Words do not exist, to express the incomprehensible outrages upon the Muses, which this dread darkness usher'd in. Classical Corinthian columns upholding arches half Gothick and half Romanesque! God's blood, Sir! I am put in mind of the description of Mrs. Ogle in the School for Scandal—an Irish front, Caledonian locks, Dutch nose, Austrian lips, the complexion of a Spaniard, teeth a la Chinoise . . . . in short, a face 'that resembles a table d'hote at Spa, where no two guests are of a nation, or a congress at the close of a general war, wherein all the members appear to have a different interest.'[8] Aye, Sir, that, or some great shapeless building of the Middle Ages, where the construction cover'd many centuries, and caus'd a round-arch'd Romanesque foundation to uphold a Gothic sett of towers, each of which receiv'd an early renaissance roof. I am glad to observe, that many horrors of this sort in Providence have been alter'd or demolish'd within the last score of years, or else will be in the near future. When you come here, I will shew you a most interesting corner, where one Victorian house hath been perfectly sett back to the stile of 1780, with Colonial doorway, whilst the house diagonally across the street is midway in a similar course of change, furnishing a very diagram or object lesson in architectural taste. Our worst Victorian monstrosity is the Butler Exchange, in Westminster St., built in 1872 opposite the purely Grecian Arcade (1826). I often ask myself, how any man cou'd build so hideous a thing after having look'd upon the beauty of the older Providence; and can answer only by admitting candidly, that the aesthetick sensitiveness of the Anglo-Saxon world was utterly stifled or exhausted from 1830 or 1840 on, to be reviv'd only by the influence of that school, in itself so extravagant and comical, of which the late Oscar Wilde was the nucleus. But, thank the gods, we are recovering. The twentieth century is a mighty renaissance of all the intellect and the imagination save (so far) the creative faculty, and in all our old towns a new growth of Georgian architecture is rising to salute the skies. You shou'd see the new Sturges mansion (half done) or the Arnold chemical laboratory of Brown University, (just finish'd) neither of which wou'd be pronounc'd—save by an expert—as of later dates than 1780 and 1730, respectively.

I will send you—to be return'd with reverent care, since 'tis absolutely my only copy—a leaflet on the Colonial houses of Providence. I am certain you cannot be insensible to their traditional beauty, and will promise you a good sight of them (if they please you) when you come to this town.

I cou'd, if I chose, devote pages more to the superiority of eighteenth century decoration, china, and furniture, to those of any other aera; but will forbear lest I weary you more than I have already done. Besides, I shou'd by that process fan myself into a flaming feud against the older members of my family, who have permitted the dispersal among relatives, one by one, of those Georgian household antiquities which shou'd have been zealously cherish'd for the furnishing of one household. I will only ask you, when I take you to the Pendleton House of the Rhode-Island School of Design, to contrast the simple yet classically opulent beauty of that splendidly adorn'd Georgian mansion, with what you may remember of Victorian parlours of the ghoulish haircloth age, or of the age of plush and antimacassars. The Pendleton House is a fireproof museum built in 1906 to reproduce with loving exactness a typical Providence mansion of about 1780, and containing what is universally admitted to be the finest collection of Colonial furniture, silver, china, and general household antiques, in the United States. This collection was the life work of that distinguished dilettante and connoisseur, the late Charles Leonard Pendleton, Esq., of Providence, and was conceiv'd with the notion of including the best and most sumptuous specimen obtainable of each sort of object represented. When Mr. Pendleton obtain'd enough articles exactly to furnish a mansion in proper taste, he ceas'd collecting new types; and began to look about for more luxurious specimens of articles he had already. When in this way he would discover something incomparably fine, he wou'd buy it and discard the corresponding object in his former collection. Thus was assembled a sett of choice antiques to which no rival exists, and which ought to convince any gentleman of taste, of the peerless supremacy of the eighteenth century in all matters of household embellishment. Mr. Pendleton, upon his death, bequeath'd his treasures to the Rhode-Island School of Design, on condition that they erect a Colonial mansion to house it, which they did.

In another letter I may add some remarks on the superiority of eighteenth century costume, and the barbarousness of the nineteenth century with its whiskers, short hair, and ugly long trousers. But this can wait. Meanwhile I am all agog for Friday, when I will board the Boston train at five-fifty-six!

I am ever, Sir, yr. most resp and obt Svt
Lo.

Notes

1. HPL would not visit the Fairbanks house until 1929. See the essay "An Account of a Trip to the Fairbanks House . . ." (1929; *CE* 4.62–66).
2. The First Baptist Meeting House (1775) at 75 North Main Street, designed by Joseph Brown.
3. John Holden Greene (1777–1850), celebrated Rhode Island architect who designed many notable public buildings and private homes in Providence from 1806 to 1842.
4. "I fear Greeks, even when bearing gifts." A celebrated line (referring to the Trojan Horse) in Virgil's *Aeneid* 2.49.
5. St. John's Episcopal Church at 271 N. Main Street, designed by John Holden Greene.
6. Grace Church at 175 Mathewson Street in Providence, built in 1845–46 in the Gothic style by Richard Upjohn.
7. Charles William Eliot (1834–1926), president of Harvard (1869–1909). Gore Hall (1838), Harvard's first dedicated library building, was built in the Gothic style by Richard Bond. In 1913 it was demolished and the Harry Elkins Widener Memorial Library (1913–15) was built in the Georgian style by Horace Trumbauer & Associates.
8. HPL refers to a scene in Act 2, scene 2 of *The School for Scandal* (1777) by Richard Brinsley Sheridan (1751–1816). HPL owned an 1874 edition of Sheridan's *Works*.

[23]   [AHT]

Old 598
Aug. 19 [1923]

Mocrates, My Son:—
              Tuesday I made the Portsmouth trip according to schedule, and oh, Boy! what a survival of the past I found! I'll be shot if it doesn't knock Salem off the map, and dangerously challenge Marblehead for the champeenship! Fancy a living town of some 13,569 inhabitants—almost purely old Yankee stock—with a dominant industry over a century old, and an array of buildings practically the same as in the decade 1800–1810! It is a dream—a vision—the experience of a lifetime! Man, man! Why didn't someone shoot me while I was happy—there amidst the atmosphere of Georgian days! I can't describe the trip except lyrically—but I enclose a folder (for you to keep) showing the route I fully and faithfully follow'd. Boy, what a town! Vistas of endless ancient roofs, steeples, and chimneys, with not a modern feature in sight! Labyrinths of quiet streets and lanes lined with *Colonial doorways* and innocent of sidewalk or paving—streets redolent of an elder world, and communicating their old-Yankee air even to their inhabitants. How can I put across the magick of those streets ..... I grope for words and phrases ..... white houses with green blinds and small-paned windows; sprawling flagstones and jagged doorsteps; glimpses of old gardens with tall hollyhocks; glints of the sea down long narrow lanes where grasses grow around the iron-railed steps that lead to high colonial doorways ..... it's the whale's pocket-flask, kid! And I went across on the ferry (to be abandoned this week when the $2,000,000 bridge is opened) into Kittery, Maine (my first contact with Maine soil—I bought some ice-cream for twelve cents at a village shop, to say I had eaten in Maine) obtaining on the way some glimpses of the ancient Portsmouth waterfront which recalled with eery fidelity the great old days of the Colonial sea-trade. Where can one find another such waterfront? I show'd you the old Providence warehouses (1816) and adjacent things, but that is cheaply modern compared with the harbour of Portsmouth, where warehouses of 1750–1800 rub elbows with still older gambrel-roofed dwellings, and crown a moss-grown bank wall rising partly from the water and partly from still grassy banks. O happy town! O felicitous freedom from smoky factories! No need for me to use my imagination in describing a prosperous eighteenth century seaport—*I have seen one!* Oh, man! What alluring crooked waterfront streets with painted advertisements on buildings and swinging signs over Colonial doorways—my gawd! But for marine stuff, it knocks hell outa Marblehead! Boy! But yuh'd orta see Market St., Daniel St., Bow St., and a few others! It's the salamander's fire-extinguisher, kid! I wished to Pegāna you could have managed by hook, crook, or miracle to stay over another day and lap it all up! I went over (tho' unconverted) on the Christian Shore and lamped the oldest dump in the burg—Jackson House, 1664—and took off

my hat before the Earl of Halifax Tavern, where the loyalists and crown officials used to congregate. I did the Thomas Bailey Aldrich house with extreme thoroughness, and revelled in the colonial substratum underlying the base Victorian gewgaws—and too, St. John's Church, which overlooks a bluff above the quaint waterfront section and has a delectable churchyard. In the athenaeum—1803—I stopt to write post cards, and looked up at the portraits of many of His Majesty's officers concern'd in the taking of Louisburg (1745)—and at the Warner house (1718–23) I beheld a lightning rod put up by the ingenious hands of Dr. Franklin himself. And the old mansions! Boy, boy! What magnificence! Say, kid, even the Lee Mansion is nothing extra beside the Gardner-Wentworth house (unfortunately unfurnish'd) and the Moffett-Ladd house.[1] This last is the cobra's radio set—take it from me! Oh, boy, what luxury! Pipe the pictorial wall paper, and the exquisite staircase, and the carved doors—no two alike—and the magnificent mantels—one of 'em carved *by Grinling Gibbons himself!* But hell, what's the use of describing? I sure have gotta swell 1924 itinerary planned out fer youse, kid! This same joint has gotta garden what is the ibex's hair-tonic. Man, man! The winding paths amidst the tall flowers—the circular seat round the antient apple tree—the bird fountain in the hedged enclosure—the sundial on the grapy terrace—the shady walks and festooned arbours—the sodded [?] steps from terrace to terrace—honest to gawd, I'll be damned if I know whether I dream'd it or not! Why the deuce weren't you along to stick a pin into me and prove I was awake? Say, it cost me a pang to hop the eight-forty-two freight homeward!

    I gotta do Portsmouth a helluva lotta times more—but Pete, what a expense! They soak ya $2.06 from Boston for B. & M. fare, which same makes $3.66 from Providence, or $7.32 round trip! But it's worth it! I'll announce to the yawning gulph!

    Well, ol' sport, howja come out with N.Y.? Didja see Van Cortlandt Mansion, Old Mill, Flatbush Churchyard, Dyckman Cottage, Jumel Mansion, Metropolitan Museum, American Museum, N.Y. Historical Society Museum, Hispanic, Geographic, and Numismatic Museum, Brooklyn Museum with Japanese garden, Fraunce's [*sic*] Tavern, Schenck homestead (the one thing I didn't get wise to whilst I was there, damn the luck!) (1656), Poe Cottage, 59th St. bookstalls, Inwood????

    No? . . . . . and this guy thinks he's ben stayin' in N'York!

    It ain't no use, kid! I gotta rake up the jack nex' year and show ya Li'l ol' N.Y. myself! Nobody knows it like me!

    I dunno what your posolutely ultra-final decision about going home was, but whatever it was, I hope you're having a helluva good time about it—or as good a time as any bimbo can have going away from the big town. If ya hits Nia-ga´-ra (cf. Goldsmith, "The Traveller"),[2] go acrossed to the loyal side and chant gawd save the king (not queen) for me.

    I am, Sir, for cosmick aeternity,

Yr most oblig'd, most obt Servt
LO.

Notes

1. The Jackson House (c. 1664), 76 Northwest Street; the Earl of Halifax Tavern (1766; now the William Pitt Tavern), 416 Court Street; the Thomas Bailey Aldrich house (1797), 14 Hancock Street; St. John's Episcopal Church (1807), 101 Chapel Street; Portsmouth Athenaeum (1805), 9 Market Square; the Warner house (c. 1716), 150 Daniel Street; the Wentworth-Gardner house (1760), 140 Mechanic Street; the Moffatt-Ladd house (1763), 154 Market Street; all in Portsmouth, NH. The "Lee Mansion" is the Jeremiah Lee Mansion (1768), 161 Washington Street, Marblehead.
2. HPL refers to l. 412 in Oliver Goldsmith's *The Traveller* (1764), "And Niagara stuns with thund'ring sound," in which Niagara must be accented on the first and third syllables.

[24] [AHT]

Usual Sepulchre
4th September [1923]

Mocrates, my Son:—
And did I tell you about the Moffat[t]–Ladd house in Market St.?[1] 1763—with a mantel carved by Grinling Gibbons himself. I found there the finest woodwork interior I ever beheld, save possibly in the Lee Mansion. It was a dream—a visual orgie. There are pictorial panels beyond descriptions, and carvings that transport the fancy. And the grand staircase! It is an ecstasy . . . . . a sonnet! The arched window on the landing is one of the most beautiful things ever glimpsed by human eyes, though perhaps not superior to similar colossal windows in the Lee Mansion and the Gardner–Wentworth house.

But the garden behind the house! May the mantle of Aristaenetus descend upon me, that I may draw in moving numbers a terraced paradise more lovely than ever the garden of Phyllion was.[2] Mehercule! Not L. Licinius Lucullus himself could dream such a garden![3] It is of the *eighteenth century*, and of that alone! It is a lyric of sensuous colour and plastic form, moulded and tinted with a thousand subtleties of grace and feeling, and vivid with an atmosphere in which line, hue, odour, and sound are blent to a potent and opiate climax that expands the soul and annihilates time and reality. It is deep—a whole large city block in depth—and in width it takes nearly a block as well. Here one may stray in perfumed dream for long summer hours, loitering in the shade of vast arbours, ascending and descending gentle steps of verdant turf, watching the aërial minstrels as they carol and chatter around the bird-fountain on an obscurely hedged inner lawn with settees and flower-beds, or marking the sun's progress on the antique dial amidst the central riot of passionate blooms—rose and white, violet and blue, purple and pink, gold and green—and of dionysiac scents and symbols—lilac and lily, lavender and valerian, polychrome and swelling fruit, scarlet berries, and in the distance the diamond music of an hyaline fount in whose pool an universe of gay petals drifts and drinks. To sit here through eternities of visioning, here on an ancient circular bench beneath a gnarled and venerable apple-tree under a sinking August sun, when all the world of faery—that lovely elder world which stays only in the most delicate dreams—is turning from white to gold, from gold to vermeil, and from deepening ruddiness to the cool purple and ineffable shadow of star-gemmed night . . . . . Hei! but that were happiness in truth . . . an happiness in which the ecstasy of the mere senses is lifted into the highest exaltations of the spirit, and by infinite wonder and the mystery of dim worlds and centuries made one with the rapture of Pegāna's gods. When it is twilight in the worlds, there are heard in that garden the invisible steps of MĀNA-YOOD-SUSHĀĪ who is weary of Sardathrion's gleaming walls and onyx lions, and would gaze softly and gently on that loveliness he hath created in his dreams. It was very beautiful in that garden.

And in that dying light I made another and final circuit of the cryptical, that prehistoric town; beholding the ancient mansions as sunset gilded their gables and reddened their roofs, lit witch-fires in their age-old windows, and drew their grotesque chimneys in black, fantastic outlines against the west. And besides the mansions I looked at the little lowly streets with flagstones and cottage doorways, peopled now with those Georgian shades that loom out of the dusk when it is quivering, violet, and ambiguous. When I was at the hoary Point of Graves on the harbour-front, watching the shadows dance sarabands amongst the low slate slabs, I saw a tenuous thread of lucent selmite tremble above the far-off Christian Shore, and melt even as I glimpsed it, into the deep, shimmering western mists that still echoed with light. Evening had come, and through silent, unillumined Colonial streets I made my way back to the station, glancing now and then at the arabesques of the tenebrous steeples and Gothic vanes and singular chimney-pots as they stood limned before the inscrutable and immemorial stars; the pale, languorous stars that saw Portsmouth born, and that without a smile will see Portsmouth die. A century is not much in Portsmouth—I was sorry to leave it.

I beg leave to subscribe myself, Sir,
 Yr most hble, most obt Servt
  LO.

Notes

1. The Moffatt–Ladd House, also known as the William Whipple House, stands at 154 Market Street in Portsmouth, NH.

2. HPL refers to the Greek writer Aristaenetus (5th–6th c. C.E.), author of two books of love stories in the form of letters. One book is entitled *The Garden of Phyllion*.

3. L. Licinius Lucullus (118–57? B.C.E.), Roman politician and gastronome. He amassed a vast fortune that allowed him to erect extensive gardens in a villa outside Rome.

[25]   [AHT]

November 24, 1923

Mocrates, My Son:—
       Tho' by no means wishful to obtrude more verbiage upon one whom I have already delug'd with so many harangues, I cannot resist relating the scenick and antiquarian voyages which I took on Wednesday and Thursday without quitting the boundaries of this village. I am now become definitely an antiquarian, rather than a general student of letters; for in truth I find all fascination to proceed from the past in general, and the eighteenth century in particular. On Novr. 21st I resum'd my delvings, walking with my daughter Mrs. Clark thro' the most antient part of Providence, and visiting the one museum which I had never before inspected—the new private museum of Col. George L. Shepley, in Benefit-Street, where may be found the greatest of all collections of Rhode-Island relicks and antiquities.[1] I regret that you cou'd not have seen this place when in Providence, and vow, you must do so when next here; for truly, I got from it more data regarding the early days of the town, than I had ever before gain'd from any one source. There are records, samples of papers and broadsides, advertisements, maps, pictures, books, proclamations, (one by Gov. Ward,[2] 1762, with GOD SAVE THE KING at the bottom!) letters, autographs, diaries, miniatures, and miscellaneous articles of every sort, giving a very compleat picture of Providence throughout its existence, and shewing the handwriting of all the principal publick men from Roger Williams down. Of much interest are the books, almanacks, and maps printed in French by the naval forces of King Louis, the occupy'd Newport in 1780 and 1781, during the late insurrection. The fleet had its own press—L'Imprimerie Royale de l'Escadre—and produc'd not only isolated works, but a regular newspaper, *Gazette Francaise de Newport*. Its typography was excellent, and its maps both accurate and artistick. As a repository of Georgian architectural designs, this museum hath not any equal in this town. It contains the full Mason collection of photographs of Rhode-Island Colonial doorways, shewing thousands of these classical portals in Providence, Warren, Bristol, Newport, and other ancient towns, (circular enclos'd) together with magnificent sets of etchings and displaying all the Georgian master-pieces of architecture, both publick and domestick, in the American colonies. These latter sets have convinc'd me of something I but vaguely suspected before; namely, that the finest 18th century buildings on this continent are yet unseen by me, being in the original colonial metropolis Philadelphia, to which my peregrinations have not yet extended. This city was very populous, wealthy, and finely built up when Boston and Providence were scarce more than villages, and when New-York was uneasily divided betwixt Holland and English architecture. It accordingly contains Georgian edifices of a splendour unapproach'd by anything I have seen, and will henceforward form a goal of travel, from which only poverty can keep me. I also discover,

that Connecticut, and Staten-Island in New-York, abound with Colonial reliquiae of uncommon interest. I must some day see all these things, for I am certain, that nothing interests me so vastly as the scenes and landskips of my 18th century. But of paramount immediate interest to me, were the illuminating views of Colonial Providence, which I shall employ in the essay or book I am planning on the subject. There is one monstrous fine drawing of the town in 1762, as seen from the hill where Prospect-Street now runs, wherein may be observ'd the tangle of antient roofs in Cheapside and Town Street, the houses in Gaol-Lane,[3] the new colony-house, just finish'd, and looking as it does today, the Market-Parade without the new (1773) market house, the narrow bridge across the river that preceded the Great Bridge, and the opposite shoar, with a few houses scatter'd along Weybosset-Street (the old Pequot path) and the line of the future Westminster-Street, which was platted out across the place where Mr. Staples had shovell'd down Weybosset Hill in 1719 to get clay for his brickyard. It was truly a remarkable view—precisely what I had long wish'd to see—and I shall certainly refer to it when writing on antique Providence. There is a possibility that I may be able to get a copy for myself, for the curator at the museum told me I cou'd have one if another exists in the archives. Still more important, however, is the crude but striking plan or bird's-eye view of Providence in 1777, which Stephen Avery, a rebel soldier, engrav'd upon his powder-horn. The practice of defeating homesickness by drawing one's native town upon one's powder-horn was not uncommon in the late provincial uprising, and in this same museum there is an excellent rendering of Boston in the same manner. But the Providence view is of greatest interest to me, insomuch as it very accurately pictures on contemporary evidence just how much of the town was built up in 1777. The Great Bridge had been enlarg'd, the market-house built, the college set up on the hill, the Baptist church erected in all its London grandeur, and all the hill settled by the thick building up of Benefit-Street, and of Rosemary-Lane (now College St.) that leads to the college. But the greatest changes were on the west side of the bridge, where Westminster-Street was now cut through and solidly built up, and Weybosset-Street settled very thickly, together with the region southward along Richmond-Street, Chestnut-Street, South-Street, and the like. (of which much more anon) In a word, the town had in 1777 begun to cover the area now forming the business section; an area but sparsely inhabited before the filling of the salt marshes and widening of the bridge. Of this quaint powder-horn view I was lucky enough to obtain a copy, which now lyes before me. As I contemplate it I am fill'd with Georgian pride and pleasure, that the town shou'd have kept so many of the buildings, streets, institutions, manners and customs which flourisht when it was design'd. The Baptist church was then but two years built, and each night at nine curfew was rung there by a bell-ringer pay'd by the town. That curfew is still rung every night at nine, by the same bell in the same steeple; and the town still pays its bell-ringer.

What are 150 years in antient, Georgian Providence, where the past never dyes, and where Colonial doorways look out at the same shady streets they us'd to know when the Georges reign'd? GOD SAVE THE KING! Before going home, my daughter and I sat at a new ordinary down town; and perceiv'd with pleasure, that it was panell'd and furnisht in the Georgian manner. 'Tis one of the greatest coincidences in the world, that Providence shou'd be returning so markedly to the 18th century, when I wish'd for it so violently years before 'twas ever publickly thought of. Only a year ago the Citizens' Bank put up a new building of great size and splendour, with fine Colonial columns and white belfry, for all the world like the colony house built in 1760.

Animated by these reflections, I joyn'd my adopted son Eddy on the following day (22nd November—my grandfather's birthday) for a tour of exploration of certain parts of Colonial Providence which I had never before seen or more than vaguely heard of. I refer to the southerly section west of the Great Bridge, around Richmond and Chestnut Streets; now sunk to slums and on that account avoided by me, but prov'd by the 1777 view to be genuinely Colonial. Here indeed I found a world of wonder that for 33 years I had ignor'd! Not a stone's throw from the travell'd business section, tuckt quietly in behind Broad and Weybosset Streets, lurk the beginnings of a squalid Colonial labyrinth in which I mov'd as an utter stranger, each moment wondering whether I were in truth in my native town or some leprous distorted witch-Salem of fever or nightmare. I had not thought my own city to be so large and vary'd—so London-like in containing separate worlds unsuspected one by another. This antient and pestilential reticulation of crumbling cottages and decaying doorways was like nothing I had ever beheld save in dream—it was the 18th century of Goya, not of the Georges; of Hogarth, not of Horace Walpole. Eddy knew it, and was my guide. Led by him, I wander'd up hills where rotting Dorick columns rested on worn stone steps out of which rusted footscrapers rose like malignant fungi. Dirty small-pan'd windows leer'd malevolently on all sides, and sometimes glasslessly, from gouged sockets. There was a fog, and out of it and into it again mov'd dark monstrous diseas'd shapes. They may have been people, or what once were, or might have been, people. Only the gods know who can inhabit these morbid mazes—Eddy spoke of Cape Verde Portuguese blacks, of Swedes, and of a few decadent Yankees; but I saw a great Greek church of brick and stone, which suggests a putrescent Hellenism. This was a new church, and Eddy said that two incredibly archaick houses had been torn down to make room for it. On thro' the fog we went, threading our way thro' narrow exotick streets and unbelievable courts and alleys, sometimes having the antient houses almost meet above our heads, but often emerging into unwholesome little squares or grassless parks at crossings or junctions where five or six of the tangled streets or lanes meet and open out into expanses as loathsome as Victor Hugo's *Cour des Miracles*.[4] Eddy inform'd me, that these little squares are characteristick of the old west side of Providence, but I had never heard of them. Then, when we wou'd reach the crest of some eminence in this uneven ground, we wou'd see on every hand the strange streets stretching down silent and sinister to the unknown elder mysteries that gave them birth.... grotesque lines of gambrel roofs with drunken eaves and idiotick tottering chimneys, and rows of Georgian doorways with shatter'd pillars and worm-eaten pediments ..... streets, lines, rows; bent and broken, twisted and mysterious, wan and wither'd ..... claws of gargoyles obscurely beckoning to witch-sabbaths of cannibal horror in shadow'd alleys that are black at noon ..... long, long hills up which daemon winds sweep and daemon riders clatter over cobblestones ..... and toward the southeast, a stark silhouette of hoary, unhallow'd black chimneys and bleak ridgepoles against a mist that is white and blank and saline—the venerable, the immemorial sea; the ancient harbour where pirate barques once rode unquietly at anchor. Many of these places—especially a "Gould's Court" of black, gnawing hideousness which I call'd "Ghoul's Court" upon seeing it in the lone pallid lamplight after the sun had set—Eddy tells me are famous in the annals of crime—but I do not read police reports. There must be crime where so many dead things are ... the mass'd dead of Colonial decay .... the dead that draw shapes out of the night to feed and feast and fatten.... No, I had not thought that Providence held such places as this. We came out silently.

Thus imprest with the metropolitan variety of a town which I had always deem'd a village because I had never seen more than the business and good residential parts of it, I decided to have Eddy guide me thro' the vast and celebrated Italian quarter—Federal Hill—which I had heard him so often describe and extol as quainter even than the Boston Italian quarter—which you did not get to see. Italians are the most numerous foreigners in Providence, and they have a separate place of habitation in which they spend all their lives, with shops, restaurants, and theatres of their own, seldom going "down city" (as they phrase it) from their isolated elevation. Federal Hill was sparsely settled in the Colonial period, a church and a few houses being shewn in Avery's 1777 view. It was later a stronghold of the Irish, till after 1870 the Italians drove them down the northern slope and took the crest for themselves, finally occupying the whole, almost to the foot on all sides.... the legions of a Caesar victorious over the Celts. On this occasion we ascended the south slope in the darkness, soon coming upon odd groups of people—old peasant men in corduroy cloaths, and old women with kerchiefs over their heads. The houses, built by the Irish, are of the cheap American type of the middle 19th century. Only on the north slope, in the dark winding alleys by the railway, will one find any of the remaining Colonial houses. But the strange life of the community is in itself sufficiently interesting. Atwell's Avenue, the principal thoroughfare, is a gaudy Italian Main Street with glittering signs and brightly lighted shops whose signs are in the mellow Tuscan—"G. Narducci, Pasticceria" etc.

Parts of it, especially near the intersection with the broad arterial Arthur Avenue, rise definitely above the slum class into a sort of exotick brilliancy—it is here that La Sirena theatre sends forth its polychrome lure, and the principal ristoranti flaunt their electrick signs. We stopt at one of these to eat, and obtain'd the first real Italian spaghetti I have had since I was in New York. Seated in this foreign eating-house where only ourselves spoke English, and looking out into the bright street with the glittering Italian signs, we cou'd only with difficulty believe, that the main business section of Providence lay scarce a mile to the southeast. To me it was utterly and absolutely new; tho' I had once ridden thro' it without getting off the coach, when I shew'd a visitor the Church of the Blessed Sacrament, with the LaFarge windows and mural paintings, in the Irish district beyond.[5] Finally we decided to return to reality and America, which we did with appropriate deliberation, setting as a time and place of next meeting December 2nd, 6:45 a.m., west facade of the Federal Building—whence leaves the coach for Chepachet and the Dark Swamp.

Providence is in truth a more extensive, vary'd, and colourful city than I had ever suspected; and I mean to see more of its curious wonders. There is much of the antient waterfront to explore—the east front where *all* the houses and warehouses are Colonial, and the west front where Colonial vestiges lurk furtively amidst the factories, coal-pockets, and gas works. Coincidently with this adventurous policy of mine, the general interest in the town's oddities is rising, as shewn by a series of articles and quaint etchings appearing in the *Evening Bulletin*, intitul'd "Corners and Characters of Providence."[6] This series starts with the market place and its 1773 market house and 1816 warehouses, which I have pointed out to you. I will send you a set if you are interested—I mean to get several copies of each issue containing this department. Yes—Providence is a very antient and spreading town, and full of weird marvels and elder mysteries. And it is small enough not to have its marvels vulgarised by wide fame.

Well, ol' timer—that's that! I won't bore yuh with any more cheap Socony, but will lay off till I get a line of dope from 2303. But say—howja like Grandpa's yarns? . . . . One thing more . . . Cook, now United Off. Pub., may pass thro' Prov. next week, so that I can see him for the first time in nearly three years. But I promised to dry up.

    Yr. obt. Servt.,
        H. PAGET-LOWE

Notes

1. George L. Shepley (1854–1924), deputy governor of Rhode Island (1902–03), established a library at 292 Benefit Street. Annie Gamwell worked for Shepley in his library for a time. It was mentioned in "The Shunned House" (*CF* 1.465) and *The Case of Charles Dexter Ward* (*CF* 2.221, 235). It is no longer in existence.
2. Samuel Ward (1725–1776), governor of the colony of Rhode Island (1762–63,

1765–67). HPL alludes to him in his mention of the "Ward party" in *The Case of Charles Dexter Ward* (*CF* 2.240).

3. Meeting Street in modern Providence.

4. The phrase "Cour des Miracles" (court of miracles) referred to the slum districts of Paris. One specific district, between the Rue de Caire and the Rue Reaumur, served as the inspiration of Victor Hugo's *Notre-Dame de Paris* (1831; *The Hunchback of Notre Dame*) and *Les Misérables* (1862).

5. At 239 Regent Avenue in Providence. In 1904–05, the artist John La Farge (1835–1910) created six stained glass windows representing Angels of the Adoration for the round-arched windows in the upper register of the apse.

6. A long-running column in the [Providence] *Evening Bulletin* written mostly by George D. Laswell.

[26]   [AHT]

598 Angell St.,
Providence, R.I.,
Inauguration Day [4 March], 1924

Sieur St. Maurice:—

So this is the end! It is all over! He casts us aside like roses that are faded and leaves us to plod over the world's weary paths alone an' forsooken for ever! Twin rivers of tears from Appleton and Providence mingle to form a new ocean, whereon float barques of sorrow. Eheu! Why, oh why did the artist Mocrates leave the paths of fancy and settle down to be a "solid citizen" with a thoroughly adult life whose functions are all "definitely purposed?" With H. L. Mencken I weep at the great American mania for "right-thinking" and "forward looking".[1] If everybody is going to be so damned adult, then who the h. will sing in gardens at evening when the moon is tender and the west wind stirs the lotos-buds? (Once there came into the stern granite city of Teloth a youth, vine-crowned, his yellow hair glistening with myrrh and his purple robe torn with briers of the mountain Sidrak that lies across the antique bridge of stone; and he sang of the twilight, and the moon, and soft songs, and the window where he was rocked to sleep as the lights came out one by one and shadows danced in the marble streets below, and the sun of morning bright above the many-coloured hills in summer, and the sweetness of flowers borne on the south wind that made the trees sing. And when the archons bade him cease his songs and apprentice himself to Othok the cobbler he said, "Wherefore do ye toil; is it not that ye may live and be happy? And if ye toil only that ye may toil more, when shall happiness find you? Ye toil to live, but is not life made of beauty and song? And if ye suffer no singers among you, where shall be the fruits of your toil? Toil without song is like a weary journey without end. Were not death more pleasing?" Thus spake the youth crowned with vines and scented with myrrh, who came into Teloth from the hills and told men that he was Iranon, who had been a Prince in remote Aira, the city of marble and beryl.)[2]

H. PAGET-LOWE.

Notes

1. Favorite expressions of the satirical journalist H. L. Mencken (1880–1956). See "Professor Veblen" in *Prejudices: First Series* (1919; New York: Library of America, 2010): "To it Prof. Dr. Dewey was elected by the acclimation of all right-thinking and forward-looking men" (36).
2. The parenthetical text is a compressed version of HPL's "The Quest of Iranon."

[27]   [AHT]

The Old Ash-Pile
19 October, 1924

Shantih, Shantih,[1] Mawine ol' Sport!

Weird Tales—ee—yow! Boy, yuh'd orta give the retinal review to the letter I got from Ye Ed yestermorn! Mmman! Say, that guy says he wants to use *all* the stories I can send him, one right after another; since the flattering letters "Dagon" drew prove 'that my work makes a peculiar appeal to his readers' ...... you tell 'em, Archibald! "The Picture in the House" went to press last week for the November issue, "The Hound" is slated for December, and "Arthur Jermyn" for January. Jumping hell! but that mag sure was cooked to order for your aged grandpa! I gotta new way to get all my old manuscripts retyped in double-spacing, too. It's that new local boy Eddy, what I was tellin' ya about. I revise his stuff; and for every story I jazz up, he types one for me. Could aught be sweeter? I ask ya if it ain't the lynx's snowshoes! If *W.T.* plays up my stuff, some other editors may gradually become willing to give my little dark chilluns a home, for they do say the taste for the spooky is staging a comeback. If so—O cheques, come to papa! I sure can manage to accomodate the jack without materially altering the annual reports of the local banking institutions!

With sincere adjurations to be alike merry and industrious, believe me, Sir, yr most devoted and docile menial—

Grandpa Theobald.

Notes

1. The Sanskrit word for peace, tranquility, or bliss. From the final line of T. S. Eliot's *The Waste Land* (*Dial*, November 1922). HPL's satirical "Waste Paper" lampoons Eliot's opus, ending "Nobody home / In the shantih."

[28]   [ALS, JHL]

                                    169 Clinton St.,
                                    Brooklyn, N.Y.,
                                    June 15, 1925.
Mocrates, My Son:—

Well, may Petrus charge a double war-tax on my immortal psyche! Hath it indeed come to this—this—that sour, peppery old Theobald, well-known author of "The Isaacsonio-Mortoniad", (1915) & "Medusa, a Portrait", (1921) must deliver a didactick addreſs on the easy-going dismissal of nugatory nuisances to cool-headed, sensible, analytical Bre'r Moses the Prophet? Gawd! Ya could knock me nor'sou'eas'wes' for a sextuple relay of 1907 almanacks! In short, what in Pegāna's name d'ya mean by trying to take serious-like the priceless, inimitable, & delicious absurdity of that gold-medal Torricellian vacuum Wit-acher[1] the Ark Purser? Why, my dear boy, I thought you'd be splitting your sides over that Keith–Barnum–Bailey melange of fabulae Atellanae;[2] for truly, the sole net effect on the impartial bystander is to provoke a most gamesome wonder at the illimitable extent of Noachic naivete & crudity. In other words, what the poor old mutt really did was merely to make a gorgeously hilarious damn'd fool of himself—or rather, to call attention to Nature's accomplishments in that direction—without injuring anybody else in the least so far as the publick judgment is concern'd! Great Gad! So little did I think the incident would do other than amuse you, that I believe I dropt you a postcard about it, to shew mine own appreciation of Frere Noë's rhinocerian ludicrousness! Hell! When it comes to real cause for serious offence, how the devil can you think this farce even half as grave as that other old Ohio slush-brain's attack on me in 1921?[3] Boy, there isn't half the real poison in the whole damn carcass of Peg-Ass-Us, that there is in one ophidian strand of the false hair of that fat cow-hippopotamus in Columbus! Put the li'l' ol' memory to work, Kid! Whilst all Witless-Cuss has done is to fume picturesquely under deserved criticism, that 'Idra Hot-One monster ran the very gamut of abuse & positive insult—culminating even in an aspersion on my stewardship of the United funds! If ever anybody had cause for a demand such as your present one, I had in that memorable autumn of 1921—& yet I didn't consider such a step except in the most fleeting, tentative, & instantly dismissed fashion. Instead, I decided to fight back & give the old gal Hades—which I did, much to the horror of your chivalrous protege Lemon-Cooler.[4] And so it goes. Great Scott! If I were you I wouldn't expect the National to work up the nerve to can an active publisher; for it takes a lot of legislation & machinery & guts to pull anything like that, & you know what amateurdom is today. No, ol' Soak, that ain't the way at all! Just think up a few mean cracks on your own account, & let 'em loose at the old scoundrel—start something snappy, & you'll not only put him in the shade beneath an avalanche of superior satire, but arouse throughout amateurdom a breath of controversial vigour well-calculated to punctuate & perhaps banish the prevailing lassitude. Oh, for a good scrap! Not a private fight, but a real Donnybrook free-for-all that anybody kin git in!!

And now about this United business. It's this-a-way. Wisely or not—that's all past now—I took the damned editorship on my hands in 1923 & the frau took the presidency. That may or may not qualify us for the squirrel's cafeteria, but anyhow, we're in charge, & it's up to us as a definite obligation not to sneak out the back door or lower our trunk from the window at 2 a.m. I have some $39.50, if memory plays no tricks, in the official organ fund; & it'd be a damn sight harder to hunt up the original sources & return it piece by piece than to dump it into one farewell issue of the U.A. Besides, that U.A. would help just so much more in the last desperate efforts to salvage the institution—yuh can't tell what'd turn the tide! Of course, you may remark that the same dodge netted no percentage a year ago when I tried it—but I would counter your objection by laying the defect to a subsequent slip . . . the total absence of follow-up work. I was too bally busy to engineer an election—so the whole thing slid! Now this year I'm conserving & correlating my activities a bit better. For one thing, I've cut out absolutely all social engagements except the hebdomedal meetings of the local pseudo-literary gang, so that I have at least a fraction of a second per annum for writing an epistle or two. And as a result of this much-needed reform, I very early resolved to wind up my amateur affairs decently & honourably or die in the attempt. Now I define decency & honour in this case as (a) keeping all promises to write things—in particular, a critique of Bullen's verse,[5] (b) putting current Association cash into a final *United Amateur*, & (c) leaving the ghost of the official framework in the hands of a duly elected board composed of as truly active youngsters as a thorough & conscientious search would reveal. These steps I have been taking with relentless deliberation. I wrote the Bullen critique a couple of weeks ago, & have been rewarded by the gurgling ecstasies of the Aonian subject, who tells me that it met with the wild applause of the Toronto literary world—or such of that world as heard it read by him. Two days ago I finished *The United Amateur*, & shall send the copy to Cook this very afternoon if all goes well. And as for the future board—well, I've dug up two live wires, & am writing laboriously to others in an effort to procure their official services. The prize packages are young Davis & Bacon,[6] the latter of whom (whether you recall him or not) you met in person at the Hub Club gathering in 1923. He has since moved to St. Louis, but is more active than ever, & bids fair (if plans succeed) to accomplish an actual revivification of the United, for a time at least. If he keeps up his present activity, he'll be third in the dynasty of benevolent bosses whose earlier representatives are Edward F. Daas & Grandpa Theobald. I'll enclose a few random missives from Davis & Bacon for you to look over. Don't you think there's a sort of half-chance for the United to come back with two such cherubs as its leaders? With Davis's brains, & Bacon's restless egotism & energy to prod those brains into action, we certainly have a team whose possibilities are not to be sneez'd at.

The following ticket will be placed in the field at a mail election to be held July 15:

  President— Edgar J. Davis
  1st V P— Paul Livingston Keil (?)
  2nd V P— Grace M. Bromley
  Laur. Rec.— Eugene B. Kuntz (?)
  MS. Mgr— B. Coursin Black*
  Directors { —Sonia H. G. Lovecraft
      —Maurice Winter Moe (we fondly hope)
      —Frank Belknap Long, Jr.

Bacon will be Official Editor—appointed by Davis. For Sec. Treas. we may try to get Conover,[7] or if he won't serve, promote Miss Bromley & get another 2nd V.P. If you finally decline to take the directorship, I suppose we'll have to scour to plain for somebody else—mayhap amiable George Kirk would fall for it if I swore on the Greek testament that he wouldn't have to do any work. Now in cold reality, all this hinges on young Bacon's organising & epistolary energy. At present, my Ld Verulam[8] seems indued with that same daemonick activity which enabled others to keep things going a decade or two ago. Unless this flags, he stands a chance of rousing & getting together enough surviving "live ones" to resist the decadent tendencies of the age, so ably adverted to in your communication; so that we may be able to postpone hiring the mortician for a year or two more. At any rate, I feel a damn sight more comfortable in handing the sceptre down to a willing & vigorous heir, than I would in tossing the bauble nonchalantly into the sea. So that, in a manner of speaking, is that.

And now for the news reel. My Gawsh in Halifax, but it must take noive for a full-panoplied eldest son of the Sphinx to get off that easy line about receiving only baffling &c. scraps from his Grandpa Theobald!! I han' it tuh youse! But after all, there's nothing like a swell example, so here goes for a chronological survey of the House of Paget-Lowe since last aestival advices— prefaced by the statement that current revenue (meagre as it is) comes from the same damned revisory & allied sources, but that there is a prospect (dim as all worldly prospects are for the unworldly) of my getting a more regular connexion with a financial & commercial paper, to do hack write-ups.[9]

News, as I recall it, came last through about midsummer, 1924, when the household at Parkside Ave. was ambling along in accustomed domestick pla-

---

*A new & ultra-enthusiastic youth of Chautauqua, N.Y.

cidity, vext only by a losing financial venture of 'the' wife's in the domain of independent millinery manufacture. In September we enjoyed a visit from my younger aunt Mrs. Gamwell, during which I exercised anew that penchant for antiquarian guiding which hath become of late years my most salient characteristick. The August–September period markt also the beginning of that wave of Cleveland immigration whose effects on our local gang have been so great. In August Kirk blew in, taking a room up in 106th St. & setting up as a free-lance '[']gentleman who deals in books". Shortly afterward the blond & boyish Edward Lazare[10] (ever meet him on Erie's templed shore?) floated hither, tarried with us a while, & then drifted subtly out of our ken without actually quitting the metropolis as a place of residence. Then, with a fanfare of elfin horns atop Helicon, Samuelus Lovemanus the poet drew nigh in his chariot, tarried a while with Kirk in 106th St., & then set up for himself in a magnificent room in Columbia Heights, Brooklyn, with bow-window overlooking the whole cosmic focus of New-York Harbour & the faery pinnacles & minarets of lower Manhattan. Here he tarried till two weeks ago, sustained by a steady tho' very uncongenial position in a downtown bookstall. Finally the idiosyncrasies of his testy & humoursome employer wore too much upon him, & he resigned with dignity & finality—returning for the nonce to his old Cleveland address, though with every intention of Manhattanising again in the fall, when he can bring more of his belongings with him. Kirk's settlement has been less interrupted. From 106th St. he moved over to this house after I did, & now occupies the room directly above me. This, however, he will soon quit; for he has taken a partner (a new Cleveland importation whom you haven't met) & opened a bookstall at 97 Fourth Ave., & when that partner starts housekeeping with his wife, (a matter of 3 weeks hence) Kirk will board with them. They will probably live in the famed Greenwich Village. With all this new Cleveland blood, you can imagine how large & important our local gang has grown! For a long period I let its assemblages, both regular & informal, monopolise much of my time; till finally I found my room overrun almost daily by pairs & trios of members, urging me to go here or there, or to loaf artistically about this or that coffee-house, cafeteria, or Greenwich-Village restaurant. Kirk, Loveman, & Kleiner in particular seemed to have acquired an almost morbid gregariousness; as if their own resources of personality were so slight that they must needs dread solitude & rush at any cost into the society of others whether or not possessed of anything to say! Thus my own time was preyed upon beyond all endurance, till about a month & a half ago I had to call a halt; limit my engagements largely to the Wednesday night meetings, & restore my daily programme to that uneventful literary concentration which befits a constitutional recluse. Whatever society I have outside my home & the weekly conclaves is now mainly confined to little Frank Belknap Long & his household. Belknap is really the most congenial to me of all the local group—he has my own tastes, & a remarkably similar family background—so that our trips to museums, bookstalls, & rural spots, & the visits of my wife & me to his house, (his mother is a delightfully pleasant person) form the major unofficial items on the Theobald calendar. But to return to chronological order—in October, not long after my aunt's departure for Providence, the indifferent health of my wife culminated in a double breakdown, nervous and gastric. Being without servants in the apartment, my wife did not wish to eke along with any home treatment—especially since an operation for removal of the gall-bladder was threatened—so she took up her quarters on the fourth floor of the Brooklyn Hospital, in a sunny room whose windows opened on a spacious balcony and overlooked both the verdant hills of Fort Greene Park and the picturesque steeples of eastern Brooklyn. Expert medical advice from three leaders of the profession—Dr. Westbrook, a general practitioner descended in direct line from my architect-hero Sir Christopher Wren, Dr. Kingman, a nerve specialist, and Dr. Crane, a nasal specialist who thought some of the nerve trouble came from a misplaced septum—did much to mitigate the acuteness of the trouble; and after three weeks of dieting and reclining the patient was discharged with instructions to rest at least six weeks in the country. Westbrook wanted to operate on the gall-bladder, but layman that I am, I urged my spouse not to let him without the concurrent opinion of several first-rate physicians. Such an operation was the immediate cause of my mother's death, and I had heard of other methods of dealing with obstinate liver complaints. Later I was very glad I thus held out—for a subsequent physician, a woman graduate of the Sorbonne with a high Paris reputation, has done wonders with milder dietetic methods, and advises against surgery. During this hospital period I had my first experience in lone housekeeping. Aided by the written instructions of my wife I made coffee that I could actually drink, and cooked spaghetti that I could actually eat—and as I matter of personal pride I kept the house swept and dusted. I may have said that after my advent the furnishing was changed; the dining-room which you saw becoming my study, with all my own things from Providence, and the living-room becoming a combination dining-living room after a plan first adopted by Frank B. Long's mother. I visited the hospital each day; bringing books, papers, and such edibles as were permitted, and meanwhile gained a practice in solitary food preparation which was later to serve me in good stead. On Hallowe'en I welcomed back the mistress of the manse, having previously decorated the living-room with appropriate black and orange streamers, and paper witches at strategic points. As soon as possible after this, we located what seemed to be a good rustic retreat for an invalid or convalescent; and one evening in early November set out for the agrestic acres of one Mrs. R. A. Craig in South Somerville, N.J., something over half way to Philadelphia. Reaching the farmhouse by motor from the station, we found it quite tolerable though somewhat lonely; and to my mind vastly enhanced by the lively presence of a large family of irresistible gray kittens. The next day we explored the surrounding country, which proved rather flattish as compared with New England, yet which was by no means unattractive. The nearest village—Somerville—possessed considerable quaintness and charm. Now as just mentioned, this region is more than half way from N.Y. to Philadelphia—so that I thought the opportunity for further antiquarian exploration in the Quaker metropolis too good to miss. Accordingly it was not for N.Y. but for Dr. Franklin's thriving town that I set out when I finally took my leave of Somerville, where the superior nine-tenths seemed comfortably settled. I arrived at the P. & R. station at 9 p.m.; & following jointly a suggestion of the wiff's & a remembrance of thine own godly procedure, set out to obtain lodgment at the hospitable tavern of the Y.M.C.A. And a good idea it was—for they placed me in a clean room in convenient proximity to a delectable shower-bath, & with fine ice-water on tap in the hall just opposite my door—all this for only *$1.50* per! And the location is positively idyllic for the sightseer—Arch St. right near Broad, within walking distance of everything, & scarce a pebble's cast from the principal station. Well, Bozo, ef ya asts me, I'll slip it to youse dat it was some li'l' ol' spree! I hung around for 5—count 'em—5 diurnal epochs, & what I left unknown about that burg ain't worth telling to the devil-dawg! Remember that I had already taken one general orientation tour thither, & that I had studied maps & guide-books very thoroughly, so that I knew exactly where I wanted to go & what I wanted to see. And Oh, Boy! did I go there & see it? I'll hint to the celestial sphere I did! The first two days I put in solidly on the ancient city proper—the pre-Revolutionary town lying roughly between the Delaware River on the east, 13th St. on the west, Christian St. on the south, & Poplar St. on the north. And as Pete is my witness, I never before suspected that so much of colonial antiquity could survive in a city of nearly two-million! There are row on row of solid brick blocks absolutely unchanged since Franklin's time—seas of slate roofs which were old when His Majesty's officers staged the Meschianza![11] Some of these ancient alleys have sunk to nigger slums, but the solidity of the architecture has preserved them from decay. One or two are tolerably kept up—Great God! shall I ever forget Elfret Alley, near the river, where the *original pavement with central gutter* remains, & where every door retains the panels & knocker of George the Second's reign!? And the churches & publick buildings! And the ancient squares! One late Georgian section around 11th, 12th, & 13th Sts, built up about 1790 or 1800, has been artistically reclaimed as a sort of refined & diluted Greenwich Village; & presents a highly captivating aspect. It is here that we find the Centaur Pub. Co.,[12] which next autumn is to issue Loveman's book on Edgar Saltus. Ah, Philadelphia! After thee how cheap & parvenu New-York seems! The third day I spent in museums, in odd parts of the newer town, & in a scouting expedition to Fairmount Park, where most of the fine colonial country-seats are. The fourth day I visited the more distant country-seats & suburbs—John Bartram's house (1731) & botanick gardens,[13] the ancient town of Chester, Pa., & the like—& upon my return covered that part of Fairmount Park which lies on the town side of the Schuylkill. Among the splendid manor-houses here situate—all on grassy bluffs overlooking the windings of the stream—is Mt. Pleasant, for a time the home of the hapless Benedict Arnold. I explored till dark overtook me, then paying a call on our placid & well-disposed United poet Washington Van Dusen, who gave me many tips for the next day's sightseeing. He's a nice old chap, of an old Philadelphia family, & lives in the colonial paradise of Germantown—a suburban village founded in the 17th century by German Moravians & Dunkards, but now long since overtaken & engulfed by the city—though preserving vastly more of its old personality & identity than the similarly engulfed village of Flatbush, Brooklyn does. The fifth & last day I began by finishing Fairmount Park—the trans-fluminal part—& thence proceeded to tackle Germantown in detail. Man, what a place! As different from brick Philadelphia proper as Marblehead is from Manhattan . . . . gambrel-roofed houses of grey stone, with green yards & gardens—& *what* an historical museum! I'll send you a descriptive folder of sights, which please return. The best part of it is that they still maintain the old traditions, building new houses in exactly the same colonial fashion. Even in Victorian times the lapse was only partial. After Germantown I explored as much as possible of the famous Wissahickon valley, a deep wooded gorge whose scenery is absolutely the finest I have ever beheld. That evening I returned home—& shortly afterward my wife returned also, deciding that Somerville was more dreary than restful, & that one's own apartment isn't a bad place to get rested. Shortly afterward my elder aunt Mrs. Clark came for a visit, & we had a glorious time of leisurely exploring. Later she went to visit old family friends in the suburb of Mt. Vernon, where she stayed till the middle of February, though making frequent trips to the sights of N.Y. Meanwhile my wife was improving so much that she began to take notice of professional things; & when, in December, she received a sudden offer of an important & highly salaried post in the largest department-store of Cincinnati, she determined to try it for a while—I to engage a room until some permanent system could be devised. Looking about for quarters with the assistance of my aunt, we finally hit upon this old place in the Brooklyn Heights region of brick & brownstone, within sight of the sea, & with an old-world air of musty stateliness which to many suggests parts of London. Since my wife was, as part of her new work, to be in N.Y. frequently for a week at a time, we had to secure arrangements large enough for two. This we did by taking a spacious corner room with two alcoves, one for dressing materials & the other with washing paraphernalia, so that nothing of the bedroom would mar the tasteful library-study effect of the room proper—which is furnished throughout with my stuff from Providence. I will append a diagram of the place:

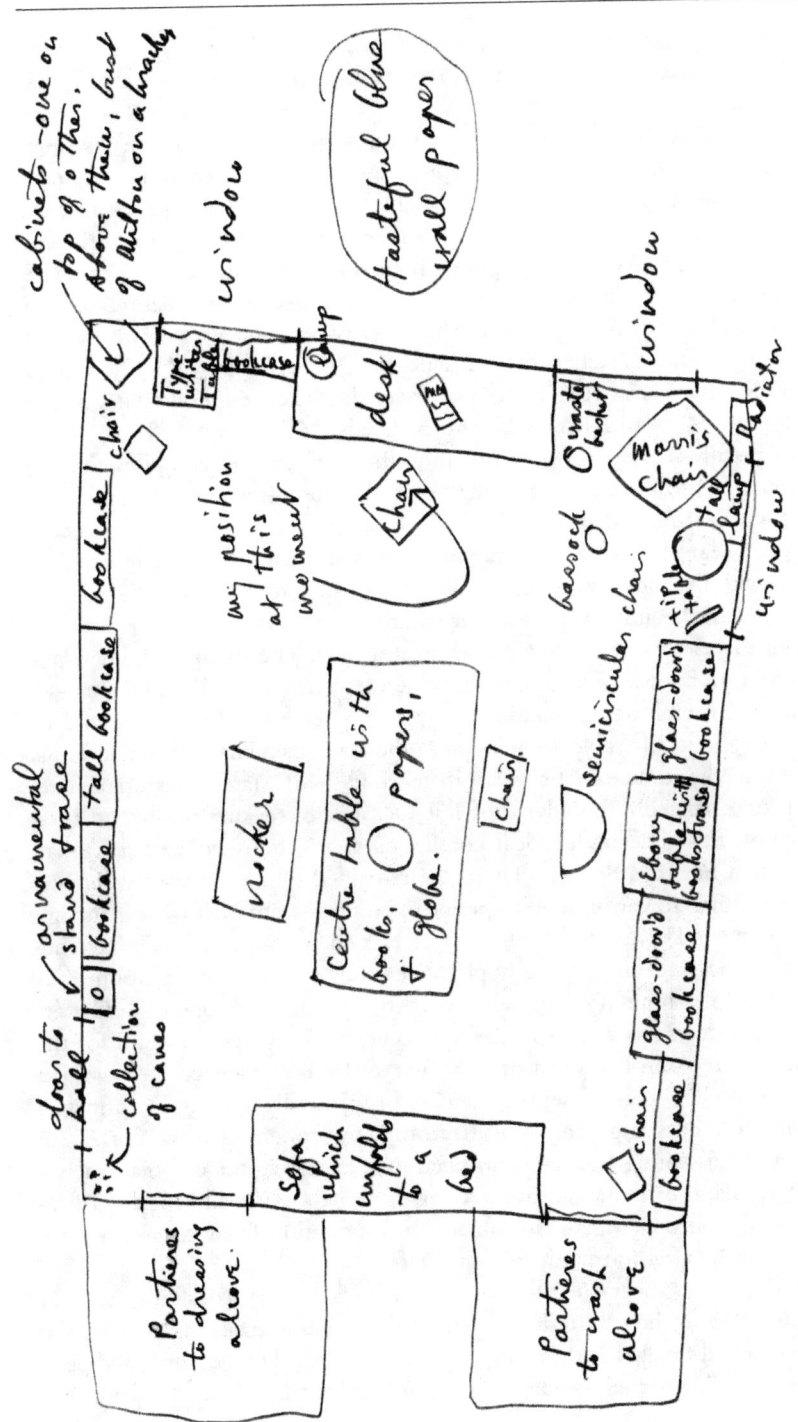

The room is early-Victorian—1845 period—tall, with tasteful white woodwork, & deep window-seats. It reminds me of my birthplace at 454 Angell St., & suits me admirably, though I'm not fond of the general seediness of the neighbourhood; an evil to which the leanness of my purse just now condemns me. Shortly after my advent here I persuaded George Kirk to take the room above me; and when Loveman dwelt only a few squares off, we certainly had the makings of quite a little literary colony. On Dec. 31st the last load left Parkside Ave.—some goods here, some in storage,—and my wife took the train for Cincinnati, where she had found an excellent boarding place—an almost family-like circle where her two principal associates were a pair of high-school teachers from Maine, the Misses Parington and Curtis. I began the new year at 169 Clinton St., exceedingly active in the affairs of our local gang—Morton, Kleiner, Loveman, Leeds, McNeil, Long, Kirk, etc.—and frequently serving as host to them in the quarters they complimented so generously. They do me the honour to say that my place looks exceptionally classic and restful, and that its mellow sedateness suggests continuous occupancy for years if not for generations. When my wife visited, she acted as hostess with the most extreme graciousness; & all agreed that we did remarkably well with the limited space at our command.

But this exact state of things was not for long. The strain of the new position told on my wife's health; so that she was twice in a private hospital—a well known establishment conducted by a Dr. Beyer—in Cincinnati, and finally thought it advisable to relinquish the responsibilities of her arduous post. From the middle of February to the middle of March she rested here, then taking belatedly the advice of last October & seeking prolonged rural retirement; this time under ideal conditions in the household of a woman physician at Saratoga Springs. There she remained till a week ago, when she returned hither for an indefinite period. She now seems fairly well, though easily fatigued. The turmoil & throngs of N.Y. depress her, as they have begun to do me, & eventually we hope to clear out of this Babylonish burg for good. I find it a bore after the novelty of the museums, skyline & bolder architectural effects has worn off, & hope to get back to New England for the rest of my life—the Boston district at first, & later Providence, if I ever get the money to live there as befits a member of my family. As it is, my principal pastime these days is getting away from the atmosphere of New York. Last summer & this spring I have spent much time exploring the colonial reaches of Staten Island & the adjacent New Jersey shore—especially ancient Elizabeth-town, a pure Georgian city which I haunt continually, & where my wife and I spent the afternoon only two days ago.

But my most spectacular feat of the season is *reducing*. You know how fat I was in 1923, & how bitterly I resented the circumstance. In 1924 I grew even worse, till finally I had to adopt a #16 collar! During the combined period of my wife's hospital sojourn & my Philadelphia trip, I had the opportunity of regulating my own diet for the first time in my entire career—eating just as much as I wanted, rather than as much as someone else thought I ought to have. Upon the close of this period I had thinned perceptibly, returning to a 15¾ collar .... I don't know how much I lost, for after passing the 193 mark on the upward course a year before, I had refused to mount a pair of scales! During the winter I kept a sterner guard of my diet, & managed not to regain the tonnage I had lost—and then, when in January I became absolute autocrat of my breakfast, dinner, & supper table, I flung my hat in the air—or ring—and started reducing *in earnest!!* And oh, Boy!!! what results! D'ya know, I didn't even need to be fat at all! It was all the result of acquiescing spinelessly in the dicta of one's solicitous family! How the pounds flew! I helped the course along by exercise & outdoor walks, & every time my friends saw me they were either pleased or frightened at the startling shrinkage. Fortunately I had not been fat for so many years that the skin must needs suffer radical distension. Instead, it shrunk neatly along with the tissue beneath, leaving a firm surface & simply restoring the lost outlines of 1915 & before. And what a story the scales & my clothing told! The latter had to be thoroughly retailored, whilst every week I bought smaller & smaller collars. It was dramatic—breathless—sensational—this reclamation of a decade-lost statue from the vile mud which had so long encrusted it! As you may imagine, my wife protested fearfully at what seemed an alarming decline. I received long scolding letters from my aunts, & was lectured severely by Mrs. Long every time I went up to see Little Belknap. But I knew what I was doing, & kept on like grim death. I had simply changed my dietetic standard to the normal, &—as I hope—permanently broken the fat-accumulating tendency. When I had condensed to my old pre-war figure, I ceased to apply the extremes of my method—yet not only did I escape a subsequent increase, but have even lost nine additional pounds—this last year without even trying. I now publickly avow my personal mastery of my diet, & do not permit my wife to feed me in excess of it. If you were to meet me on the street tomorrow you would not know me except from the very earliest pictures you ever saw—the story is told by figures like these: weight, **146** lbs.; waist with shirt and underclothing on, **30** inches; collar (and a loose fit at that) 14¾. And I mean to stay that way a long, long while! Here is a snapshot of Little Belknap & me, taken a month ago when my weight was 154. Some difference from the old porpoise you saw a couple of years ago, eh? And as Fate would have it, Sonny is beginning to get fat!

I think I mentioned the Great Robbery on my card of t'other day. Yes—on Sunday, May 24, thieves operating from the next room (which they had hired) cleaned out my dressing alcove, with which their room has a perpetually locked door in common. They picked the lock & made a thorough job—leaving me not a rag to my name save the old blue suit which you saw me in in Providence—but which I changed before we went to Boston because I didn't think it was good enough to wear there! I had hung that carelessly on a chair in the room proper, which they didn't enter—noble argument for carelessness, since if I'd hung it up where it belonged, in the alcove, I'd be parading around in a barrel these days! It was a fearful financial blow—my whole wardrobe wiped out, & just after everything had been tailored over to fit my reduced figure. Nothing has turned up from the police—the whole loss included a blanket, a suit case of my wife's, & an expensive radio set I was storing for Loveman.

Well—now it's your turn to tell the sad, sad story of your life. I've purposely omitted an account of my Washington excursion of April 12, because I'm going to enclose a full carbon of the travelogue I wrote my elder aunt.[14] Please return it—& don't bother to finish it if it begins to bore you too badly. Sechrist is a good scout—he's coming to N.Y. soon, & has also invited me to Washington for a week some time this summer. ¶ And so it goes. For Yahweh's sake forget old No-account W. & take that Directorship! I'll live in hope till the last glimmer fades.

And meanwhile pray consider me Yr. most obt. Servt.

Lo.

P.S. Pardon the awkward paper. This is a batch Kirk has given me—queer shape, but darned good writing surface

Notes

1. The amateur journalist Noah F. Whitaker, editor/publisher of the journal *Pegasus*, to which HPL contributed a few poems. As HPL states later in the letter, Whitaker erroneously pronounced the name Pegasus with the accent on the second syllable.
2. *Fabulae Atellanae* ("Atellan plays") were rustic improvisational farces originating in the town of Atella in Italy. By the first century C.E. they had become a literary genre. Some of the characters were resurrected in the *commedia dell'arte* of 16th-century Italy.
3. The amateur Ida C. Haughton (1860–1933), a member of the Woodbees, an amateur journalism club in Columbus, Ohio. During the 1920–21 term, she accused HPL (then Official Editor of the UAPA) of various malfeasances, including the mishandling of the Official Organ Fund, a fund to which members would contribute for the publication of the *United Amateur*. In response, HPL made Haughton the focus of his vicious poetic satire, "Medusa: A Portrait."
4. The amateur Harry N. Lehmkuhl (1890–1973) of Milwaukee.
5. "The Poetry of John Ravenor Bullen." Later adapted as the preface to Bullen's *White Fire* (1927). Bullen (1886–1927) was a Canadian amateur journalist and poet.
6. Edgar J. Davis and Victor E. Bacon in fact became President and Official Editor of the UAPA for the 1925–26 term, but they published only a few issues of the *United Amateur*, after which the UAPA became moribund.
7. Howard R. Conover of Cincinnati. He was the head of the UAPA ticket that ousted HPL's administration for the 1922–23 term.

8. HPL makes a punning reference to Sir Francis Bacon (1561–1626), who became Baron Verulam in 1618.

9. HPL alludes to a scheme conceived by a man named Yesley (a friend of Arthur Leeds) whereby HPL and others would write brief flattering articles on various shops and companies with the intent of having the companies purchase them for publication in magazines. The venture never materialized, but HPL wrote five such articles, now published under the title "Commercial Blurbs" (*CE* 5.180–84).

10. Edward Lazare (1904–1991), member of Hart Crane's literary circle who met HPL occasionally in New York. He was later editor of *American Book-Prices Current* (1940–65).

11. An elaborate fête in honor of British General Sir William Howe in Philadelphia on 18 May 1778.

12. Initially Centaur Press. See SL 6 herein.

13. John Bartram (1699–1777), early American botanist, horticulturist, and explorer. His house is at 54th Street and Eastwick Avenue in Philadelphia.

14. See HPL's typed letter to Lillian D. Clark, 21 April 1925; in *Letters to Family and Family Friends*.

[29] [AHT]

June 30, 1927

Great Lord of L'arnin'!

Another interesting—and still sooner—visitor is from your own golden west—my latest discovery in infant prodigies. This youth, whose years number nineteen and whose education has just survived the junior year at the University of Minnesota, is one Donald Wandrei of St. Paul, Minn.; a genius in weird fiction and an encyclopaedick reader of everything connected therewith. By a somewhat circuitous process, both Clark Ashton Smith and I were instrumental in his discovery, and he has taken a definite place amongst my adopted grandchildren. His poetick horrors have a quality of authentick bizarrerie seldom found in contemporary writers, and I predict that he will go far. Just to prove that latter point he's making a walking (or rather, a begged-motor-lift) trip East at the present moment, being now in New York, where the gang—Kirk, Loveman, Little Belknap, etc.—are keeping him busy. He'll probably be here in about a week, and I expect to give him a good glimpse of ancient sights in Providence, Newport, Boston, and their respective environs. He hated Chicago when he passed through it, and didn't get to liking the landscape till he struck Pennsylvania. New York, I predict, will disgust him; and I fancy he'll appreciate New England quite keenly. He wouldn't stay in Chicago but two days—one of which he spent at the *Weird Tales* office. This is his first trip of any distance from his Duo-Urban place of nativity.

Yr most oblig'd, most obt Servt

Lo.

[30] [AHT]

10 Barnes St.,
Providence, R.I.,
July 30, 1927

Rhetor Clarissime:—

I hope you can find a way of slipping me that snap of ol' Мікрот Мократол, before the missus finds it out—for I'd sure like a glimpse of the li'l rascals, and my actual sight of their sprightly grace in 1923 would prevent my being deceiv'd by the unfavourableness of the view. Is either—or are both—in long trousers yet? I assumed that dignity at thirteen and one-half, being tall for my years; but I am sensible others are occasionally less precocious with the toga virilis of modernity. As for athaletics—you needn't worry about being outdistanced in the brine when you're still half laid up with a set of game vertebrae! Once you get the old postern colyum limber'd up, I'll wager you can still give the younger generation a run for its money at a heap of things besides ping-pong. Apropos of the latter—it's news to me that they still make sets! Or are your games played by means of some still surviving relicks of the dear old 1900's? Golden days! Naivete and primitive syncopation—cake-walks and the first horseless carriages—romantic costume novels and residual Spanish-near-war glamour—"Florodora" and the "Prince of Pilsen"[1]—early marvels of radium and the Xray, and the absurd failures of flying machines. McKinley and Roosevelt—down with Free Silver!—Shall it be a Panama or Nicaragua canal?—the Queen is dead, long live King Edward!—Boxer rebellions and Russo-Japanese mutterings—the latest from Praetoria and Bloemfontein—nameless author of "Lady Windermere's Fan"[2] dead in Paris—pyrography—mandolins—"Good Bye, Dolly Gray",[3] Dewey and Hobson, Sampson and Schley, Aguinaldo and Funston[4]—Charles Dana Gibson—"To Have and to Hold",[5] "Quincy Adams Sawyer"[6]—Galveston flood[7]—Martinique eruption[8]—Jeffries, Corbett, Fitzsimmons[9]—the biograph pictures after the real shows at Keith's[10]—Pan-American Exposition[11]—"Put me off at Buffalo"[12]—the scandalous new novel of that impossible young Theodore Dreiser,[13] who they do say is Paul Dresser's brother[14]—"Quo Vadis"[15]—Peter F. Dailey[16]—Stanley J. Weyman's new serial in *The Munsey*[17]—sets of De Maupassant: is it quite proper to read him?—Haeckel's "Riddle of the Universe" . . . . . don't read it, my dear, it's almost as blasphemous as "Robert Elsmere"![18]—the new interurban trolley line with double-truck cars and real air brakes—Kipling and Stevenson—The Simple Life[19]—Emperor William—Elbert Hubbard[20]—Mark Hanna[21]—Lord Kitchener—Dreyfus—Jack London—"I have been faithful to thee, Cynara, in my fashion"[22]—"I am the master of my fate, I am the captain of my soul!"[23]—Sherlock Holmes—"Blennerhasset[t]"[24] and "The Conqueror"[25]—the first neo-colonial houses—Renaissance post offices and public libraries—the new Boston subway . . . . .

and they say New York is going to dig one, too—Lafcadio Hearn . . . . not quite nice, but very artistic—the monkey dinner[26]—Ward McAllister[27]—Barry Wall[28]—Prince Henry[29]—flat felt hats and puff ties—turned-up trousers and football hair—Standard Oil—civic purpose—the poor, oppressed miners—Minneapolis graft—muckraking—the new fad, psychology—Ibsen—Frank Norris—David Graham Phillips[30]—the later Mark Twain—and that dear old lady William Dean Howells still lives . . . . . and who is this morbid French poet Beau de something . . . . . Baudelaire, I guess . . . . . . that Mr. Swinburne writes so much about?—"David Harum",[31] "Richard Carvel"[32]—Olga Nethersole in "Sapho";[33] Mrs. Leslie Carter in "Zaza"[34] . . . . . my dear, the stage is absolutely going to the dogs! I'm sure there'll have to be a wholesome reaction before many years!—F. Marion Crawford—good old Pope Leo[35]—that awful story by Mrs. Gilman, "The Yellow Wall-Paper"[36] . . . . . . why can't people choose pleasant things to write about?—H. G. Wells—and how long has this George Bernard Shaw been writing? I don't like him—he's so irreverent and insincere, and his paradoxes make one think of . . . er . . . . . "The Importance of Being Earnest"—E. H. Sothern—"If I Were King"[37]—the new Yerkes Observatory—Primrose and West's Minstrels[38]—the Paris Exposition[39]—Marconi and Tesla—is Mars inhabited?—Samuel P. Langley[40]—Santos-Dumont's balloons[41]—Count Zeppelin[42]—Alfonso, the Boy King[43]—Thomas Hardy . . . . . such a pessimist!—Stephen Crane—Harold Frederic[44]—"One lies down at Appomatox, many miles away"[45]—"Won't you come home, Bill Bailey; won't you come home?"[46]—"Go 'way back and sit down"[47]—Ah, me, the dear old days! Groping and grotesque, hopeful and bombastic, quaint and ingenuous, that restless turn of the century . . . . . but it was my day, and for all its defects there isn't a thing I wouldn't give to have good old 1900 back again! And all this just because somebody mention'd ping-pong (a game he never play'd!) to the Old Gentleman!

Our latest spectacular discovery has been the nineteen-year-old marvel Donald Wandrei, of 1152 Portland Ave., St. Paul, Minn.—who finished his junior year at the University of Minnesota last month. This child, who got in touch with Clark Ashton Smith and me through *Weird Tales*, is a real poet and fantastic genius—and an artist of exquisite sensibility and disillusioned power. He will be heard from yet. He is six feet two inches tall, and lean as a beanpole—quite Galpinian as to careless attire and contempt for mankind, but vastly the reverse where considerateness and good-breeding are concern'd. He has for some time been making a hitch-hiking tour of the East, (he's in Athol now, having left Providence Friday morning) so that all of us have had the pleasure of meeting him in person. Upon all who have seen him he has produced the pleasantest and most favourable of impressions. His first published story—"The Red Dust"—will appear in the October *Weird Tales*.[48]

Young Wandering Wandrei was the first to come and the last to leave. He blew in on July 12; and at once established himself in a delightful poet's garret in this very house, which the landlady let him have for $3.50 per week. The next day I took him to archaick Newport, where he wander'd through the living past and revelled in his first sight of the wine-dark sea from titan cliffs—his only previous glimpse having been the week before, from the detestably squalid strand of Coney Island. The next couple of days we spend in the exquisite Quinsnicket region north of Providence—you know my pastorals on that idyllick realm—and on Saturday the sixteenth we started out for Boston. That afternoon was spent in the Museum of Fine Arts, and in the evening we explored the colonial byways of the town. We stopped at the Y.M.C.A., (and Wandrei complained the next day of invertebrate inhabitants of his humble couch, although I found neither them nor rodentia in my monastic cubicle) and the next day set out for Salem and Marblehead. Oh, Boy—but maybe I wasn't glad to lamp those archaick realms again! Hadn't seen 'em for a year, when I show'd George Kirk around. We did Salem with extreme thoroughness, including the Essex Institute and the House of the Seven Gables; and thereafter hopped a car for Marblehead. They have some fine new trolleys on that line now, with soft leather seats like those of motor coaches. Counter-competition, as it were! Marblehead was . . . . . . Marblehead! What the hell more could be ask'd? We did most of the town, and took the ferry across to the Neck, where Wandrei communed with his beloved and newly-discover'd sea from the rugged cliffs. You didn't visit the Neck, for there's nothing colonial there—it having been an open space us'd for fish-drying in the old days. At dusk we returned to Boston via Lynn, and made it a through trip to Providence while we were about it. The next day was spent in writing, but Tuesday the big delegation came. Little Frank Belknap was with his papa and mamma in their new Essex horseless carriage, and good old James Ferdinand—needing a haircut, and with a yellowed straw hat two sizes too small for him. They came from opposite directions, Morton having been previously in Green Acre, Me., whilst the Longs motored directly from neo-Babylon. Morton stopped at his favourite local hostelry, the Crown, but Sonny's party had a couple of rooms at #10 Barnes, right across the hall from me—the landlady's study and reception-room, obligingly vacated for the occasion and rented for the astonishing pittance of a dollar a night each. The next day was spent in local sight-seeing, and that evening we had a regular old-time gang meeting—even hunting up the local scribbler C. M. Eddy, Jun. to pad out the personnel. On Thursday all hands took a trip to Newport—the Longs remaining on the cliffs and at the beach whilst Morton, Wandrei, and I took a hike into the Bishop Berkeley country (cf. a former travelogue of mine) and wrote verses on the Hanging Rocks. Through all this sightseeing poor philistine Dr. Long was atrociously bored, and I was at my wits' end devising means to palliate his patient misery. At length, in the evening, the

Fates intervened in my favour—in the form of an electric-appliance shop from whose broad doorway the Dempsey–Sharkey[49] returns were in process of broadcasting. Doc was happy at last, and I felt that the day had not fallen wholly short of the elements of social success! The next morning the Longs departed on another leg of that protracted motor trip which is not to end till the last of August. They are having all their household mail forwarded in my care, and I am re-forwarding whenever they telegraph me a temporary address. They've now done Cape Cod, Salem, Marblehead, Gloucester, Portland, and Belgrade Lakes, and are on their way to the White Mountains. It's a gay life—but they deserve the outing; for Dr. Long works like a slave when he works, whilst both Belknap and his mamma are in such poor health—cardiac trouble—that they never take walks or outings in the ordinary way. Transportation is a prime essential. Well—after the Long Essex chugged off, Morton led Wandrei and me on one of his characterstick mineralogical expeditions. (I think I told you of the one last month, when the local curator took us in his car.) This time, through a singular coincidence, the designated territory was a quarry on which I hold a mortgage; so that we were received with ceremonious hospitality by the Dago owner.[50] The good old Roman set all his men to work hunting specimens, and his sportily Americanised son took us all home in his snappy new roadster—to say nothing of chugging back and fetching the geologist's hammer which Mortonius forgot. That's what I call real Latin courtesy! Later in the day we made another expedition to the exquisite scenic region north of Providence—securing no specimens, but getting a swell eye-full of landscape. Saturday morning all three of us went to Colonial Warren—down the east shore of the bay—and staged an ice-cream eating contest at the celebrated emporium of Mrs. Julia A. Maxfield—an aged matron of antient Warren lineage who has won fame by serving more flavours of ice cream than any other purveyor either living or dead. There are *twenty-eight* varieties this season, and we *sampled them all* within the course of an hour. Each would order a double portion—two kinds—and by dividing equally would ensure *six* flavours each round. *Five* rounds took us all through the twenty-eight and two to carry. Mortonius and I each consumed two and one-half quarts, but Wandrei fell down toward the last. Now James Ferdinand and I will have to stage an elimination match to determine the champion! Well—that same afternoon the next delegation arrived; good old W. Paul Cook and his weird-literary protege H. Warner Munn from Athol. They came in Munn's car, and stopped at #10 in the rooms the Longs had so lately vacated. Munn is a splendid young chap—blond and burly, and just now sporting a gold medal awarded him for saving a man from drowning in the Hudson a couple of months ago. That night we all sat till two-thirty a.m. on a flat-topped tomb in St. John's hidden hillside churchyard which Poe used to love, and the next day we lounged about the Blackstone Park woods beside the Seekonk—agrestick haunt of my earliest infancy, and true genesis of my pas-

toral soul. Cook brought with him the book of Goodenough's poems which he has just printed, as well as an unfinished copy of his coming *Recluse*—containing my history of weird literature. In the evening the Atholites had to return home—Cook leaving his raincoat behind, and Munn carrying off the garage key. My guests are apparently very forgetful—for even Little Belknap carried off the house key! Monday, Tuesday, and Wednesday Wandrei and I rested and wrote letters and scoured bookshops. Thursday we explored the Athenaeum and art museum, and witnessed a marvellous sunset from Prospect Terrace. Friday morning I saw Wandrei off toward Athol—setting him on the right turnpike for Worcester-ward lifts, since he was to meet Cook in the latter town at two p.m. The balance of that day I spent in the Quinsnicket woods—whither I now take all such work, on pleasant days, as does not require typing. Saturday I repeated the woodland programme, and am now back at my desk as a rainy Sunday sets in. Later in the season I mean to do some more hiking by myself—perhaps Plymouth, Cape Cod, Boston, Salem, Marblehead, Gloucester, Ipswich, Newburyport, Portsmouth, and Portland. There's no life for me but soaking up the scenick and architectural beauties of New England's magical past—even literature is tame as compared with getting directly next to the real thing! First I must get a hell of a lot of work cleaned up—but then, Oh, Boy! All the world of archaick glamour and sunset vistas over wooded hills and century'd roofs and cyclopean sea-cliffs shall be at my beck, and shall justify my continuance of the tedious routine known as life! Well—don't slave too hard, and drop the Old Gent a semiannual when the right moment comes.
        Yrs for better English tests—
                Lo

Notes

1. *Florodora* (1899), a musical comedy (book by Owen Hall [pseud. of Jimmy Davis], music by Leslie Stuart, additional songs by Paul Rubens), became one of the first successful Broadway musicals of the 20th century following a long run in London. *The Prince of Pilsen* is a lost 1926 silent film comedy-romance, based on a 1903 Broadway musical by Gustav Luders, directed by Paul Powell and starring Anita Stewart.
2. Oscar Wilde died 30 November 1900.
3. A music hall song written c. 1900 (lyrics by Will D. Cobb, music by Paul Barnes). It was written during the Spanish–American War but became a Boer War anthem.
4. HPL refers to individuals chiefly known for the involvement in the battle for the Philippines during the Spanish-American War: Admiral George Dewey (1837–1917), victor of the Battle of Manila Bay (1 May 1898); Rear Admiral Richmond P. Hobson (1870–1937), who was captured as prisoner of war in June 1898, taken to Cuba, and released in a prisoner exchange on 6 July 1898; Rear Admiral William T. Sampson (1840–1902), victor of the Battle of Santiago de Cuba (3 July 1898); Admiral Winfield Scott Schley (1839–1911), who also participated in the Battle of Santiago de Cuba;

Emilio Aguinaldo (1869–1964), Filipino revolutionary who battled the U.S. forces during 1899–1901 and was captured on 23 March 1901 by General Frederick N. Funston (1865–1917).

5. By Mary Johnston (1870–1936); the best-selling novel in the U.S. in 1900.

6. A novel (1900) by Charles Felton Pidgin.

7. Resulting from the Great Galveston (Texas) Hurricane, which made landfall on 8 September 1900.

8. Saint-Pierre, Martinique, was destroyed in 1902 by a volcanic eruption.

9. See MWM 64n39. Also mentioned in "An Epistle to the Rt. Honble Maurice Winter-Moe, Esq. . . ." (MWM 38).

10. HPL refers to the fact that biograph (an early form of the cinematograph or film) was replacing actual theatre productions at venues such as Keith's Theatre in Boston.

11. A world's fair held in Buffalo, NY, from 1 May to 2 November 1901.

12. "Put Me Off at Buffalo" (1895), a vaudeville song by the Dillon brothers (lyrics by Harry Dillon, music by John Dillon).

13. I.e., *Sister Carrie*.

14. The noted American author Theodore Dreiser (1871–1945) was the younger brother of Paul Dresser (born Johann Paul Dreiser, Jr.; 1857–1906), an American singer, songwriter, and comedic actor of the late 19th and early 20th centuries.

15. A celebrated novel about Jesus Christ (1894) by Henryk Sienkiewicz.

16. Peter Francis Dailey (1868–1908), an American burlesque comedian and singer popular during the Gay Nineties.

17. Stanley John Weyman (1855–1928), British novelist known as the "Prince of Romance." HPL may have been referring to his *Sophia* (1900), *Count Hannibal* (1901), or *The Abbess of Alaye* (1904).

18. A controversial but immensely popular novel (1888) by British author Mrs. Humphry Ward (1851–1920), about a clergyman's doubts about his faith.

19. *The Simple Life* (1901), a translation of a French inspirational work (*La Vie simple*, 1895) by Charles Wagner (1852–1918).

20. Elbert Hubbard (1856–1915), American writer and printer who gained celebrity with the founding of the Roycroft Press, a press specializing in self-consciously "arty" books influenced by William Morris's Kelmscott Press.

21. Marcus Alonzo Hanna (1837–1904), American businessman and Republican politician, and U.S. Senator from Ohio (1897–1904). He managed William McKinley's presidential campaigns in 1896 and 1900.

22. A recurring line in the poem "Non Sum Qualis Eram Bonae Sub Regno Cynarae" (1894) by British poet Ernest Dowson (1867–1900).

23. William Ernest Henley (1849–1903), "Invictus" (1875), ll. 15–16.

24. By Charles Felton Pidgin (1844–1923).

25. By Gertrude Atherton.

26. Harry Lehr conducted the widely publicized Monkey Dinner, at which guests were presented to "Prince del Drago," a chimpanzee in royal regalia. Other monkeys in dress suites accompanied women to their places at table.

27. Ward McAllister (1827–1895), self-styled arbiter of New York high society who coined the term "the Four Hundred," referring to the most illustrious families in the city.

28. Barry Wall, the beau of America, was a well-known dandy of the day and rival of Ward McAllister.

29. Possibly Prince Henry, Duke of Gloucester (1900–1974), third son of the Duke of York (later George V). Or Prince Heinrich (Henry) of Prussia (1862–1929), younger brother of the Kaiser Wilhelm II. Henry toured the U.S. in 1902 and was famously entertained in the luxurious bordello of the Everleigh sisters in Chicago.

30. David Graham Phillips (1867–1911), American muckraker and novelist.

31. Edward Noyes Westcott (1846–1898), *David Harum: A Story of American Life*, a best-selling novel of 1899.

32. A historical novel by the American novelist Winston Churchill (1871–1947) published in 1899.

33. *Sappho* (1900) was an American play by Clyde Fitch, based on the French novel (1884) of the same name by Alphonse Daudet and a play (1885) by Daudet and Adolphe Belot. It was at the center of an indecency trial in New York City involving the play's star and producer/director, Olga Nethersole.

34. A play originally written in French by Pierre Berton and Charles Simon; best known in the English-speaking world in David Belasco's adaptation of 1898. The title character is a prostitute who becomes a music hall entertainer and mistress of a married man.

35. Pope Leo XIII (1810–1903) reigned from 1878 to 1903.

36. HPL briefly cites the story by Charlotte Perkins Gilman (1860–1935) in "Supernatural Horror in Literature." It was first published in *New England Magazine* (January 1892).

37. Edward Hugh Sothern (1859–1933), American actor who starred as François Villon in *If I Were King* (1901).

38. Primrose and West's Big Minstrels was a blackface minstrel troupe organized by George Primose (1852–1919) and William H. West (1853–1902).

39. The Paris Exposition (Exposition Universelle) of 1900, running from 14 April to 12 November. It was one of a succession of such expositions held in Paris in the later 19th century; HPL's grandfather Whipple Phillips had attended the Paris Exposition of 1878.

40. Samuel Pierpont Langley (1834–1906), American astronomer, physicist, and pioneer of aviation.

41. The Brazilian Alberto Santos-Dumont (1873–1932) designed, built, and flew hot air balloons and early dirigibles.

42. Ferdinand von Zeppelin (1838–1917) pioneered rigid airship development at the beginning of the 20th century.

43. King Alfonso XIII of Spain (1886–1941), whose reign extended from his birth on 17 May 1886 (his father, Alfonso XII, had died six months earlier) until 14 April 1931, when he was deposed.

44. Harold Frederic (1856–1898), American journalist and novelist.

45. The first line of the chorus of "The Blue and the Gray (or, a Mother's Gift to Her Country)" (1900) by Paul Dresser.
46. "Bill Bailey, Won't You Please Come Home?" (1902), written by American songwriter and pianist Hughie Cannon (1877–1912).
47. A song published in 1901 (lyrics by Elmer Bowman, music by Al Johns).
48. *WT*, October 1927, contained Wandrei's "The Red Brain" (original title "The Twilight of Time").
49. The bout between Jack Sharkey (1902–1994) and William Harrison "Jack" Dempsey (1895–1983) was held 21 July 1927. Dempsey won by knockout.
50. Mariano de Magistris paid HPL $37.08 every six months as a mortgage payment to mine the quarry in question.

[31]   [ALS, JHL]

Thursday, August 4th[, 1927]

Aristotele Secunde:—
          Congratulations on the quick-time authorship! May the eggs soon become a basket-full! Yes, in future may a fenestral orifice of Bascom Hall become celebrated as the Window to Poeticks! Here's hoping the publishing fraternity may take kindly to the finisht product.[1] Damn it all, if they don't, we'll get good old W. Paul Cook to publish it as the piece de resistance of the Recluse Press! Good luck, too, with the book tests—to which I trust the printers may do reasonable credit. I'll wager your lecture was both comprehensive & absorbing—if you ever get to broadcasting these events, I shall have to get a radio set after all . . . . . by mail-order, no doubt, from the Trumpeter of Judgment Day.
    And now, Sir, for the heavy stuff! As to metres—I think you are safe in assigning a prime literary antiquity to the dactyl, since all the most antient Grecian poets employ'd the dactylick hexameter. It must at the same time be observ'd, that the earliest surviving poems show so great a degree of artistick perfection, that they cannot be other than the last of a long line of development, during which the dactylick foot took shape out of a multiplicity of antecedent experiments. All sorts of hymns & ballads & songs for ceremonial observances (like the Linus-songs, dirges, & epithalamia whereof mention is frequently found in the later writers) must have existed long before the birth of the hexameter epick; & 'tis not to be thought that all of these things were coucht in a dactylick measure. That the dactyl emerg'd as the first visible metre of Grecian poesy, must be reckon'd as due very largely to chance. I doubt very greatly that it was in truth unique in the Homerick aera, but conceive rather that it was merely the only sort of measure to survive from that period, being that which was chosen for the most dignify'd & permanent sort of compositions. 'Tis scarce to be assum'd, that the lyrical measures of the age of Archilocus, Theognis, Simonides, Alcaeus, Sappho, & Anacreon were pure

inventions of the time; (tho' the *elegiack* measure is clearly a new shortening of the epick hexameter in alternate lines) & we must rather believe that they form'd the maturing of tendencies long current in the poetry of the region. The lack of all *written* literature at this period, is amply sufficient to account for the total submergence of the earlier & more ephemeral specimens of non-hexameter Greek verse. We may, then, declare with confidence that the dactylic hexameter is the earliest sort of poetick numbers which we possess; but must beware against assigning to it any specifick character of natural primitiveness. There is no proof that it was the first spontaneous measure to be hit upon by the rude dawning strains of European song.

Now as to your second point, I must reluctantly dissent from your assumption that the dactyl bulks largest in the poesy of Greece. 'Tis true that the dactylick hexameter is the standard *epick* or *heroick* measure of the Greeks; as also that the dactylick *elegy* (alternate hexameter & pentameter) of Callinus, Tyrtaeus, (who likewise imploy'd the *anapaest* in his marching-songs) Simonides, and the Alexandrians was extremely popular. The overshadowing supremacy of Homer, moreover, brings the dactyl very prominently to the mind of the learner; so that it is easy to fall into the habit of taking it as a type of all classical antiquity. In truth, however, it cannot be said that this metre enjoyed any such universal dominance amongst the Grecians. Perhaps the most striking single disproof is the case of the Attick tragedy, which is generally allow'd to be the greatest expression of the Hellenick genius after Homer. As you must indeed be sensible, this form of literature develop'd out of the Dorian choral ode in its most elaborated form, the Dionysiack dithyramb; & had its dialogue parts in the IAMBICK *"hexameter"* (or *trimeter*, in the reckoning of the antients. The form now known as "Alexandrine" which, passing thro' the Latin,* became in the end the fixt form of French heroick verse) whilst the strophes & antistrophes of the chorus follow'd a variety of lyrical patterns. Milton, in his "Paradise Regain'd", alludes to this circumstance in the following lines:

> "Thence what the lofty, grave Tragedians taught
> In Chorus or Iambick . . . . . ."[2]

Comedy follow'd the same pattern, & the Latin dramatists adopted without change the measures of the Greeks; so that we must realise that all the immortal drama of antiquity—Æschylus, Euripides, & Sophocles, Aristophanes & the lost Philemon & Menander, Plautus, Terence,† & Seneca—was writ in an alternation of lyrical choruses (tho' these things disappear'd from the New

---

*The directness of this descent—Greek to French—is perhaps doubtful—but I think Seneca must have influenced the French dramatick poesy during the Renaissance.
†However, Plautus & Terence used great licence in varying their flow of metre.

Comedy & were not taken into Latin comedy) & iambick "hexameters" of the Alexandrine sort. This surely makes out a strong case against the supremacy of the dactyl, even for serious themes; tho' we may say that it remain'd the dominant *epical* measure to the last; couching such heroick poems as the "Argonautica" of Apollonius Rhodius, the "Æneid" of Virgil, Statius his "Thebaïs", & the tragicall "Pharsalia" of Lucan. 'Tis also to be noted, that Virgil retain'd this measure in his Georgicks & Eclogues; shewing perhaps that it possesst a higher importance amongst the Romans than amongst the Grecians. This also couch'd Ovid his Metamorphoses, such didactick pieces as Lucretius' "De Rerum Natura", (whose use of it was probably what fixt it finally upon the language, since the early saturnian had occasionally persisted till then) & the immortal satires of Horace, Persius, & Juvenal. Against the hexameter let us observe the amount of antient poesie produc'd in other measures, even beyond the iambick drama. We must first note the dactylick elegy, or alternate hexameter & pentameter verse; which, tho' deriv'd from the heroick hexameter, clearly has as different an artisticall & emotional effect as the English elegiack measure of Mr. Gray's poem has from the standard heroick couplet of our British epicks & satires. Amongst the Grecians we behold a very great use of the elgiack form; beginning with Callinus of Ephesus, & continuing with Tyrtaeus, Solon, Theognis, Phocylides, Simonides, Xenophanes, & such typical Alexandrians as the celebrated Callimachus. Amongst the Romans it flourisht no less; being the chief measure of Catullus, (tho' of course 'twas only one department with him) Propertius, & Tibullus, & the customary habit of Ovid except in his Metamorphoses. Then of course the amount of important work in measures not dactylick is enormous. I need only mention Archilocus & Simonides of Amorgas (not the great Simonides of Ceos) Mimnermus of Smyrna, & Hipponax of Ephesus, as examples of great workers in iambick forms. Alcaeus invented a stanzaical fashion all his own, which your good friend Mr. Tennyson has reproduc'd in English with some success; whilst the piquant uniquity of the Sapphick mode is known to every schoolboy. Anacreon likewise imploy'd the lyricall measures of the Æolians; whilst the Dorick strains of the choral lyrists Alcman, Stesichorus, Arion, Simonides, Bacchylides, & the great Pindar, are all in irregular numbers far remov'd from the stately march of the Homerick hexameter. Pindar, indeed, hath become a byword for the irregular ode; the term "Pindarick" being now apply'd to any lyrick production whose metre (like that of Mr. Gray's "Progress of Poesy") involves a complex pattern of lines of unequal length. The lesser poets amongst the Grecians went even further than Pindar with their study'd want of evenness; producing sometimes a poem whose lines, arrang'd on paper, form'd the outline of some such object as an egg, an axe, a pair of wings, an altar, or a shepherd's pipe. Mr. Addison, in those numbers of his *Spectator* (58–62) which deal with false wit, hath very aptly pointed out some of the trivial characteristicks of this species of versification; as well as many other puerile affectations of the post-classical Grecians. Amongst the Romans a variety of important metrical forms are found. Catullus was particularly versatile & inventive in this regard, his hendecasyllabick numbers being held characteristick of him, & emulated in the Victorian age by Ld Tennyson & Mr. Swinburne—yea, & by Mr. Coleridge in the age just before it. Horace, with a curious felicity, indulg'd in the most vary'd forms of the Grecian lyrists; producing verses in the Alcaick & Sapphick manner, which posterity has universally adjug'd to be not unworthy of their original sources.

We may say, then, as a summary, that whilst the dactylick hexameter was the acknowledg'd *heroical* or *epical* metre of classical antiquity, (being imploy'd in epick, didactick, & satyrick verse, & probably getting wider usage from the Romans than from the Grecians who devis'd it) it was by no means the dominant measure of that period. The whole of the classic drama was in *iambick* numbers, whilst the elegiack couplet, & the vary'd forms of other lyricall measures, are represented by figures as titanick as Alcaeus, Sappho, Simonides, Pindar, Catullus, Propertius, Tibullus, Ovid, Horace, Phaedrus, (who writ in trimeter iambicks) and Martial. (who employ'd a variety of measures, mostly irregular.) Comparing the place of the dactylick hexameter in the ancient world with that of the iambick pentameter in the English world, I think we can trace some general parallelism, at least so far as epick & didactick poesy are concern'd. We cannot, however, trace the analogy too far; for whereas the Greeks & Romans did not carry their dactyls into the drama, we have indeed made the heroick line not only a common, but virtually an indispensable, feature of the poetick play. The antients did not, clearly enough, esteem their heroick hexameters essential to high & serious thought; as their non-use of them in tragedy well proves; but with us the iambick pentameter is indeed link'd powerfully in the general mind with any attempt at sustain'd gravity or loftiness. Just as the Romans were more inclin'd to an epical measure than the Grecians, so are we more inclin'd to ours than were the antients as a whole to theirs. The superficial observer may seek to establish a false generalisation from the circumstance that the measure of the Greek drama was *what we call* an iambick "hexameter"; deducing therefrom that serious Grecian thought ran toward hexameters as a whole. I scarcely need say that this fallacy results wholly from thinking in terms of meer names instead of in terms of the actualities behind them. There was *nothing at all* in common betwixt the dactylick *hexameter* (the six measures being of *quantity* only, & not of syllabick feet) of the epick, & that iambick *trimeter* (as reckon'd by quantity, & recognis'd by the antients) of the drama *which we, viewing it from the purely modern angle of accentual metre, un-Hellenically* call *"hexameter".* In other words, to a Grecian, the "Alexandrine" measure of the drama was *not "hexameter"* at all, & was not in any way associated with the Homerick epicall measures. The following parallel shews the difference:

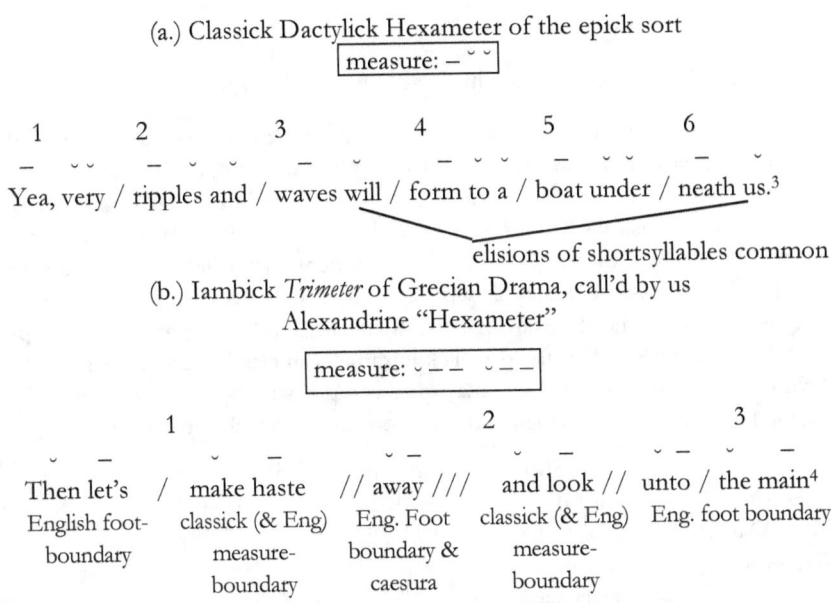

Observe, roughly speaking, that the "measure" in this sort of trimeter consisted of *two* iambick "feet" in the modern sense. Thus the verse *tended to be* six-stress'd & equivalent to the modern hexameter Alexandrine. But it was really rather different in rendition, since each two-foot measure had only one stress. We of this aera of accentual verse can think back only with difficulty to the conditions of purely quantitative verse. If we cou'd recite the foregoing line thus: "Then LET'S make haste aWAY and look unTO the main", we might (provided our emphasis was of vocal prolongation rather than accent) obtain some *theoretical* notion of the composition of a classick trimeter line, tho' the process wou'd probably end in chaos rather than true enlightenment. There are Latin lines which (because of their greater familiarity than Greek to most of us) offer intermediate stepping-stones in the matter of comprehending classick iambick trimeter. The following standard quotation from Horace is a case in point:

Beatus il/le qui procul / negotiis[5]   N.B. In Latin, this sort of verse was term'd "senarius".

Here we behold the three measures of classick quantity, less confus'd with the idea of six accentual feet which tends to come up in the English mind. ¶ And since writing the previous English Alexandrine, I have thought of *another* which shews *much better* (by virtue of the parts which chance to be stress'd) the nature of classick iambick trimeter. It is from Spenser, & I will mark it for scansion in the antient Graeco-Roman fashion:

⏑ _́ ⏑ _ ⏑ ⏑ _́ ⏑ _ ⏑ ⏑ _́ ⏑ _
When Phoebus lifts / his head out of / the winter's wave[6]

But I have say'd enough upon this topick. 'Tis very clear, that the iambicks of Grecian drama were *not true hexameters* to the Grecian mind, & held no community with the Grecian heroick measure. In the idea of hexameter quality, there was nothing intrinsically serious to the Greek. It meant simply epick or didactick matters. Just where the appeal of our heroick pentameter lies, 'tis very hard to say. I think the *iambick* quality is with us more closely associated weith serious use than is the numerical status of the *pentameter* line. A diagram can perhaps best illustrate the status of the dactylick hexameter in classical poetry as a whole. From a survey of this chart, you may quickly judge whether you feel justify'd in calling the measure as dominant a thing as our own iambick pentameter:

(Supreme figures underlined)

DACTYLICK HEXAMETER (Heroick)	ELEGIACK DACTYLS (Hexameter & Pentameter alt.)	IAMBICK TRIMETER	OTHER METRES	
Homer	Callinus	Aeschylus	Archilocus	
Hesiod	Tyrtaeus	Sophocles	Simonides of Armagas	
Apollonius Rh.+	Solon (lost)	Euripides	Mimnermus+	various
Theocritus	Theognis	Aristophanes	Hipponax+	iambick
Lucretius	Phocylides+	Philemon (lost)	Alcaeus	forms
Virgil	Simonides	Menander (")	Tyrtaeus (anapaests et al)	
Horace Satires	Xenophanes	Plautus	Sappho	
Ovid. Metam.	Callimachus	*Terence*	Anacreon	
Valerius Flaccus+	Catullus	Seneca+	Alcman	
Silius Italicus+	Propertius	(Seneca as a tra-	Stesichorus	
Lucan+	Tibullus	gick poet had not	Arion (lost)	
Statius+	Ovid (exc. Met.)	a high status)	Simonides	
Persius			Bacchylides	
Juvenal			Pindar	
			Catullus	
			Phaedrus+	
			Horace	
+Essentially a minor figure			Martial	

Returning to matters exclusively English—I do not think that any such thing as an entire pentameter line in spondees is possible to the genius of our language & prosody. Your line, I conceive,

IAMBUS   SPONDEE   SPONDEE   IAMBUS   SPONDEE
ᵕ —   —   —   —   —   ᵕ —   —   —
While ten / slow words / oft march / in one / dull line*

has at least two inescapable iambi in it; such accent being distinctively determin'd by relative importance of words even when apparently equalised. Even when one tries with extream care to produce an wholly spondaick pentameter line, as

Thus with / weak wings / that thrush / seeks out / far lands[7]

there is very great difficulty in preserving the character of the metre. The first foot tends to become either a trochee or a pyrrhick, whilst the third & fifth have iambick inclinations. Perhaps you can excel me in an ingenious coinage of this sort, but I vow, the task will be one of no small difficulty. As for the deliberate introduction of the spondee for rhetorical effect—I believe Mr. Pope, in his Essay on Criticism, furnishes as good specimens as are to be had; the following seeming to fulfil the conditions with some exactness:

The hoarse / rough verse / shou'd like / the tor/rent roar (369)

When A/jax strives / some rock's / vast weight / to throw

The line / too la/bours and / the words / move slow

Milton has instances of spondaic effects:

So he / with dif/ficul / ty and la/bour hard

Mov'd on / with dif/fi cul/ty and la/bour he

                                                                     Par. Lost. II-1021

    A specimen very familiar to me, but which I can't quite place at the moment, is this:

Up the / high hill / he heaves / the hea/vy stone[8]

    As for antepenultimate—or fourth-from-end—rhymes—like you, I do not see that Mr. Browning's specimen is properly one; for accentual stress is a sine qua non with truly rhyming syllables, (tho' I will at once transmit to you

---

*As Mr. Pope hath it: "And ten low words oft creep in one dull line." [*An Essay on Criticism* 347.—ED.]

any I may discover hereafter* but "Hudibras" is of course rich in antepenultimate specimens of varying correctness. I suppose you have the best-known ones already recorded—but I will add a few at the risk of parallelling:

> Remember how in arms & *politicks*
> We still have worsted all your *holy tricks.* II, II, 519

> They'll write a love-letter in *chancery,*
> Shall bring her upon oath to *answer ye.* III, III, 501

> Sir, quoth the lawyer, not to *flatter ye,*
> You have as good & fair a *battery* III, III, 675

> Us'd all means, both direct & *sinister,*
> I' th' pow'r of gospel-preaching *minister.* I, II, 583

> And laid about in fight more *busily*
> Than th' Amazonian Dame *Penthesile.* I, II, 377

> There was an antient sage *philosopher*
> That had read Alexander *Ross over.* I, II, 1

Shelley, in his Letter to Maria Gisborne, hath the following:
Then comes a range of *mathematical* Instruments for plans nautical & *statical.*
The place of the rhyme in the lines, however, is not as it ought to be.[10]

Byron, in Don Juan, has this rather poor triple rhyme—
Have spent my life, both interest & *principal*
And deem not, what I deem'd, my soul *invincible.*[9]

As for false rhymes in great poems—well, Sir, I conceive you do not place *allowable* rhymes in this class, hence will not cite any of the extreamly numerous instances of the sort. The following, both from Mr. Dryden, I deem definitely false:

> Our thoughtless sex is caught by outward *form*
> And empty noise, & loves itself in *man.*[11]

> My parents are propitious to my *wish*
> And she herself consenting to the *bliss.*[12]

Mr. Addison hath writ, in his version of Ovid,

---

*Later—as we go to press! HURRAH! Here is a really *fine quadruple rhyme* at last, from Byron's Don Juan:
> So that their plan & prosody are *eligible*
> Unless, like Wordsworth, they prove *unintelligible.*)

> One sees her thighs transform'd; another *views*
> Her arms shoot out, & branching into *boughs*.[13]

Mr. Pope rhym'd *thought* & *bought* with *fault*, as in the couplet:

> Before his sacred name flies ev'ry *fault*,
> And each exalted stanza teems with *thought*.[14]

He also writ:

> Wit kindled by the sulph'rous breath of *vice*,
> Like the blue lightning, while it shines *destroys*.[15]

Mr. Keats's debatable rhyme, which I do not allow to be incorrect in practice for Southern England & the Eastern part of America, is in the Epistle to George Felton Mathew, lines 21–2:

> I shall again see Phoebus in the *morning*,
> Or flush'd Aurora in the roseate *dawning*.

Mr. Poe has a similar instance in "A Valentine", addrest to Mrs. Frances Sargent Osgood:

(a diagonal acrostic)
> For her this rhyme is penn'd whose luminous eyes
> Brightly expressive as the twins of *Leda*
> Shall find her own sweet name, that nestling lies
> Upon the page, enwrapp'd from ev'ry *reader*.

Shelley teems with bad rhymes, especially rhymes on unaccented syllables & rhymes of syllables with themselves. For instance—

> That is another's, could dissever *ours*,
> We love not."—What! do not the silent *hours*
> 						(Ginevra)[16]

> On the level quiv'ring *line*
> On the waters crystal*line*
> 			(Euganaean Hills)[17]

Elsewhere Shelley rhymes *pass* & *surpass*, *clips* & *eclipse*, & so on ad infinitum

> What hand would crush the silver-wingÈd fly,
> 	The youngest of inconstant April's *minions*,
> Because it can not climb the purest sky,
> 	Where the swan sings amid the sun's *dominions*?
> 						(To Mary)[18]

John Greenleaf Whittier, Esq., of Tryout-Land,[19] is especially prone to the kind of rrrr....less rhyme you do not relish. Here is a stanzaick beginning from "The Lumbermen":

> Wildly round our woodland *quarters*,
> Sad-voiced Autumn grieves;
> Thickly down these swelling *waters*
> Float his fallen leaves.

A really false rhyme occurs in what the poet writ for an occasion in this very town; a levee of the president of Brown University held on June 29, 1870:

> Is't fancy that he* watches still
>   His Providence *Plantations?*
> *That still the careful founder takes*
>   *A part in these occasions?*
>
> Methinks I see that rev'rend form
>   That all of us so *well know:*
> He rises up to speak; he jogs
>   The presidential *elbow.*[20]

In "St. Martin's Summer" Mr. Whittier writes:

> O gracious morn, with rose-red *dawn*,
>   And thin moon curving o'er it!
> The old year's daughter, latest *born*,
>   More lov'd than all before it.

Byron, in "The Vision of Judgment", rhymes *suspicion* & *vision*, (xxxiv) *insertion* & *reversion*, (vi) *saints* with *contents* & *scents*, (cii) & *yours* & *allures* with *reviewers*. (xcix)

In truth, I fancy that a full hour's search of nearly any bard might bring to light some gem of imperfect rhyme well fitted to adorn your prosodicall chamber of horrors. I will try to encounter more & communicate them to you as I find them.

Now as to Boeotian extracts from the amateur press—I'll try my best to discover something choice as soon as I get some especially insistent labour (hopeless revision, as usual) off my hands. My vacation of last month congested my programme to an alarming degree, so that I shall have to perform prodigies of celerity & industry if I am to have any breathing-spells in the near future. Meanwhile I am enclosing some current amateur matter, which cannot fail to exhibit some specimens of immortal dulness, unless the associa-

---

*Roger Williams

tions have changed most marvellously since last I pay'd attention to them. In a later epistle I will send what further gems I unearth in my back files. Another peculiarly fertile source which I advise you to tap is the collection of *James Ferdinand Morton, Paterson Museum, Paterson, New-Jersey*, wherein is a special class devoted to the ludicrously impossible in verse. Mortonius hath made a specialty of grotesque extremes in this direction, & I am certain he wou'd be glad to lend you such screamingly comick items as the epicall "Bride of Gettysburg",[21] sundry Bushiana, & the priceless "Selected Gems" of P. J. Pendergast, which I gave him five years gone. Pray write Jacobus Ferdinandus without delay, explaining your immediate need; & I am confident he will send you samples precisely fitted to your purpose. Another thing which I may be able to find hereabouts, & which I will surely send you if I do, is the unbelievable (yet serious) magazine of a prosodical paranoiack in New-York, intitul'd *Poet & Philosopher*.[22] This is almost too exquisite for verity, & nearly eclipses the rarest effusions of the Baldwins & Whitakers—deriving all the more charm from the circumstance that the editor undertakes to *teach* the poetick art compleat by mail for a consideration. I pray Heav'n it may yet come to hand!

Well, Sir, if you care to behold any recent fictional work of Old Theobald, procure the new issue of *Amazing Stories* & note "The Colour Out of Space". My copy arriv'd only today, & I have not yet receiv'd my cheque for the tale. My task of editing the posthumous Bullen verse grows in magnitude as Culinarius urges haste,[23] but I yet hope to discharge the responsibility with honour. Cook & Munn design to pay me another visit a week hence, & I may accompany them back to Athol for my first visit thither; perhaps taking the Codex Bulleniensis along & doing some rapid editing & proofreading on the very scene of publication. My late guest Wandrei is on his homeward journey, having had unexceptionally pleasant sojourns both at Athol & at West Shokan. His weird-artist host at the latter place, Bernard Dwyer, Esq., turn'd out to be a gentleman of the most interesting & attractive sort—a youngish athletick giant of rural environment, whom it will be a pleasure for me to meet later on, as plann'd.

I sincerely trust that your book may mature in brilliant fashion, & hereby offer my name as a subscriber for the very first copy! I'll wager it will cover ground, & combine elements, which no previous volume hath ever treated in an unify'd way; & believe the paedagogicall fraternity will hail you as a leader & pioneer in the exposition of prosodick truths, & the right guiding of poetick taste. I only regret that I cannot offer more assistance at this juncture, than these my rambling observations & disjointed recollections. ¶ Hop'g to hear from you at y^r leisure, & extend'g the choicest comp'm'ts to ye Season,

I am, Sir, ever y^r most hble ob^t Servt—

Lo

Notes

1. HPL refers to MWM's work on a treatise, *Doorways to Poetry,* on which HPL assisted him significantly over the next several years. It was scheduled for publication by Macmillan, but the book never appeared and the ms. is now apparently nonextant.
2. *Paradise Regain'd* (1671), 4.261–62.
3. Arthur Hugh Clough, *The Bothie of Tober-na-Vuolich* (1848), l. 866.
4. Shakespeare, *2 Henry VI* 1.1.206.
5. Horace, *Epodes* 2.1.
6. Michael Drayton, *The Poly-Olbion* (1612–22), 13.41.
7. This line is of HPL's invention.
8. HPL appears to be referring to the line "Up the high hill he heaves a huge round stone," from Alexander Pope's translation of Homer's *Odyssey* (1726), 11.736.
9. Byron, *Don Juan* (1819–24), Canto 1, 113.7–8.
10. Percy Bysshe Shelley, *Letter to Maria Gisborne* (1820), ll. 82–85.
11. John Dryden [and Nathaniel Lee], *Oedipus* (1679), 1.1.93–94.
12. From "Garth's Ovid" (Ovid's *Metamorphoses,* ed. Samuel Garth), 9.931–32.
13. "Garth's Ovid," 2.421–22.
14. *An Essay on Criticism,* ll. 422–23.
15. This is in fact from John Brown's *An Essay on Satire* (1745), 3.488–89. The poem was written upon Pope's death and is frequently found in editions of Pope's poetical works.
16. Shelley, "Ginevra" (1821), ll. 68–69.
17. Shelley, "Written among the Euganean Hills" (1818), ll. 63–64.
18. Shelley, "To Mary" (prefatory poem to *The Witch of Atlas* [1820]), ll. 9–12.
19. I.e., Haverhill, MA.
20. John Greenleaf Whittier, "A Spiritual Manifestation" (1870), ll. 9–16.
21. By J. Dunbar Hylton.
22. *The Poet and Philosopher: A Quarterly Magazine Devoted to Poetry and Philosophy* (New York: F. L. Schmidt, 1913f.), edited by Fritz Leopold Schmidt.
23. *White Fire* by John Ravenor Bullen, published by W. Paul Cook.

[32] [AHT]

Friday, August 12, 1927

Quintiliane Maxime:—

Now about English iambic verse—a matter of *accents* and very different in laws from the classick—certainly you're one hundred per cent O.K. in assuming that the iambick plan is often dropped for the nonce in the interest of richer and more varied cadence. The accent never falls where it would not in good rhetorical prose; and when you behold an unsuitable word in a place where the conventional iambic stress would ordinarily occur, you may be sure that the accent has moved as taste demands, and that the foot in question has consciously assumed a non-iambic character. When we speak of iambic verse, we refer simply to the metre whose spirit predominates. Variant individual feet are common—I might say frequent and universal—nor could any poem of permanent merit be created without some latitude of the sort. Only well-meaning and technically immature poets, like good old Dr. Kuntz of Colorady, think they must stick unswervingly to exactly the same foot. Let's see what your chosen line reveals:

$$\_\ \smile\ \smile\ \_\ \smile\ \_\ \smile\ \_$$
Cloth'd in / white Sam/ite, Mys/tick Won/der ful[1]

Yes—we have a trochee tacked on to a line otherwise all iambic: The same (or perhaps we might better say that the odd foot in this other line—"out of"—is a *pyrrhick* rather than a *trochee*) is the case with the other line—of which more anon. All the older manuals of rhetorick—the good old volumes I used to find and gloat over in the dark attick "trunk room" of the old home (454 Angell St.) back in the '90's—were very copious with their illustrations of lines with artistically mixed feet, and soon taught the learner to distinguish betwixt these subtle modifications of conventional versification. I fear no such helpful volumes are published now—indeed, whenever I have occasion to give advice to a revisory client, I invariably bid him procure my favourite book of the sort; which was widely esteem'd in its day, and which my grandfather study'd to great advantage in the East Greenwich Academy in the early fifties, when it was quite new (it was first published in 1844). I allude to the famous "Aids to English Composition" by Richard Green Parker, Esq., of Boston, which ran thro' nearly thirty editions, and was in common use and favour till long after the Civil War, when the age of correct taste and linguistick elegance in America commenc'd its present decadence. No better exposition of the details of poetick practice hath ever appear'd in print; and were I in your place I wou'd procure a copy and reprint the section on poesy intact as an appendix to the new book. I obtain all the copies I can at the bookstalls, later giving or lending them to persons who show a need of their perusal. You may recall that this was amongst the books I procur'd for our now evaporated colleague *Co* back in 1915, when I was so set upon embellishing the lustre of his refulgent native genius with the elegant adornments of rhetorical precision. If you have any wish to examine this indispensable vade mecum, and cannot find copies in your part of the world, I shall esteem it an honour to lend you my personal and hereditary copy—which is now wearing out the new leather binding I had made for it a quarter of a century ago. You will find it an invaluable aid in the formulation of those nice principles of composition which were, in a sounder and more polished age than the present, justly deem'd alike essential to the accomplishments of a gentleman, and to the right instruction of youth. But to return to the subject of variety in versification, which Mr. Parker illustrates with such generous examples, it is well to consider the more common orders of such genteel diversity, as practic'd by the choicest and most correct poets of the Golden Age, in the formation of their spirited and pleasingly modulated heroicks and other iambick lines. Here we have frequent *spondees*, to import an agreeable and proper stateliness:

> ‒ ‒ ᴗ ‒ ᴗ ‒ ᴗ ‒
> There soon the suff'rer sinks to rest
>
> ‒ ‒ ᴗ ‒ ᴗ ‒ ᴗ ‒
> There too was he, who nobly stemm'd the tide
>
> ‒ ‒ ᴗ ‒ ᴗ ‒ ᴗ ‒
> That breast, the seat of sentiment refin'd
>
> ‒ ‒ ‒ ‒ ‒ ‒ ᴗ ‒
> Hail, long-lost Peace! Hail, dove-ey'd maid divine!²

We here encounter several judiciously inserted *pyrrhicks*:

> ᴗ ‒ ᴗ ‒ ᴗ ᴗ ‒ ‒
> If aught be welcome to our sylvan shed
>
> ᴗ ᴗ ᴗ ‒ ᴗ ᴗ ᴗ ‒
> Be it the trav'ler who has lost his way
>
> ‒ ‒ ᴗ ‒ ᴗ ‒ ᴗ ‒
> I sought the beauties of the painted vale
>
> ᴗ ‒ ᴗ ‒ ᴗ ᴗ ᴗ ‒
> The flow'rs I often water'd with my tears
>
> ᴗ ‒ ᴗ ‒ ᴗ ᴗ ᴗ ‒
> And loaded with my sighs the passing gale³

Both *spondees* and *pyrrhicks*, and one *trochee*, are mixed with the iambi:

> ‒ ‒ ᴗ ‒ ᴗ ‒ ᴗ ‒
> Go, pious offspring, and restrain those tears;
>
> ᴗ ‒ ᴗ ‒ ᴗ ᴗ ‒ ‒
> I fly to regions of aeternal bliss.
>
> ‒ ‒ ᴗ ‒ ‒ ‒ ᴗ ‒
> Heav'n in your favour hears my dying pray'rs;
>
> ‒ ᴗ ‒ ᴗ ᴗ ‒ ᴗ ‒
> Take my last blessing in this clay-cold kiss.⁴

Parker gives a case which he calls a *dactyl* amongst iambi; but I conceive that it becomes a *trochee* by the contraction of the first word to its usual poetick form of a dissyllable: *murm'ring*

> ‒ ᴗ ‒ ᴗ ᴗ ‒ ᴗ ‒
> Murmuring, and with him fled the shades of night

We here behold an *amphibrach* in the midst of iambi: (Tho' it can be made wholly iambick by pronouncing *many a* as a dissyllable—thus: man'-y'a)

$$\smile\ —\ \smile\ \smile\ —\ \smile\ \smile\ —\ \smile\ —\ \smile\ —$$
O'er many / a fro/zen, many / a fier/y alp

Here, again assuming that we do not run any syllables together, we are rewarded by the spectacle of a *tribrach* and an *anapaest* amongst iambi:

$$\smile\ —\ \smile\ \smile\ \smile\ —\ \smile\ —\ \smile\ —$$
Innu/merable / before / the Almigh/ty throne[5]

(Parker scans this line differently, but this is one of the very rare instances where I am unable to follow him.)

I have sav'd, for final consideration whilst upon this topick, that Alexandrine out of Spenser which I chose with particular care (and not without having previously chosen a less apt instance) to illustrate, in easily comprehensible fashion, a metrical point which is *not English at all*, but *classically Graeco-Roman*. I am now wondering whether I made myself perfectly clear in that impromptu 'master's thesis'—clear, that is, regarding the fact that I chose this particular line because of a *purely accidental* resemblance to a *Graeco-Roman* metre *which is not the English iambus*. This line, *Englishly scann'd*, is truly an hexameter of iambi with one *pyrrhick:* (or possibly a *trochee* if one say "OUT of" instead of "out of")

$$—\ —\ \smile\ —\ \smile\ —\ \smile\ \smile\ \smile\ —\ \smile\ —$$
When Phoe/bus lifts / his head / out of / the win/ter's wave

But I did not select it for its English scansion at all—as you will see by observing the infrequency of the syllables I emphasised. Those marks of emphasis were not for the actual English stress-accent at all, but for the *Graeco-Roman quantiative ictus in the senarian iambick trimeter (not hexameter* as *classically* scann'd, but the complex dipodick *trimeter* of the Graeco-Roman drama) *to which this specimen bore a chance but very illuminating resemblance*. In this line, certain words of particular importance chanced to fall in places perfectly coinciding with the theoretical position of the ictus in a classical dipodick trimeter iambick line of the same number of syllables. To give a concrete illustration of the place and infrequency of this quantitative stress in classical iambicks, and thus to show why the antients regarded iambick lines of *twelve* syllables as *trimeter* instead of *hexameter*, I put this convenient line to a fortuitous metrick use never dreamt of by the author—following a precedent of Harkness[6]—but perhaps I did not make the wholly arbitrary and un-English nature of my illustration sufficiently plain in the garrulous explanatory text.

But lest this be so, permit me to summarise the classical point once more. It is, that the old Graeco-Roman iambick measure *was not our modern iambick foot of two syllables at all*, but an affair of *four syllables*, with the ictus of quantitative stress on the *second*, thus: *an-TIP-a-thy*. (In digesting this illustration, remember of course that any illustration from English verse is at best only an affair of *analogy*, since *accent* and *quantity* are different things). Of course, in a line of this sort there must necessarily be a secondary ictus—and this fell on the final syllable, thus making the measure roughly a combination of *two iambick feet in the modern sense*. Well—what I tried to do was to find a line where I could illustrate the seat of the main trimeter ictus (without paying attention to the second) without having the source of emphasis as purely accentual as in the instance (an-TIP-a-thy) which I have just given. The Spenserian line in question seemed to form the best possible case, due to the location of the most emphatick idea-syllables; (*idea* here serving instead of *accent* as a substitute for the classical *quantity* so hard to reproduce in an English instance) so I proceeded as best I might to adapt it to my purpose. I trust I have now made it clear—but will add some parallel classic specimens to illustrate my point better. First of all, get the exact form and dimensions of the Graeco-Roman dipodick iambus fixed in your mind. Here is how Harkness delineates it: u –́ u –. Well—now for the specimens. Here's a fragment—no—I see on scansion that this line is irregular—with the free-and-easy license so common to comedy. Better luck next time. Here's something from mawkish old Rippy[7] with the correct precision: (Note difference of *accent* and *quantity*)

Εν ελπισιν / χρε τους σοφους / εχειν βιον

Moreover that it is proper the wise, to have long life shall expect

Εν ελ πι σιν / χρε ΤΟΥΣ σο φους / εχΕΙΝ βιον

And in Latine, Horace giveth us the following: (I'd give a whole sestertius to hear old Quint reel this off himself!)

qvid OB se ra / tis AU ri bus / fun DIS pre ces?[8]

(Arranging this in the comparative manner of my invention, to show the difference betwixt *accent* and *quantity*, and adding musical notes to show the time value of each syllable, we have the following:

Accent—QUID / ob / se RA / tis / AU / ri / bus / FUN / dis / PRE / ces?

Quantity: quid / OB / se / ra / tis / AU / ri / bus / fun DIS / pre / ces?

Well, now at last we're prepared to see what I was driving at in my special use of that Spenserian line. *Quantity*, Kid, *quantity!* Here it is, doctored up in my patient way to show the difference betwixt accent and quantity:

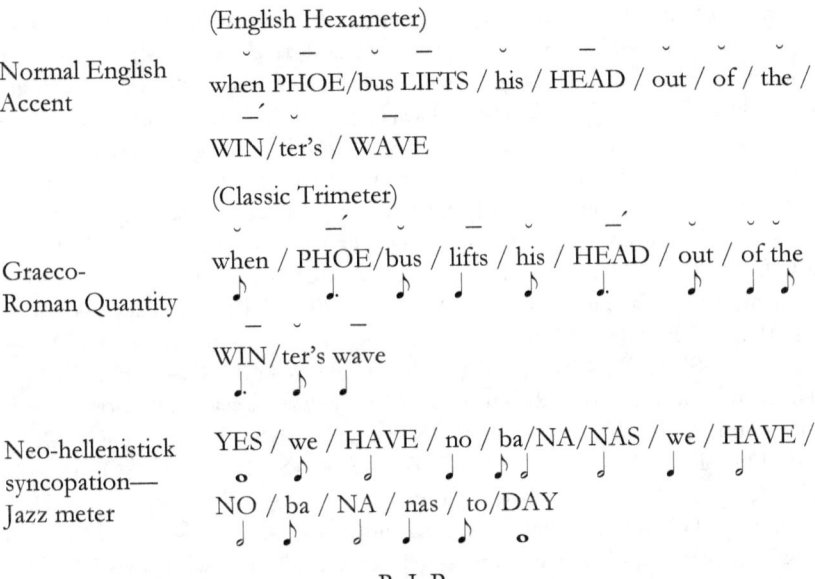

R. I. P.

I absorb with proper receptivity the additional data regarding the tests, and hope your bosses won't make too ruthless cuts, or let the Columbia and other education sharps transmute 'em too extensively. So you ain't read a dam thing of Adam Bede,[9] eh? Well—it's a great and standard book, and all that, but I can sum up my advice about perusal in the Lacedaemonian manner of another eminent authority on another topick—*don't*. There are too many interesting things to read, to warrant any guy's putting in a day on Mary Ann Evans' seriousminded yeomen! Arthur Machen, in his critical volume "Hieroglyphics", about sums up my own candid tho' not candy'd opinion of that eminent and hipposprosopeian she-Victorian. I am much more interested in your coming volume on poeticks; and am sure I shan't mind the elementary tone, for surely yuh gotta begin at the beginning of the subject for the practical instruction of the average Boeotian citizen. Considering the authorship, I'm a bit sceptical about the amount of Bush-work the volume will need; but send it along if you're flush; for I love soft snaps, and just dote on drawing pay without labour!

As for the word mania—it's certainly damn odd how such a thing can flourish in one part of the country and be virtually unknown in another! I shall watch the local press and see when it lands here, but so far there are no signs. The old *Chitrib* is a great paper, and its Line[10] bespeaks a popular mental activity and easy diffusion of wit and learning which seem rather absent in the East—at least in decaying New-York, where most Eastern columnar activity originates. I think I'm slowly acquiring the this-to-that bug. Only last night my aunt was looking at my desk, and wanted to know the meaning of the lines of short words scribbled over the backs of the envelopes in my lawless and perniciously tall heap of unanswered mail! I have perused with great interest all your cuttings—both vert and argent—on the subject, and have come to the melancholy conclusion that I'm not a *lugan*—whatever that means. Let's see if I can get from HIDE to SEEK in eight, like Edgar the Ph.D. HIDE—BIDE—BIDS—BEDS—BEES—SEES—SEEK!!! *EIGHT* your grandmother! What are our Ph.D.'s a-comin' to, when a poor old illiterate like I be kin beat 'em right off at the first crack! I did that in *six*, or else my elementary mathematicks are all scattered away! There's another way to do it in six—HIDE—HIRE—HERE—HERD—HEED—SEED—SEEK. Hell! What jerkwater academy gave that bimbo his Ph.D.? As for TEACH to LEARN—lessee—TEACH—PEACH—PEACE—PLACE—PLANE—PLANS—CLANS—CLAMS—SLAMS—SEAMS—SEARS—YEARS—YEARN—*LEARN*. Thirteen! And that bozo Raveurwood El took *twenty-seven!!!!* Oh, boy—this is pie! And now WEEKS to MONTH. WEEKS—REEKS—REEDS—READS—ROADS—ROODS—ROOTS—SOOTS—SOOTH—SOUTH—MOUTH—*MONTH*—in *eleven!* Migord! And this egg called Swanee the Hick gave it up! Hot dorg! In half an hour I did it two ways in *twelve* and then cut down to *eleven* another way. Nguess [?] Scotch 'n' Irish, who boasted of his *twelve*, was so glad to do it at all that he didn't try again. But what's this? He says he did HIDE to SEEK in *five*. Houzat, when I took six? Lessee—Oh, hell—too much bother! Hecarne does SHIP to LAND in five. How come? SHIP—SLIP—SLID—SAID—SAND—LAND. Done! And BAIT to FISH also in five? Well—BAIT—WAIT—WAST—FAST—FIST—FISH! Easier and easier! CLOUD to CLEAR in eleven? CLOUD—CLOUT—FLOUT—FLOAT—BLOAT—BLEAT—CLEAT—CLEAR. *Seven!* Who said come 'leben? Ah done got sebben! Dis yeah is de golf fo' dis chile! But am I one of those mysterious lugani whom E. B., the eleven cloud-clearer, wants to keep out? B. T. W.—I see by another cutting that an Hoosier schoolmaster has tied me. He proposes ROOT to BUSH—not that I like Bush work, but I gotta see how few I can give it—ROOT—LOOT—LOST—LUST—LUSH—BUSH—five. Nothing to it, Oswald! Now howbout Andy Tucker? PULL to DRAW in eight? DRAW—DRAG—BRAG—BRAT—BEAT—BELT—BELL—BULL—PULL at last! Nobody HOME! Got it time and again in nine, but it took me a full hour to boil it down to eight, and then I had to do it backward—DRAW to PULL. And this same goof proposes ALL to WET in five. Well—ALL—AIL—AIT—WIT—WET. Hee haw! *FOUR!!* I done it in lessen than what Andy done it in! Oh, babby—I'm a lugan, I guess! M. Annaeus Luganus! I'll send all these Pompeys down to their Pharsalia!

That's pretty good about the "intelligentsia"—I heartily believe it, too, for in my opinion the cerebral left wing which arrogates this title to itself is a faddish upstart train, too little grounded in the ancient foundations of eternal beauty to derive much benefit from the traditional shelves of a real bookshop. And speaking of the foundations of beauty—Heinie's article and your comment interested me exceedingly.[11] I have a great respect for Hank's philosophy, though I loathe his taste and manners; but fancy that he now and then errs in the same way as his adversaries, by proffering a deceptively simple explanation for the exceedingly complex. In the present matter I'd say offhand that you're both right in your respective ways—but you are far ahead of H. L. in establishing the point that the various aesthetic standards are psychologically built up through individual or group experience. As a matter of fact there are no basic standards of beauty, any more than there are basic standards for anything else in an infinite, purposeless cosmos of alternate building up and breaking down. That supreme dissociater of ideas, the late Remy de Gourmont, had the right idea when he said "there is no such thing as beauty—there are only beautiful things."[12] In the last analysis we may say with Heinrich Ludwig that all aesthetics are physiological, since of course all sense-perceptions and appreciations are physiological. But in practice there is of course a vast difference between the directly physiological—as expressed in terms of purely sensory reactions like eye-motion—and the psychologically physiological, where the filtration of cerebral cell-action is involved. Now as a matter of fact, there is no one aesthetic principle. Our artistic appreciations are tremendously complex affairs, nearly all of them being an inextricable synthesis of sensory pleasure, associative emotion, and a tertium quid best described empirically as a love of pattern (i.e., fixed symmetrical relationship—rhythmic conformity—regular disposition or recurrence) for its own sake. It is right here—on this third and last point—that the question becomes quasi-metaphysical and starts the heavy controversy; for all persons generally concede the two former elements as colouring most common aesthetic judgments. Indeed—as Mencken shows, there is even much tendency among some to deny the whole existence of the Pythagorean element, (if I may so denominate a feeling much allied to the mood of Pythagoras' harmony-worshipping followers) and to attribute every part of an aesthetic impression to pure physical sensation plus associative emotion. To me, however, this latter position seems to lack strength; since there does not appear to be any well-defined set of purely physical sensations, or any constant and coherent group of strong emotions, capable of seeking with such unfailing persistence the element of symmetry in environment and experience. The abstract quality of rhythm or pattern is too remote from the immediate contacts causing agreeable reaction to be logically considered as operating solely through simple sense and emotions in producing its aesthetic results. We must, then, in my opinion, concede the existence of a special department of brain-cells whose neural satisfaction depends on the reiterated presentation of impressions of harmonick pattern—in other words, an "aesthetic sense" distinct from all others. I do not think this sense is as clearly isolated and strongly specialised as many groups of experimenting moderns—groups who preach new doctrines of abstract form as divorced from content and association, and who produce theoretical works of "art" like the sculptural brass of Brancusi*[13]—believe, and I doubt if there are any aesthetic judgments in real life in which it operates unsupported. Art based on the sole appeal of "significant form" (to use a catchword of the after-1920 group of "ultras") must necessarily be freakish, chaotic, and to a large extent unappealing and incomprehensible—except, ironically enough, to its own devotees, for whom it has acquired enough associative emotion to cause a complex reaction which they mistake for a pure reaction! But in spite of all this, the rudimentary abstract sense is really there, and we find the fact repeatedly proved by the gradations of response to avowedly aesthetic offerings in which the symmetric element is present in varying quantity. Nothing absolutely without it can ring true as art, as we see clearly exemplified by the total dulness and aridity of all pseudo-artistic attempts in which the intended appeal is laboriously calculated, without aesthetic feeling, on an intellectually estimated basis of pure physical comfort or pleasure, or of pure emotional gratification. Aside from the unconscious residuum of the symmetrical which may inhere through accident, such stilted attempts invariably lack true beauty, and fail to impress any spectator who may have true taste or sensitiveness in any appreciable degree. The great examples of this awkward comfort-emotion substitution are didacticism and ethics in literature, and luxurious ostentation in architecture and furnishings. (This particular type of defect must not be confused with sheer *false taste*,— i.e., the spirit of Victorian decoration—which is a decadent and clumsy misapplication of the genuine aesthetic impulse, occurring when that impulse is *not felt*, but painstakingly *imitated* from a merely empirical or academic conception of it.) Well—so far, so good. We now agree that Heinie is wrong, and that there *is* an aesthetic sense. But *what* is that sense? Surely no active mind can rest till it has tracked down the elusive tertium quid and connected it up with the general cell and nerve and gland mechanism which forms the whole of the human personality. Now my own explanation is simply this: that the artistic sense is basically rooted in a natural *inertia* of the more delicate cerebral cells, purely physiological, and absolutely of a piece with the natural inertia manifested in other phases of the economy of life. In other words, whilst all aesthetic *standards* are artificial, fortuitous, and variable—born of varying racial and individual experiences—the aesthetic *faculty* which assimilates the ingredients of these standards, and which later formulates and applies them, is natural, constant, and physiological. The gist is, that one department of our mind demands an environment more or less homogeneous with whatever

---

*The most colyum-worthy item of straight news that I've seen in a decade was the refusal of the U.S. Customs Dept. about three months ago to admit some of Brancusi's "sculpture" duty-free as "works of art". They charged duty, as on *metal in ingot form!* Pretty damn good, I'll say! Now the moderns can sneer about Mummius and the sculptures of Corinth!

preceding environment it may have happened to acquire. Since harmony and rhythm, as expressed in the tides, seasons, alternations of day and night, biological and mineral formations, and so on, are universal and inevitable ingredients of all terrestrial life—being constantly ground into the mind through millions of years of evolutionary development and the whole of individual life—it follows that they have become the dominant and indispensable environment of every human mind; and that departures from them, either actual or symbolic, will necessarily have a strong automatic resistance to overcome, so that the process of departure will actually be attended by a marked degree of instinctive, habit-bred conflict and true physical fatigue amongst the delicate cells and filaments of the brain-lobes concerned. Here we have a direct and coherent explanation, on a strongly physiological basis, of that aesthetic longing for symmetry which is common to all mankind so far as general background (i.e., the shared experience of terrestrial origin and habitation) is concerned, but whose details differ amongst various races and individuals according to their respective local differences of immediate heritage and influence. The *material* of aesthetic standards let us concede is external, accidental, and variable. It is the *faculty* of inertia which causes standards to be formed of whatever material is offered, which is natural, fundamental, inherent, and constant. Harmony dominates the faculty because it is the moot universal, insistent, and outstanding principle in Nature as viewed by mammal primates in this particular part of space, and is therefore an environmental essential which cannot be violated without a physiological fatigue of certain nerves whose manifestations are psychological. This about sums my aesthetic position up—but be sure you do not mistake it for a vague endorsement of Mencken's. Hank assumes that the seat of all aesthetic pleasure is the obvious and elementary system of the five visible senses—i.e., that it is the actual organ of the ear which loves music and poetry, the tangible retina of the eye which enjoys architecture, sculpture, and painting, and so on. To me this is an inadequate and impossible explanation, hence I believe that the prime cause is a *cerebral habit*—physiological, of course, but not connected with the specialised nerve-groups serving the visible senses—which enjoys the confirmation, and resists the violation, of subtle environmental conditions to which its protoplasmic locale is sensitive in varying degree amongst individuals of varying fineness of organisation. This conclusion seems almost inescapable when we reflect on the supremacy of harmonic pattern in all aesthetic feelings, realising at the same time how little this abstract quality has to do with purely sensory comfort or pleasure, or with any definite titillation of the complex system of general emotional nerve-action. So much for theory. In practice, we must continue to recognise common and visible aesthetic preferences as highly complex phenomena, into which sentiment and sensuousness enter largely. Indeed, I fancy that amongst commonplace or coarse-grained people nearly all alleged artistic feelings can be traced to bodily and emotional gratification.

But the subtler quality exists, none the less; and as we ascend in the scale of mental calibre we behold it as sharing increasingly in all aesthetic perceptions.

Yes—I'm sure you've undermined Heinie right and proper, and don't see why your argument can't go straight into the book 'as is'. Just now I'm lending H. L.'s essay and your epistle to Little Belknap—with whom I constantly discuss aesthetick theory—but I've told him to return them, and will restore them to you if you wish them back—as I imagine you will. Incidentally—the extract from your book gives me a very enthusiastic notion of its style and scope. I shall probably recommend it to all my poetick satellites when it is published—just as I now invariably recommend Brander Matthews' "Study of Versification." But say! Thinking of old Brander made me recall another *quadruple rhyme* for you! My own, at that—and not a perfect one, nor really quadruple if the constituent lines be taken as pentameters. (It's heroick verse). It's quadruple—legitimately—only if its couplet be regarded as tetrameter. I pulled it at the end of my "Simple Speller's Tale" in that first fearful and wonderful loose-leaf, blue-paper *Conservative* of April 1915, and it reads as follows:

> But why on us your angry hand or wrath use?
> We do but ape Professor Brander Matthews![14]

As for "Dolly Gray"[15]—it referred to the Spanish War but was slightly subsequent. Songs didn't fate quite so quickly then—there was something of a genuine folk-strain in the naive old ballads which modern trash utterly lacks—and "Dolly" wasn't a real chestnut until '02 or so. Ah, those gems of yesterday! Can't I hear the overture of "The Burgomaster"[16] once more—week of Oct. 20, 1900, Providence Opera House . . . . . and Pete Dailey singing "My Sunflower Sue" and "Cindy" . . . . . ah, what a cake-walk that was! There's an exercise in scansion for you, which overleaps all the hexameter doctrines in Aristotle's "Poeticks"—not a word forgotten after these twenty-six years (for Dailey's "Hodge, Podge, and Co." came in '01.)[17]

> Cindy, Ah dreams about yo', Cindy,
> Cain't lib without yo', Cindy,
> How can ah doubt yo' w'en yo' smahles awn me-e-e-e-e
> Ah longs to wed yo', honey,
> Take mah heart, my lahfe, mah money,
> Only promise yo' will be mah Ci-i-i-i-i-in-dee!

And all the others—"When the Blue Sky Turns to Gold",[18] "When the Harvest Moon is Shining",[19] "Jessie Dear",[20] "The Blue and the Grey",[21] "Just as the Sun Went Down",[22] "Creole Belles",[23] "Georgia Camp Meeting",[24] "Smoky Mokes",[25] "Coon, Coon, Coon . . . ah wish mah colour would fade—Coon, Coon, Coon, ... ah'd lahk a different shade! Coon, coon, coon . . . . mo'nin', nan-haht an' noon; ah wish ah was a whaht-man 'stead ob a Coon, Coon, Coon!"²⁶ "Oh, Oh, Miss-a Phoe-boe-boe-bee . . . . . don't nebbah-ha le-he-heabe me . . . tell me yo's mah honey gal, an' true to me yo' ebbah, ebbah, ebbah bee . . . . an' oh, oh, say-a yo-ho'll be true; fo' oh, oh, Phoe-boe-boe-boe-boe-boe-boe-boe-boe-bee!"²⁷ "The Bird in a Gilded Cage"²⁸ . . . . and oh, Man! that smashing song hit that struck town in November '03 . . . . . . "Bedelia"!²⁹ Golden days! And yet some folks think "You're the Flower of My Heart, Sweet Adeline"³⁰ is a venerable folk song . . . . base tonsorio-choral parvenu, which wasn't out till the spring of '04!! "Oh, Josepine-a, mah Jo . . . . . don't tease yo' ba-ba-by so; ef dat's yo' oh, oh, oh, speak, dear, an' let me know" . . . . . alas! there's not a hurdy-gurdy today that could grind out the lively Dorick melody as the products of G. Molinari, Milano, used to grind 'em out in 1900!³¹

YOUR-oour-obur-obdr—OBD'T—sbdt—srdt—S'RV'T—Hink—Ill—Luck.

Notes

1. Alfred, Lord Tennyson, "Morte d'Arthur" (1838), l. 31 (and elsewhere).
2. These four lines were cited in Richard Green Parker, *Aids to English Composition* (New York: Harper & Brothers, 1845), 237. The first line can be found in an anonymous poem (signed "M."), "Addressed to a Branch of the River Avon," *Monthly Magazine* 20 (1 October 1805): 235; the other three appear to be of Parker's invention.
3. Cited in Parker 238.
4. Cited in Parker 238.
5. The above three lines are cited in Parker 238.
6. Albert Harkness, American classical scholar, educator, and professor of Greek at Brown University. HPL owned his *Latin Grammar for Schools and Colleges*.
7. The lines are from Euripides, Fragment 408 (χρὴ for χρε and ἄγειν for εχειν in Euripides). It is unclear where HPL found this fragment.
8. Horace, *Epodes* 17.53.
9. The first novel of George Eliot (pseudonym of Mary Ann Evans [1819–1880]), published in 1859.
10. "A Line o' Type or Two" was a popular column in the *Chicago Tribune*, edited by Bert Leston Taylor until his death in 1921, followed by Richard Henry Little.
11. HPL refers to an article by H. L. Mencken (HPL jokes about Mencken's German heritage by referring to his first name, Henry, as Heinrich). The article in question is unknown. Mencken wrote occasionally on aesthetics; possibly the reference is to "The American: His Ideas of Beauty," *Smart Set* 41, No. 1 (September 1913): 91–98.
12. Remy de Gourmont (1858–1915), *Philosophic Nights in Paris*, tr. Isaac Goldberg (Boston: John W. Luce, 1920), 178: "There are beautiful things, but there is no such thing as Beauty: that is an abridged expression." The work is a selection from Gourmont's *Promenades philosophiques* (1905).
13. Constantin Brâncuşi (1876–1957), Romanian sculptor, painter and photographer. In October 1926, U.S. customs officials refused to recognize his sculpture *Bird of Space*

as a work of art, and imposed the standard tariff for objects manufactured of metal: 40 percent of the sale price, or $240 (approximately $2,400 today).

14. HPL only gave Matthews's initials in the poem.

15. See MWM 30n3.

16. *The Burgomaster* (1900), a musical comedy (book and lyrics by Frank S. Pixley, music by Gustav Luders). "My Sunflower Sue" and "Cindy" were songs in this work.

17. *Hodge, Podge & Co.* (1900), a musical comedy (words by Walter Ford; music by John W. Bratton and Harry Pleon; adapted from the German by George V. Hobart), in which Peter F. Dailey starred.

18. "When the Blue Sky Turns to Gold" (1901), words and music by Thurland Chattaway.

19. "When the Harvest Moon Is Shining on the River" (1904), words by Arthur J. Lamb, music by S. R. Henry.

20. "Jessie Dear" (1901), words by Howard Graham, music by Harry von Tilzer.

21. "The Blue and the Gray" (1900), words and music by Paul Dresser.

22. "Just as the Sun Went Down" (1899), words and music by Lyn Udall.

23. "Creole Belles" (1901), words by George Sidney, music by J. Bodewalt Lampe.

24. "At a Georgia Camp Meeting" (1899), words and music by Kerry Mills.

25. "Smoky Mokes" (1899), words and music by Abe Holzmann.

26. "Coon, Coon, Coon" (1901), words by Gene Jefferson, music by Leo Friedman.

27. "Oh, Miss Phoebe" (1900), words by Andrew B. Sterling, music by Harry von Tilzer.

28. "The Bird in a Gilded Cage" (1900), words by Arthur J. Lamb, music by Harry von Tilzer.

29. "Bedelia" (1903), words by William Jerome, music by Jean Schwartz. HPL discusses the song in detail in letters to J. Vernon Shea. See *Letters to J. Vernon Shea, Carl F. Strauch, and Lee McBride White*, ed. S. T. Joshi and David E. Schultz (New York: Hippocampus Press, 2016), 196–97, 229–30.

30. "(You're the Flower of My Heart,) Sweet Adeline," words by Richard H. Gerard, music by Harry Armstrong. The song dates to 1903, not the spring of 1904 as HPL states.

31. G. Molinari & Sons, a firm based in Brooklyn, manufactured barrel organs, music boxes, and other items.

[33] [AN, *Marginalia*]

[Postmarked c. 12 August 1927,
Providence, R.I.

The law, despite its show of awe, a soft thing to infract is,
And crime, mere theory in its time, too soon is put in practice!
My soul, now on its downward roll, in crafty scheming romps on,
And ne'er will rest till I can best a Bickford or a Thompson.[1]

Notes

1. HPL had wagered MWM that two letters could be sent for the price of one. He steamed open a letter he received, crossed out his house address, addressed it to himself, now "% M. W. Moe / University W.M.C.A., Madison Wisconsin," enclosing a card with the verses above. Now published as "[On Cheating the Post Office]."

[34]   [AHT]

Oct. 6, 1927

All Hail!

  As for the trip . . . . . oh, boy! Hot dawg! I haven't had such a good time since the golden 1900's! I spent five days with Cook in Athol, and was tooken around to all the adjacent mountain vistas and agrestick landscapes—AND DEERFIELD! Man, them blasphemously primordial ellums and unwholesomely archaick houses! It's all there, kid—every inch what it's crack'd up to be! But the big trip in the Culinary chariot was the northward one—Vermont as far north as Bellows Falls, and then N.H. to Lake Sunapee. It was on this jaunt that we stopped to discover that last of nineteenth century Novanglia's Puritan Pleiade—Arthur Henry Goodenough, Yeoman, unspoil'd amidst his native rural shades, and favour'd nursling of th' Aonian Maids. Honustly, 'bo, I never seen no country niftier than the wild hills west of Brattleboro, where this guy hangs out. Brat itself is the diplodoccus' gold molar, with its works of pristine Yankee survival, but once you climb the slopes toward the setting sun you're in another and an elder world. All allegiance to modern and decadent things is cast off—all memory of such degenerate excrescences as steel and steam, tar and concrete roads, and the vulgar civilisation that bred them. Evoë! Evoë! We wind rapt and wondering over elder and familiar ribbons of rutted whiteness which curl past alluring valleys and traverse old wooden bridges in the lee of green slopes. The nearness and intimacy of the little domed hills become almost breath-taking—their steepness and abruptness hold nothing in common with the humdrum, standardised world we know, and we cannot help feeling that their outlines have some strange and almost-forgotten meaning, like vast hieroglyphs left by a rumoured titan race whose glories live only in rare, deep dreams. We climb and plunge fantastically as we thread this hypnotic landscape. Time has lost itself in the labyrinths behind, and around us stretch only the flowering waves of faery. Tawdriness and commerce, futile activity and urban smoke, greasy filling-stations and ugly billboards, are not there—but instead, the recaptured beauty of vanished centuries; the hoary groves, the untainted pastures hedg'd with gay blossoms, and the small brown farmsteads nestling amidst huge trees beneath vertical precipices of fragrant brier and meadow-grass. Even the sunlight assumes a supernal glamour, as if some special atmosphere or exhalation mantled the whole region. There is nothing like it save in the magick vistas that sometimes form the backgrounds of Italian primitives. Sodoma and Leonardo saw such expanses, but only in the distance and thro' the vaultings of Renaissance arcades. We rove at will thro' the midst of the picture; and find in its necromancy a thing we have known or inherited, and for which we have always been vainly searching. At the heart of this weirdly beautiful Arcadia Vermont's gentle poet dwells. Good ol' Arty! We found him in overalls and a bristle of bucolick whiskerage; but he insisted on a ceremonious toilet before greeting his distinguished guests, and appeared later in all the radiance of a rusty black Prince-Albert, misfit collar, and gay tie with enormous opal pin in its northern hemisphere. Sunday best or nothin', b'gosh! And what a delectable atavism the old boy is! Old New England forever! His wife, an ex-teacher, and his prepossessing son Rupert, have seen a little of the outer world; but Squire Goodenough knows only the paternal Sabine farm. He has never set eyes on a city, and goes but once or twice a year to quaint Brattleboro, three miles distant. In speech, thought, and gesture he reflects only the days that were, the simple Saturnian reign of our fathers, when primal Virtue hung o'er Tempë's slope, and swains and ploughmen dwelt in faith and hope. One with his hereditary hills and groves, with the spreading, venerable trees and the antient peaked roofs of the vine-bank'd cottages, he sounds the elder strain, and sings as the last of the long line of Puritan Oracles. Tilling his ancestral hearth in the good old way, and keeping alive beside his daily hearth the well-lov'd thoughts and customs of our Golden Age, he is vastly more than a retrospective teller of bygone tales. Alone amongst the surviving choir he truly leads the pastoral life he breathes; so that we need not wonder at the flawless authenticity of his Dorick reed. He has prolong'd our old New-England in himself, and his stately charm and genial hospitality are as truly poems—if not more so—as anything his oaten pipe could sound 'neath beechen shade. Happy Tityrus![1] Lovely beyond words is the realm whereover the poet wields his rural sway. The antient house on the hillside, embower'd in greenery and shadow'd by a lone leafy monarch peopled by the feathery train; the dream-stirring slope to the westward, where earth's beauty melts into the cosmick glory of sunset; the narrow, beckoning road, the outspread, dew-glistening meadows, and the hint of spectral woodlands and valleys in the background—all these mark out a perfect poet's seat, and cause us to thank Fate that for once in history a man and his setting are well-matched. Cook took several pictures with a brand-new camera he had bought that morning, and I'll send you a set as soon as he furnishes me with some promised duplicates. I know you'll enjoy an intimate glimpse of the half-fabulous old faun whose simple strains you have seen for a quarter-century in the piquant pages of amateurdom. Northward from Brattleboro the charm still holds. There are glorious sweeps of vivid valley where great cliffs rise, New-England's virgin granite showing grey and austere thro' the verdure that scales the crests. There are gorges where untamed streams leap, bearing down toward the bordering

Connecticut the unimagined secrets of a thousand pathless peaks. Narrow, half-hidden roads bore their way thro' solid, luxuriant masses of forest, among whose primal trees whole armies of fauns and dryads lurk. Archaick cover'd bridges of a sort wholly extinct in Rhode-Island linger fearsomely out of the past in pockets of the hills, and here and there a summit bears a tiny hamlet of trim, clean old houses and steeples that time has never been able to sully. Idyllick Vermont! Fit cradle for Imperial power, and native seat of the sturdy Consul C. Culigius Calvinus, whom Pollux bless! I'm writing up my general impressions of the province for the new amateur Walter J. Coates of North Montpelier, whose magazine—*Driftwind*—is devoted to Vermont and its literature.[2]

Athol itself is no slouch—a delightful hill-and-valley town of 10,000, with decent architecture and pleasing prospects on every hand. I ascended a majestick eminence west of the village, and enjoy'd a highly agreeable vista of outspread roofs and spires, the circumjacent countryside, and the distant glint of Lake Rahonta amongst its enfolding summits. From Athol to Boston I had a magnificent stage-coach ride thro' quaint Massachusetts towns, and on the following day rejoiced in an auspicious northward journey to Portland. And what a pippin Portland is! On the whole, aside from Providence, I like it the best of all the sizeable cities I've ever seen . . . . . and how an old Y-hound like you would rave over the immaculate, just-completed GEORGIAN Y! Portland, antiently call'd Falmouth, is situated upon a loftily elevated peninsula stretching southward into Casco Bay; and is adorn'd with the choicest gifts of Nature and of art. Its maritime bluffs are finely developed as promenades, whilst its streets are so thickly lin'd with the unslain titans of the primal grove, that it will merit the affectionately colloquial appellation of "the Forest City." On every hand are the most majestick panoramas imaginable; those of the harbour to the south, with its antient forts and lighthouses, and of the outspread country to the west, culminating in the distantly glimps'd White Mountains, being deserving of the most spirited panegyrick. I beheld all these things, not only from the promenades, but from an antient observation-tower on Munjoy Hill, put up in 1807 for purposes of marine signalling. The town itself, alas, hath lost many of its original Georgian buildings; but enough remain—especially in the elder parts toward the river—to preserve the most lively memories of better times. Both the birthplace and early residence of Prof. Longfellow, once a noted poet, are in good condition and open for inspection as musaeums—the residence being the better kept and managed.[3] The birthplace is a square wooden house built in 1784, once on the shore, but now in a slum fronting the Grand Trunk station and railway yards, built on made land. The other house is of brick, built in 1786 and enlarged in 1815—now sandwiched in between a Keith theatre and a business block on the main thoroughfare of the town. With Portland as a base I took several absorbing side-trips—to Portland Head Light, (1791) the sleepy colonial suburbs of Yarmouth and Strondwater, and the widely celebrated White Mountains of New-Hampshire. The latter were very impressive—especially so since I had never beheld real mountains before. In Crawford Notch the mystery of the overshadowing steeps became acute and portentous, whilst the outspread Presidential Range as glimpsed from Bretton Woods is something to dream about. I ascended Mt. Washington by cogwheel railway; and when cut off from the living world below by the bleak mists of the summit, could sense the terror of outer space in the cold, cosmic winds that swept from nowhere to nowhere. Some experience!

Well, from Portland (after three nights at that exquisite new Georgian Y in Forest Ave.) I descended the coast by stage coach, reaching again a stamping-ground more familiar to me. Good old Portsmouth—which I first saw in 1923, on the day after I bade you a reluctant adieu at Bostonium's South Station. The old place was just the same—without a doubt the most unchangedly colonial of any large town in the United States. I retraced all those paths made familiar to me four years agone, and enlarged my radius by a hike to the famous Benning Wentworth "mansion" at Little Harbour—scene of the late Prof. Longfellow's w. k. verses.[4] The place was an atrocious disappointment—but I'm glad I saw it (which I'll bet is more than H. W. L. ever did!) as a matter of record. Postero die ad Newburyportum profeci—striking that venerable burg in the afternoon and making the main rounds before dark. Old Newburyport can give Portsmouth a run for its money in the matter of archaism, and the utter, hushed stagnation of the place is impressive and unparallell'd. It ain't never ben the same senct "Lord" Timothy Dexter croak'd![5] The main business section is precisely the same as it was a century and more ago, the omnipresent edifices being shapely brick blocks put up just after the Great fire of 1811. South of the central district are marvellous slum labyrinths of narrow, unpaved, sidewalkless streets with antediluvian gambrel-roof'd houses—streets absolutely unalter'd from their pre-Revolutionary state, and elsewhere to be rivall'd only in archaick Portsmouth. After soaking up all of this dump, and pumping 'em dry at the Historical Society, I took a side-trip to old Newbury (and got a peach of a view from a weird rural hill) and set off for Haverhill to call on good old Tryout Smithy. The Y there is the rottenest I've yet struck—no real building, but scatter'd amongst a lot of seedy Victorian joints. Newburyport's—donated by a *Providence* man—is a palace by comparison . . . . . although intrinsically it's nothing to erupt into quantitative dactyls over. Haverhill sure is quite a city—it looks as big as Providence, tho' it's only a fifth as large. As for nice old Smiffkins—believe me, he's a hardy perennial! The gnarled old faun hasn't aged a day in the five years since I saw him last, but is the same eternal boy . . . . . tough and spry, and deep in his printing, hiking, and stamp-collecting, tho' he turns seventy-five on the twenty-fourth of this month! Long may he wave—content amidst his native bow'rs! He is, as I have told you aforetime, stone deaf; but on this occasion I made good conversational progress with pad and pencil, instead of shouting in his ear as I did in 1921 and 1922. I shall pay him another visit next summer—unfading genius of the untam'd grove! Returning to Newburyport by another route, I entrain'd for archaick Ipswich; where I went over the awesomely antient and collaterally* ancestral Whipple homestead, a relique of the peaked, pre-Georgian, house-of-VII-gables period.[6] Thence I proceeded to Essex, where I hopped a Gloucester stage-coach. And at Gloucester—oh, Boy! Maybe I didn't lap up the living residue of Novanglia's seagoing picturesqueness! I didn't half do the place justice in my former visit of 1922, but this trip I left nothing to the imagination. Do I know Gloucester? Be yourself, buddy! It's a great old port, and I took in both interiors and exteriors. The old mansions in Middle St. are superb, and I went all over the Sargent–Murray–Gilman house—1768. In side-trips I explored Annisquam and Rockport—the latter ineffably quaint—and renew'd my antient acquaintance with Magnolia's titan cliffs. From Gloucester I proceeded southward thro' Manchester and Beverly to Salem—good old Salem, whose venerable ways and lovely doorways you cannot but remember—and thence cross'd over to ever-alluring Marblehead, apex of surviving colonialism and home of my spirit. There I wander'd about the time-hallow'd lanes and alleys—the same yesterday, today, and forever, and drank in the aura of surviving history. But I don't need to tell you about Marblehead, with its glory of sea and sky and antiquity—you have seen it, even if youse guys—Carbo, Bozo Sandy, and Mocrates—did line up on that bank-wall down in Barnegat behind the hill, and refuse to let Grandpa take you on a real walk after the introductory practice was over! Yea, 'bo, it's the same ol' Marblehead, and I shed a tear over the cenotaph I have erected on Old Burying Hill to the memory of that scion of the house of Waterman whose gold and caoutchouc[7] skeleton lies bleaching somewhere . . . . . somewhere . . . . . on those shifting sands and frowning cliffs. Memorials to the lost are not unaccustom'd sights in that venerable town, so many of whose sons have never return'd from the cryptic sea. After a flaming and mystical sunset had lighted western windows with ethereal flame, and the red and gold had subsided into twilight's violet wonder, I began that series of consecutive stage-coach journeys which deposited me at mine own humble hearth not far from Friday midnight, the second of Sept. It was a great old spree, I'll reveal to the astigmatick planet; and if I haven't laid in enough accumulated imagery and picturesqueness to last me thro' the winter, I sure am a glutton for sights!

    Yr obt hble Servt
        Lo.

---

*I thought this joint was *directly* ancestral till a coupla weeks ago, when the young genealogist Talman induced me to get out and overhaul my dust-cover'd family archives. I then found that my Whipples were related to those W's only back in Norfolk, England.

Notes

1. Tityrus is a shepherd cited in Virgil's *Eclogues*.
2. Much of the above paragraph was reworked into the essay "Vermont—A First Impression."
3. Longfellow's birthplace is at the corner of Fore and Hancock Streets in Portland. The other house is now called the Wadsworth–Longfellow house (1785–86), at 489 Congress Street.
4. Now called the Coolidge-Wentworth Mansion Historic Site (1750) at 375 Little Harbor Road in Portsmouth, NH. It was the home of Benning Wentworth (1696–1770), governor of the province of New Hampshire (1741–66). Longfellow's poem "Lady Wentworth" (in *Tales of a Wayside Inn*) deals with the house.
5. "Lord" Timothy Dexter (1747–1806), as he was known to his contemporaries, was an eccentric American businessman and author of *A Pickle for the Knowing Ones* (1805), who dubbed himself "first in the East, the first in the West, and the greatest philosopher in the known world." He was a source for the character Obed Marsh in "The Shadow over Innsmouth."
6. The John Whipple house (1677), at 53 S. Main Street in Ipswich. Captain John Whipple (1625–1685) was HPL's great-great-great-great-great-great-grandfather.
7. Unvulcanized natural rubber.

[35] [ALS, JHL]

Decr. 13, 1928

Magister Omnis Sapientiae:—

I am indebted to you, Sir, for an exceeding agreeable session deriv'd from both sides of the ochraceous pages which reach'd me not long ago. Lud's death, but I had no notion your reading-book was to be such a bibliotheca in parva![1] 'Tis not enough you put in half the good reading of the ages—besides that, you must needs supplement it with Mocraticall booktests & enlightening exercises till the result is not only a young gentleman's compleat library, but an entire liberal education as well! Sink me, Sir, but I regret I had no such aids to learning when I was young. At this rate, what sort of young prodigies will the schools be turning out a generation hence? I hope the Mocratick tests may receive proper identification *as such* in the preface, so that the book will in some manner form an advertisement for the quizzes. Likewise, I hope that your colleagues are seeing fit to obtain Mocratick tests for the *other* volumes of the series: a thing they really ought to do* (save perchance in the very lowest primers for small infants) not only in the interest of uniformity, but in the interest of good education as well. The more I inspect

---

*notwithstanding the paſsage in "Say's" letter which seems to imply that he thinks the 9th grade the earliest fit for such auxiliary devices.

your table of contents, the more I am mov'd to admiration of the extent & variety of the coming work. Gad's blood, but I never heard of so great a range of writers, old & new, drawn upon for the for the instruction of youth; tho' I myself fed early upon the solid compilations of Abner Alden, Lindley Murray, & others of my day who furnish'd decent & ample reflections of Dr. Johnson, Mr. Addison, Mr. Pope, & the generality of good writers in prose & verse. I am given a very humble sensation of ignorance when I behold the nurslings of the future drawing draughts of intellectual nectar from sources as widely separated as Don Marquis, Old Italian Tale, Firdausi, William Beebe, & A. Cherry-Garrard—none of which I had ever heard about in good old 1900. I note with much interest the appended comments of "Say",[2] but cannot affirm that I agree with all of them. However, I trust he has not proved a great hindrance to you in your labours. I am inform'd, that "Say" & his staff have approached our honest old friend Everett McNeil concerning the use of one or more of his short tales for the readers. Good old Mac knows not what books they are wish'd for, but I presume 'twould be those of a more elementary nature than that which you are preparing. Let us hope that the delay in the iſsuance of your volume will not be too great.

I am even more interested—because of the more originally Mocratick nature of the body of the work—in your forthcoming "Doorways"; the pluralisation of whose title is permissible enough, though I scarcely think it was actually necessary. Pray don't allow any other concernments to hinder the completion of this treatise—yet on t'other hand don't hurry it out if additional delay wou'd give you time to incorporate added matter or new & illuminating devices in the way of imagery tests or such. I lately came upon the inclos'd review of a book by one Baldwin, which wou'd open up rich paths of study in the matter of antient & mediaeval verse, (a topick we so extensively discuſs'd last year) had you not decided to omit such antiquarian considerations from your volume. As you see, the work review'd is one upon mediaeval rhetorick & prosody; but there is mention'd *another* book by the same author—"Antient Rhetorick & Poetick"—in which you wou'd indubitably find a full & masterly treatment of all those points—claſsical hexameter & iambicks, & quantity versus accent—which I so amateurishly spoke upon, out of my meagre & fragmentary layman's knowledge. Now I wou'd advise you to employ them in the construction of your present treatise; for truly, they cou'd not but enrich your familiarity with the whole history of poesie in such a way as to make you a more aſsur'd master & expositor of the subject. I have not my self beheld them, but all the indications in the review point to their remarkable excellence. "B. C. C." is Benjamin C. Clough, Esq[r], Profeſsor of Greek in Brown-University.[3]

And now, Sir, permit me to congratulate you upon your newly discover'd system of *primary image cards;* which I believe cannot fail to be of vast aid in habituating the novice to the anfractuosities of poetick symbolism. It seems to me that "Say" is correct in believing there will be a ready market for them, & I trust you will lose no time in devising & publishing the contemplated set of an hundred. They ought to serve not only in paedagogy, but in social converse as well; as a drawing-room diversion akin to the crofs-word puzzle, the questionnaire, & the institution of this-to-thatting. One might devise a parlour game upon this basis, with fixt rules & scores bas'd on correctnefs of analysis & interpretation. In such a contest, I wou'd not hesitate to award the consolation-prize to that youth who conjur'd a brace of evicted wanderers out of a freezing, agitant, & fragrant breeze! I still wonder how extensive was the investigation thro' which you absolv'd this young gentleman of satyrick subtlety! Pray let me know how this device turns out, as tested by the intellects of your tender charges. The adult senior ought to furnish a good beginning, tho' the irresponsible generality of pupildom will doubtlefs form a more exacting & characteristick field for experiment.

I am gratify'd to learn, that the Mocraticall book-tests are still in wide demand; & believe they will become still more universal in the course of time & judicious advertising. Their propos'd use in studies other than English is indeed an opening of the most auspicious sort, & I doubt not but that their basick principle cou'd be adopted to a surprising diversity of purposes outside their originally conceiv'd radius. Truly, you have in your hands the nucleus of a great industry, which I trust the future will see develop'd to Gargantuan proportions. I am pleas'd to hear how well Mistrefs Caution Slicegood spoke of the tests at the Pf... atchew!.... Pfister banquet, & hope that her recommendation may produce a sure, even if slow, reaction in the conservative brains of her academick auditors. I am astonisht to hear of the *suocephalick*[4] pertinacity with which the W. D. tutorial train resist the boon you have devis'd for their easement, & griev'd to reflect that the departmental chamber is amongst the obtuse dissenters. But sure, you are here encountering only a sample of that fate which confronts all innovators, from Socrates to Copernicus, & Galileo to Einstein! But the dawning good sense of the nation at large, puts to shame the angustious pusillanimity of the Zythopolitan[5] potentates; & I feel confident that posterity will vindicate & enthrone, what Hesperio-Schismatick[6] dogmatism now regards with reserve. Permit me, by the way, to congratulate you upon that self-pofsefsion & ready wit which enabled you at one stroke to save the day at the preceptorial lecture session, & to announce to the world your discovery of the poetick image-card. I hope to hear of great results from your point of view—& I think there is no doubt but that the results were great from the point of view of the programme-arranger.

And now, Sir, permit me to extend my sincerest sympathy concerning Mrs. Moe's talarial fracture.[7] I can imagine the disastrous nature of the event; both as regards the pain of the actual sufferer, & as regards the disruptive transference of domestick burthens. But lud, Sir, you ought not to let the jentacular responsibility remain permanent! Zeus knows you are weigh'd down enough with your usual work—which is more than two men ought to do anyway! Let us hope you will in time find a tactful way of retreating from the trying innovation—tho' not, of course, till the distaff side of the household is fully able & actively eager to effect the re-transference. I am glad to hear that the injury is mending in a thoroughly satisfactory fashion, & hope that the tramway company can be held fully liable. Tram-cars, Sir, are implements of the devil; & 'tis Heav'n's own revenge which is pushing them off the landskip in favour of resurgent stage-coaches. My mother was, in the year 1906, thrown to the floor of a car which started prematurely; & sustain'd a nervous shock whose effects never wholly left her. The company made a moderate settlement out of court, after a litigation had been prepar'd against them.

Of the progreſs of Οἱ Μίκροι Μόκρατοι I always hear with acute gratification, & it does not surprise me that Robertulus hath become the scientifick mainstay of the archangelical loud-speaker. His recent feat with *quadratick equations* turns me sick with envy & humiliation; [?] for it was at just about this stage of mathematicks—back in dear old 1906—that I finally saw I had no natural head for figures; & that I wou'd be wasting time if I attempted to continue my ambition to be a profeſsor of astronomy. And to think a smart little atom that I held on my knee from the South Station to Cambridge five years ago, hath become a daily & facile practitioner of that which finally convinc'd the Old Gentleman he was floor'd . . . . in those dim, far-off days before the atom himself was born or dream'd of! Ah, me, what smart children there be nowadays! They've left Grandpa behind altogether! I hope that Robertulus & Azrafil betwixt 'em will make such radio history that the daintiest devices of today will soon be fit for James Ferdinand Morton's museum—yet to think that, at the same time, the child remains an appreciative authority upon P. Maro & Q. Flaccus![8] That damn me, Sir, is *brains!* I t'other day found use for Flaccus myself, in sympathising with a correspondent who fretted at the growing use of *garlick* in our ordinaries, as introduc'd by cursed dago immigrants. Get Robertulus to read you the third Epode, addreſs'd to C. Cilnius Maecenas.[9] I trust, by the way, that he may engage himself pleasantly & profitably with the Extension Division work, unleſs indeed an alteration in family fortunes takes him elsewhere.

As for this poſsible alteration—why, sink me, Sir, but I believe it wou'd be a monstrous wise move to quit the high for the normal field![10] You have, besides your aptitude in literary subjects, a phenomenal knack & knowledge in the principles & practice of pedagogy; so that it is truly a cursed waste of brains to have you applying your special ability to your own work only, when you are so manifestly fitted to disseminate the teaching art to others. Your plan to take an examination at Chicago is highly to be commended; & I hope emphatically that your technical lack of an advanced string of more or leſs meaningless letters will not affect your chances with a hide-bound & myopick board of judices. But sure, it wou'd be delightful to complete the high-degree process at the University, & I hope to Pegāna that you will do it unless all doors are freely open'd to you without it.

I shou'd, Sir, be vastly beholden to you, were you to send me the Junior magazines of which you have from time to time made mention; & will promise their safe return in such an event. I am not insensible of the young genius which frequently shews itself in things of the sort, & do not doubt but that you have amongst your nursling prodigies many a future *Atlantick* & *Harper's* contributor. *The Eclectick*, I vow, must be a compilation worthy of a place in any gentleman's or institution's library.

Yes—I recall your occasional mention of the monthly poem comments; for was it not in connexion with these that the incidents of *Ibid*,[11] & of the confusion of the deceased helpmeet & the dismantled stanelizabetha,[12] occurr'd? I believe that, after the suitable elimination, a group of such poems with student comment wou'd be admirably deserving of permanent binding as a book—& eventually of actual professional publication. Sir, you have a future before you! A man of ideas, by Gad, a man of ideas!

As for this new definition of a school as a place for the self-education (with minor tutorial suggestions!) of the young—well, Sir, it sounds damn'd smooth, but I was born a cynick! A devilish hard cynick, Sir! Shew me the brats that go to school eager to fill themselves & their playmates with learning, & I'll shew you a monstrous small fraction of the smiling morning faces that look trustfully into yours each day! But it sounds well, & mayhap the young rascals will study & behave the better for thinking that their rever'd masters believe it of them. Anyway, if the conceit works, it proves its worth most abundantly—especially to one whom like yourself, (I speak on antient Kleicomolo evidence) professes a pragmatical philosophy. Good luck with your free-lunch counter—noble relique of pre-war liberty & Zythopolitan fame—& may the tables & their leaders become equally famous as archetypes of a broader & finer educational order! Pray keep me inform'd of the progress of the innovation.

And now, Sir, let me thank you most exceedingly for that pleasing Old Testament outline, which I shall paste with gratitude in that paternal bible whose literary worth hath ever kept it upon my nefandous atheistical shelves. Sir, I wish you all success with the fraternity of Gideons—how adroit you were to give them a free mention (albeit not in your largest type) in your second column! Actually, I conceive the outline to be of the utmost possible value to the scriptural student; insomuch as it reduces to a coherent system a loose congeries of disjointed & repetitious matter out of which it is almost impossible for a novice to extract a connected & orderly narrative. I trust you will not fail, in time, to provide an homologous clue to the jumbled gospels of the New Testament—a work of considerable interest in the King James translation, notwithstanding the vile vulgar Greek of the original.

As for mine own concernments—'Zounds, Sir, but the short & simple annals of the poor sound but anticlimactick after a brilliant chronicle of ambitious progression! I have not, in truth, done one curst thing that merits recording since last I writ you; so I can only say that all goes along as usual from day to day, that my elder aunt is slowly getting better, & that the recent autumn hath been the finest I have known in years, so that all thro' September & October I took my work out to the antient woods & groves north of the town on almost every clear afternoon. Yes—& I made one trip—incredibile dictu—as late as the 16th of November last! I have also made many trips of architectural exploration around the venerable town itself; discovering regions & vistas I never beheld before, & renewing my pleasure in those already familiar to me. The charm & beauty of Old Providence never lose their hold; & were you to visit me today, I cou'd treat you to a much fuller & quainter course of sights than that on which I regal'd you five years ago. For example—I have come upon an altogether unsuspected country lane which winds up the ancient hill by the falls of the Moshaſsuck (where John Smith built his grist mill in 1646) not a quarter of a mile from this very house, yet which I never knew of prior to this September! From one point along this lane (which is call'd *Bark St.*,[13] & which is lin'd on one side by abandon'd gambrel-roof'd houses of the vintage of 1740 or 1750) there is obtainable a glamorous view of Smith's Hill—with the dome of the marble State House & the tower & transept gable of St Patrick's Popish church in singularly felicitous juxtaposition above the treetops—which reminds one of the citadel of some fascinating Renaissance hill town, & which cannot be obtain'd from any other point. It so overwhelm'd me with an aesthetick extasy when first I glimps'd it, that I was impell'd to exclaim out loud, & whip forth my tatter'd note book to make a crude sketch. Then later, I told of it to an attendant at the local art club; in the hope that he might paſs on the information to some artist capable of making proper use of the scene. I will here endeavour to shew, in my clumsy manner, what so poignantly enraptur'd me, & prompted so many fascinated revisitations.

I might mention, that this same art club lately hous'd an exhibit which proves that I am not alone in viewing Old Providence with an enraptur'd eye. The exhibit, of which I enclose a catalogue, was of drawings & etchings by one Henry J. Peck;[14] & reveal'd the archaick loveliness of the antient town in such a way as to excite the acutest phases of my commingled envy & admiration. This artist, when he looks at the story'd scene, beholds the same cryptick overtones of brooding elder magick that I behold—& happily unlike me, has the divine faculty of transferring his vision to paper. Lud, Sir, but what views he did have on display! Huddles of ancient roofs, vistas of grass-grown colonial lanes & Georgian flights of railed steps, glimpses of tarry ghosts along the Indies-dreaming waterfront . . . . . Gad sink me, but what wou'd I not give for that lucky rascal's power to put Old Providence on paper! I had the honour of meeting him in person, & told him, I wou'd not be satisfy'd till he had publisht a book of his collected urban sketches. The whole exhibition reaffirm'd my steady conviction, that Providence is one of the best surviving of the large colonial seaports of New-England. No such variety of pure Georgian scenes cou'd ever be cull'd, for example, in Boston. The drawing reproduc'd in the catalogue is #30 of the exhibit—the antient inn-yard of the Franklin Tavern (circa 1770) on College Hill—one of that row of venerable houses which I photograph'd on the day I was there with you in 1923. Providence has four or five of these inn-yards still remaining, though even Philadelphia hath retain'd but one—that of the Black Horse Tavern in Second Street. (which, incidentally, is boarded up, whilst all the Providence specimens are open & permeable) Such arch'd yardways, when unlighted within, present the most spectral suggestions conceivable at night. There is one on the hill in antient Thomas St. on my diurnal way down town, which I have always regarded as the orifice of some fathomlefs dream-gulph of namelefs elder mystery. There stood always, until lately, a very venerable black cat as guardian of this primordial portal; a mystick beast for whom I had the greatest pofsible friendship. He belong'd to a market at the foot of the hill; & not knowing his specifick appelation, I was wont to call him simply "Old Man." He us'd to greet me with an hoarse, friendly *"eaow"*, & rub purringly about my aged ancles [*sic*] . . . . fellow-grandsires & colonial archaists! Often I fancy'd he wisht to invite me to primal nocturnal mysteries in the unfathom'd gulph beyond the yawning archway. Well, I was griev'd to find him absent one day from his accustom'd hill—& at his market I learn'd he was indeed no more. He had gone back to those palaeocosmick abysses out of which he came in a mystick kittenhood near a quarter of a century ago. Vae mihi—the old hill is not the same now, without Old Man! But I find I dream of him often, & only a few nights ago he came to me in sleep & rubbed purringly about my ancles & bade me (in his hoarse, friendly "eaow") follow him thro' the yawning arch into the nighted kingdom of Azathoth & Yog-Sothoth, Nug & Yeb, Bugg-Shoggog & Shub-Niggurath. On that occasion I awak'd too early to do so; but each time I retire I have hopes of another apparition, & am eagerly expectant of the ethereal marvels my black, vanish'd old friend will unfold to me. Good Old Man!

I am next week going to Boston to behold one of the finest new musaeum exhibits in the country—the just-open'd decorative wing of the Musaeum of Fine Arts, wherein are contain'd typical rooms transplanted from antient houses in England, France, & New-England, & extending in date from 1490 to 1805. The Pendleton House in Providence (that furnish'd colonial mansion attach'd to the art musaeum which I took you thro') will furnish you a vague notion of what it is like; & you can form a still better idea if you have ever seen pictures of the American Wing of the Metropolitan Musaeum in New-York. But this new affair surpasses anything of the kind ever before install'd in a place of publick resort, so that I am tingling with expectancy of the antiquarian feast before me. I shall go in the morning, & may spend the afternoon in that supreme home of my spirit—*Marblehead*—where I had so much trouble restraining you & Sandy & Eduardus Carbo from taking a longer walking itinerary from that which I had plann'd. I first saw Marblehead in the sunset under a shroud of snow, (on Dec. 17, 1922) & I am wishful to do so again. It has, under such conditions, so compleat an effacement of modern stigmata, & so happy a freedom from parasitick aestival sojourners, that it then seems even closer to the living past than it does under more genial skies & in more populous seasons.

And now, Sir, allow me to indulge in as much of the amiable pastime of trumpet-sounding as my pathetically meagre honours will permit me to do. I shall begin with enclosures. Note (a) the marked Meredith Janvier catalogue, (Gad, Sir, but I am become a collectors' item, worth all of fifteen shillings!)[15] & (b) the not less marked *Transcript* page shewing my proud listing by the omniscient O'Brien. Shou'd you care to amplify the (b) point, & see what mine Hibernian friend & pathron is afther sayin' av me in his "Best Short Stories of 1928," you have but to repair to the nearest bookstall or library & look alphabetically into the Biographical Roll of Honour in that volume. You will there find Grandpa writ up in 18 lines of the usual type, as conscientiously computed by that young friend whose omnivident literary glance marks him ever first to apprise me of any mention in the publick prints—August William Derleth of Sauk City (res.) & 823 W. Johnson St., Madison, (coll. soj.) in your own historick & cultivated Wisconsin Free State. But since your heavy duties may preclude an early glance at the volume, I will take it upon myself to transcribe here what Derleth says is recorded. I have not, incidentally, as yet beheld the printed reality myself. Attend, then—& glimpse Grandpa in a nutshell:

> Lovecraft, Howard Phillips. Was born of Old Yankee-English stock on August 20, 1890, in Providence, Rhode Island. Has always lived there except for very brief periods.* Educated in local schools and privately; ill health precluding university. Interested early in colour and mystery of things. More youthful products—verse and essays—voluminous, valueless,† mostly privately printed. Contributed astronomical articles to press 1906–18. Serious literary efforts now confined to tales of dream-life, strange shadow, and cosmic "outsideness," notwithstanding sceptical rationalism of outlook and keen regard for the sciences. Lives quietly and eventlessly, with classical and antiquarian tastes. Especially fond of atmosphere of Colonial New England. Favourite authors—in most intimate personal sense—Poe, Arthur Machen, Lord Dunsany, Walter de la Mare, Algernon Blackwood. Occupation—literary hack work including revision and special editorial jobs. Has contributed macabre fiction to *Weird Tales* regularly since 1923. Conservative in general perspective and method so far as compatible with phantasy in art and mechanistic materialism in philosophy. Lives in Providence, Rhode Island.

*Take that, Brooklyn!
†Byronick comma-for-and effect

But, Sir, the half of it is as yet unheard by you! Latest Derleth bulletins apprise me that my "Pickman's Model" is included in a list of third-quality American tales in the 1928 volume of the O. Henry Memorial Prize Short Stories. Not much of a distinction, but something for an insignificant novice.[16]

Residual current honours are purely anthological. I believe I last winter appris'd you, that my "Horror at Red Hook" had been included in the British weird anthology "Not at Night"—published by the now unhappily deceased London firm of Selwyn & Blount. Well, Sir, that anthology has just been republished in America, (Macy-Masius, $2.00) & I am still in it.[17] So much that for that. The rest is that my "Call of Cthulhu" is about to appear in a future anthology of unusual tales, edited by one T. Everett Harré & published by the Macaulay Co. This Harré is an amiable & interesting gentleman, & has ask'd my advice very flatteringly concerning some of the older standard items he wishes to include in his book. He is also about to include "The City of Spiders" by H. Warner Munn of Athol[18]—that youthful protege of Cook, Orton, & myself, whose work in *Weird Tales* your small & sapient Robertulus may have notic'd. And these are all the honours. As a quaint practical aside I may add (tho' possibly I have mention'd this before) that my last fictional effort, "The Dunwich Horror", has brought a greater amount from *Weird Tales* than I ever receiv'd before for any one story—the princely sum being exactly *$240.00*.

But I am not alone amongst our gangsters in my tenure of minor recent distinctions. If you are a careful reader of your valu'd *Litdig*, you must have beheld on the 19th ult. a sequence of three free-verse effusions, intitul'd "Translations from the American", by one "Brest" Orton—a name which your knowledge of typographical uncertainties may have rectified itself in your mind as that of my excellent acquaintance & quondam Vermont host, Vrest Teachout Orton.[19] The pieces were copy'd from Coates's faithful *Driftwind*. And I enclose a brief N.Y. Times note referring to the exploits of our honest old friend Mac[20]—whose connexion with your Macmillan reader series I have mention'd earlier in this document.

And now, Sir, I must close & adopt a posture of recumbency if I wish to nip in the bud the Baal-blasted headache which hath been insidiously marshalling its forces during the past hour. Desirous of avoiding delay, I will place this instalment in the mails as it is, rather than lay it by for future augmentation. And when I do get to augmenting, I trust that I may have before me another chapter of the semi-annual for inspiration.

I am, Sir, ever y^r moft oblig'd, moft ob^t Servt
Lo

Notes

1. "A small library." HPL alludes to the series *Junior Literature,* ed. Sterling A. Leonard and Harold Y. Moffett (New York: Macmillan, 1930; 3 vols.). MWM is listed as a co-

editor only on Vol. 3, but he appears to have assisted in the compilation of the other two volumes as well.

2. Presumably a nickname for Sterling A. Leonard, based on his first two initials.

3. The review by Clough of Charles Sears Baldwin's *Medieval Rhetoric and Poetic* (New York: Macmillan, 1928) presumably appeared in the *Providence Journal*.

4. I.e., pig-headed, or stubborn.

5. *Zythopolis* (beer-town) was HPL's humorous epithet for Milwaukee.

6. HPL's coined Latin for "West Division [High School]," where MWM taught.

7. I.e., of the ankle.

8. I.e., Virgil (P. Vergilius Maro) and Horace (Q. Horatius Flaccus).

9. "Parentis olim siquis inpia manu / senile guttur fregerit, / edit cicutis alium nocentius" (If any man, with impious hand, should ever strangle an aged parent, make him eat garlic). Horace, *Epodes* 3.1–3 (tr. A. S. Kline).

10. I.e., HPL endorses MWM's plans (never apparently realized) to give up teaching at the high school level in order to teach at a "normal school" (a school that trains teachers).

11. I.e., HPL's story about the fictional character "Ibid," written c. December 1927.

12. MWM has annotated this invented word with the note "Ford" (i.e., automobile), but the exact signification of the word is unclear.

13. It ran from Mill St. to Stevens St. at the foot of Constitution Hill. No longer extant.

14. Henry J. Peck (1880–1964), *Glimpses of Providence: From Crayon Drawings, with Notes* ([Warren, RI: Henry J. Peck, n.d.]).

15. HPL's "collector's item" probably was the *Recluse* containing "Supernatural Horror in Literature." See W. Paul Cook, *In Memoriam: Howard Phillips Lovecraft* (1941; LR 137-38).

16. See Blanche Colton Williams, *O. Henry Memorial Award Prize Stories* (Garden City, NY: Doubleday, Doran, 1928), 294.

17. In fact, Herbert Asbury compiled an anthology titled *Not at Night* for Macy-Masius that pirated the contents of several volumes of the Selwyn & Blount *Not at Night* series. The volume was later withdrawn from circulation.

18. *WT*, November 1926.

19. See "Translation from the American," *Literary Digest* 99 (17 November 1928): 44 (as by "Brest Teachout Orton"). Another group of poems, "Translations from the American: White Birches," appeared in *Driftwind* 5, No. 1 (July 1930): 20.

20. See "Books and Authors," *New York Times Book Review* (2 December 1928): 73, about McNeil's completion of the novel *The Shores of Adventure*.

[36] [AHT]

[January 1929]

Turning to the consideration of your appreciated epistle—permit me to enclose all that my limited and laymanlike erudition can do toward supplying the classical data you solicit. Had I present access to the publick library, I might do better; but my amateurish home library is very meagre, and much less ample on the side of Greek than on the side of Latin. The reason that I have not *made up* lines to suit the unsupplyable metres is this: that I'm not sure the metres themselves exist in practice; and that, having no guide to usage, I cou'd not hit upon the exact right form (for you are sensible each variety in actual usage has individual characteristicks which cannot be guess'd from a general numerical law) if any such form does indeed exist. Furthermore, I doubt the advisability of depicting any theoretical metre which did not occur in the actual poetry of the antients. Such are the resources of my personal library, that I can be tolerably sure these unsupply'd measures *did not* occur in *Latin* literature. As to *Grecian* literature, I cannot be so positive; but I imagine you (or I when I break quarantine) might find information conclusive one way or the other in some such encyclopaedick treatise as Schmidt's "Rhythmick and Metrick of the Classick Languages", or that new book I mention'd to you not long ago. As for concocting you illustrative specimens to replace those found to be tangled up in the copyright law—lead me to it, 'bo! Just shoot me the sort of thing you want parallell'd—with enough of your explanatory context to show exactly what point you wish principally brought out—and grandpa will do the rest! I'll be delighted to see the whole manuscript of "Doorways"—the special carbon you mention—and don't believe I ought to charge any vulgar fee for giving it the once-over. I can't imagine that anything from your pen would need a reviser's services. If it were a profesh job, I fancy the charge wouldn't be very formidable—I always go by the magnitude of the task, and never quote figures till I've seen what sort of a manuscript I'm handling. Shoot along your sample poem orders whenever you like, and follow up at will with the bulk of the manuscript. Just to show you that Grandpa's heroick-couplet will isn't quite obsolescent even at this advanced stage of senility, I think I'll repeat for you the lines I wrote last month to my modern and sophisticated young grandchild Francis, Lord Belknap—otherwise Frank Belknap Long, Jun.—to accompany an appropriately sophisticated Christmas present—a copy of Proust's "Swann's Way":

An Epistle
to
Francis, Ld. Belknap,
With a Volume of *Proust,* presented to him by his aged
Grandsire, Lewis Theobald, Jun.
Christmas, MDCCCCXVIII

>   Ingenuous Age once more essays to find
>   A proper Gift for Youth's sophistick Mind,
>   Well tho' he know how bootless 'tis to send
>   Aught that his own Head can comprehend.
>   Perplext, the Grandsire scowrs the Stalls to chuse
>   Some Spawn of Chaos and the bedlam Muse;

Some complex Fruit of multiple Dimensions,
With modern outlines and remote Pretensions,
Which, scorning *Euclid* and the pedant Race,
Revolts from Time, and flings a Sneer at Space;
Of Wit and Beauty keeps discreetly chary,
And forfeits Sense to be contemporary.

What best can suit so deep a Disillusion,
And cater to such civiliz'd a Confusion?
Whose Pen indeed the wrought-steel Crown deserves
As Chasm of Cubes, and Arbiter of Curves?
For sure, 'twere vain on normal Art to lean
In Youth's jazz'd World of Concrete and Machine!
Gods of the Waste-Land! say what Monster new
Shou'd grace a Shelf by Benda or Leleu?[1]
What best befits a Book-Case carv'd to ape
An Air-Plane's Angles, or a Subway's Shape?
Subtile the Stile that fits our motor Nation,
Smooth as a Ford, prim as a Filling-Station,
Mass'd and severe as yonder office Tower,
Short in its Wave-Length, statick in its Power;
High as the Crown of *Mencken's* scornful Hat,
Objective as a *Time-Square* Automat;
Devoid of Pomp as *Woolworth's* or *McCrory's*,
And cerebral as *Vogue* or *Snappy-Stories*:
Mature as moonshine Booze, and free from Bunk
As the frank Perfume of the candid Skunk;
Gay as a Billboard, ardent as the *Graphick*,[2]
And muddled as a Stream of *Broadway* Traffick;
Firm as a Gangster or a stick-up Man,
Ironick as an old tomato Can,
As Radio loud, as Movies democratick,
Symbolick as a *Greenwich-Village* Attick;
Bright as the Tungstens of a *Wrigley* "Ad",
And settled as the latest side-burn Fad—
Thus the deep Lines that may alone express
Our whirling Epoch in its rightful Dress!

But who, midst our Embarrassment of Riches,
Wears the true Laureat's four-plus flannel Breeches?
See in what Throng th' ambitious Candidate
Crashes and storms—and sometimes gets—the Gate!
Here Joyce appears with Odysseys demure,
His Prose a Sunk-Pile, and his Mind a Sewer;

Hard on his heels the Hecht-ick Hero hurtles,[3]
With rose-tipt Beak, and twin'd with Paphian Myrtles.
While Eliot stalks in State—no Friend of Cant he—
And stores a Cosmos in a triple "Shantih";
Cursing all caps, the comely cummings comes,
And Lindsay[4] pounds his syncopated Drums;
With Run and Folklore struts romantick Cabell,[5]
Chalking his half-hid Smut behind the Stable;
Stein formless foams, and chants the tender Button,[6]
Whilst Arlen's Wise-Cracks[7] knowing Saps may glut on.
Cubist and Futurist combine to shew
Sublimer Heights in *Kreymborg* and *Cocteau*,[8]
The Shade of *Huysmans* reddens Prose and Rhyme,
And Fiction soars in *Burke* and *Bodenheim*.[9]

Assist, ye brazen Nymphs of *Mont-parnassus*,
To chuse a Chief from the bold Hordes that gas us;
Say what pied Knight of these assorted Lots
Outshines with broken Lines or Rows of Dots?
Tell aged Ignorance what Seer to pick
As Symbol of a World gone lunatick.
Count them allo'er, and find a Name to lead
A dizzy Universe of aimless Speed.
How shall we do it? Simple as the Day!—
Listen intent whilst modern Criticks bray.
Weigh the wild Clamour, and proclaim as proudest
The jumbled Scribe whose Name is heard the loudest.
Him we elect, and to the Heights promote
As Kind Sophisticate by true straw Vote.
His Words alone we hold supremely fit
To feast a flaming Youth of modern Wit.
Hark! One-two-three!—the long-ear'd Herd decide
On a vague Ghost to be their Æsthete-Guide:
Hail to the Chief their phrensy'd Plaudits boost—
And take, young Man, a Tome by Marcel Proust!

Raymond's additional reflections pleased me greatly, and I certainly think he is a better general commentator than the great H. L.—since the latter has tended to crystallise his thoughts into a fixed convention and manner which never had the merit of grace, and now have not even the merit of novelty. I distrust anyone with a mannerism. As for Raymond's opinions—I fancy that in the end I agree with more than I disagree with. I think no rabble is fit to govern a nation, and believe that the best government is that which gives the power—legally or otherwise—to a cultivated group, no matter what its numerical magnitude. If an oligarchy can't be managed, I prefer Fascism to democracy. Somebody's got to dictate—and it had better be somebody who knows at least a little of what he's about. I'm not so keen on *liberty of action*, but believe that *liberty of thought* ought to be scrupulously maintained as an essential of true civilisation. I enjoyed Raymond's reference to collegiate sport, and quite thoroughly agree with it. Overemphasis on sport is the feature of our true hereditary civilisation about which I am least enthusiastick, and when that overemphasis advances from its former amateur proportions to the status of a feverish professionalised focus of interest—especially in connexion with institutions which ought to be educational—I am ready to join the lachrymose chorus and set down another evil victory for the age of machinery and democracy. Regarding *censorship*—I think the whole question is really too complex to be dealt with in summary terms, or to be expressed in a few expansive generalities. Frequent or widespread censorship is certainly bad—because essentially futile and ridiculous. But I still think the power to guide utterance at certain times, and to regulate many forms of public taste within certain limits at all times, ought to lie in reserve as one of the theoretical potentialities of government. I would apply it to architecture in particular now and then—as indeed the zoning boards in many cities do. As for language—I fancy that general taste is the best guide for it. A certain amount of the emphasis naively classified as profanity is normal under many conditions, and has always characterised the speech of virile men in every class of society except during the brief farce of Victorian repression. I am for it—for its attempted total deletion was a mere grotesque gesture unwarranted by the history of our language and culture. Nothing is more cursedly sissified than a magazine which prints "d—n" with blanks, or a six-foot milk-sucker who is afraid to say "oh, hell" in stag company. But that's not saying that all times and companies are equally suitable for the airing of a hairy-chested vocabulary—or that all the current extremes of racy diction are of equal aesthetick value. However—you can't pick and choose by censor. Better leave up the lid and let good breeding muddle slowly through its efforts to reformulate a rational code of conversational standards. There are more important things for legislation to control. I return the collegiate cutting as per request, hoping that you may find it an inspiration for the more concrete article you are planning. As to suggestions for that article—I don't know whether you'd find anything available in the dicta of one holding my views of life and the social fabric. In the first place, I consider it absolutely immaterial whether the numerical majority of boys go to college or not. In the second place, I consider the only proper function of a college the training of a young gentleman in the art of enjoying life as his birth or acquired taste entitles him to enjoy it—the sharpening of his sensitivities and his sensibilities, and the leading of his mind toward harmonious contacts with the mental and aesthetic stimuli of the past and of the surrounding world. All this has not the slightest connexion with business or professional life—because a gentleman's private mental and imaginative life is utterly apart from any profession or business. If lack of inherited money compels a man to labour, his professional training ought to be a thing wholly apart from his liberal education—whether or not it is acquired at the same institution. College and business are ideas which ought never to be bracketed, since college is properly a man's preparation not for trade, but for the art of making his life worth enduring. I don't see why a gentleman need enjoy his orientation to the cosmos less, in cases where his necessary toil is of a sort widely different from the collegiate atmosphere. What a man *does for pay* is of little significance. What he *is*, as a sensitive instrument responsive to the world's beauty, is everything! That is his true measure; and whatever contributes toward its refinement is of intrinsic value to him, no matter how little it may affect his material or industrial status. A poor but cultivated man is, absolutely, the superior of a *rich* boor whose responses to the cosmos are limited to a few stereotyped physical and emotional reactions. I never ask a man what his business is, for it never interests me. What is ask him about are his thoughts and dreams. Now as for colleges, I think the only ones that really matter are those with liberal cultural courses, and with the ability to control their attendance and governance in such a way that the social and educational standard may never fall below the best English standard. I think a young gentleman ought to have an education in an atmosphere not inferior to that of his own home, and according to traditions not inferior to those whereby his father and grandfather were educated. We need an urbane and homogeneous upper class to maintain a real civilisation amidst the decay of the machine age, and the best group of our universities are the right force to ensure it. As for the majority of colleges and the majority of youths—I don't think it vastly important whether or not widespread collegiate education exists, but I do think it is *distinctly preferable* that it exist. Though no democrat in theory, I certainly prefer to see any young man enjoying life decently, than to see him drifting dumbly and blindly in a half-animal state; hence I really think it is an excellent idea to offer the opportunities of mental and imaginative cultivation to all whose natural parts in any way fit them for such development. It is a sort of elimination test—for some will use these opportunities as a stepping-stone to real heights of mental-aesthetic life, thus entering the upper class of traditionalists, whilst others will remain content with a more moderate enlargement of sensitivities, or perhaps be wholly untouched, and fall back into the general mass. I don't think anyone will be harmed, and fancy that many will be helped. Moreover, I think the net effect on civilisation will be good rather than bad. But all this education must not be mixed up with industrialism. Men must be directed toward positions in consonance with their natural aptitudes, and this will often mean positions wholly disconnected from their holders' cultural lives. The idea of incongruity between certain kinds of endeavour and a cultivated mind ought to be dispelled as far as possible. The only limitation I would place on collegiate attendance would be in the case of youths obviously lacking either the desire to go, or the natural mental cast to derive any good therefrom. I think high school teachers ought to study their pupils, and issue college certificates only when they think a continuance of general education is of real advantage. This would rid the colleges of a vast amount of deadwood—though of course the first year of college itself does a good deal of riddance for the later and more vital years. In a way, I think all schools ought to exercise an eliminative function regarding the more advanced schools just ahead of them—that is, beginning with the grammar schools. There are thousands of dullards or coarse-grained, material-minded churls who have no business inside a high-school. Grammar schools ought to recognise these types, and arrange courses for them, so that their liberal education need go no farther. Upon leaving grammar-school, the only education of any value to them—or to the community through them—is a special industrial one designed to adjust them to the life and environment which will necessarily be theirs. An analogous phenomenon on a much higher plane is likewise the logical thing for those leaving high-school. Pre-war Germany with its industrial education for the industrial classes had the right idea. But, as I also say, I don't think there's any harm in giving culturally qualified high-school graduates a chance to continue the general liberal education which broadens and heightens their mental-imaginative lives. The only thing one ought to be sure of, is that the students *are* continuing for that purpose. To effect that surety, I wish that some of the athletick fripperies and purely artificial glamour could be stripped away from "college life"—and also, that it could be made very clear that college is *not* to be considered as a road to industrial or professional preferment. College is to make thinkers and appreciators—to make connoisseurs in the epicurean art of living. Let that sink into the publick! If a boy doesn't care for what that implies, let him attend a technical or industrial school, a business "college", or something else. I might add, that I believe the business of *scholastick research* ought to be left to the great private universities of the upper or traditional class. It is burden enough for the publickly-supported or minor colleges to attempt the task of placing youth in contact with the standard accumulations of the ages and the time-tried quickeners of mentality and responsiveness. Altogether, I say let any boy go to college if he wants to and seems mentally and culturally likely to be helped thereby; but don't let him lose the idea of education amidst a chaos of sport and frivolity, or fancy that he is fitting himself for some special occupational niche when he is merely *learning how to live as a fully-functioning and intelligent organism*. What Raymond says of the democratick political control of state-supported colleges is all too true, and one can only rely on chance to ensure that such institutions will teach a reasonably civilised curriculum. But at worst, the majority will be better than nothing; and intelligent parents can choose colleges in comparatively enlightened communities, where a population of generally superior cast causes the institutions to represent the real scholarship of the day. Such, I believe, is the case with your own U. of Wis.—a truly great, tho' state-managed, seat of learning. The Rice linguistic articles interested me greatly. My own position has never been one of close grammatical pedantry. Usage by the best writers, and intrinsic value in forming an artistick medium for thought, have always formed my supreme criteria of language. I have not even try'd to remember many of the technical minutiae I was taught in youth, and write altogether spontaneously—without thought of rules of any kind. My conservatism has to do with basic things—word-meanings, major syntactical practices, and so on—things which do reflect standard usage and aesthetick value rather than Priscianick purism.[10] I think some sort of academy ought to be establish'd to safeguard these things—though of course that academy would necessarily vote in a new word if one arose very spontaneously and widely in response to some actual need, and if it possessed a reasonable conformity with the genius and principles of the language. I am wholly with Rice on relative clauses—and with him on adverbs whenever the really adverbial nature of such a word can be established through good precedent. As to *whom* and *who* I am less liberal. I do not think the instances of lax usage by good authors are sufficiently numerous to form an adequate authority. Very clearly, certain standards of uniform usage *must* be maintained if English is not to become a chaos of awkward illiteracy. The need is greater now than ever, when more and more of our publicly noted writing and speaking comes from uncultivated and undereducated persons. It would, to my mind, be foolish to pay any attention to shifting usages which concern only the illiterate rabble in an age of unmistakable cultural decay. You are perfectly right in adhering to Webster's unabridged as a standard of pronunciation, and I hope you will not allow any transient fashion to swerve you therefrom. What does it matter to you that dirty truck-drivers take down an *ad'dress* instead of an *address'*, or that feather-brained clubwomen discuss the evening's *pro-grum* instead of *programme*? Amidst the sea of conflicting usage, the man of sense will pronounce as his father and grandfather and conservative dictionary pronounced before him! I use a Stormonth's Dictionary which was my father's—recommended to him by his father. And I shall use it till I die, Sir! A fig for your momentary fashions!

With every assurance of distinguisht consideration, I am, Sir,
    Ever yr most oblig'd and obt Servt
        Lo.

Notes

1. Władysław Teodor Benda (1873–1948), American illustrator and designer. Jules Leleu (1883–1961), decorative artist and furniture designer.
2. The *Graphic* (1869–1932), a London illustrated weekly paper.

3. Ben Hecht (1894–1964), American novelist and playwright whose novel *Erik Dorn* (1921) HPL regarded as the epitome of "literary modernism" (*SL* 2.96).
4. Nicholas Vachel Lindsay (1879–1931), a founder of modern singing poetry, the verses of which are meant to be sung or chanted.
5. James Branch Cabell (1879–1958), American author of fantasy fiction and belles lettres. His novel *Jurgen* (1919) was the focus of a celebrated obscenity trial.
6. Gertrude Stein (1874–1946), American novelist, poet, playwright, and art collector. HPL alludes to her *Tender Buttons* (1914), a book of Modernist poems on mundane subjects.
7. Michael Arlen (1895–1956), Armenian essayist, short story writer, novelist, playwright, and scriptwriter, famous for his satirical romances set in English smart society.
8. Alfred Francis Kreymborg (1883–1966), American poet, novelist, and playwright. Jean Cocteau (1889–1963), French writer, filmmaker, playwright, designer, and artist.
9. Kenneth Burke (1897–1995), leading Modernist critic and fiction writer, author of *Counter-Statement* (1931). Maxwell Bodenheim (1892–1954), American poet and novelist who gained international notoriety during the Jazz Age.
10. HPL refers to Priscian (Priscianus Caesariensis, fl. c. 500 C.E.), a Latin grammarian whose *Institutiones Grammaticae* was a standard textbook in the Middle Ages.

[37]   [AHT]

Visitation B. V. M. [2 July] 1929

To Athenodorus Kosmokrates, All Hail!

As for domesticity—I'm no dealer in dogmatisms and blanket generalities.[1] Some things suit some temperaments, others others. I haven't a doubt but that matrimony can become a very helpful and pleasing permanent arrangement when both parties happen to harbour the potentialities of parallel mental and imaginative lives—similar or at least mutually comprehensible reactions to the same salient points in environment, reading, historic and philosophic reflection, and so on; and corresponding needs and aspirations in geographic, social, and intellectual milieu—but I must add that I don't see how the hell any couple outside of professional psychiatrists can ever tell whether or not they possess this genuine parallelism until the actual test of two or three years of joint family life has brushed aside all the transient and superficial reactions due to novelty and rashly assumed adaptability, and revealed the basic, rock-bottom motivating mental and imaginative influences on each side—the influences actually constituting the inmost respective personalities involved, and forming inviolable nuclei of identity whose safeguarding is the inevitable and fundamental aim of every human being's intellectual-emotional mechanism. It is all a matter of chance—in greater or less degree as the parties have or lack a lifelong acquaintanceship, or are naturally good or poor judges of human temperament—whether a given marriage will develop into a true and lasting domestic harmony, or become an intolerable mental irritant until cancelled by a sane and benign court action. Fortunately people are beginning to realise this as time passes and philosophic outlooks broaden, so that in most enlightened states like Rhode Island the divorce laws are such as to allow rational readjustments when no other solution is wholly adequate. If other kinds of states—such as New York or South Carolina, with their mediaeval lack of liberal statutes—were equally intelligent in their solicitude for the half-moribund institution of monogamy, they would hasten to follow suit in legislation; for certainly, the disillusioned future generations will never tolerate a blind trap which offers ten chances of disaster to one of success. If the divorce laws of a region be not sufficiently intelligent to provide for the necessary readjustment of lives misplaced in good faith, then the result will be a gradual disuse of legal marriage and an almost complete reign of that type of semi-clandestine extra-legal relationship which has indeed already displaced the older system to some extent, yet which is infinitely less desirable from a social, political, economic, and aesthetic point of view. To my mind, any acceleration of this "new morality" is an unwise thing, even though the new system may be the normal rule in the remote future. Too quick a transition tends to uproot some of the deepest emotional anchorings of the Anglo-Saxon race—and the loss of the well-known values of domestic tranquillity seems very likely to outweigh the corresponding gain in erotic normality to such an extent that the net result will be an impoverishment rather than an enrichment of life as a whole. No—I am in favour of the established order; old-fashioned marriage with its Roman regularity of registration and its wholesome absence of the element of furtiveness. But if it is to survive, it must clean house—must purge itself of primitive superstition and Victorian hypocrisy, and reorganise itself as a rational institution adapted to human needs rather than remain an impossible Procrustean bed to which all human temperaments must be fitted through crippling and torture. It must allow for the mistakes and false starts which all but savants and clairvoyants are certain to make now and then, and must not pose as a romantic ideal when in truth it is at best merely a social compromise. The very intelligent and conscientious Judge Lindsey has about the right idea. Marriage should *aim* at permanence, but should not be bound to it—especially in the case of the young and the inexperienced—with superstitious rigidity. And if any shudder at the possible abuses of such a liberalised system, let him reflect that an occasionally abused system is vastly better than a system contemptuously discarded in favour of no system at all. Nothing is abuse-proof, and the true conservative would prefer to see an intelligently historic background, possibilities of family harmony, and favourable conditions for offspring, even if it did lead to occasional cases of premeditated consecutive polygamy; rather than witness the total collapse and repudiation of lawful wedlock, and the adoption of an unregulated type of companionship perilous to posterity and to the state. Under a rational regime, a very fair number of persons would—according to the laws of chance—need only one plunge in order to hit the target of a passable permanent marriage. More, perhaps, would succeed at the second plunge—having learned much of their orientation-possibilities from the first. Others, like Paul J. Campbell, would ring the bell only on their third shot. And anybody that tried more than three shots would be the sort of person to experiment anyway—under any system, or outside all systems! A good way to cut down the percentages of abuse would be to make divorces for purely temperamental reasons (i.e., for reasons other than those specific and acute ones already recognised by the laws of most states) available only for couples married long enough (say two or three years) to have truly demonstrated their essential incompatibility. The one kind of divorce which sometimes strikes me as a bit fishy and premature is where the marriage date itself is only a year or less in the past. Weed these out, and there is not the least modicum of sense in denying divorce to any couple who mutually desire it—custody of offspring to be determined by the court if not decided by the joint petitioners. And *alimony* is a relique of obsolescent economics and a source of ridiculous extortion which ought to be laughed off the statutes in favour of a very restricted programme of financial responsibility to be applied by the court when called for in a few individual cases. Ho, hum—it's easy to be a Lycurgus on paper! Descending to the merely concrete—I've no fault to find with the institution, but think the chances of success for a strongly individualised, opinionated, and imaginative person are damn slender. It's a hundred to one shot that any four or five consecutive plunges he might make would turn out to be flivvers equally oppressive to himself and to his fellow-victim, so if he's a wise guy he "lays off" after the collapse of venture #1 . . . . . . or if he's very wise he avoids even that! Matrimony may be more or less normal, and socially essential in the abstract, and all that—but nothing in heaven or earth is so important to the man of spirit and imagination as the inviolate integrity of his cerebral life—his sense of utter integration and defiant independence as a proud, lone entity face to face with the illimitable cosmos. And if he has the general temperament that usually goes with such a mental makeup, he will not be apt to consider a haughty celibacy any great price to pay for this ethereal inviolateness. Independence, and perfect seclusion from the futile herd, are things so necessary to a certain type of mind that all other issues become subordinate when brought into comparison with them. Probably this is so with me. And yet I didn't find matrimony such a bugbear as one might imagine. With a wife of the same temperament as my mother and aunts, I would probably have been able to reconstruct a type of domestic life not unlike that of Angell St. days, even though I would have had a different status in the household hierarchy. But years brought out basic and essential diversities in reactions to the various landmarks of the time-stream, and antipodal ambitions and conceptions of value in planning a fixed joint milieu. It was the clash of the abstract-traditional-individual-retrospective-Apollonian aesthetic with the concrete-emotional-present-dwelling-social-ethical-Dionysian aesthetic; and amidst this, the originally fancied congeniality, based on a shared disillusion, philosophic bent, and sensitiveness to beauty, waged a losing struggle. It was a struggle unaccompanied by any lessening of mutual esteem or respect or appreciation, but it nevertheless meant the constant attrition and ultimate impairment of two personalities revealed by time to be antipodal in the minor overtones and deep hidden currents that count. I could not exist except in a slow-moving and historically-grounded New England backwater—and the hapless sharer of the voyage found such a prospect, complicated as it was by economic stress, nothing short of asphyxiation! Trying to exist in N.Y. drove me close to madness, and trying to think of living in Rhode Island drove the late missus equally close to despair. Each, obviously, formed an integral and inextricable part of a radically different scene and life-cycle—so the distaff side of the outfit, for whom the initiative in such matters is traditionally reserved, proffered increasingly forcible arguments in favour of a rational and amicable dissolution. Without wishing to retreat from any historic responsibility of an English gentleman, I could not for ever be deaf to such logic; hence last winter agreed to do what I could to further a liberation and a fresh start all around. Rhode Island, as a really civilised commonwealth, did its duty—so oil returns to oil and water to water! And I would, despite my profound theoretical regard for the custom of wedlock, be rather a Nilotic saurian if I used peeled onions to register my emotions at getting back to the comfortable old Rhode Island basis of contemplative independence with congenial blood-kinsfolk hovering benignly by! After all, when a guy has been a secluded and set-in-his-ways bachelor for thirty-three-and-one-half years, as I had been when I risked the plunge in 1924, the chances are that he won't take kindly to any radical domestic change. A bird as old as that is past the age of weaving new kinds of nests, and had better not try it. Be a Benedick[2] before twenty-five or not at all, is my grandpaternal advice to conservative youth. I don't try to advise the "flaming" kind, because I don't understand 'em.

By the way—our fellow-amateur Edward Lloyd Sechrist of Washington also emerged from a sadly ill-assorted union last winter; an union which he had endured for nearly a quarter of a century for the sake of providing his three children with a settled home until the adulthood of the youngest. One anecdote is enough to indicate what he—an enlightened and sensitive aesthete—had to put up with . . . . . . his prim and acidulous spouse, chancing to read "The Fall of the House of Usher" in his library, considered it so "morbid and horrible" that she *burnt his entire set of Poe*—or rather, made him burn it to avoid a scene! Sechrist surely was a gentleman down to the inmost fibre to stand a life like that for two decades and more; and no one begrudged him the waning residue of his life (for he is over fifty now) when, upon the maturity of all his children, he decided to come up for air. Nevada fixed him up . . . . but alas, there's nae fu' like an aud fu'—and last month the poor devil took a *second* plunge! At over fifty! But in all seriousness I don't think he's made so bad a mistake this time, for the new Mrs. Sechrist is a gentlewoman of taste and intelligence from Richmond, and appears to understand him pretty well. I hope he has a happy and peaceful afternoon of life—he's a real white man, and gawd knows he's earned it!

More anon—
Yr obt Servt
LO.

Notes

1. This letter was written a few months after HPL and Sonia concluded divorce proceedings in Rhode Island (March 1929). But since HPL never signed the final decree, he and Sonia were not legally divorced.
2. A character in Shakespeare's *Much Ado about Nothing* who marries Beatrice at the end of the play and also offers the advice, "Get thee a wife" (5.4.607).

[38]   [AHT]
July 25[, 1929]

Ave, Sapentissime!

    Sonnets   (a) Dago Stuff

Sonnets are sighs, breath'd beautiful and brief
From spirits sober'd by their weight of dreams;
Figures in jade whose perfection gleams
A tortur'd thought too luminous for grief,
Shap'd with that ecstasy which brings relief
And rest, distill'd from woe's encircling streams.
Solemn and high the poet's chosen themes,
Their stray tones gather'd to a stately sheaf.
Not mine to mould such Tuscan symphonies,
Wherein each note must sound the singer's mood;
Octave advance and sestet retrogress
In subtler turns than common vision sees:
Dulness stands lost in an enchanted wood
Pathless to eyes untouch'd by loveliness.
                —Al Capone (Cashen Carey's Tr.)

The Elizabethan Sonnet   (b) White Man Stuff
by
B. Jonson Flomont-Betcher[1]

The subtle mind in subtle tones can speak,
   Nor trip in paths Italianate;
Finding the door for which his wishes seek
   In the slow sonnet which made Petrarch great.
Such order'd shadings, drawn with grave intent,
   A thousand charms of musing bring to sight,
As brooding dusk reveals in his descent
   The countless day-enshrouded orbs of night.
But we, of plainer, hardier metal wrought,
   A straighter path demand, whose hedge and goal
May suit the Saxon's undivided thought,
   And guide his changeless impulse, warm and whole:
Summing his message in one final shout
   That speaks his mind, and drowns all wav'ring out!

An Epistle
to the
Rt. Hon[ble] Maurice Winter-Moe, Esq.,
of Zythopolis,[2] in the Northwest-
Territory of
His Majesty's American Dominions.
By
L. Theobald, Jun.

Thanks for the gift, nor blame me if I TETER[3]
And slip into mine antient vice of metre,
For sure, your kindness piles Temptation on
With this new Handy Guide to Helicon!
Tho' brief, 'tis clear, with no false precepts strown,
Nor fashion'd for the pedant's mind alone;
Each turn of stile, and each mechanick art,
The cogent author can with skill impart:
Bright beyond rivals, peerless three or four ways—
A fitting pair of steps to reach your Doorways!

   Yet such a tome must take its proper place,
Nor vie with your own volume in the race!
Lud, Sir, but what new marvels daily come

Full-arm'd from the MOCRATICK cerebrum!
Tests, outlines, drills—and now your genius adds
New leaves of wonder in your sep'rate pads!
Macmillan sure would prove a brainless dolt
Did he not vie in eagerness with Holt—[4]
But be their sense of judgment more or less,
You need not care—for you've the Kenyon Press,
Nurse of the arts—hail, Mater Gloriosa!
The press that carry'd fame to Wauwatosa![5]

    And now in meekness let my fancy glance
At these sly tests which prov'd my ignorance—
Those tricky snares which ev'n Mortonian mind
Could scarcely meet and scatheless leave behind!
The prose I view with less disorder'd pride,
And by my pristine verdicts still abide:
D may be Tark's[6]—but still I vow it groans
With needless weight, and talks in cumbrous tones;
Labours for pow'r, forgetting to be neat,
And trades its birthright for a cheap conceit.
As for trite F, I censur'd not its stream
Of thought, nor held it faithless to its theme;
My wildest wish was for less verbal pelf,
And for more freshness from the scribe himself!
But E—oh priceless pearl! how quick mine eye
Caught the bright vision from an age gone by!
Past my pleas'd mind in long procession ran
The assembl'd genius of the a. j. clan:
Lynch, Haughton, Fritter, roving Henness[e]y;[7]
Hasemann—don't choke!—and deathless David V.—
Lehmkuhl[8] and Crowley, and—young imps of hell—
Porter and Moitoret and Kid Dowdell—[9]
Woodbee and Warrenite the foreground take,[10]
Whilst over all immortal soars Our Jake!

    Dropping to poesy—my head drops, too,
As my illit'rate score I dumbly view!
(So dumb, eheu, my mental equipage,
I think Iambus was a Grecian sage!)
What can I say when here I stand confest,
I can't pick Shelley in a blindfold test?
How can I face the world—a crawling midge

Who puts a Wordsworth tag on Coleridge?
I say no more! May all the Muses chide me . . .
But, damn it, Morton's in the soup beside me!

           I now with pleasure hear, whilst you relate
Your recent deeds, and how you aestivate.
Pox on't, but how you crown the flying hours
With new-made proofs of your scholastic pow'rs!
Your leisure's like my toil—and when *you* labour,
You rise to heights that leave you not a neighbour!
I still await my cherisht chance to quaff
The nectar of your class-day *Moe-Know-Graph*.
Ah, me! can't be that twenty years and more
Have pass'd since that blest Golden Age—'04?
A quarter century! And old and grey,
We see it still as if it 'twere yesterday!
Old Nineteen-hundreds! What would we not give
Once more amid your artless hours to live?
Puff ties and cake-walks, cloak-and-sword romance,
And Teddy fighting back the trusts' advance;
Queer horseless carriages on cobbled streets,
And new-found radium in the science sheets:
Wireless—the latest—(never'll be much use!)
Japan—not yet a mark for our abuse—
"Bedelia" light on ev'ry whistler's lip,
And rearward seating still the smartest quip:
St. Louis' glory—crowds in fairward push
To rest beneath the broad Anheuser Busch.
Edwardus Rex on Britain's antient throne,
And "Hiawatha" on the graphophone:
Hope still triumphant, and the cold grey morn
Of Mencken, Krutch, and Einstein yet unborn:[11]
Harper's chaste leaves with polisht mildness rife,
And prim McClure's a stranger still to life.
Gilder still gilding with decorous mien,
And Winter freezing o'er the painted scene;[12]
Van Dyke and Aldrich[13] saying in fresh rhymes
The borrow'd thoughts and saws of other times—
Vague pleasing dreams of futures ever young;
"The Simple Life" on ev'ry trusting tongue;[14]
Graft and muckraking in their genial fights,
And prophets soon to set the world to rights;
Dowie, Lyme Abbott, Parkhurst,[15] and the rest

With various plans to put us 'midst the blest;
Bryan and Hanna, nigger-minstrel shows,
Elb Hubbard posing o'er his Windsor bows,
Corbett, Fitzsimmons, Sharkey, and Old Jeff,[16]
Pete Dailey, Weber-Fields, and Fritzi Scheff,[17]
Young Buster nosing out the Yellow Kid,[18]
And ev'ry newsboy in an "Old Coon" lid;
"Extry—Port Arthur Falls"—we stand aghast—[19]
But "Russia's Czar has got a son at last"[20]—
Santos-Dumont displays a fresh balloon,
And Langley vows his gliders will fly soon.[21]
Bill Pick'ring vainly tells a sceptick nation
Of finding signs of lunar vegetation,
Nor can Park Lowell gather many pals
To hear about his precious Mars-canals![22]
Dear bygone days! Could modern genius hatch
A Mrs. Wiggs from any Cabbage Patch?[23]
Could modern talent make us gape and marvel
At Zenda, Haddon Hall, or Richard Carvel?[24]
'04 *produced* what modern throats but whine—
The Flower of My Heart—Sweet Adeline!
Then Pilsen's Prince in tuneful splendour reign'd,
And "Woodland" bloom'd, by jazz yet unprofan'd:[25]
Boston was still a sep'rate realm from Cork,
Whilst English yet was spoken in New York!

         Shades of the past! And have I liv'd to view
A scene so diff'rent, and a world so new?
Have five and twenty years in truth gone by,
While still the old days seem so clear and nigh?
'Zounds! 'Tis a dream—this is not I at all—
This greybeard in the mirror on the wall!
What nonsense—when but lately I dar'd don
A derby hat, and put long trousers on!
Of course 'tis dreaming—merely look about
And see how all reality's in rout!
Autos in droves, men flying o'er the mist,
And talk of things that simply *can't* exist! . . .
Shucks! There's the proof! Sure, we need fret no more,
Because it *must* be still our old '04!
We're merely dizzy—say, from overeating,
Or from some thought of Time's relentless fleeting:
Sing, boys, in chorus—put the nightmare down

With "Bluebell", "Creole Belles", or "Nancy Brown".[26]
All—one—two—three—nor let your voices fail ye—
"Won't you come home"—here, mind the pitch!—"Bill Bailey?"
No—that won't do—try this: "O Karama,"[27]
(Too high, I fancy) "be my guiding star!"
What's this? No rhyme? O damn such close precision!
I hold these Western rrrrrh's in deep derision!
Not on your life—I vow you're off your trolley
To think I'd listen to such upstart folly!
A fight! A figh! Here, knock his block off, Joe!
Eat him up, Jack; dump him at Buffalo!
But in his coc'nut! Lam him on the bean!
Go bite his head off! Puncture his canteen!
Bats in your belfry—you're another, Jack!
Bum—bughouse—looney—go sit on a tack! . . . .
Thus down the years the virile echoes pour,   )
Fresh with the vigour of the days of yore:)
While such survive, it is not still '04?   )

      Oh, yes, those magazines which presently
Will saunter westward to 2303:
In one vast packet safely I'll return all—
Mags, Doorways, and that pleasing *English Journal*.
The latter—thanks—sheds an informing blaze
On your young charges' editorial ways:
I see—I know—and with new zeal extend
Congrats on what each hopeful chick hath penn'd.
So gifted Franklin turns the other Cheek   )
In fistick fashion, vigilant to seek   )
Ways to knock guys to the middle of next week!   )
Attaboy, Frank! An' don'tcha let no bimbo
Knock ya down hill into de has-been's limbo!
Keep right and left glov'd, dauntless and on edge,
Till ev'ry knuckle grows to be a sledge:
Punch 'em to pulp, and let Manila's shoar
Grow vocal in one tributary roar;
But keep art's cunning in the mitt that slugs—
Pug among painters, painter among pugs!

      I thrill with joy if Rems devoid of sound[28]
Will bring Mocratick lines more frequent round!
For my part, nothing like a damn'd machine
Will give my thought a free and fair demesne.

'Tis too unnatural for an old man still
A dweller in the realm of script and quill—
Words pause embarrassed, images depart
At sight of such an enemy to art:
When thoughts pile up, a *pen* must set 'em free—
My grandsire's ways are good enough for me!!

  Well, Sir, my days in wonted fashion run
Beneath Rhode Island's classick Georgian sun.
Last week a guest adorn'd the local strand—
Victor E. Bacon of the a. j. band;
Fresh from convention, he declar'd his fellows
Had nurs'd the dying flame with frantick bellows:
An happier twelvemonth he discerns ahead,
The National still declining to be dead.
Six years had pass'd since I the youth had seen
In visual form, and I recall'd him lean;
Fancy my thoughts to find *him* deck'd today
In all the poundage *I* have cast away!
His stay was brief, yet fill'd with lib'ral cheer
And season'd with our Georgian atmosphere.
To Newport's antient shoar I bade him rove,
And old Pawtuxet, dreaming by its cove.
Of much we spoke, the past more than the present—
So that the passing hours to both were pleasant.

  And so it goes. But Lud! you must be yawning
At these misshapen lines my quill is spawning!
Pardon, Sir—pardon—yet pray don't omit
To mind that TETER set me doing it!
A brief recess—now back to art's dim last row,
To doctor that curst junk by old De Castro![29]
Hail and farewell—and may my trembling hand
Clasp yours some morning in a better land—
Some Delian isle or mild Ionian shoar
Where 'twill be ever summer—and '04!

Notes

1. A parodic pseudonym on the names of English dramatists Francis Beaumont (1584–1616) and John Fletcher (1579–1625), who collaborated during the reign of James I of England.
2. See MWM 35n5.

3. Referring to George E. Teter, an associate of MWM. HPL owned his *An Introduction to Some Elements of Poetry*.

4. Both Macmillan (for whom MWM was editing a reader series) and Henry Holt had considered publishing the book.

5. Kenyon Press, based in Wauwatosa, WI, published some booklets by MWM and also by Teter.

6. The letters D, E, and F in the the following lines seems to refer to examples of writing, as if in a quiz, such as MWM employed in his various test exercises. Tark may refer to American novelist Booth Tarkington (1869–1946).

7. James J. Hennessey. In "News Notes" (*United Amateur*, January 1921), HPL says that he is an "old-time United member [who] is now returning to the fold and delighting his correspondents with some artistic penmanship second only to the Samples brand" (*CE* 1.270).

8. Harry N. Lehmkuhl.

9. Wesley H[ilon] Porter (1898–1972), editor of the *Toledo Amateur* and Secretary of the NAPA (1922–23). Anthony F. Moitoret (1892–1979), co-editor of the *Cleveland Sun* and an amateur journalist with whom HPL engaged in various disputes during the 1910s and 1920s. William J. Dowdell (1898–1953), amateur journalist who abruptly resigned as president of the NAPA in late 1922, leading the executive judges to appoint HPL as interim president.

10. The Woodbees, a group of amateur journalists in Columbus, OH, included such figures as Arthur Ziegfeld, Edith W. Fowler, Henriette Ziegfeld, Norma Sanger, Ida C. Haughton, and Leo Fritter. Warren, OH, was home to another group.

11. H. L. Mencken (1880–1956), Joseph Wood Krutch (1893–1970), and Albert Einstein (1879–1955). All were living but not yet famous.

12. Richard Watson Gilder (1844–1909), American poet and the editor of *Scribner's Monthly* (later *Century Magazine*) from 1881 to 1909. William Winter (1836–1917), American drama critic.

13. Henry Van Dyke (1852–1933) and Thomas Bailey Aldrich (1936–1907), American poets.

14. See MWM 30n19.

15. John Alexander Dowie (1847–1907), a Scottish evangelist who had been preaching in the U.S. since 1888; Lyman Abbott (1835–1922), American Congregationalist theologian; and Charles Henry Parkhurst (1842–1933), American clergyman and reformer.

16. The boxers James J. "Gentleman Jim" Corbett (American, 1866–1933), Robert James "Bob" Fitzsimmons (British, 1863–1917), Tom Sharkey (American, 1873–1953), and James Jackson Jeffries (American, 1875–1953).

17. Weber and Fields, the comedy duo of Joe Weber (1867–1942) and Lew Fields (1867–1941); and Fritzi Scheff (1879–1954), American actress and opera singer.

18. Buster Brown (1902f.) and the Yellow Kid (in *Hogan's Alley*, 1895–98) were comic strip characters created by Richard Felton Outcault (1863–1928).

19. In Battle of Port Arthur (8–9 February 1904), the Japanese army defeated the Russian army at Port Arthur, Manchuria, thereby initiating the Russo-Japanese War (1904–05).

20. Czar Nicholas II of Russia was the father of a son, Alexei Nikolaevich, born on 12

August 1904. He had previously fathered four daughters.

21. The Brazilian Alberto Santos-Dumont (1873–1932) and the American Samuel Pierpont Langley (1834–1906) were early pioneers in aviation.

22. HPL refers to the astronomers William H. Pickering (1858–1938) and Percival Lowell (1855–1916). HPL's astronomy columns of 1906–18 refer often to Lowell's hypotheses on the Martian canals.

23. *Mrs. Wiggs from the Cabbage Patch* (1901), a sentimental novel by Alice Hegan Rice that was turned into a play in 1903.

24. HPL refers to the popular novels *The Prisoner of Zenda* (1894) by Anthony Hope; *Dorothy Vernon of Haddon Hall* (1902) by Charles Major (turned into a play in 1903); and *Richard Carvel* (1899) by the American novelist Winston Churchill (turned into a play in 1900).

25. *The Prince of Pilsen* (1902) (AHT erroneously reads "Pilen's") and *Woodland: A Forest Fantasy* (1904), operas by Gustav Luders and Frank S. Pixley.

26. "Blue Bell" (1904), words by Edward Madden, music by Theodore F. Morse; "Creole Belles" (1901), words by George Sidney, music by J. Bodewalt Lampe; "Nancy Brown" (1902), words by Clifton Crawford, music by J. W. Myers.

27. "Karama: A Japanese Romance" (1904) by Vivian Grey (pseudonym of Mabel McKinley).

28. I.e., the Remington Noiseless typewriter, introduced c. 1928.

29. HPL refers to revisory work for Adolphe de Castro, possibly "The Electric Executioner."

[39] [AHT]

July 27, 1929

Pantheon of Prosody:—

[. . .]

A third suggestion—or string of suggestions—has to do with the chapters upon triteness and insincerity; and here again I apologise if I recommend as new any point which you have actually cover'd unseen to the rheumy eye of the grandpaternal senility. You have spoken at due length of *trite words and phrases*, (to which you apply the fashionable word *cliché*, a which I dislike tho' I admit its recent permissibility) and of those "emotional short-circuits" whereby certain facile feelings are call'd into play by the mechanical serving-up of standard stimuli, be they words, images, incidents, or sentiments. What I wonder is, whether you cou'd not add a passage to warn readers against a subtler form of the same hollowness—i.e., a kind of imposture wherein not the bald *language*, but the less obvious *substance* of a ready-made stock stimulus is provided; as in mediocre magazine poetry of the third and fourth grade above Mr. Guest.[1] You cover some of this ground in the section on insincerity—i.e., "burning love" and "the open road", but it strikes my dull brain that you might in a new section suggest *more* of the uses of *false appeal*, and place the learner more definitely on guard against it. What I mean, specifically, is simply the selection of a certain sentiment, *type of scene*, object, situation, etc.

etc. for versify'd treatment, without the addition of any original vision, ecstasy, arrangement, or personally selective touch to it; depending wholly upon the *general associative value of the subject* for emotional effect, and thus really approaching creative art no more closely than it would be approach'd by a recital of the title or a statistical cataloguing of the subject-matter. The language may be as fresh, direct, unhackney'd, and graceful as one might wish—thus giving a sort of secondary art to the outward eye—but the "short circuiting" is there just the same, since the reader is reached solely through the unindividualised dishing-up of conceptions made familiar to him by previous reading; conceptions too general for vitality when connected with something particular and individual. To be specifick—this class of false appeal wou'd include all such verses as make their bid for approval through such things as unvitalised and catalogue-like *images* of garden stiles, gates (especially lynch-gates or wicket-gates) thatched roof'd cots, valleys, lanes, hedges, church-bells, mountain peaks, vine-clad walls, firesides, roses, lilies, violets, hillsides, old mills, distant steeples, (a particular vice of mine own, which I constantly combat with varying success) moonlight, (especially on ruins or gardens) cliffs, sea-beaches, swelling sails, castle turrets, crowded streets, and the like; *mechanical celebration of abstract emotions and conceptions* such as grief, wonder, right, beauty, courage, and so on; and glibly *ready-made incidents* such as death, sacrifice, amatory phenomena, passing of time, growth, decay, survival, cycle of seasons, bird-song, homecoming, homeleaving, etc. etc. I know that all this is included under *insincerity*, and an Havelock Ellis wou'd challenge my right to suggest a separate catagory; but I do think that this *systematick and vary'd use of standardis'd fancy-ticklers* has in it something transcending the mere directional and quantitative insincerity of Arab-sheikism and Whitmanesque open-roading. In your place, I wou'd certainly expand the volume sufficiently to accomodate a separate notice of this urbane and unobtrusive fakery. Of course, it must not be suggested that the subjects mention'd are ineligible for poetick use. It must merely be shown, that they are *insufficient for poetick completeness* unless linkt to life and reality by some quality of personal vision, individual selectiveness, or actually vital relation to specifick concrete objects or occurrences. They are not intrinsically unpoetick, but they need *something more* to make them poetry. The general type of spuriousness involv'd is what you less specifically touch under the heading of *insincerity*—padding, "short-circuits"; words and phrases whose associations and connexions are too generalised to imply any artistick selection or personal vision of the rhymester's, and whose mere catalogue-value is unadorn'd by any of that genuine deep feeling on the poet's part from which alone true poetry proceeds. This sort of thing, I believe, ought to be treated as an extension of the chapter on artistick sincerity toward the end of the book. Attention to this point would explain the crucial weakness of much of that vague, "correct", urbane, and cultivated verse which somehow can't 'get across'.

A fourth suggestion which I might make, is one likely to be rul'd out by you as too purely *technical and trivial* for consideration in an avowedly elementary treatise, and as too closely connected with the art of verse *writing* to be pertinent in a guide to *reading and appreciation* alone. In defence of it, I wou'd merely say, that the subject cover'd is one of increasing surface magnitude as the evolution of technique unfolds itself; and moreover, that it is not very generous to overlook the wou'd-be poetick *writer* altogether. You must surely be sensible, that a work of such uniqueness and merit will—despite its precise purpose—undoubtedly be recommended to many incipient writers of verse, and diligently study'd by them. It is in every respect qualify'd to aid in their development, and will in all truth be far more helpful to them than any other volume publisht—so that it wou'd be a pity to omit any easily-manag'd feature which might benefit them without injuring its primary function as a reader's manual. What I suggest is, that you append a section covering the topick of *poetick diction and so-called licence*—calling attention to certain characteristick archaisms, liberties, inversions, and mannerisms practic'd by the bards of former times, *and to the fact that at present nearly all of these devices are forbidden and ridicul'd by conservative technicians as silly affectations, "short-circuits", and confessions of linguistic limitations.* I need not point out the class of diction to which I refer—the *o'ers* and *ev'ns*, *'tis's* and *'neaths*, interchang'd parts of speech, noun-following adjectives and verbs, and other paraphernalia of my own Georgian aera; plus the *far more tawdry and extravagant* follies of Victorian times, wherein all manner of promiscuous and unnecessary archaisms were fish'd up from mediaeval and Elizabethan literature and woven into a tissue of mincing preciosity which had almost no point of contact with living speech, but which brought the reproach of imbecility and effeminacy upon the whole poetick art—the *glaives* and *eftsoons*, *yblents* and *weens*, *kens* and *sooths*, *lilied streams among's*, *right well's* and *full soons*, and all such damn'd nineteenth-century pre-Raphaelite maundering. I do not think it is merely my hatred of the puling nineteenth century which makes me consider this Tennysonian and Rossettish play-acting a vastly more contemptible kind of fakery than the archaisms and pseudo-classicisms of my own eighteenth century. There is a very important distinction involv'd—namely, that the artificialities of the eighteenth century were largely those of *legitimate survival* and *unconscious* preference; whereas those of the nineteenth century were *outright, deliberate, and intentional departures from life and reality,* involving an open-eyed and sophisticated plundering of closed historical chapters in the interest of empty decoration, and a puerile and mechanical employment of dead words in connexions which fail'd utterly to bring them to life. It hardly needs to be pointed out that the pseudo-mediaevalism and pseudo-Elizabethanism of the sanctimonious and didactick Victorian "uplifter" had not the slightest real kinship to the actual thought and feeling of the Middle Ages or Renaissance period. The whole imitative process was a kind of childish cambrick-tea affair whose only effect was to widen the gap betwixt language and life. Waving crests and mailed hands, ladyes fair and tables round, warriours bravely bedight and roses this, that, and the other . . . . . Hell's bells, what slop! Thank gawd this stuff was at least on the wane—Kipling'd into sedately respectable retirement—before my Golden Nineteen-Hundreds! Otherwise all the glamour of my youth wou'd be vitiated by the miasmata of namby-pambyism! Well—so much for that. This tirade is really a digression, since the point I wish to make operates as much against my eighteenth century survivals and formalisms as against the nineteenth century's simperings and ruff-and-farthingale dressings-up. The point is, that today the whole institution of poetick diction has risen above the level of affectations and mannerisms, and has adopted *the plain, simple, and straightforward speech of ordinary cultivated conversation*—a *living* idiom with a direct relation to reality—as its unvarying and inflexible standard. *O'er* and *e'en*, *'neath* and *'gainst, charger black, distant turret spy'd*, etc., are to all intents and purposes *absolutely and definitely tabooed;* as are likewise such flashy "poeticisms" as *beauteous, ensanguined, guerdon, saith, hath, walketh, thou, winged*, and the like. It was Rheinhart Kleiner—good old Klei, bless his heart—who first strongly impress'd this truth upon my archaick soul; and once I had learnt the lesson, I clearly beheld it illustrated in all the really important poetry of the present. The twentieth century, in truth, has effected a poetick revolution of no less magnitude than that which Wordsworth, Coleridge, and their contemporaries effected at the close of my own classick aera; a more quiet revolution, and one less advertised by didactick heralding, yet a thorough and genuine one for all that. For proof, study the more conservative specimens in any modern anthology from nigger Braithwaite's down. Artificiality and posing are out—and honest human speech is in! In mentioning this trend, I of course confine my remarks to that normal and conservative poetry which carries on the main stream, emotionally and technically, of the great English tradition; modern, but not "modernistick", verse. The latter really does not count. Let us remember, then—no more obsolete contractions; no more archaick words or verb-forms; and no more tortur'd inversions of the *meadow green, a ship discern'd*, and *garden paths between* sort. There is no question but that this great development is essentially a sound one; based upon the truest aesthetick and psychological laws, and forming just as great a permanent advance in man's mastery of poetick expression, as the discovery of aerial perspective form'd in man's mastery of the art of painting. In the language of painting, both Georgian and Victorian poems must be regarded essentially as "primitives". I cou'd not with good conscience enjoin any course upon a poet or critic, save to recognise and practice this great advance in the art; and I have accordingly been at great pains to amend my precepts and cancel my former tolerances and recommendations in the case of such prosodical satellites (Doc Kuntz, for example) as have depended upon my advice since the days before my own Kleinerian conversion. No one living intellectually and emotionally in the twentieth century can afford to speak in an idiom now universally recognis'd as tawdry, artificial, obsolete, and ridiculous ..... Having utter'd which dictum, I proceed to relapse into mine own Georgian mannerisms and inversions, and forget all that I have ponderously and conscientiously said! What saves my position from inconsistency, is the fact that I *do not pretend to live in the twentieth century* except so far as academick science and philosophy are concern'd. My perspective and emotions are too firmly and instinctively grounded in the eighteenth to make any other allegiance other than a mockery.

Now the reason why you ought to mention the nature and decline of artificial mannerism in verse—aside from the need of guiding incipient poets aright—is that most of the standard specimens used in ordinary school and college curricula, and copiously cited in your book itself, are survivals from the older phases of technique, and consequently contain frequent instances of the inversion, contraction, and pseudo-archaism now frown'd upon. It would not be well to omit these older selections; because they form the bulk of the poetick material in our cultural background, and must be made familiar and intelligible to the learner. Moreover, the time since the fall of the artificial speech-tradition has not yet been long enough—or environmentally favourable enough (there is grave doubt whether any really great poetry—or art of any kind—can be produced in a mechanical, commercial, or scientifically-minded age; or indeed any age given to democracy)—to produce any poets of the natural calibre of the best bards of the past. The older poets must still be depended upon to display the art of emotional utterance at its height, just as the primitive thirteenth and fourteenth century artists have to be depended upon to illustrate the apex of certain emotional qualities which decreased after the technique of painting reached its zenith in the fifteenth or early sixteenth century. We cannot abandon the past as a background for emotional training and a source of examples of supremely great imaginative and emotional formulation. It must continue to hold chief place in any general system of appreciative reading, and its methods must be understood. But just *because* of this fact, there ought to be an increasingly explicit recognition of the past's linguistick idiosyncrasies, and a clear understanding that such devices are inadmissible in the poetick composition of today. Otherwise, the preponderance in all curricula of highly-prais'd and strongly-recommended verse-specimens which abound with archaistic and artificial devices will set up such an image in the reader's mind, that it will require a vast and painful amount of *unlearning* to bring him vitally face to face with the best linguistick standards of contemporary versification. I know this from personal experience, for all my poetick habits were form'd at the age of six from the reading of a book on rhetorick publish'd in 1797[2] and us'd by my great-great-grandfather, and confirm'd by a reading of all the poets recommended in that work—plus the late seventeenth and early eighteenth century verse translations of those Grecian and Roman classicks which then form'd my chief interest. It was not till much later that I realised there *was* any well-regarded poetry (outside the light nursery-rhymes and ephemeral balladry encounter'd by all children) other than in the Georgian tradition; and even then I cou'd not take *seriously* the odd and watery Longfellonious and Tennysonorous stanzas which my grandfather, mother, and aunts presented to me as antidotes for the growing eccentricities and archaisms of my taste—a taste of which my attempts on paper made them at length conscious. Early receptiveness and first impressions had done their work—and I was, am, and always shall be a Georgian of Georgians; one with the pilaster'd steeples and fanlighted doorways of my own old Providence—that old Providence whose visual influence undoubtedly helped to confirm me in the periwigg'dness of my ways as my infant eyes widen'd at the cobbled lanes, gambrel roofs, and iron-rail'd flights of steps on the ancient hill. Today I know—objectively—all about the newer standards of technique . . . . . but what good does that do me? I can't *feel* in the contemporary media about which I have such exact information, and to which I accord so much intellectual admiration! *Emotionally and imaginatively* I am still what first impressions made me—I can see my present self clearly, albeit on a smaller scale, in a series of letters which I wrote between 1896 and 1899, and which my younger aunt lately exhum'd from storage to show me. Now the moral of all this senile rambling is this: that it is important to start the young poet or poetry-reader right, lest he form mental and aesthetic habits based on obsolete schools of technique and unfitting him for authorship or appreciative reading in contemporary media. Therefore, it you are to give him as a main pabulum the poetry of a less naturalistick period, it seems as though you ought to point out the differences of form which separate that material from the poetry now written—the poetry which he himself will have to write if he would really fit into his own age and express it. As for me—I fortunately happen to be so archaistick in *all* my tastes, that this rhetorical separation from my chronological period does not worry me. After all, the Georgian stile is the only one appropriate to a thoroughly Georgian mind and spirit, and I'd probably seem like a clown if I try'd any other. What I am thankful for, is that it is in the Georgian rather than in the Victorian past that I am stranded. The nineteenth century never existed so far as I am concern'd—its smugness, affectation, decorum, purposefulness, preciosity, mock-mediaevalism, optimism, hypocrisy, progressivism, inhibitions and so on having rebounded from me as an 1870 rubber ball might rebound from a 1720 brick wall. My spirit is of the eighteenth century—my scientifick information and philosophick perspective of the twentieth. Between them yawns a void—a gulph of nightmare symbolised by French roofs, side-whiskers, "limbs," "gentlemen-cows," "moral purpose," bustles, "elegance," unreality, and pose. Of its feelings and outlook I have less genuinely sympathetick knowledge than I have of the feelings and outlook of Tyre and Persepolis, Bactria and Sogdiana, Sabo and Palmyra, Timbuctoo and The Solomon Islands. It was, to me, just an interlude—an interregnum—a blind spot—O gawd, why did it ever fasten a city hall and an Infantry Hall on Providence? I always pitied poor John Ravenor Bullen for his inextricable habitancy of this Dark Age—pity'd him so genuinely that I faked up an euphemistick defence of his amiable inanities to console him whilst he liv'd. After his demise I chang'd it to serve as a preface to his collected poems—edited by me, as I must have told you, and publish'd by W. Paul Cook at the expense of a wealthy Chicago friend and admirer of Bullen's. Did I ever send you this book—which really forms the mechanical tour de force of the *Recluse Press?* If not, pray don't fail to tell me, and I will include a copy in the express package I am about to send. It is *suppos'd* to sell for two bucks, but is really a drug on the market—so that Cook, the last time he came down here, brought me a dozen copies to give away to anybody who might care for one. Hell, what rambling! *Ad nostras carnes ovillas redeamus!*[3] Anyway, the big idea is that you had orta slip in sumpun to tip the reader off, that the frills of pre-1890 or pre-1885 verse—no matter how "standard" such verse may be—form an outmoded technique which ain't stood for in 1929, no matter how common and excusable it was in its day. A few parallel passages—arrang'd in your inimitable manner—would hale a helluva lot to get the idee acrost in quick, nifty fashion. You might line up a bird like William Morris beside a modern egg like Bob Frost—Matt Arnold beside Ed Robinson—Alf Tennyson or Henry Longfellow alongside of Jack Masefield or A. E. Housman, Al Swinburne over-against Conrad Aiken—yuh get what I mean. See how the years have given the razzberry to the *'gins* and *yons* and *methoughts, oh's* and *ah's* and *meseems's*. I leave it to you, kid. If it's a bum steer, just pass it up and forget it. If it strikes yuh as a hot top, go to it! Them's my sentiments—thass all! Oh, wait, though! You'll find a swell paragraph on this subject in Clement Wood's booklet on poetry-writing in the *Haldeman-Julius* series. It's No. 514—why not get it and take a look?

July 29, 1929.

Well, fer the luvva gord! Loquacity delay'd this sage bulletin of lofty precepts, and now wot do I see in me matin post? Some *Moe-Know-Graph*—but then, young reprobate, what meanest thou by exposing an old man's random and careless metrick extemporaneousness to a highly critical circle of intelligent '04 grads? Lud, Sir, I blush, I shrink, I retreat! Reel'd off at ordinary prose speed without attention to rhetorical niceties, what bold exposure hath o'erta'en me haphazard and uncoördinated couplets? But stay! To know all is to forgive all. I've just seen how damn cleverly you've selected passages less pointless and inane than the majority, and with what uncanny skill you've pieced 'em together without leaving any telltale marks of patching and soldering. That's what I call art! If all editors cut down one's effusions with such taste and ingenuity, there'd be fewer broken hearts amongst the Grub-Street train—and I could afford to rescind my inflexible contributing proviso that ev'ry comma and semicolon must appear "as is", or else the item must come home to grandpa. Sir, there's more of your art in this assembling job than there is in the majority of pomes wherein the author synthesises the ready-made short-circuit phrases he finds lying about! You had orta of sign'd it yourself! As for the *Graph* itself—I have perus'd it with the most extreme edification and admiration, and am sensible how pleasing a celebration your class achiev'd on the occasion of its semi-semi-centennial! The festivities live again in my imagination, convey'd as they are by your polished periods, and I can but regret that I had not the good sense to enter University of Wisconsin back in dear old 1900, in order that I might be one of you! Good old 1900—will I ever forget it? My mother gave me my first bicycle on Aug. 20 of that memorable year—my tenth birthday—and I found myself able to *ride* it without lessons..... although I *couldn't get off*. I just rode around and around until pride vanished and I confest my technical limitation—slowing up and letting my grandfather hold the wheel still whilst I clamber'd down with the aid of the horse-block. But before the year's end I was master of my steed—burning up all the roads for miles around. Hell, but I wish an old man cou'd ride a bike today without getting stared at! Good old 1900—my only mistake was not entering the University of Wisconsin! Yes—that's the year they electrified the N.Y.N.H.&H.'s lines to Bristol and Fall River, and tried to run the new trains through the city streets but found the flanges too deep for the local trolley tracks..... and "The Burgomaster" came to the Providence Opera House..... "O moonbeams light and airy, O moonbeams soft and blue, pray be my good kind fairy, for I've work tonight for you....." and the East Greenwich trolley line was opened—big double-truck open cars (light green) number'd 740, 741, 742 etc.—and the old Abbott house, last seventeenth century building in Providence, was torn down, gawdam it!—and the new marble state house was finished, and Newport stopped being one of Rhode Island's joint capitals—and I wrote the first volume of my "Poemata Minora"[4] ... and succeeded in enforcing my ultimatum that I *would not* wear any more babish blouses with sailor collars..... and the Publick Library mov'd up to its present building from Snow St...... good old 1900! Some day I shall have to undertake a systematick recapture of early memories in the Proust manner, beginning with the first flash of permanent record in the summer of 1892. Or perhaps I shall boldly attempt to recapture the past,[5] moment by moment, through a system of mnemonick stimulation like that of the hero of poor Leonard Cline's "Dark Chamber." Anyhow, those were great days back around 1900—and they all troop back in a glorious procession whenever I get a stimulus as graceful and potent as your *Moe-Know-Graph!* I shall have to stage a class reunion myself—for the Slater Ave. Grammar School, to whose Class of '03 (dear old '03) I manag'd to belong despite a woeful lack of continuous attendance. I even have a class photograph to start with! If any year was more glorious than d. o. '00 or d. o. '04, it surely was d. o.

'03. My first astronomical telescope ..... the completion of my treatise "Pleasant Ways in Astronomy" (still unpublished) ..... my establishment of the hectographed *R.I. Journal of Astronomy* ..... Borelly's Comet ..... the glorious trip to Willimantic with my mother and grandfather ..... the long open-car rides (alone, in proud adult self-sufficiency) to Taunton, Fall River, Bristol, East Greenwich, Riverpoint, Buttonwoods ..... the bicycle rides to quaint Georgian villages amongst Rhode Island's ancient hills and vales ..... Blackstone Park and the Swan Point river road, (still, the gods be thanked, absolutely unchang'd, and still visited by me in the same old way on most pleasant summer afternoons!) where I used to take books, magazines, and writing-materials for studious or literary afternoons ..... my introduction to Prof. Upton of Brown,[6] and my glorious permission to visit the Ladd Observatory whenever I liked! ..... my odd, shy private tutor Arthur P. May[7]—a theological student whom I loved to shock with my pagan materialism ..... wonder where he is now? ..... Prof. Willett,[8] with his Vandyke beard, whom my grandfather allow'd to store books (most of which I read—they were admirably vary'd and pleasing!) in the attick of the stable ..... the chap with the new-fashioned *auto* (no longer call'd "horseless carriage" save by the elderly!)—a red Winton—who stored the queer thing in the carriage-room (no longer us'd, alas, for our last horses went in 1901) of our stable. It had a very high licence number for Rhode Island—782! Black on white, just as in 1929, for we've always alternated with a single scheme—black on white odd years, white on black even years. 782—high number. And now we have 'em up to 200·000. O tempora, O mores![9] An old man can't cross the street without getting run over ..... but the durn'd things will get in one another's way and come to a Kilkenny cat's ending[10] if they get much thicker, confound 'em! Dear old '03. And in those days you and Zimmy and Loren Blackman and Vic Marquissee and John Andrews and Willis Whitby and Bill Bradford and all the rest were carefree Juniors at the Alm. Mat. out in the Northwest Territory. But I *did* know of Wisconsin in those days. It was in my geography, and I'd heard of it as a place where some people my family once knew had gone. It seemed almost as real as heaven or hell. Mostly like the latter in my imagination, because there were tales of its *winter cold*. Ugh! My attitude toward *temperature* was just the same then as now. Good old '03! And who could have suspected what those Wright boys were doing down at Kitty Hawk? By the way—the physical aspect of the *Moe-Know-Graph* makes me think of the "books" which I us'd to make back in those very days of the golden nineteen-hundreds! I had a Simplex Typewriter, and used to conduct very ambitious experiments in bookbinding. No year went by without a formal publication from my "press"—variously call'd "The Royal Atlas Co.", "The Providence Press Co.", "The R.I. Journal Co.", "The Royal Press", etc. In '01 it was "Poemata Minora". (verse—heroicks, elegiack quatrains, et al.) In '02 "The Mysterious Ship", (fiction) and also "Ross's Antarctic Voyage",[11] "Wilkes'

Explorations", and the (relatively) ponderous "Antarctic Atlas" . . . . . oh, yes—I almost forgot "The Royal Atlas of the World"! In '03 it was an abridged version of my Astronomy . . . . . and so on. Lud, but the energy young folks will spend on things! I don't think I ever equall'd *The Moe-Know-Graph*, unless it was in my almost adult "The Moon", published in '06. But no—as I recall, I didn't justify the right-hand margins! That was my first job on my *present* Remington, then a new-bought wonder. I remember the July ('06) day it came. The slim young Remington clerk who brought it and show'd me all its ins and outs—Francis H. Neilan—is fat, bald, (on top and back) middle-aged now . . . . . and runs the leading typewriter establishment in town! I'm going down to his joint later this week and have him send up a man to fix the spacing mechanism on *that selfsame* Remington. Good old '06! Not a bad year, but getting too near modernity to have the fullest charm. That's the year I first broke into *print*—monthly astronomy articles etc. Also, the year I got my *present* telescope. *Providence Journal* moving into its new building . . . . . little old open cars (converted horse-cars!) still on a few of the local lines, but a legislative act passed requiring *vestibules* on the closed cars . . . . . had a fine new grey suit and ruin'd it the first day I wore it, in a spill from my bike on Irving Ave. hill in September . . . . . but after all, only the trousers got the worst of it, and the tailor did a marvellous job on the right knee. Damn the slipping handlebars that caused it! . . . . . Oh, yes, and '06 was the year I tried out an acetylene bike lamp instead of my old oil one . . . . . Hope St. High School . . . . . back in September despite the breakdown which took me out the preceding spring . . . . . pleasant new physics-teacher—Brown student named H. W. Congdon . . . . . wonder where he is now? . . . getting interested in chemistry—my old specialty of '99—again—new laboratory down cellar in 598 Angell like the old one at 454 . . . . . fitting up a summer-house and landskip garden in the vacant lot next the house . . . . . San Francisco earthquake . . . . . theatre (New Park) opened with *nothing but biograph pictures*, hitherto us'd only to chase late lingerers out of Keith's—illustrated songs— "When the Whippoorwill Sings, Marguerite" . . . . . "When the Mocking-Bird is Singing in the Wildwood" . . . . . "A Picnic for Two" . . . . . "She Waits by the Deep Blue Sea" . . . . . "If the Man in the Moon was a Coon" . . . . . "The Moon Has His Eyes on You"[12] . . . . . Belasco's "Darling of the Gods" gets around to the local stock company[13] . . . . . wonder what's become of the guy that play'd the hero? . . . . . Sayonara! Sayonara! . . . . . his name was William Ingersoll,[14] and he was no youth even then . . . . . *Another* theatre with *nothing but biograph films* . . . . . the Scenic—made over from the old Westminster Unitarian Church in Mathewson St., and *gawd damn* the vandal who took down the marvellous Ionick portico—Providence's closest approach to the Parthenon—to make way for that cursed foyer with the cheap electric sign! This dump has an *Orchestra*—not merely a piano like the New Park. Leader is a fat little fiddler named Charley Miller . . . . . wonder if he's alive now? New illustrated song howled by a duet—"Aren't You Coming Back to Old New Hampshire, Molly?"[15] New flash sayings ..... Oh, you Kid! ..... Skiddoo ..... twenty-three for you ..... Hell, how sophisticated '06 was! Not like my real old Golden Age of 1900! Something rare and naive must have gone out of the world about '05. But you're safe, bo ..... on record as belonging to good old '04! Only trouble is that us old guys have to see the cosmos going to the dogs right under our noses. Sure is hell to outlive one's period!

Addendum—tell this Saccherine bimbo[16] to send along his Injun-day reminiscences in the fall if he wants 'em doctor'd up. I'll ferment 'em into A-1 hootch if I'm still alive after de Castro—and if I *do* survive that bird there ain't nothin' but what'll seem like pie in comparison!

Well, Kid, that's the way I get going when somebody brings up the g. o. nineteen-hundreds! No help for it ..... just humour me and conceal your yawns with a graceful gesture. But let's see where we were anent the *Ars Poetica et al.*

Yrs for 1900–04
Lo.

Notes:
Random—touching queries in your epistle.

There is no law of "allowability" in rhyme, except that all the variation must be in the vowel rather than the consonant sound.[17] The latter admits of no variation. In many cases the variation arises from an original identity of sounds—(say, tea—carve, serve)—but in other cases (sigh, tender*y*—flung, along—vice, destr*oys*—power, secure) no such relationship is conceivable. In this latter case it is fair to suppose that authors, noting cases of discrepancy in once-perfect rhymes made imperfect by orthoëpic change, and not realising that such change had occurred, fancied that a certain amount of latitude was allow'd them in rhyming; and thus took deliberate liberties which time has made as classick as the once-perfect "allowables".

As for "limits of poetick licence"—hell, one can't even begin to establish anything of the sort! Usage—precedent—general principles of tests and moderation—roll your own, 'bo! But all this applies only to archaic verse anyway. In contemporary verse there is no such thing as poetick licence. Straight, pure, idiomatick and conversational English or nothing!

Religious cliché explanation O.K. if subject is of sufficient magnitude to warrant so much space. Page Song damn good.

Harris's praise of "action no stronger than flower" is superficially clever,[18] but personal—subjective—and probably of no vast general significance. It shows too great admiration of the psychology of the Elizabethan "conceit"—not enough appreciation of genuine insight and poignant imagery. I wouldn't take it very seriously—Harris is a senile lunatic and perverted egomaniac anyhow.

Notes

1. Edgar A. Guest (1881–1959), British-born American poet whose work was widely syndicated in newspapers, but who was criticized for the mundane and hackneyed quality of his verse.
2. I.e., Abner Alden's *Reader*.
3. "Let us return to our sheep meat!"
4. Elsewhere (and later in this letter) HPL dates Volume 1 of *Poemata Minora* to 1901. It is nonextant, but Volume 2 (1902) survives.
5. HPL undertook no such project, but later in the year he wrote, in much shorter compass, the sonnet "Recapture." Note that his "List of Certain Basic Underlying Horrors Effectively Used in Weird Fiction" contains the following passage (a synopsis of Leonard Cline's *The Dark Chamber*): "Man tries to recapture *all* of his past, aided by drugs and music acting on memory. Extends process to *hereditary* memory—even to pre-human days. These ancestral memories figure in dreams. Plans stupendous recovery of primal past—but becomes sub-human, develops a hideous primal odour, takes to the woods, and is killed by own dog."
6. Winslow Upton (1853–1914), professor of astronomy at Brown University.
7. Of his tutor, Arthur P. May (1880–?), HPL wrote in a sarcastic ad in the *Rhode Island Journal of Astronomy* (3 January 1904): "HIRE ME. I CAN'T DO THE WORK BUT I NEED THE MONEY."
8. Allan Herbert Willett (1865–?), professor of political economy at Brown University. Cf. the character Dr. Marinus Bicknell Willett in *The Case of Charles Dexter Ward*.
9. "Oh the times! Oh the customs!" A sentence by Cicero in the fourth book of his second oration against Verres (chapter 25) and First Oration against Catiline.
10. According to legend, two cats fought to the death and ate each other up such that only their tails were left.
11. In a later letter (see MWM 64), HPL titles this work "Voyages of Capt. Ross, R.N." In a letter to Marian F. Bonner (26 April 1936), HPL cites the title as "Ross's Explorations." See *Letters to Family and Friends*, 1024.
12. "When the Whippoorwill Sings, Marguerite" (1906), words by C. M. Denison, music by J. Fred Helf. "When the Mocking Birds Are Singing in the Wildwood" (1906), words by Arthur J. Lamb, music by H. B. Blanke. "A Picnic for Two" (1905), words by Arthur J. Lamb, music by Albert von Tilzer. "She Waits by the Deep Blue Sea" (1905), words by Edward Madden, music by Theodore Morse. "If the Man in the Moon Were a Coon" (1905), words and music by Fred Fischer. "The Moon Has His Eyes on You" (1905), words by Billy Johnson, music by Albert von Tilzer.
13. *The Darling of the Gods: A Drama of Japan* (1902), a play by David Belasco.
14. American actor William Ingersoll (1860–1936) did not play any role in the two Broadway runs of *The Darling of the Gods* (Belasco Theatre, 3 December 1902–May 1903, 16 September 1903–July 1904), but may have played it elsewhere.
15. "Ain't You Coming Back to Old New Hampshire, Molly?" (1906), words by Robert F. Roden, music by J. Fred Help.
16. Lucien J. Sweet (1877–1947) of Wauwatosa, Wisconsin, ran the Kenyon Press. See

also "Saccharissus" in letter 58.
17. Cf. HPL's "The Allowable Rhyme."
18. The line is from Shakespeare's Sonnets 65.4. British critic and biographer Frank Harris (1855–1931) discussed the line in "The True Shakespeare: An Essay in Realistic Criticism—Part IV," *Saturday Review* (London) 86, No. (16 July 1898): 72.

[40]   [TLS, JHL][1]

> 10 Barnes Street
> Providence, Rhode Island
> August 1, 1929

My dear Mr. Moe:

    I have just finished examining your *Doorways to Poetry*, and so far as I can see, it is by all odds the most nearly perfect and effective treatise of its kind I have ever encountered--touching upon more truly salient points, and illuminating each topic with more truly analytical and constructive precepts and exercises, than any manual hitherto written. I shall recommend it without reservation to every poetic client in my circle, and believe it will do them more good than all the admonitions and emendations I could supply in a year's time. Up to now I have had to content myself with recommending the late Prof. Matthews's *Study of Versification*. I am, in fine, so taken with the work that I can say nothing but praise concerning it.

    It must be evident to you that this study—despite its stated purpose of serving as an aid toward the more appreciative reading of literature—can be strongly recommended to incipient writers of verse for diligent study and assimilation. It is in every respect qualified to aid in their development, and will in all truth be far more helpful to them than any other volume published.

    I wish to thank you for the pleasure it has given me to look through this manuscript, and I hope it will soon be possible for me to use it in print as an important adjunct to my work.

> Cordially yours,
> H. P. Lovecraft

Mr. Maurice W. Moe
~~2303 Highland Avenue~~[2]
Milwaukee, Wisconsin

Notes

1. This letter apparently was written as an endorsement of *Doorways to Poetry* to be sent to publishers evaluating the book.
2. Presumably cancelled by MWM some time after he had moved to a new address, his own cover letter to a prospective publisher containing his current address.

[41]   [ANS, JHL][1]

[Postmarked Providence, R.I.,
3 August 1929]

Both envelopes of additional material arriv'd simultaneously safely SATURDAY, AUG. 3, at 10 a.m. Greetings! And not in the Caledonian sense, at that! I'll get busy beginning *Tuesday,* for today & tomorrow are all shot to hell with stuff to do, & Monday is listed for a glorious *vacation*—an all-day trip to Sudbury, in the Province of the Maſsachusetts-Bay, to visit the Red Horse Tavern,[2] popularly known as the Wayside Inn, & now own'd by a rich coachmaker named Ford, who dwells at the army post of Detroit, lately taken from the French king by His Majesty's troops. ¶ I shall attend to Doorways items before looking over that Salick test stuff. ¶ As for incomprehensibilities in my '04 epistle—I don't recollect saying a word about *winter!* And *"rearward seating"* might be more glibly comprehensible if I explained that the period cover'd is not merely '04 itself, but all the space—'00–'04—represented by your class's collegiate experience. The quip belongs to *1900,* & might be more easily recognisable if given in literal, original form "Go 'way back & sit down." I forget just when *McClure's* stopped. I know it was going in '03.[3] ¶ Say, LEAD ME TO THAT SIRENICA![4] I'm drooling, too! ¶ About *commerce*—of course, my unwillingness to charge money applies *only to friends.* Do you suppose I'd let De Castro get away free with the curst nightmares of labour he inflicts on me? ¶ Your metrical samples are OK. ¶ Hope the old Providence booklet interests you. I'll put Bullen in the express package. More anon.
Yr obt
Lo

[P.S. on front:] Now—12 noon Saturday—I gotta box Morton's mineral & shell specimens & call up the express office. I got about all in yesterday toting a coupla heavy boxes up from down town to pack the damn things in. ¶ Our old amateur side-kick Wash Van Dusen of Philada. has just had a small volume of his mild, sedate verses printed—my copy came yesterday.

> "The sun is sinking in the West,
>   The birds in leafy coverts rest" . . . .[5]

But you shan't have any specimens for your Doorways, for Wash is a nice old man, & I won't see him held up to publick reprobation!

Notes

1. *Front:* University Hall and Manning Hall Brown University.
2. HPL describes the visit in "An Account of a Trip to the Antient Fairbanks House..."
3. *McClure's Magazine* ran from 1893 to 1926.

4. By W. Compton Leith.
5. The lines do not come from Washington Van Dusen's *Sonnets on Great Men and Women*. They may be a misremembering of ll. 1–2 of "The Wife's Prayer" by Annie de G. Van Sickle: "The sun is sinking in the west, / The song-birds have all gone to rest . . ."

[42]   [ALS; AHT]

September 1, 1929
Melancholy harbinger of
autumnal chill!

Magister:—

Another instalment! Little drops of Carter's, little grains of prose, make the mighty volumes stack'd in endlefs rows! Your latest hath duly blow'd in, & I guess the enclosed about fixes you up for Doorways proper—apart from the Standards—unless you intend to send those Sidney & Keats sonnets for grandpaternal comment. Use all the stuff just as you like—change, amplify, transpose, or delete at will—for I send it only as rough source-material; amorphous notes & glofses for you to decipher, collate, interpret, arrange, & apply just as you chuse. As for giving credit—my gawd! What do you suppose a disillusion'd cynic whose 39th birthday occurr'd week before last wants with publicity? If I haven't shed the puerile love of fame at my age, by St. Paul, I ought to be studying a primer instead of helping on a learned treatise! Seclusion & privacy, not notoriety, are what a gentleman seeks. You know how to fix up acknowledgments in the preface—

"Thanks are hereby extended to the Singlenight, Raywalked Co., Shortboys, Red, & Co., & the O'Factoryan Co. for permission to reproduce certain of the poems in this volume; to Edgar A. Guest, Esq., & Mifs Fanny Hurst[1] for literary specimens to be us'd as models, & to several persons (including John A. Doe, Esq., Prof. Gorham A. Leagenes, L. Theobald Jun., & R. Anthony Roe, Esq.) who have kindly read the manuscript & furnisht helpful suggestions."

That's the sort of dope to dish out—& if any guy complains that you ain't gave 'im big enough electrick-sign display, you can crofs him off your list as a vulgar pusher & climber of no background or sophistication. Incidentally, I'm glad you find the old man's comments useful & of at least high-school intelligence. When they fall below par, don't hesitate to use plastick surgery or euthanasia! Wish I cou'd have speeded 'em up a bit better, but this was my extream limit. Apologies & all that understood. Now lemme know of any 23d-hour tinkering you want afore I shoot the precious first folio back.

I'm gonna save the Standards for a sep'rate job, beginning tomorrow, although I advise their inclusion in the main work. At present all I've done is to afsemble the several sections (including the verse-test part of the Codex Salicianus) in what I conceive to be their proper order—saving out the nifty Jane test as a final & presumably less hurry'd matter. I'll do all the tests in order—

first yours, & then the Salicianae; constructing key-comments wherever your letters or annotations appear to demand them. Then I shall add the Standards pages to the back of the Doorways MS.—considering the whole as one monumental work; a truly unique, long-needed, marvellously effective, & potentially clafsick manual on a subject whose subtleties & anfractuosities have hitherto defied concise, concrete, & systematick exposition.

Oh—about Exercise V, I gotta disappoint you about my non-recognition of the pafsages treated; for if your memory of 5:30 a.m. Si-Reen performances were more retentive, you'd recall that you gave away the whole businefs in advance! But I don't think I was much influence'd by awesome names—& I'd have spotted some of the authors anyhow. I recognise about half the items, I think, in the bunch herewith treated—Ex. 40. Too bad you mislay'd the portfolio of top-notch poesy comment, but I trust the stuff will turn up in time for the volume's ifsuance.

Glad you got some heavy dope from your Chicago conferee. What's his idea about the pads' killing the book? Does he think that, since the pads embody the most unique & indispensable features of your system of instruction, the average school-board will be content to purchase *pads only* & get along without the text proper—or at least put the text proper only in the hands of teachers? There's something in such a notion, I suppose—which illustrates how vilely different commercial enterprise is from the straightforward business of aesthetick creation or intellectual instruction. All I have to say about the matter is what I said before—that I think you ought to have the test matter in the main book *as well as* on separate pads, in order to make the volume a complete, self-contain'd, compact unit for the private lay student & for purchasers at second-hand. But use your own judgment—gord knows I haven't even a five-year-old's quota of business sense & practical acumen. As for a good firm to tackle—I've heard very favourably of the A B C, & have many volumes of theirs on my shelves right now. Ginn & Co. of Boston have quite a rep for schoolbooks—you might try them as second choice if A B C doesn't pan out.[2]

As for *floating accents* in poesy—I think there's a good deal to Brother Hat's theory, especially when consider'd in its historick relationship to clafsical quantitative verse. At the same time I believe the whole point is so damn'd subtle & technical—so much a matter of mature aesthetick imprefsion & so little a tangible matter of metrical mechanicks—that it would be simply nonsense to burden any beginner's head with it. Certainly, if you think that matter of not rhyming two secondarily accented syllables is too abstruse for your clientele, you ought not to vex their Arcadian simplicity with this *infinitely more tenuous & technical* consideration.

As for Hat's refusal to discriminate betwixt *sentiment* (real emotion) & *sentimentality*, (depicted emotion out of keeping with its subject) I don't follow him there at all! Of course the line of demarcation is *not clear*, because no two persons agree exactly about the precise quantity or nature of the emotion suited to any given subject; but beyond this necessary twilight zone there surely extend vast hemispheres in both directions, concerning whose classification there can be no reasonable doubt or divided opinion whatever among the average cultivated members of the same race & culture-stream. Everyone knows that Eddie Guest is not a poet & that Keats is, even tho' there may be considerable legitimate doubt about figures like James Whitcomb Riley & T. S. Eliot, N. P. Willis[3] & H. W. Longfellow.

About trochaick metre—well, I guess everybody can be right without much mutual contradiction. It all depends on how you use it—how long you make your lines, what sort of sounds you dump into the mould, what you write about, & what imagery you use. You can trip amiably along as Klei's idol Fred'k Locker-Lampson does in "At Her Window"—[4]

> "Sing thy song, thou trancèd thrush,
>   Pipe thy best, thy clearest—
> Hush, her lattice moves, oh, hush—
>   *Dearest Mabel!—dearest* . . . . ."

Or you can thunder out as Tom Campbell does in translating a chorus from Euripides' Medea—

> "Hast thou, on the troubled ocean,
>   Brav'd the tempest loud & strong,
> Where the waves, in wild commotion,
>   Roar Cyanean rocks among?"[5]

Write your own ticket—& draw your own conclusions! As for me, I'm so dumb I think a trochee is a cough-drop!

As for your Chi trip—I'll bet you & Donaldulus got an eyeful, & am cursedly sorry that the junior voyager had to be laid up for repairs at the medical garage immediately afterward. Trust he's all well & skipping about by this time. I'll have to see Chi some day, tho' naturally there are a lot of ancient burgs (e.g. Quebec, Charleston, St. Augustine, New Orleans) I wanna see a helluva lot more. Large cities ain't just my specialty, as my ultimate "reaction" to—or from—Manhattan amply illustrates. But at that there's 2 or 3 points about Chi worth dodging a few bombs for—& one of them's that planetarium, which sure does appeal to my constitutionally astronomico-cosmick soul. I may make Chi the objective of one of my annual sprees some day—if 'bus fares stay down at a decent level—& if I do I'll probably give Zythopolis the once-over too. Indeed—whilst about it, I'd probably take in Madisonium & get my money's worth. I ought to see Illinois, for the central part of the state is full of my collateral kinsfolk—almost every inhabitant of Delavan (near Bloomington) probably having something of Phillips blood in him. Of the four sons of my great-great-grandfather Asaph Phillips, (1764–1829) one (James) went there himself, whilst two more (Benoni & Whipple) had children who went. For years the mayor of Delavan was Louis Lawton, son of Whipple Phillips' daughter Mary & therefore my mother's second cousin. Louis' brother Samuel has just been visiting here—hence my reminiscences. It will amuse you to hear that *he does not roll his rrr..'s,* & says that none of the pioneer stock in Delavan do! The place was all filled up with Rhode Island Yankees from 1830 to after 1850, so that New England speech & folk-ways became firmly seated there despite the midwestern locale. I wish I could have seen this visitor, but I was at Onset during his unexpected & regrettably brief sojourn. My aunts, however, report his speech & observations with intelligent fidelity.

Well, well! So the author of "Sirenica" is an ex-curator![6] I must tell Mortonius—tho' I'm afraid good ol' James Ferdinand will never shine in any sort of prose except his own ponderous argumentative style! "Compton Leith"—you surely must find out his real name from this egg Spaulding,[7] & pass it on to Grandpa. Not that it wou'd necessarily be familiar, but that I'd like—merely as a matter of record—to know the straight handle of any bimbo who can turn out a line of Socony as slick as that paſsage you quoted! And of course I must see the book itself—such prose has no right to exist unperus'd by me! This guy Spaulding turns out fair stanzas—I'm glad to see how keenly he appreciates Leith (but why does he end up elegiacally, as tho' his hero had croak'd?)—though I'd hardly call him a new Swinburne or Shelley. His letter sounds oddly ordinary for a real poet's product—tho' the list of his habitual markets explains much. I wish I could rake in junk as he does, but somehow I feel damn sure I couldn't. Prose is my natural medium, & all my forc'd verses have a stilted quality which even cheap editors cou'd spot. Besides, I'm so completely out of sympathy with the popular moods reflected in saleable fugitive verse, that I could only thro' great effort think of anything to write about .... & when I did think & write, the reluctant, artificial, tongue-in-cheek eſsense of the job would inevitably peer revealingly from behind whatever camouflage of surface glibness I might be able to supply. No use talking—a guy can't put across stuff unless he has some real interest in it.

Incidentally, I'm repudiating my own pre-1927 prose style after a close examination of all my printed stories. I find in all my tales prior to the "Colour Out of Space" a certain naively pompous & incipiently melodramatick quality which annoys me increasingly as I get older & read more widely. That damned "Hound" just reprinted in W.T. almost knocked me cold with its high-flown rhetorick when I saw it again after seven years. If I ever had a collection publish'd, I'd go over all the early items stylistically—do Bush-work on myself, as it were. By the way—your admiration for A. C. Benson is undoubtedly well-founded. My kid cousin Phillips Gamwell—who died in 1916 & whom I probably mention'd often to you back in early amateur days—was especially stuck on his "From A College Window", & I found no reason to dissent from his verdict.⁸ My favourite stylist is Edward John Moreton Drax Plunkett, 18th Baron Dunsany; but I can see where Ex-Curator Leith is likely to give him a run for his money! I was greatly entertain'd by the portrait of Mr. Poe's taxidermical kinsman⁹ & his eminently appropriate profeſsional subject! There are many Poes today—descendants of the poet's uncles—but so far they have done little to augment the treasury of Columbian song.

Well—my ancestral pilgrimage of last Wednesday was a highly pleasing event, & one which I design to repeat in amplify'd form ere long. It was only three years ago that I decided to begin a systematick study of the lovely rural realm of Foster whence all my maternal forbears came, & where they were predominant in the 18th century; & you will recall my travelogue of the expedition which my younger aunt & I took in October, 1926. I had at that time intended to revisit the region soon, but chance caus'd the second trip to be deferr'd till now. My 1926 voyage was to territory largely connected with the Place, Casey, & Tyler streams of my heritage. Now, to equalise matters, I chose a region in which Phillipses & Howards were thickest—the lovely slopes of Howard Hill, which on the N.W. merge into the Place country—Moosup Valley—cover'd by my earlier trip. This is not the *oldest* Phillips region; for that terrain, containing the very ancient homestead now falling to ruin, lies to the south, on the old abandon'd section of the Plainfield Pike, & is being sav'd by me as a climax. In the graveyard there I shall find the early Georgian slabs of James Phillips Jun., my great-great-great-grandfather, & probably that of my great-great-great-great grandfather James Phillips Senior; which I have never seen, but of whose carven cherubs others have told me. For this trip I took a region easier of access, (tho' never before seen by me) where between 1788 & 1790 my great-great-grandfather Asaph Phillips settled, & where his descendants are represented both by permanent residents & by persons who spend only their summers there for old heritage's sake. The day was ideal, & my aunt & I had an exquisite rural walk from the stage-coach on the Plainfield Pike to the idyllick reaches of Howard Hill. We alighted at the semi-abandon'd village of Mt. Vernon, whose chief house has a splendid Georgian doorway with festoon'd fanlight, & which still holds the crumbling cellar walls of the ruin'd bank where my great-uncle Raymond Place was cashier in the 1830's. Helpful rusticks—who remember'd my grandfather well—directed us to the proper road, & we were soon rambling northward along one of the loveliest country lanes I have ever seen—a lane which now & then dipt into oak copses, & now & then emerg'd to graſsy heights whence one might survey the countryside for miles around, spying distant farmhouse gables, lines of stone walls, winding brooks, & gnarl'd hillside orchards whose combined glamour produc'd a picture finer than anything in any eclogue I ever read. This lane at length debouch'd upon the Howard Hill Road thro' a picturesque farmyard with an old mill & mill stream close by. Then came a walk along the hill crest, where every land ended in a noble prospect of distant horizons & where sentinel elms & pines, swinging meadow gates, walls & bars, & a little old white schoolhouse with small-pan'd windows, help'd to promote the pastoral beauty of the scene. At last the site of the Asaph Phillips homestead hove in sight, (recognis'd by my aunt, who had been there before) & we knew we had arriv'd at the focal point of our journey. The old house, built about 1790, was some time ago burn'd down; but the present owner of the estate, William Henry, Esq., a civil-engineer of Providence (who marry'd the great-granddaughter of Asaph Phillips) who dwells there summers, hath erected a new house of antient design, with interior woodwork taken from demolish'd colonial buildings of the region. There are lovely orchards, picturesque old barns & byres, rambling stone walls, noble groves, & magnificent prospects on every hand; so that, recalling that my grandfather (Whipple V.) & great-grandfather (Capt. Jeremiah) were both born here, & that the seat of my Place ancestors down the slope toward Moosup Valley is equally beautiful, (cf. travelogue of Oct. 26, 1926) I again assur'd myself that I come naturally & honestly by my pastoral predilections & love of fine bucolick landskips. The old Phillips graveyard, which I have long'd to see for years, is situate on the crest of a meadow hill which drops abruptly to an exquisite wooded valley with a brook. It is girdled by a low stone wall, & commands a splendid vista of woods & groves—one particularly imprefsive cluster of trees lying shortly westward. On its hillward side it drops to a lower terrace which juts boldly out from the slope & ends in a high bank wall—a terrace devoted to the newer interments, & maintain'd in as elegant & sophisticated a state as the smartest urban cemetery; with close-shav'd lawn, trim beds of gay flowers, tasteful urns, & polisht granite monument & markers of the most metropolitan pattern. In this lower terrace area are interr'd many Providence Phillipses who cherish a wish to lie on ancestral soil despite their lifetime separation from the ancestral scene. It is very lovely in its way, but forms a rather incongruous note in the agrestick Foster landskip. Naturally, my chief interest lay in the upper & older burying-ground with its Georgian slate slabs bearing weeping-willows, cinerery urns, & neatly rhym'd epitaphs, & its white marble slabs of the 1840's with their brief, pious, & sentimental observations. This place was much like the old Place cemetery in Moosup Valley, which I describ'd in my 1926 travelogue. I now copied with great pains several ancestral epitaphs—in some cases having to clear away moss, earth, & creepers in order to reach the bottom lines. Here are a few:

Asaph Phillips (1764–1829) [my gt-gt-grandfather] The sweet remembrance of the just Shall flourish when they sleep in dust.	Esther Whipple wife of Asaph P. (1767–1842) Blessed are the pure in heart, For they shall see God
Capt. Jeremiah Phillips (1800–1848) [son of Asaph—my gt-grandfather. Kill'd in his own mill.]* This mortal shall put on immortality.	Rhoby Rathbone† wife of Capt. Jeremiah (1797–1848) O ye mourners, cease to languish O'er the grave of those you love; Pain & death & nights of anguish Enter not the world above.

Susan Esther Phillips
[dau. of Capt. Jeremiah—1827–1851. my grandfather's favourite sister, who dy'd at 24, & after whom my mother was given her second name of Susan.]
      Thou art gone to the grave, but we will not deplore thee,
      Tho' sorrows & darkneſs encompaſs the tomb;
      The Saviour has pass'd thro' the portals before thee,
      And the lamp of his love is thy guide thro' the gloom.

Seth Whipple Phillips
[1825–1829]
[Son of Capt. Jeremiah—dy'd at age of 3 yrs. 7 mo. 22 d., before my grandfather was born. When (1833) my grandfather was born, he was given the first name of Whipple, which had been borne as a 2nd name by this tiny brother he had never known.]
      Parents, weep not for thy son,
        Who is early call'd away;
      His better life is now begun,
        Where youth will ne'er decay.

---

*he was inspecting a mill he own'd on Nov. 20, 1848, & caught the skirts of his voluminous frock coat in a whirling belt. This was 4 months after his wife's death, so that my grandfather grew up an orphan.

† whose sister Sarah marrying Capt. Stephen Place Jr. was the mother of Rhoby Place, (named after her) my grandmother. cf. 1926 travelogue

> Zilpha Ann Phillips
> [dau. of James, son of Asaph & brother of Capt. Jeremiah, who later went to Illinois & became a fellow mid-Westerner of yours, tho' he never roll'd his rrr...s. He owned the Hotel at Delavan, Ill. where Abraham Lincoln often stopp'd, & knew Lincoln well. My grandfather met L. whilst visiting his uncle James at Delavan in the 1840's.]
> (died Sept. 23, 1824
> aged 10 mo. 20 d.)
> Our short-lived idol, our sweetest flow'r,
> Is call'd by death's all-conquering pow'r,
> To leave a world of grief & pain:
> We part, but soon shall meet again.

Tho' the head of the household was absent in town, his visiting daughter (my 3d cousin) from New-Jersey & several grandsons extended pleasing hospitality. I had met none of them before, & was very favourably imprest by their kindliness & cultivation. They produc'd some genealogical books & charts which help'd me very materially in defining my exact relationship to several collateral Phillips lines, & I in turn was able to tell them much they did not know about the Whipples (whose blood we get thro' Asaph's wife) & their descent from the Whipleys of Norfolk in Old England. I blazon'd the Whipple arms for them—a thing they were very grateful for, insomuch as they had not previously known the exact design. Here the heraldick knowledge taught me by my young friend Talman stood me in good stead . . . . .

Phillips

Whipple

Casey

Place

Rathbone

Howard

. . . . tho' I must concede that his precepts in the art of actual heraldick delineation were lefs succefsful, as the above bunglings attest! Being regal'd with cordiality, coffee, data, & pears from a tree planted by Asaph Phillips, we departed over Howard Hill in quest of a short road to Moosup Valley & the Place country, insomuch as I wish'd to behold again the antient & sightly birthplace of my mother, grandmother, & Place great-grandfather. At the top of the hill we paus'd at the newer Howard homestead, where we made ourselves known to the gentleman of the estate, Whipple Howard, Jun., son of Whipple son of Leonard son of Judge Daniel Howard, whose wife was Asaph Phillips' daughter Anna—my third cousin by that link, & a remoter cousin by an earlier link. He prov'd a man of middle age, wide information, & much affability; who remains on his ancestral soil in the manner of those who went before him. His house is of early 19th century date, & in fine repair—one of the most attractive New England rural places I have ever beheld. By his directions we found the Moosup-Valley short cut, & at once plung'd into a deserted countryside of utterly dreamlike lovelineſs. The lane we follow'd was formerly the main high-road to Moosup Valley & the country westward, but was abandon'd about the time of the revolution in favour of the present route. During its existence houses had been built upon the Howard Hill half of it, so that the perpetuation of that part as an acceſsible lane was neceſsary. The other half, in the valley beyond the Lyon burying ground & toward the James Phillips place, was suffer'd to fall into desuetude; so that today not a trace remains of it. Entering the still-preserv'd part of the route from the top of Howard Hill, we found ourselves in the most marvellous & magical colonial territory it hath ever been my good-fortune to behold. Other old roads have such signs of modern decadence as telegraph-poles & mail-boxes, but here nothing of the kind had intruded. Just the quaint, narrow, stone-wall'd line of the antient road, now carpeted with soft, delicate graſs & moſses & rambling in curves & twists through an incredibly exquisite variety of meadows, orchards, woods, valleys, & sleepy Georgian farmsteads. Birds sang, & the westering sun pour'd a flood of almost unreal & theatrical glamour over the graceful verdure & undulant pastures. The feeling that one walkt in a sheer vision became more & more intense as the chromatick pageantry of fresh greenery, deep-blue sky, & fleecy cumulus clouds spread more & more thoroughly within one's consciousneſs. The grace of the antient farms with their white-gabled houses, old-fashion'd gardens, stone walls, sloping orchards, & picturesque lines of barns & sheds became so overwhelmingly pervasive that one felt almost opprest for lack of opportunities for instant lyrical utterance. Here, indeed, was a small & glorious world of the past *completely* sever'd from the sullying tides of time; a world *exactly* the same as before the revolution, with *absolutely nothing* changed in the way of visual details, currents of folk-feeling, identity of families, or social & oeconomick order. Where Howards or Lyons or Phillipses & Places settled in the first half of the 18th century, there Howards & Lyons & Phillips & Places live now—tilling the same fields in the same way, living in the same houses & thinking the same thoughts. Horse-drawn vehicles predominate still, & the drowsy hum of summer is unvext by any discordant note of urbanism or mechanism. A gentle, elusive fragrance unknown either to towns or to ordinary countrysides pervades the whole scene, & so stimulates the imagination that even I, whose fancy is so preponderantly visual, found myself living with several senses rather than with one. The lines of Milton came into my head, & I found myself muttering:

> "As one who long in populous City pent,
> Where Houſes thick, and Sewers, annoy the Air,
> Forth iſſuing on a Summer's Morn, to breathe

> Among the pleaſant Villages, and Farms
> Adjoyn'd, from each Thing met conceives Delight:
> The Smell of Grain, or tedded Graſs, or Kine,
> Or Dairy, each rural Sight, each rural Sound."[10]

Verily, I told my aunt, there is no need to marvel at that circumstance notic'd by Horace, when he say'd:

> "Scriptorum Chorus omnis amat Nemus et fugit Urbes."[11]

Such, without the least difference in aspect or mood, is the agrestick realm thro' which my forefathers rov'd in the Golden Age of the Georges. It is beyond question that young Asaph Phillips must have strid along its length on many a sunny afternoon whilst bound for his kinsfolk's abodes in the valley beyond, & here my great-grandfather Jeremiah must often have pluckt blossoms & lain on the sward looking up at the mysterious sky & elfin clouds & fantastick treetops in the days just after 1800, when as a little boy he play'd truant from the trim white schoolhouse with its neat belfry & small-pan'd windows. Today either young Asaph or little Jeremiah & his brothers & sisters—Benoni, Betsey, Waity, James, Whipple, Anna & Esther—could roam thro' these selfsame meads & lanes & groves without finding anything amiſs or thinking that anything had happen'd to their small, simple, Arcadian world in the interim. For after all, the antient New-England of the Magnalia, the Pilgrim's Progreſs, the Bible, the Farmer's Almanack, the New-England Primer, & the elder poets *is not dead.* It has merely *retreated from visibility* & from oeconomic predominance—from the dirty fringe of foreigniſed cities & the squalid length of cement state roads with their billboards, roadhouses, hot dawg stands, & tourist cabins. Quietly, in the tranquil & lovely by-roads where vulgar wealth & aimless progress never intrude, it still lives on in its own old way—with narrow winding roads, lovely rock-&-turf slopes, gnarl'd brooding orchards, & maſsive, smoke-wreath'd farmhouse chimneys. There is no paradox or deception in the statement that the old Foster scene shrined in my ancestral memories is likewise a reality of the 20th century, & that the piled-up squares & rectangles on my genealogical charts represent not a dynasty & milieu that are extinct, but a breed & life which exist today as truly as they existed in those glamorous 1700's & early 1800's. The only difference is in *the relative place which these people & this life occupy in the nation and world as a whole*—& as you may easily imagine, this difference is trifling indeed to one who repudiates *in toto* both the entire machine culture of the present, & the personality-stunted Babbitt-warren of American commercialism, size-worship, & time-table servitude to which that accursed bastard-culture has now reduced these once glorious colonies. God Save the King! I am happy to say that the peril of Finnish immigration, which was an active threat to Foster when I writ my travelogue three years ago, is waning rather than increasing.

The intruding Finns were mainly summer pests who spent their winters in diverse labours around the wharves of New-York, & as time goes on, they seem to gravitate more toward New-York than toward Foster. It was their old Finland peasant heritage which made them seek the soil upon first reaching America, but as they become assimilated into the mongrel proletariat of the usurping machine-civilisation of this continent, they gradually adopt its rat-like urbanism. Many farms, Finn-own'd a decade ago, have now return'd to Anglo-Saxon hands. Howard Hill never had other than its old colonial stock, & now the whole South Foster region seems afsur'd of an indefinite English future. The Italian wave from Providence stops ten miles east of this terrain, with a great reservoir system & barren belt as a buffer. Most of the home-keeping old folk have never seen a foreigner save for the few intruding Finns, & are inclin'd to call all foreigners "Finns." If any ingulphment ever comes, it will probably be from the towns of Connecticut across the state line rather than from Providence—but even that menace is obviously far distant. At present, Foster is an all-Yankee colonial town carrying on the original New-England tradition of agricultural simplicity. There is less danger of change now than in the middle 19th century, when everyone flock'd to the towns & dreaded the notion of being thought countrify'd.[12] The good families send their sons to Providence schools and Brown University, and sometimes (as in the case of Mr. Henry) engage in business or professional occupations in town; but their anchorage always remains on their paternal soil—they are on their old farms all summer, and choose (as the lower terrace of the Phillips burying ground attests) to be laid to rest in the end beneath the calm skies and waving grasses of the meadows their fathers knew and lov'd. For two hundred years these people and their lands have always been the same—and I hope they will always be. I am sorry that my direct personal line did not stay on the antient soil; for as it is, my affection and loyalty are divided betwixt these pastoral meads of ancestral memory, and the ancient hill and Georgian spires and roofs of that Old Providence to which my own infant eyes were open'd. By birth urban, I am by every hereditary instinct the complete rural squire. God Save the King!

Well, having loiter'd as long as possible along the old road, we finally came to the hilltop farm of the Lyons which marks the end of its accessible part. Inquiring the way to Moosup-Valley of a kindly antient gentlewoman, we struck out across thinly path'd hills and dales of the greatest conceivable beauty; skirting the Lyon burying ground and traversing the pastures where the kine of Howard Hill and Moosup Valley meet on common territory. The way became increasingly difficult as we proceeded, paths being obscure and thorn-choak'd, and valleys being exceedingly marshy. At one point an enormous black snake glided across our path, causing my aunt to advance with added caution. The last barrier was a brook which separated a wooded swamp from a rising meadow—and having edg'd across this on planks, we stood at the edge of Moosup-Valley, where the exquisitely lovely James Phillips place dreams on as of old at the road's bend; nestling in the lee of its rocky hill, and looking across the elm-arcaded way at the green lower meadow, where graceful alders nod above a crystal, convoluted stream. Of this place I spoke at some length in my 1926 travelogue, telling how I visited there for two weks in August 1896 when my grand-uncle James Phillips (my grandfather's brother—Capt. Jeremiah's eldest son) was alive, and how it is now in the hands of a local couple named Bennis, both collateral kinsfolk of mine. On this occasion we paus'd only for brief civilities, proceeding at once to the neighbouring Place homestead whose picture (a crayon drawing by my mother after a painting by my late great-aunt Sarah Place Vaughan[13] of East Greenwich) hath ever hung upon my wall, and beneath whose roof my mother, my grandmother, and my great-grandfather Stephen Place Jun. were born. Of the loveliness of this house, landscape, and roadside burying-ground I have spoken in the earlier travelogue, so that I need not describe in detail my pleasure at beholding the time-weather'd gables, the climbing ivy, the stone-wall'd road, the verdant vale behind, and the downward-sloping meadows to the northwest, where the modest white belfry of Moosup-Valley village gleam'd thro' embowering boskage. Even A. C. Benson, in selection F of Exercise V, couldn't describe a landscape more hauntingly sightly and healingly restful than this! Despite the mediocre newcomers who have inhabited the place since it left our family in 1870, we on this occasion decided to inspect the interior; which I had not seen since my sixth birthday, Aug. 20, 1896, which my aunt *had never seen in her life*—at least with conscious eyes, since her only entrance to the house was as a toddling infant in the last days of its Place tenure. Beholding it thus as a relative novelty, we were very favourably imprest with the evidences of what had been—though the present inhabitants are slovenly householders with far from old-Novanglian standards of neatness and decoration. The Place who built the house toward the end of the eighteenth century (Stephen Sr., 1736–1817) must have had something of the mediaeval-manorial in his taste, insomuch as he provided an enormous central room or "great hall" with fireplace, out of which many smaller rooms open'd—a design which I have never seen in any other old New England farmhouse. The interior woodwork, tho' not treated as well as it deserves during the last sixty years, is still excellent; and I wou'd give much to have the carv'd white Georgian mantel to sit by of an evening as the logs blaz'd behind colonial andirons! The six-panell'd doors are finely wrought, and equipped with latches and hinges of a type already old-fashion'd when the house was built. Old Stephen was a man after my own heart and I have reason to know that he fully appreciated his exquisite rustick environment. It is his file of Farmer's Almanacks which begins my own collection, and in those numbers publish'd toward the close of his life I find marginal notes indicating timid poetick attempts based upon the agrestick scene—or more, perhaps, on the conventional literature of agrestick scenes. In the 1815 issue I find the following not very original bit—

"Hark from the copse a tuneful sound,
My ears attend the cry"[14]

which makes me regret that no more of the text is accessible. He was evidently unwilling to have any of his manuscripts survive for the edification of his posterity, since I have never seen any complete poem of his. Incidentally—the rhetorical text book us'd by his son Stephen Jr. (my great-grandfather) at the old Kent Academy in the 1790's (*The Reader;* by Abner Alden, A.M. Boston, 1797) is the very volume out of which I first picked up the rules of prosody myself—by coincidence, in the same year of 1896 wherein I visited Foster. I found it tucked away with other Georgian reliquiae in a windowless attick room of my birthplace—454 Angell St.—and was fascinated by its long ſ's, well-stated precepts, and Dryden–Pope–Thomson–Addison–Johnson selections. I have it before me now as I pen these lines—faithful guide and companion of my youth and old age alike! God bless it—a worthy praecursor to the Mocratick "Doorways"! It has the same sort of definitions and specimen lines that your volume has, and not a few highly philosophick observations—obviously cribb'd from the elder Sheridan.

"Poetick numbers", (it saith), "are founded upon the same principle with those of the musical kind, and are governed by similar laws. Proportion and Order are the sources of the pleasure we receive from both; and the beauty of each depends upon a due observation of the laws of Measure and Movement."

After a time the author observes:

"There are eight different kinds of feet admitted into English verse; viz.

The Iambus ˘ –	The Dactyle – ˘ ˘
The Trochee – ˘	The Amphibrach ˘ – ˘
The Spondee – –	The Anapaest ˘ ˘ –
The Pyrrhick ˘ ˘	The Tribrach ˘ ˘ ˘

The Iambus is a foot of two syllables, the first short or unaccented, the other long or accented. This foot is most congenial to English heroick verse, because it is the only one of which an heroick line can be wholly composed.

EXAMPLES
All Iambicks

˘   –   ˘   –   ˘   –   ˘   –   ˘   –
"Above / how high / progres/sive life / may go,

˘   –   ˘   –   ˘   –   ˘   –   ˘   –
Around / how wide / how deep / extend / below!"[15]

Behold the influences which made Old Grandpa Theobald what he is! How I lapt this up in '96 and '97! No wonder "Doorways" finds me in my element. And little Steve Place Jun. lapt this same material up at Kent Academy in another good old '97 or '98—*1797*! Same stuff—same book—same spirit—and here I was in the same house on a glorious August afternoon; the house where little Steve was born, where he grew up, and where he dy'd full of placid rural memories in 1849—the year after his brother-in-law Capt. Jeremiah Phillips was killed in the old mill down the Moosup Valley Road. Old days—old days—and old ways! Here I sit with Steve's old book before me a score of his other books on my shelves, his file of Farmer's Almanacks (following his father's) in my lower table drawer, his blood in my veins, and the glowing memory of his house and native landscape in my mind and fancy. God Save the King! Who says the Georgian past is gone? Bring on your damn'd years—a helluva lot they can modernise this tough old Georgian bird!

> Nor can decadent Change unchalleng'd thrive
> Whilst Foster and Old Theobald both survive![16]

Well—we broke away from the hallow'd spot at last, and walked amongst lengthening shadows in the golden light down the old road, the narrow, stone-wall'd road, the bending, mead-flanked road, through vary'd rustick vistas to the huddle of old gables and chimneys, barns and byres, elms and orchards, that is antient Mount-Vernon on the Plainfield Pike. There, as twilight stole upon us, we took the Providence stage-coach; thereafter rumbling back thro' the fine old villages of Clayville and North-Scituate, and finally entering the mongrel chaos of the urban penumbra. Jangling, bustling down-town was a sad anticlimax after Foster—but balm came when I turn'd toward the antient hill and saw the great square of Pegasus shimmering over the shadowy Georgian roofs and steeples on the wooded crest. Old Providence! Here, too, the ancient colonial life and spirit survive amongst the hillside lanes where double flights of steps rise from brick sidewalks, and the early lights evening gleam soft and yellow from arching fanlights and small-paned windows. God Save the King! If one must dwell in a town, then surely there's no place like Old Providence, round which all the memories of my youth are cluster'd! Thank Heav'n I reside in a quiet by-way on the crest of the hill; where all is as it us'd to be, and no sight or sound suggest anything that one might not find in a placid New England village of two or three thousand population.

My next ancestral pilgrimage will cover the *earlier* Phillips region south of Howard Hill—on the *old* Plainfield Pike; a section cut off from offensive traffick when the highway was re-located to banish a bend. Here I hope to find living and discursive a very distant cousin nam'd Frank Phillips,[17] who can show me where my great-great-great-grandfather James Jun. (died 1807) (Asaph's father) is bury'd—in an old god's-acre which may possibly harbour my great-great-great-great-grandfather James Sr. (died 1753) as well. I want both their epitaphs. (I may find the old (early eighteenth century) Phillips homestead in a state of abandonment and decrepitude. I am told that the chances are even for its being still a tottering entity or a heap of ruins.) James Sr.'s father Michael (1642–1689) rests at Newport, and I still hope to find his mortal remains amidst the populous slate acreage of the Farewell St. burying-ground.¹⁸ Mike was a townsman—I'm asham'd of him!—for Newport was a great and cultivated seaport in his day. His father Rev. George (prais'd in Cotton Mather's "Magnalia") dy'd in 1644 and is bury'd where he preach'd, in Watertown, in yᵉ Massachusetts-Bay—a place I have never seen, but which I have all my life been meaning to visit. And Rev. George's father Christopher—and all the still earlier fathers—Elizabethan, Tudor, and Plantagenet gentlemen of Old England—sleep on still holier soil—beneath the ivy'd and crumbling parish church of Rainham, in Norfolk. They never saw New-England—and with lov'd, blest *Old England* stretching delectably about them they never needed to!! The main line—by primogeniture—of these Norfolk Phillipses now sports a baronetcy; the present baronet being Sir Lionel Phillips, of Boxford, unless he was kill'd in the war or somehow return'd to dust since the last account I read. And so it goes. Now to revision and *Doorways*—but more ancestral travelogues soon.

      Yr obt Servt
      H. Phillips Lo.

Notes

1. Fannie Hurst (1885–1968), American novelist and short story writer.
2. When Macmillan returned *Doorways to Poetry* to MWM in 1930, he immediately sent it to American Book Company, best known for publishing the McGuffey Readers. It, too, rejected MWM's book.
3. N[athaniel] P[arker] Willis (1806–1867), an American author, poet, and editor who worked with Edgar Allan Poe and Henry Wadsworth Longfellow. He was the highest-paid magazine writer of his day.
4. Frederick Locker-Lampson, English man of letters, bibliophile and poet. The poem is in *London Lyrics*, the quoted lines (27–30) on p. 51.
5. "The Speech of the Chorus" (ll. 89–92) in *Medea*. In *The Poetical Works of Thomas Campbell* 249–50.
6. W. Compton Leith is the pseudonym of Ormonde M. Dalton (1866–1945), a British writer who worked for many years at the British Museum, becoming the head of the department of British and medieval antiquities (1921–28).
7. Unidentified. A Mrs. Spaulding is mentioned in a letter to the Coryciani, but she too is unidentified.
8. A[rthur] C[hristopher] Benson (1862–1925), British essayist, poet, author, and the 28th Master of Magdalene College, Cambridge. Like his brother E. F. Benson, A. C. wrote ghost stories. *From a College Window* is a collection of essays.

9. Unidentified.
10. Milton, *Paradise Lost* 9.445–51.
11. "The entire band of writers loves the woods and flees the city." Horace, *Epistles* 2.2.77.
12. Ms. at JHL ends at this point; balance taken from AHT.
13. Older sister of Robie Alzada Place Phillips, HPL's maternal grandmother.
14. Isaac Watts, "Hark! From the Tombs a Doleful Sound," *Hymns and Spiritual Songs* (1707–9), Book 2, number 63. This hymn was sung at the funeral of American president George Washington. *Copse* is probably an error by the transcriber.
15. The above quotations are from Abner Alden, *The Reader* (Boston: I. Thomas & E. T. Andrews, 1802), 112–14.
16. Also in HPL to FBL, 1 September 1929 (AMS, JHL).
17. Frank Darius Phillips (1872–1958) of Potterville, Scituate, Rhode Island.
18. Michael Phillips was actually dead by 1676. Most references give a probable birth date of ca. 1630. No authorities seem to support HPL's claim that Michael Phillips was the son of Rev. George Phillips (d. 1644) of Watertown, MA. Some assert that Michael was one of three brothers who emigrated from Wales.

[43] [AHT]

[November 1929?]

LINES
Upon the Magnates of the Pulp.
by
Lewis Theobald, Junr.

In former Times our letter'd Brethren sought
To starve their Bodies while they fed their Thought;
Unaw'd by Wealth, unbought by Luxury,
They own'd their Brains, and scorn'd the Slaver's Fee.
Poor, modest, proud, they held the princely Pen,
Masters and Peers, and conscious Gentlemen;
And who, unbow'd, would not their Place prefer
To the rich Tradesman's—harness'd, fawning Cur?
But Time, the Goth, each pleasing Virtue blights
As his curst Legions storm our guarded Heights;
Behold! where Bards free Musick once outpour'd,
A Crowd of Lackeys cringe around their Lord:
From gold-stain'd Pockets beg their tawdry Doles,
And stuff their Bellies as they sell their Souls.
What shall they write? 'Tis not for them to say—
King Mob will give them Orders for the Day!
Scrawling what's bid, they woo the unwash'd Throng
In chap-book Prose, and loud illit'rate Song;

Themselves in Boasting, not in Art, express,
And reckon Worth in Terms of Gainfulness.
See! see! where once the honest Dreamer try'd
To scale the Slopes of Loveliness and Pride,
To cast off Earth, and reach th' aetherial Mead
High o'er the Slough where wallowing Porkers feed,
Our newer Band opposing ways pursue,
And lose the Freeman in the grasping Jew.
'Tis theirs to shine in Tests of haggling Skill,
Their bulging Purses, not their Heads, to fill;
To drown their Yearnings and their Freeman's Bent
In sticky Swamps of servile Excrement.
Hail to the Carcass, fed, tho' bound in Chains;
Pox on your Dreamer's or your Poet's pains:
We drink to Flesh in one black Stygian Gulp,
And sink our Spirits in a Grave of Pulp!

    By the way—Belknap, young August W. Derleth, and L. Theobald Jun. are gonna be mention'd soon in the daily lit'ry colyum of the *Providence Journal*—"The Sideshow", conducted by the critick Bertrand K. Hart.[1] The cause is this: that Bre'r Hart began the other day to discuss the question of the *greatest horror-story in all literature*, and named such commonplace and mechanical specimens as the choices of himself and his friends that I couldn't resist sending him my *Recluse* article, plus some lists of "Best horror tales" compiled by Sonny, Derleth, and Grandpa. It seems he was interested—for today I had a note from him, asking permission to transfer the discussion to his colyum, and to mention Grandpa and his boys by name! Fame, gents, fame—a prophet with honour in his own burg! I'm letting him. Of course, in giving Belknap's and Derleth's lists of favourites, I omitted such tales as I wrote myself. I'll shoot ya any spicy items in the discush which may appear.
        Yr obt Servt
            Grandpa

Notes

1. B[ertrand] K[elton] Hart (1892–1941), was literary editor of the *Providence Journal* and author of the column, "The Sideshow." HPL refers to "The Sideshow," *Providence Journal* 101, No. 285 (29 November 1929): 12.

[44]   [AHT]

Thor's Day
[4 January 1930?]

Apex of Academick Acuteness:—

About your Lit Guild letter—I'm damn sorry, for my natural and superficial sympathies are all on your side; but I can't so well 'see what you see' in giving mature consideration to profound and complex matters like this—matters which compel us to embark upon a long and involved course of standard-tracing. A decade ago, when I was less soberly analytical and more governed by personal prejudice and experience than today, I would have reeled you off a one hundred per cent endorsement very cheerfully—and probably in heroick satire quite annihilative to your adversaries—but Grandpa is an old man now, and looks back upon life and the stream of history with an old man's impersonal detachment and all-inclusiveness. I don't get perspectives tangled and blurred by local and transient impressions as I used to—indeed, I often smile ruefully at some of the emphatick dogmatisms and indignations of my early Kleicomolo period. Indignation is a naive and absurd emotion at best—but then, young philosophers were naive and absurd creatures in the dear old 1900's, when the fog of Victorian unrealities still hung over the scene and blurred the hard, clear outlines of things and trends and standards as they are. The baker's dozen of years since 1916 have given Old Theobald plenty of time for reading, reflection, and observation—and the old boy's eyes and faculties still hang on after a fashion.

The fact is, that before passing judgment on the taste of any work of art, we must establish *the validity of the standard by which we judge it*—establish that validity *abstractly* and *impersonally*, without the least reference to what we ourselves may happen to like or dislike, or what we may have been taught at our mothers' knees or by the especial transient milieu surrounding our early and impressionable years. The "good" of one era may be the "evil" of another, and we must not use such expressions as "filth" and "smut" irresponsibly. Before adopting a nomenclature, we must see whether it has any reasonably universal meaning or not.

Now when we come to the question of that peculiar rage felt by persons over forty (persons, that is, educated well before the wartime period) concerning the free presentation of erotic matters in art and literature, there are two points visible at the very outset which make us feel that there must be something erroneous and abnormal about it. First—its very *degree and venom*, as contrasted with the comparatively mild attitude of its possessors against such other doubtful trends as democracy, machine-standardisation, futurism, general and violent lawlessness, etc., excite our suspicion. Why all this abnormal, hair-trigger touchiness and *interest* in one particular subject out of many? And second—we are so plainly aware that the people of the generation in question were educated under a system whose position regarding the given subject was flagrantly and fundamentally erroneous. We don't have to be told nowadays that the whole structure of Victorian art and thought and sexual morality was based upon a tragic sham—a criminal denial of the facts and relative values of Nature as they are, and a wholesale conspiracy to represent mankind as being governed by thoughts, standards, wishes, and motives essentially different from his real thoughts, standards, wishes, and motives. Part of this, of course, was pre-Victorian; and honestly inherited from the natural system of standards evolved from the social needs of earlier ages—a system which indeed had genuine value until the discovery of effective contraceptive methods removed its primary basis and made the formation of a revised system increasingly necessary as the aesthetic influence of the original system wore thinner and thinner—but the gravest exaggerations, distortions, and hypocrisies were the fruit of that most despicable of centuries—the unreal, prurient, nineteenth. It was this lousy, hollow period which made the whole subject of sex such an alluringly hidden mystery that its dupes acquired an itching curiosity and abnormal interest in the subject—something which it will take a quarter-century of open air and sanity to wash and aerate and fumigate away.

Now what about standards? Clearly, the feelings of Victorian-born people can't be used as a guide. Their capacity for judgment has been damaged by a very definite cause. Nor can old-time Georgians and classicists like me be really valuable judges, either—for although we ancients have not the Victorian's preoccupation with sex, (I, for example, am much less annoyed by the rise of promiscuity than by the rise of democratic standardisation and the gospel of efficiency, although I heartily dislike both) we do inherit a tradition of sexual ethics based on social, philosophic, economic, medical, biological, political, and aesthetic foundations which modern phases of western civilisation have largely overthrown; a primal Roman-Nordic and adoptively Hebraic tradition which was real in its day, but which is now increasingly unreal as civilisation moves farther and farther from the conditions on which it rested. This old Roman-Teuton-English tradition—the pre-Victorian Anglo-Saxon main stream as touched by the habits of elder New England—is what I inherit, and what is likely to govern my own personal conduct and feelings (so far as an analytical philosopher may have feelings as a vital psychological factor) during my few remaining years; but I am not too blind to perceive that it is merely an attribute of an aera now in its final phase—an aera whose knell was sounded a century and a half ago, when scientific knowledge was first applied on a large scale to the daily affairs and utilities of life. We are the Boethii and Claudiani and Symmachi and Cassiodori of a dying world.[1] That old world still exists for us, and will exist in part for our children—but will not exist for our grandchildren. For them will be the real machine age, together with the code of ethics produced by its conditions. Thus as a man of sense I don't try to project my own personal aesthetic "reactions" out of their own period into an hypothetical universal time-stream. I don't like modernistic geometrical art, imagistic poetry, erotic emphasis, or democratic social-political organisation—but what the hell of it? It would be infantile in me to label all these things as intrinsically and universally "bad" merely because they are out of place in the obsolescent world which bred me and my prejudices. The modern age is none of my goddam business—I am an old man lingering amongst the good old 1900's and the eighteenth century and the Ciceronian aera at Rome. And, as I have said, the prurient reticences, hollow "idealism" and hypocritically trashy sentimentalities of the Browning–Tennyson period simply don't count. The nineteenth century was a mistake—to my mind far more disgusting (because more subversive of that straight thinking which is man's only real dignity and claim to respect) than the Restoration or the age of Juvenal and Martial. I had much rather take up wenching or pornography than spout the degrading pap of Victorian idealists and Baptist or Popish obscurantists. An honest whore is less of an insult to humanity than a sanctimonious prig who ignores the truth and fosters error and illusion.

Who, then, *is* capable of guessing at possible standards of taste in matters erotic? Well—I'd say, after careful reflection, that the only competent bozo is the cool, impersonal analyst who has shaken free from the *local* influence of any particular age or culture or thought-stream, and surveyed the whole problem of interacting historic and psychological forces in the most panoramic possible way—envisaging man as a unit coextensive with the whole reign of his species, past and future. In this way only can one plot a sort of curve roughly answering for a norm in each of the component groups of the race; and finally devise a complex series of approximate value-systems, each good for one especial age in the history of one especial culture. It's a full-sized man's job to do this—but boys like Lecky laid the foundations for some future work of the kind.[2]

Having established this basis, let's see how the present age stacks up . . . . . . let's see what, in terms of normal contemporary life, we are justified in saying about the various forms of erotic presentation now current. First, of course, we must classify our subject-matter—seeing how much really comes within the field of our survey, and how many separate categories are embraced in that section which does fall within. We must get rid of the ignorant inclusiveness and unanalytical empiricism of the Victorian obscurantist, eliminating such superficial and meaningless catchwords (terms without foundations in reality) as "dirt", "morality", "propriety", "decency", etc. Now taking the whole world of erotic literature and iconography as defined and reprobated by the Victorian maiden-aunt class, we find that it falls into several sharply differentiated and in some cases *diametrically opposite* groups—which only the morbid lubricity of a repressed Puritan could possibly be stupid enough to confound as one. Here is an offhand list:

1. Impersonal and serious descriptions of erotic scenes, relationships, motivations, and consequences in real life.

2. Poetic—and other aesthetic—exaltations of erotic feelings.
3. Satirical glimpses of the erotic realities underlying non-erotic pretences and exteriors.
4. Artificial descriptions or symbols designed to stimulate erotic feelings, yet without a well-proportioned grounding in life or art.
5. Corporeal nudity in pictorial or sartorial art.
6. Erotic subject-matter operating through the medium of wit and humour.
7. Free discussion of philosophic and scientific issues involving sex.

Of course, the boundaries of these groups frequently overlap, but the distinctions are none the less clear. We can illustrate (1) by Theodore Dreiser or Ernest Hemingway or James Joyce, (2) by Catullus or Walt Whitman, (3) by Cabell, Voltaire, Fielding, etc., (4) by Pierre Louys or Marquis de Sade, (5) by Giorgione or Praxiteles or modern bathing-suit designers, (6) by the dramatists of the Restoration, and (7) by the work of men like Havelock Ellis, Forel,[3] Krafft-Ebing, Freud, etc. etc. Now is any one of these things intrinsically bad in the light of the civilisation of 1930? *Certainly not #1*—for no sane adult since 1910 could possibly wish life to be depicted in serious art in other than its true proportions. Any other sort of depiction would be as meaningless as Victorian literature. Since we now know that the habits of ordinary people are so-and-so, and that the amount of mental and emotional and motivating attention which they give to this-or-that subject is such-and-such, we have come to realise as a matter of course that no artist can give any real or valid interpretation of life without drawing conditions as they are, *and with the same relation to the whole life and motivation of the race which each set, respectively, actually possesses* as judged by the most profound and serious evidence. What do people *really* think and do? And *why* do they think and do thus? If we cannot seriously and honestly touch upon these basic things, *whether or not* they lead us into fields which our grandparents might have disliked, we might as well relapse into savagery and not think about mankind at all. And the most contemptible form of that thoughtless savagery is a blind, ostrich-like retreat into the outmoded prejudice and residual seventeenth century cosmic philosophy of the Victorian age. The only truly valid objection against an erotic theme or description in serious literature, is one attacking its proportioned truth to life. This of course brings up a whole cycle of psychological and sociological investigation in itself—but when all is said and done, the results are not unfavourable to men like Hecht and Dell and Dreiser and Hemingway. We are less taken in than of yore about what average people really say and think and do under veils of varying thickness. Today we don't make the mistake of judging aimless, stupid, physically overdeveloped man-in-general by the relatively fastidious, aesthetically governed, and interest-preoccupied minority of students and dreamers whose etherealised personalities have hitherto (i.e., during the Victorian age) been permitted to stand as typical of society as a whole. It is not the hazily immaculate teacher or antiquarian, but the hard-headed business-man with his stenographers and "canaries",[4] and the stolid clerk or mechanic with his "dates" and "girl-friends", who must be said to constitute that society-in-general from which the material of art is drawn. To this overwhelming majority must be conceded the function of representing the vast, blind, deterministic trends of the race. And what they think and do, must be spoken and written, if we are to have any sound realistic art or understanding of life. Personally I am a fantaisiste and cosmicist, and don't care much about realism—but I certainly loathe sentimental hypocrites like Dickens and Trollope far more than honest portrayers and intelligent interpreters like Zola and Fielding and Smollett and Flaubert and Hemingway. Crude workmanship can produce unpleasant or exaggerated effects with erotic material, just as it can with any other kind of material—but why get unduly excited about it? I find cubist painting much more deserving of active disgust! No—the anti-truth fanatic in serious literature simply hasn't a leg to stand on. Intellectually, he simply *ain't!*

As for point #2—erotic lyrism—one may regard it much as one regards point #1. So long as it rests on genuine human feeling, there's nothing sensible to be said against it; and all our legitimate protests must rest on one of two questions—(a) whether (cf. case of #1) the motivating phenomena be genuine, and (b) whether they be proportionately typical of the culture-group from which the lyric manifestation is evolved. Only a fool talks against Catullus or Whitman on subject-grounds in 1930.

Point #3 is analogous to Nos. 1 and 2. There is art and sanity in psychological deflation, and a touch of healthy shit to offset stinking gallons of bad patchouli and eau-de-cologne cannot but be welcome to a man of sense and perspective. He may not want to read it all the time, but he is glad it has existed at certain periods when its sanifying effect on a romanticised cultural stream was peculiarly needed. Hence "Candide"—which I own, have read, have admired, and have almost completely forgotten. Hence Rabelais—whom all men whom I respect revere, but whom I haven't ever bothered to read myself. One of the most contemptible ostentations of the human primate is a priggish dignity and particularity about non-essentials of form, custom, convention, regularity, and so on. It is this devastating pusillanimity which has created the repulsive beast called Babbitus Americanus, and which has paved the downward path toward standardisation, time-table helotry, and glorified mass-mediocrity. No saviour is more deserving of praise than one who can jolt and kick these cow-like conformers into something like a semblance of vitality, individuality, and well-proportioned perspective—who can air out their stuffy and meaningless primness and precision, and give them at least a pinch of that basic sense of humour, proportion, relativity, and cosmic irony which makes real *men* as distinguished from grotesque sawdust-stuffed homunculi. All hats off to the lusty deflater! Our only just criticism of a work of deflation is whether or not its content is suitably proportioned to its theme, or whether its theme involves a vital and necessary piece of bubble-puncturing. Judged by this test, Cabell has a sort of half-and-half status. Much of his work is sound and admirable, whilst other parts (notably "Jurgen") slop over into an extravagance of innuendo which amounts to no more than an inverted sentimentality.

Group #4—artificially aphrodisiac works of "art" not grounded in nature or in normal harmonics—is where you and I meet. These things are like Harold Bell Wright[5] and Eddie Guest in other fields—pap and hokum, and emotional short-circuits and fakes. They are certainly not genuine art, and may therefore be ranked as just so much waste material. Personally, I don't get as excited and indignant about 'em as a younger or naiver aesthete might—but for me they simply don't exist . . . . any more than the advertisements which come in my mail and go unread into the waste basket. If someone were to give me a sealed copy of Sacher-Masoch's "Venus in Furs" for Christmas, I certainly wouldn't get het up and call in the repressed perverts of the Watch and Ward Society of Boston.[6] Instead, I'd thank my liberal benefactor and sell the damn thing in its original seals for a young fortune!

Point #5—the matter of nudity—is in truth *wholly outside the present question,* because it is not, primarily, an erotic phenomenon at all. No one but a ridiculous ignoramus or a warped Victorian sees anything erotic in the healthy human body, either as revealed in Nature, or as depicted in its normal proportions by painting and sculpture. It is, on the other hand, a basic and powerful form of abstract beauty; to withhold which from appreciative contemplation would be an act of unprecedented clownishness. Only fools, jokers and perverts feel the urge to put overalls on Discobolus or tie an apron around the Venus of the Medici![7] A beautiful human body is just as necessary and non-erotic a part of life's aesthetic perspective as a beautiful feline, canine, equine or elephantine body. Only old dogs over fifty—sly reliquiae of Victorian suppression—get any real erotic kick out of a classical gallery or bathing beach. As for objections—here again we have the sole test of *proportion and truth.* Iconographic pornography in its true sense is limited to the tinsel tawdriness of such effects as depict nudity *out of its normal setting,* or with its sexual aspects slyly exaggerated. For instance—I agree perfectly with you that the covers as well as contents of rags like *Snappy Stories* represent true pornography. The most repulsive forms of pornography are those which bear a veil or an excuse—"art", double entendre, "moral purpose", "intellectual instruction", and so on. But in such cases it is not so much the pornographic content as the obvious sneaking *insincerity* which alienates us. We are equally alienated by the obvious insincerity of Victorianism.

Point #6—Eroticism operating through wit and humour—is probably the most genuinely debatable of all the seven I am listing. *Absolutely,* I don't think we can make much of a case against it—but we have more available objections than we have against serious erotic literature, since here only the light overtones of the spirit are involved. Our verdict on a bit of risqué wit must always be provisional and tentative—resting wholly on the dominant aesthetic mood of the place and moment. Clearly, there is bad taste in the overdoing of any subject *not necessitated by the laws of truth-telling*, which may contravene the sensibilities of a large proportion of the possible audience. At present, the dying anti-erotic age is not (in my opinion) quite dead enough to make Restoration wit wholly acceptable to our older generation. But I think this wit was all right enough in its day, Jeremy Collier to the contrary;[8] and that it would be O.K. in France now.

Point #7, on the other hand, is not *debatable at all*. No full-witted adult outside the Popish church or the vestigial backwoods of Georgia and Tennessee could wish to limit the sober scientific investigation of any subject whatsoever, from the geology of Antarctica to the cosmic ray and inner structure of the electron. A puritan who would limit the discussion and study of any phase of biology is simply outside civilisation—outside any argument which can take place among civilised men in 1929 or 1930.

And so it goes. I'd like to be with you, but I can't be. And I predict that you'll "see what I see" before many years are over. I've been through much the same cycle of shifting opinion as fresh data has appeared and old prejudices have slowly revealed their hollowness, subjectivity, and essential localism in space and time. As for the relative debatability of Restoration and recent literature—I think the recent is franker because the age is franker, but that both are equally authentic. And I don't know about that "franker" either, on second thought . . . . . . have you seen the less-known "poems" of Dean Swift—especially the one intitul'd Celia ———*?[9] That was a typical piece of sentimental deflation that even an Hemingway cou'd scarcely lead to! One thing about frank writing—remember that the authors and admirers of it don't expect anybody to read it all the time. It's only a fraction of the whole aesthetic field, and I can't yet understand why Victorians continue to single it out and make such a cursed hullaballoo over it! But I ought not to wonder about any attitude connected with the generation that produced cast-iron lawn deer, the Boston city hall, the poetry of Robert Browning, and sidewhiskers. As for me I don't give a god damn one way or the other. I *own* Boccaccio—and *read* Poe, Dunsany, and Arthur Machen. What t' hell!

Be good
  Yr obt Servt
    Grandpa Lo.

---

*Rhymes with WITS.

Notes

1. Anicius Manlius Severinus Boethius (480?–524), Roman senator and author of *De Consolatione Philosophiae* (The Consolations of Philosophy). Claudius Claudianus (370?–404?), Latin poet. Q. Aurelius Symmachus (345?–402), Roman statesman and author who sought to combat the spread of Christianity. Flavius Magnus Aurelius Cassiodorus Senator (485?–585?), Roman statesman and author who attempted to preserve the legacy of classical literature.
2. William Edward Hartpole Lecky (1838–1903), Irish historian and political theorist, author of *A History of European Morals from Augustus to Charlemagne* (1869).
3. Auguste Forel (1848–1931), author of *The Sexual Question: A Scientific, Psychological, Hygienic, and Sociological Study* (1908).
4. A female singer, especially with a dance band.
5. Harold Bell Wright (1872–1944), bestselling American novelist generally scorned by critics as a purveyor of hackwork to the masses.
6. The Watch and Ward Society (founded in 1878 as the New England Society for the Suppression of Vice) sought to censor books, magazines, and other literary and artistic works in the name of promoting virtue. Under various reincarnations, it lasted into the 1970s.
7. The Discobolus of Myron (discus thrower), a Greek sculpture completed c. 460–450 B.C.E. The original bronze is lost, but the work is known through numerous Roman copies in marble. The Venus de' Medici or Medici Venus is a lifesize Hellenistic marble sculpture depicting the Aphrodite. It is a first century B.C.E. marble copy of a bronze original Greek sculpture.
8. Jeremy Collier (1650–1726), English theatre critic, non-juror bishop, theologian, and author of *Short View of the Immorality and Profaneness of the English Stage* (1698).
9. The poem is in fact titled "The Lady's Dressing Room." It contains the line "Oh! Celia, Celia, Celia shits!"

[45] [AHT]

Thor's Day Again
[18 January 1930]

Salvator:—

One really sad announcement that you'll be pained to hear is that our good old friend Everett McNeil—author of "Tonty" and so on—is no more. I think I told you of his collapse with diabetes last spring, and of his move across the continent to his sister's home in Tacoma two months ago. Belknap and I were afraid that trip might be a strain, and we advised him to rest up at a hospital in preparation; but he did not deem it necessary or feasible. Now it seems he had a relapse soon after reaching his destination—with the melancholy result announced in Sunday's papers.[1] Good old Mac! It is an infernal shame that he couldn't have had a longer period of emancipation from Hell's-Kitchen squalor at the close of his career. The N.Y. terrain will never seem the same to the gang without him, for his naive, characteristic note was so inextricably woven into our folklore. He forms a vital part of that first, fresh, fantastically marvellous impression of the metropolis which I receiv'd before familiarity bred disgust—that elusive, ecstatically mystical impression of exotick giganticism and Dunsanian strangeness and seethingly monstrous vitality which I picked up in 1922, before I knew it too well ...... Cyclopean phantom-pinnacles flowering in violet mist, surging vortices of alien life coursing from wonder-hidden springs in Samarcand and Carthage and Babylon and Ægyptus, breathless sunset vistas of weird architecture and unknown landscape glimpsed from bizarrely balustraded plazas and tiers of titan terraces, glittering twilights that thickened into cryptic ceilings of darkness pressing low over lanes and vaults of unearthly phosphorescence, and the vast, low-lying flat lands and salt marshes of Southern Brooklyn; where old Dutch cottages reared their curved gables, and old Dutch winds stirred the sedges along sluggish inlets brooding gray and shadowy and out of reach of the long red rays of hazy setting suns. And I remember when good old Mac display'd Hell's Kitchen to Little Belknap and me—a first glimpse for both of us. Morbid nightmare aisles of odorous Abaddon-labyrinths and Phlegethontic shores—accursed hashish-dreams of endless brick walls bulging and bursting with viscous abominations and staring insanely with bleared, geometrical patterns of windows—confused rivers of elemental, simian life with half-Nordic faces twisted and grotesque in the evil flare of bonfires set to signal the nameless gods of dark stars—sinister pigeon-breeders on the flat roofs of unclean teocallis, sending out birds of space with blasphemous messages for the black, elder gods of the cosmic void—death and menace behind furtive doors—frightened policemen in pairs—fumes of hellish brews concocted in obscene crypts—49th St.—11th Ave.—47th St.—10th Ave.—9th Ave. elevated—and through it all the little white-hair'd guide plodding naively along with his head in a simpler, older, lovelier, and not very possible world ..... a sunny, hazy world of Wisconsin farm-days and green shores of romantick boy-adventure and Utopian lands of fixt, uncomplex standards and values ..... good old Mac! When will there ever be another like him?

I remember the first time I ever saw Mac—shy and silent, at the now-deserted Dench cottage[2] on the strange, wharf-tangled waterfront of old Sheepshead Bay. He liked to visit there, and used to have subway races with Mortonius on the homeward trip over the old B.R.T.—not the B.M.T. in those days. When they got to DeKalb Ave. the dashing meliorist used to race across the platform with the herd to catch the bridge express, while good old Mac stay'd on the plodding tunnel local—Borough Hall, (no Lawrence St. station in those days) Whitehall St., Rector, Cortlandt, City Hall, Canal, Prince, 8th, 14th, 23d, 28th, 34th—and then the two used to meet on the Times Square platform and compare notes ..... and found that Mortonius never saved more than eight minutes at best by changing to the bridge train.

Hare-and-tortoise stuff—and bravo for little Mac, less touched of the two by the meaningless time-concept of the machine age! Yet to this day you'll see the blindly frantic herd racing across the platform at DeKalb from the tunnel trains to the bridge trains which may save them those eight minutes and may save them nothing at all! One wonders what those droves of mongrels do with their possible eight minutes . . . . . . But anyway, as a rule it paid Mac to stay on the tunnel trains, for they went up to his 49th St. station whilst the expresses had a Times Square terminus.

Good old Mac—I can see him in the 1924–5 period, too—modest host to the gang in his device-crowded Hell's Kitchen eyrie. The same modest refreshments—the same doubtful coffee—the same stock gang arguments—Arthur Leeds and the historic feud—the hilarious night when poor Wheeler Dryden[3] tried to refute an argument about cosmick values—the glimpses of the Hudson and the New-Jersey lights—faint bell-notes and puffings from the freight locomotives in 11th Ave.—glitter of passing boats—the old gas heater—the little arm-rests and book-supports that sprang from Mac's mechanical ingenuity—the reference volumes crowded with slips—the lists of "hard words" like *des´-o-late* pinned up around the walls to defeat Mac's orthographical difficulties (he never could forgive the forces of custom that shaped our spelling!)—the simple, ingenuous chromos and photographs—the scrap books and copies of Mac's novels—*Lost Nation, Totem of Black Hawk, Kit Carson, Treasure Cave*—the chapters of "Tonty" read aloud for gang criticism[4]—Kleiner's growing ennui—the hectic prohibition arguments—the tales of lawless doings and police visits elsewhere in the building—the gang adieux—and our increasing repulsion at the gauntlet-running walk through no-longer-novel squalor to the relatively less obnoxious precincts of Broadway. I saw Mac's later places, too. The Brooklyn roost was neither filthy nor noisy (save for dogs' barking—Mac called the place "Dogtown")—merely grey and depressing. And Mac was too naively Victorian to realise that it *was* grey and depressing. The dogs were all he objected to. And Astoria—the ground-floor flat in the new apartment-house at the foot of Ditmars Blvd., with parlour windows looking out over the shore drive and park-fringed seawall to the blue East River where it lay in the shadow of that vast Roman viaduct—the Hell Gate Bridge. Good old Mac—he couldn't get far from Hell—from the Kitchen to the Gate! But here he had rest and beauty—magick casements of Providence-bound sound steamers by night. I was damn glad to see Mac in such a peaceful, lovely place at last—and am damn sorry to think he couldn't have stay'd there longer. I'm glad I got there twice to see him—pure chance that my N.Y. visit of last spring came at the right time. And I recall Mac's typical ways at the other fellows' quarters. He had a special, favourite chair at Sonny's, (good old 823 West End—now torn down) and always took my great morris-chair (I glance now at its vacant seat!) at Parkside and Clinton. But curiously enough, I think of him most often on the long Blue Pencil hikes over the ancient, misty, sedgy marshes and flat lands of southern Brooklyn . . . . the little, grey plodding figure against that grey twilight background of Dutch lore and immemorial antiquity which is, after all, my acutest N.Y. memory. The frail dreams and presence of man against the infinite . . . .

Well—be good, and pardon that boner about page twenty-five!
Yr obt Loavus. [?]

Notes

1. McNeil had died 4 December 1929. See "H. Everett M'Neil, Author, Dies in West," *New York Times* (15 December 1929): 60.
2. The home of amateur Ernest A. Dench.
3. Wheeler Dryden (1892–1957), British actor and film director and half-brother to Charlie Chaplin. It was he who informed Sonia Davis in 1945 of HPL's death.
4. HPL refers to McNeil's novels *The Lost Nation* (1918), *The Totem of Black Hawk* (1921), *With Kit Carson in the Rockies* (1909), *The Lost Treasure Cave* (1905), and *Tonty of the Iron Hand* (1925).

[46] [AHT]

Sunday the 22nd
[March 1930?]

Illustrious Doorkeeper:

I perus'd that Sat Rev article with the most extreme interest, and am mov'd to wonder just how much significant evidence supports its contentions. That the vulgar herd is without a true sense of rhythm, I am not surpris'd to hear; but I had not thought this typical of those persons of cultivation who form the body of our actual civilisation. I had assum'd, on the other hand, that the civilis'd publick were not only keenly responsive to fine rhythms, but so sophisticated in this field as to revolt against simple measures and seek for delicate and elusive beats of sound more closely linkt to turns of thought and feeling. I was not, I must own, much impress'd by the results of their experiments; but I at least conceiv'd them to be born of a too-keen rather than too-blunt sense of tone-colour. However, it is possible that Dr. Canby[1] is right—tho' I think he seeks too simple an explanation when he lays the declining state of rhythm to the influence of jazz. If such a decline has occurred, I would trace it rather to the absence of artistick feeling in common thought—an absence caus'd by the predominant modern inclination to pierce through forms toward realities, and to spend the best brain and feeling of the age on the intellectual adventuring of pure science and philosophy. Still, it is *absurdly easy* to find the cause of that decay in *prose* rhythm of which Dr. Canby speaks—so easy, indeed, that I marvel at his failure to dwell upon it himself. I allude to the *use of the typewriter* in the original composition of manuscripts; a practice which not only discourages good workmanship through its undue speed, distracting noise, (for not everyone hath a SiReen!) and division of the attention, but which insidiously tempts a writer to condone hasty crudities in rhythm on account of the extreme difficulty of making adequate interlineations, corrections, and recastings in the sentences of the rough draught. No writer ought ever to consider a rapidly written sentence as a finished product. It may be that four or five verbal transpositions will be needed to produce the desired effect; or that wholesale substitutions of words of diverse length—often demanding still further textural changes for their perfect accomodation—will have to be effected. These needs may be obvious at once, or not until some later passage brings out the asymmetrical quality of the first-evolved version. In any case, an artistically conceived prose manuscript must be in a perpetual state of flux; with unlimited opportunities for every kind of shifting, interpolation, and minute remodelling, and with no sentence or paragraph accepted more than tentatively until the very last word is set down. Now it is clearly impossible to adhere to this standard of *ultimate perfection at any cost,* unless the writer is able to correct and re-correct his manuscript with the utmost thoroughness and intricacy—adding here, striking out there, substituting here, transposing there; and now and then transforming whole passages of varying length by recasting operations which involve the sacrifice of all the original wording and the substitution of a differently-cast paraphrase. On a hand-written manuscript this process is easily managed through finely-written interlineation, marginal insertions etc. etc.—but when one tries it with a typewriter a vast number of difficulties arise. Only a limited amount of the correction can be done by the machine itself, even when triple-spacing is used; yet the trouble of removing and reinserting the sheet acts as a deterrent to the proper hand-correction—which of course must be made whilst the creative impulse is fresh, and not postponed till the completion of the page. In other words, no decent prose—or rather, no prose of permanent rhythmical value—can be produced except on a sheet which can *at any moment be subjected to instant emendation in any degree of extensiveness, in any of its parts whatsoever;* a set of conditions which cannot be met on the typewriter. Of course, it is possible that occasional typed products—casual letters, and so on—of persons with an already-implanted rhythm-sense may accidentally achieve a fair grade of harmoniousness; just as an accomplished musician's idle strumming of piano-keys may produce a chance bar of fair quality. But in this case the merit will be due to a long previous saturation with good melody and cadence, such as can be obtained only through habits of deliberate, fastidious, and constantly-amended longhand composition. Only the generation of writers brought up on cautious pen and ink methods can have any chance of clicking out passable rhythm on a typewriter. This is indeed already sadly obvious—for the newest crop of adults contains from fifty to seventy-five percent of lifelong typewriter-addicts whose tempo and mechanically imposed limitations can be readily traced in short, jerky sentences, staccato near-rhythms, and an utter ignoring of periodic beats and modulations in favour of ideas and images presented by direct intellection and without the aid of sound-appeal. These people often show a perfect *natural* sense of rhythm when they write *in verse* and are *obliged* to keep the prosodick element paramount; but when they turn to prose, the discouraging effect of their mechanical incubus grows too much for them, and they soon succumb to the deadening staccato and careless structure inevitable in not-easily-corrected and over-speeded writing. This is my constant quarrel with Belknap and Loveman—both splendid *poets*, yet each with characteristick limitations in prose which proceed from a one hundred percent and lifelong use of the machine. If I had a son I would not let him see a typewriter till he had formed a natural and rhythmical prose style of such strength and persistence as to be beyond harm from any source. I myself would no more think of composing any original work on the typewriter, than I would think of composing it in a printing office with galley and type-case or linotype machine. The only stuff I have ever clicked off in rough-draught has been the casual Kleicomolo and travelogue material—not destined for print, and requiring carbon copies. I'll wager you can see the inferiority in style of this over my other writing—and you can well imagine how much *worse* it would be if I had never formed and practiced any other habits of composition. Here, then, is the great cause of the contemporary decline in prose rhythm. It is not so much that the young writers spend their nights amidst the bleat of jazzing saxophones and the jangle of syncopated cow-bells, as that they approach their tasks with a tool which handicaps instead of serving them—that, and a mood attuned to standards of haste and realistic thinking which measurably clashes with the sheerly aesthetick mood. I'd hate to think of what "Sirenica" would have been if W. Compton Leith (and don't forget to tell me this bird's straight moniker when you worm it outa Spaulding!) had been brought up on Underwoods and Remingtons! As for the astonishing results of your accent-tests with words like *invincible, trolley-car, evidence,* etc.—well, my vocabulary breaks down! What sort of back alleys formed the speech-moulding background of these poor gamins? *Dii Immortales!* Will tendencies like these ever rise to affect the speech of civilised persons? There must be some sinister current behind phenomena like the acceptance of *ad´dress* and *ac´climated, kew-pon* and *shōne,* by more and more persons of at least ostensible and self-regarded semi-literateness! Here's hoping that your "Doorways" and class-room work may do much to stem the tide—but I thank gawd I'm an old man who ain't long for this goin'-to-seed world!

I have perus'd with keen interest the folder of *Instructions to English Students,* and must pause in breathless admiration of the precision and mastery with which you have work'd out your system! Lud, Sir, but what we old folks have miss'd by not having been born late enough to enjoy these enlighten'd methods! The question of the effect of classification on C-students is, I fancy, something which only experience can solve. It is of course the one weakness of all intelligence tests of known results that they tend to inspire a fatalistic apathy in the tail-ender, which sometimes leads him to do worse than he might have done if spurr'd on by powerful and hopeful emotion and will-born application. The tangible successes in this ironick world are seldom the result of the keenest abstract intelligence. Yet the share of the intelligence is *so great* in everything pertaining to instruction, that it would seem foolish and wasteful not to take advantage of reliable classifying methods, but instead to hold down the bright and overstrain the dull in an effort to judge all by an uniform set of standards and requirements. In the case of these grades, I think you avoid all psychological errors by making it seem as if *voluntary studiousness* were the passport to A and B rating. The C-student will probably feel merely that he isn't willing to be such a "grind" as the A's and B's. Or else he'll simply assume that his talents lie in another direction—as indeed they may, since often a high intelligence shows singular slovenliness in fields remote from its natural tastes and interests. Effective work always demands emotional driving-power behind it; and when a superior brain possesses a profound indifference and distaste for a given subject, the results are often curious to behold. It certainly is a cinch that you can make your classes to some extent self-propelling; and I'll bet you occasionally get some pretty useable book-tests from the Class A Galpinii who choose that method of piling up credits! Some system, kid—right down to the gum-chewing! I suppose you tolerate tobacco-chewing because of its historick colour as the dominant habit of the fabulous 'forties—when all the most palatial eating-saloons and most elegant tonsorial parlours were equipped with numerous, spacious, accessible, and tastefully decorated cuspidors. Yea, bo, yuh cer'n'y gotta swell racket worked out, and I hope the rulin' scholastick powers prop'ly appreciate it. Things wasn't done so in my day—so that I was always bored to death by English classes, even tho' I was grinding out Jawjun varse and macabre hell-raisers on my own hook at the very same time!

   Well—go to it, kid!
    Yr obt Servt Lo.

Notes

1. Henry Seidel Canby (1878–1961), critic book reviewer, and editor of the *Saturday Review of Literature* from 1924 to 1936. The article in question is an unsigned piece, "The Decay of Rhythm," *Saturday Review of Literature* 5, No. 12 (13 October 1928): 207–8.

[47]   [AHT]

> Y.M.C.A. Tavern,
> Charles-Town, in His Maj'ty's
> Province of South-Carolina,
> 4th of May, 1730.

Sapientissime:—

Confronted by a dizzying embarrassment of colonial riches which I must needs despair of ever weaving into a suitable travelogue, I take my pen in hand to convey at least a microscopick notion of what I am exploring, and of the extent to which antient Charles-Town hath captivated me. Lud, Sir, but this place was meant for my old bones—to say nothing of my old tastes and historick yearnings. I did not, I vow to God, Sir, know that such places still existed!

As I think I wrote you on a postcard, I travell'd day and night from New York by stage-coach; stopping nowhere save to change vehicles at Washington, Richmond, Winston-Salem, N.C., and Columbia, S.C. This procedure turn'd out to be very well-advis'd, insomuch as every moment spent away from Charles-Town betwixt Sept. 15 and May 15 must be accounted a sheer waste of time. Never in my eighty or ninety years of existence have I beheld a place which wou'd appeal to me so much if it were more like Providence! The climate is marvellous and summerlike—palmettos, live oaks, creeping vines, wisteria, jasmine, azaleas, etc. etc., everywhere, and the thermometer up around seventy-five degrees and eighty degrees. Near everyone is array'd in a straw hat, and it is possible to sit outdoors all day and enjoy it. Right now I am in antient Battery Park looking out across the harbour at Ft. Sumter of Civil War fame. The atmosphere makes me feel twenty years younger and one hundred percent better—and I really seem to have a surplus fund of energy for the first time since last August. The sea breeze is always blowing, and I have become as tanned as an Indian in less than a week—I say less than a week after consulting the calendar; tho' I have seen so many sights since arriving on Monday last, that I feel as if I had been here a full decade.

But the climate, O Sage, is *only the beginning* of the miracle from an antiquarian point of view. Indeed—there is nothing about the place so wholly important and distinctive as the astoundingly eighteenth century atmosphere—for in all verity I can say that Charleston is the best-preserv'd colonial city of any size, without exception, that I have ever encounter'd. Virtually *everything* is just as it was in the reign of George the Third—indeed, 'tis easier to count the houses which are *not* colonial, than to attempt to count those which *are*. The inhabitants are by nature conservative, and have never chang'd their way of building houses thro' all the years—save for a trifling Victorian lapse in extending the northern fringe of the city, and in replacing the buildings burnt in the fire of 1861. (An event *not* connected with the Civil War.) On account of the climate, these edifices differ somewhat from the structures of the Northern colonies—usually having piazzas on all three storeys of the southern or western side. This is a feature develop'd shortly after 1750; houses before that date being more of the general colonial or British Georgian type. There are even a few cases of the familiar New England gambrel roofs—a design perhaps pick'd up by Charleston mariners on voyages to Salem or Newport, but soon abandon'd because of its unsuitability for a warm climate. Houses here are generally of brick with stucco exterior, and the general details and contours show more latitude and individuality than elsewhere. Tiled roofs are a distinctive feature—this fashion having been introduc'd subsequently to 1735. The publick buildings—dating from 1760 to 1800 and after—are of monumental magnificence; all in the classick Grecian manner, and of such solid workmanship as to be aeternal in duration. There are likewise many excellent churches and steeples—of which my favourite is St. Michael's, set up in 1762, whose sweet-ton'd chimes dominate the aural atmosphere of the city. This is visible from my Y.M.C.A. window. The most glamourous of all is the old Unitarian Church which I discover'd only this morning. This is one of those *very rare* specimens of *revived Gothick* built in *Georgian* times—perhaps as an echo of the antiquarianism which produc'd Mr. Walpole's Strawberry-Hill. It was erected in 1772, yet is in every detail a fine type of English pointed Gothick. The churchyard is the last word in glamourousness—a perfum'd green tropick twilight of overarching live-oaks and hanging vines, with antient headstones peeping through a vivid, odorous undergrowth threaded by curious winding walks. It is really something out of a *dream* of my oddly prescient "Randolph Carter"—such things do not belong to the waking world! In this enchanted spot are interr'd the last mortal reliquiae of the Rev'd. Samuel Gilman, author of the college hymn "Fair Harvard,"[1] who was long pastor of the church, and whose birthplace I beheld in 1927 at Gloucester, in the Province of the Massachusetts-Bay.

One of the most famous features of Charleston is its profusion of wrought-iron work—gates, balconies, window-grilles, railings, and the like; all of the finest craftsmanship. I will enclose among other views, a card showing one typical gate. These gates are especially numerous because of the prevalence of high-wall'd gardens in this land of luxurious flowers, rambling vines, and opulent trees that weave an omnipresent green twilight. Charlestonians endeavour to secure privacy and the open air at the same time.

Another phase of Charleston is represented by the sea islands that bound the harbour, one of which—the Isle of Palms—is reputed to possess the finest beach on the Atlantick Coast. Of these, my own chief interest centres in Sullivan's Island, which contains Ft. Moultrie, where Poe served in 1829 as "Corp. Edgar A. Perry" of the Quartermaster's Corps. Many of the scenes of "The Gold Bug" were laid upon this island, and it gave me a thrill to visit in person a region familiar to me in literature for above thirty years.

Of the general history of Charles-Town, I presume you have long been sensible. The original settlement was made in 1669 or 1670 on the west bank of the Ashley River, by some colonists under Col. Wm. Sayle. Ten years later they mov'd to the present location betwixt the Ashley and Cooper rivers, and founded the still-existing town. This new founding is the event whose two hundred fiftieth anniversary is commemorated by the new special stamp—one of which will adorn the exterior of this modest communication.

The colony prosper'd exceedingly despite war with pirates, Florida Spaniards, and the adjacent redskin savages. In the course of time it receiv'd many valuable accessions—gentlemen-adventurers from England, Ireland, and Scotland, oppressed Huguenots from France, and solid planters from the West Indies. The best settlers established themselves inland as planters; raising rice and indigo, but living much in salubrious Charleston because of the malaria infesting the interior lowlands in summer. Their wealth and taste built up an extremely rich and mature civilisation—surpassing anything in Virginia so far as I can judge. Just before the unfortunate revolt against His Majesty's lawful authority, Charles-Town was one of the foremost cities in all America, sharing honours with Boston, Newport, New York, Philadelphia, Annapolis, and Alexandria. During the trouble the town was long besieg'd by His Majesty's forces,[2] but held out for the rebels till 1780, when the forces of Sir Henry Clinton and my Lord Rawdon mov'd in, taking up headquarters at the old Brewton–Pringle house in King St., a mansion of much splendour, which I explor'd on Tuesday last.

After the disastrous termination of the treasonable uprising in 1783, the town (now charter'd as a city and changing its name from *Charles-Town* to the present form of *Charleston*) regained its prosperity; having meanwhile suffer'd but little change in manners and customs. It was still discriminating, aristocratical, and cultivated in temper, notwithstanding the democratick fallacies into which its politicks had been betray'd. The invention of the cotton-gin gave the planters a new source of revenue, so that from 1800 to the Civil War there was not a prouder or more cultur'd city in the Western Hemisphere. But the war produc'd collapse and stagnation, and since then the material importance of Charleston has been less great. It has, however, retain'd its eighteenth century standard of taste and learning; so that I doubt if there be at this moment a more suitable place in these colonies for a gentleman to dwell. It forms the last stand of our genuine hereditary civilisation—agricultural, individualistick, qualitative, and leisurely—as distinguished from the intrusive mongrel barbarism brought about by the new aera of speed, quantity, time-tables, trade, and machinery.

As in Newport and Salem, relatively few of the antient houses are ever demolished; and the population appear to appreciate their history and background very keenly. Unlike many other historick cities—including Providence, Richmond, and Newport—Charles-Town hath an excellent array of postcards and guidebooks to offer the visitor. I spent one day at the publick library accumulating historical and architectural data in order to make my enjoyment as full and comprehending as possible. The odd ramifications to follow up are almost numberless—the subject of *street-cries* alone being worth a full volume of close anthropological research. Niggers are exceedingly numerous and almost incredibly black, but know their place to perfection. Foreigners are happily absent—or at least gratifyingly scarce.

Of course all this tarrying and postcard-purchasing is eating up my cash; but I shall make up by eliminating other features of my contemplated Grand Tour—e.g., the long sojourns I had plann'd at Richmond, Fredericksburg, Annapolis, Philadelphia, and so on. I shall, however, manage to stay a bit with Little Belknap in N.Y., and shall probably repeat my last year's visits to Bernard Dwyer in Kingston and W. Paul Cook in Athol. I am paid up at the Y. here till tomorrow night—and may venture a night or two more. Whatever way it develops, though, it'll be a great trip, all told!

In June the East may get a glimpse of our little prodigy-friend Galpinius, who has hopes of a stay at the MacDowell colony at Peterborough.[3] Grandpa's young composer! In August he, Belknap, and I may try to stage a triangular reunion somewhere on the Massachusetts coast—at antient *Marblehead* if the children take their old Grandpa's advice!

   And so it goes! More anon. Be good—and don't work too hard!
    Yr obt Lo.

Notes

1. Samuel Gilman (1791–1858), American clergyman and author. The song is set to the traditional Irish air best known in early 19th century America as "Believe Me, If All Those Endearing Young Charms."
2. AHT has "rebels," an apparent error.
3. The MacDowell Colony is an artists' colony founded by Marian MacDowell in Peterborough, NH, in 1907.

[48] [AHT]

                 Mercury's Day
                 [June 1930?]

Ave, Jazzbo the Great!
    And as for the phase of ugliness called "indecency"—I haven't had much chance to get shocked by the wholesale, because the direction of my strongly fixed interests doesn't often lead me up against such specimens; but now and then I naturally find a passage or two which I consider a bit thick. Parts of Huysman's "A Rebours" and "La Bas" could have been modelled in a way more pleasing to Anglo-Saxons without any subtraction from the substance or proportioning—yet do you find me ringing the burglar alarm or summoning up the flames of Savonarola? Be yourself, 'bo! I don't

consider either my own distaste, or Br'er Joris-Karl's possible carelessness or poor taste or difference of nationality, of sufficient importance to read the riot act about! Neither do I throw away the whole apple merely because one spot chances to be a trifle mellow. I just let it go at that—conceding, so far as I stop to analyse my own opinions at all, that I don't like this or that point, and then going on with the reading of the bulk of the work. By another day the whole matter of the doubtful passage is relegated to the background of negligible things. Now I don't like to hold myself up as a model—but that's what I call the normal attitude of a realistic and liberal-minded man of sense in the year 1930. Indeed, I don't have to brag personally in giving this definition, because as a matter of fact it's the lifelong and habitual attitude of most of the people I know and of most of the writers and critics I admire. Little Belknap, Cook, Morton, Loveman, Clark Ashton Smith, Sechrist, Kirk,—virtually ninety-eight per cent of the gang—are just the same, as are such larger literary figures as "B. K. H." and the still more prominent examples whom you know as well as I. The whole sane temper of a civilised age is on my side—so why try to cling to the illusory criteria which 1930 has long outgrown? None of the people I've mentioned care a damn for pornography, and at least three of them—yes, I think as many as four—happen to have tastes and interests as accidentally within the circle of traditional approval as my own . . . . or your own. But we of the majority simply keep our grip on a sense of facts and of proportion. Speaking of facts and proportion—don't fancy that we consider all the erotically-minded writers of the past and present non-morbid merely because we feel no urge to blot them off the earth. Undoubtedly the emotional stresses of many great and little artists display traces of one-sided education, warped mentality, ill-proportioned impulses, or such things—but does this necessarily make them candidates for the stake or gaol or waste-basket? On the contrary many of these definitely diseased minds have produced much material of the highest artistic value, which only requires the proper mental discounting and interpretation of the reader in order to possess the highest importance as an expression of life and a key to the riddle of human personality. Writers I'd call morbid are D. H. Lawrence and James Joyce, Huysmans and Baudelaire. Yet every one is an indispensable figure in the expression and interpretation of Western Europe between 1850 and 1930. Writers I *wouldn't* call morbid are Theodore Dreiser and Floyd Dell and Ben Hecht. These men simply try to tell straightforwardly what they see and what they think this data signifies in relation to the acts and motives of all people. Dreiser is a really titanic figure—*the* novelist of the United States. And so it goes. The only rational attitude of a civilised man is to let all the evidence about life go on record impartially, and not try to tamper with the books. We each have our own likes and dislikes, but they're of importance only to ourselves individually. Nor need we fear that the free circulation of all the evidence is going to have any especial effect on the direction of the civilisation, one way or the other. That's an exploded psychological fiction, although I believed it once myself. Trends come from deeper sources than what is written on the surface of literature, and the average domestic adjustments of 1980 or 2030 will not depend on the question of whether Ernest Hemingway is suppressed or encouraged in 1930. Indignation, in the light of contemporary knowledge, is a naive and juvenile emotion in any field. All that anyone of us has to bother about is to obey such practical laws as are generally agreed upon, to be true to the traditions of beauty as perceived through the lenses of one's own personality, and to leave others free to follow their visions as one follows one's own. There are not many absolute or basic or intrinsic values, so that a critical or censorious attitude does not well become a philosopher. Amidst the disillusion'd mellowness of my present old age, I smile at some of the bigoted middle-aged carpings I used to pull off in the old Kleicomolo days! I *do* and *like* the same things now that I did and liked then—but with grey hairs has come a knowledge that this is a very diverse world, in which many different systems of action and preference have an equal right to existence.

But all this business is only a drop in the bucket as scaled against other vital trends in civilisation. Here again is a case of old Grandpa Theobald gradually getting adjusted to a new set of facts as unwelcome horizons open up. The more I analyse the future of Western Civilisation, the less hope I see for the survival of any of the conditions and values which for me invest life with what little zest and piquancy it has; yet as my wrinkles accumulate and my shoulders increase their stoop I see increasingly that there is no possible way to alter the chain of inevitable circumstances which arose from the accidental development of the power machine. The natural adjustment of man to the earth, to the landscape, to the conceptions of time and space and proportion, to the social group, to the struggle for existence, to his fellows, to himself and his own imaginative life—all this will inevitably be uprooted by the changes accruing from a mechanised regime which destroys familiar dependences and limitations and economic balances, and substitutes a new set unlinked with that age-long conditions have crystallised, and wholly dependent on a complex technological organisation that ennui or revolt or conquest or natural convulsions will sooner or later destroy. From now until the next Spenglerian[1] collapse of civilisation we shall have an increasingly grotesque and unsatisfying type of life—a type without sufficient points of contact with ingrainedly hereditary conditions to provide any first-class emotional satisfactions. But I no longer deem it possible to avert this, nor do I think there is any reason to waste breath in whining over it. What must come, must come. New sensations will arise to replace the old; and even if their pleasing poignancy is less, their possessors will have no basis of comparison wherefrom to reckon their inferiority. There will be a deadly stagnation punctuated by a few morbid nervous revolts. Sovietism and capitalism and fascism will meet in a curious triangular paradox to solve the enigma of a culture in which constant machine overproduction will have destroyed the law of supply and demand and made the individual's relation to the economic fabric an arbitrary, unstable, and difficultly determined problem. And sooner or later some revolt, aided by modern mechanism, will play hell with the whole mess. One of the troubles will be that goals and preferred lines of action will have become exceedingly confused and obscure under the strongly artificialised conditions and relations to nature and sensation. Eventually the comedy will be over, as the comedies of Ur and Babylon, Thebes and Memphis, Tyre and Sidon, Cnossus and Carthage are now over, and after that there will be another simple world with simple ways and few facts and childlike beliefs. There will be shepherds on the hills, and walled towns of homes on the rivers and seacoasts. Men will pray again to the personified emptiness of space, and the smoke of the sacrifice will ascend. Armies will follow great-bearded priest-kings in defence of primal rights and imagined dignities. Bards will chant to queer pipes and flutes and tympani, and the graver will carve his dreams upon dolomite and chrysoberyl and chalcedony. And then the towns will grow, and the inventions of man multiply. The bow will give way to the bomb, and the skin-saddled horse to the wheeled chariot. Smoke will arise from tall chimneys, and the forge of the smith give way to the vault of the guild. And ways will grow devious, and knowledge great; and what was once known and forgotten will be known again. Steel shall multiply the bodied dreams of men, and clangour and ugliness come once more. And there will again be speed and confusion, futility and alienation. And what was the doom of the world we know, will be the doom of the world by whom our world can scarce be remembered. Then anew there will be shepherds on the hills, and walled towns of homes on the rivers and seacoasts . . . .

 Now for work, dammit!
  Yr obt Servt
   Lo.

Notes

1. See Dwyer 3n3.

[49] [AHT]

      Briefly stopping at 10 Barnes St.,
       Providence, R.I.,
        July 3, 1930

Magister Sapientiae:—

 So you are a popcorn-hound, eh? Bless me, but I thought that was largely a Vermont habit! My friend Orton is a nut about corn-popping, and always has some new-popped stuff lying about, which he expects his friends to appreciate. I don't mind a kernel or two once or twice a year, but as a steady diet the delicacy tends to afflict me with ennui. The only three nutritive principles I ever get really enthusiastic about are cheese, chocolate, and ice-cream. But any ornamental diet is useful in promoting an idyllic domestic atmosphere, and I can well imagine how the popping makes home attractive for the sprightly Mocratuli. Glad to hear these Dioscuri[1] aren't wasting valuable time on sentimental sighs over the Zythopolitan fair. In this generation, when more is known of motivations than formerly, a whole lot of the fluttering glamour of Victorian philandering simply dies a natural and unlamented death—restoring the more rational realism of the eighteenth century in the attitude of nubile youth. Here's hoping Robertulus does well at Madison next year. If he wants to know a bright young chap who will probably be there as a post-graduate student, tell him to write my adopted grandchild August W. Derleth, Sauk City, Wisconsin. There's a great kid—who can turn out ten reams of hack tripe with his left hand every day, and get one and a half cents or two cents a word for it in pulp magazines, while his right hand is performing serious literary work—Proustian reminiscent fiction—of a sort which promises a really brilliant future. You and the Mocratuli ought to know this fellow-citizen of your virile and boreal commonwealth. He is twenty years old, and has just received an A.B. on Mendota's templed shore. He may have a minor instructorship as well as post-graduate work next year. I've never met this little rascal in person.

Yr obt Lo.

Notes

1. In Greek mythology, the Dioscuri were the twin brothers Castor and Pollux. Here (as with *Mocratuli*) HPL refers to MWM's two sons, although they were not twins.

[50] [ANS, JHL][1]

[Postmarked Providence, R.I., 10 July 1930]

Ah, there, old-timer! I did attend the Convention, & I'll tell the flat & cock-ey'd world[2] that it was a surprising success! The turnout of veterans astonish'd me—Edwin Hadley Smith, Wylie, Suhre, Haggerty, L. C. Wills, Morton, Cole, Sandusky, Lynch, Mrs. Sawyer, Thom[p]son, Tilden,[3] &c. &c. Cook & Mrs. Miniter too ill to attend. Had a great time, including boat trip up the Charles, banquet, & the usual accessories. Bacon elected Pres, & St. Louis next Convention Seat. Young Spink, reëlected Off. Editor, is a great kid. We made trips—with Suhre—to Salem & Marblehead, & he is going to stop in Providence on his return trip. ¶ The Hub amateurs are a bit changed in the 6 yrs since I last saw them. Cole has grown fat, & Lynch has been through a nervous breakdown. Morton was the centre of things, as usual. ¶ Today I took a solitary trip to Quincy to see the Adams house. Home tomorrow. Also went over a reproduction of the ship Arbella, on which my revered great-

great-great-great-great-great-grandfather the Rev. George Phillips (1594–1644) came to Salem in 1630. Too bad you couldn't have been present at the festivities. I boasted your tests & Doorways with Cole & others. More anon.
Yr obt
Lo

Notes

1. *Front:* Old State House, Boston, Mass.
2. A phrase going back to wartime slang of 1917–18. *The Cockeyed World* (1929), a sequel to *What Price Glory?,* was a popular war movie.
3. HPL refers to the amateur journalists Willard Otis Wylie (1862–1944) of Boston, noted philatelic writer, editor of *Our Compliments,* and member of both the NAPA and UAPA; Edward F. Suhre (1879–1939), editor of the *Missourian* and *Occasional Press,* and president of the NAPA (1910–11); Louis Charles Wills (1884–1975) of Brooklyn; Laurie A. Sawyer, member of the Hub Club and president of the NAPA (1909–10); and George A. Thompson of Fairhaven, WA. For the others, see Glossary. For Leonard E. Tilden, see MWM 17n2.

[51]   [AHT]

10 Barnes Street
Providence, R.I.
[July 1930?]

[. . .]

About rhyming secondarily accented syllables—hell! I can't give the page and volume where the rule is stated, for I've no kind of a technical rhetorical library. But I know it's O.K.—I would never have the brains to think up a point like that myself, and you can see for yourself that it's sound. Try it over on your piano! No question—the point must be cover'd in print in a dozen places. I'd almost swear it's in ol' Bran Matt[1]—which reminds me that I *must* buy a copy of that "Study of Versification" to have on hand to overawe clients with a display of indisputable authority!

[. . .]

Notes

1. I.e., Brander Matthews.

[52]   [AHT]

Aug. 9[, 1930?]

Ave!

About that synthetick verse—when I read in your letter of the changes, I endors'd 'em without looking to see what they were, because I knew my version was a rough impromptu, and that that "pelf" was as brazenly a rhyme-word as the homologous "elf" which old Walt Scott so annoyingly pulled in a more classick specimen. But after looking at the revision and checking up with the free-verse prototype on the details of *meaning*, I feel impell'd to make the respectful queries indicated by notes on the enclosed text. Your verse is better than mine as verse, but how about those details of sense? Are they important enough to matter? You know a book like this is likely to have some damn'd critical readers. Possibly you cou'd think of a third version better than anything heretofore devis'd. I leave it all to your judgment—go to it, 'bo! Not but what 'twould get by all right as you have it. As you say, the piecing in the rhymed version is not beyond conjecture, and the improvement *as a conveyor of the idea* is distinctly doubtful. That is because verse was *never meant* to convey *ideas*, but only *moods, images, and sensations. Prose* is the normal medium of ideas, *and that is just what "free verse" is!* No wonder the jazz'd lines beat the real couplets when they're applied to something distinctly calling for *prose rhythms!* When will poets ever learn that their province is that of the emotions and the imagination—*not* the intellect?

Glad that dope on *straightforward poetick diction* was useful. It's a damn hard principle for an old-school guy to get hammer'd into him—as I know from the slowness of my response to Klei's kindly efforts at enlightenment. But once it's across, a guy never slips back into the ah, oh, doth, and armed Knights among stuff. Doesn't ol' Bran Matt have something to say on this theme? It's getting to be a sort of Kleicomolo institution—Klei to Lo, Lo to Mo—and alas! that good ol' Co isn't on deck to get the transmitted impact! Good old 1916! Really, come to think of it, my early amateur days are now getting far enough into the past to qualify as a sort of second order of "good-olds"—a lesser nobility as compared with the supreme "good-olds" clustering around 1900.

Yrs for better metricks—
    Grandpa Lo.

[53] [AHT]

                      Thursday
                    [4 September 1930]

Epitome of Erudition:—
    Well, well—and so the good old Kleicomolo hath been brought again to the daylight for the edification of your little senate! I must get out my carbon copies—in a box now stored in a stable about a mile from here—and see just what my endless rambling of that period really was like. I haven't changed much, either in manner or opinions; but I have a sort of vague idea that I don't write quite so much damn'd nonsense as I used to. It may be that this subtle progress is but a complacent illusion—in fact, I feel

sure that it is upon considering much of the recent epistolary verbosities I have perpetrated. But anyhow, my present nonsense may not be quite so damn'd, even if its volume be undiminish'd. I don't take the dysoptic world as seriously as I did in 1916, hence don't make the amusing excursions into political and sociological fields which I made once upon a time. Also, I know enough to keep my metrical mouth shut except when somebody drags an elegy out of me. I don't try to spread myself over so wide a range of interests, don't labour to be enthusiastick over what I don't really give a hang about, and don't get attached to opinions for arbitrary or whimsical reasons any more. I change my mind oftener, and accept the results of new scientific discoveries with greater readiness. The unimportance of life and effort, and the purposelessness of the whole cosmos, are closer realities to me than they were then, even though I fully realised them and upheld them in argument. I don't get excited about things as readily as I did; for I realise that every different individual has his own subjective world of perspectives and values, and what is it to me whether or not other people's worlds resemble or coincide with mine? I am less attached to mannerisms, and more attached to simplicity. *Style* I now conceive to be a personal property of mind rather than an art to be learnt; and I deem that man wisest, who writes most plainly in the exact language most descriptive of his actual thoughts. My valuation of the element of *sincerity* in works of art and literature has increas'd to such an extent that I now esteem it a necessity to perfect expression. In taste I am coming to value the local more than the universal, a sign no doubt of provincial old age. My standard of literature has slightly risen; so that I impose upon my serious writing a closer censorship than formerly, taking care to delete that which is trite, commonplace, artificial, affected, ornate, or rhetorically involv'd. I demand a more cleanly-cut visual image than formerly, before I will commit any picture or conception to paper. *The Conservative*, were I editing it today, wou'd have a very perceptible difference from those issues which saw the light in Kleicomolo times. Editorials wou'd be shorter in length and less florid in tone, whilst contributions wou'd be sifted and selected with greater care. The Kleicomolo itself wou'd be perhaps less rambling and buoyantly irresponsible in diction. And so forth, and so forth, and so forth. It is at least amusing to fancy that one has lost a trifle of one's naive ridiculousness. The great lesson of age, and of cultivation, is the better apportionment of one's emotions and their expression to the various objects around which they centre. Triviality, sentimentality, gush, pose, and rhetorical hollowness are among the things a man ought to leave behind as he grows older or advances in the comprehension of life and art.

By the way—do you know of any book which has a detailed exposition, with illustrative tables, of the precise usage of the *hyphen*? I'm sure I don't see what *general* laws there could be for anything so arbitrary, for of course the use of a hyphen in a compound word is something determined by the very vaguest and most delicate kind of rhetorical equilibrium—representing an uncertain middle ground where two elements are slightly more than one word and slightly less than two words. Usage and precedent would seem to me all-powerful in each individual case. The reason I ask is that I have just received an inquiry on this subject from Mrs. Paul J. Campbell, who avows that hyphens form her especial stumbling-block. I've told her to ask you about it, for you know more about current manuals—and what they do or don't contain—than I do. All my old books say that each individual case ought to be looked up in the dictionary. In practice, we may group instances of hyphen-doubt into two classes—cases where one wavers betwixt hyphenation and fusion into one word, and those where the debate is betwixt hyphenation and the use of the two or more words unconnected. If there's anything I hate, it's the silly modern fashion of joining up compounds like *oldfashioned*, *broadminded*, etc. Ugh! If they keep that up they'll soon have High-Dutch-like strings of syllables *pennyintheslot*, *nevertobeforgotten*, *Newcastleontyne*, etc. Bah! And hell!

Yrs for more classick readers—
Wash: Irving, Gent.

[54] [AHT]

Jan. 18[, 1931]

Magister Sapientiae:—

As for the subject of Victorian re-ti´-cence (as the amachoor Charles W. Heins pronounces it)—I'm sorry to say I don't getcha a-tall, 'bo, because I can't see the slightest connexion betwixt the aesthetick of conversation and the aesthetick of serious written litrachoor. Youse conventional guys have the most maddening habit of tryin' to dispose of complex subjects with simple formulae and ready-made taboos! Hell! The cold fact is, that *conversation and serious literature are as far apart as any two branches of expression could possibly be*—the one having surface elegance, lightness, custom, ease, and immediate pleasure as essential desiderata, to say nothing of having its place as regards time and occasion fixed in advance; whilst the other is basic, impersonal, universal, and non-chronological; and with the time and occasion for its absorption left to the option of the ultimate consumer. Why, damn it all, man! Where in thunder *do* you get your parallel betwixt conversation and writing? You wouldn't blame prose because it doesn't meet the requirements of verse—and if conversation ain't more diff'runt from litrachoor than prose is from verse, then, by god, Sir, my name is Elbert Edgar Hubbard–Guest! *Conversation* is a light, personal, decorative art, whose sole aim is to give transient pleasure, through intensifying the hearer's sense of ease, superiority, and security. As such it has a thousand Dresden-china graces wholly unknown to the serious arts—indispensable, of course, to its own suave and delicate essence; but having nothing to do with any other art except such superficial fringes of written literature as professedly imitate it. There are scores of tacit taboos besides the sort you mention—one must not be inquisitive, one must not mention things likely to make others feel awkward, one must not argue on serious topics about which anyone may feel deeply—in short, one must be eternally careful to suit all decorative conversation to the likes of those participating in it, and (as a corollary) to the dominant conversation-tradition in which these participants are likely to have been brought up. The conditions of oral conversation—utterly unlike those of reading—are so diffusive, direct, unalterable, and personal, that it would obviously be unwise to let it transcend generalities in any casually selected group. It must not defeat its own object, which is to please and to promote a feeling of easiness. Therefore it excludes whatever would be reasonably likely to have unpleasant associations for anybody present. No balanced or conservative thinker disputes this judgment, even though a few ultra-moderns may challenge certain parts of it. Special conversations among special groups, of course, present exceptions—and naturally, different ages and nationalities afford considerably different applications of the rule. For example—in a greatly mixed group which might contain religious believers, one does not discuss cosmic philosophy; but special groups of the present generation can freely analyse these things because everyone is approximately disillusioned and in agreement. Likewise—what would shock an Englishman in twentieth century conversation would not necessarily have shocked a Frenchman in Rabelais' time ..... and might not, in some cases, shock a Frenchman or other Continental today. To the Continentals, Rabelais and Boccaccio are not the bogey-men that they are to us—one reason being that Continental intellectual society is not so annoyingly mixed as ours is. Despite encroachments, it tends to preserve the sound all-masculine complexion of Graeco-Roman times. However—this has nothing to do with our argument. I grant as freely as you that the art of *conversation* demands a careful selectiveness depending on the background of those participating—and since I represent the same old-school Anglo-Saxon background that you do, it is probable that our views on oral tastefulness in general company are virtually identical.

But I can't follow you at all when you apply these urbane rules to *serious written literature*. If you were to confine the extension merely to jesting and light literature, I might be with you, for nothing bores me more than the cheapness of casual and unmotivated bawdry; but with serious literature there is no conceivable linkage. The material of solid literature is life, and whatever is in life must be in solid literature. This is an absolute necessity, because we can never achieve authenticity in depiction unless we recognise genuine rather than feigned motivations. When science tells us that this or that cause produces this or that effect, or when mere observation reveals that this or that element occupies this or that proportion in the thoughts and acts of a given character, there is absolutely nothing for an author to do but set the facts down. Otherwise he gives a false and confusing fake—a phantom shadow without relation to life, art, or anything else—which is far more harmful and reprehensible than any amount of unpleasant truth could be. Victorian "literature" foisted on the reader a whole faked world of impossible thoughts, values, motivations, and proportions which did nobody any good and accomplished no result save that of making life a thousandfold harder to understand than it ever was before—not that the job was ever especially easy, at that! Every person brought up in the Victorian tradition has remained more or less of an intellectual and emotional cripple unless he instinctively resisted the poison in youth or cast it off by dint of vast travail in later life. If you want a damn good definition of a *total loss*, it is the Victorian's pretence at portraying life through art! Actually, the sound brains of the Victorian period all went into *pure science*. It is *there* that we see the "lost age" redeemed—and redeemed damn well, too, for there's no denying the tremendous power of thought that went into the nineteenth century's great literal onslaught against the unknown. When we want to take off our hats to somebody in side-whiskers and barrel pants we don't have far to go[1]—Darwin, Huxley, Tyndall, Faraday, Lecky, Lubbock, Kelvin, Clark Maxwell, Tylor, Frazer, Haeckel, Freud, Mill, Buckle,[2] Herbert Spencer, Mendelejeef, Mendel, Quatrafages, Geoffroy St. Hilaire, Geikie, Kirchoff[3]—hell! the woods are full of 'em—we'd be damn glad of as fine a bunch today! But the fact is, that all this profound truth-delving was through the medium of *literal intellection* and *not* through *artistic interpretation*. That is the whole key to the nineteenth century. It was profound and literal and esoteric in its approach to truth—keeping its facts in the classroom and the laboratory, but sedulously excluding them from the studio and the drawing-room. Life was regarded as something to be analysed by scientists and historians, but hidden from everybody else. Art and literature were left to fakers and sentimentalists and doctrinaires until the sanifying revolt of Swinburne and Samuel Butler (of "Erewhon") and Wilde—itself grotesque in many ways—let in a little brains and fresh air and cleared the way for a fresh start. Ah, me! I think the reason I have such a love for science is that I was born toward the tail end of an aesthetick tradition which no adult could take seriously . . . . . and which I certainly never took seriously, since I gave it a nose-thumbing from the start and went back to the daylight of the eighteenth century! Anyhow—all that is past. Now we know again, as we did in the days before Victoria, that *no subject exists which cannot be seriously treated in literature*. There are no exceptions—indeed, there could be no exceptions according to any soundly impersonal and universal view of the organic history of this planet. Each of the subjects you cite, inadmissible as they are in conversation, can conceivably find a place—appropriately proportioned—in the grimly serious and impersonally artistic portrayal of the tragedy of human consciousness. I don't recall all the specific instances on your list, but I can easily see where any one of the points might form a single glancing note in some dark, minor passage of a verbal symphony based on the complex and varied agony that is human life. Of course, as with all topics from planets to colonial doorways and from steam-shovels to china teacups, there are artistic and inartistic ways of handling these themes; nor would I venture to say that all the well-known robust writers have hit upon exactly the best way in every case. But what of this? Why get excited? What is all the circus about? Don't boobs like Eddie Guest and Harold Bell Wright make just as bad a mess with common questions of taste as ol' Doc' Rabelais and Herr Remarque[4] and Mons. Arouet de Voltaire, and Dago Johnny Boccaccio do with their special questions of taste? It's fifty-fifty dope, bozo, and I can't see why people want to pick on one set of poor guys with vitriol-dipped pens while they're content to laugh the others off lightly and easily. I suppose there's lots of delicate stuff mishandled and ill-exploited by various authors, even when their intentions are perfectly abstract and artistic; but that's no reason for clamping a blanket taboo on them and all their subjects. Do you outlaw every subject that Ed Guest ever made an ass of himself over? Do you demand the suppression of all the silly and tasteless slush ever pulled by geezers like Browning and Tennyson and Longfellow? Probably not. You doubtless argue that the reader has sense enough of his own to laugh at the tawdry junk and pick out the solid parts as he goes. And so it ought to be with Chaucer and Boccace, D. H. Lawrence and Dreiser, Remarque and Huysmans, and so on. Gawd knows they aren't cosmically perfect creators of one hundred percent successful art—any more than Shakespeare or Homer or Praxiteles or Michaelangelo or Rembrandt were. Everybody nods now and then—so why expect any special group to keep up a one hundred percent batting average all the time? They blunder as we all do—and it is rather naive and pusillanimous and ungenerous to cavil at the blunders of those who work in a difficult province, more than we cavil at the blunders of those whose field requires less skill. I call it downright unsportsmanlike—although in the narrow ignorance of my younger days I used to do it myself. Even now I have no use for a fellow who simply sets out to violate people's inherited sensibilities for no adequate reason—such swine as you'll see listed in book-catalogues under the euphemism of "curiosa"—but in my intellectual maturity I refuse to commit the blunder of confusing these leprous scavengers with honest men whose affronts to convention are merely incidents in a sincere and praiseworthy struggle to interpret or symbolise life as it is. Of course it is possible to make mistakes in classification, for border-line and ambiguous cases always exist; but when we are considering figures of the stature of Voltaire and Rabelais, Lawrence and Fielding, we would be simply foolish not to recognise the vigorously honest intent to see and depict life as a balanced whole, which everywhere animates their productions. When they commit a blunder in technique or proportioning, it is our place to excuse it—whether it concern a difficult or a common theme—and not to adopt a leering or sanctimoniously horrified attitude if the theme happen to be difficult. A case like that calls for more, rather than less, of our sympathy. It no more hurts us to stumble on a brothel or backhouse slopping-over in Remarque, than it does to stumble on a didactic or sentimental slopping-over in Browning or Longfellow. Both sorts of slopping-over may be unpleasant—I like neither myself—but we oughtn't to get any more stirred up over the one than over the other. This, of course, as applied to *serious written literature*. Nobody wants to judge *conversation* by the same standard—and so far as that goes, I'll wager you'd find the oral discourse of Floyd Dell or Ben Hecht or Theodore Dreiser just as normal and pleasant as anybody else's . . . . . and perhaps even more so than the speech of the sainted Alfred, Lord Tennyson, who is said on credible authority to have disgusted many of his intimates by the dirty stories he loved to tell. And that's that. Grandpa's too old and detached a spectator to hold subjective prejudices nowadays. I'll endorse a censorship of the blunders of Boccaccio only *after* the Watch and Ward Society have disposed of the blunders of Eddie Guest and of the designers of houses and public buildings of the 1860–1890 period. *There* is some ugliness that *ought* to be abolished by law in the interest of the good life! Down with French roofs and imitation Norman Gothic . . . . . keep the children from the degrading contemplation of scroll-saw porch trimmings and octagonal cupolas and Richardsonian quasi-Romanesque . . . . . fie on the immorality of cast-iron lawn deer! As for governmental censorship as distinguish'd from aesthetick reticence—one might be in favour of any system calculated to diminish actual crimes of violence and perversity, but the best psychologists agree that censorship has little to do with these things. The creatures who perpetrate aggressive crimes of abnormality are generally defective from the start, and but little motivated by what they read. Conversely, normal persons are rarely moved to overt anti-social acts by any amount of reading. Censorship as now administered is a joke and a minor publick nuisance—touching as it does standard books which the impressionable rabble never read, and wouldn't understand if they did. It is not, however, anything to get wildly excited about—any more than the frankness it opposes is. The liberals who waste time and wind-power howling against the fools in Boston and elsewhere who interfere with the sale of necessary classics are themselves fools in a lesser degree; since anyone knows that a man of wit and resources can buy a book secretly or in another city even if he can't do it openly or at home. No censorship law ever kept any high-grade scholar from reading and owning all the books he needs—Bostonians read Dreiser and Lawrence and Tennesseeans understand the principles of biology—and it does not matter whether the rabble read these things or not. As a matter of fact, the current type of ignorant censorship by Victorian left-overs and Irish Catholic grafters is really a practical benefit despite its absurdity of principle and infantility of psychology—for what it does is to keep a lot of wholly unimportant and banal sewer-effluvium off the cheap news-stands whilst having very little effect on the purchases and perusals of men of taste. One may be highly grateful to be rid of the ugly and worthless pornography which might otherwise clutter up the low-grade stationery shops—and through a law which in practice does not make it impossible for scholars to own Ovid's *Ars Amatoria* and the *Decameron* and the *Old Testament* and *Candide*. The only real hardship ever worked, is in connexion with the drama—as, for instance, when the primer-puzzled, rosary-fingering nitwits of Providence and Boston officialdom banned Eugene O'Neill's "Strange Interlude" a few months ago. And even that wasn't so bad—for the play was put on in Quincy, Mass., whither repaired all the studious Providentians (myself not among them) and Bostonians who cared to sit through its five or six hours of almost unrelieved taedium. Ho, hum! But life is a bore! And I don't know but that the frank expressers are about as damned a bore as the vacant-skull'd suppressors! That's why I light out for the fifth dimension and the galaxies beyond the rim of Einsteinian space-time—to escape the concentrated ennui to which all phases of objective life, flexor-minded or extensor-minded, Apollinian or Dionysiac, ultimately boil down. To hell with mammal primates—I'm sure the articulata will do a damn sight better when they inherit the aging planet and give us the air as we gave it to the dinosaurs! The first intelligent civilisation on this planet will probably be one of the formicarinae, the coleoptera, the aphidae, the muscidae, or the culicidae.

Yr most oblig'd, obt hble Servt
H. Paget-Lowe.

Notes

1. Most of the following are well-known Victorian-era scientists and writers.
2. Henry Thomas Buckle (1821–1862), British historian, author of the unfinished *History of Civilization in England*.
3. Étienne Geoffroy Saint-Hilaire (1772–1844), French naturalist; James Murdoch Geikie (1839–1915), Scottish geologist, professor of geology at Edinburgh University (1882–1914); Alfred Kirchhoff (1838–1907), German geographer and naturalist.
4. Erich Maria Remarque (1898–1970), a German novelist, author of *All Quiet on the Western Front* (1928).

[55]   [AHT]

19 Ianuarii [1931]

Doctissime:—

Ecce! Last Wednesday was published, for the exclusive perusal of its author, (like his earlier works, circa 1896–7–8) the following important historico-geographical work, in an edition of one copy—with one hundred thirty-six pages of Theobaldian cursive text:

A
Description
of the
Town of
Quebeck, in New France,
Lately annext to His Britannick Majesty's
Dominions.

By H. Lovecraft, Gent.,
of
Providence, in New-England.

Design'd for the Information of the Curious, and the Guiding of Travellers from His Majesty's New-England and other American Provinces. To which is added, an Historical Account of New-France.

———————— * ————————

The Whole embellished with Maps and Designs illustrative of the Text.

———————— * ————————

CONTENTS:

Book I. An Historical Account of Quebeck
- A. The Founding of New-France...1
- B. The Company of an Hundred Associates.......................7
- C. New-France as a Royal Province 15
- D. The Struggle for North-America..
    1. King William's War..26
    2. Queen Anne's War. 32
    3. King George's War...35
    4. The Old French War. 37
    5. The Fall of New-France..49
- E. Canada under His Britannick Majesty's Rule 56

Book II. The Present State of Quebeck
- A. The Province, and Approaches to Quebeck...................78
- B. The Aspect and Architecture of Quebeck...........................
    1. Architecture. 86
    2. Atmosphere and Topography................................ 93
- C. Modes of Observing Quebeck ....
    1. General Considerations..97
    2. An Orientation-Tour of Quebeck........................100
    3. A Series of Pedestrian Tours...................................108

         4. The Suburbs of Quebeck.........................132
    Appendix: Tables of Place-Names & Origins.............135

                Providence, in Rhode-Island,
    Printed by John Carter, at Shakespear's-Head in Gaol-Lane
    over-against the Court-House, and sold by Booksellers and
    Stationers generally. MDCCCCXXXI.

Which same, tack'd onto a helluva potery doctoring job, will account for Grandpa's time around the turn of the year! As for my correspondence—well, Sir, for the first time I've come damn near adopting the desperate tacticks of W. Paul Cook—who has fled Athol and left all his unclaim'd mail at the P.O., giving no forwarding address. What I've done is to leave a good three hundred fourteen of my recent letters *unopen'd*—tho' the semiannual did not share that treatment. I owe about twenty right now. 'Sa grea' life! Speaking of congestion, tho', I'm never within even approximate hailing-distance of you! Some "vacation"! Gawd—if I were you and Morton, I'd sure find some damn way to tone down the grind and get some time to live in! You two birds are the limit for programme-crowding!

An' on toppa all this, to think ya hadda set down and copy that old *Ibid* spoof![1] Hell—I sure do feel the compliment! I'd almost forgotten the thing, and it brought back golden memories of the past (dear old 1927) to peruse it once more. Yet out of its original setting and contemporary motivation it really is kinda a drug on the market. A clever bozo would know how to doctor it up and give it real pep—but as I scan its sonorous periods I'm hang'd if I know just how to start it in or end it up. Ya see, all that Prairie–Highland stuff means nothing except in connexion with the personal circumstances of the correspondence.[2] To make it any good, a *whole new idea* has gotta be thought up as an adequate climactic punch . . . . . and at this moment I can no more think of anything zippy than I can square the circle! We gotta form a *whole new conception* of how such a wheeze had orta wind up and snap—and all I can suggest now is that it ought to have something to do with the way the thing begins—a new beginning, too, for the present one lacks the air of having an adequate raison d'etre. The snap of the ending depends on having Ibid's skull in some *particular place*—but how the hell is this snap gonna be retain'd when the thing is depersonalised and delocalised? One thing that occurs to me is to have the whole article ostensibly written by some very-small-town museum curator (no, I'm *not* thinking Jim Ferd!) who—having read an allusion to *Ibid*—corrects it because of personal interest inspired by possession of the skull. The town must be small and commonplace enough to make its possession of any important museum (give it a high-sounding name) seem absurd. Just how the opening reference to *Ibid* can best be made, is another question. It may be better to let the slip be made by a small-town editor in the course of a bombastick and sententious editorial—for no stranger would be likely to see a schoolboy howler in such a way as to inspire instant scholarly correction. To promote the air of whimsical humour, the editor's small town may be in the same state as the curator's small town—the two being natural rivals and enemies. In opening the harangue, the curator expresses surprise that the editor should have made such a slip about *Ibid*, when that great sage's very skull rests within the confines of the same glorious commonwealth. But then—what can one expect from an editor in a place like Blankville? By playing up the rustick hostility betwixt Wauklecatchee Four Corners and Blankville, it might be possible to give the article the added motivation of being a *pure bluff* on the curator's part—an attempt to "put one over" on the ignorant editor and his fellow-townsmen. What d'ya thinka this idee? I don't wanna waste time on it unless it looks oke to you. Of course, this is only half the problem. After this beginning is adopted, we gotta finda way of giving the skull a decently snappy and climactick mode of landing in the Wauklecatchee Four Corners Museum of Anthropology, Fine Arts, Science, Industry, and Okkagama County Local History—involving one more step of transportation after it has been in the possession of Herr Zimmerman of Zythopolis. This means a wholly new comick idea or image—of which I am dismally dry at the moment. As a matter of fact, the whole thing might be a damn sight more homogeneous. When I started spoofing about *Ibid* I had no idea of even mentioning his skull—but as I got reeling off biographical ponderosities, I kinda hated to stop, hence kept on until it occurr'd to me to carry the linkage straight through to good old Qzoz. [*sic*][3] In these grey after-years, without the spontaneity of the occasion, I can't get the same old mood. The old man has aged and dry'd up since good old 1927! Well—let's think on the subject at our respective leisures, (if such exist) and maybe one of us will get an idea and go ahead with the goat-gland surgery.[4] I'm carefully filing my copy, and will make a try sometime when my dulness is less assertively dominant than it is this week. Meanwhile if you have a sudden inspiration go ahead with the thing yourself. I shall certainly be marvellously glad to evade the responsibility. Whether any periodical would print the thing even as a gift is another matter entirely. Stuff that goes oke in epistles, ain't so hot by a damn sight when ya try to mine it out and smelt it for the public's consumption—as I've just said to my new correspondent Doc Whitehead (who turns out to be an alienist and psychiatrist—just the boy to keep our gang out of the booby hatch in the cud!) upon his suggestion that I let him jazz up and peddle a coupla pages of random observations on the future social, political, and economic fortunes of the poor old U.S. I can't think of any rag that would care much for the venerable *St. Ibidus*, but if anybody wants to waste postage, there ain't no law agin it. Well—as I says afore—take Grandpa's emendation-

suggestions for what they're worth; and lemme know whether there's anything I can do—at a more humoursome and leisurely moment—about acting on 'em. That pupil-typed page sure is a bird—I wonder what that guy would make outa a *really* difficult manuscript of mine—say one of the intricate chapters of my treatise on Quebeck?
  Well—rye-toodle-inkaday!
    Yr obt Grandpa Lo.

Notes

1. See letter 35n11.
2. MWM lived on Prairie Street, renamed Highland Avenue. See "Ibid": "In the roseal dawn of the burghers of Milwaukee rose to find a former prairie turned to a highland!" (*CF* 2.416).
3. It is uncertain what the stenographer mistyped—perhaps "Hans" Zimmerman (*CF* 2.415).
4. HPL alludes to the practice of John Romulus Brinkley (1885–1942), who fraudulently claimed to be a medical doctor (he had no legitimate medical education) and became known as the "goat-gland doctor." He became wealthy through the xenotransplantation of goat testicles into human males to treat impotence, and then numerous other maladies.

[56] [AHT]

Freyr's Day
[February 1931]

Doctissime:—
  As for this neogalpinius of the classroom—bless my old bones, but he does look like the real Kleicomolo timber! Even his name will be oke as soon as returning spring makes me less sensitive to polar suggestions![1] Rebel against dull order, thoughtless myth, and meaningless convention—'fore gad, Sir, a lad after me own heart! By all means tell the child to write Old Grandpa Theobald! I'm all out of touch with real youth these days, for even my latest crop of grandchildren—the Wandrei–Derleth generation—has come of age and is out of college; whilst the original generation itself is stolid and middle-aged now, clutter'd up with excess fat, wives, moustachelets, worldly-wisdom, and all the other excrescences which ruthless time brings in its train. Great god, to think that Grandpa's scintillant little Alfredus will be *thirty* next November, and that tiny Sonny Belknap (whose moustachelet can now be seen without magnification under favourable illumination) has a distinct bay-window and second chin, and will be *twenty-nine* in April![2] The years, the years, the years! And still Zaro Agha and Old Grandpa Theobald hang on! Yes, damn it, this youthful Amundsen person sounds like the real stuff! Glad he likes the Kleicomolo—or at least the more opinionated and articulate part

of it. Good ol' Klei never did go in much for views and argifyings, being of that serenely civilised poise which recognises the futility of all belief and utterance. At times, I have rather envy'd him his quasi-Chinese detachment—but we're all as hell slung us together, and there's no use of any one bimbo quarrellin' wit' his own architecture! Wish Klei'd start up writing again—but these days he finds social contacts, urban contemplations, and senescent gallantries more in his line. Wonder which type stands old age the best—his'n or ourn? But young John looks to be in our division. There's some damn good reprint dope in the H. J. nickleodea[3]—only trouble is keepin' em stacked for easy use. I must have two hundred or three hundred of 'em—never go off without a batch in my flask pockets. Psycho-analysis is undoubtedly a damn sight more important than I believed in Kleicomolo days. Ya see, despite my years, I ain't no guy to get his mind set in a rut and do the ostrich act toward evidence. Modern psychology, put to the test, has shown it's got the goods—it explains things and fulfils conditions as nothing else does—hence even an antient Georgian has no reason for not recognising it. Naturally, details are still obscure. Pavlov, Watson, and the behaviourists generally, form an important modifying influence to correlate with the Viennese school; whilst the dream-symbolisms of Freud still seem, to the impartial eye, as carried beyond reasonable likelihood and existing evidence. But take modern psychology as a whole, and anybody can see that its now-irrefutable nucleus of truth has utterly altered our knowledge of our own emotions, mental processes, and adjustments, and shed floods of blinding light upon our relationship to the external world. What was formerly merely adumbrated by the wise, is now open to the every-day perception of all. Mankind is saved from countless hoary absurdities by the deflation of flatulent sentimentalities, illusions, attitudes, and spurious apparent values. No sane adult of the general Browning–Tennyson calibre could ever again throw the bull they threw. That pap is now left to the tenth-raters and the soulful hangers-on of correspondence Poetry Circles. Of course, I never fell for the worst of Victorian slush even in Victorian times; but I did carelessly and passively tolerate a cursed lot of bunk (so long as it meant nothing in the cosmic problems with really interest me) as late as the early Kleicomolo Period. It took little Alfie to start the old man on his second wind of self-debunking, which is still in progress. Thus I was most distinctly *not* one of the pioneers in accepting the newer psychology—a fact I confess without shame merely because shame is a meaningless and uncivilised pseudo-emotion. But John is more fortunate intellectually in having been reared in a saner world than the pre-war world of my youth—just as he is more unfortunate culturally in belonging to a world farther removed from the old non-mechanical and aesthetically-integrated past. He won't have as much to unlearn as Grandpa Theobald did—and is that much to the good. His sizeup of his fellow-infant from extemporaneous unconscious scribbling—be it a luck shot or the real thing—did surely form a highly dramatick perfor-

mance; and I hope you'll set him to work on something of the sort again. Glad the other kid took the unflattering analysis in good part. Modern youth, on the whole, has a sounder perspective and less meaningless egotism than we used to have—tho' there are exceptions, as my young Derleth-grandchild (aet. 21) proves. Well, anyway—don't hesitate to sic Parvulus Johannes on to Grandpa. One can always ditch something to make room—gawd, but I must manage to can about half a dozen dumbbells whom I keep on the correspondence-list more through irony or inertia—or both—than through anything else. Did I say half-a-dozen? I really mean nearer twenty-five. I gotta quit tryin' to be so damn civil!
        Yr obt Lo.

Notes

1. HPL apparently refers to a colleague of MWM's named John Amundsen (whose name made HPL think of the Antarctic explorer Roald Amundsen). It does not appear as if Amundsen ever joined in a Kleicomolo-like correspondence cycle.
2. Actually, FBL would turn thirty. HPL mistakenly thought him to have been born in 1902.
3. I.e., booklets published by the Haldeman-Julius Co., costing 5¢.

[57] [AHT]

                                                            Sun's Day
                                                         [March 1931?]
Hail, O Mokrates, Prince of Light:—
                    [. . .]
    BUT—don't fancy for a moment that anybody thinks a literary artist need know no more than the single jargon of his chosen province. When a critic praises the rough vigour of a really unlettered author he is simply taking what value he finds, and not inquiring into what value the same aestheticK attempt would have had if made by a cultivated person using the patois consciously (but sincerely) and able to think beyond it in modulating the flow of narration and enlarging the scope of the illustration by calculated departures from simple fact-relation. He is not trying to say that the crude writer is a real author merely because one piece of real literature has been achieved. This kind of literature is literature by accident—each creator is able to create just one genuine piece because of its relation to his personal experience. Outside that one shot, he is just as helpless as the next gutter illiterate. The object of literary training is to overcome this limitation—to make a writer know what he is doing, and to reproduce with equal effectiveness all those phases of life to which he is sensitive, whether or not they have any place in his personal history. Training emancipates the writer from the cramping chains of sheer fact-narration, and gives him the flexibility to make writing an art instead of

an accident. It is no attack at all on literary scholarship to admit that an illiterate may sometimes write better prose than a scholar—since this admission has a string to it; to wit, that the dumbbell can thus excel only once in his whole life, when getting his chief obsession off his chest. The use to which conscious scholars can put this circumstance is that of recognising what kinds of language go naturally with certain kinds of experience-presentation. In a scholar's hands, the illiterate language of the street may take on vast poignancy, as indeed it has repeatedly done throughout the history of literature. In reproductions of conversation, this patois is used with folklore fidelity. In concomitant third-person passages, its basic spirit, simplicity, and angle of approach are preserved, though with rectification to the normal syntactical laws of the language, and an intellectual oversight which may guard the text from ignoring real distinctions of meaning and from reflecting a perspective contrary to mature knowledge. It does not take a microscope to perceive that Ernest Hemingway and John V. A. Weaver[1] have a much greater intellectual command of their material than would the kind of people they depict! But they are right in stripping down to vulgate essentials when they wish to say what they have to say. Life could not possibly be interpreted without this intelligent adaptation of medium to subject matter . . . . . indeed, the blank record of the nineteenth century in saying anything of real significance or reality is sufficient proof of the validity of the assumption. The eighteenth century—in its earlier half before the falling of the curse of "elegance and chaste refinement"—did not fall into this trap of false diction and spurious emotional values . . . . . hence the immortal prose of everybody from Defoe to Swift, and Steele to Smollett. After that, the twilight, and the curse of Latinity and namby-pamby . . . . . Richardson, Johnson, Fanny Burney, Mackenzie, Mrs. Radcliffe—and the nineteenth century. I can never forgive Fate for fixing upon me some of the typical rhythms and mannerisms of the later eighteenth century and 1830's. I have tried to shake 'em off and get back to Addison and Swift, but indolence, the Poe tradition, and such-like get in the way and drag me back to the abyss. But thank gawd my conscious mind is not as enslaved as my aesthetick habits are! Anyway—the big idea is not that authors should grow up illiterate, but that they should be conscious of the value and appropriateness of adapting their carefully managed style to the matter and point of view they are presenting. It is utter puerility to think that a single standard of diction can cover all the modes in which diction must be used—even by the same person. But hell, this isn't any kick-in-the-ass for scholarship. Rather is it a severer demand on scholarship! The intelligent litterateur, instead of getting one conventional jargon by rote and rule and applying to every goddam thing he tackles, must know every type of natural diction as a vital, orgnaic thing in relation to the psychology of the types and moods involved. Any other kind of utterance is deadwood and dry bones, without the stamp of personality, perception, and proportion. Study and training? Cripes!

It means a study and training which begin when the conventional study and training (all very well and indispensable as an elementary start) leave off! When the bolsheviks enjoin a proletarian style, their real blunder is not in postulating a relationship betwixt style and substance, but merely in prescribing what the substance of an artist's efforts shall be. A free and intelligent author might conceivably choose a style much like the "proletarian" in depicting a scene and group of people animated [by] modern proletarian ideals—but he would of course use this style flexibly and consciously instead of naively; retaining his realistic and artistic perspective on the universe, and not falling into the error of agreeing in the third person with the narrow and artificial ideology of the characters.

Well, that's the way it is. The intelligence of the present demands a perception of the relation of style to subject matter; hence dictates the use of varied manners of expression for material of widely different content and psychology. To suppose a man with the aesthetick and philosophick vision of Hemingway could say anything in the French pastry jargon of Thornton Wilder, or that a sensitive perceiver like Marcel Proust (the one real novelist of the last decade or two) could get anything at all over in the stereotyped phrases and attitudes of the "great tradition", is to miss the whole point of the purpose and mode of functioning of language. What any guy has to say, is what's in him—and every fresh combination of a guy and wot he's got on his chest calls for a distinctly individual use of language. If anybody feels perfectly at home in some other bimbo's shiny coat and pants, that's a proof of one of two things—either that he is, by accident, a dead ringer for the other guy; or that he hasn't a damn thing of his own to say. Standardised manners and perspectives are natural in literature only during ages so un-analytical and unreflective that they can't depict human character; or during other ages when the art of drawing individuals is more or less voluntarily passed up in favour of a sketchy art confined to rough universals. The latter set of conditions is what we tend to recognise as "classicism" ..... the former is mediaevalism and its Victorian flareback. Romanticism, that is. Of these two positions, romanticism and classicism, the first is a disease and a defect whilst the latter is a discipline verging dangerously toward being a pose. In fact classicism can't helping being a pose in this age of psychological understanding and poignant perception of human differences. Honest depiction of life must be based on realism, no matter how much that realism may be suffused with imaginative overtones derived from subjective attitudes toward reality and dream.

But what I can't see, is where you find anything radical or confusing in all this. Doesn't the ordinary theory of pedagogy practically say the same thing today? In all this business, I can't see a single contradiction of those various distinctions betwixt strong and feeble utterance, real and insincere utterance, original and stereotyped utterance, etc., which you bring out with such magnificent and unparalleled concreteness in your Doorways. Any of the various modern prose styles could be tested successfully by the tests accompanying your book, or by the Abbott–Trabue[2] tests. There's nothing new—all the moderns, even to Joyce and T. S. Eliot, recognise certain differences betwixt inane and hollow sound, of the Bush–Whitaker–Duffee[3] type, and the emotionally authentic use of word-symbols which appears equally in Milton, Proust, much of Walt Whitman, Herman Melville, Dunsany, Dean Swift, Carl Sandburg, or Virginia Woolf. If anything, the modern standard means a more intense rather than less intense application of these laws of substance and quality; for it picks up instances of masked Bushery and camouflaged Duffee-ism in the emptily sonorous prose and verse of former idols who were once able to get away with it . . . . . as in the Thackeray crap cited in the article, or in some of the meaningless slopping over of Dickens, Tennyson, Wordsworth, et al. Who today could read Bulwer-Lytton without a laugh? Maybe he was never taught in schools, but I can testify that he was taken damn seriously around Victorian firesides with their ugly marble mantels and tasselled lambrequins that matched that stuffy paterfamilias's Dundrearies.[4] Under the gaslight, boys! Ho, hum!

The whole issue is that of clarification—a getting down to hard pan and trying to dope out the realities behind the traditional facades called standards. That's the task of the twentieth century as it cleans up and disinfects the sickroom litter of the unsound nineteenth. Standards are oke when they mean anything—and it's the present's job to find out what ones do and what ones don't. As applied to language, it seems pretty clear that sincerity and congruity—rhythmic harmony and atmospheric aptitude—are the real criteria to judge by. These are nothing new—indeed, they are among the oldest of standards. They have proved their worth and have earned acceptance. But the standard of "dignity" or "refinement" which temporarily tagged along with these things between 1760 and 1920 has not come out from the analysis quite so well. It has not been found to correspond to any fixed universal reality, or to dictate any mode of writing of more than local and limited application. Obviously, it was enforced through a basically mistaken idea regarding the values and relationships of things, and was a fatal handicap largely responsible for the slender success of nineteenth century literature in reflecting human life. It propped up a false and artificial view of man and of the cosmos, and was thereby inherently ridiculous. Instead, the standard should have been one of disinterested force, spontaneity, vitality, congruity, appropriateness, directness, and simplicity—a standard implying as by-products, in their proper and natural proportions, many of the graces which artificial standards enjoined awkwardly and grotesquely as mere mechanical tricks. The natural standard takes harmonious rhythm for granted; and in the close relationship of the words and rhythms to the personal and individual thought-turns and feeling-twists of the utterer, involves imaginative figures and vigorous collocations of words and phrases far sounder than those taught by rote for conscious trick employment. Not but that harmonies and figures of rhetoric ought to be taught and recognised, but that their use ought to be determined by the spontaneous personality of the artist rather than by consultations of rules and traditional precedents. It is easy to spot the difference between a vigorous artist's use of language as his own living and personal medium—a use including original comparisons and imagery, unique ways of stating or implying things, authentic modulations of tone and tempo to suit the shifting of the artist's mood, and so on—and a Victorian purist's mincing adherence to a set of rules which unsuccessfully try to conceal his lack of any distinctive thoughts or feelings. When a chap tries to be correct, elegant, and refined, he invariably succeeds in being nothing at all. If, on the other hand, he tries sincerely and artistically to be himself—in the immortal verbiage of our li'l' pal Sandusky—he often achieves through unconscious appropriateness (if the theme happens to justify it) the selfsame refined musick and delicate imagery which the conscious plodder tried his damndest [*sic*] to get but couldn't! And of course, the natural and rational literature has dozens of sources of strength which are forever closed to the inhibited Howellite—healthy surges of rhythm and burst of iconoclastically direct vocabulary; mordant ironies and sanifying sham-penetrations; clarifying analyses and unhackneyed relationship-perceptions . . . . . dozens of sound linguistick attributes which he uses in accordance with the laws of rational proportion, and which have as clear a discipline of their own—the discipline of eurythmy and appropriateness—which guards against triviality, namby-pamby, bombast, extravagance, sentimentality, and slopping-over—as have the hollow, arbitrary, and artificial attributes of Victorian "elegant" writing.

It's a good idea to give "eloquence" a black eye, since the word has come to imply more liabilities than assets. "Eloquence" inclines the novice to trust in empty symbols and tinsel-pretty jugglings of symbols instead of buckling right down to life and refusing to dally with meaningless jigsaw ornaments. Not that one wants to write uncouthly for uncouthness's sake, but that one wants to make one's beauty the beauty of perfect functional proportion and adaptation instead of the birthday-cake beauty of plastered-on curlicues. God, if somebody could only drown half the teachers of elocution! This *Curry System* that James Ferdinand and Ma Renshaw dote so beatifically upon gives me dull, boneless ache betwixt the shoulderblades.[5] Flatulent belchings of spurious, worked-up emotion, hand-wavings based on cockeyed myths regarding emotional values (like a Jew ragman or like the opponent of Cicero, Q. Hortensius, who had invisible strings tied to parts of his toga so that he could manipulate the falling of the folds at different periods of his Asiatically florid harangues in the praetorium), trite conscious manipulations of the supposed ebb and flow of climatic or dramatic pulsations, phrases and antitheses in whose hoary whiskers Isocrates used to get tangled up—oh, hell! What wouldn't I give if I could take Jim Ferd in hand and loosen and liven his style and imagination up a bit! And in the short story field, how many promising imaginations have been melted into inane caramel by the school-of-journalism radiation of unctuous, second-hand Rudyardery and Ohenricism! Right now I'm trying like blazes to save little Sonny Belknap from the Kipling stereotype. The child is getting so infatuated with words and phrases, and poses of urbanely ironic sophistication, that half the guts are getting let out of his tales. Back to earth—down with the gingerbread facade—to the swill-cart with refined smartness—thus the grandpaternal exhortations of a blunt old man who wants the boys to deal in life and art and genuine emotions and imagination-vistas instead of sounding rhetoric and popular pastry. Of course it's too late to save Grandpa himself, since the poor old duffer has always been a perfect 1830 stereotype so far as serious fictional utterance is concern'd. All that can be done is to prevent the younger folks from following the same road to ruin . . . . . and at least one kid is indeed escaping the wreckage; to wit, that young Wisconsin prodigy I've occasionally mention'd—little Augie Derleth, whose serious Proustian work would surprise anybody who had seen only his disavowed pot-boilers in *Weird Tales*. That child, as an artist, doesn't take orders from any guy or any guy's textbook . . . . . and mark Grandpa's words, he'll be heard from. BUT—he of course bases his spontaneous artistic attitude upon a sound objective knowledge of the principles of language and literature as taught in the schools and at your own University of Wisconsin. Without that knowledge he would be too hopelessly reduced to a blind, bungling system of trial and error. The mind must be opened up to perspectives and rhythms, and there will always be a need to teach the difference between false utterance and direct, emotionally authentic utterance. All that must be scrapped is the already vanishing tendency to teach "elegant writing" for the sake of elegance instead of expression. The thing to do is to teach each person to say exactly what that person, as determined by temperament and experience, really has to say.

I don't see anything especially off with modern curricula except perhaps that they put too much emphasis on certain glibly unsound nineteenth century models—unctuously hollow or mawkish things which will either sap the student's rugged creative vitality or send him off into a healthily barbaric reaction against all formal literature. How anybody can read Tennyson's *Idylls of the King* without puking is more than I can see. Old Alf had to tell dirty stories to compensate for drooling such tripe—and I'd rather omit both the story-telling and the tripe-writing. And some of the mincing prose they used to feed me back in the dear old 1900's—but then, I was already corrupted in a far more antient direction, that of Sam Johnson; so that I escaped the smallpox of Victorianism through having the cowpox of late-Georgianism. What I'd do if I were the big sho[t?] in the head-dope racket is to teach the same basic principles of language, but with a little more vital range of models. Early eighteenth century—Elizabethan, immediate twentieth century, etc. And of course, whatever good stuff the nineteenth century did manage to pull. One of my theories is that the universal aesthetic debacle of the nineteenth century was caused by the transfer of all the really first-rate brains to the scientific field; thus leaving the arts for drooling sentimentalists and ethics-hounds to maunder over. By that token, we ought to find some of the best, simplest, and unconsciously sincerest prose among those serious scientific writers who happened to have the gift of expression as well . . . . . and hang me if it isn't so in a good number of cases. Huxley's "Man's Place in Nature" and Tyndall's "Fragments of Science" have lots of parts that would make good school reading where prose structure is to be inculcated. Some of this honest, direct prose would be a good balance wheel for any extravagances which an age of individualism may tend to foster.

One thing I shake with the moderns on is the utter banality and bad artistry of *plot* in the conventional or fiction-correspondence-school sense. It doesn't take half an eye to show how blatantly false to life such cheap event-juggling is—indeed, I can't think of a thing more obviously and essentially meaningless and hollow than this idol of the Dickenses and LeFanus, the Walter B. Pitkins and Thomas H. Uzzells[6] . . . . . to say nothing of that Newspaper Institute whose yellow dodger you lately sent me. A story ought to be a fragment of life and just that—life of the external form or of the imagination, but in any case authentic and normally proportioned life, without any artificial values and stock conceptions of events and motivations thrust in to spoil the coherence of the fabrick. I often feel hellishly cheap when some vestige of my nineteenth century environment impels me to wind up a yarn of mine with a cheap little twist of event. Not that climax itself is inherently inartistic in its proper place—but it is inartistic when it coincides too patly with certain streams of events or volitional elements. The whole Victorian idea of a "story" is rotten to the point of Valdemarian liquescence—and yet that is just what the punk Saddypost-feeding schools of journalism peddle even to this day. Thank gawd, I believe the standard school and college curricula go fairly easy on this fallacy. You can't tell me that this hokum will ever come back in serious literature. Five years from now the Priestleys and Herberts[7] will be on the shelf with the incipiently dated Thornton Wilder. Life is vague and tangled and groping—an endless dissatisfaction which begins nowhere and ends nowhere, has no values and means only a dull pain of frustration as all imagined goals recede farther and farther out of reach into the alluring, tantalising sunset. The writer who catches this authentick outline and serves up episodes from it in poignant fashion cannot dally with arranged-to-order coincidences and synthetick happy endings. He need not be cramped to greyness, for the imaginative phenomena of escape are always legitimate material for artists built that way—but when he tries to remodel the workings of the cosmos to suit an infantile idea of how events ought to dovetail together, he has no further right to call himself an artist.

And so it goes. A vital writer doesn't have to be a roughneck—except when his theme dictates it—but he has to repudiate the silly notion that there is no place for roughneckery. He may, as prompted by natural temperament, be the most delicate of ethereal fantaisistes, or the most analytical and precise of intellectual psychologists—in both of these latter cases departing as far as imaginable from the uncouth in manner—but he must at all times be one thing if he is to be anything at all—and that is himself. He must think of his subject and creative urge first—and of his language and rhetorical machinery only later on. What he must fling off like a poisoned garment is the whole psychology of convention, verbal tradition, elegance, refinement, primness, purism, artificiality, and kindred bullshit. Let the refinement come when it wants to, where natural art suggests it and makes it appropriate—but let it keep out of the way otherwise, lest it serve not as an asset and adornment, but as a grotesque sham and target for the jeers and healthy reactionary coarseness of sound masculine thinkers and artists. It took a "Pamela" to breed a "Joseph Andrews"[8]—and a Victorian era to breed a Joyce and a T. S. Eliot. And another thing, as I keep trying to remind young writers like Sonny Belknap—it's utterly silly to get self-conscious as a writer, and invest the process and profession of writing with a kind of spurious sentimental glamour. That kind of thing breeds a false mood and motivation in art. Young whippersnappers try first to pose as "I, Marmaduke Esme Yellowbook, the writer" ..... and only afterward think of their inward and immortal urge to record some image which is the only excuse for a gentleman's bothering with the messy boredom of setting down words. No man ought to be "a writer". Conscious "writers" spew out words. But when a man has to say something because he'll be uneasy if he doesn't, the thing for him to do is to say it. And very possibly the result may be art.

Hell, but I've covered a lot of paper—and ain't sure that I've said much at that! But you get the idea—that there ain't nothing really radical about Bob Holliday's little sidelight.[9] Or if there is, as I said before, you can give me a kick in the behind as a dumbbell. But to my eye, there ain't a damn thing about the modern position which conflicts in the least with the basic standards of discrimination between real and spurious expression as set forth in your *Doorways*—and, by inference, in your daily W. D. H. S.[10] classes. So much for that.

        La de inka day!

              Grandpa Lo.

Notes

1. John V[an] A[lstyne] Weaver, Jr. (1893–1938), poet, novelist, and screenwriter.
2. See Allan Abbott and M. R. Trabue, "A Measure of Ability to Judge Poetry," *Teacher's College Record* 22, No. 2 (March 1921): 101–26.

3. Amateur poets David Van Bush, Noah F. Whitaker, and May M. Duffee.

4. Long flowing sideburns.

5. Samuel Silas Curry (1847–1921) founded the School of Elocution and Expression (now Curry College) in Milton, MA, in 1879.

6. Walter B. Pitkin (1878–1953), professor at the Columbia University School of Journalism (1912–43). He wrote self-help books such as *Life Begins at Forty* (1932), as well as *A Short Introduction to the History of Human Stupidity* (1932), the latter of which HPL often mentioned in letters. Thomas H. Uzzell (1884–?) writer, editor, and teacher in New York City during the 1920s and '30s. He was fiction editor at *Collier's*, taught seminars on fiction writing at New York University, and published several books on the craft of writing, including *Narrative Technique: A Practical Course in Literary Psychology* (1934), *Writing as a Career* (1938), and *The Technique of the Novel* (1947). FBL was a pupil of his, but HPL considered him a charlatan.

7. The British fiction writers J. B. Priestley (1894–1984) and A. P. Herbert (1890–1971).

8. Samuel Richardson's sentimental novel *Pamela; or, Virtue Rewarded* (1740) was parodied by Henry Fielding in *Joseph Andrews* (1742).

9. Robert Cortes Holliday (1880–1947), American writer and literary editor, co-author of *The Business of Writing: A Practical Guide for Authors* (1922).

10. I.e., West Division High School, in Milwaukee.

[58] [AHT]

April 5, 1931

Hail, O Sage—

Young Talman—the gang's arch-genealogist—hounded me into getting out all my fam'ly charts on both sides three years ago, and when I waded through 'em for the first time in years I couldn't find a goddam thing to account for such a nut as Grandpaw Tibbald.[1] The whole keynote of my personality, aside from my antiquarianism, is individual revolt against meaningless convention; yet the whole family's branchage behind me is about as solidly conventional a mess as you could well imagine. Any sort of aesthete is rare as a hen's tooth, and intellect doesn't sparkle a bit—but that's to be expected, since I ain't no arc light myself. The overwhelming majority—virtually totality—of my ancestry on both sides is of the staid and stolid country-gentry class, with an abnormally high percentage of *clergymen* droning their amiably well-meaning matins and liturgies across the well-clipt hedges of a subdu'd and commonplace rural mead. I can scare up a full-fledged clerick—the Rev. Francis Fulford, Vicar of Dunsford—in four generations—that is, he is my great-great-grandfather—and by two generations behind him they come up thick and fast. Then on my mother's side, also, they rant and rave—only here they tend to be Puritans and other freaks instead of sober Anglicans. That screechy old Quaker gal hang'd in Boston Common in 1660—Mary Dyer—is among my doubtfully revered progenitrices. Mediocrity seems quite the rule; for the three or four really great lines I touch—Musgrave of

Edenhall, Cumberland, Chichester; Carew of Haccombe; Legge, Lord Dartmouth; etc. etc.—are so far back that no trait from them could conceivably have any perceptible share in moulding me. When one's chart gets so far back as that, one can't be sure of having any more of this blood than any common churl may have; since of course the peasantry were constantly fertilised left-handedly by just the same people who handed right-handed blood along the chart lines. When you get back to two or three key ancestors, any one of these can connect you up with half the worthies of Plantagenet times and before—thus there probably isn't any Englishman living who *isn't* descended from Charlemagne or at least from half a dozen of William the Conqueror's companions. All of which took the kick out of my rediscovery on the chart of bimboes like Thomas, Earl of Warwick, the lines of Beauchamp, Clavering, de Clifford, Moreton, St. Albyn, Fitzurse, Challons, etc. etc. One of these guys may have meant a lot in 1850, but in 1550 or 1450 they are just decoration. I can raise both a knight (Sir Lancelot Allgood of Nunwick) and a Baronet (Sir John Morris of Clasemont, Glamorganshire, Wales) in the fifth generation back—that is, these guys are my great-great-great-grandfathers—but when you come to analyse 'em you find they are very ordinary specimens of their kind—the Knight being merely a small-time Tory (High Sheriff of Northumberland) knighted by George III, upon his accession, for Tory loyalty during the preceding Whig regime. And Sir John is merely a first baronet—a novus homo whose old man wasn't any more than a simple gentleman of Tregedar. In direct male line, I can't get back to the Conquest at all; the family of Lovecroft (early spelling) first appearing in Devonshire, in the valley of the Teign, circa 1450. I can't push my own lineal stem back to 1560 plus or minus, when John Lovecraft (present spelling) of Minister Hall near Newton-Abbot bore the present arms of the family: a chevron, engrailed, Or, between three foxes' heads, erased, Or, on a field Vert. Following his progeny down the line, I don't find a single mark of distinction above the mediocre country-gentry average. Clergymen to burn (though there was no Queen Mary to get it done), just plain squires who probably talked with a dialect almost as broad as their tenants', Captains, Colonels, occasional marriages into old lines but mostly marriages into small-time lines whose charted antecedents don't reach the Domesday Book—that's the bulk of the germ-plasm that made up Grandpa's paternal half. One curious strain is that of Washington—a branch with no discoverable relation to that which emigrated to Virginia and produc'd the arch-rebel. But not a damn thing to indicate a revolt against commonplace unintelligence or a taste for the weird and the cosmic. No philosophers—no artists—no writers—not a cursed soul I could possibly talk to without getting a pain in the neck.

In 1745 we find born a restless egg who probably felt the blind stultification of all this oppressive respectability; for according to common report this Thomas Lovecraft struck out to live where he lived, aided by wine, horses, and the fair. I hope he had a good time, for his legacy to posterity was a general property scattering which shot everything to hell before he croaked—so that he had to sell even his family seat in 1823 . . . . . historick date, on which the Lovecrafts ceased to be gentlemen according to the original and technical definition. Possibly the shock killed the old reprobate, for he himself bumped off three years after that. Out of the wreckage climbed sundry of his numerous lawful progeny—I can't answer for the doubtless numerous rest—including his sixth child and their son Joseph; already married and with six children of his own. This bird Joe, gentlemen, was the great-grandfather of your Grandpaw Tibbald. Casting around for a possible comeback area, he lit in an evil hour on these revolted colonies, whither he transported himself, wife (daughter of the Vicar of Dunsford), and offspring in the year 1827. Or more exactly, he meant to settle in still loyal Upper-Canada—the present Ontario—but found nothing doing, so filtered across the line to the Province of New York, in whose northern reaches he settled down on an experimental farm and promptly died, leaving his heirs to worry along as best they might. As it happened, all of them—John, William, Joseph, George, and Aaron—and a sister Mary—managed to keep above water; improved in some cases by advantageous marriages. Of these lines, however, all but two are definitely extinct, and even one of these two probably is. Joseph had a grandson who went west in the 1880's and dropped from sight. And George, marrying the daughter of a transplanted Allgood of Nunwick, had a son Winfield—who married into the old Yankee stock of Rhode Island and left one good-for-nothing descendant to close the family history of these colonies . . . . . H. P. Lovecraft of Angell Street Grange and Tenbarnes Manor, author of those numerous works so conspicuously unmention'd in the annals of fame. George also had daughters, whose childless next generation complete the dead-ending. Hence—unless that lost western grandson of Joe Junior managed to keep alive amidst the wild and woolly—you behold in Old Theobald the Last of a Dynasty . . . . . that is, so far as the States are concern'd. If I can ever get over to Devon I may try to see what sort of cousins I can unearth there aside from those planted beneath and around the parish churches of the Newton-Abbot region. I came across the name about twenty years ago in an advertisement of estates tied up in chancery in London—heirs wanted, and all that—but recalling the futile claims put in by other lines for similarly advertised fortunes great and small, (my maternal grandfather tried for a Rathbone fortune back in 1878, in a mild way, but nothing doing) I let chancery take care of its own. In America, the Lovecraft line made some effort to keep from becoming nasally Yankeeised—and here for the first time we see an influence which may have directly affected me. Hence, almost without a doubt, stems my lifelong Toryism. This resistance may have been stronger in the equally-British Allgoods than in the Lovecrafts; for while the Lovecrafts were not university men, my Grandmother Allgood's father and maternal grandfather were both Oxonians. At any rate, my father was constantly warned not to fall into Americanisms of speech and provincial vulgarities of dress and mannerisms—so much so that he was generally regarded as an Englishman despite his birth in Rochester, N.Y. I can just recall his extremely precise and cultivated British voice, and his immaculate black morning-coat and vest, Ascot tie, and striped grey trousers. I have myself worn some of his old Ascots and wing collars, left all too immaculate by his early illness and death . . . . . for in my youth I, too, resented being called anything but an Englishman. Now right here appears some of the force of sheer traditional influence operating in a blind way, as opposed to any of the obvious tags of conscious instruction. My father was stricken when I was less than three years old, and ever after that I was brought up in the utter and engulfing midst of a typical old Rhode Island family whose direct line came to these colonies in 1630 on the Arbella and who have not any link beyond the sea of a later date than 1658—of which more hereafter. According to all accepted rules, I ought to be as Yankeefied as any person living—for I was out of touch with any line other than Yankee, and a purely English line domiciled in New York state since 1827 is hardly bizarre or different enough to give a small child any great feeling of half-alienage. That is, by ordinary reckoning. And yet it did . . . . . and how! I suppose I heard people mentioning that my father was "an Englishman"—and of course my mother now and then brought up ideals of unbroken traditions as the base for a proper self-respect and a gentleman's attitude of delicacy and mutual non-encroachment . . . . . ideals naturally drawn from both sides of the stock I represented, and including mention of Minster Hall and the Lovecraft past as well as of Greene, Foster, and South County, and the Phillips past. Be that as it may, some inner force set me at once singing "God Save the King" and taking the opposite side of everything I read in American-biassed child books on the Revolution. My aunts remember that as early as the age of three I wanted a British officer's red uniform, and paraded around the house in a nondescript "coat" of brilliant crimson, originally part of a less masculine costume, and in picturesque juxtaposition with the kilts which with me represented the twelfth Royal Highland Regiment. Rule, Britannia! Nor can I say that any major change has ever taken place in my emotions. As I was then, so am I today. All my deep emotional loyalties are with the race and the empire rather than with the American branch—and if anything, this Old Englandism is about to become intensified as America grows more and more mechanised, standardised, and vulgarised—farther and farther removed from the original Anglo-Saxon stream which I represent. I could very well use Rupert Brooke's famous lines . . . . . "If I should die, think only this of me; that there's some corner of a foreign field that is for ever ENGLAND."[2] My attitude is, however, not so crudely material and naive as it was in 1893. In early youth, indeed, it operated so strongly as to exclude my American side from the innermost region of my interest—so that my New

England antiquarianism is really to some extent a new growth. Even when you first knew me my Novanglianism was of a rather passive, unobservant sort—I had a layman's vague familiarity with my own soil because I had always lived on it and been used to its ways and aspect; but it did not play a large part in my imaginative life except when curiously translated into terms of the Old English countryside or the pastoral Italy of Virgil. The only clear-cut New England emotion I had till about 1910 was one of Gothick *horror*—connected with the little brown farmhouses of the remote country, huddling furtively in the lee of overshadowing hills with great rocks. Their terrible age, potential secrecy, and frightful isolation from common thought and common ways haunted me fiendishly and uniquely. Puritanism—unnatural belief in monstrous powers—uncouthness—this was what provincial Yankeeism meant for me in youth. The quaint Georgian streets of Old Providence, and the exquisite rolling countryside and spaciously benign farmsteads of the more civilised hinterland, were for me Old England and nothing else but. Then, after the age of twenty, I began to develop a slow interest in New England for its own sake—culminating in the veritable explosion of 1922, when I had my first sight of SALEM and MARBLEHEAD. You know the rest—or if you don't, look at your postcard files! Today, amusingly enough, early-Americana comes way up near the top of my list of interests.

And whence came this new impulse—which certainly did not coincide with any new environmental influence, or any other new influence? Was it an outcropping of my maternal hereditary strain? What were my maternal strains—and how were they environed during their approximate three centuries in New England? Lumping them, we find a few points in common. They were, to begin with, wholly local. No American ancestor of mine (ruling out my whole paternal side as spiritually British) ever lived in any part of America but New England. Narrowing further, they were predominantly the quickly-rebellious strain of originally-Puritan colonists who came to the Massachusetts-Bay in 1630 and reëmigrated to Rhode Island within the next ten or twenty years. I have not a single drop of Mayflower-Pilgrim blood—Plymouth being as remote from my veins as Quebec and South Carolina notwithstanding the fact that I have never lived in any house from whose roof the former soil of the Plymouth Colony is not visible—and near enough to count houses without a telescope. As to origin—most of the lines have an amusing resemblance to just the kind of lines encountered in my paternal ancestry—giving me a curious accidental homogeneity. Small rural gentry, without distinction, but nearly all armigerous. Not the meek and pliant stock of the Pilgrims, nor yet the haughty and expansive stock of Virginia. The Phillips line here begins with the Rev. George Phillips, son of Christopher Phillips, Gent., of Rainham St. Martin's in Norfolk, who came on the Arbella in 1630 and settled in Watertown, Mass. From his eldest son Samuel comes the founder of the Exeter and Andover academies; but I come from his youngest son Michael who emigrated to Newport in 1668. Michael's sons (from two of whom I am descended) crossed the bay and settled in the Narragansett Country, which differed radically from any other part of New England in being divided into rather large patriarchal estates with slaves, large houses, and a non-Puritan Church-of-England civilisation of the Virginian sort. Horse-breeding and dairying were the great industries, Narragansett pacers and cheeses being objects of familiar admiration even in distant countries. The quaint customs of this region would fill books—and has done so . . . . . but the unhappy revolt against His Majesty's lawful authority set it into a decay from which it has never recovered. The youngest children of Narragansett planters generally moved north to smaller farms in the exquisitely idyllic Scituate–Foster country—and there we find my Phillipses after 1750. I have told you of my two pilgrimages to this region—1926 and 1929—and of my researches amongst the gravestones there. Life in Foster was conducted on a reduced scale, but never involved dropping from the status of gentry. Money was not free, but children were educated in good academies and reared with a proper regard for pride and taste. My great-grandfather Jeremiah Phillips owned a mill which supplied the neighbouring countryside with grain. My grandfather, moving southward to a small village which he renamed Greene, engaged in lumbering and milling industries and ended by acquiring all the land in and around the village. He built the local hall, founded the local Masonic lodge, saw to the various educational enterprises of the region, and in general reëstablished the magnate-like status of the pre-revolutionary south county; but in 1870 was overtaken by sudden collapse financially—a thing he could have averted by disavowing responsibility for a signed note, but which as a gentleman he refused to evade. This moved the family to Providence, where an happy financial recovery took place; so that I was born into a very comfortable home in the best part of the city—you saw the house on its terrace in 1923, though both it and the locality are not what they were in 1890. Other maternal lines had a very similar history—several having been larger and more important planters in the south county than the Phillipses. The Hazards and Rathbones, I may say without exaggeration, were great houses even in the full Virginian sense—a resemblance obvious even in the old colonial days, when relations between Narragansett and the South were very close. It is no mere caprice which turns my aging fancy toward Charleston. Many a Rhode Islander before the Revolution went there before me as health declined—so that some Whipple blood still survives there, though not in the male line. It was the congeniality betwixt Narragansett and the South which first exploited Newport as a watering place—the earliest visitors being southern families. Newport, of course, was "the town" frequented by Narragansett planters; Providence being relatively small and crude before the revolution, whilst Newport was a centre of cultivation and the arts. My principal non-Narragansett maternal strains are from the Providence area—Whipple, Field,

Clemence, and Mathewson. The Whipples are a Norfolk line who first came to Ipswich, in the Massachusetts-Bay, where one of their branches settled whilst Capt. John Whipple came to Providence and founded the Rhode Island line. The antient Whipple homestead in Ipswich still stands and is used as a museum—a seventeenth century building with an overhang like that of Salem's Seven Gables. In the revolution this family were all damn'd rebels, including the famous privateer Abraham, Capt. Benajah, and my lineal ancestor Capt. Benedict. My ancestor Benjamin Whipple married a daughter of the celebrated Huguenot Gabriel Bernon, who in 1723 founded King's Church (now St. John's) in Providence, but—haw! I caught you there—she is not my ancestress, since he had a second wife Esther Millard from whom I am descended. No curst French in Grandpa!

But I do have a single strain of Irish—Casey—coming in as follows. In 1641 Thomas Casey, Gent., of the Caseys of Tyrone who (by virtue of O'Neill descent) used the bloody hand of the O'Neills as their coat-of-arms, was a Protestant resident of Dublin, and marry'd to a gentlewoman of Gloucestershire. In that year came a frightful massacre of the papists, wherein all of Casey's household were butcher'd in cold blood except for his six year old son, also named Thomas, who was taken by his nurse to the seat of his mother's family in England. Hence, growing up as an Englishman, he emigrated to Newport in 1658; marrying an Elliott and founding a line which includes Gen. Silas Casey (killed in the Mexican War—author of *Casey's Military Tactics*), Gen. Edward Casey, the engineer who started the Washington Monument, Edward Pearce Casey (still living), architect of the Congressional Library, and so on. This celebrated military-engineering line descends from his middle son Adam. I am descended from Samuel, the youngest son. Also descended from Samuel, though not a lineal ancestor of mine, is a delightful artist-scoundrel forming the only aesthete I can scare up on my family tree. He was Sam's own son—Sam junior, whose older brother John is my ancestor. A still older brother, Thomas, migrated to the province of New York, remain'd loyal to our rightful king during the treason of the 1770's, and after the war migrated to Colborne, in Upper-Canada, where his posterity still hold positions of honour and respect.

Samuel Casey, Jun.—my great-great-great-granduncle—deserves a paragraph all to himself. He was a silversmith of such art and skill that pieces of his work are in both the Boston Museum of Fine Arts and the Metropolitan Museum of New York; and originally held a good estate in the Narragansett Country. In 1764 the burning of his house with valuable contents threw him into poverty ..... but his notions of honour were more elastick than those of my grandfather Whipple Phillips in an hour of adversity. In short—mov'd by the easy morals which enabled many colonists to tolerate piracy, smuggling, coining, and rebellion against their lawful king—Uncle Samuel turn'd his silversmithing skill to counterfeiting, and produced some masterly Spanish milled dollars and Portugese moedores before the long arm of the law reached out for him. Being sentenced to be hang'd on Nov. 4, 1770, he was rescu'd by a band of neighbours with black'd faces (cf. Boston Tea Party) who storm'd the gaol and supply'd him with an horse for leaving the colony. Last seen riding west with coattails flapping in the wind, he leaves the history of Rhode Island and the pages of my pedigree. His brother John's daughter Sarah (whose mother was a Dyer of the Quaker martyr's line) marry'd John Rathbone and had two daughters, Sarah and Rhoby. These marry'd, respectively, Stephen Place and Jeremiah Phillips—and in the next generation Sarah's daughter Rhoby Place (nam'd for her aunt) marry'd Rhoby's son Whipple Phillips . . . . . these espoused cousins becoming my mother's parents and thus giving me two lines of Casey–Rathbone blood.

Mention of this cousinly alliance calls to mind many similar occurrences in my ancestry, so that consanguinity may be set down as one hereditary influence in me—if it is that. I might also remark that longevity is very rare. Most of us tend to shuffle off around seventy, though the Place strain is long-lived (my elder aunt looks like the Places, and I therefore have high hopes of her long survival despite her poor health), and one of the elements behind the Place strain involves the sole real centenarian in my stock—Mary Brownell, wife of Thomas Hazard, who lived from 1623 to 1723. Physically I favour the strain running through my Phillips line back to the Whipples; indeed, almost everyone remarks a resemblance to me in the painting of Commodore Abraham Whipple at the Rhode Island Historical Society.

But is Grandpa yet accounted for after all these words? Whence the weird and cosmic inclinations? Whence the predilection for dabbling in these floods of words and sentences? Whence the disgust for blind beliefs and meaningless conventions? Certainly, it is in personal experience rather than in heredity that we must look for the answer.

Weirdness? Well, my Grandfather Phillips used to tell witch stories with vast gusto, and would relate a certain western tale of antelope-hunting which involved a sudden surprise climax. But have not other grandfathers done much the same? Why did little rock-hill farmhouses arouse horror in me? Why did I pore over *Grimm* and the *Arabian Nights* and the Greek myths with an ardour given to nothing else? Why did I think that Providence's antient Georgian hill was a haunted place, connected with some memory just eluding me? Why did the sunset, seen beyond the mystical spires and domes of the lower town from Prospect Terrace, always fill me with a curious sensation of opening gates and about-to-be-revealed wonders? Don't ask me—for I haven't a shadow of an answer! It is clear that the centring of my attention on literature as a whole is due to my mother's friendship with the poetess Miss Guiney, and my winter of 1892–3 at the Guiney home, when I heard a constant stream of casual and of course uncomprehended literary conversation and was encouraged to recite poetry standing on a table . . . . . but what has this to do with the especial *direction* which my literary interests assumed the first moment I had any interests at all? And whence my restless curiosity about the basic question of "what is anything"? And my innate and instinctive disgust at the orthodox Christian influences around me at home and at Sunday-school—a disgust which left me free to be a Graeco-Roman pagan without the slightest emotional tugging from the direction of the obsolescent Christian faith? No—I don't think any *basic* quality of mine has any *visible* source either in heredity or experience. Grandpaw jest grow'd!³ How, for example, does a pure Nordick come to possess a fully-develop'd ROMAN patriotism—when nobody around me ever gave Rome any particular notice?

Regarding a general taste for phantasy, it is barely possible that the amount of *Celtic* blood in me—an amount I never fully realised till Talman set me to reviewing my charts—may have something to do with it. From Ireland I have only the single Casey strain—already half-English in 1641—previously described, and of Scottish blood I have not a drop; but Wales and Cornwall have certainly put a marked Cymric element into my grand total. My father's mother—Rachel Morris—came from the Morrises of Clasement, Glamorganshire; and though this is a Norman house with Musgrave and other English strains, it also has many Celtic components—Parry, Rhys, Jenkins, etc. etc., whereby I can claim descent from Owen Gwynnedd, Prince of North Wales. Then the Edgecombes, of whose blood I have a double dose through a cousinly alliance, are half Carew; a stock with much Cornish blood, including lines as typically Cornish as Trefusis. And besides this, it is certain that most of the native stock of Devonshire have a greater Celtic admixture than is commonly suppos'd; the conquest of that region by the Saxons involving far more mixture than outright massacre. In the light of the charts, as study'd in latter years, I can certainly no longer lay claim to that pure Teutonism of which I carelessly boasted in days when my ancestral knowledge was of a more generalis'd and hearsay type. I am, assuredly, mainly a Teuton—and indeed the Allgoods have Northumbrians and Yorkshiremen to some extent—but the preponderance of South-English strains in my paternal line make the Celtic dilution far more than a nominal shadow. The mystic Druids, as well as the thundering gods of Asgard, come legitimately into my blood heritage.

Any strains of the sombre or the melancholy in me must be attributed to a variety of circumstances. Poor health and a sort of low vitality may form a starter; and the early death of my father and slightly melancholick cast of my mother cannot be overlook'd. There is, too, the element of economic decline to be reckon'd with. Whether any echoes of declines before my time—the collapse of my paternal line in Devon, the passing of the Narragansett Country, or the failure of my grandfather's enterprises in 1870—had an influence upon me is distinctly doubtful. It is barely possible that such things filtered into my consciousness and gave me the habit of thinking of time as a downward rather than upward process, but I have my distinct doubts. All was comfortable again by the time I was born—my father had regained a modest prosperity tho' he left only ten thousand dollars, and my grandfather was fully on his feet again, and President-Treasurer of a company promoting land and irrigation in Idaho. My array of toys, books, and other youthful pleasures was virtually unlimited; and I doubt if I ever thought of such a thing as varying prosperity or instability of fortune. The poor were simply curious animals about whom one spoke insincerely and to whom one gave money, food, and clothing . . . . . like "heathen" about whom the church people were always talking. Money as a definite conception was wholly absent from my horizon. Rather was I a simple, unplaced entity like the carefree figures moving through the Hellenick myths. But actual decline did set in when I was about ten years old; so that I saw a steady dropping of servants, horses, and other adjuncts of domestick management. Even before my grandfather's death a sense of peril and falling-off were strong within me, so that I felt a kinship to Poe's gloomy heroes with their broken fortunes. And of course the frightful crash itself—in 1904, when the death of my grandfather broke up all his recuperative plans and forced the sale of the old home—gave me a tremendous and positive melancholy. All the air rotted with decay, and the moon itself was putrescent. I had been vastly attached to my grandfather and to my birthplace, and when both—to say nothing of my beloved cat Nigger-Man—were swept away in the course of a few months, I was about ready to cash in myself. I actually thought of bumping off, and used to ride my wheel down to the shallow Barrington River and wonder how painful it would be to wade into the warmish water, lie face down, and get rid of the useless and absurd thing called consciousness. But I didn't—for I was only fourteen after all, and had my first pairs of long trousers and the prospect of high school to think about . . . . . besides which, 598 wasn't exactly a slum or gaol, even after 454. And there was the mystery of the limitless cosmos to penetrate . . . . . the tantalising void with the unknown circling orbs, and the power of imagination to piece out what science couldn't tell. Thus I jogg'd along and managed to have a fairly good time in spots despite rotten health, headaches, and a sort of sense of decline in everything. But without doubt, my aesthetick sense worked more in the line of escape than lyric exultation; with the macabre then and ever its long suit. And economic decline continued steadily—without a break to this day, and with several sharp jogs downward, as when an uncle lost a lot of dough for my mother and me in 1911, and (of course) when my poor health and jazzed-up nerves made it clear that I was not going to be any wow at sestertius-scraping myself. Lately I have become so harden'd to poverty that ironick amusement is mixed with the melancholy. Indeed, I can live on less than anybody I know of, and have developed economies I couldn't have thought of twenty, fifteen, ten, or even five years ago. But I'm about at rock-bottom as I am, and I guess any fresh tobogganing would send me back to the Barrington river—without the bicycle, but with no need of any means for a return trip. I certainly shan't keep on the existence-farce if I have to give up living in an aesthetic neighbourhood, or have to lose the books and familiar objects of furniture and decoration which constitute my concrete as distinguished from my abstract universe.

As for a physique—I didn't inherit a very good set of nerves, since near relatives on both sides of my ancestry were prone to headaches, nerve-exhaustion, and breakdowns. My grandfather had frightful blind headaches, and my mother could run him a close second; whilst my father was stricken with paralysis in the early forties. My own headaches and nervous irritability and exhaustion-tendency begin as early as my existence itself—I, too, was an early bottle baby with unexplained miseries and meagre nutriment-assimilative capacities; though I got along excellently after a time except for nervousness and headaches ..... and bad digestion ..... and heart and kidney trouble due to nervous malregulation of automatic organic functions ..... and poor eyesight ..... and dizziness ..... and abnormally ready fatigue ..... yeah, outside of this I was quite okay. School had to be irregular, and I undoubtedly had too little physical exercise because I hated exercise for its own sake, and was bored to death with all games. I loved the summer countryside, however, and was constantly in the open in warm weather ..... my old home then being close to the edge of the primal woods and fields and ravines, most of which are now built over. Of course my abnormal sensitiveness to the cold has always existed—though always compensated for by a power to enjoy any amount of mid-July heat. My leading pleasures were books, pictures, walks in ancient places, museums, writing, music (until my violin experience soured me on the latter), and such playing with other children as involved the making-up and acting-out of plots. I was not, like many neurotic and bookish children, essentially solitary by nature. I liked to play war and Indian and policeman and railway man and all that, though I could not abide a mere game which involved no imagination or dramatic unfolding. I liked a flexible and extemporaneous plot-element, and baseball, football, and all that simply left me cold. Nor was this because of my poor physique. Sedentary games, if they were games only, made me yawn just as widely. And still do. I have not the least trace of sporting blood in me. The lure of gambling is as alien to me as the love of gawd. My dizziness made me tremendously afraid of heights, but I deliberately conquered that by repeated experiments of wall-walking at increasing altitudes. Finally I took a post-graduate course in railway trestles. Having weak ankles, I never skated; but I loved the woods and their traditional associations. The lore of hunting allured me, and the feel of a rifle was balm to my soul; but after killing a squirrel I formed a dislike for killing things which could not fight back, hence turned to targets until such a time as chance might give me a war. But I had bad luck in wars, for I was only eight when the Spanish came, and was discouraged with more eloquence than urbanity when I had almost persuaded a world war examiner that I was Hercules Secundus. My greatest exercise was bicycle-riding, which I pursued from 1900 to 1913. I cultivated high speeds, and managed to cover a large and picturesque area of countryside—perhaps forming in this way that close acquaintance with rural New England which made me a local antiquarian in the end. It is in this period that my typical love of white village steeples in distant vales, and farmhouse roofs beyond gnarled hillside orchards, became so prominent a feature. Most of my cycle trips were made in quest of new and surprising landscape vistas—for I always sought the element of surprise—unfolding—the unexpected—the edge of the unreal, where anything is possible—. My eyes troubled intermittently, and I wore glasses most of the time. Around 1906 I was a good rifle shot, but by 1910 my skill had declined. Nervous breakdowns were frequent, and that of 1908 caused me to adopt a sort of hermitage and withdrawal from the world which only the influence of amateur journalism dispersed. College was found impraticable—and meanwhile my interests had veered away from literature to science and back to literature again. Cosmic mystery was always my goal in one way or another—but I saw that the pen would get me a bigger slice of it than would the more exacting telescope, mathematical formula, or laboratory. I was a devotee of the drama, though this interest has waned in later years. Never was I any good mechanically—making things, and all that. And I have no drawing skill. All the effective use I ever put the old lunchhooks to was writing and map-drawing. As for family attitudes toward reading, pleasures, society, and church—nothing unusual in any way. Liberal, urban, tolerant—sound conservative culture, pride, honour, good taste, and non-encroachment may be recognis'd as cardinal principles. (And I ought to mention the scholarly uncle, Dr. Clark, among family influences.)

Well, you know all there is else to know about the old man. I might remark that my tendency to endless correspondence is a relatively late growth. In youth I scarcely did any letter-writing—thanking anybody for a present was so much of an ordeal that I would rather have written a two hundred fifty-line pastoral or a twenty-page treatise on the rings of Saturn. Not until I was twenty years old did I write any letters worthy of the name—and my beginning then was due to the fact that my well-beloved little cousin Phillips Gamwell (died 1916) had reached the age of twelve and blossomed out as a piquant letter-writer eager to discuss the various literary and scientific topics broached during our occasional personal conversations. Four or five years of Johnsonese periods loosed upon this youthful and encouraging audience form'd the preparation for the verbal deluges which you first sampled in the 1914–15 season.

Latter chapters need no recapitulation. My health improved vastly and rapidly, though without any ascertainable cause, about 1920–21; and still further (in connexion with my reducing) in 1925. In that latter year I left off the full-time use of glasses, though I shall probably have to go back shortly. In these latter years I don't know but that age is beginning to counteract the improvement—

winters seem to get at me about as badly as imagination can picture—but compared with the early years Grandpa is a pretty tough old bird.

And so—after some nine pages—the explanation may rest for a while. A fine explanation, except for two things—first, that it doesn't explain anything; and second, that the personality it tries to explain amounts to too little to need explanation. But outside of that it's quite all right. Orta get me theme credit in the class, if credit is due for quantitative allotments of verbiage. No—on the whole, I'm afraid that all this prose doesn't tell half so much about the old man as certain of his quasi-sonneteering Fungi from Yuggoth. But that doesn't matter a damn when the subject is of complete and carefree insignificance. Nine pages of ancestry and environment—to define Old Theobald. *Montes laborant—nascitur ridiculus mus!*[4]

Rye toodle inkaday!

Grandpa Lo.

Notes

1. Some of the information on HPL's ancestry provided in this letter—especially relating to his maternal ancestry prior to his great-great-grandfather Asaph Phillips and to the remoter reaches of his paternal ancestry—cannot be verified, and other information is demonstrably wrong. See, in general, Kenneth W. Faig, Jr., "Quae Amamus Tuemur: Ancestors in Lovecraft's Life and Fiction," in *The Unknown Lovecraft* (New York: Hippocampus Press, 2009), 14–49.
2. Rupert Brooke (1887–1915), "The Soldier," ll. 1–3.
3. A parody of "Topsy just growed." Topsy is girl in the novel *Uncle Tom's Cabin* (1851–1852) by Harriet Beecher Stowe. When asked if she knows who made her (i.e., whether she has heard of God), she replies "I expect I grow'd."
4. "The mountains labor—an absurd mouse is born!" From Horace, *Ars Poetica* 139 (where the passage is "Parturient montes, nascetur ridiculus mus").

[59]   [AHT]

Home at last—
August 3d. 1931

Hail, O Sage!

But it certainly was too bad about S. A. L.[1] Hope the event will make a minimum of difference to publishing plans—though as you say, the chances in some directions are rather doubtful. The day of the services surely was a crowded one for you—and I'm positive no one but a season'd activity-hound like yourself could have swung the full programme. Your address is a delectably appropriate piece of work, and I don't wonder that it went over big. I doubt if S. A. L. would have objected to your use of the immortality-myth so long as you kept it a personal sentiment and did not imply that *he* harboured such a primitive delusion. This ancient legendry has much poetick value and decorative grace when rationally used in the manner of all such legendry—as historic ornament recalling the moods and convictions of our uninformed ancestors in situations similar to those which evoke the citations. I have no patience with untraditional moderns who resent all primitive survivals in nomenclature and folklore; and am just as glad to tolerate Christian vestiges like Candlemas, Whitsuntide, the A.D. chronology, etc., as I am to tolerate those more authentic Aryan vestiges exemplified by names of the planets, constellations, and days of the week. Immortality is a pretty conception, and was natural enough to believe in when almost nothing was known of the details, relationships, relative nature, and proportions of the various objects and modes of motion in the universe. It still serves as a poetic symbol for those comparatively lasting effects produced by an exceptional individual on his environment, and as such has a permanent place in literature beside Pegasus, the Nine, Apollo, and other bits of obsolete imagination. Incidentally—I suppose it is very liberal in a surviving Protestant believer to accord a wicked infidel a place in Elysium! The papists would admit rascals like me and S. A. L. and Galpinius to purgatory, but to a reactionary hard-shell we are all foreordain'd to aeternal roasting. I think I'll have to go Calvinist, so that I can kid myself into thinking there's a place where I can *always* be warm enough! Seriously, though, this kind of thing is dead as a doornail among normal adults with a sense of humour and even the rudiments of a contemporary education. Even those who still hang on to theistic illusions have let most of the damnation trimmings go by the board. Whitehead—an actual Anglican cleric—is a good example. He realises the silliness of "doctrines", and takes the mummery of churchianity as the mere allegory it properly is. It is amusing how closely Whitehead and I agree on almost all social and political points—splitting up only when a scientific view of the causes and directions of natural action are concern'd. The dull and devastating piety and literalism of the backwoods evangelical are destined to survive only in intellectually retarded areas like Tennessee, Mississippi, Iowa, etc., once the elder generation of childhood-biassed standpatters dies off in the ordinary course of events. That lower class among whom contemporary education is not diffused—and who will therefore continue to hand down a naively theistic tradition—are now overwhelmingly Catholic. To think clearly about the cosmos in the light of contemporary information is to abandon any possibility of believing in the fantastic and capricious orthodoxies of yesterday—be they Buddhistic, Judaic, Christian, Hindoo, Mahometan, or any other brand. More liberal wish-delusions, however, will undoubtedly last for several generations more—or until the race has lost that emotional dependence on mythic values, and elogies, [?] and immortalistics which the earlier centuries of primitive ignorance and fanciful speculation have bred into it. Some of us—as individuals—have lost this primitive dependence already; but we can more or less understand its survival in others—especially since we are ourselves full of primitive and vestigial feelings in other directions ..... feelings which (like worship of pageantry, exaltation of the family, love of hunting and fishing, etc.) are no less poignant because of our understanding of their purely mundane and fortuitous origin, and purely relative and transient significance as environmentally adjustive factors. Thus I know what you *mean* when you speak of the illusion of immortality as something emotionally "satisfying"; though to one of the contemporary milieu the element of emotional satisfyingness or its reverse *has nothing whatever to do with the question of a theory's truth or falsity* ..... experience and observation having taught us the complete unreliability of the emotions (which bring different and sometimes opposite conclusions to different persons) as a guide or interpreter of the external world. Moreover—the conventional emotional biasses toward immortality and cosmic purpose are themselves very largely accidental results of traditions rather than basic attitudes, as we may see by comparing the moods of different types and individuals—older and younger, unsophisticated and sophisticated. No level-headed modern either wants to be "immortal" himself (gawd, what boredom!) or to have his favourite characters immortal. Each appears for a second in the pattern and then disappears ..... and what of it? What more could anybody not filled up with infantile myth expect or even dream of? It is overwhelmingly true that no sane adult, confronted with the information of today, could possibly think up anything as grotesque, gratuitous, irrelevant, chimerical, and unmotivated as "immortality" unless bludgeoned into the ancient phantasy by the stultifying crime of childhood orthodox training. Religionists openly give away the fakery of their position when they insist on crippling children's emotions with specialised suggestion anterior to the development of a genuine critical faculty. We all know that *any* emotional bias—irrespective of truth or falsity—can be implanted by suggestion in the emotions of the young, hence the inherited traditions of an orthodox community are absolutely without evidential value regarding the real *is-or-isn'tness* of things. Only the exceptional individual reared in the nineteenth century or before has any chance of holding any genuine opinion of value regarding the universe—except by a slow and painful process of courageous disillusionment. If religion were true, its followers would not try to bludgeon their young into an artificial conformity; but would merely insist on their unbending quest for *truth*, irrespective of artificial backgrounds or practical consequences. With such an honest and inflexible *openness to evidence,* they could not fail to receive any *real truth* which might be manifesting itself around them. The fact that religionists do *not* follow this honourable course, but cheat at their game by invoking juvenile quasi-hypnosis, is enough to destroy their pretensions in my eyes even if their absurdity were not manifest in every other direction. Of course, their policy is the habitual ostrich-act of all primitive thinkers. When they see that honest openness to evidence does not incline their children toward the preferred system of myths, they do not behave like civilised beings and question the validity of the myths, but turn about and try to cripple the mental receiving apparatus of their children until the poor mites duplicate the accidental bias of their misinformed elders and forcibly acquire the same set of meaningless moods and obsolete prejudices. Thus each of the deeply-seated myth-systems carries on—the little Hindoo becoming a Brahma-worshipper like papa, the little Moslem continuing the ancestral whine to Allah, the little Yankee intoning nasal psalms to the god or demigods of the Christians, the little Jap burning more and more incense at Shinto shrines ..... and so on ..... and so on ..... ad infinitum ..... ad absurdum ..... and pretty soon the solar system will play out, and nobody in the cosmos will know that there has ever been any earth or human race or Brahmins or Moslems or Christians or Shintoists or such ..... dust to dust ..... and the ironic laughter of any entity which may happen to be watching the cosmos from outside ..... ho, hum! But as I said, your tribute to "Say" is damned graceful, and exceedingly clever in every turn of thought and imagery—not excluding the citation from "Lycidas". How you ever concocted[2] such a prize-winner under such brief and tumultuous circumstances is beyond me! You have Grandpa licked at the start in that line!

    Yr obt
        Grandpa Lo.

Notes

1. MWM's associate Sterling Andrus Leonard (1888–1931) died on 31 May in a drowning accident in Lake Mendota in Madison, WI.
2. AHT reads "corrected," an apparent error.

[60]   [AHT]
        The Antient River-Bank—Unchang'd since the Golden Nineties
                              August 30, (can it be?) 1931

Migrant Sir:—
    As for your reaction to Mr. Darrow's earnest and well-meaning effort to teach the world that snow is white and that it's colder in winter than in summer—it certainly gives me a kick to encounter the Cotton Mather psychology in a bodily contemporary! How do you get that way? Still—it is easy to understand the inhibiting effect of biassed emotion upon the reason and sense of proportion in even the highest-grade minds. Unless one is steeled against the ascendancy of the capricious and meaningless subjective feelings, he is lost so far as the power of rational appraisal of the external world is concerned. Thus poor W. E. Leonard sees and feels things that aren't there—and knows he does—yet continues to see and feel them just the same. That shows the power of irrational mood over rational perception.[1] Your case is less spectacular—especially since your bias coincides with a former perspective of the majority—but it is bizarre enough for all that! A man with the intelligence of a savant in

dealing with every aspect of the world but one—and in that one matter using the primitive psychology of a Salem bigot or Georgia cracker!

So far as the matter of the growth of organic forms from one another is concerned, it is simply quibbling to insist on the word "theory" to describe what is as near *fact* as *any* recognised fact in our possession. It is simply a matter of using one's sense of proportion. We can see around us organic forms whose anatomical homologousness and adaptive capacities are so marked that it would be insane to try to account for them in any way but the obvious way. Nobody pretends to account for every detailed step in the growth of one species from another, or to insist that any one single factor like natural selection is the sole one. There is room for infinite future research. But enough is perceived even now to show plain linkages over very wide areas of the organic kingdoms; and every fresh discovery in biology and palaeontology is so much direct expansion. In the face of what is known and plainly visible, it is no longer an adult possibility to deny the general fact that life-forms arise from gradual differentiation. It is not an exaggeration to say that the general evolutionary nature of life is *unanimously* recognised by all persons competent to express any opinion whatever. By this I mean that *no living being* who has, on the one hand, given evidence of a high-grade mind as measured by his general achievements and status; and who has, on the other hand, studied the sciences of biology, anatomy, physiology, zoölogy, and palaeontology to what may be called a professional extent, regards it as other than frivolous to deny the virtual certainty of the broad evolutionary principle as applied to organic forms. When probability is so overwhelming, objections never come except from the ignorant or the biased. That this is so is shown by the fact that these same objectors (lacking the herd stimulus) never bother to challenge the virtual truth of *other* overwhelming probabilities. If they see a footprint, they believe a person has passed by—although of course something else *may* have made the footprint. You can see the same ignorant bigot psychology at work on a lower plane by surveying the case of Zion City—the Dowie–Voliva flat-earth-ites.[2] They, like you, refuse to apply a sane sense of proportion to the data supporting the overwhelming probability of the earth's sphericity and solar revolution. Others, no doubt, refuse to believe in the glacial periods—attributing boulders, drumlins, moraines, etc. to this or that absurd and capricious source. As a matter of fact, bias and bigotry can arbitrarily challenge almost any fact outside the realm of the easily visible. Indeed—they don't even confine themselves to what is outside that realm—for look at the Christian scientists! Suppose anyone asked these people to produce even .00000000001 as much proof for their religious delusions as they demand for some of the simplest and most obvious probabilities of nature! Ho, hum, but the world is an amusing madhouse! Why all the pother about evolution? Don't ask me! Sane teachers and textbooks merely present it along with the other facts of nature, (and it would be silly to pause and analyse the exact, minute metaphysical and epistemological basis for each of the overwhelming probabilities we regard as fact) when lo! some bunch of corn-fed illiterates pipes up and demands that this particular thing be suppressed, whether it's true or not! By cracky, the good Lord ain't a-goin' to let nobody tell me my gran'ther was a monkey! No, sirree, Sir! of all the bullshit! The whole thing boils itself down to a matter of the human faculty for weighing evidence and preserving a sense of proportion. When strong emotion acts on a narrowly informed mind, no real judgment is possible—and there we see the circus in the backwoods districts. One glance at the cultural status of all groups of "anti-monkey folks" is enough to tell the tale. Over against them stands the whole of civilisation—including normal theists as well as rationalists. Thus when one from civilisation gets infected with the poor-white mountaineer complex, he may be very legitimately said to form a rather picturesque case! Hell knows I'm not trying to convince you of anything—but you must admit that it doesn't show a very rational attitude to boast in advance that you will never be convinced! A man of sense believes what normal evidence indicates—and if new evidence appears, he changes his belief to match. My own beliefs depend merely on what is presented to my senses and reason, and every one of them is liable to change (as many of them have indeed changed in the past) upon the introduction of fresh evidence. If anybody ever discovers any real probability of the existence of such a cosmic will as primitive myth depicted, then I shall certainly be a theist. I am the reverse merely because the probability has not yet appeared. I simply recognise, honestly, the dominant probabilities about the is-or-isn't-ness of things. The trouble with you is that your theism is of the most primitive archaeological form. You could easily cling to the deity-illusion while allowing your powers of observation and rational sense of proportion a more normal latitude. Many forms of modern religion have none of the rank grotesqueness and absurdity of yesterday's dead orthodoxies—and many of those orthodoxies (especially Anglicanism) have acquired a civilised mellowness which redeems them from the blind plebeian insanity of camp-meeting gospel. Why, you ought to hear me argue with the Rev. Henry St. Clair Whitehead, orthodox, high-church Anglo-Catholic . . . . . and some boy, I'll say! The really serious religious thought of the day is that of informed mystics like Harry Emerson Fosdick[3] or the theist-scientists Eddington and Jeans. They seem to me to reason erroneously—or rather, to venture unjustifiably beyond reason—but they do not try to contract the facts of nature, or to lose their sense of proportion in primitive emotional extravagances surviving from bygone epoches and sets of conditions. They are at least worthy of serious adult consideration. I haven't seen that Darrow film,[4] but fancy it must be rather informative. Darrow takes the herd too seriously, though. As if it mattered what primitive junk stevedores and Kentucky hill-billies believe!

As for your reader job—godelpa ya! But of course it all adds to the Mocratick prestige. I take a personal interest in them readers since they deigned to include me[5] and my gang—me and Wash Irving and Walt Scott and the rest. I hope to see any of the series that has your name on the cover and your notes in the back. Further congrats and commizes anent your chairmanships etc. in the Teachers' Council. Hope it gives you enough of a kick to pay for the bother! You'll sure get a rep—and all that kind of thing will be useful later on in floating *Doorways* etc. But bless my soul—such a whirl of activity would get Grandpa Theobald so dizzy he'd forget his specs and false teeth and ear-trumpet!

And now for the interesting exhibits—though you haven't yet told me what you thought of my senile floundering with these tough units at the end of the analogy test in the last semi-annual. I'd say that Exhibit A was a darned good test if ya ast me—the authors represented being respectively Haverhill John, Concord Ralph, Chicago Carl, Nick Vach, Spoon River Ed, Henry D., Old Faker Roycroft, and Gnalterius Bombastes, in the order given.[6] I don't think anybody would be likely to mistake one bozo's spiel for another's—and my only kick is at the inclusion of that cheap ass Hubbard, who has no more place in literature than the guy who writes Old Gold Cigarette ads. Which reminds me, through a process of association, that from now on I am going to conceal my birthday from the publick. Gawd, but this is arful! Who else do you think was born on August twentieth? Steady, boys,—don't faint—*Edgar A. Guest!!!* There, there, ... just give him air ..... Draw your own astrological conclusions if astrology be among your archaic credulities ... Aug. 20 .... Sun in the whatever-it-is house of Leo, moon in ascendant or descendant or some such thing .... stars all set .... and behold two Great Men .... I got this from one of the Bekes.[7] Heretofore I've been content to share my date with the austere statesman who was celebrating his own birthday in Washington's executive mansion at the very hour that I blew in—Benjamin Harrison—but now the day is simply ruined.[8]

As for Exhibit B—the superiority of the second selection is so obvious that comment is scarcely necessary. #1 is simply a collection of sure-fire phrases in my own best 598 Angell style, with all the individuality and specific sincerity of a multigraphed form-letter. #2 has specific images in unhackneyed language, and the figures and rhymes show a perceptible amount of genuine feeling. There is none of the hit-or-miss ready-made generalisation which reveals dull and casual carpentry, and which strikes one so offensively in #1. And to think that a class of future teachers could be inconclusive in a vote on the two! O gawd, O Montreal![9] Pity the next or post-Mocratick generation of schoolboys! The annotation by S A surely has a melancholy enough interest now, and I return the sheet as per request. Sorry to hear, incidentally, that poor Saccharissus is in such bad financial shape. Hope he pulls through—even if all the pedagogues of the land don't flock to the *Kenyon Press* to have their immortal thoughts crystallised with the aid of Mokrates the Great, Little Sonny Belknap, and Grandpa Theobald! Your transparency device sounds like the gun's goatee, and I certainly hope it can find a commercial outlet somehow, whether through *Glykeros* or another. Speaking of profesh matters—did I tell you that Little Belknap and his Grandpa are both to be represented in the coming weird anthology—"Creeps by Night"—edited by Dashiell Hammett and published by the John Day Co.? Sonny's story will be "A Visitor from Egypt", and mine will be "The Music of Erich Zann"—a favourite of my own, by the way. We got only twenty-five bucks apiece, but the prestige may be helpful in dealings with editors.

Returning to exhibits—glad to see the *Highland Prairie*[10] so long honour'd by Mocratick tenacity, even if it does represent merely a closed chapter. No doubt the clatter was damnable, but I'll bet the street didn't look half bad in summer when those tenderly nurtured trees were doing their stuff. Exhibit D surely does excite philosophick reflection. Time, time, time! Well—it's a good central setting for the future bronze tablet. Incidentally, I am mourning the destruction of the old stable at my own birthplace, and the erection of some damn modern thing on the rear half of the grounds. I think I showed you the old place—454 Angell—and told you that the land was now dividedly owned. The *house* still stands on its terrace as a doctors' building; but the separately owned stable and rear grounds are going the way of all real estate. To think I should live to see such chaos and decay! The stable was newer than the house—built in 1881. My aunt Mrs. Gamwell has just salvaged, through the obliging vandal labourers, the baking-powder tin full of historic data (her tintype, a newspaper page, and a couple of "to whom it may concern" letters) which she placed in the foundation walls as a kid. Alas, that she herself should have to be the claimer of that which was design'd for the archaeologists of a future aera!

Exhibit E surely displays a commendably bright and thoughtful youth, and I am glad you were able to enlarge his horizons as indicated.

As for Exhibit F—oy, I shood get famous a'ready when effery schoolboy like a Klessick kvotes me! Me and Dick Gilder[11]—ve iss guys vot makes it opinions yah kent kest aside lightly! Guys vot iss for our lit'ry vork acclaimed a'ready! Ven ah men like Gilder or ah men like Luffkreft says ah pome iss ah sunnett, I esk you, aindt it ah sunnett? But det fella Voidsvoit—oy, vot ah oilcan! He shood write aboudt lying ahvake end call it ah sunnett![12] Oy! Such ah men! He so dumb iss, he t'inks it ah sunnett is ah kind uff straw het! Now det Meestah Moe, he ken make it ah sunnett vot shood make ah men get trenqvil inside uff him. Who, I esk you, cood so nize make voids ahboudt ah gret luff like dis a'ready?

> Seenze foist your reddient booty's luffly star
> Pegun to tveenkle by mine heffens dear . . . . .

ah, Moses, dot iss boetry! Ken't you see it how urritchinal iss effery immitch? Ah leedle star it shood mek de voild more bright den de sun—det is pretty, I esk you, ain'dt it? Den det nezst lest line—

Uff ethereal soul-shine in your luffer's eyce!¹³

Nize, yes? Det soul-shine—vot ah immitch! End de vey dot void e'the'-real gets voited into det metre! Now, why coodn't det feller vit de sleep sunnett urritchinal like det get a'ready? By de mesters vee gotta judge 'em—and I esk you, iss you got enny choice? Petruck, Dente, Sheksper, Meelton, Pup, Svinebun, Russetti, Lunkfella .... no, Voidsvoit iss gotta get outa det bunch. He vass in der moodt, but he didn't mek it an sunnett!

Oy, soch an med voild! But it sure ain't much of a credit to the nation's degree-mills that the preceptorial bas-bleu¹⁴ outa Marquette shoulda fell down on the same quiz. If that's the kinda dumbbell they're gonna have in the schools of the future, they'd better furnish 'em with a chart of what to praise and what not to praise, and forbid 'em to pass judgment on other material till given special instructions . . . . . and then, in another generation, the nitwits'll be getting on the boards that make the charts . . . and so on, and so on . . . . O Tempora, O Mores! One never saw such chaos looming ahead in dear old 1900! By the way—how come you say that golf doggerel is practically perfect technically? Look at that Georgia-cracker "like" in line four, and lamp the *octosyllabic* length of line seven!

As for Exhibit G—I can see that forty percent of your class are in dire need of "Doorways"!

> Annanguls through thuh silunt night
> Keep lovin' watch till mornin's light.

Smooth—sincere—imageful—ow!

By the way, I'm going to spring those Abbot-Trabue tests on a new young correspondent of mine—one J. Vernon Shea of Pittsburgh, aetat XIX—and see how he stands up under 'em. He's apparently very bright, though scarcely Galpinian—but I recall that even Sonny Belknap slipped up on a few back in 1922.

Ho, hum—what a thing is taste . . . . and what a goddam bluff in many cases! Why, damitall, d'ye know that at this minute, despite all the objective rules I outwardly acknowledge, I can get a bigger kick (as determin'd by symbolick associations reaching back to my early years) out of a good Georgian pastoral than out of any other kind of metrical composition. *With me,* such a pastoral is really a sincere form of expression. Take the exquisite antient landscape now spreading around me—the scene of my earliest rambles, and unchang'd since my boyhood. I simply *can't think of it* except in terms of eighteenth century verse. *No other medium* could convey to me the sensations I derive from the verdant and azure prospect itself. It wouldn't be a matter of *words,* but of associative mnemonick stimuli. Listen to the kind of stuff I shall grind out by just looking around and letting myself go . . . . this kind of thing simply weaves itself spontaneously and endlessly . . . .

On an Unchang'd Rural Prospect[15]
by L. Theobald, Jun[r].

How tranquil spread these sloping Meads
    That glow as Evening gilds the West,
And verdant from the River's Reeds
    Ascend to join the Beech-crown'd Crest!

Yon bosky Vale, where lily'd Streams
    Glide on to shadowy Glens unknown,
Seems drowsy with the ling'ring Dreams
    Of Ages happier than our own.

For here the Breeze with soften'd Strain
    Salutes a Scene of changeless Grace,
And Spring on Spring returns again
    As to a lov'd, remember'd Place.

These Oaks and Elms seem echoing still
    To Pipes that bygone Shepherds play'd,
As resting on this selfsame Hill
    They grateful scann'd the neighb'ring Shade.

Notes that cou'd please the Naiad Band,
    And charm the Dryads of the Wood,
Sound soft once more along the Land
    When Twilight looms on Solitude.

The winding Walls that Vines enfold,
    The mossy Roofs beyond the Mere,
Shine antient, as the Sunset's Gold
    Recalls each long-departed Year.

Here the encumb'ring Weight of Age
    Its bitt'rest Force a while resigns,
For sylvan Spells reverse the Page,
    And bare the long-hid earlier Lines.

In aureate Floods o'er Grove and Field
    The vandal Æons sink from Sight,
Till Time and Change, dissolving, yield
    A Breath's Eternity of Light!

GOD SAVE THE KING

Hell, but it's getting cold! I'll have to beat it indoors—fingers damn near freezing. But visually, this vista is every inch as above depicted.
And so it goes. Bekes soon.
                    Yrs for higher temperatures—
                              Grandpa Lo.

Notes

1. William Ellery Leonard (1876–1944), professor of English at the University of Wisconsin (1906–44), author of *The Locomotive God*, which describes his distance phobia.
2. Zion is a city in northern Illinois, near the boundary with Wisconsin, founded in 1901 by John Alexander Dowie (1847–1907), a Scottish evangelist, on theocratic principles including the prohibition of smoking, drinking, and the practice of modern medicine. When the city ran into financial difficulties, Dowie was ousted by Wilbur Glenn Voliva (1870–1942), a proponent of the flat earth theory.
3. Harry Emerson Fosdick (1878–1969), central figure in the Fundamentalist-Modernist controversy within American Protestantism in the 1920s and 1930s.
4. *The Mystery of Life* (Universal Pictures, 1931) directed by George Cochran; starring H. M. Parshley and Clarence Darrow as themselves. Parshley also wrote the script. The aim of the film was to explain the theory of evolution.
5. "Sleepy Hollow To-day."
6. The poets are John Greenleaf Whittier, Ralph Waldo Emerson, Carl Sandburg, [Nicholas] Vachel Lindsay, Edgar Lee Masters, Henry David Thoreau, and Walt Whitman. For "Roycroft" see MWM 30n20. Gnalterius Bombastes is unidentified.
7. As HPL put it, "our local colloquialism (based on the sketchy phonetic value of the signatory initials) for the diurnal columnar essays of Bertrand Kelton Hart, Esq. I always peruse these with extreme pleasure when they are passed down to me—& I, in turn, pass them along to a learned friend of mine in the distant metropolis of Milwaukee. He—a teacher of English in the West Division High School—uses many of them as a basis of classroom exercises, saves many in a scrap book, & constantly carries a pocketful for reading in odd moments. He has come, after many years, to measure distance by 'Bekes'. Thus the trolley trip from his home downtown is 2 Bekes. The train ride from Milwaukee to Chicago is 10 Bekes, &c." *Letters to Family and Friends*, 1021.
8. Guest was born in 1881, Harrison in 1833.
9. The expression "O God! O Montreal!" is a refrain found in the poem "A Psalm of Montreal" by Samuel Butler (1835–1902), first published in the *Spectator* (18 May 1878).
10. West Division High School, where MWM taught, was at 2300 W Highland Avenue (formerly Prairie Street).
11. See MWM 38n12.
12. HPL refers to William Wordsworth's sonnet, "To Sleep."
13. This line and the couplet above are of HPL's composition (containing hackneyed poetic images).
14. I.e., a bluestocking; an educated, intellectual woman.
15. In other mss. the poem is titled "On an Unspoil'd Rural Prospect."

[61] [AHT]

Oct. *30* (eheu!) 1731

Doctissime:—
(1) There *is* without doubt a real difference in the sort of self-revelation inherent in a *positive statement* of tastes, and in that effected by passages of writing which *unconsciously indicate* the author's tastes and temperament. *That is*, such a difference exists *if* we mean, in the former case, to accept the author's statement at face value. With such acceptance, this sort of revelation is almost invariably *less* genuine and valuable than is the unconscious sort. If, on the other hand, we treat such a statement merely as material for psychological conjecture—judging it on its own internal stylistic evidence and refusing to be swayed by the author's conscious claims—it may often be as effective as the other sort; *veritably becoming, indeed, that other sort itself,* and thus eradicating the difference formerly existing. In such a case, naturally, the indicated results may either confirm or contradict (in varying degrees) the conscious claims of the author.

(2) As just stated, the unconscious self-revelation of implication is *overwhelmingly* more reliable than that purporting to come by direct statement. No person can speak impartially of himself, and all his statements about himself are biassed in the direction of qualities which his heredity and environment have happened to make him feel are favourable—i.e., likely to win the approval of the given audience, and to cause a magnification of his ego in their eyes and in his own. This bias may or may not be conscious. It is conscious in relatively crude, realistic or purposefully insincere types, but unconscious in types with one degree more of imagination (fanatics, dogmatists, idealists), or with a sort of selective art-in-life sense which may be coupled with the most sincere *external* disinterestedness. When a writer describes himself as possessing what are regarded as *faults* by the surrounding code, he must not thereby be thought to show any greater reliability than the writer who lays claim to approved qualities. In many cases, his unconscious mind realises that the alleged "faults" are secretly regarded with approval by the group which professedly condemns them, whilst in other cases it recognises the popular dislike of perfection, and thus claims minor unfavoured qualities in order to seem the more "human" and "lovable". Moreover, a limited number of persons hold a scale of values *opposite* to that of the community, hence derive their maximum ego-satisfaction from appearing as deep and thorough violators of the established code. Such were the French decadents—Baudelairians—of the later nineteenth century. In certain rather rare cases a person *will actually* convey an accurate image of himself by conscious statement—these cases being most often found in very listless, prosaic, and unimaginative folk. True conscious images may also proceed, occasionally, from more intellectual and imaginative persons whose interests happen to be *overwhelmingly generalised and objective,* and who are therefore more interested in the cerebral feat of

achieving accurate statement, than in the process of *direct* ego-exaltation. That is, they obtain their ego-exaltation through an objective demonstration of successful portrayal as such, and do not feel any need to overcolour the image in order to gratify their ego-feeling. *However*—it is not likely that they (or the prosaic type either) would persevere in their conscious and unconscious accuracy if the revelation-demands touched on really ponderable flaws and smallnesses (so regarded by them or by the community or both) of theirs, or interfered with any mental images of themselves which they might happen to cherish. It is hardly necessary to add that in most cases the distortions of high-grade persons are largely unconscious, and to some extent limited to matters of *degree* rather than of *kind*. Thus a man who hates dogs in a conventional dog-loving environment will not say (or think) that he *loves* dogs, but will *tend* to exhibit his hatred as a sort of whimsical, humorous, and good-natured *dislike of certain qualities of most dogs*. If he lets his real state of mind appear, it will be in the inadvertent choice of an adjective, the sly use of a veiledly unfavourable comparison, or even some minimising quality in the proportioning of material or management of cadence and rhythm.

(3) Yes—a piece of bad reasoning or faulty observation is so plain and accurate a self-revelation that it should certainly be marked as such—*provided* the mark is *not* intended to be one of *merit*. This forces us to go over the whole ground from the start, and inquire *just what this test is for*. *If* it is to check up the character of the pupil, the foregoing affirmative emphatically stands. If, however, the test is designed purely to show the pupil's *degree of self-projection in art*, we must pause a bit and see whether or we're oversimplifying our concepts and methods. It becomes a bit doubtful whether we can, as you wish, get at the gist of the thing without veering toward the "master's thesis" atmosphere. How about it? First—we must say flatly, from common sense, that nobody shows any real art-power of 'putting himself across' if he merely gives himself away as a damn fool by pulling a line of D. V. Bush or John H. Hasemann Jr. or Noah Whitaker tripe. He is revealing himself, to be sure, but he isn't getting anything over. We know he is an ass in the same way that we'd know it from a vacant eye or drooling mouth or abnormal facial index. Clearly, *if this test is for the purpose of ascertaining the subject's power to use language as an active revelation of his conscious or unconscious personality*, we've got to call a halt and reconsider. That "yes" back there beside the figure (3) must give place to a "no". The old "yes and no" stuff! Nope—we can't *credit* a pupil with self-revelation just because he obviously can't reason or remember whether the sun rises out of Lake Michigan or from the far end of the Madison state road. When we come up against a naive boner we gotta stop and see whether it's just a dumbbell giveaway or some unconscious elliptical trick connected with an unique way of marshalling words, ideas, and images. Chances are nine to one it's the former—hence no credit work. But before swinging the axe we wanna look sharp and see whether the queer passage *is* just another flop or whether it has some redeeming quirk.

(3a) Here's a free extra topic—volunteer stuff—no charge. When (if (1) and (2)) we take a writer's statement as mere analysis-material and draw personality-revelation from it in a direction contrary to the purport of the statement, *we must not think that this unconscious betrayal is necessarily a mere dumb or neutral giveaway to be marked by a demerit or not marked at all.* That's the hell of it—we gotta think sharp and draw fine "master's-degree" distinctions! Certainly, the betrayal *may not* be any more than just such a giveaway. But then again it *may!* Each case must be studied *individually* if we are to award marks on a basis of *vital self-projection in art.* Now take this pupil whose paper you sent—the wholesome angel child who doesn't like the cinema and reads only good uplifting books and yearns for educational and helpful things. Clearly; she has let drop an unconscious revelation of amusing smugness—but are we to think that (a) she has painted a picture with subconscious art, that (b) she has simply displayed a trait casually, without either art or real stupidity, or that (c) she has idiotically babbled out an evidence of inferiority? Well—we have to stop and use common sense and individual observation. A second's study shows that both (a) and (c) are ridiculous interpretations. The wench is not [an?] artist, neither is she a fool. The whole thing tells of bland, self-satisfied, neutral mediocrity. Therefore, *if the grading is for merit,* she gets neither a plus nor a minus mark. But of course, if you're looking simply for *instances of revelation* (perhaps we oughtn't to call the neutral and dumbbell giveaways 'self-revelation', since *the subject puts nothing positive across,* but is merely shown up by some accidental trait or commitment), you'll have to record a very plain one. Not that Sister Bernadine has told anything, but that her plain, prosaic, boldly recorded (*yet still aesthetically unexpressed*) opinion of herself has afforded unmistakable evidence. Get this distinction, O Sage?

Now let's see what a concrete example of (a) really would be like. We can dismiss (c) as easy and self-evident. Bush—May M. Duffee—we all know how to recognise a nitwit from a plainly nitwit job. Just a matter of *evidence without real expression.* But *what is the kind of unconscious betrayal that really counts as artistic self-expression while it contradicts the conscious claim of the writer?* Well—let's get back to the bozo that hates dawgs but *says* he merely gets fed up on ugly Airedale faces etc. etc. etc. Perhaps he cracks jokes about dachshunds being pulled out by being half-caught in a sausage-machine—or talks about manufacturing a modernistic perfume from the stink of unwashed collies—that kind of catchy dope which doesn't offend the Victorian readers of "Beautiful Joe",[1] yet which lets the guy blow off steam just the same. In trying to judge whether his self-betrayal is an (a), (b), or (c) case, just stop and see *what has betrayed him.* Has he shown an utter absence of correlative power like Jawn Hasemann? Hell no! Then (c) is out. Has he dully and prosaically, in undistinguished language, let fall *mental opinions* which indicate a dog-hating type? That would put him in class (b) along with Cousin Bernadine. How about it? Isn't there something different? Let's look at the text closely and see *how* the bimbo *does* let out the true state of affairs. (Imagine a theme before you—in a virile, intelligent handwriting (you'll need imagination) and couched in a vivid prose of real subtlety (take another shot of cannabis indica!), with unconsciously frequent mention of the *coyote* and *dingo*, with many *good-humoured* allusions to clumsy peasant demonstrativeness, vile odour, greedy habits, slavish, fawning temperament, etc. etc.—and with frequent *playful* use of such phrases as *whipped mongrel, 'you cur!'* as a cry of reproach to despised human beings, *'dog of an infidel!'* . . . . . *snarling pup* . . . . . *slavering bitch* . . . . . . *doglike stupidity* . . . . . *dirty dog* . . . . etc. etc. etc.) Well—how about it? This guy has let something out, but he seems to have done it differently from the righteous Bernadine. The fellow has accidentally let drop *images, word-choices,* and *rhetorical parallels* which show that his secret of unconscious personality *has a natural tendency to express its strong genuine emotions by the instinctively selective use of such symbols*. And what does this mean? Can we (b) the boy on this point and pass along? Be yourself, Oswald! Hell! If this gink ain't spilling (accidentally, but who cares?) dope through *real self-expression,* then what in the name of Brahma, Vishnu and Siva *is* aesthetic self-expression? Eh, Mawruss, ah-gen I esk it by you—vot iss? Well—to make a long story short, *this* is the kinda case what yore Gran'paw Theobald would tag with an (a) . . . . . or with your beneficent star *even in case merit, or actual artistic personality-projection, is the basis of marking*. This egg *has put himself across*. I may add that he didn't have to turn the trick in *just this way* in order to cop a plus rating. He could have omitted the *words* of unconscious hatred and let boldly narrated *but slyly chosen* anecdotes and illustrations do the work. But you get the big idea. *Real self-expression* or revelation demands the handling of language or marshalling of ideas and images *according to principles of sincere emotional selection, conscious or unconscious*. Just sloppily letting fall opinions that reveal where one really stands doesn't turn the trick. That's mere Bernardism. Just (b) stuff. But of course you may not have this sort of criterion in mind. If you merely want to see whether pupils have any tastes or not, and if so what—and whether they know it—why, the simpler system is quite oke. Personally I rather lean toward the qualitative idea. The mere hunt for personal characteristics seems to have a sort of very-clever-but-what-the-devil-of-it quality. As our li'l fren Sandy says, there ain't no percentage in it . . . . . except, of course, as a classroom index for the teacher's benefit.

(4) Self-revelation *can* be achieved in any non-statistical form of writing known to the human race.

(5) Is real self-revelation synonymous with style? Have the two any inherent connexion? Can journalese reveal personality? Go slow, Joe! It's 'yes and no' again. Let's see. First—*if we mean aesthetic self-revelation,* I'd say that there can't be any without "style" (in the broadest possible sense) and that it would be hard to imagine any style which is not at least subtly revelatory of its author to those equipped with an adequate interpretive background. I'd say that journalese is *not* theoretically a *style*, but simply *an impersonal conventional*

pattern—though it frequently *becomes* a style (against its own rules) in the hands of men with sufficient personality to override its sterile limitations. It then really gives self-expression to its writers. The seeming dilemma about journalese which has a *typical form* but does not *reveal* is simply a *verbal* one—residing in a dual use of the *word* style. *True* style *must* involve individual expression, subtle or otherwise. Will Rogers[2] *has style.* Humour is self-revelation the moment it leaves the Joe-Miller-echo class and reflects the individual perspective of its creator. The *form* is not revelation *per se,* but almost any conceivable *application of it* is.

(6) And now Grandpa's gonna givya another free pearl of elder wisdom. Hark back to topic (2) where I say that a few very prosaic or objective people can really delineate themselves by conscious statement. *This sort of delineation may or may not be real artistic self-expression.* It can be (and usually is with the prosaic clods) *mere correct statement*—a neutral (b) on the qualitative or art scale. It can, however, sometimes be a really artistic thing—an emotionally motivated and selectively marshalled array of symbols, images or cadences. In that case it gets my (a) and your star without a dissenting vote. The same with an artistic passage *indirectly* expressing personality—whether or not intended to express such.

(7) Now the pink paper. With *mere character-gauging in mind,* I'd give Sis Bernie a star, since the letter clearly reveals much about her temperament. With the qualitative basis, I'd pause for a fresh survey. I wouldn't award a star on the basis of the *previously mentioned* revelation—i.e., smug self-righteousness as expressed in good book and helpful bike [trike?] stuff—but perhaps I might on other points. The one-meal-a-day spoof is old stuff—I think it goes back to Hellenic days when the Greeks made a crack at the changed habits of the once-ascetic Persians—but this fresh selection of it is probably motivated by something like a real (though rudimentary) aesthetic process. I might give this thing a grudging star—but hell, how different Little Alfie, Sonny Belknap, and Grandpa's other young prodigies! *There* are some kids who have always *really* had something distinctive to put across. But I think the whole letter is revelatory both to friends and to strangers. Subject is Pride, wholesome, active, convention. As to whether self-revelation *must* be recognisable by strangers—I'd say that it must *in theory,* but that *in practice* it may depend on the length, nature, and completeness of the given extract. I'll add, though, that *in any case everybody ought to recognise that something is being said,* even though conditions may not let the whole message get across.

Remarks: No—I'm not chuckling at your "ignorance", but merely at your idea that any real comment could be made *concisely.* Look at the nice nuances, 'bo!

Well—I done me best—albeit late. Here's hoping your pal is slow, too. Forgive and remember!

No time to read over and revise—this goes special.

Book job laid me flat with headache, then digestive trouble supervened.

Then *another* rush job. But Orton is effusive about the big job, and promises me all the work of his firm.[3]

Going to Boston tomorrow for another weekend with Cook. Get his new address—7 Hancock St.

As for religio magistri[4]—read over my text again before dragging out the theist's old shield. I'm asking you to indicate even the merest probability that anything as notoriously unreliable as hand-modelled blind emotions has any evidential value in determining the facts of the cosmos and I get no answer. You use the *word* "spiritual" without indicating any reality which could possibly correspond to the primitive concept. And you say I "revile" when I merely *compare*.

Your form letter is very piquant and interesting. Congrats on the youth. More than I could regain despite a visit to old Ponce's fountain at San Augustin!

I agree with that other Dept. member.

Well—I'll try to have the new address handy when I dropya card.

Remorse and lah de inkaday!
Loavus Senex.

Notes

1. Margaret Marshall Saunders (1861–1947), prolific Canadian writer of children's stories and romance novels, and an animal rights advocate. HPL refers to her novel *Beautiful Joe: An Autobiography,* as by Marshall Saunders, the purported autobiography of a dog that had been mistreated by its owner and was rescued by the father of Saunders's sister-in-law.
2. Will[iam Penn Adair] Rogers (1879–1935), American humorist, newspaper columnist, cowboy, vaudeville performer, social commentator, and actor.
3. HPL had recently edited Leon Burr Richardson's *History of Dartmouth College* (1932), for Orton's Stephen Daye Press (Brattleboro, VT). As it happened, HPL did no other work for the publisher.
4. "The religion of a teacher"—a play on John Dryden's poem *Religio Laici; or, A Layman's Faith* (1682), a defense of the Christian religion against Deism.

[62] [AHT]

March 26, 1932

O Sage:—

As for the personality quiz—hot dawg, bozo, but you sure are the protozoon's front claws when it comes to dishing out cerebrometrical novelties! Pretty damn clever—although I'll admit that the superficial 'yes and no' character of the answers limits its usefulness and indicativeness considerably .... as in the classick case of the question 'Have you stopped beating your wife?' As a matter of fact, in some of the matters covered, exceptions and qualifications can be fully as important as dominant trends. I've always maintain'd that the fatal flaw in many psychological tests (as well as intellectual inquiries of every sort) is an oversimplification which misleads utterly through its neglect of vitally significant gradations and distinctions. It would be impossible for a genuinely analytical person to answer this Norris noseying except through the addition of copious marginal notes—unless, of course, he set "?" to 0.9 of his replies and was willing to be adjudg'd a dumbbell in consequence. Well, of the two possible alternatives I chose the former—whether the quizzer likes it or not. If you pass the thing on, do it notes and all—including the preliminary note wherein I outline my position. With this additional feature, the test ought to be quite a help toward complying with ol' Pop Solon's Γνοθι σεαυτον injunction[1]—although as a matter of fact the words "introvert" and "extravert" are used damn loosely and carelessly. Many an aesthetick dreamer is not a *true* introvert, but rather (as Aldous Huxley points out in "Proper Studies") a *sensationalist-extravert* who derives his emotional satisfactions from the visible world viewed purely as an impersonal decorative spectacle, instead of from an inner world of his own subjective synthesising. Wilde, Flaubert, Gautier, and many others were sensationalist-extraverts. I am inclined to think I am—and that Little Belknap is. As for the verdict labelling you an extravert, I think it's essentially correct, even though you do find primary interest in your own activities. The question hinges on the *nature* of those preferred activities—and here certainly you can see your emphatic extraversion. You spend very little time in an unique inner world (emotional, imaginative, and wholly subjective) of your own, but demand ceaseless contact with practical outside matters—showing a relish for these matters far beyond the radius of survival-necessity. Another typical extravert is our old pal Jim Morton. He, too, fills his time with activities in the world of affairs instead of taking prime satisfaction in imaginative reflection and expression. To the true introvert, any switching of time and energy from the process of imagining, inwardly savouring beauty and wonder, and uttering the wholly unique things which his inward syntheses and compulsions force him to utter, is time and energy wasted. To him the objective world is a thing of very secondary interest—merely an unpleasant annoyance to be endured. He mixes in its turmoil only so far as is necessary to keep him alive, and takes no satisfaction in any achievement apart from the perfection of his own dreams, or the perfect utterance of those dreams. Keats, Baudelaire, Swinburne, Cowper, Collins, Blake, Shelley, and most of the major poets are introverts. Loveman is one. Some introversion, indeed, is necessary to any aesthetic temperament. It also figures in the most unadulterated forms of religious illusion—especially in that hallucinative mood to which the popish church is most inclin'd to accord the dignities of sainthood. Ira A. Cole with his present Pentecostal aberrations and former poetic etherealities is as typical an introvert as one might wish to see. But you and Morton, with your practical executive enthusiasms, fall outside this category. So do many poets—Pope, Holmes, etc. etc.—whose concern is with the external world and not with an individual world of beauty and phantasy within. Poe, on the other hand, was the absolutely perfect introvert. As for me—I have some qualities of introversion, and I might possibly show up as an intro on Doc Norris's smugly graded system; but am really a sort of fifty-fifty proposition with a hell of a lot of extraversion. You'll notice that although my yarns reach out to the nameless abyss, they always take off from the spring board of a realistic setting. Poe has his haunted regions nameless, and peopled by mysterious beings with unknown pasts—but I make mine minutely typical of old New England, and give my characters (by implication and sometimes in detail) characteristic New England genealogies. I don't weave dreams absolutely out of nothing, (i.e., out of material wholly in the subconscious) but need the spur of some actual scene or object or incident to set me off. Like Gautier (tho' on a microscopically reduc'd scale) I am 'one for whom the visible world exists'. In short, I probably form—roughly speaking—what young Huxley calls a *sensationalist-extravert*. The visible world is my circus and prompt-book, but I don't take it very seriously and don't give much of a damn what becomes of it. To me the most important thing—and the most primarily interesting thing—is opportunity to think and dream and express myself as I please. Worldly activity like yours and Morton's would be to me a poignant and unendurable hell—something which no compulsion, not even the threat of starving, could induce me to undertake. But on the other hand I am more extraverted than Loveman and Sonny Belknap; since they are aesthetically self-sufficient without travel, whereas I crave a diversity of objective scenic and architectural impressions. Amidst all these subtle gradations, he would be an ass indeed who tried to group all mankind into two compartments—extraverts and introverts. By the way—can you get more of these quizzes? I wouldn't mind trying 'em on various members of the gang—James Ferd, Sonny, Loveman, etc.—just as I tried those poetry appreciation quizzes back in good old '22.

Speaking of quizzes—I'm dead agin your infant charges in the matter of the rival paragraphs of Exhibit E. While it is damn true that of two statements the more *direct, caeteris paribus,* is the better, it does not follow that a skeletonic structure is the prose ideal. There are limits—and euphony must not be sacrificed for headline brevity. The sort of superfluous stuff that needs clearing away is what dilutes the thought by removing the closely-knit relationship of cognate parts. It isn't wholly a matter of the number of words; and often a smooth, ample passage is actually more *direct* than a chopped-up, rugged hash of conscious Carlylese which shows less words by mathematical count. Then again, actual phonetic harmony means a lot in itself. Good prose needs *rhythm* as much as good verse, and anybody who thinks that the style of *Time* is real prose is a sucker. Of course, one oughtn't to strike a cloying sing-song like Thrift's pale-Hubbardesque iambicks in the *Lucky Dog*,[2] or like some of my own "and"-balanc'd periods of yesteryear; but just the same, there's no excuse for barking out an Hemingway machine-gun fire when one could weave prose which can be read aloud without sore throat or hiccoughs. I refuse to be taken in by the goddam bunk of this aera just as totally as I refused to fall for the pompous, polite bull of Victorianism—and one of the chief fallacies of the present is that smoothness, even when involving no sacrifice of directness, is a defect. The best prose is vigorous, direct, unadorn'd, and closely related (as is the best verse) to the language of actual discourse; but it has its natural rhythms and smoothness just as good oral speech has. There has never been any prose as good as that of the early eighteenth century, and anyone who thinks he can improve upon Swift, Steele, and Addison is a blockhead. On the other hand, the affectations of the late eighteenth and early nineteenth centuries are very bad; good prose not appearing again until the eighties or nineties. I had hopes that the improv'd prose of my youth wou'd prove permanent, but I find to my sorrow that it is sinking into a slough of abbreviated affectation. However, *verse* is spectacularly and paradoxically *improving;* so that I do not know any age since that of Elizabeth in which poets have enjoy'd a better medium of expression. One can but wish that a race of major bards surviv'd to take advantage of the post-Victorian rise in taste and fastidiousness. Now, returning to the paragraph in question, and the possible justification of intentional roughness in view of the subject-matter, I am sensible that your babes have *theory* on their side. As Mr. Pope hath pointed out:

> But when loud Surges lash the sounding Shoar,
> The hoarse, rough Verse shou'd like the Torrent roar.
> When Ajax strives some Rock's vast Weight to throw,
> The line too labours, and the words move slow;
> Not so when swift Camilla scowrs the Plain,
> Flies o'er th' unbending Corn, and skims along the Main.[3]

Too, Mr. Broome, in preparing the eleventh book of the Odyssey for Mr. Pope's edition, confirms this precept in speaking thus of Sisyphus in Hades:

> Up the high Hill he heaves a huge round Stone.[4]

But if you will give careful attention to these cases of intelligent onomatopoetick usage, you will observe that their roughness is wholly a matter of judicious consonantal collocation, and in no way related to the neatness of the syntax. It is going too far to break up good syntax for the sake of dramatising a hard climb; tho' one might very well give the consonants a more rugged grouping, and perhaps make the sentences generally shorter—more panting and toilsome, tho' by no means stript and skeletonick. I can see how one might tend momentarily to prefer your B passage over A, but the fact remains that I get a clearer and quicker visual image from A than I do from B. (Let us now see what gently-sighing Alfie himself had to say—since you assure me the source lies with him.) Personally I wouldn't have placed the extract in the absence of identifying names; for as you are well aware, Mr. Tennyson's pallid pseudo-Arthurianisms never produc'd in me anything save a protracted yawn, and have not been open'd by me in these last twenty-five years. Yet I'll own that for all his languishing and aqueous Victorianism Little Alf had a preternatural skill in juggling aural effects. That's probably the reason that he is still a favourite teacher's poet—serving as an illustration of many important technical points even when his soulful slop is thoroughly debunked. Therefore—let's see how the boy tackled his job.

 . . . . ah . . . . here we are! . . . . . gawdam me, but I begin to remember this stuff now that I lamp it again! Who'd a thought it . . . . me, that ain't saw Art pass since good old '07 or '08 at the very latest! . . . . Not so damn bad, at that! Hell—why couldn't the boy have stuck to descriptive themes, where he really did have the goods? As well ask why old lady Hen Longfellow didn't stick to its really effective sea-pomes! What a world! Well—here's how Alf tackles it:

> Dry clash'd his harness in the icy caves
> And barren chasms, and all to left and right
> The bare, black cliff clang'd round him, as he bas'd
> His feet on juts of slippery crag that rang
> Sharp-smitten with the dint of armed heels—
> And on a sudden, lo! the level lake,
> And the long glories of the winter moon.[5]

By god, that's good, even if Alf did pull it! Yep—plenty of A-1 onomatopoeia, especially in the fourth line—yet nothing of bareness or barrenness. Nope—this doesn't represent the stripping illustrated by specimen A. This is real English, rough'd up to just the right degree. Alf hasn't sacrificed the *pictorial* quality for all his scraping consonants. You see the *scrambler basing his feet* and *slippery juts*—and have actual words of action to drive the image in. Well—so have you in specimen A. Your climber *catches* at roots and jutting boulders. But in B the process of stripping makes the action *abstract and passive.* Your climber there merely has 'rocks and roots for handholds' to keep him upright etc. See the falling-off in visual effectiveness and dynamic punch? Contrast these two phrases—(a) 'catching at roots and jutting boulders to steady himself', and (b) 'rocks and roots for handholds kept him upright.' Gawd, man, don't you get the falling-off in real guts and punch? Without question, this laconick compression bug defeats its own ends. My vote stays on A—be it senile dementia or not!

Vell, I hope yet shoodn't get much trouble wriding oudt det Neshunul Council speech by Mexie Hoishboig. Mebbe the publicity iss voit de voik, but

Mexie he ought to feegs it you shood get some money or etverdisingk sbace. The *Poetry World* puff, I fancy, was well worth the deadhead copy of "Imagery Aids". All in the name!

B. t. w.—That Snyder anecdote is pretty good, and tallies up fairly well with my own maturer views on literary appreciation and creation. It's quite possible to get a very fair objective slant on literary values through scholarship and taste alone—enough, certainly, to help one pick out real stuff from hokum—but at the same time, it isn't likely that anybody can get full value out if any artistick manifestation unless he's been through actual first-hand experiences (at least to some extent) paralleling those of the artist. I recognise that my own subjective indifference to realistick literature (an indifference, however, which in no way dulls my intense objective appreciation of the realistick masters) depends very largely on the circumstance that I have had a comparatively small range of worldly contacts and experiences. Little Belknap is circumscribed in the same way, but the trouble with him is that he doesn't yet know it. Sonny still thinks that he—who has never spent a night except under the same roof with papa and mama, and to whom nothing but measles and appendicitis operation has ever happened in the changeless course of his little life from his zero'th to his approaching thirtieth birthday (migawd, *can* the kid be that old?)—can branch out and write a convincing, sophisticated novel just like Waldo Frank and Floyd Dell and Ted[6] Dreiser, and Ben Hecht and Louis Bromfield and all the big boys! When Grandpa tells him he can't, and that his pseudo-sophistication sounds like a small boy playing pirate, he simply strokes his 12½ upper-lip down wisps superciliously, points to the omnipotent omniscience of the truly sensitive subjective imagination, and tells Grandpa that old gentlemen can't possibly envisage the creative scope of abstract aestheticism! Maybe so .... maybe so .... but just the same Grandpa notices that Sonny Belknap doesn't make any such strides toward reality as does that other little marvel out in your own subarctick commonwealth—young Augie Derleth of Sauk City, who pries into the texture of real life until his fellow-townsfolk look upon him as almost a tasteless and impertinent nuisance! Gad, but the way that child is getting along! He has things habitually in *The Midland* and kindred sheets, and is perfecting a Proustian insight and poignancy which at times leaves me quite breathless. Take an old man's tip—your state is going to boast a new literary figure to match its Zythopolitan educator and its Appletonian composer! But Little Belknap can't make this grade in realistic writing; so if he's a wise young man he'll heed his antient Grandpa and stick to the poetic and fantastic—fields in which there is indeed much latitude for those who lack worldly knowledge but have a compensating imaginative sensitiveness. I myself clearly recognise the limits beyond which I cannot successfully go, and have no thought of doing anything serious except in the domain of phantasy. (And that's not saying I'll do anything really important in that domain either!) Well, anyway, as I doze off on the rear seat of the amphitheatre I can realise that Say pulled a good anecdote! More power to its echoes!

    Etaoin shrdlu!⁷
     —Grandpa Lo.

Notes

1. "Know thyself."
2. Timothy Burr Thrift (1883–1947?), editor of *Lucky Dog* and the *Mailbag*, with Ernest A. Edkins, co-editor of the *Aonian*.
3. *An Essay on Criticism*, ll. 368–73.
4. From Pope's translation of the *Odyssey* 11.736. Books 2, 6, 8, 11, 12, 16, 18, and 23 were translated by William Broome (1689–1745).
5. Tennyson, "Morte d'Arthur," ll. 186–92.
6. AHT reads "The."
7. Linotype and Intertype machines, letter were arranged by frequency: e-t-a-o-i-n s-h-r-d-l-u were the lowercase keys in the first two vertical columns on the left side of the keyboard. If an operator made a composing error, he often finished the line by running a finger down the first two columns of the keyboard and then starting over. The faulty line of hot-metal type sometimes was overlooked and printed in error.

[63] [AHT]

                  July 12, 1932

O Sage:—

  I am sure that you will, upon learning the melancholy circumstances attending its writing, excuse the striking inadequacy of this attempted reply to your piquant and well-supplemented epistle of the first. Only the pressure of extreme nerve-strain could excuse the superficiality and neglectfulness I shall probably exhibit.

  My return to Brooklyn from Richmond—via Fredericksburg, Washington, Annapolis, and Philadelphia—was carried out according to schedule; but upon the sixth day of my visit to Loveman I received a disastrous telegram which sent me hastening home on the first train, and caused 1932 to take its place as a black year for this household. It told of the sudden sinking of my semi-invalid aunt Mrs. Clark, (age seventy-six) whose decade-long neuritic and arthritic pains had produced an unexpected weakening and collapse of the general organic system. Hope of survival had been abandoned—though the pains themselves, after a burst of extraordinary acuteness, had mercifully subsided. When I reached home—eight hours after receiving the telegram on the morning of July first—my aunt was in a semi-coma out of which she never emerged. The next day showed no visible change, though the doctor thought she was weaker and gave her but twenty-four hours to live. Sadly enough, his prophecy was correct; for the end came at one-twenty p.m. Sunday the third—

so peacefully and imperceptibly that I could not for some time believe that the dread change had actually taken place. Services were held on the sixth—for traditional reasons, according to the ancient Anglican ritual, though my aunt had no more belief in childish theology and immortality-myths than I have—and interment took place in the Clark lot in old Swan Point Cemetery (in another lot in which I shall myself be buried) among the sepulchres of Clark ancestors extending back to 1711. Green wooded slopes rise beside the mournful spot, and close by is a great hollow tree inhabited by a woodpecker whose quaint twittering my aunt would have loved to hear in life.

The vacuum created in this household is easy to imagine, since my aunt was its presiding genius and animating spirit. It will be impossible for me to get concentrated on any project of moment for some time to come—and meanwhile there intervenes the painful task of distributing my aunt's effects . . . . whose familiar arrangement, so expressive of her tastes and personality, I dread to disturb. The family is now reduced to my younger aunt—living a mile from here—and myself.

I note with great interest the memory passages—which indeed are excellent things to know, though one ought to avoid peppering one's writing and conversation with them. It is a curious commentary on the times that these reliques from English literature have now come to supplant the Greek and Roman tags which were upon the lips and pens of our forefathers. Your list seems to me well-chosen—though I must protest against the total misquotation of the first line of Mr. Dryden's famous couplet:

(Correct version)   Great Wits are sure to Madness near ally'd,
                     And thin Partitions do their Bounds divide.[1]

The perverted line, as given, violates subtly every tradition of the vigorous verse of its period. It has a flatness which proclaims to every lover of the late seventeenth and early eighteenth centuries that it could not have been written in that Augustan aera. I have seen at least part of the *Percy Papers* before, and am glad to behold the present amplification. I don't believe I could excel you—if indeed I could equal you—in the production of such material, though I may try my hand at it during some future period of greater tranquillity than the present. The same postponement holds good for the exercise in "roughening up"—a process much easier to theorise about than to accomplish effectively. However, in view of the urgency of the appeal, I have just tried an experiment on a small, tentative scale, which I will enclose for whatever it is worth . . . . probably not much. I merely took a passage—virtually at random—from a juvenile classic, and reproduced the sense and imagery in the most inept language (short of *strained* and grotesque ugliness or actual bad syntax) my weary head could think of at the moment. I fear this specimen is far inferior to what you could produce. Actually, a passage of this sort ought to be patched together at very great leisure—for notably harsh passages are as much a matter of sudden and spontaneous inspiration as notably smooth passages are. By the way—I duly note your reversal of this process—i.e., the toning up of an inadequate theme—as exemplified in the *Comet*. You certainly illustrate very effectively the sort of colouring and subsidiary images needed to produce a real narrative instead of a mere synopsis. The only criticism I could possibly offer is that the expanded version has a touch of complacent conventionality about it—but of course high school students cannot be expected to discriminate betwixt this urbane orthodoxy and actual first-hand realism. In my old age I am making violent warfare upon the usual, the unctuous, and the *unmotivatedly* sunny.

Glad to hear that the Bekes continue to have an appreciative audience. As soon as I am less ingulph'd in the present chaos I will send another lot, including those which accumulated during my absence, and which I have not yet had a chance to peruse. Regrading the doubtful idiom "in back of"—I must confess myself lacking in historical and etymological information. It is an ancient colloquial form, especially common in rural New England, but I have not yet heard any serious attempt to defend it as an ingredient of serious written literature. Beke's occasional employment of this and other rustic phrases has always struck me as being a *conscious* and artistic one—carrying with it no trace of ignorance or carelessness on the one hand, and no certificate of classicism on the other hand. He is using a very light, sprightly, and informal prose, like that of many modern columnists and reviewers; and in such a medium, there may legitimately be imbedded many scraps of popular speech—whether or not violative of academic rules—whose status in relation to the whole fabric is no more than that of a *quotation*, even though inverted commas are not used. Rich and vital prose demands a faithful reproduction of what people actually say, no matter how the formal rules read. We may guard the purity of formal expository prose if we wish, but in any homely presentation of a homely theme we must practice a greater flexibility. When a writer places colloquialisms in his own mouth, it is generally for the purpose of establishing an intimate rapport betwixt himself and the subject he is treating. Thus one who writes much of old New England's byways may often advantageously allow himself to fall into the century-grounded (even if unclassical) idioms of these byways. Beke, as you can see, always makes much of his rural origin and affiliations. He was born and spent his childhood in an hereditary Concord farmhouse, and is rather proud of that fact when he surveys the parvenu and traditionless megalopoltanism which has usurped so great a place in American life. Better a rustic Yankee with the tang of the soil—a legitimate outgrowth of the region—than a slickly educated city foreigner whose flawless English cloaks a complete lack of homogeneity with our thoughts, feelings, history, and institutions. New England has outgrown its anti-rustic attitude of the '70's and '80's, when people flocked to the towns and tried to forget their agricultural pasts. Nowadays those of us who have a rustic ancestry or background are damn'd proud of it—for we realise that the backbone of our traditional culture was proud and refined agrarianism, and that unctuous megalopolitanism belongs to the mongrel, mechanised culture of the future, against which we are arrayed in a death-struggle. Ancient rural folkways have come into fashion along with ancient rural furniture, china, and pewterware. It may be a sterile and Alexandrian sort of prolongation of the old tradition, but to us it represents the lesser of alternative evils. Worst of all would be a surrender to the alien mechanicality of Babbittesque, quantitarian, commercialised neo-America. God Save the King!

I have examined with keenest interest the documents of the Gunville–Prokosch case, and hardly know what kind of a verdict to bring in.[2] I get the author's idea now that I have read his explanation; but just what my final impression would have been without that guide, I am not egotist enough to say. It would have been easy to form the notion of tapestry panels—which would not be incompatible with a meaning beyond the pictorial conception. Still, it seems to me that the impression of *relentless hounding* would have remained paramount. Roughly, I'd have said that the black hound meant death—though Freddy is 'way ahead of me when he suggests a balancing pursuit of death by life. Since he isn't quite sure what he does mean, I fancy we are all safe enough. As a matter of fact, it is often damn near impossible for a poet to know exactly what he's writing about. He deals in moods and impressions, usually pictorially symbolised; and very frequently the elusive mood or impression does not correspond to any one definite thing in objective reality. When, for example, we observe the golden light of late afternoon upon a quiet meadow at the edge of a wood we feel a variety of vague sensations of which a sort of hushed expectancy is the strongest. We cannot trace the affiliations of all these sensations; and if we could, they would be so diverse and heterogeneous as to possess no significance. We do not know what it is we 'expect'—for as a matter of fact, there is nothing in the real cosmos corresponding to the hypothetical fulfilment of that expectancy. All we can do is to depict the *mood;* using the appropriate pictures and trusting to luck that the discriminating reader will find in these uncomprehended glimpses an echo of similarly visualised moods in his own experience. Poetry is the groping exploration of an unknown and unseen country whose wonders can never be conceived in terms of the visible world. The poet is a man desperately driven to express in some way a series of insistent, unplaced impressions which relentlessly haunt him. Often he cannot tell what they mean, but they are none the less real to him. His task is to set down the vague symbols of these impressions as they come to him—leaving all interpretations to others. In former times, poets sought an appearance of clearness by falsifying their moods just enough to make them correspond with known and simple things. Nowadays the sincere artist scorns such artificialities and subterfuges, and is determined to say what is in him regardless of his audience. We realise in this age as never before the confused, irrelevant hodge-podge of complexities which constitutes our real inner cerebral life behind the mask of conventional simplicity and coherence. However—the skilful artist does his best to minimise the chaos of natural moods through the assumption of a plan and the visible linkage of symbols as far as they can be linked. We have a right to object to the *deliberate* suppression or wilful neglect of links between a primary image and any comprehensible 'reality' which the poet may himself envisage as the source of the image. But we must not forget that in many cases a powerful and clear-cut primary image may exist without being referable to any single source in reality. In such cases, the want of a concrete interpretation ought not to chain the poet down to silence. Perhaps his readers can interpret what he cannot—and perhaps there are as many possible (and equally valid) interpretations as there are different persons in the world. One must use one's taste, sense of proportion, and individual judgment in appraising such matters. Incidentally—I'm hanged if I know the original source of that Browning anecdote. I think it's reasonably old, though.

And so it goes. Again let me ask pardon for this inadequate letter—which is probably full of inexcusable omissions. Hope I've returned all the desired material.

Yr obt Servt—Lo.

Notes

1. *Absalom and Achitophel* (1681–82), 1.163–64.
2. HPL apparently refers to a controversy pertaining to the American writer Frederic Prokosch (1906–1989), who was born in Madison, WI. Prokosch's poem "Persian Idyll," *Harper's Monthly Magazine* 164 (April 1932): 533, begins: "The black hound flees and noiselessly, rapidly flees / Over the flower-white hill . . ." "Gunville" is unidentified. It is possibly a mistranscription for "Granville" (i.e., British playwright and critic Harley Granville Barker [1877–1946]), although Granville-Barker is not known to have engaged in any controversy with Prokosch at this time.

[64]   [AHT]

Sept. 18, 1732

Greetings, O Aristoteles Rhetor!

I found your pleasing epistle upon my return from the trip whereof frequent postal echoes have undoubtedly reach'd you—a trip which was follow'd at once by a ten-day period of guest-receiving. First came a new correspondent of mine—the young Allentown, Pa. poet (and Asst. Librarian of Muhlenburg Univ.) Carl Ferdinand Strauch, a close friend of the youth Harry Brobst who mov'd here last winter—and then came my young friend of six years' standing, Donald Wandrei of St. Paul,

Minn., whose contributions to *Weird Tales* and its congeners can scarcely be unknown to the Mocratuli. I shew'd both of these boys around the antient city—taking each to the justly celebrated Harris Collection of Am. Poetry (finest and largest in the world) in the John Hay Library of Brown University. Too bad their visits couldn't overlap, for they would have prov'd vastly congenial. Wandrei, you may remember, was here for a fortnight in 1927.

As for my trip—it was a delightful success from start to finish, and the eclipse was absolutely oke despite the failure of eclipse expeditions elsewhere. Cook and I picked antient Newburyport as a post of observation; and although there were clouds in the sky, the sun and moon were entirely clear of them at the climactick moment of totality. We reach'd Newburyport long before the eclipse started, and chose an hilltop meadow with a wide view—near the northern part of the town—as our observatory. Naturally the clouds made us anxious, but the sun came out every little while and gave us long glimpses of all stages of the phenomenon. The landskip did not change in tone till the solar crescent was rather small, and then a kind of sunset vividness became apparent. When the crescent waned to extreme thinness, the scene grew strange and spectral—an almost deathlike quality inhering in the sickly yellowish light. Just about that time the sun went under a cloud, and Cook and I commenced goddamming the rooster-optick'd cosmos in seventeen different languages including the Assyrian! At last, though, the thin thread of the pre-totality glitter emerg'd into a large patch of absolutely clear sky. The outspread valleys faded into unnatural night—Jupiter came out in the deep-violet heavens—ghoulish shadow-bands raced across the winding white roads—the last beaded strip of glitter vanish'd—and the pale corona flicker'd into aureolar radiance around the black disc of the obscuring moon. We were seeing the real show! Tho' Newburyport was by no means close to the line of maximum duration, the totality lasted for a surprisingly long time—long enough for the impression to sink ineffaceably in. It would have been foolish if we had gone up to the crowded central line in Maine or N.H. The earth was darken'd much more pronouncedly than in the eclipse of 1925, tho' the corona was not so bright. There was a suggestion of a streamer extending above and to the left of the disc, with a shorter corresponding streamer below and to the right. We absorb'd the whole spectacle with the utmost impressedness and appreciation. Finally the beaded crescent reappear'd, the valleys glow'd again in faint, eerie light, and the various partial phases were repeated in reverse order. The marvel was over, and accustom'd things resum'd their wonted sway. Considering my advanc'd years, I may never behold another; yet 'tis not every old gentleman who hath witness'd *two* total solar eclipses. On our way to Newburyport we stopt in Haverhill to call upon good old Tryout, (whose eightieth birthday comes on the 24th of next month) who is not chang'd a bit since my first sight of him in 1921. Happy Tityrus! We cou'd not persuade him to accompany us to our destination, (where the totality was longer than in Haverhill) but he hath since writ that he beheld the celestial prodigy under perfect conditions.

My subsequent trip to Montreal and Quebeck was distinguish'd by an uniform interest and agreeableness. Montreal is more Anglo-Saxon than the antient capital, and does not seem at all foreign except in the French section east of St. Lawrence Blvd. It is an highly attractive city, well set off by the towering slope of Mt. Royal, which rises in its midst. The antient part is that closest to the southern waterfront—where may be found the great Gothick Cathedral (1824), the quaint sailors' chapel of Notre-Dame de Bonsecoeurs (1771), the old governors' house or Chateau de Ramazay (1705—now a publick museum), the venerable Marche Bonsecoeurs with its crumbling dome, and numerous other architectural monuments of former times. Montreal wou'd seem much like any other high-grade American city but for the profusion of horse-drawn vehicles. I explor'd it as thoroughly as limited time wou'd permit, and also took a coach trip to the adjacent rapids of Lachine, where antiently was situated the seigniory of the illustrious explorer La Salle. But I was glad to get to hoary QUEBECK at last, for that is unique among the cities of this continent. As in 1930, I revell'd in the atmosphere of mass'd antiquity—and I also, as my card indicated, took a coach excursion around the neighbouring Isle of Orleans, where the old French countryside remains in a primitive, unspoil'd state. I hated to go home—for I always feel a peculiar exaltation when on soil still loyal to our rightful Sovereign and Parliament—and when re-passing thro' Boston (curses on which for its damn'd treasons of 1775 and later) eas'd the transition by making a side trip to antient MARBLEHEAD . . . . around which I took a brief walk only about five times longer than the preliminary jaunt of 1923 which so cruelly fatigu'd three delicate gentlemen! And now a dispiriting autumnal chill is in the air, so that outdoor events are nearly over for Grandpa. Farewell to the world—tho' perhaps the old man will survive for one more year, and behold once more the vernal sun upon the faun-haunted wold.

I was, needless to say, greatly pleas'd at hearing the details of your all-too-brief vacation; and will vow that you are becoming a formidable figure in the contemporary revival of ping-pong! Ah, me—the simple sports of idyllick 1900! Who wou'd not, in an aera of unrest and disillusion, exchange all the maturity, taste, and penetration of today for the innocent, expansive dreams of our century's infancy? Ping-pong . . . . a ride in an open trolley-car with striped flapping awnings . . . . . . a glass of Phosa at the Wheelmen's Rest after a fifteen-mile spin[1] . . . . hansom cabs in front of Boston's new Hotel Touraine[2] . . . . . . headlines of the Boer War . . . . . those new-fangled suburban cars with vestibules . . . . . necks craned to see the steam-propelled horseless phaëton (last week in Boston one saw a very clever electric carriage!) . . . . sportsmen in trim gigs bound for the trotting at Narragansett Park . . . . . the Function House, Patrick J. Cronin, Prop., Ales, Wines, and Liquors . . . . . Jerome Kennedy and Son, All-Wool Suits, $9.00 . . . . . Providence Opera House, Week of September 8, John

Cart presents Richard Gold in a new Musical Comedy, *The Burgomaster*, Words by Frank Pixley, Music by Gustav Luders .... new electric trains to Bristol and Fall River ..... talk of electrifying the New York elevated and using Sprague's new multiple-unit system[3] .... some of the very new houses wired for electric lights just like the down town shops ..... fine, brilliant 16 c. p. bulbs ..... Vote for McKinley and Roosevelt ..... will the Pan-American be as good as the Chicago Fair? ..... put me off at Buffalo! ..... what kind of a King will the sporty Prince of Wales make now that Victoria is dead?[4] ..... telephones are getting common in private houses ..... successful wireless messages from Block Island ..... Nikola Tesla reports signals from Mars ..... this new metal Radium seems to be queer stuff—actually shoots off X-rays! ..... prudish whispers—the nameless author of "The Importance of Being Earnest" has just died in a cheap Paris hotel[5] ..... collegiate sofa-pillows—"Reflections", "Pipe Dreams", "The Summer Girl",[6] "The Touch-down" ..... recitations of Kipling ..... "I have been faithful to thee, Cynara, in my fashion" ..... "David Harum" ..... "Caleb West"[7]: ..... "To Have and to Hold" ..... E. H. Sothern in Justin McCarthy's Romantic Drama, "If I Were King" ..... "Way Down East"[8] ..... "Sag Harbor"[9] ..... "Sky Farm"[10] ..... "York State Folks"[11] ..... Neil Burgess in "The County Fair" ..... Mrs. Leslie Carter in "Zaza"[12] (shocking!) ..... Maude Adams in "The Little Minister"[13] ..... quartette at Keith's Continuous Vaudeville—"When the Harvest Moon is Shining on the River"[14] ..... Aguinaldo captured ..... *Life of Admiral Dewey*,[15] fully illustrated, special subscription edition, only $3.75 ..... that awful book by Paul Dresser's queer brother—"Sister Carrie" ..... Peter F. Dailey at the Opera House in "Hodge, Podge, and Co." ..... Copeland's Livery Stable ..... cake-walks ..... "Oh, Oh, Miss Phoebe" ..... Gilmore's Band[16] ..... Life's Gibson Calendar for 1902—A Handsome Gift or Souvenir ..... Edison Phonographs ..... the new gramophones that use flat discs[17] ..... T. & C. pyrography outfits, $1.80 ..... Braun's Carbon Prints ..... Famous Fasso Corsets ..... Studebaker Carriages and Wagons ..... Angelus Pianola ..... the new cat book by Agnes Repplier[18] ..... Hand Sapolio, just on the market ..... "Good Morning! Have you used Pears' Soap?" ..... go 'way back and sit down ..... Mt. Pelee ..... Chauncey Olcott[19] ..... new strike in the Klondike ..... "Ale that is Ale, from the Highland Spring" ..... Anti-Imperialism ..... "The Riddle of the Universe"[20] ..... Nova Persei[21] ..... disturbing works on sociology by that fellow Lester Ward[22] ..... the Sunday sermon ..... Sweet Caporal[23] ..... Egyptian Deities ..... these new houses with colonial gambrel roofs ..... McClure's Magazine ..... Lincoln Steffens ..... "The Shame of Minneapolis"[24] ..... moral purpose ..... B. & L. Cut Plug[25] ..... germs ..... The Open Door ..... Hague Conference ..... anti-trust act ..... Our New Possessions[26] ..... cable to Hawaii ..... going down to Virginia to see the eclipse of May 28, 1900, as total? ..... Dreyfus's book[27] ..... monster G. A. R.[28] proces-

sion..... talk of building a subway in New York longer than Boston's.....
"ideals"..... "Georgia Camp Meeting" on the mandolin..... those new
flat felt hats the college boys are wearing..... peg-top trousers..... tan
topcoats..... rag-time..... "Hello, Mah Baby"[29]..... Lombroso.....
translations of that terrible, irreverent person, Anatole France..... who is
this 'Baudelaire' that the fast literary set are talking about?..... and who *could*
have written that nasty, cynical "Book of Jade"?—internal evidence indicates
a Harvard student[30]..... Ibsen..... do you *approve* of Shaw?..... Santos-
Dumont..... Boxers..... Tien-Tsin..... Siege of the Legations.....
bold Kaiser Wilhelm, Champion of the Western World..... the Coal Strike
..... new type-writers with visible writing..... Remex Fountain Pen.....
Carter's Black-Letter Ink..... Teddy!..... Senator Aldrich..... Platt
..... Hanna..... Norris's McTeague—so unpleasant and unwholesome!
..... Carrie Nation..... Doxie..... Lyman Abbott..... New York res-
ervoir at 40th to 42nd St. all gone, to make room for new library..... Is
Doyle going to write any more Sherlock Holmes books?..... "In the Good
Old Summer Time"[31]..... "Just as the Sun Went Down"..... Stephen
Crane..... W. C. Morrow..... Richard Harding Davis[32]..... Jack Lon-
don..... have you heard of that queer old codger Ambrose Bierce, who
writes the awful morbid stories syndicated in the papers?..... *The Yellow Kid*
..... Buster Brown..... smart boy named Henry Louis Mencken—lives in
Baltimore—contributing light verse to *Bookman, Leslie's, New England Magazine*, etc.—wonder if he'll amount to much?[33]..... Paul Elmer More, leading
critic of serious people.... note from *Appleton Crescent*—Mr. and Mrs. Alfred Galpin of 536 College Ave. are receiving congratulations on the birth of
a son, Alfred Jr., on November 8th—1901..... Harlem note in the *New
York Tribune* for 1902—"Dr. and Mrs. Frank Belknap Long are receiving
congratulations on the birth of a son, Frank Belknap Jr., on April 27th"[34]
..... "Poemata Minora", by H. P. Lovecraft (pencil—one copy) published
by the *Royal Press*, Providence, Sept. 1902..... other works by the same author, "The Mysterious Ship", "The Secret of the Grave", "Antarctic Atlas",
"Voyages of Capt. Ross, R.N.", "Wilkes's Explorations", "Mythology for the
Young", "Chemistry", etc. etc. sold by the *Royal Press* at reasonable rates in
exclusive editions of one copy each..... M. W. Moe piles up brilliant record
at University of Wisconsin..... isn't that new sea author Joseph Conrad
gloomy?..... Hardy is *such* a cynic, too bad!..... *The Cosmopolitan*, edited by
John Brisben Walker[35]—so much more staid and dignified than *Munsey's*, with
all those cheap pictures..... *Browning and King's Magazine*[36]..... "I Want My
Clothes!"..... prize amateur photo by Nick Breuhl, Sherwood, Wis......
"At the Sign of the Sphinx",[37] conducted by Carolyn Wells..... the new
cheap Brownie Camera..... Sen-Sen..... Munyon's Inhaler..... "There
is Hope!"[38]..... all the fashionable 1894 Vandykes shaved off..... "A Bird
in a Gilded Cage"..... Jeffries knocks out Fitzsimmons[39]..... Terry

McGovern[40] ..... Kid McCoy[41] ..... that silly, affected painter Whistler, who was flunked out of West Point, has just died![42] His freakish stuff won't last! ..... They say the St. Louis fair is going to beat the Pan-American ..... new stamp albums with space for Pan-American and King Edward stamps ..... such trouble negotiating a Panama Canal treaty with Colombia! ..... football haircuts ..... "Coffin-nails" ..... bars to lower on the left-hand side of open trolley-cars ..... acetylene bicycle lamps ..... autoscopes at the shore resorts ..... new biograph travel films to chase the audiences out of Keith's at six o'clock ..... *Harper's Round-Table*[43] has failed ..... premiums for *Youths' Companion* subscriptions ..... everybody is getting interested in colonial houses and antique furniture—as if they could compare with French roofs and golden oak! .... Red Trading Stamps ..... "The Prince of Pilsen" ..... "Babes in Toyland"[44] ..... "King Dodo"[45] ..... "The Sultan of Sulu"[46] ..... the Invicta steam roller ..... "get a horse!" ..... "The Lightning Conductor", by C. N. & A. M. Williamson[47] ..... "Janice Meredith"[48] ..... "Richard Carvel" ..... "The Prisoner of Zenda" ..... Stanley J. Weyman ..... Yeats and Synge—queer fellows ..... Josiah Royce ..... new interurban trolley lines ..... "can you make anything of this new fellow Santayana, with his 'Interpretations of Poetry and Religion'? Queer stuff—but he's only a foreigner! I'm sure I much prefer dear William James—though even he isn't as sure about ultimate things as our pastor, Dr. F. Latt Uhlance. For real spiritual satisfaction, give me Dr. Uhlance every time!" ..... "Smoky Mokes" ..... Weber and Fields ..... Edna May[49] ..... Charley Grapewin[50] ..... Buffalo Bill ..... who are these people—Schopenhauer and Nietzsche—that the collegians discuss? ..... they say that Krutch boy is getting mighty studious for a ten-year-old[51] ..... Have you read John Dewey's "Studies in Logical Theory"? Pretty heavy reading—he's a middle-aged professor at Chicago—and what do you think of the odd things that young fellow—the Hon. Bertrand Russell—has been writing? A mighty queer kind of mathematician, I say! But then—he's the son of that horrid *free-thinker* (yes, really!) Viscount Amberley ..... How fortunate that all the foundations of our moral beliefs are secure!! ..... And permanent prosperity will be assured under Roosevelt and Fairbanks ..... 1900 ..... 1901 ..... 1902 ..... 1903 ..... 1904 ..... ping-pong ..... puff ties ..... "Darktown is Out Tonight"[52] ..... Hay–Pauncefote treaty .....

> "The Golden Age was first, when Man, yet new
> No rule but uncorrupted Reason knew,
> and, with a native Bent, did Good pursue .....
>
> E're Sails were spread new Oceans to explore,
> And happy Mortals, unconcern'd for more,
> Confin'd their Wishes to their native Shoar."[53]

As for my old friend *Erisichton*[54] . . . . . gordelpus! Art serious in claiming you'd never heard of this hungry boy till Beke tipt ya off? Holy Mackerel! I soaked up all about him from Bulfinch back in '97, and by good old 1900 had been right to the fountain head in Ovid's *Metamorphoses* (the seventeenth to eighteenth century Translation by Various Hands), whose eighth Book (ll. 738–878 of the Latin original) gives the whole sad story as a narrative related to Theseus by the river-god Acheloüs—the same divine bimbo who pulled the immortal tale of *Baucis and Philemon*, as well as the standard accounts of the death of your solar friend Herakles. Hell—for a pious guy you sure do neglect your theology! Fancy not knowing about poor Sikky! If you don't believe that impious egg was some hungry, just read what old Publius Naso had to say about him—as render'd into English poetick numbers by Mr. Vernon:

> "Straight he requires, impatient in Demand,
> Provisions from the Air, the Seas, the Land;
> But tho' the Land, Air, Seas, Provisions grant,
> Starves at full Tables, and complains of Want:
> What to a People might in Doe be paid,
> Or victual Cities for a long Blockade,
> Cou'd not one wolfish Appetite assuage,
> For glutting Nourishment increas'd its Rage . . . .
>
> Food raises a Desire for Food, and Meat
> Is but a new Provocative to eat!
> He grows more empty, as the more supply'd,
> And endless Cramming but extends the Void.
> * * * *
> At last all Means, as all Provisions, fail'd,
> For the Disease by Remedies prevail'd;
> His Muscles with a furious Bite he tore,
> Gorg'd his own tatter'd Flesh, and gulph'd his Gore:
> Wounds were his Feast; his Life to Life a Prey,
> Supporting Nature by its own Decay."[55]

Nearest contemporary parallel—James Ferdinand Morton at a restaurant with a dollar to spend.

Regarding Παν and Βυχυ [*sic*][56]—I must own, that I do not recall the latter's reference to the former; but at any rate I can assure you that you are entirely correct regarding the origin of *panick fear*. By all the antients Pan was allow'd to be a creature of peculiarly affrighting nature; not alone as concern'd his grotesque outer aspect, but in some subtle, mystical way undoubtedly connected with man's early fears of the deep untrodden groves and what they hide. When his mother (according to the dominant legend as given in an

Homerick hymn, a nymph of Arcadia) first beheld him, she fled away in fright; but his father Hermes bore him off to Olympus, where his singularities are said to have greatly delighted the gods. He was first worship in his native Arcadia, and introduc'd among the Athenians at the time of the Persian wars. Pan's time of sleep was mid-day—the heat of noon—and it was thought dangerous to disturb or intrude upon him at this hour. Accordingly the mid-day lull became a period of vague fear amongst the Grecian rusticks, who at such a time avoided so far as possible the shady sylvan coverts. Both the sight and the voice of Pan were capable of producing terror. With the latter he frighted the Titans during their war with the gods of Olympus; whilst he promis'd Pheidippides to employ all his horrors in disconcerting the Persians, if the people of Athens wou'd establish his worship. He not infrequently terrify'd lone travellers by appearing to them in wild and remote places—and this species of frightening was totally different from that occasion'd by his constant amorous pursuit of the nymphs. To certain men Pan was dispos'd to be kindly and amicable; thus he liked the poet Pindar, singing and dancing the bard's songs, and receiving in response a votive sanctuary. I was my self a worshipper of Pan in the year 1897; building to him an altar in an oak grove not far from my abode, and offering up such things as he was reputed to relish—cows, rams, lambs, (i.e., pieces of beef, mutton, and lamb when obtainable) milk, and honey. When the pyre fail'd to consume such materials, I left them as they were; confident that the god and his Panisci wou'd come at the proper time to enjoy them. The oaken copse is still in existence; and if old age ever causes me to resume the belief and practice of religion, I shall undoubtedly sacrifice to Pan on the selfsame spot, and in a much more impressive manner! To conclude—the name of panick fear is no modern coinage, but something as old as the love of the god himself. The Greeks had a word for it—two words, in fact—calling it Πανικον δειμα.

Regarding your solar-myth parallels—I see relatively little amiss with them, and in any case I am no authority on the legends of the eastern races. Regarding Herakles, I think you might insert *more*—for his servitude to Emystheus is closely duplicated in his other servitude to Omphalé. Also—he was *twice* heal'd of ills of body and mind—first after he had slain his three children in a fit of madness (before his servitude to Emystheus), and second, when disease had been sent upon him in later life in punishment for his mad slaying of Iphitus. It was—somewhat indirectly—to secure this second healing that Herakles (by order of the Delphick oracle) bound himself out to Queen Omphale. In your parallel I would advise your not coupling the *Nessus-shirt*[57] with Gilgamesh's disease unless you think the *motive* is more important than the *circumstance*. To parallel the *scaly disease*, you had perhaps better use the second *illness* of Herakles; that impos'd on him as a penalty for killing Iphitus. The *sending of the wild bull to destroy Gilgamesh* is perhaps the best parallel of the *Nessus-shirt*—in that it implies *external injury* rather than *disease*. On the other hand, the Nessus-shirt represents not the wrath of the goddess, but the vindictiveness of the slain centaur. Use your judgment. Dejanira's innocent offspring of the poison'd shirt to Herakles may possibly form a very rough parallel to Delilah's intentional injuries to Samson—i.e., the injurious effect of a consort, whether wilful or not. However, *perfect parallelism must not be expected* among nature myths whose development has been largely independent despite occasional mutual borrowings.

In the matter of your *interpretations* of various myth-phases, I am dispos'd to challenge you more often. You incline to an excessively *utilitarian and humanocentrick* type of allegory, whereas the primitive Aryans (so vastly superior to the Semites in nimbleness of mind and imagination) conceiv'd of the solar drama as something wholly celestial and apart from earth and mankind. To our race, the solar drama represents not the sun in relation to the earth, but the sun in relation to the vicissitudes which beset it on its journey (probably both diurnal and annual—these elements being confus'd in the myths) thro' the heavens. The sun's *long yellow hair* indeed represents its rays, but its great strength signifies its power *to overcome heavenly obstacles*—not to vivify the earth. The *overcoming of lions*, and kindred feats of violence and valour, do *not* signify the *terrestrially* 'slaying power of the sun'; but instead allude to the *coelestial monsters—rain clouds and the like*—with which the sun must always contend. The part play'd by *man* in such adventures is always diminutive and passive—it being said, whenever humans are introduced at all, that the solar hero rescues people opprest by (cloud and frost) monsters. The *enmity of a goddess* (or woman) to the sun-hero is *not reckon'd as having to do with terrestrial fertility and the decay of the sun's power over the earth, but is interpreted as simply the opposition of darkness to light.* The hostile god or goddess of the solar myth (often the *parent* of the sun-hero) is the *eastern darkness* out of which the sun is born. If a parent, the deity is hostile *because he or she knows that the offspring will eventually form his or her death*—the slaying of the night by the day. Thus many solar heroes are exposed to die at birth by their fearful and therefore hostile progenitors. As for the sun-hero's amours and marriages—it is generally held that they do *not* typify aestival vegetation on the earth, but that they have to do with the sun's close association with the beautiful *twilight* of dawn (Eos, Jocasta, etc.) or evening (Œnone, Iolë, etc.). The *dawn-maiden* is a clearly recognisable fixture of Aryan myth, and is always the bride and sometimes the mother, as well, of the solar hero. When such a maiden is (in place of *night*, for the sun is both of violet and rose *dawn* as well as of *blackness*) the hero's mother, he is represented as incestuously wedding her either unknowingly (Œdipus-Jocasta) or knowingly (as the Hindoo Indra weds, at evening, that twilight-mother Dehava who bore him in the morning.). The *injuries, defeats, and diseases* of the solar hero are (except sometimes toward the end) probably to be consider'd as results of a combin'd struggle with the original darkness-enmity and with the cloud and storm monsters or obstacles encounter'd along the way. The idea of a sort of *doom* or *fate* no doubt proceeds from the knowledge that darkness will eventually triumph, and of course the *final* feeblenesses of the hero are probably often suggested by the decline in his lustre and obvious approach of his end. At the same time, this ultimate merging with twilight and darkness is frequently given an interpretation savouring of triumph rather than defeat; this coalescence (vide supra) being taken as the nuptials of the hero with a long-wish'd bride. Whether this circumstance has any bearing on the oft-recurring *destructiveness* of a solar hero's bride, I am not certain; but it seems to me highly probable. The *recovery* of the hero from ills and injuries may signify either his emergence from obscuration by clouds, or his return to life after the dormancy of night or of winter. It may be noted, that the *diurnal* behaviour of the sun is undoubtedly more potent than its *annual* behaviour in shaping the standard solar myth. Indeed, I wou'd not be surprised if many anthropologists deny'd altogether the participation of the annual element. This annual course of the sun, with its mark'd effects upon terrestrial life, seems to produce a wholly independent cycle of myth in which the central figure is not the sun-hero himself, but a weak, lovely youth typifying terrestrial fertility—Dionysus—Iacchus—Zagreus—Adonis—Linus—Hylas—Taunming [*sic*] etc. etc.—who is annually slain but later resurrected from the tomb to a new and glorify'd existence. There is scarce any doubt but that this myth, engrafted upon the Jewish legend of a coming Messiah and the feminine ethical notions of Syria in the age of the earlier Caesars, form'd the basis of the Christ-legend which wove itself about some itinerant Syrian enthusiast or enthusiasts of the time of Augustus, Tiberius, Caligula, or Claudius—indeed, many of the earlier forms indicate the beautiful youth as meeting his cruel but temporary death *for the sake of mankind;* it being assumed that the perishing of autumnal things is needful for the new vivifying of the earth in the spring. Returning to the diurnal myth—I think you are right in associating the flaming pyre of Herakles with the flaming lines of the sunset. Indeed, in this especial legend the pyre takes the place of the usual wedding; for the violet-twilight bride Iolë (cf. ιον, *violet*) marries his son instead of himself. His own final bride is Hebe, whom he marries in Olympus after his resume from the pyre. Roughly tracing the history of Herakles, we see him as an infant hated by an Heré who sends serpents of darkness to strangle him. He overcomes them and shines clear, but clouds and storms hold him in subjection until he works off the burthen feat by feat. Certain of the feats have very marked individual allegorisations of the struggle betwixt light and darkness—especially that of the seizure of the bright oxen (of the Sun) from the dark monster Geryon. In the *Latin* myths which became merg'd with the Grecian, there is added to this tale the incident of the robber *Cacus,* (not from *Kakos, bad,* since the legend is *not Greek;* but from *COECIVS, he who blinds or darkens*) who steals from HERCVLES (a name of different origin from Ἐρακλες, deriv'd from Hercere, to enclose, whereas Ἐρακλες means "Hera's glory"—the name Ἐρακ (= Ἐρε) plus the word κλεος) some of the bright cattle taken from Geryon. The import of a darkener who steals *bright* cattle, and is overcome by the hero, is obvious. Cacus hides the bright cattle in a dark cave beneath the Mons Aventin on the future site of Rome, but *Hercules* (who ought, strictly, to be distinguish'd from *Herakles*) tracks them down, recovers them, and slays the miscreant. Cacus was the original hi-jacker! In the later life of Herakles Nessius is undoubtedly a storm-cloud myth—the slaying *with arrows* being especially significant of other myths symbolick of the solar rays. And at the end, as we have agreed, the pyre is the flaming glory of sunset. I return herewith, as per request, the very clever synopsis. I'll leave further procedure to you—just ponder on Grandpa's ramblings and use your judgment. The subject is, as you doubtless realise, infinitely complex; and really deserving of far deeper research than you or I will ever be likely to give it.

Sept. 21

God Damn! Had to call a halt to instalment I, and have been further delay'd by one of my old-time sick headaches—which had me down for two days. The minute autumn chill appears, the old man begins to go to pieces! Well—anyhow, I don't have as many of those cursed things as I used to. About library research—I can surely agree with you concerning its charm, tho' I think its apex of pleasure is obtainable only if the library be one's own private collection, so that no formalities regarding hours need be observ'd. Also, publick research can never be quite as effective as that conducted in an atmosphere free from distraction. However—in most fields the average student must of necessity depend on publick facilities; since home libraries cannot be exhaustive in all directions. Thus Wandrei, whilst in Providence, took advantage of the Harris Collection to unearth two obscure poets (Frederick Tuckerman[58] and Park Barnitz) about whom little can be found in ordinary channels. I resort to publick libraries when I have to; yet on account of my native indolence am dispos'd to slight subjects which drive me to them, and to concentrate on subjects cover'd by my own collection. Thus a man's learning is often determin'd by the nature of the books he happens to possess—tho' of course, his original selection of them (or of such as are not hereditary) is dictated by his unguided inclinations. My books are such as will settle most *common* problems in astronomy, chemistry, natural philosophy, classical literature, or English literature prior to 1820. For other matters I am forc'd to ampler collections than my own.

News from Sauk City upholds the reputation of the youth of your sub-arctic commonwealth—my grandson August W. Derleth has just had one story three-starred in O'Brien's 1932 annual, and *another* two-starred in the same austere volume![59] Good for little Augie! I hope you'll meet the kid some day—he is often in Madison, from whose university he graduated not so many twelvemonths ago.

The blessing of Pan upon thee!

Yr obt Loavus.

Notes

1. Herb-O Phosa was a soft drink marketed as "a sweet bitter nerve drink" and "a true fruit phosphate drink." It was manufactured in Providence, RI.
2. A residential hotel (1897–1966) on the corner of Tremont and Boylston Streets, near the Boston Common.
3. Frank Julian Sprague (1857–1934), American naval officer and inventor. He devised a multiple unit system of electric railway operation.
4. Queen Victoria had died 22 January 1901. She was succeeded by Edward VII (1841–1910).
5. Oscar Wilde died 30 November 1900.
6. A concert piece (1901) by John Philip Sousa.
7. Francis Hopkinson Smith (1838–1915), *Caleb West, Master Diver*, a novel; the best-selling book in the U.S. in 1898.
8. A play (1898) by Charlotte Blair Parker (1858–1937).
9. A play (1900) by James A. Herne (1839–1901).
10. A play (1902) by Edward E. Kidder (1846–1927).
11. A play (1903) by Arthur C. Sidman (1863–1901).
12. *Zaza* (1899), a play by Pierre Berton and Charles Simon, starring Mrs. Leslie Carter (1862–1937).
13. *The Little Minister* (1897), a play by J. M. Barrie, starring Maude Adams (1872–1953).
14. A song (words by Arthur J. Lamb, music by S. R. Henry).
15. Louis Stanley Young, *Life and Heroic Deeds of Admiral Dewey* (1899), a biography of Admiral George Dewey (1837–1917).
16. A band founded by Irish-born American composer and bandmaster Patrick Gilmore (1829–1892) in 1858. The band dispersed in 1898.
17. Initially, the gramophone played a rotating tin cylinder.
18. Agnes Repplier (1858–1950), *The Fireside Sphinx* (1901).
19. Chauncey Olcott (1858–1932), American stage actor and singer of Irish descent.
20. A philosophical treatise (1899; Eng. tr. 1900) by Ernst Haeckel (1834–1919) that significantly influenced HPL.
21 A bright nova in the constellation Perseus that flared up in 1901. HPL mentions it in "Beyond the Wall of Sleep" (*CF* 1.85).
22. Lester Frank Ward (1841–1913), American botanist and sociologist and first president of the American Sociological Association (1906–07). Ward challenged the prevailing Social Darwinism of the period in such works as *Neo-Darwinism and Lamarckism* (1891) and *Outlines of Sociology* (1898).
23. A brand of cigarette manufactured by the Kinney Brothers Tobacco Company, beginning in 1878.
24. A muckracking article by Lincoln Steffens (*McClure's Magazine*, January 1903) about the system of graft in the administration of Albert Alonzo Ames, mayor of Minneapolis. It was included in Steffens's *The Shame of the Cities* (1904), about corrupt political machines in major American cities.

25. A container for holding "cut plug" tobacco (tobacco leaves pressed into the shape of a brick) manufactured by Bausch & Lomb.

26. By Trumbull White.

27. Alfred Dreyfus (1859–1935), *Cinq années de ma vie, 1894–1899* (1901), translated as *Five Years of My Life* (1901). Dreyfus, a French Jewish army officer, was convicted of treason in 1895, in a trial that was widely seen as an instance of blatant anti-Semitism.

28. The Grand Army of the Republic, an organization comprised of veterans of the Union Army and other groups that had served in the Civil War. It held marches every year from 1866 to 1949.

29. "Hello! Ma Baby" (1899), a Tin Pan Alley song by Joseph E. Howard and Ida Emerson.

30. Park Barnitz (1878–1901), a Harvard graduate, died shortly after his book was published.

31. "In the Good Old Summer Time" (1902), a Tin Pan Alley song (words by Ren Shields, music by George Evans).

32. Richard Harding Davis (1864–1916), journalist, writer of fiction, and dramatist, known foremost as the first American war correspondent to cover the Spanish-American War, the Second Boer War, and World War I.

33. Mencken's verse is now gathered in *Collected Poems* (Hippocampus Press, 2009).

34. FBL was actually born in 1901.

35. John Brisben Walker (1847–1931) purchased *Cosmopolitan Magazine* in 1899 and sold it to William Randolph Hearst in 1905.

36. Browning, King & Co. was a clothing manufacturer in New York. The reference is to *Browning, King. & Co.'s Illustrated Monthly* (1890–1901), later titled *Browning, King & Co.'s Monthly Magazine* (1901–02) and still later as *Browning's Magazine: A Periodical of Fashions and Fancies* (1902–20).

37. Carolyn Wells (1862–1942), American writer and poet. *At the Sign of the Sphinx* was published in 1896.

38. James M. Munyon (1848–1918) was a popular manufacturer of homeopathic patent medicines. His slogan was "There is hope."

39. James J. Jeffries (1875–1953) knocked out Bob Fitzsimmons (1863–1917): once in 1899, but HPL alludes to the second time on 25 July 1902.

40. Terrible Terry McGovern (1880–1918) was an American professional boxer who held the World Bantamweight and Featherweight Championships.

41. Charles "Kid" McCoy (born Norman Selby; 1872–1940), American world champion boxer.

42. James Abbott McNeill Whistler (b. 1834), American artist, died on 17 July 1903.

43. *Harper's Young People,* founded in 1879, later became *Harper's Round Table.* It ceased publication in 1899.

44. An operetta (1903) composed by Victor Herbert (1859–1924).

45. *King Dodo: A Musical Comedy in Three Acts* (1901) by Gustav Luders and Frank S. Pixley.

46. A musical (1902): book and lyrics by George Ade; music by Alfred G. Wathall; songs by Nat D. Mann.

47. C[harles] N[orris] Williamson (1859–1920) and A[lice] M[uriel] Williamson (1869–

1933), *The Lightning Conductor: The Strange Adventures of a Motor-car* (1903).
48. A play (1900) by Paul Leicester Ford and Edward Everett Rose.
49. Edna May Pettie (1878–1948), American stage actress and singer known as Edna May.
50. Charley Grapewin (1869–1956), American vaudeville performer. He later appeared as Uncle Henry in *The Wizard of Oz* (1939).
51. Joseph Wood Krutch was born in 1893 (d. 1970).
52. A song in *Clorindy, or The Origin of the Cake Walk* (1898), a one-act musical by composer Will Marion Cook and librettist Paul Laurence Dunbar.
53. Ovid, *Metamorphoses* 1.117–19, 130–32 (tr. John Dryden in Garth's Ovid).
54. In Greek mythology, Erysichthon (anglicised as Erisichthon and sometimes called Aethon), son of Triopas, was a King of Thessaly.
55. Ovid, *Metamorphoses* 8.1269–76, 1285–88, 1330–35 (tr. Thomas Vernon in Garth's Ovid).
56. So transcribed by AH. HPL may have written Βεκε or Βηκη (= Beke), referring to a clipping from Bertrand K. Hart's "Sideshow."
57. In Greek mythology, the shirt (chiton) daubed with the tainted blood of the centaur Nessus that Deianeira, Heracles' wife, naïvely gave Heracles, burning him, and driving him to throw himself onto a funeral pyre.
58. Frederick Goddard Tuckerman (1821–1873), remembered mostly for his sonnet series. Apart from his *Poems* (1860), which included roughly 40 percent of his lifetime sonnet output and various other poetic works, the balance of his poetry was published in the 20th century. For Barnitz, see n30.
59. The three-star story was "Old Ladies"; the two-star story was "Nella."

[65]   [AHT]

Prospect Terrace—with the sunset expanse
of the Lower Town outspread before me.
VIth Day before the Kalends of Quintilis.
[26 June? 1933]

O Sage:—

Glad that Robertulus has landed something not only in his line but containing possible avenues of advancement. It is certainly fortunate when one possesses a real aptitude and training in some field involving a constant commercial demand. Glad you could get off for the commencement at Madisonium, and that the ceremonies unfolded themselves with appropriate pomp and pageantry. I imagine that Glenn Frank's[1] oration must have been very good—for his published writings are usually eminently sensible. There was certainly no inconsistency in the two points which you line up—the need of a flexible intelligence amidst changing foundations of knowledge, and the parallel need of caution against ephemeral fads. These points, far from being mutually exclusive, are really only facets of one very sensible underlying attitude—that of true sanity; which refuses on the one hand to base actions on premises found to be definitely false or obsolete, and on the other hand to disturb the equilibrium of things through sheer restlessness before their falsity or obsolescence has been demonstrated. Any belief justified only by tradition is silly—but our discarding of false beliefs must not become a blind rush away from all landmarks, since many of the landmarks are indeed founded on demonstrable realities. The whole point of Frank's position is that we must face the world as alertly thinking men rather than as emotional children—either of the reactionary or the radical sort. Test everything. Hold nothing which does not meet a real test; but do not reject things which meet the test, merely because they happen to be old. The assumptions and ideals of the past are not all true—but neither are they all untrue. Some were true according to former conditions and are so no longer. Others were never true, but were wholly products of error and undisciplined emotion. Still others both were and are true. The emotional child, senile reactionary, or blind rebel chooses the old or the new according to his own subjective caprice—and such a choice is of course wholly valueless. Frank—and any man of sense—would urge us to leave caprice and the age-element out of our choices; accepting merely *what meets the test of reality* and paying no attention to the matter of whether it is old or new. In the interest of an harmonious and reposeful culture, it is advantageous to hold over from earlier usage whatever is not proved false by the evidence of discovery and clarified thought. This means that old *folkways and aesthetic perspectives* can be held much longer than old *intellectual beliefs*. We cannot hold a *belief* when we know it to be false. A man who claims to be a "traditionalist" in *belief* is simply a paradoxical ass. But we *can* often hold an *attitude or custom or aesthetic method* long after the disappearance of the conditions which gave rise to it. There is really no connexion between stupid *intellectual reaction* and well-considered *emotional artistic conservatism*—and it only beclouds the issue to pretend that there is. *What is and what isn't* and *what we like and don't like* are two antipodally different propositions. Artistic and cultural change should be slow and gradual—old forms dying only after their foundations have become thoroughly ridiculous and instinctively discredited. What *must* change in consonance with changes of human knowledge are those practical matters of social and economic organisation which require an absolute adjustment to objective reality. It is simply infantile to advocate any social, political, or economic policy which is based on assumptions contrary to what we now recognise as fact—or on assumptions true only amidst industrial and commercial conditions no longer existing. Our general culture belongs as much to the world of dream as to the world of reality; hence must take into account not only *facts*, but certain racial *attitudes* on which hinge the illusions of purpose, direction, value, and interest in the cosmic flux. But our social policy and jurisprudence deal primarily with *hard facts*, hence cannot but suffer in proportion to their removal from objective truth. Any social or economic measure not founded on the *real facts of existence*, as best we know such, is not only foolish but essentially harmful.

Travelogue material will be scarce this year, but I can at least record a sort of local convention which coincided in date with the N.A.P.A.'s big show. This pleasing event revolved around the visit to these Georgian abodes of one whom your gifted young Mocratuli will at once recall from their *Weird Tale* reading—to wit, Edgar Hoffmann Price, Esq., fantaisiste and Orientalist, late of New Orleans and recipient of my famous twenty-five and one-half hour call a year ago. Price has come north in a shady 1928 Ford Juggernaut, and is staying with a friend who conducts a school near the Sleepy Hollow country—Irvington, N.Y. On June 30, he blew into antient Providentium for a sub-visit of four days (while my aunt was still at the hospital)[2]—during which time festivities were plentiful.[3] Cook stopped in on his way to the convention, and young Harry Brobst (whom I've described to you) was over twice—on one occasion staying all night for a session of triangular literary and philosophical discussion punctuated by a trip to an antient churchyard (the one I shew'd you in '23—completely hidden from all highways by bank walls and century'd houses) on the hill (somewhat north of here) at about three a.m. What we saw, whisper'd, and inton'd in that nighted and legend-haunted necropolis is not for the timid pen to record . . . . . "You fool, Harley Warren is dead" . . . .

On July 2, Price brought his Juggernaut into the service of antiquarian exploration by taking me to a Rhode-Island region which—despite my life-long residence less than thirty miles from it, and my one-third ancestral connexion with its antient families—I had never (thro' lack of publick transportation facilities) seen before with the physical eye. This was the historick "South County" or "Narragansett Country" west of the bay, where before the revolution there existed a system of large plantations and black slaves comparable to that of the South. Happy days! In that Golden Age Narragansett cheeses and Narragansett pacers were fam'd in all the markets of the world; whilst the culture of the planters (most of whom had fine houses across the bay in Newport, so that they mingled in the literary and philosophick society adorn'd by Dean Berkeley) was ample and distinguish'd. Cordial ties with the kindred regions of Virginia and the Carolinas were maintain'd; tho' in building their manor-houses the planters did not copy the architecture of the South, but us'd the New-England gambrel-roof'd design on an unprecedentedly large scale. The abode (now long vanish'd) of my own lineal ancestor Robert Hazard (who own'd at least one hundred thirty-three niggers) was so large, that a physician calling there once ask'd, 'whether he had any conveyance to take the occupants from the front to the rear door!' This house had a wing for the black domesticks, the fireplace of which was so large that the pickaninnies us'd to sit on stone benches inside it. The blacks were very well treated, and once a year were allow'd a kind of Saturnalian festival at which they elected one of their number to be the "Black Governor" or "King of the Congo" for the ensuing twelvemonth. Their attachment to their masters was extreme, and after they became free they clung round the old estates as of yore. Some of the free blacks developed into unique and picturesque local characters—like Old Guy, who had fought in the Revolution, the prophetess Silvia Torrey, who had the "evil eye", the fiddler Polydore Gardiner, and old "Gambia", who claim'd to have been a prince in Africa. This region was never blighted by Puritan barbarism, but was Cavalier and Church-of-England from the first—with a Quaker admixture later on. Christmas (rejected by the snivelling Puritans) was observ'd in the lavish fashion of Old England, and hospitality (as in the South) was a sacred tradition. As in Virginia, the churches were not in the villages but in the open country, being attended in coaches by the local gentry. The chief fane was the old Narragansett Church, built in 1707 under the patronage of Her Majesty Queen Anne, and presided over by the jovial, dearly lov'd, and broadly cultivated Reverend MacSparran. This church is still in existence in the best of condition—tho' moved up to the village of Wickford in 1800, after the ravages of rebellion and mob government had ruined the plantation system and thinn'd out the population of the countryside. Besides the seaport of Wickford, the chief town of this region was the inland hamlet of Little Rest (now call'd Kingston), seat of King's County and a centre of much cultivation. Here a group of silversmiths flourish'd and attain'd a vast degree of artistick eminence, among them being my great-great-grand-uncle Samuel Casey, who is today represented by pieces in the Boston Museum of Fine Arts and the Metropolitan Museum in N.Y. It was this artist who (having been ruin'd in 1763 by the burning of his house) turn'd to counterfeiting, and in 1770 was sentenc'd to be hang'd—only to be forcibly liberated by his neighbours who black'd their faces, storm'd the gaol, and provided the prisoner with the swift horse on which he vanish'd for ever. I am lineally descended from his elder brother John, whose wife was Mercy Dyer, a descendant of the Quaker Martyr. The scenery of this unique region is ineffably fine, as I had long realis'd from reading, tho' none of the choicest areas can be glimps'd from the main trunk highways. On this occasion we began with the marvellously unspoil'd colonial seaport of Wickford, and work'd southward thro' the magical land of yesterday. Wickford—with its sleepy streets, great elms, finely-kept Georgian houses, and picturesque wharves—I describ'd to you some years ago when I visited it with James Ferdinand Morton. It was antiently known as Updike's Landing, after a celebrated South County family of Dutch origin, descended from Dr. Gysbert op Dyke, who came from Nieuw-Amsterdam at an early period. Here is now to be found the old Narragansett Church once'd rul'd by genial Dr. MacSparran.

After Wickford we went south on the post road and soon turn'd into an exquisite winding highway which, rambling amongst stone-walls, gentle hills, pleasing farmsteads, and venerable groves, leads eventually to the rambling old snuff-mill on the Narrow (or Pattaquamscutt) River where in 1755 the great painter Gilbert Stuart was born. This mill was built in 1750 by Dr. Moffett of Newport, who sent to Scotland for Stuart's father as an expert snuff-miller. Both Moffett and Stuart were loyal to our rightful Sovereign during the tragedy of 1775–83, and thus property was seiz'd by the rebels and suffer'd to fall into decay. Only two or three years ago a memorial association reclaim'd the ancient mill and restor'd it to its original state as a museum. We were shown about by a highly intelligent old yeoman who started the vast water-wheel and deftly-repair'd machinery. All is in perfect condition, and its simple effectiveness forms a tacit rebuke to the needless complications of our decadent and false-valu'd machine age. God Save the King!

Our next objective was the great gambrel-roof'd mansion of Rowland Robinson, Gent.—the last perfect example of the typical South County plantation-house with gambrel roof and neighbouring slave-quarters. This mighty edifice stands amidst a grove of uncannily antient and gigantick willows, and well justifies all the spectral legends clustering round it. It was built in 1705 and enlarg'd in 1740; and possesses a fine early-Georgian door with segmental pediment, above which is carv'd the heraldick escallop of the Hazard arms—the Robinsons, like myself, being ally'd to the antient Hazard line. This device was of especial interest to Price, who till the day before had not known what a scallop was, but who had then sampled the mollusc at my suggestion. The interior carving and panelling of the house are very fine, being in parts so archaick as to approach the Jacobean. Rowland Robinson, Esq., from whom this mansion is chiefly known, was a son of Governor Wm. Robinson and himself High-Sheriff of King's County. He liv'd in good style, having an household of forty-one persons including slaves, and generally dressing in a dark velvet coat, light plush waistcoat with wide flaps, velvet small-cloaths, white-top boots, and ruffled cambrick shirt. He wore his own long hair, suitably powder'd when occasion demanded. His cheeses and pacers were the finest in the world, and his herd of cows was the pride of all the countryside. No man kept Christmas more lavishly than he, and tho' not without sternness, was a kind master to his blacks. On one occasion, when he sent to Africa for a cargo of slaves to sell as a speculation, he kept them all himself—feeding them well and giving them light labour—he so pity'd the wretched state of the negroes. As a Sheriff, Mr. Robinson was distinguish'd for vast ability and bravery—as display'd in 1751, when he track'd to Newport and captur'd single-handed the murderer Thomas Carter, who had kill'd a companion for his money on the Tower Hill Road. Robinson had a daughter Hannah, born in 1746, who fell in love with a worthless French tutor in Newport. He forbade the match, but with the aid of an Updike aunt in Wickford the couple eloped to Providence. Robinson then disown'd her till such a time as she wou'd leave her husband. Not long afterward, ill-treated and deserted by the disappointed fortune-hunter whose affection had been more for the Robinson fortune than for Hannah, this hapless young gentlewoman fell ill and was promptly succoured by her anxious parent. Borne back to the old plantation by coach and litter, poor Hannah felt that she was not to live long; and ask'd on the journey to be taken to a certain high rock off the Tower Hill Road, whence she cou'd obtain a last view of her native countryside. This was done—and ever afterward the spot has been known as "Hannah Robinson's Rock." True to her melancholy prophecy, she died not much later in her old room at home. Robinson was a Churchman and parishioner of Dr. MacSparran, but his descendants are now Quakers. The sole bearer of his name is an antient gentlewoman now resident in Philadelphia, who spends her summers at the old Robinson town house (circa 1750) in Water St. (now Washington), Newport. The old plantation-house, after many vicissitudes, is again inhabited by gentry—the present occupant being one of a junior Hazard line, accomplish'd in many arts, and the conductor of a poultry-farm in the true tradition of the gentleman-agriculturist. He is, incidentally, a keen connoisseur of colonial architecture and furniture, and an enthusiastick exhibitor of his venerable abode. On August 4, this century'd manor-house will be the scene of an operatick pageant, writ by a Providence author, depicting the tragical history of poor Hannah Robinson.[4]

Well—having pay'd our respects to the shades of the Robinsons, we travers'd a mile of sandy road to the bluff overlooking the bay, where (above the site of the antient South ferry to Conanicut Island) stands the deserted, white-steepled outline of the old Ferry Church, a landmark for miles around. The South ferry is now abandon'd—traffick depending altogether on the North ferry from Saunderstown.

We now struck inland thro' the wildly beautiful woodland roads of MacSparran's Hill, coming at length to the spectral lich-gate and crumbling stone steps which—tho' visibly back'd only by a tall wall of lush, neglected vines and trees, leads through an almost sinister-looking series of damp-flagg'd, briar-grown courtyards and tunnels of overarching greenery to the lone, decrepit, long-abandon'd "glebe" or rectory of Dr. MacSparran (1727). This decaying gambrel-roof'd cottage was for many years us'd as a granary, so that an ugly *barn-door* replaced the once sightly Georgian portal which the good pastor knew. In the untended garden, however, there still bloom the wild and aristocratick scions of the flowers which Dr. MacSparran planted— together with the mulberry-tree which attests his vain attempt to introduce silk-culture. Good old MacSparran! He was a native of the North of Ireland, and came to Rhode-Island in 1720. Smibert of Newport painted his portrait, so that he still lives for us today as a fat, merry soul with huge curling periwig. He was by all accounts a man of the greatest taste, kindliness, and cultivation.

Having seen the glebe, and taken samples of its flora, we climb'd the hill to Hannah Robinson's Rock and enjoy'd what I confidently believe to be the finest landscape vista in Rhode-Island, if not in all New-England—winding blue river far below, rich green meadows and woodlands, white headland church in the distance, and the remote gleams of the half-glimps'd sea. Great stuff—I don't wonder that poor Hannah wanted to see it again before she dy'd! A pocket telescope which I had with me (a small dollar affair replacing that which was stolen from me in Kingston, N.Y. in 1929) greatly aided to our appreciation of the pleasing prospect.

But the climax of our trip was the wholly unspoil'd colonial village of Little-Rest (now call'd Kingston), previously mention'd in these pages. Tho' the site of Rhode Island State College, this antient hamlet remains virtually the same as when men in knee-breeches and periwigs congregated there for the quarterly assizes. Absence of publick transportation is undoubtedly the secret of its preservation . . . . and the well-kept, centuried houses, the enormous shade-trees, the venerable court building, and the quaint 1746 inn all remain as of yore to fascinate the beholder. Such is the old Narragansett country—and to think I had never seen these gems of antiquity before! On our way back Price obtained a typical Rhode Island shore dinner (clams etc.—ugh!) at the antient fishing village of Pawtucket (six miles south of Providence)—whilst I (of whose loathing for all sea-food you have doubtless long been sensible) got something fit to eat at a Waldorf when we hit town.

Probably I described Price to you last year—slim, dashing chap of thirty-five; dark, with small moustache. West-Pointer, war veteran, amateur Arabic student, Persian rug expert, swordsman, gourmet, and a lot of other things. One of the most likeable and fascinating fellows I have come across in years. He is now going in for commercial writing—as the declining quality of his tales sadly attests.

Only convention news comes from Sonny Belknap, who seems to have had a great time. Lots of old-timers present—Wylie, Boechat,[5] Klei, E. H. Smith, Murphy, Haggerty, Heins, Jim Ferd, Cole, etc. etc. I could give Fate a sock on the beezer for keeping me away from it!

Thine for the glories of other days—
Grandpa Lo.

Notes

1. Glenn Frank (1887–1940) was a president of the University of Wisconsin–Madison and editor-in-chief of *Century Magazines*.
2. Annie Gamwell had broken her ankle 14 June 1933 falling down the stairs.
3. Price chronicled the event in "The Man Who Was Lovecraft" (1949; *LR* 292–94).
4. *The Legend of Hanna Robinson* by George Spink (1873–1936) was produced in 1933 at the Robinson homestead in North Kingston.
5. The amateur journalist Michael Boechat (1863?–1949?).

[66] [AHT]

Home again, and on the old River-bank—
July 17, '34

Hail, Lord of Larnin'!

Your welcome holiday bulletin awaited me as I blew into

the home harbour on the morning of July 10th—and amidst what a profusion of neglected tasks, piled-up periodicals, accumulated epistles, and the like did I find it! Ædepol! I'm not half straightened out even now! You last heard from me, I conceive, in antient San Agustin—where I had a delectable week amidst facades and gables half a century old when the first Pilgrim landed on Plymouth Rock. After that came two days in immortal Charleston, one in Richmond, one in Fredericksburg, two in Washington, and one in Philadelphia. It was devilish hard getting used to northern scenery after my habituation to the lush subtropical landscape—but about the time I got to Fredericksburg, the subtle charm of traditional oaks and elms and maples and grassy pastures had wholly recaptured me. After all, this is the landscape that lurks in our blood—the sort our fathers knew in the Old World, and that most of us have always known in the New. In Richmond I stopped at a cheap hotel only two doors from the site of the Allan mansion where Poe grew up. In Washington I did several things I had never done before—(a) explored the interior of the capitol, (b) ditto the Pan-American Union, (c) visited Rock Creek Park, (d) ascended the Washington Monument (and *what* a view!), and (e) inspected the furnished interior of Arlington, the old Custis-Lee mansion on the Virginia heights across the river. This latter forms the finest and most satisfying restoration of an early XIX century plantation home that I have yet beheld. I explored the *unfurnished* house in 1925 on my trip with Kirk, but this is the first time I ever saw it properly equipped. It was like pulling a tooth to start north for Philadelphia, but the weather was with me—giving me temperatures of ninety-six degrees and ninety-seven degrees right along. In Philadelphia I went my usual antique rounds—including Germantown and the Wissahickon and visited the modest home of Poe (1842–44) at Seventh and Spring Garden Sts., lately open'd as a publick museum. It is a neat brick cottage with a tasteful garden, and is furnished precisely as during Poe's occupancy—with even two or three pieces which he actually owned. In the adjacent building is a well-stocked museum of reliques with the first printing of several tales and poems. The air of the place is highly captivating, and one half expects to see the dark-brow'd bard appearing through a doorway!

In decadent Manhattan I found Sonny Belknap and his parents about to leave for Asbury Park and Ocean Grove, N.J. over the week-end; and at their invitation went along with them—arguing with the child amidst the rhythm of the broad Atlantick's waves. I had not cash enough to stay in N.Y. long, hence looked up no one else save Loveman, with whom I spent a pleasant evening. Fra Samuelus quite overwhelm'd me by making me another gift from his private musaeum—a slim conventionalised bird of carv'd and polish'd horn, with a black lacquer'd surface. It is a typical specimen of the carving of Yankee sailors in the India trade a century ago—made under the influence of Sino-Japanese craftsmanship traditions. It stands as if pois'd for flight thro' gulphs beyond the galaxy—I call it "The Bird of Space", and feel damn lucky to have it. Loveman certainly is a philanthropist!

Well—I came home on the midnight coach July 9–10, and struck the first disconcertingly cool weather since last May. Damn the northern climate! Dawn came near the R.I. line, and it was surely good to behold once more the rolling hills, stone walls, great elms, and white village steeples of my native sod! Then there loom'd up before me a distant prospect of the spires and domes of antient *Providence,* all golden in the morning light. Home! God Save the King!

I found my aunt in splendid health—going everywhere without a cane. And at the boarding-house across the back garden I found something else of infinite interest and grace—something small and coal-black and furry, that is still a bit wobbly on its little legs, although already beginning to be playful. Just a double-handful with great eyes undecided whether to turn green or yellow . . . . Mrs. Spotty Perkins's latest child, born last month and known as Samuel. Yesterday young Mr. Perkins spent a couple of hours at #66, crawling all over Grandpa, chewing the old gentleman's fingers and coat-lapels, and finally dropping off to sleep whilst Grandpa read the *Evening Bulletin.* He hasn't begun to purr yet, but probably will shortly. Grandpa's little niggerman! He looks like a bear cub of paperweight size . . . . I must get a photograph of the microscopick rascal! He's certainly slated to spend a lot of time over at 66! When he grows up he'll doubtless join the Kappa Alpha Tau on the shed roof beyond the side garden.[1] Incidentally—Mrs. Spotty's February kitten—Betsey Perkins, an almost precise black and white duplicate of herself—is getting to be quite as big as mamma, though she still seeks nourishment at the maternal bosom along with little brother Sam.

As usual, I do my reading and writing outdoors whenever possible; and am now on the wooded bluff of the antient Seekonk, which hath chang'd so little since my earliest infancy. A marvellous golden sunset has just settled into twilight, and a lovely crescent moon hangs delicately in the west. But a chill wells up from the river, and the dusk makes this pen-steering more and more uncertain. I must close this instalment, pack my stationery for a Waldorf-Lunch-and-homeward stroll, and resume later with the aid of the midnight juice.

And so it goes. Blessings on thee!
       Yr obt grandsire—Lo.

Notes

1. Because 66 College Street was on Brown University's fraternity row, HPL devised the Greek name K.A.T. (standing for *Kompsōn Ailurōn Taxis,* or "band of elegant [or well-dressed] cats") for the array of cats at the neighboring boarding house.

[67]   [AHT]

Theobald Grange—
July 29, 1934

Ave, Imperator of Intellectual Inculcation!

Now about this Beke–Bridges business—damn it, boy, but what a stir you raise!¹ D'ya know, I've been raking over those stanzas for about an hour trying to see what the least illogical way of doping them out is ..... since I assume that a complete scansion is what you're asking for under the name of a "form appraisal". I've totally forgotten what I did for "Doorways" five years ago, so any uniformity with past performances will be strictly accidental. But god, what a job! Ya see the fact is, that all these damn technical terms—feet, accents, metre, and what the hell—are simply academick devices to account for something already existing; something so vague, flexible, and irregular that it can never be captured in exact rules and names. As a result, schoolbook precepts and definitions are always incomplete, ambiguous, varied, and even conflicting. The irregular lines of a guy like old Bridges—that is, a good part of 'em—*can be scanned in more than one way* according to how one interprets the foot-boundaries. Take that hellion near the beginning and look at the two interpretations you can get:

— ˘   ˘ —   ˘ —   ˘   ˘ —   ˘ —   ˘ —

Leaning / across / the bo/som of / the ur/gent west   (Alexandrine)
Trochee   Pyrrhick

— ˘   ˘ —   ˘ —   ˘   ˘ —   ˘   —

Leaning / across / the bosom / of the ur/gent west   (Pentameter)
Trochee   Amphibrach   Anapaest

I am choosing the latter interpretation because of the obviously pentametrical nature of the whole poem. As for the downright contradictions in definition—take the matter of poetick feet. The modern smart alecs, who despise the honest syllable-counting of my good old eighteenth century, tell you that every foot must have a long or accented syllable. Now in direct contradiction to that we have the good old Pyrrick (˘ ˘) and the Tribrach (˘ ˘ ˘) of standard rhetorick; each a fully-accredited "foot" and employ'd as such by the best authors. As for the *spondee*, about which you enquire, you're right in saying that the double accent does *not* properly count as a separate "beat" or whatever they measure metre by. Nor do I think that Bobby B. has attempted to use it so—you'll see presently how I interpret the old coot's apparently defective lines. What has happened is not that any single foot is taken as two feet, but that in certain cases whole "feet" or "beats" are *dropped altogether*. This sort of thing is sometimes done—look at Pope's ᵕ   —   ᵕ   —   ᵕ — ᵕ — ᵕ —

        Which Jews / might kiss, / and in /fidels adore   (four beats)[2]

or Shakespeare's

        — ᵕ   ᵕ —   — ᵕ   —   ᵕ

        Than the / soft myr/tle. / But more / proud man[3]   (four beats)
        Trochee

This latter case is more extreme than the former, since not only a beat but a syllable is missing. If we accept the older and more traditional definitions allowing "feet" without "beats", the Pope line is not defective, since the pyrrhick brings the number of feet up to five. Shakespeare's line, however, has a foot that is clearly defective by any definition—a single short syllable (-tle).

                                      ᵕ   — ᵕ

Or if we interpret it another way and call "soft myr-tle" a single amphibrach, we can say that the foot is simply rubbed out—taken for a ride. Or I suppose you could cook up an altogether different interpretation also coming short a foot, or rather part of one:

        ᵕ   ᵕ   —   —   ᵕ   ᵕ   —   ᵕ   —

        Than the / soft myr/tle. / But more / proud man

The first interpretation seems to be the commonest one. Anyhow, a heavy accent or beat is missing. What is theatrically left in exchange, of course, is the same kind of a lull that you constantly find in irregular metres where unaccented or short syllables are suppressed. The only difference is that poets don't so often kill an accented syllable in exchange for such a lull—or "compensating pause", as I believe they call it. Occasionally the reality of the omission depends on a fine point of classification—as to whether a given syllable can or can't be counted as accented . But even if they don't do it often, they do it sometimes—no matter what certain textbooks may say as a rough generality..... for here is another fruitful source of ambiguity, since accent and lack of accent have a twilight zone of secondary or subsidiary accenting betwixt them. (Some might call that Pope line regular in beat by counting the *secondary* accent of *"in-fi-del'"* and making the Pyrrick an iambus.) In other cases, the omission is absolutely conclusive according to *any* possible interpretation ... thus the above-cited Shakespeare line. It is well to cut loose from cut-and-dried pedantry and misleading dogmatism and accept the liberal statement of good old Gummere (*Handbook of Poetics*, 1885) which I shall herewith quote:

> "When we say that a verse has five accents, we mean that the metrical scheme calls for five stress-syllables; but we do not expect the concrete verse to show five strictly equal stresses. We do demand, however, that the concrete verse shall give us the *general effect* of five stress-syllables; shall make us feel the uniform metrical scheme underlying the rhythm."

It is elsewhere pointed out that Chaucer is by no means regular in his number of beats and stresses per line. Well—I'll tell the cockeyed world that Bob Bridges ain't, either! Of course, I don't know what the old buzzard's theory was. As I tell you, it's anybody's guess how to interpret easy-going lines of that sort. The technical rules and names are merely afterthoughts devised to explain preëxisting realities of composition, so that it's no wonder they're ambiguous and contradictory half the time. Then again, they were concocted in the first place for a kind of verse—Graeco-Roman quantitative stuff—wholly alien to our own; so that the use of those pompous laws and terms in dealing with English poetry is largely a matter of inept substitution to start with. For all I know, Bobby *may* have considered himself as very bold counting both beats of a spondee in metre now and then—he being dead, I can't very well ask him. All I can say is that you don't *have* to interpret his lines that way if you don't want to. He evidently wrote largely by ear to please a sensitive aesthetick sense, so that it would take quite a bit of figuring to reduce his subtle melody to visible rules and diagrams. Therefore when I try to dope out my idea of the technical scansion, don't for Pete's sake fancy I'm presenting anything absolute or conclusive. I'm merely giving one of many interpretations which small-time dryasdusts could cook up. But you're welcome to the suggestions—look closely at the way I try to explain the lines which have especially puzzled you.

"The Passer-By",[4] [*sic*] though unmistakably iambick as a whole, represents an extreme form of metrical flexibility and irregularity. The proportion of such substituted feet as anapaests, spondees, amphibrachs, trochees, tribrachs, and Pyrrhicks is very high, so that a careless reading will result in much confusion. A skilful reader, however, will find the undercurrent of symmetry very strong; and will appreciate the vivid variety of a melody which enhances greatly the pictorial and imaginative charm of the substance. The scanned text follows:

Whither, / O spleen / did ship, / thy white / sails crowd/ing,
Trochee   Spondee   Spondee

Leaning / across / the bosom / of the urg/ent west,
Trochee   Amphibrach   Anapaest

That fear / est nor[1] / sea ris/ing[,] nor[1] / sky cloud/ing,
   Pyrrhick Spondee   Pyrrick   Spondee

Whither / away, / fair ro/ver, and what / thy quest?
                          Anapaest

Ah! soon, / when Win/ter has all / our vales / opprest,
Spondee   Anapaest

```
         ᵕ    —    ᵕ   —     ᵕ    —     ᵕ   ᵕ    —  ᵕ
```
When skies / are cold / and mis/ty, and hail / is hurling,
                              Anapaest

```
  —   ᵕ      —    —    —     ᵕ     —   ᵕ    —    ᵕ
```
Wilt thou / glide on / the blue / Pacif/ick[,] or rest
Trochee   Spondee   Anapaest

```
 ᵕ  ᵕ   —    ᵕ    —   ᵕ  ᵕ   —    ᵕ     —    ᵕ    —
```
In a sum/mer ha/ven asleep, / thy white / sails furl/ing.
Anapaest   Anapaest   Spondee

```
  —    ᵕ    ᵕ    —   ᵕ   ᵕ   —   ᵕ    —    ᵕ  —
```
I, there / before thee, / in the coun/try that well / thou know/est.
Spondee Amphibrach Anapaest   Anapaest

```
 ᵕ   —    ᵕ    —   ᵕ   ᵕ   —  ᵕ      —    ᵕ
```
I watch / thee en/ter unerr/ingly where / thou go/est,
                Anapaest Anapaest

```
  —   ᵕ   —   ᵕ    ᵕ     —     ᵕ     —    —
```
And an/chor, queen / of the* / strange shipp/ing there,
                  Pyrrick   Spondee

```
  —   ᵕ    ᵕ   —    ᵕ    —      ᵕ    —   —
```
Thy sails / for awn/ings spread, / thy / masts / bare.†

```
 ᵕ   ᵕ    —   ᵕ   ᵕ   —    ᵕ  ᵕ   —   ᵕ   —
```
Nor is aught / from the foam/ing reef / to the snow/capt, grandest
  Anapaest   Anapaest   Anapaest

```
    —     ᵕ   ᵕ   —    ᵕ    ᵕ  ᵕ      ᵕ  —
```
. . . . Peak,‡ / that is o/ver the feath/ery palms / more fair
             Anapaest   Anapaest   Anapaest

```
 ᵕ    —   ᵕ   ᵕ  —   ᵕ    ᵕ   ᵕ  —   ᵕ  —  ᵕ
```
Than thou, / so up/right[,] so state/ly, and still / thou stand/est.
             Anapaest   Anapaest

```
  ᵕ   —    —     —    ᵕ   —    ᵕ    —   ᵕ
```
And yet, / O splen/did ship, / unhail'd / and name/less,
        Spondee

*Possible compensation pause—if the theory of five beats must be sustain'd. Each of these Pyrricks *might* have been an anapaest.

†Two possible interpretations. We may say that a stressed syllable has been suppressed after the unstressed *thy*, thus wrecking an iambus, and making *masts bare* a spondaick foot; or we may group *masts* with *thy* in a perfect iambus, putting *bare* in a separate foot—presumably with the unaccented syllable suppressed.

‡We may consider *peak* as the stress'd member of an iambus whose unstress'd member hath been suppress'd.

⏑   —   ⏑   ⏑   —   ⏑   ⏑   —   ⏑   ⏑   —
I know not / if[,] aim/ing a fan / cy, I right/ly divine
Amphibrach   Spondee   Anapaest   Anapaest

⏑   ⏑   ⏑   ⏑   —   ⏑   —   ⏑   ⏑   —   —
⁴That thou hast / a pur/pose joy/ful[,] a cour/age blame/less,
    Tribrach*   Anapaest

⏑   —   ⏑   —   ⏑   ⏑   —   ⏑   —
Thy port / assur'd / in a hap/pier land / than mine.
                 Anapaest   Anapaest

⏑   ⏑   —   ⏑   ⏑   —   ⏑   ⏑   —   ⏑   ⏑   —
But for all / I have giv/en thee, beau/ty enough / is thine,
Anapaest   Anapaest   Anapaest   Anapaest

⏑   —   ⏑   —   ⏑   ⏑   —   ⏑   —
As thou,† / aslant / with trim tack/le and shroud/ing,
                 Anapaest‡   Anapaest

—   ⏑   —   —   ⏑   ⏑   —   —
From the / proud nos/tril curve / of a§ / prow's line
Trochee   Spondee   Pyrrick   Spondee

⏑   ⏑   —   ⏑   ⏑   —   —   —   —   —
In the off/ing scat/terest foam, / thy white / sails crowd/ing.
Anapaest   Anapaest   Spondee

* Those who refuse to admit feet without stress'd syllables may consider a beat as here suppress'd.

† We may here consider an entire foot, with its accented syllable, to have been omitted, or replaced with a "compensation pause".

‡ A different scansion can be given by regarding *aslant with* as an amphibrach, and having *trim tack* . . . constitute a spondaick foot.

§ We may assume, if theory forbids the acceptance of a Pyrrhick as a foot, that a stress'd syllable has here been suppress'd.

Is this a juicy item for "Doorways"? I'll say it is! And if it ain't *final* in its way, I'll go back to primary school! Boy! I need air! I guess I'll go and read a horror-story and return to my epistolation in the evening!

    I note the note from Gustavus Osculus—whose period of activity would appear to be just prior to my amateur advent in 1914—and the extremely interesting extract from *Time*. Who the author of the latter could be, I'm hang'd if I know. Someone fairly in touch with amateurdom, I fancy, yet not close enough to get Tryout's age (he'll be eighty-two on Oct. 24) or Moi-toret's middle initial or the period of the *Pippin* and *Odd One*⁵ right. In the case of good old Smiffkins there was an interesting sequel. A fortnight ago 408 Groveland received a long-distance telephone call from New York, and somebody asked Smithy's daughter all about him—whether he published *Tryout,* how old he was, and so on. Then a week later a reporter from the *N.Y. Tribune* called and asked for an interview—anticipating a feature writeup in the magazine section! He had seen the *Time* article, with its piquant references to the old boy, and thought he had a rich field for quaint exploitation. But he didn't know his Smiffkins! Honest Tryout is no peasant clown, to sell his picture for a shilling and prattle artless quaintness for the amusement of city slickers. Nothing doing! Smithy told the fellow that he didn't care for publicity—that he simply printed his paper for personal pleasure, and was not ambitious to be featured as a "character". So the vanquish'd news-hound walked on into the night, and slunk back to Manhattan with a better idea of the dignity of a civilised Novanglian. Good for the old fawn of the groves! However, I'm glad that somebody's putting amateurdom on the map. The *National* is getting famous in its old age—there was a picture of young Babcock in the rotogravure section of the *Providence Sunday Journal!* Glad you accepted the important "advisory" post along with Grandpa Theobald. I fancy our duties will be mainly to look wise and send out cerebral waves of encouragement to young Master Adams.[6] Glad you had some old-time material to send the kid, and hope you'll be able to dig up some more—in or out of gaols. Incidentally, convicts in amateurdom aren't new. Look back in the *U.A.'s* for 1915 and 1916 and you'll find in the Ohio section of the membership list the name of *William Harris, No. 41323, State Penitentiary.* He was a find of Melvin Ryder[7] (later prominent in doughboy journalism in France), who was in turn a find of some of those damn'd Woodbees. I was never in touch with him, and don't recall anything he ever wrote; but at least he was a genuine representative of amateurdom in the "big house". At the time I wished that many other Ohio amateurs could share his fate . . . . . but instead of going to gaol they've merely gone to oblivion. I doubt whether #41323 had the unmistakable genius possessed by Faville's protege. You really ought to recruit that bird if he's still accessible—outside or inside stone walls. And Faville may be able to scare up some more gifted yeggs and gunmen . . . . . go to it, boys! No—I never saw "Contrasts" in the *Magazine World.* The comic-contrast bit by the same author has a good image or two near the start, but is hardly what I'd call major poetry. Yes—Parker still publishes *L'Alouette* as a professional magazine of high standards. It comes out irregularly, and a subscription is for a certain number of issues, not a certain span of time. He also publishes many brochures for amateur, semi-amateur, and not-so-amateur bards—and does it tastefully and well. I'd recommend him to you as a typographer if Saccharissus weren't on the docket. Did I tell you, by the way, that Snowball, our coal-black furry friend of '23, was still going strong when last I called on Parker a couple of years ago? Whether he remembered Grandpa I don't know—but he still had a cordial purr for the old gentleman! You certainly had quite a time at the banquet, and I'm sorry you had to flee the scene so soon. The glimpse of Father Davis, or whatever he calls himself, must have been interesting. Sink me if I know anything about his son[8]—legitimate, natural, adopted, step, or what the hell! Possibly he was being modernistically candid about what most priests call their "nephews"—though Pete knows he might well have sandwiched a wedding or two into a career as varied as his! Sorry to hear that old P. J. is piling up such a rep. Mortonius mentioned something of the sort, but I fancied it was exaggerated. He has been in trying straits, and borrowed a fiver (he asked for ten) of me a couple of years ago, but has never shown any inclination to disavow his indebtedness. A card from him in Chicago, postmarked July 5, led me to fancy he had sampled the convention. The Brodie–Hyde anecdote was wholly new to me—and quite typical of the Shillalabite! What I heard at the time, I imagine, was just the shocked reaction—not the shocker itself.

   Hoping the Robertopontick[9] scansion ain't too raw—
    Yrs for the Pierian Millennium—
     Grandpa Lo.

Notes

1. Presumably a discussion by B. K. Hart of the poetry of Robert Bridges. Bridges (1844–1930) was Britain's poet laureate from 1913 to 1930.
2. Alexander Pope, *The Rape of the Lock* (1714), 2.8. Clearly there are *five* beats.
3. Shakespeare, *Measure for Measure* 2.2.117.
4. "A Passer-By," in *Poetical Works of Robert Bridges* (London: Oxford University Press, 1912), 244. HPL, or AHT, omits line 10: "Already arrived am inhaling the odorous air:" Bridges himself indicates a stress on *thou* in l. 7. The ellipses in l. 15 are HPL's.
5. A publication of Frank A[ustin] Kendall (1884–1913) of Prairie du Sac, WI. Kendall was Official Editor of the NAPA in 1908, and its 47th president. He also published the *Torpedo* and the *Booster*.
6. Presumably John D. Adams (see Glossary).
7. Melvin Ryder (1893?–1979) was sent to France as a member of the staff of *Stars and Stripes*. He later became the founder and chairman of the board of the Army Times Publishing Co.
8. Alexander Voigt Davis, briefly in amateur journalism after his father's death (1938). Whether natural or adoptive son of Rev. Frank Graeme Davis is unknown. He returned with Davis from Davis's sojourn in European sanataria in 1932.
9. Pertaining to the poet Robert Bridges (*pons* is Latin for "bridge").

[68] [ALS; AHT]

              Antient Nantucket
              —Sept^r· 2, 1934

Hail, Spicus Sapientium:—[1]

   If everything has been duly forwarded at your end,

you are already aware of the final 1934 jaunt on whose tail end I now am. Last week with Cole & Cook in Boston—& now antient Nantucket, climax of all—an elder world brooding unchang'd since the days of the Yankee whalers! I simply haven't words to convey the ineffable fascination of this place—there is absolutely nothing else like it. Other towns have old houses—but Nantucket has nothing else but! And all the *accessories*—cobblestones, silver doorplates, hitching-posts, horse-blocks, &c. &c. The percentage of colonial & early-republic houses undoubtedly runs higher than in any other place in America—a combined result of insular isolation, commercial decline, & appreciative preservation & restoration by summer visitors. It is Salem & Marblehead intensified—the general suggestion being perhaps more of Salem than of Marblehead. Though smaller than Salem, it was nevertheless a great port & the abode of much wealth & culture—thus being sumptuous & regular in its main parts, rather than haphazard in the Marblehead fashion. I've done quite a bit of browsing as to its history & architecture & traditions at the local Athenaeum (now a publick library)—& amusingly enough, the best book on old Nantucket life is by a resident of *Providence* about whom I have always known—Joseph Farnham, who was born & educated in Nantucket. I've also bought two small Nantucket books by a local historian—one of the Nantucket Macys. The great names on this island are Macy, Folger, Coffin, Hussey, Gardner, & Starbuck. Dr. Franklin's mother was a Nantucket Folger. All these families still flourish on their native soil. During the unfortunate rebellion of 1775–83 Nantucket was neutral ground, & many residents were loyal to our rightful Sovereign. Admiral Sir Isaac Coffin, Bart., of His Majesty's navy, who in 1826 endow'd a school in the town, was a scion of the antient Nantucket line. The island—like my own Colony of R.I.—was peopled by Massachusetts men fleeing from the bigotry of the Bay . . . . in this case families fined for the "crime" of harbouring distress'd Quakers during a storm. From its settlement in 1660 till 1692 Nantucket was part of the Province of New-York, but since 1692 it has belong'd to Massachusetts. Nantucket folk, like other islanders, have distinctive ways & idioms of their own; but because of their excellent academies & aristocratick social order they never became odd or quaint characters like the Marbleheaders. Here again we find the *Salem* resemblance very strong . . . . though their opposition to bigotry links them more with Rhode-Island. Of the mainland cities, New Bedford & Providence are probably most esteem'd by Nantucketers. I find the Providence Journal on sale here. It is really almost comical to reflect that this utterly colonial world has existed virtually under my nose (90 miles—a 6-hour trip—from Providence) all my life without my ever seeing it before—but such are the ironies of existence! Close tho' it is to my doorstep, Nantucket *seems* in many ways as remote as Charleston or Quebec. Its architecture, tho' derived from that of the Merrimack Valley, has many features all its own—which I am studying in detail. Generally, the houses follow styles long obsolete on the mainland. Thus the old 17th century "salt-box" type, with a roof almost reaching the ground in the rear, was quite dominant in Nantucket till after 1750. As late as 1790 old Richard Macy protested when his son Job built a regular two-story house—vowing that unless it were of the old style he would never enter it. He never did! (I've seen the house in question.) The Georgian style continued to rule long after architecture had all gone to seed on the mainland—three of the finest specimens (which you'd swear dated from about 1810) being as late as *1837*. The oldest surviving house is of 1686 (vide enc.), & has been finely restored. I've been all over it—& over all the other houses which are open as museums. I've also explored the 1746 windmill & its mechanism—the first I ever studied at close range, though a couple survive in R.I. The hotel I'm stopping at—The Overlook in Step-Lane, on Beacon-Hill over-against the North Church—is obviously of ancient date; with small-paned windows, wide-floor-boards, [*sic*] & 6-panel doors. Monday night I observed Saturn through the 5″ refractor at the Maria Mitchell Observatory in Gaol-Lane—securing a fine view of the planet & its ring system. This observatory adjoins the birthplace of the eminent female astronomer Maria Mitchell, whose father, W$^{m.}$ Mitchell, Esq., a gentleman of Nantucket, was an amateur of no mean attainments & the owner of a telescope still shewn in the observatory. Mifs Mitchell, as is well known, was a professor of astronomy at Vassar College.

 The only flaw in my present sojourn is the cold, from which I have suffer'd considerably. This tavern is not heated, & I have to drape a blanket around myself (thereby getting a cursed lot of lint on my 1928 best store clothes!) in order to keep warm enough to write. It is not now, however, as bad as day before yesterday. In the daytime I do most of my writing on benches in antient Main St. or just outside the town on the top of Windmill Hill.

 One of the greatest kicks of the visit is that of *hiring a bicycle*—a common Nantucket custom. I had not been astride a wheel for *19 years* when I first took one t'other day, & was in doubt whether I could ride with old-time ease—but I quickly found that time had made no difference. I simply got on & rode off as though I had put my old Corp Bros.[2] bike in the cellar of 598 only the night before. Nothing was unfamiliar—the sense of balance & adjustment was as in 1913 & before. I have often said that the years slip by so fast that events of 10, 20, & 30 years ago are simply as of yesterday. Thus with the bicycle. I wish to gawd it weren't conspicuous for a man of my years to ride one in Providence! It put new life into me to hop on & spin off—all the atmosphere of youth was restored . . . it became 1910 . . . 1905 . . . . 1900 . . . . And what a glorious spin I had*! All around the outskirts of the town &

---

*I think I made 25 or 30 m. per hr. on one stretch when the wind was with me. I passed two motors!

the neighbouring countryside in the good old way. (It was the bicycle which made me so closely familiar with the New England countryside & its typical villages in youth.) I was not sensible of any fatigue or after-effects—for the truth is that I am vastly stronger today than when I spent so much time awheel. The sense of rejuvenation does not wear off—at this moment I can scarcely believe (in the absence of a mirror) that the head bending over this sheet is an aging & greying one. It seems about '07 or '08 . . . . . as if I would be going back to Hope St. High School next week! Hell, but I wish I could adopt the bike again as a regular pastime! I drew a very good one at the livery-stable—an easy-running specimen with a coaster-brake. I see that nowadays they all have *mud-guards* . . . in my time such things existed only on girls' wheels. The bike I'm now riding would have stamped me as a damn sissy in good old '04! How Chet & Harold Munroe & Ken Tanner & Percival Miller & Perry Locke & Ronald Upham & Stuart Coleman & Sidney Sherman & all the rest would have jeered![3] Ah, me—the old days! Well, anyhow, Grandpa can still keep balanced & moving on the inseparable steed of his youth!

Only one more full day in Nantucket. If I can spare the 70¢ for a couple of hours, I think I'll take a bike trip to antient Siasconset on t'other side of the island—which I briefly explored last Monday as part of a rubberneck jaunt. Home late Septr. 3—& the next day my aunt starts off for a fortnight in Ogunquit, Maine—fancy going to *Maine* at *this* time of year! I hope we shan't have an early autumn—some years I've been able to take enjoyable walks way up till November. But hell, I wish I could take to cycling again! Modern traffick—fairly representatively heavy in Nantucket because of the summer people with cars—doesn't seem to bother me at all—I dodge & fit in with *many* vehicles just as I used to do with a *few* vehicles. It is amusing, after years of pedestrianism, to have to pay attention to 1-way streets. They were a rare innovation in my day.[4]

Well, well, well—how the old man rambles! The electrick light in this hotel room is so dim and lousy that visions of 1904 become more real than the objective scene around me! But let me proceed to congratulate you on your own outing, the account of which interested me vastly. Your Madisonian pastimes seem to have been piquant and varied—and the reunions with A. H. S. figures must help to bring back old days. I'm on the lookout myself for that cinema you saw—"Treasure Island"[5]—since from all accounts it's just my eighteenth century sort of thing. A friend whets my interest by telling me that one of the characters (Dr. Livesey) looks and talks and acts *exactly like me*.[6] Poor devil! Probably my informant exaggerates, however. The only cinemas in the last two years that have produced any impression on me are "Cavalcade" and "Berkeley Square"[7]—but then, I scarce ever go save when somebody like my grandson Belknap drags me.

Concerning Word Hunts—bless my soul, Son, but what an institution you've founded! The present condens'd form is admirable from every point of view, and you certainly have the mechanical end worked out to perfection. I can see that your hectograph system is a bit different from mine in the old days. I simply wrote my copy with hectograph ink and placed it face down on a tray of the gelatine for a few minutes. Then I took it up, leaving a negative impression from which copies could be pulled by contact and pressure. I forget whether the pad or tray had to be heated—or moistened—or not. When the copies were taken, the pad was washed blank—whereupon (after drying) another page could be reproduced in the same way. Of course, the gelatine got thin and vanished pretty soon—and then I'd exchange the empty tray for a full one for fifty cents. That was the way back in good old '04—and perhaps these simple models are still made and used for some purposes. Well—anyhow, I hope you have good luck with the marketing. Your circular seems to me the acme of effective persuasiveness, and the new instruction wrapper is the last word in snappy efficiency. Here's hoping the jack pours in—and that the right kind of publisher will become interested. I presume poor old Saccharissus couldn't be of much use in his present fiscal state.

But damn the delays in *Doorways!* Here I get all worked up and set to spring this life-saver on the Kuntzies and their congeners—when flop! Another time-stretch falls across the path. However—I'm a patient old cuss! Tough luck, by the way, that you didn't freeze to that job with the Waukeshau [*sic*] dame which is now netting her the heavy sestertii!

Well—behave!
                                                                    Grandpa Lo.

Notes

1. *Spicus* means "point" (as in the point of a spear). Hence, *spicus sapientium* would roughly mean "the sharpest of the wise."
2. Corp Brothers is a Providence company (still in operation). It was founded in 1893 as a machine tool shop and later manufactured bicycles for a short time.
3. HPL refers to his boyhood friends Chester and Harold Munroe (see Glossary), Kenneth [James] Tanner (1890–1979), Ronald Kingsley Upham (1892–1968), Stuart Tiepke Coleman (1892–1969), and others.
4. ALS ends at this point (end of sheet II). Balance of text derived from AHT.
5. *Treasure Island* (MGM, 1934), directed by Victor Fleming; starring Wallace Beery, Jackie Cooper, Lionel Barrymore, and Otto Kruger. Based on the novel by Robert Louis Stevenson.
6. The actor who played the role of Dr. Livesey was Otto Kruger (1885–1974). His resemblance to HPL is not especially strong.
7. *Cavalcade* (Fox Film Corp., 1933), directed by Frank Lloyd; starring Diana Wynyard, Clive Brook, and Una O'Connor. *Berkeley Square* (Fox Film Corp., 1933), directed by Frank Lloyd; starring Leslie Howard, Heather Angel, and Valerie Taylor. Based on the play by John L. Balderston. HPL saw the latter four times, and it clearly helped to inspire his "The Shadow out of Time."

[69]   [ALS, JHL]

                                    Theobald Manor—
                                       Thanksgiving Day
                                    [29 November 1934]

Hail, Mighty Mocrates!
             I found the welcome semiannual upon my return from that Boston trip whereof the card from Culinarius & me hath already appris'd you. As trips go, this was a very modest one—for the goddam cold kept me from anything requiring outdoor tramping. We didn't get to see Parker, either—for after the cards were mailed Cook decided he was too shaky to attempt the trip. He is in rather bad shape this autumn, but I hope a few weeks at his sister's in Sunapee will set him up in good style. Cole was the same pleasing host as always—& we likewise saw Lynch, whose ego hath suffer'd no impairment with the years.

The old papers from Mrs. Miniter's family proved tremendously impressive—bringing the past right under our noses, so to speak. I have them here now, awaiting the discovery of a blood-heir capable of appreciating them. Meanwhile the plans for a memorial brochure go forward. I suppose you received Tryout's crude attempt at such.[1] Cook's will be infinitely more ambitious—containing articles by all the prominent old-timers & perhaps attaining the proportions of an actual book. An article from you is very ardently desired—its nature & length to be left entirely to your inclination & judgment. There is no space limit—&, very fortunately, no time limit. Forms [?] are not likely to be closed in a year.

About the chairmanship of the N.A.P.A. Critical Bureau—including the handling of verse criticism—I was rather afraid that you'd turn down my plea, since Ye Ed keeps calling for copy. I told the kids—Babcock & Bradley—that I'd keep on functioning (& also keep the rest of the old bureau functioning) until they found another easy mark to saddle the job on. Evidently they ain't found such—so Grandpa & Uncle Ed & little Spink are plodding along as in 1933-4, & will probably have to finish out the year. Thanks for the offer to criticise a bunch of pomes—I may take you up on that for the March or June N.A. It would be a great idea to have some typical specimens dissected & explained in the good old Mocratick way—object lessons not only for the authors but for kindred bardlets as well.

Sure, I'm the guy what switched the Bishop job[2] your way—didn' I tell ya I was agonna? But whether ya have me to thank or have me to curse, only time will tell. Remember that I warned ya to look sharp for your pay. The old gal is honest, & will come across in the end; but so far as promptness goes, the proverbial snail is a streamlined flyer in comparison. Make her cough up a good bit before you deliver the job. Hope you like the way the opening threads of the novel are woven together—blending the fortunes of Our Hero with those of the Ross or Wellington or whatever-it-is clan—because the plan is yore Gran'paw's. Ye authoress was all foundering around in vacuo, with dates hashed up so badly that a 1725 colonist had grandchildren living today, whilst poor li'l Alan took 11 years to become 9 years old! You may recognise a few of the old man's touches here & there. It was a hell of a job, & I socked the dame 15 bucks—which I ain't seen yet. Gord 'elp us all! And now old de Castro is trying to saddle a purely speculative job on me—a sort of philosophick tome which he vows will make us both rich & famous—despite my inability to assume any heavy task of doubtful remunerativeness. I shall let him down easy—reading the text & giving him some free corrections in stylistic externals—for the old reprobate is in a bad way .... 74, destitute, half-blind, & with a wife gravely ill of tuberculosis. You must recall who this bird is—the old coot who collaborated with Ambrose Bierce in the 1880's, & who wrote a charlatanic biography of him (revision of which I turned down) in 1928. I did several jobs for him between 1927 & 1930, & Sonny Belknap wrote the preface for his Bierce book. A learned cuss, but a born egotist & faker. Honest in financial matters, but willing to do anything for a sensation.

Well—so another old-time Appletonian has turned up? I recall seeing the name of Evelyn van Stratam [?] in *The Pippin,* though I believe she dropped out of amateurdom just before I got in touch with your infant train. I recall, too, your mention of "Grapes of Eschol"[3]—though I wouldn't say whether I read it or not. Always glad to hear of old-time children turning out well—which reminds me that Little Alfie's pa's estate is getting settled at last, so that Master Consul Hasting may get 2000 bucks a year from a trust fund.[4] Hot stuff! He's fixing up the old home (726 E. College Ave.—formerly numbered 536 College Ave) in good style, & his ma is turning out the boarders as fast as she can—& his wife is giving up her job in Chi. He'll probably chuck his own Lawrence job & spend some more time musicalising in Paris before long, the lucky young divvle!

I learn of the prospective near-Kleicomolo with considerable interest, & have informed Br'er Adams that I'll try my hand at participation if the requirements aren't too exacting for an old geezer. He dropped me a card about it, saying that you'd furnish particulars. All that you say sounds extremely sensible & promising, & I fancy the epistle itself—when it reaches me—will still further explain itself. Good idea having duplicates—though that'll make it necessary to be damn careful about what one writes. I wonder if the bull I'm throwing today will sound as callow & asinine to me 20 years from now (if I hang on that long) as the crap I pulled in the Kleicomolo Æra sounds to me today? Probably it will—for stuff of mine as late as '27 or '28 sounds sappy to my elderly taste of the present. It takes years to make a realistick man of sense if he ain't quick at l'arnin'—& I'll probably be dead of old age before I'm thoroughly sensible & hard-boiled! Yes—I hope young Adams follows your recommendations as closely as possible .... & say! if you wanna do that kid a real kindness, back me up in my efforts to jolt him out of the silly affectation whereby he signs his alleged pomes *"Jon" Adams*. He thinks "Jon" is more classy & distingué than just plain *John* . . . . whereupon Grandpa snorts with the disgust of a plain old Georgian at such neo-Victorian prettifying! I suppose the young squirt got that "Jon" out of Galsworthy, or from the second Lindbergh infant. Gad's blood, but there were no such foolish goings-on when I was young! In those days a man was content to use the honest name his parents gave him!

I have perus'd your enclosures with the most extream pleasure, & must repeat those expressions of admiration which I have formerly made, concerning your ability to excite interest in scholastick matters thro' novel & agreeable modes of presentation. The epistles to disabled veterans, & the many individual magazines, are both devices of the greatest brilliancy; whilst the plan of compelling the students to perform difficult & potentially embarrassing acts (acts which I myself dread with all the shrinking of a born hermit) is little short of a stroke of genius! Do not again tell me, Sir, that I exaggerate when describing the distinguish'd & inexhaustibly versatile endowments which you bring to bear upon your paedagogical labours!

Regarding literary contributions to the various magazines of your infant charges—bless me, but I don't know whether I'll have time to write anything fresh! I am having to curtail on extras, for the number of obligations surrounding me wou'd otherwise become all-ingulphing. Would *old* material do? For example, I could send my 1921 elegy on Tryout's cat[5] to the young editor who wants something on pets, whilst any of the Fungi from Yuggoth could go to the two who desire respectively "any poem suitable for a magazine of literary & general interest" & "poem on any suitable topick for poetry". Or possibly my themes & efforts lack suitability! The one bit of *new* writing which tempts me is that which I'd produce in response to the request for something on *Roman architecture*.[6] There's a theme I'm really keen about, tho' I've never written on it. But I doubt whether I'll have much time before mid-December. Anyhow, let me know whether old & published stuff can be accepted. If so, I'll surely be able to dig up something . . . . . tho' I *will not* do any great amount of *typing*. Not that! God, not that!

I trust you duly receiv'd the Bekes sent in mid-October. Here's another batch—under separate cover—& with them I am enclosing an issue of a little magazine—dedicated to the Old Gent—which may be of some slight interest.[7] Needn't return it.

Well—I guess it's time to go across to the boarding house & gorge on white meat & mince pie! Blessings—Grandpa Lo

Notes

1. *In Memory of Edith May Miniter: A Coworker in Amateur Journalism—1884–1934* (Haverhill, MA: C. W. Smith, August 1934). A special issue of Smith's *Tryout*. It contained HPL's poem on Miniter.

2. Presumably a revision job for HPL's client Zealia Brown Reed Bishop (1897–1968), for whom he revised several weird stories as well as romantic and historical stories. The item discussed here appears to be one of the latter.

3. Emily Huntington Miller (1833–1913), "The Grapes of Eshcol," *Century Magazine* 85, No. 1 (November 1912): 94.

4. Galpin's wealthy banker father, who died in May 1924, had left him only $300 in his will. See Galpin, "Portrait of a Father," *Wisconsin Magazine of History* 63, No. 4 (Summer 1980): 276.

5. "Sir Thomas Tryout."

6. "A Living Heritage: Roman Architecture in Today's America."

7. HPL was the dedicatee of the October 1935 issue of the *Fantasy Fan*.

[70]   [AHT]

Art Antique
Time of the Lupercalia
[15 February 1935?]

Rever'd Sage:—

Well, well—the welcome semiannualette blew in only a day after my despatch of an epistle to Mocratulus Maior¹ . . . . . inviting him to explore the Georgian antiquities of these parts, and containing a pair of crude charts to guide the indomitable Skippy over the intervening space and through the century'd labyrinths that lead to the precipice-crowning Theobald citadel! It surely was a pleasant surprise to learn yesterday of Robertulus's presence in venerable Novanglia. Good boy—I hope he stays! He spoke of a wish to see what Grandpa looked like after all these years, and I hastened to furnish all possible information about travel conditions. I certainly hope he gets up this way early and often—and as I told him, he ought to arrange to get to antient Bostonium some time and let me reintroduce him to Cole and the Myers household—and display to him once more the winding lanes and huddled gambrel roofs of Marblehead. I'll bet he wouldn't squat down on a stone wall and refuse to go any farther, as a gang of bimbos once did . . . . . long, long ago! He doesn't recall Grandpa very distinctly, even tho' he rode on the Old Gentleman's knee from the South Station to the Myers dump in Cambridge on that far-distant August day. Well—it's just as well; since if he *did* remember the fat, bespectacled, dark-thatched behemoth of '23, he wouldn't find much to recognise in the lean, un-gloss'd, grey-headed old dodderer of '35! I'm asking him how much he recollects of the whole Boston expedition. I'm assuredly glad to hear of his promotion (for a testing-to-designing move could scarcely mean less than that), and congratulate him on his acumen in picking a better field than Schenectady. He is certainly slated for soaring in the world—as I realised years ago when your first bulletins of his tastes and progress began to reach me. In my letter to him I mentioned something which I've been meaning to mention to you for a full year, but have always forgotten when actually writing. Do you recall his idea for a gigantically powerful *television telescope* in the winter of 1927–8? He called it the *telemegascope*, and its principle was the conversion of light rays into a current of electricity, the amplification of this current and the subsequent reconversion of the electricity into luminous energy in the form of a prodigiously magnified image at the receiving end. You sent me his carefully written explanation early in 1928, and I have always kept it on hand with the vague idea of using it in a story—assigning him credit for the idea. Well—just a year ago the press carried accounts of a *television microscope* invented by one Dr. V. K. Zworykin[2] *and depending upon what seems to a layman the exact principle enunciated by our young scientist six years before.* It was stated that the principle, while most immediately acceptable to microscopy, might ultimately be applied to telescopy. Can you beat it? Robertulus, without instruments or laboratory exercise, intellectually anticipated the intricate actuality just as Democritus, Epicurus, and Lucretius, in antient times, anticipated the atomick theory of matter now establish'd by exact and instrumental experiment! Whether he recalls or attaches any importance to the matter I know not—but I am now reminding him of it. Bless my soul, but I shall be glad to see him! I'm also giving him the addresses of the leading gangsters in and near New York—Belknap, Klei, Talman, Mortonius, Loveman . . . and a new chap named Herman C. Koenig, who will be especially congenial because he is both an electrical engineer (holding down an important executive post in the Electrical Testing Laboratories at 540 E. 80th St.) and a well-inform'd and enthusiastick weird fiction fan whose library of spectral source-material (including things like the "Malleus Maleficarum",[3] Boguet's "Examen of Witches", Summers' books on vampirism and witchcraft, etc. etc.) is most generously at the disposal of all borrowers. Robertulus will undoubtedly be getting around Manhattan way repeatedly, and it will be pleasant to have so many congenial spirits on tap. I'm telling him that Sonny Belknap will probably form his best guide to the local museums, art galleries, bookstalls, and such like. Bridgeport is about sixty miles from New York—a thriving, neat city, tho' not—apparently—very replete in colonial antiquities. I've never been off a wheel'd vehicle in that town, but the stage-coach route through it affords some very fair glimpses of both commercial and residential sections. Well—I hope I shan't bore the child to death . . . . . I won't launch him on any foot-wearying Georgian explorations unless he displays a spontaneous interest in the antient scenes about him. I'll tell him what the prime attractions are, and he can use his own judgment (a damn good one, according to all available evidence!) regarding what to see. I'm telling him we can park him here if an army cot will suffice him—and will point out other places of lodgment (the excellent boarding-house across the back garden from 66, or the Y which you patronised) if he craves a more restful slumber. I don't think his views of the cosmos will be modify'd much by anything I shall have to say. In the first place, he's probably a keener thinker than I am, and a vast number of years past the age when the emotions can be steered and fixed—independently of truth or falsity—in arbitrary, previously selected patterns. He's a highly intelligent grown man; and at his age—and with his keenness—nobody forms ideas except through the disinterested observation and individual appraisal of such really relevant evidence as is available. When a chap like that acquires a *new* idea (no matter how many fallacies are *held over* from previous crippling received before the mind had acquired its independent powers, and before the emotions had lost their infantile extra-rational plasticity), it isn't because *anybody else* can influence him, but because *he himself* has formed a fresh conclusion based on additional evidence. In the second place—extensive analyses of the cosmos don't often arise unless one or more of a company holds ideas contrary to the rational conclusions of the existing generation. You must recognise that today virtually nobody under thirty-five who shows any signs of an active, disinterested, and philosophically exercised intelligence (i.e. exercised in fields involving a comparison of ideas and investigation of the sources and processes of our conceptions, as distinguished from fields involving simply the handling of a single line of ideas, the amassing (without digestion or correlation) of a single body of facts, or the accomplishment of specific material objects) believes any longer in the theistic conception. *Tempora mutantur, et nos in illis.*[4] It would be an eye-opener for you to read an article in last August's *Harpers*, refuting the artfully deceptive claim of evangelistic enthusiasts that superstition is increasing instead of decreasing. It is by James H. Leuba, Professor of Psychology at Bryn Mawr, and is entitled "Religious Beliefs of American Scientists"[5]—though college students are also included in its scope. Leuba made two general surveys of scientific men in several distinct fields—one in 1914 and one in 1933—picking his subjects at random from Cattell's *American Men of Science*. He also prepared tables in which the men were classified (according to the Cattell book's own rating) as *lesser* and *eminent* scientists. But the most significant classification of all was his own—*according to the subject's field of work and thought*. He argued very sensibly that the practice of the *different* sciences equips man very differently for the task of drawing rational conclusions on a subject involving on the one hand a close consideration of human vital and psychological processes, and on the other hand a profound analysis of the psychological and anthropological laws by which beliefs (whether true or false) come into being and establish an instinctive sway over the emotions and faculties of individuals and groups. As he viewed it, practitioners of single physical sciences (astronomy, geology, physics, chemistry, botany, meteorology, etc.) are *least* likely to be specially qualified for rational cosmic views. The intelligences of these men are engrossed in specific lines, and their range of information and reflection naturally tends to be biassed in the direction of those lines. For purposes of cosmic appraisal, only *two* factors are in their favour: (a) intrinsic intelligence, and (b) the habit of scientific method. Otherwise, they are laymen. In order to be very liberal, Prof. Leuba selected his subjects of this class from that branch *most* likely to be qualified for acute general reasoning . . . . . i.e., the physicists, who deal with the most generalised and least narrow aspects of material entity. (A meteorologist or dendrologist—or other narrow specialist—

would clearly be no more truly fitted for philosophic reflection than an artist or engineer or business man.) So Class I was the *physicist* group. Next in order of logical qualification for judgment, Leuba chose the *biologists*, who have studied the nature of life and have investigated the physical bases of all human thoughts and moods and beliefs. Above them he placed the *sociologists*, whose knowledge of *human relations and motives* enables them to test the arbitrary claims and values of orthodox theism and supernatural ethics. At the top, of course, came the *psychologists*, who understand how human beliefs are formed, and why the emotions tend to retain certain types of belief irrespective of their truth or falsity. Well—Leuba picked an immense number of names in every class—absolutely at random—from Cattell's *Who's Who* book; and submitted questionnaires to them in 1914 and 1933. He considered that the intervening nineteen years ought not to be without significance in estimating any trend which might exist. The questionnaire specialised in two major points—belief in the popular "god" ..... i.e., a conscious entity that understands and answers prayers ..... and belief in the immortality-myth. He did not attempt to plumb the later phases of supernatural belief—that is, vague faith in more or less ethereal and impersonal elements of consciousness or purpose in the cosmic cycle. Well—here are the results. The figures indicate not numbers of individuals, but *percentages of very large numbers interrogated*. B—believer; D—disbeliever; U—doubter or uncertain. The first table aims simply to show the *present* opinions of the different groups of scientists (1933).

	Belief in "God"			Belief in Immortality		
	B	D	U	B	D	Combined D & U
Physicists	38	47	16	41	32	60
Biologists	27	60	13	29	44	71
Sociologists	24	67	9	25	48	75
Psychologists	10	79	12	9	70	91
			All together	33	41	67

It is to be noticed that Leuba did not attempt to classify these men by *age*. This might have been significant, although of course the generation least predisposed and emotionally crippled—the generation of post-war education—is only just beginning to be represented in the ranks of "arrived" scientists. Next Leuba considers the present (1933) beliefs of the various types of scientist with the element of *eminent ability* (as classified by Cattell) taken into consideration. Here is his table—using the same nomenclature.

	Belief in "God"			Belief in Immortality		
	B	D	U	B	D	U & D
Lesser Physicists	43	43	58	46	29	55
Greater Physicists	17	60	83	20	43	80
Lesser Biologists	31	56	69	32	40	68
Greater Biologists	12	76	88	15	62	86
Lesser Sociologists	30	60	70	31	40	69
Greater Sociologists	20	70	80	10	60	90
Greatest Sociologists	5	95	95	10	70	90
Lesser Psychologists	13	74	87	12	65	88
Greater Psychologists	2	87	98	2	79	98
All Lesser Scientists	35	51	65	37	36	62
All Greater Scientists	13	71	87	15	56	85

These figures speak for themselves. Finally Leuba gets to the matter of a *trend* during the past twenty years. Here are his tables—with a somewhat different system:

	Believers in "God"				Believers in Immortality			
	Lesser Scientists		Greater Scientists		Lesser Scientists		Greater Scientists	
	1914	1933	1914	1933	1914	1933	1914	1933
Physicists	50	43	34	17	57	46	40	20
Biologists	39	31	17	12	45	32	25	15
Sociologists	29	30	19	13	52	31	27	10
Psychologists	32	13	13	12	27	12	9	2

This concludes the survey of men of science. Prof. Leuba's inferences are as follows: that belief is less in men of science who (a) are of distinguished ability, (b) are concerned with life, human behaviour, and thought-processes, and (c) tend to belong to the present rather than the past. The number of outright disbelievers in immortality is less than that of the disbelievers in a traditional "God", but the number of doubters is greater.

We now come to Prof. Leuba's extension of his survey to college undergraduates. Here he introduces three factors of classification—type of institution, academic rank of student, and period (1914 or 1933). His survey was made in two colleges, each typical of a tendency. *College A* is a conservative and aristocratic institution of Protestant auspices and with a personnel drawn from traditional native-American families where religio-emotional crippling of the young is most common and rigid, and where the fetish of conformity and convention is most sedulously worshipped at the expense of pungent and disinterested truth. *College B* is a large university of heterogeneous personnel and liberal leanings, where the student body has fewer artificially predisposing factors, and is in general animated by a sheer desire for knowledge rather than a wish to conform to a chosen artificial mould. Leuba mentions neither institution by name. The first table represents *percentages of believers in "God" in 1933*.

	College A	College B
Freshmen	34	20
Sophomores	37	14
Juniors	30	6
Seniors	20	5
All together	31	11

(an *incomplete* survey was made in 1914, and indicates a substantially larger number of believers then—in both institutions—than now).

The second table is the only one in which the *period element* is statistically shown. This represents *percentage of believers in immortality in College A*—the exclusive, Protestant, old-American institution.

	Believers		Disbelievers		Disbelievers Plus Doubters	
	1914	1933	1914	1933	1914	1933
Freshmen	80	42	15	33	20	58
Sophomores	76	50	19	30	24	50
Juniors	60	37	32	37	40	63
Seniors	70	27	24	47	30	73
All together		39		37		61

Here again is something which speaks for itself. It may be noted that a 1914 tendency to recover belief in the senior year—presumably under the influence of involved traditional metaphysics—has totally vanished in 1933. Leuba's final table concerns *percentage of believers in immortality in College B in 1933*—this being the heterogeneous liberal college representing the increasing "new American" element as opposed to the dwindling old-American aristocracy:

	Believers	Disbelievers	Disbelievers Plus Doubters
Freshmen	29	44	72
Sophomores	20	44	80
Juniors	14	63	86
Seniors	5	68	95
All together	18	55	83

No open-eyed observer can escape the significance of figures such as these. Prof. Leuba's conclusions are obvious—i.e., that belief in both "God" and immortality grow less (a) when non-intellectual traditional influences are less, (b) as the student advances in learning, and (c) as the years of human knowledge and experience move forward. There's no need of my trotting out any personal arguments in the face of this dispassionate evidence. Of course, it may be said that human belief has nothing to do with the absolute truth or falsity of the object of that belief. Thus in 1400 all respectable people believed in witches and devils and the Ptolemaic theory of the universe, and were appalled and unconvinced when anybody challenged those delusions. But draw your own conclusions. Even you don't believe in witches and devils and the Ptolemaic system today . . . you don't try to defend them in the face of lapsed public belief. Well—so it is with the *next* set of illusions to be sloughed off. People who specialise in the analysis of nature and of thought—and virtually all young thinkers maturing in an age of decreased mass-crippling of the infant emotions—are gradually getting rid of the residual stigma of primitive myth typified by the "personal god" and "immortality" delusions. You can claim that all these alert modern thinkers are wrong, if you like . . . . . but it doesn't get you anywhere! The real facts are the same, whatever people think or wish . . . . . and when we notice that *every increase of knowledge and every increase of honesty and thoroughness in mental training leads more and more people to modify their always changing* (compare 1900 with 1850 and 1650 and 1450 and B.C. 200 and B.C. 4000 and the evidence of Cro-magnon and other carvings back to B.C. 30,000 or so . . . . .) *opinions in a certain direction,* we cannot escape certain definite conclusions. Selah. In connexion with the statistics just presented, you really ought to read the whole *Harpers* article from which they came. That will attend to many of the points you might tend to bring up. Unfortunately I haven't it here—I merely *borrow* the magazine, and in this case copied for my files nothing but the bare tables. Incidentally—I'm not trying to corrupt your beliefs, but am merely showing once more that rational scepticism is no patented private foible of my own. Go ask Prof. Leuba—or George Santayana—or John Dewey—or Bertrand Russell—or Hugh Elliott—or Dr. Freud—or Prof. Pavlov—or Dr. Adler—or Joseph Wood Krutch—or anybody who throws all his mental and scholarly energies into the single, absolutely disinterested task of *discovering and recognising truth for its own sake.*

Thanks abundantly for the stamps—always usable . . . . . and how!—but hell's bells! don't think I gotta be reimbursed for the perennially congenial task of Shastia' off we went'! [*sic*] Glad my sloppy architectural screed wears well on re-reading—but cripes! I shake in me brogans when I think of the careless way it was really composed . . . . . the loose diction, unrhythmical paragraphs, unverified statements, general lack of planning, and what-all! The extent to which you have deciphered the introductory part quite floors me . . . . . I'll bet I couldn't make as much out of the original manuscript this minute! Actually, I've forgotten so damn much that whenever I make a correction it's in a spirit of fresh revision—not memory of what I wrote. Of such corrections I have thus far found only *seven* necessary. The reasons will be obvious when you come to apply them. In their absence, the manuscript would convey ideas which I do not mean to convey. So please see—if you can—that all the copies uniformly embody the following emendations:

p. 2 l. 5—insert comma after *interest*
p. 3 l. 8—delete *of* after *despite*
p. 5 l. 9—for *Madigliani* read *Modigliani*
p. 6 l. 15—insert *ancestors'* before *tenacious*
p. 9 l. 6—delete superfluous *and* at end of line
— l. 11—insert the words *do what they* between *simply* and *feel*
p. 11———in the final line insert *our* between *upon* and *natural*.

If I find any more slips, I'll let ya know—but hades, I don't see how you ever got the copy as slick and accurate as you did! And I'm hang'd if I thought that introduction ran to *thirteen pages*. Holy Yuggoth! If the mere prologue spins out that long, what sort of a young book will the whole thing be? Godelpya in the task of decoding and transcribing the rest of it . . . . . when ya get through, you might tackle Mayan hieroglyphs or Etruscan inscriptions just for a little relaxation and light practice! But if you'll let Grandpa proofread, you needn't be so damn careful—I can spot and amend any obvious boners. Some of those proper names and technical terms may ball things up,—though I'm hang'd if I recall just what is or ain't in the thing. Poor old Archbishop Cranmer[6]—wotta load his inoffensive sheet has gotta carry! Well—he ast for it . . . . . whaddya speck wenya bring up a big subject? As for actual magazine submission—I don't believe it would have a chance in a billion. Nothing fresh or timely in it. There have been dozens of slaps at modernistick henhouse and water tank pseudo-architecture, and dozens of defences of the classick, and dozens of reminders that the classick still lives in whatever is vital of modern art. And as for the mere recital of facts concerning Roman architecture and its influence—probably any textbook would have the essentials, and any dozen or half dozen books on the subject and its ramifications would contain virtually the same story. Nowadays magazines never handle straight standard information—with the sole exception of certain types of geographical description which form a basis for picture or travel notes. What they want is something definitely related to the present moment. What ain't, they argue, is stuff for a book if its worth dirtying up type for at all. An explanation of some new and imperfectly understood architectural development—even a trend book toward a classick form (if it really *were* an authentic trend and not a mere excuse to float a hackney'd description of the classick form in question)—would be likely magazine material. But nix on the textbook and museum manual kind of thing. So take an old man's tip and don't waste postage! Incidentally, I'll be on the lookout for your *Eng. Journal* article.[7] The damn scoundrels, not to letcha in on the contest! I'll bet the article is full of rare suggestions and effective synopses. Which reminds me that I'm still sighing for the day when "Doorways" will be available in one form or another!

Don't hurry with the neo-Kleicomolo. I'll probably add some dumbbell trifle—but of course there'll be some guide in what I find already added. Yes—seven or eight members do make for thinness. There *could* be that many different views if every member were a Belknap or Galpin or Edkins or Mocrates or Augie Derleth or Bob Howard or E. Hoffmann Price or J. Vernon Shea or Jim Morton—but unfortunately we ain't got no such all-star cast of original thinkers and viewers! Young "Jon", bless his naive heart, ain't so hot as a critic and chooser of critics—but I'm for anything that can help to put the lit'rachawer back in amachawer-dumb! Hope the inspissated mediocrity won't get so thick as to drive you out ..... an occurrence which, I fancy, would form the opening ceremony of the letter's funeral. By the way, I may dump some N.A.P.A. verses on ya for official criticism next spring—you know you said you'd be willing to tackle one batch. There appears to be quite a fight on in the National—some bozos are out for young Babcock's scalp—but I trust it won't disrupt the designs for literary improvement.

Well—I slipcha some Bekes yesterday, and will enclose a couple more. Am also enclosing two or three other oddznends—linguistick and otherwise. None of these need be returned except the more'n-a-year-old snaps of 66 and vicinity. As I raked a snap of 66 out to send your young hopeful (I thought he'd like to see where he was gonna visit) it occurred to me that I may not have show'd you this set taken a year ago last October. I've just suggested their return—but if any of 'em look especially suited to your files I won't be too harsh in enforcing that dictum, for I s'pose I still got the negs somewhere. Incidentally—those things was took with a #2 Brownie which I bought for two fish in *1907*. Same camera that took the first snaps of me ya ever seen, nigh onto twenty year ago! The strap rotted off in 1921—at the Boston N.A.P.A. convention—but outside that the ol' boy's pretty much okay ..... as I fancy the pitches prove. The one showing the high marble wall was taken from the courtyard of our next door neighbour the Jawn Hay Liberry (that houses the Harris Collection of Am. Poetry—greatest in the world). The pitches of folks against a very small-paned window was took in the neighbouring college grounds—the building being University Hall (1770). The dame is my aunt, who ye'd orta remember from 1922.

Well—if memory plays no tricks, the last bulletin I slipcha was around the pre-Yule season. Did I tell ya I had the first Christmas tree I've had since boyhood? Laid in a whole new stock of tinsel gewgaws and lights at Woolworth's—and ef y' ast me, the result was something to issue anextry about! Boy! did it glitter? And remember that it was set in front of a *genuine* colonial fireplace with antient candles 'n' everything, and an oval family painting hanging above it. Hot stuff! We'll have to revive the custom permanent! Well—around New Year's I paid my (latterly becoming) usual visit to Sonny Belknap, naturally seeing all the rest of the gang. The presence in Manhattan of my young Florida host of last spring—little Bobby Barlow—and the simultaneous arrival of both Wandrei boys (Donald from California, where he visited Clark Ashton Smith; Howard directly from St. Paul. They've jointly taken a flat in Greenwich Village.) gave the event something of the aspect of a convention. At a general meeting up at Sonny's Jan. 2, fifteen were present—Morton, Loveman, Klei, Barlow, the Wandreis, Kirk, Leeds, Talman, Koenig, etc. Later we met at Loveman's, where we saw the vast collection of Clark Ashton Smith's drawings lately brought from Cleveland. I had seen it in 1922, but it was wholly new to Belknap, Barlow, and the Wandreis. On another occasion Koenig show'd Belknap, Barlow, and Grandpa over his Electrical Testing Laboratories—a fascinating place full of outré devices resembling space-ships, atomick ray projectors, and what the hell not. This joint is for testing the safety and durability of every sort of common domestic electrical appliance—and ya'd orta see the grotesque devices concocted for the purpose of duplicating and intensifying the average conditions of household wear and tear! One machine repeatedly crumples up an electrick cord and straightens it out again—another knocks around a common plug in a sort of young ferris-wheel device . . . . . and so on. Mocratulus Major would be fascinated by some of the more intricate appliances. During our visit Koenig shot off some artificial lightning—of the sort devised by Steinmetz[8]—for our benefit. We also haunted the museums, library, and bookstalls—picking up quite a few bargains at the latter. This was Barlow's first visit to N.Y. since infancy, hence Belknap and I introduced him to all the high spots. The weather was quite semi-civilised . . . . . only two days being so cold as to give me serious inconvenience.

I returned home Jan. 8, and have ever since been wrestling with one thing or another. A lousy snowstorm Jan. 23–4—tied up traffick, and is scarce melted off even yet. Damn cold, too—down to -nine degrees one day. I was tied indoors eight days in succession. After all, this cursed winter is nearly as bad as its loathsome predecessor! However—I have managed to soak up two of the poetry readings by authors at the college—Susanna Valentine Mitchell[9] (now of Providence) and Archibald MacLeish, author of "Conquistador". Mac is getting to be about as serious a poet as this continent can boast!

News item—to accomodate my teeming and chaotick files, I've picked up a couple dark walnut chests of drawers at a fire sale. By piling one atop t'other I get a neat single cabinet—so mellow and colonial looking that it accords well with the Georgian atmosphere of an old gentleman's study. The outfit stands on the south wall beside my tall glass-door'd bookcase—encroaching only slightly on the window near the Morris chair, and displacing no previous piece of furniture. Those ten capacious drawers ought to take care of a lot of now-scattered papers.

And so it goes. I'm certainly looking forward with the vastest eagerness to the visit of Mocratulus Major, and hope antient Providentium will contain enough of interest to make him feel repay'd for the trip. I hope, too, that his settlement in New-England will be permanent enough to cause his paw to visit him—in which case a repetition of 1923 would surely have to be arrang'd! What an event to drag the two of you around century'd Marblehead—with Cole to add a touch of the old days!

Benedictions and obeisances—

Grandpa Lo.

Notes

1. The elder of the two sons of MWM; i.e., Robert. Donald was Mocratulus Minor.
2. Vladimir Kosmich Zworykin (1888–1982), Russian inventor, engineer, and pioneer of television technology who played a role in the development of the electron microscope.
3. By Heinrich Kremer and Jakob Sprenger.
4. "The times change, and we [change] in them." A Latin adage more customarily written as *Tempora mutantur et nos mutamus in illis.*
5. James H. Leuba, "Religious Beliefs of American Scientists," *Harper's* 169, No. 3 (August 1934): 291–300.
6. Thomas Cranmer (1489–1556) Archbishop of Canterbury during the reigns of Henry VIII, Edward VI, and, for a short time, Mary I, and a leader of the English Reformation. He helped build the case for the annulment of Henry's marriage to Catherine of Aragon, one cause of the separation of the English Church from union with the Holy See. With Thomas Cromwell, he supported the principle of royal supremacy, in which the king was considered sovereign over the church within his realm.
7. "First Steps in the Appreciation of Poetry." See Appendix.
8. Charles Proteus Steinmetz (1865–1923), Prussian-born American mathematician and electrical engineer. He fostered the development of alternating current, which made the expansion of the electric power industry in the U.S. possible.
9. Susanna Valentine Mitchell (1896–1979), author of the poetry volumes *Journey Taken by a Woman* (1935), *In the Bright April Weather* (1952), and *Make New Banners* (1954). Her *Collected Poems* appeared in 1966.

[71] [AHT]

The Antient Citadel
—3d Day of Spring
[24 March 1935]

Hail, O Sage!

Well—the guest of honour blew in at one p.m. Saturday, March 2, and the first thing I did was to guide him to a tangle of semi-rural alleys just a bit north on the hill, where Skippy could be tethered indefinitely to rest and graze. We then returned briefly to the house, chatted a bit with my aunt, and set out on an antiquarian tour of the ancient hill—after a pause at some bookstalls downtown, where Mocratulus wished to purchase a volume of soulful lyrics for some young gentlewoman of his acquaintance. We followed the general course of sprints through which I put you in '23—first north, by the 1775 church, the 1783 Golden Ball Inn, the 1761 court and colony house, the 1769 schoolhouse, the 1760 newspaper office, the street with steps,[1] the colonial doorways of old Benefit St., the 1809 Sullivan Dorr mansion, the hidden 1723 churchyard (with its 1810 church), the Sarah Helen Whitman house, the Roger Williams spring, home-site, and original burial-place, and (an added attraction which I didn't know about in '23) the 1801 Halsey Mansion near 10 Barnes St. I also briefly pointed out good old #10—hideous Victorian dump that it is! And was the boy tired? Not a bit of it! Returning to College St., we examined the ancient buildings on the N. side below #66—with the venerable archways to interior courtyards .... only thing of their kind in the U.S. to remain in their original condition. (Alas—this historic row of crumbling facades hath a doom upon it—tho' the depression hath so far held up the wou'd-be marauders.)

But this was merely getting warm'd up! Now for those parts of the antient hill *south* of College St.! Before proceeding thither, though, I dragged my victim thro' the art museum and furnish'd colonial house which I show'd you—but which now has a splendid new (1926) building, of which the older part forms a minor wing. Also took in the antient Athenaeum. Then south along Benefit St. past colonial doorways and the 1816 Unitarian Church, noting the 1786 John Brown mansion, the 1795 Joseph Nightingale mansion, the 1811 Carrington mansion, etc.[2] Then through some quaint lanes which I didn't discover till after your visit, and back over Brown and Benevolent Sts., seeing the Ives mansion (1806) and kindred sights. Then the college campus with its 1770 main edifice, the 1820 dormitory, where John Hay roomed, its Grecian-Dorick Manning Hall (1830), etc. etc. At this point I had mercy on the poor lad, and let him rest a bit at #66 (which is just across Prospect St. from the campus) instead of dragging him along the S. Main St. waterfront. We then went down to one of the cheap joints where I eat, and tanked up on a heavy feed; after which we climbed the hill to #66 again—but not till I had pointed out the 1828 Arcade and other downtown details. Back at the house we talked with my aunt, fixed up a camp cot in the living-room for the guest, looked over my library, wrote postcards, began a long discussion which cover'd everything from the telemegascope to the cosmos. At about one-thirty a.m., we sought our respective hay-piles—resting well on the whole, though Mocratulus was a bit chilly because we forgot to have blankets to go *beneath* him on the mattress-less canvas surface. It was the first time my aunt or I had ever manipulated a camp cot—hence the mistake. I bought this one on purpose to accomodate the few overnight guests by whom I thought 66 might be honor'd, and ὁ Μικρος Μοκρατες was the first to try it out. He readily forgave us the error—and seemed just as spruce the next day as if all had been perfect!

Well—on the third we lit out early in Skippy, and covered a number of urban high spots awheel. Along the waterfront, through that curious poor-farm within its high wall which stands in the heart of the best residential district,³ past a complete old farm with 1735 house imbedded in the midst of one of the newer sections, past an Italian villa and garden, past one of the first two brick houses (1750) ever built in Providence, past the vast cemetery of Swan Point, where my more recent forbears and kin repose, past wooded Blackstone Park, where I roam'd in youth, past 598 Angell, where you called in '23, past 454 Angell, where the old gent first saw the light of day in a vanish'd elder world, and around through some ancient and tortuous alleys to the great new (1931) Washington Bridge over the Seekonk River. It now became our design to behold some of the antient seaports down the eastern shore of Narragansett Bay, and the relative mildness of the day (despite an high wind) made this quite feasible. Traversing the sightly Barrington Parkway, we reach'd the village of Riverside and thereafter struck out into the wholly primitive countryside. Tho' spring was eighteen days off, there was a touch of subtle vernal magick in the awakening meads and groves; so that the occasion seem'd an highly auspicious one for the breaking of Grandpa's hibernation. Passing the white steeple we soon cross'd the two bridges leading to antient Warren—but left the exploration of this century'd part for a later occasion. This part of the country was formerly in the Plymouth colony, and was settled after 1676, when King Philip's War clear'd the region of redskin savages. It had previously been the chief seat (call'd Sowans) of the Wampanoags, where in his day the virtuous Massasoit held his court. The towns of Warren and Bristol, which began to flourish before the opening of the eighteenth century, have several architectural and other characteristicks to distinguish them from places originally Rhodinsular. The type of doorway, the habit of leaving an elm-shaded common, and other details, are more suggestive of the Massachusetts-Bay than of our own colony. The Bay, of course, took over the Plymouth colony in 1691—and in Jan. 1746–7 this western strip was transferr'd to Rhode-Island by an order of His Majesty George the Second. At this period the village of Brooks' Pastures, heretofore in the Massachusetts town of Swansea, received its present name of Warren, after Admiral Sir Peter Warren, commander of His Majesty's fleet in the glorious victory of Louisburg in 1745. Well—on this occasion Skippy proceeded onward toward Bristol—soon deviating toward the right thro' the bay-skirting driveway of the extensive Colt estate, which the kindness of the proprietor hath thrown open to the publick. This route affords many pleasing marine vistas, and my youthful guest seem'd very well dispos'd toward it. In endeavouring to emerge at its south end, which joins the antient Popesquash Road, we became slightly twisted, and continu'd on along Popesquash Neck (vide a good map) without meaning to. As it turn'd out, we were very glad of the error, since it took us through an admirably picturesque and unspoil'd region which we wou'd not otherwise have seen. At one point we came out on the eastward shore of the Neck, and beheld in the distance the ethereal Mount Hope Bridge (1927) from the Bristol peninsula to the island of Aquidneck or Rhode-Island (from which the colony is nam'd), on whose southern end the antient town of Newport (1639) is situated. I had never been so far south on the Neck before, so that the scenes were equally new to both occupants of the coach. Soon, however, we gain'd the Popesquash Road, and steer'd toward the antient spires of Bristol. This town, founded in 1680, was in the eighteenth and early nineteenth centuries a great centre of whaling and privateering; and many marks of its former prosperity are manifest. We travers'd the crumbling and deserted waterfront as well as the elm-shaded inland streets, and beheld the well-preserv'd 1780 court house. It is a pleasing and singular circumstance, that all five counties of Rhode-Island still possess their eighteenth century court-houses—at Providence (1761), Newport (1739), Bristol (1780), Kingston (1780), and East-Greenwich (1750). Of these edifices, those at Bristol and East-Greenwich still serve their original purpose.

Returning to Warren, we tether'd Skippy near the antient waterfront and prepar'd to explore the village on foot. Warren, like Bristol, was a great whaling and privateering port, but is equally fallen into a decline. There is, however, a residual oyster industry—of course the inevitable manufacturing and foreigners. Both towns were fir'd upon by His Majesty's arm'd sloops during the treason of 1775–83. To my mind, Warren is superior to Bristol in picturesqueness; an opinion in which I believe Mocratulus Major concurs. We stroll'd along the rotting wharves, paus'd by the boats drawn up for the winter, and threaded the antient lanes where giant elms cast a pleasing shade upon venerable gambrel roofs. I had hop'd to show the visitor the famous ice-cream joint—Maxfield's, in the rear of [a] classick pillar'd mansion of the 1830 period—where James Ferdinand Morton so picturesquely tanks up on twenty-eight or so varieties each summer; but unfortunately it was clos'd for the winter . . . as it never was before. We had by this time re-mounted Skippy—so, smarting beneath this disappointment, we steer'd northward for Providence. Our return route was a different one—involving a dip into the antient Province of the Massachusetts-Bay. Approaching the city over Red Bridge, we glided down Angell St., stabled Skippy on the hill, and proceeded to #66. Shortly afterward we descended to "Jake's"—the famous stevedore restaurant at the foot of the hill which Wilfred B. Talman (then a Brown student) discover'd in 1926 and introduced to the gang. Here have gorg'd such dignitaries as W. Paul Cook, James Ferdinand Morton, Donald Wandrei . . . and now Robert Ellis Moe. This is the joint where good food is serv'd in such fabulous quantities. We chose sausage-meat and johnny-cakes, with stupendous bowls of short-cake (R. E. M. banana; H. P. L. peach) and whipped cream for dessert. Then up the hill again, stopping in at the antient art club building (1795), tinkering a bit with Skippy, washing up at 66, parking Skippy (alas!) for the visitor's all-too-early departure, and looking over the collection (including the 1808 curtain of the old Providence Theatre, with a view of the town on it, and the apple-tree root which enter'd Roger Williams' coffin and is said to have follow'd the lines of the skeleton) at the century-old R.I. Historical Society. (I took you there, didn't I?)

It was now past three in the afternoon, and the western sunlight was assuming its glamourous golden aspect. I hated to see the welcome guest depart, and decided to accompany him on his way as far as the antient seaport of East-Greenwich, on the bay's west shore—taking a stage-coach back. We went out Broad St., cut thro' Roger Williams Park (one of the finest publick parks in the world), and thereafter travers'd Auburn, Norwood, Hillsgrove, Greenwood, and Apponaug. Finally approaching East-Greenwich (founded 1677), we turn'd to the right and explor'd some of the picturesque inland streets. On the east the village slopes steeply down the Greenwich Bay, an arm of Narragansett Bay. (vide map) We saw likewise the 1750 courthouse, a hill street with steps in it, the old East-Greenwich Academy—attended in its day by my grandfather, great-aunt, mother, and elder aunt (for we have relatives in East-Greenwich)—and other points of interest. Then, at the waiting-point of the return coach, I was forc'd to speed the youthful traveller on his way—through antient Wickford and Narragansett Pier. I gave directions for exploring unspoil'd Wickford (formerly Newton or Updike's Landing—an exquisite seaport virtually unchang'd since 1800), and was pleas'd to learn later that the voyager avail'd himself of them—incidentally photographing one of the most typical colonial houses. He also, I find, enjoy'd the seaside drive south of there—once pausing to photograph the ocean and a sailing-vessel in the golden sunset light. Bridgeport was reach'd without mishap at nine p.m.—and now I am hoping that the young traveller will be covering the same terrain again!

Possibly you have had all this news from a younger and sprightlier source—illustrated with suitable photographs—but I could not refrain from adding my quota of quavering garrulity. It surely was a festive occasion for the old man, and I can but hope I did not weary my lively guest too extensively with demonstrations and reminiscences of antiquity. He seemed admirably appreciative of the historick scenes around him, and was always ready with interested and intelligent comment. A great boy, by gad, and once more I must congratulate you on the quality of the Mocratick product! The gang in N.Y. are eager to meet him—indeed, Koenig (the electrical engineer) has just asked for his address in order to extend him a first-hand invitation.

Well—this delightful pre-vernal event seems to have waked both Grandpa and the season up from their long wintry lethargy . . . for lo! the following Wednesday the mercury went up to *sixty-five degrees,* and old Theobald totter'd forth on his first *pedestrian* (overcoatless, of course) outing of 1935. On this occasion I took a twelve-mile walk thro' the northern suburbs to my favourite Quinsnicket countryside—which I enjoy'd despite leaflessness overhead and slush underfoot. Something vernal seem'd somehow in the air—and when sunset came, the spectacle of glowing Venus and the thin crescent moon in the west was altogether irresistible.

Yr obt hble Servt

Lo.

Notes

1. I.e., Meeting Street.
2. The First Unitarian Church (1816), 301 Benefit Street; the John Brown house (1786), 52 Power Street; the Joseph Nightingale–Nicholas Brown house (1792), 357 Benefit Street; the Corliss–Carrington mansion, 66 Williams Street.
3. The Dexter Asylum was named for Ebenezer Knight Dexter, who upon his death in 1824 bequeathed a property known as Neck Farm, for a facility to care for the poor, aged and mentally ill of Providence. It operated from 1828 to 1957. Brown University's athletic complex now stands on the former asylum site on Hope Street.

[72]   [AHT]

Arx Theobald:
—II Ante Nones Aprilis
[6 April 1935]

O Sage:—

Nope—Grand'a ain't gettin' sporty in his old age! On the contrary, this yaller journalism represents the acme of conservation ... insomuch as it involves the using-up of some bargain stationery purchas'd in the year *1910!* Whilst rearranging files, I tapp'd a box containing stuff undisturb'd since the Middle 598 Period—and found therein the most astonishing array of tail ends of writing materials—composition books with a few blank pages, incomplete pads, and the like. One composition book of 1905 bears the title of a story about which I had completely forgotten—"Gone—But Whither?" I'll bet it was a hell-raiser! The title expresses the fate of the tale itself. Another book contain'd the opening chapters of "A Brief Course in Astronomy—Descriptive, Practical, and Observational; for Beginners and General Readers" (1906). That I *do* recall—it got is far as the typed and hand-illustrated stage (circa one hundred fifty pages), though no copy survives. And this old yaller paper—of which I had a dozen or more pads at a nickel each in good old '10—is simply lousy with memories. Gawd, the heroick couplets that have bounded down these ochraceous sheets! *Twenty-five years ago*—a quarter of a century—and who would have thought the old man would still be making hen-tracks on the same aureate surface in the well-nigh fabulous future year of *1935?* Hell—I don't believe there is such a year as *1935* after all! It is merely a sort of theoretical Ragnarok like A.D. 5000 or 10,000 or 1,000,000! Or if there could be such a remote age, I couldn't be living then! Gad! Isn't 1910 bad enough for one whose heyday was around '03? What a world! King Edward dead—though I suppose they'll crown the Prince of Wales as George V next year. President Taft is a disappointment—but I trust we'll get good old T. R. back at the 1912 elections.[1] And to think that a Rhode Islander and friend of my grandfather is the arch-devil behind that Payne–Aldrich tariff bill![2] What an age! Hope Premier Asquith can keep that wretched little Welsh radical Lloyd-George in check—what *will* happen if that cursed bill curtailing the power of the House of Lords goes through? And then that silly talk about a German peril! Hades—the Kaiser doesn't want any war. I'll bet some damn'd French agitation is responsible for all this talk. Men like Lord Haldane[3] and A. Conan Doyle will help to preserve the solidarity of the Nordick powers through the diffusion of better understanding. Hear of trouble in Mexico, but I fancy old Don Porfirio[4] can keep the lid down. What do upstarts like this bonehead Madero want to make trouble for? Oh, well—political affairs are no concern of a gentleman any more. All controll'd by parvenu plutocrats and corporations. But let 'em go it—the rabble would merely be worse if they did govern. Let's see—where was I . . . . .

> Yon tiny torrent, fed by swollen springs,
> Leaps in the sun, and o'er the mountain rings;
> Thro' meads below, the streamlet flows along
> With greater amplitude, and less of song.
> At length the force of thankless toil to feel,
> And strain incessant at the whirling wheel.
> Thus with mankind: the sweetest days are first;
> From youthful lips the songs spontaneous burst;
> Maturer years a graver aspect give,
> And men become more wretched as they live.[5]

Still the old yellow paper . . . . . and the dizzy wheel of time . . . 1911 . . . 1912 . . . 1913 . . . 1914 . . . I discover amateur journalism and come across a brilliant sage in Zythopolis . . . AUGUST 1914 . . . . the crash and thunder of a dying world . . . . 1916 . . . . 1917 . . . . NOVEMBER 1917 . . . a new world is born on the blood-drenched streets of Petrograd . . . 1918 . . . the armistice . . . 1919 . . . Versailles . . . the gods laugh . . . 1920 . . . 1921 . . . 1922 . . . 1923 . . . 1924 . . . 1925 . . . 1926 . . . 1927 . . . 1928 . . . 1929 . . . OCTOBER, 1929 . . . the knell of unsupervised capitalism sounds . . . 1930 . . . 1931 . . . 1932 . . . 1933 . . . 1934 . . . 1935 . . . ?????? And here, amidst the twilight of transition, sits the same old man bent over the same old yellow pad . . . . or is it not, rather, a dream? Surely it cannot be other than 1910, even if this desk before me does look a little odd. That calendar on the wall with its impossible "1935" is obviously a joke! Back to work . . . how ought the next line to go? . . . . .

> Away, Reality! and let us roam
> Quinsnicket's realm; Imagination's home.
> Let us ascend the gently rising mound,
> And from its summit view the country round.
> What city of the blest is that which lies
> Far to the south, half-hidden from our eyes;
> Whose gold-pav'd avenues astound our gaze;

>   Whose spires and domes reflect the morning rays?
>   Bewitching distance! by thine aid alone
>   The sordid town to splendour thus hath grown!⁶

And so on . . . and so on . . . and so on . . . .

Well—in view of the highly compress'd nature of all bulletins from other sources, I'm glad I *did* spread myself in a description of the festive Mocratulary event on March 2–3! It certainly was a delight to this household, and my aunt and I are both hoping to see Skippy and his pilot again ere long. When I get my roll of film developed, I'll show you some pictorial sidelights—and I trust Mocratulus Major will give you a glimpse of his prints . . . if he doesn't, I'll lend you my copies. He snapped the Whitman house, the steps of #66 with Grandpa, a typical Wickford eighteenth century dwelling, a marine vista, and a fine down-the-hill vista of College St., showing the antient archways. Had a card from M. Maior day before yesterday, telling of his week-end stop in N.Y. after a trip to Harrison, N.J. on the company's business. He looked up my friend Koenig and was taken thro' the Electrical Testing Laboratories. Later I was trust he'll look up Loveman and Belknap and Jacobus Ferdinandus and Klei and all the rest.

And now let me thank you for the snaps showing the rest of the Gens Mauritia!⁷ My guest had exhibited a few which gave me a rough idea of present aspects, but these two are far and away ahead of 'em. Egad, what an upstanding young Hylas–Adonis–Dionysus–Apollo–Hyacinthus Mocratulus Minor has grown to be! I don't wonder that the nymphs form a mile-long queue, and swell the blue Ionian Sea with tears pour'd from Leucadian heights! It's a wonder the cinema industry doesn't grab him to boost declining box-office returns! I have a snap of you with this young giant in your arms—at a time when his vocabulary was probably very limited and gurgling. And I recall an anecdote of the days when he was three, and you found him imitating a *Macbeth* scene!

> "Ith dis a dagger w'ich I thee before me?"⁸

In '23, when I saw the little towheads, I have an idea that Minor was still more diminutive than Maior—or was that just an old man's impression bas'd on a knowledge of his juniority? Well—they sure are a great brace of youngsters, and it's a damn shame circumstances won't let you keep 'em rounded up in one place! But who knows? Maybe if Maior kip in [*sic*] at Bridgeport, you can negotiate with the academies of l'arnin' there and land a nifty praeceptorate . . . . and Minor, having wed his damsel and become a noted librarian, can get a transfer to some neighbouring repository of written records. In such a case, I might put the whole triad of youse guys through the sprints[?] at Marblehead some day! I can well imagine what a jolt the flitting of the youngest chick must produce, and trust there'll be some way in which you can arrange to get a few get-togethers.

But—things being as they are—your new proposed arrangement sounds damn good! I've always thought an office or study separate from the domestick commonplaces of an household is an ideal thing, and in youth used to rejoice in vacant-lot huts, and cryptick retreats in cellar and attick. Like you, I belong to the born celibate type—and would still be such even if saddled with a string of helpmates as long as Brigham Young's or Ibn Sand's! My dump has gotta be my dump—and if anybody doesn't like my hours or the way I keep my things, it's just too bad! At 66 my study and bedroom form an absolutely separate unit—in which I do all the sweeping, dusting, and arranging. I retire and rise and eat exactly when I goddam please—and without any bother to my aunt. And yet my two rooms harmonise with the rest of the joint, so that the old-time effect of a single household is preserv'd. My aunt's living room is the family parlour, and my study is the family library. By the way—I guess my latest semiannual described the *second* set of file cabinets I've obtain'd (Mar. 23) ... six little fellows of four drawers each, which can be tucked in any old place without disturbing the general furnishing scheme. Worked forty-eight hours arranging my stuff—and at last my odd papers and pamphlets are in the best shape they've been in since the original days of these yaller pages! Yet even so, a lot of junk still remains pil'd upon open shelves!

Thanks no end for the R. H. L. about antient Nantucket![9] He certainly catches the spirit—and makes me wish I could take another trip thither! I may at that, next summer ... even if only a one-day jaunt. They sell cheap excursion tickets for a single day—and by taking a fabulously early boat I might be able to get five hours or more on the island. I'd hire a bike as I did on my '34 visit. Some place—as detached from the world as Key West—and yet with the unmistakable air of antient New-England about it! Glad I can keep the cutting. Which reminds me that them Bekes is comin' right along.

No—you had *not* previously sent Grandpa a copy of your "First Steps" article—but I'm damn'd glad to see it at last. The hectographed *Poem Comments* aid in bringing out its gist. But say—*is* that comment of Horace's *absolutely* verbatim? I s'pose I hadn't orta be sceptical in view of some of the priceless howlers I've saw in the past. Glad to see that the good ol' Abbott–Trabue tests hold their own. How many dozen folks have I sprung them on since those bygone days of '22! You'll remember I fell down on just one pome series x-13 outa the two booklets—something by that infernal bore Browning. Well, about a year ago—when I gave the tests to a new poet after so long an interval that I'd completely forgotten what the right choice in that Browning layout was—I tried the thing myself and think I picked the right one without any trouble. Query—was it subconscious memory, or is the old gent a better picker than in '22? My present choice is *A* despite the grammatical boner (up to *who*) which sidetracked me in '22. Am I right this time, or have I blunder'd again? I lost your key and made another one of my own—just relying on memory and judgment. The *Poem Comments* are all great—you do know what's what in the putting-across line! Hope this new proposition goes over big, despite the slow start. And good luck with the *Word Hunt* marketing! Ah, me—if "Doorways" would only find an opening!

Yup—I'll pass the word along to Fra Samuelus that you're after "Instruments of Darkness",[10] and hope he can land ya one. By the way—he's just got a marvellous Greek statuette of bronze . . . the real thing, fifth century B.C. Young Heracles with lion skin and (indications of broken-off) club or staff. Seven inches high on marble base. The lucky rascal—he pick'd it up at an auction for five berries! I'm all on edge to see it—or a snapshot of it.

Well—spring hasn't been as marked as these early warm days might have led one to expect. No outings since last report. Curse this latitude—I wish I could get to Charleston! Amateurdom plods along much as usual—the current scrap hasn't interfered with the lit'ry programme much. At last my amateur papers are in some sort of shape, thanks to the new filing system. A block of two little cabinets plus one drawer of the big cabinet outfit takes care of the whole kit and boodle.

Well—here's hoping the reorientation pans out brilliantly! Thanks again for the pitchers.

Yr most oblig'd obt Servt
Lo.

Notes

1. George V (1865–1936) succeeded Edward VII, who died 6 May 1910; William Howard Taft (1857–1930) was president from 1909 to 1913. The presidency of Theodore Roosevelt (1858–1919) ended in 1909. He ran for the office again in 1912 on the "Bull Moose" Party ticket, but both he and Taft lost to Woodrow Wilson.
2. The bill, passed in 1909, was sponsored by Sereno E. Payne (Republican senator of New York) and Nelson W. Aldrich, longtime Republican senator from Rhode Island (1881–1911) and one of the most powerful politicians of his day.
3. Richard Haldane, 1st Viscount Haldane (1856–1928), Scottish politician who advocated Liberal imperialism.
4. José de la Cruz Porfirio Díaz Mori (1830–1915), Mexican soldier, politician, and dictator who served seven terms as President of Mexico (1876, 1877–80, 1884–1911). He declared himself the winner of the 1910 election, whereupon his opponent, Francisco I. Madero (1873–1913), called for an armed revolution, initiating the Mexican Civil War. Madero himself served as president of Mexico in 1911–13.
5. "Quinsnicket Park," ll. 19–28.
6. "Quinsnicket Park," ll. 29–38.
7. The Moe family.
8. *Macbeth* 2.1.33.
9. I.e., Richard Henry Little. See MWM 32n10.
10. By Alice Duer Miller.

[73]   [AHT; ALS, JHL]

Kenyon Press, L^{td.}
Editorial Revision Department

Here's to good old Saccharissus;
If his Criticks shou'd die, he might possibly miss us!

Eastern Offices:
66 College Str.,
Providence, R.I.
Jan. 22, 1936

O Sage of Sages:—

HORACE

And now about this matter of Q. Horatii Flacci, Carm. III, ix . . . . . which ought to be right in my line after the Horatian lecture by Dean Laing[1] which I heard last month, and the discussion of Horatian codices I'm now conducting with Klei. Two hundredth anniversaries do stir up echoes! Well—considering what the other translations probably were, I guess you didn't do no harm in handing the heavy sugar to the authoress of the stanzas enclosed—although I don't seem to get as much het up over them as does the preceptress at W. D. Maybe I don't appreciate modern diction—but let's see what it's all about. First we will hammer out an *absolutely literal* prose translation of the lines, and compare the two versify'd texts with it:

Hor. Carm. iii, ix
Dialogue between Horace and Lydia

Horace
Whilst I was pleasing to you, not any preferable youth put his arms on your /fair/shining/ neck; I flourished more blessed than the king of the Persians.

Lydia
Whilst you did not burn more for another, nor was Lydia /placed below/after/ Chloë. Lydia of much /name/renown/ flourish'd more famous than the Roman Ilia*.

Horace
Now Thracian Chloë, taught sweet measures and expert on the cithara†

─────────

*The Roman Ilia = the Iliana or Trojan woman (alluding to descent from Æneas of Troy), i.e. Rhea Sylvia the Vestal, mother by Mars of Romulus and Remus.
†*Cithara* (Gr. Κιθαρα) not so much an *harp* as a kind of *lyre* or (vide etymology) *zither* or *guitar*. It had four or more strings, and was shaped something like a horse-shoe.

rules me; for whom I would not fear to die, if the Fates would spare her surviving soul.

Lydia
Calaïs, son of Ornithus the Thurian, burns me with a mutual torch; for whom I could bear to die twice if the Fates would spare the surviving boy.

Horace
What if our old-time love returns, and unites us, (who are now) drawn apart, with a /brazen/copper/bronze/ yoke? If golden-hair'd Chloë is driven out, and the door open'd to ejected Lydia?

Lydia
Tho' he (= Calaïs) is more beautiful than a /star/constellation/, and you are lighter than cork and more splenetick than the wicked Adriatick, with you I would love to live; with you joyful I wou'd die.

Let us now see what various hands have done with these lines, in an attempt to render them into English verse. I assume you have access to a good library, hence will make no extensive transcriptions here. Instead, I will call attention to the much-esteem'd versions of Bishop Atterbury, made in 1700,[2] of Dr. Philip Francis (father to the reputed author of the Junius letters)[3] in the middle eighteenth century, and of Dr. Badham an hundred years ago.[4] None of them is literal, yet all are a trifle more faithful to the text than are the lines of Miss Canok. On the whole, they bear out the contention of Dean Laing that *no* good translation of *Horace* exists. 'Tis to be observ'd, that Francis copy'd not a little from Dr. Atterbury—as can be plainly seen in the fifth stanza:

Atterbury
What if sweet Love, whose Bands we broke,
Again shou'd tame us to the Yoke;

Francis
Yet what if Love, whose bands we broke,
Again shou'd tame us to the Yoke;

All these gentlemen cou'd, it seems to me, have adher'd a trifle more to the Horatian text without any sacrifice of idiomatick grace. However, I am sensible how much easier it is to censure than to excel. Lest I be thought unwilling to exemplify my precepts, I will here lay open my crudeness by attempting a rough translation of my own—not literal, indeed, but reasonably faithful to the spirit of the Augustan bard:

Dialogue betwixt Horace and Lydia
Hor. Carm. Lib. III, ix
Translated by a Gentleman of New-England

Horace
Whilst I was pleasing to your Taste,
Nor likelier Youths your Neck embrac'd,
I liv'd more happy on Love's Throne
Than Persia's Monarch on his own.

Lydia
Whilst you did for no other burn,
Nor Lydia's Charms for Chloë's spurn,
I flourish'd with a lofty Name,
And envy'd not great Ilia's Fame.

Horace
To Thracian Chloë, skill'd in Song
And on the Lyre, I now belong.
For her I wou'd not fear to die,
Wou'd Death, in Payment, pass her by.

Lydia
Now Calaïs kindles my Desire,
With Torch alight with equal Fire;
For him the Tomb I twice cou'd dare,
Wou'd Death the graceful Youth but spare!

Horace
What if old Love at last be woke
To bind us in its memory'd Yoke?
If golden Chloë reign no more,
And Lydia face an open'd Door?

Lydia
Tho' he the brightest Star outbeam,
Whilst you with Froth and Choler teem,
With you my Days I'd willing spend,
And glad with you wou'd greet the End!

(Note after perusal of lines—the contention of Dean Laing still holds good!)
[5]Examining now the Canok version call'd "Reconciliation", and taking into account the juvenility of the translatress, we may upon reflection perceive the cleverness resident in these lines. They certainly argue a comprehension of the original in all its essentials; and seem to represent an effort to be as idiomatick

in vulgar English, as Flaccus was in vulgar Latin. The metre is a little too irregular to be pleasing, but (if judg'd by beats instead of syllables) nowhere falls down completely. The principal defect is at the close of the second stanza, where the words *clarior Romanā Iliā* (more famous than the Roman Ilia—i.e., than the Vestal Rhea Sylvia, daughter of Numitor and mother by Mars of Romulus and Remus, descended from Æneas of *Ilium* or Troy) are "translated":

> ". . . more glorious than any flower
> That adorns some gracious lady's bower."

To this rendering, one may reply only with the query (borrowed from the protagonists of the translator's other version) "how come?" Horace wished to have Lydia say that, when she enjoy'd his favour, she felt more famous than this historically celebrated mother of the She-Wolf's sucklings, who had had the God of War for a lover. Betwixt this and the posies adorning the retreats of the gracious fair what connexion exists? Why has the Horatian comparison been displaced by another, far feebler and less apt, and without reference to what the author intended? I ask you? Another weak spot—what is Sister Mary trying to do when she places *Căl'-ă-is* in a location metrically impossible, and appears to link it with the impossible place-name *Thurini* as a basis of some sort of rhyme? This couplet has one buffaloed. To begin with, there's no town of "Thurini". The adjective *Thurinus,* apply'd to Calais' father Ornithus, means a native or citizen of *Thurii* (med. Ital. *Terra Nueva*) (Θούριοι), that city in Lucania near the Tarentine gulf which in B.C. 443 was founded by Athenians and other Greeks near the site of luxurious Sybaris—which the Crotoniates had utterly destroy'd in B.C. 510. Among the founders of Thurii (who expell'd from the region all of the effeminate Sybarites who remain'd) were the eminent historian Herodotus and the Attick orator Lysias (then a youth). In time the city became one of the most prosperous in Magna Graecia, and (tho' badly desolated by the Tarentine war) under Roman rule it did not decline. No person ought to be ignorant of this distinguish'd place—but what can we expect of a generation that knows not Antigone herself? O tempora! O mores! Perhaps this stanza cou'd be reduc'd as follows:

> And if the Fates would kindly save
> Sweet Thurian Cal´ais* from the grave . . etc.

Harking back to Stanza II—the trouble there might be remov'd by the substitution of the following concluding couplet—where Lydia's comparison of herself to Mars' sacerdotal inamorata is emphasis'd:

---

*Used here as a dissylable with accent on first syllable (a- syllable glided over) according to occasional custom.

I dwelt content, with prouder name
Than Ilia's own, the War-God's flame.

But on the whole, this production is distinctly appealing despite its defects. Whether it merits exhibition before a distinguish'd assemblage of Latin scholars wou'd seem to me to depend greatly upon *what is commonly achiev'd by high school pupils*. In other words, leaving intrinsick merit aside, how do these lines compare with most similar strivings of the undergraduate classick muse? There are surely present a zest and native aptitude which ought to justify continu'd Latin study on the part of the translator. Certainly, no ground for discouragement exists.

Coming now to the Æthiopian version.[6] I recognise a keen wit and wide cleverness in the liberally paraphrased text, and congratulate the translator—or author—upon having achieved an excellent "Imitation of Horace" in the main tradition. I assume that these *false rhymes* (Siam-man; Jim-bin; sigh-eyes) are *intentional*—though many might challenge the adoption of this device, even in the most extreme forms of dialect verse. One colloquialism I believe to be wrongly apply'd. In Stanza II, it is not to "any man", but to *Chloë*, that Lydia ought to protest against 'playing second fiddle'. When we speak of 'playing second fiddle' to someone, we do not mean being subordinated by that person with respect to others or to the world in general. We mean only *being eclipsed in importance by that person himself*, through some rise in his status or through some decline in ours. Thus, in the poem concerned, it is to *Chloë*, not to *Horace*, that Lydia feels herself in danger of 'playing second fiddle'. Broadly surveying the two versions, I think there can be no question but that the comick paraphrase is the better—the more vigorous in style, & the more replete with original fancy. Probably the chief talents of the translator—talents which might shew to even fuller advantage in wholly original compositions—lie in the direction of the light & whimsical. At the same time, her generally good comprehension of the Latin text must be commended, & her thoughtful choice of equivalent English expressions given an appreciative recognition. Certainly, so gifted & interested a pupil shou'd be accorded all the encouragement which the school & its staff are capable of extending. It is not often in this decadent aera that young persons so faithful to the traditional landmarks of western civilisation will be found.

Yup—Leedle Hymie[7] sho' does git reckless wif he space! I indeed have a new *Californian* before me, & am properly aw'd not only by its quantitative magnitude, but by the amount of really excellent material in it despite certain crude & flatulent spots. Your own contributions are hot stuff, & I surely don't see why the hell the *Eng Journ* wouldn't want any of them which it hath not already us'd—either in existing form or in an amplify'd version. No—the clienteles of the two periodicals aren't likely to have any overlapping area. Hell's Bells—as sharp a guy as old Farny Wright of W T is perfectly willing to buy a story at full price after its appearance in amateur journalism . . . that's why I'll prob'ly let Hymie have my newest fictional lapse[8] if you can't dig up the architectural article in time for the Apr. 15 deadline. I hope, by the way, that you can manage to be well represented in the vernal issue.

Thanks for the printed dope—& hope the word hunts go over big! They sho' have got it all over crossword puzzles! That 4-part project certainly does bring the classroom close to the practical business of life—but I'd get damn low marks in the *interviewing* project. Gawd, how I hate to butt in on people or pry into their affairs! I've often wonder'd how realistick novelists can get all their dope on actual life & human motives without making cursed nuisances of themselves.

Snowbound? Well—antient Providentium ain't far behind Zythopolis. I now gaze out of my westward window at a panorama of drifts & laden roofs. O for the sight of a palmetto or moss-bearded live-oak!

I am vastly griev'd by the passing of the King Monday night.[9] Not a mighty or resplendent Sovereign, but a kindly & honourable gentleman reflecting the deepest virtues & aspirations of the world's supreme civilisation. Never again, perhaps, will there be another such amidst the chaos & disorganisation of the years ahead. I feel the weight of years as I reflect that I have liv'd under *four* monarchs—Victoria, the Seventh Edward, George, & now the Eighth Edward. I trust that the new Sovereign—no youth, heaven knows!—will appreciate his responsibilities as the symbolick leader of Western Civilisation. God Save the King!

I the other day beheld a cinema version of Mr. O'Neill's "Ah, Wilderness",[10] which brought back the dead world of 1906 with poignant verisimilitude. At times I could well believe that the past was come back, & that the last 3 decades were merely a bad dream. Good old '06! Naïve & absurd, yet having many a value which might well have been preserved had social evolution been less violently accelerated by the war. Ah, me!

    Yrs for the Old Days—
        Grandpa Lo.

Notes

1. Gordon Jennings Laing (1869–1945) was coeditor with Paul Shorey of *Horace: Odes and Epodes* (Boston: Benj. H. Sanborn & Co., 1919).

2. Francis Atterbury (1662–1732) translated two odes of Horace (including 3.9). They were included in *The Epistolary Correspondence, Visitation Charges, Speeches, and Miscellanies, of the Right Reverend Francis Atterbury* (London: J. Nichols, 1783–84; 3 vols.).

3. Philip Francis (1708?–1773) translated Horace's odes in *Quinti Horatii Flacci Carmina: The Odes, Epodes, and Carmen Saeculare of Horace* (Patingham, UK: Printed for the editor, 1753). HPL owned an 1835 and 1838 edition of Francis's translation (see *LL* 466, 467). Francis was the father of Philip Francis (1740–1818), a British politician who is the presumed author of *The Letters of Junius* (1769–72), a series of vitriolic letters at-

tacking politicians of the day on the grounds that they were suppressing personal liberty.
4. The translation of Horace *Odes* 3.9 by Charles Badham, M.D. (1780–1845) was included in *Horace,* tr. Philip Francis et al. (London: A. J. Valpy, 1831). This translation (along with Atterbury's) was included in the Francis translations of Horace cited in n. 3.
5. A single surviving sheet (III) of the ALS begins here and proceeds to the end of the letter.
6. HPL is probably referring to an African-American student of MWM's.
7. Hyman Bradofsky, editor of the *Californian.*
8. "The Haunter of the Dark," written 5–9 November 1935.
9. King George V of England died on 20 January 1936.
10. *Ah, Wilderness!* (MGM, 1935), directed by Clarence Brown; starring Wallace Beery, Lionel Barrymore, and Aline MacMahon. Based on the play by Eugene O'Neill.

Robert Ellis Moe

Letters to Robert E. Moe

[1] [ALS, JHL]

66 College St.,
Providence, R.I.,
Feby. 13, 1935.

My dear Mocratulus Major:—
　　　　　　　　　　　　　　It surely was a delectable surprise to learn this morning that the House of Moe has fastened so brilliant a tentacle in the soil of ancient New England! Bless my old bones, but I should say I *do* remember you from the old days of 1923, when you were just about knee-high to the proverbial grasshopper, & came on East with your mother & yet more diminutive brother in an expedition which gave your revered pater a glorious surprise as it met him at Boston's South Station—where he landed with me one day early in August, after I had nearly tramped him to death shewing off the precipitous hill streets of ancient Providence's most historic section. We all bundled into Albert A. Sandusky's car ("Sandy" died just one year ago today—much to the sorrow of us all), which could scarcely hold the party—& I am quite sure that you were the young towhead who sat on my grandpaternal knee whilst your brother occupied a similar perch on the paternal anatomy. As an old man's memory runs, we all proceeded to a friend's home in Cambridge (the Myers family—whose young hopeful Peter, then seven, is now quite an imposing classicist & antiquarian!), where we also met Edward H. Cole et ux—Cole being an old epistolary friend of Pater Mocrates & myself in the world of amateur journalism. I also have two later glimpses of you in mind—during the same visit. It seems that my party—your father, Cole, Sandusky, & I—toured ancient Marblehead (do you recall that centuried seaport near Boston, with the narrow hill streets & huddled, venerable houses?) separately from your party, but met yours momentarily—beside Abbot Hall, the only really ugly (Victorian) building in the town. Later I walked my associates so far that they rebelled—all lining up on a stone wall & refusing to budge an inch more except in a return direction! Well—I saw you once after that . . . the next day, I think, where you & brother & parents were at the Copley-Plaza Hotel. August, 1923—February, 1935! 11½ years surely is quite a stretch . . . with much latitude for change on either side. However, I've seen enough fairly recent pictures of you to know about what to expect—& I certainly don't expect the clocks to stop when you confront them in this ancient & humble abode! The wonder is, that they don't keep still permanently on account of the year-round resident . . . . . well, at that, two of them *do* of late! If you retain any direct memory of me in '23, you won't have much to go by

today. The grotesque entity on whose knee you sate was a fattish, spectacled behemoth of some 180 lbs, with rather thick dark hair only fairly touched with grey. Pallid complexion, long, ugly chin, & tapir-like snout. Well—of all this descriptive matter, only the contents of the second sentence holds good. I disposed of the adipose tissue exactly a decade ago in one of the most historic reducing campaigns of history. Sloughed off 10 lbs per month for 5 months. Present weight, circa 145 (height 5′ 11″). [I had gone up to almost 200 by 1925!] Have shed the goggles for all ordinary purposes. Thatch now decidedly iron-grey & of typically elderly thinness. Look every one of my 44½ years—& probably more. Am catching up to my always-chosen ideal of grandfatherly elderliness! In order that you may recognise me (if I don't spot you first) when we meet at some chosen local terminal, I'm enclosing the latest shot of myself in existence—taken by my gifted young host down in Florida last June.[1] This really looks pretty much as the old gent does look today. Your pater has a copy of this ruthless exposure—but he hasn't seen me in person since that bygone August. He (carrying an adult recollection of '23) would certainly find very little to recognise of the behemoth of yesteryear!

Well—most emphatically you must get up to ancient Providence as early & often as possible, & I only hope you won't be too badly disappointed in the superannuated dodderer whom you'll find at this end of the journey. Despite all efforts, I rather fear that I am the most monumental of bores—hence I urge you to have no compunction about shutting Grandpa up when the verbose abstractions—or antiquarian rhapsodies—billow forth too voluminously. As you probably know, I'm a confirmed devotee of the quaint & the historic—early American architecture being my dominant hobby—& when I get a victim willing to be walked & lectured through the winding streets of an ancient town, I generally rattle on until he shrieks for mercy or takes matters into his own hands. Ask Dad—he knows! About the same, too, with the pompous speculations on the dimensions, mechanism, & [lack of] motivations of the cosmos. Glad to hear that my brutal untraditionalism in such matters won't outrage your sensibilities too violently—but I fear my soporific long-windedness can be less readily endured. So don't hesitate to chloroform the old gent when he gets too noisy! So far as powers of discernment & analysis are concerned, I'm sure it is not you who need feel modest. I've followed your career—as paternally reported—with the keenest interest & admiration, & am acutely conscious of the amount & quality of cerebration involved in your activities & objectives. I doubt if you're very juvenilely indoctrinable at this stage of the game—though even so, I shan't attempt any heavy logical fusillades as a destructive corrupter of youth! Doubtless you've seen enough of my Mocratic screeds to realise that, despite my absence of supernatural belief, I'm not exactly an advocate of an overturned social order & reversed ethical tradition. After all, Grandpa is an astonishingly insipid & conservative old cuss in dozens of ways!

Your taste for weird & science fiction, as often mentioned by your proud parent, has always greatly pleased & interested me. Relatively speaking, there are so few who harbour a taste for the bizarre—though after all we have quite a little circle of congenial "nuts" who correspondent & in some cases occasionally meet .... Frank B. Long, Jun., Wilfred B. Talman, R. H. Barlow, Arthur Leeds, Clark Ashton Smith, E. Hoffmann Price, Robert E. Howard, August W. Derleth (of Sauk City in your own state, & a son of your own Madison alma mater), Donald & Howard Wandrei, Robert Bloch (of your own town—a youthful son of Shem who once called your father up & had a pleasant telephone talk with him), Henry George Weiss (Francis Flagg), H. C. Koenig (an electrical engineer after your own heart), Bernard Dwyer, & others whose names you may recall from *The Fantasy Fan* if you take that modest little "official organ" of the cult. Incidentally, if you don't know the F F, I'll let you have an assortment of copies—my stock of duplicates being very ample. A good many of the "weird gang" (as well as a good many of the amateur crowd who knew your father) live in New York City—within an easy cruising radius of Bridgeport—& I fancy you'll want to look some of them up during the months to come. Many, you will find, are delightfully interesting. The best general guide to 'put you next' to the museums, art galleries, & general advantages of the metropolis, is my sterling young (33 in April, though—how the years do go!) friend Frank Belknap Long, Jr.—230 West 97th St. (cor. of Broadway), N.Y. City. Don't fail to get in touch with him whenever in N.Y.—he can find you excellent & reasonable lodgings in the upper reaches of his apartment-house, & will in general assist you in getting oriented. Your father just missed meeting him in '23—he had gone to Maine for the summer just before the Mocratic descent on Columbia. Then there's good old Klei of the famous Kleicomolo (about which I suppose you know)—Rheinhart Kleiner, 116 Harman St., Bklyn. And the supreme amateur poet—Samuel Loveman, 17 Middagh St. Bklyn—who can be found during working hours at Dauber & Pine's Bookshop, 66 Fifth Ave., N.Y.C. Doubtless you've heard of good old James F. Morton, now curator of the Paterson N.J. Museum, & addressable at that institution. Talman lives in Spring Valley, N.Y. but commutes to his office in the Chrysler Bldg.—where he edits a group of trade papers for the Texas (Oil) Co. Address—Room 1830, 135 E. 42 St., N.Y.C. The two Wandrei brothers live in Greenwich Village—at 155 W. 10th St., N.Y.C. over the 'Bohemian' restaurant known as Julius's. Your electrical contemporary & science fiction fan—Koenig—can be reached at his laboratories—540 E. 80th St. N.Y.C. Any & all of these would be delighted to see you. Mention your father or me to any of the amateur crowd—Morton—Kleiner—Loveman—& me to any of the rest . . . the purely weird crowd. I'll be glad to drop a line of preparation & introduction to any of those whom you'd like to see—or you could go right ahead without such heralding if a sudden chance should present itself.

 Speaking of weird & science fiction—during the past year I've often thought of you in connexion with the new type of television ultra-microscope invented by Dr. V. K. Zworykin—which converts light into an electric current, then amplifies the current, & subsequently converts it back into luminous energy. Probably you've read of this—but does it evoke any reminiscence from your own past? As a matter of fact, the resemblance of this outfit to something you thought up in the winter of 1927–8 is really startling. Remember your old *telemegascope?* Your pater sent me an account of it in your own handwriting, & I have always kept it on file, with the idea of possibly basing a story on it some day & giving you credit for the conception. If you like, I'll let you see this echo of your own boyhood inventiveness—but possibly you do recall it. Of course, I'm too dense to grasp the real gist of the device, so that perhaps Zworykin's outfit differs vastly from yours—but in any case the external resemblance *is* startling. You ought to sue old Zwory for plagiarism or something of the sort. Of course he has the *microscope* rather than the *telescope* primarily in mind—though he states that the principle may ultimately be applicable to telescopy. Every time I've written Mocrates Pater in the past year I've forgotten to mention this matter despite my intention to do so!

Well now we get around to the matter of your Providence voyage, which I surely hope will be undertaken in the near future & repeated with frequency. Just as I was about to go into the matter of stage-coach schedules, a re-reading of your letter & a recollection of something in an earlier missive from 1034 N. 23 reminded me that you probably have a car of your own—hence need a somewhat different set of guideposts. To begin with—I fancy the best route to Providence from Bridgeport . . . the shortest, that is . . . . is the one extending through New Haven (they *all* go through there), Middletown, Willimantic, & Danielson. If, however, you want to see an ampler array of Connecticut cities, you could either cut up to Hartford from New Haven & thence proceed east to Willimantic &c., or follow the old shore road through New London, Conn. & Westerly, R.I. Hartford is a pleasing city, though not especially quaint—except for its delightfully ancient suburbs Farmington & Wethersfield. New London is very quaint. A trip through there could be varied by a turn up the Thames to Norwich (a quaint old town on the terraces of a bend in the river) & thence through Plainfield to Providence. Just how much you could enjoy such sightseeing would naturally depend both on your tastes & on the amount of leisure at your disposal. If you take the shore route you will probably enter Providence from the south over Elmwood Ave. If the Willimantic route, you'll arrive from the west over Hartford Ave. Routes into town are generally well marked. Now to get to my hillcrest eyrie, you'd better enquire the way to *Market Square*—an open space at the head of Narragansett Bay. On the east a precipitous hill arises—with a neo-Georgian brick court house as a conspicuous landmark—its belfry standing out against the slope. College St. soars abruptly at this point—ascending just north (left) of the court house. Your car will be able to negotiate this incline, although it was more than the trolleys could do in the old pre-tunnel days. Keep on upward, crossing *Benefit St.* At the head of the street the ancient facade & belfry of the old college edifice (1770) will confront you. But keep your eyes peeled on the left as you near the top, where College ends in Prospect St. On the left-hand corner is the John Hay Library, an imposing marble pile with a great wall extending in from College St. Close beside this wall runs a *very narrow lane,* just the width of a single car. (And pray to all the paternal gods that it won't be filled up with the parked cars of the boys at the fraternity-house on the hither side of the lane!) This is the avenue of access to Grandpa Lo's colonial hermitage. At the end of this blind alley will be spied the yellow wooden facade & fan-carved Georgian doorway of the house itself—a snapshot of which I enclose. Enter the alley if you can—& you can park there as freely as the fraternity boys, since the lane is college property & we are the college's tenants. Just now it's a bit snowed up—but every warm day helps! As for the rest—just mount the steps & ring the bell that *isn't* marked *Shepard*² .... & the portal will open automatically in response to a button-pressing upstairs. At the head of the staircase within, a guide will await you. We have the upper floor—a quaint place, as you may have gathered from my report to the elder generation. House built about 1810.

Now as to arrangements—it would be an infernal pity to limit a weekend to a *single afternoon!* My aunt & I only half keep house—we dine out, & don't even pretend to maintain a full establishment—but if you don't mind slipshod, uneven, patched-up arrangements, you must try to stay over at least one night ... or more if you can. Unfortunately we lack any spare bed or bedroom, but if you could stand a mattressless canvas army cot temporarily set up in my study, I have one around somewhere which you could probably adjust properly even if my own mechanical ineptitude bungles the job! If, on the other hand, your tastes run to comfort, the chances are 10 to 1 that we could get you a room in the excellent boarding-house just across the back garden in Waterman St. Providence also has a good Y, though it's on the other side of town ... along the route you'd be following if you came in from the shore road & Westerly. That's where Mocrates Pater stopped in 1923. But such details can be decided at the last moment, on the spot. Regarding meals—as I said, we eat dinner out (except when I patch up something for myself out of cans)—my aunt at the boarding-house across the back garden at noon, & I at some cheaper beanery downtown at night. We can steer you all right for the day's principal meal. Our smaller meals are simply snacks grabbed informally around the house—indeed, I eat only 2 meals a day, with a doughnut, cheese, & coffee for my secondary one. If such rough & ready camp-like picnic fare will do you—welcome to the trough! If less primitive conditions appeal, we can get the small meals at the same joints at which we usually get the large meals. Our establishment aims to please! Whatever programme you prefer will be quite oke with Grandpa. As your pater is aware, I keep the most irregular hours known on this planet. No kind of system—not even consistency in irregularity! Usually I'm a night-hawk—but when any reason for a reversed schedule arises, I slip into the latter without effort. Anything except pompous conventionality goes with me!

So just drop me a line when you're coming, & we'll be all set at this end. If you come by car you probably can't predict the precise *hour;* but just specify the day, & the welcoming committee will be awake & on the spot. Judging from the usual coach schedules, it takes about 4 hrs. to motor betwixt Bridgeport & Providence under normal conditions. By now the main highways ought to be reasonably free from major niveous obstructions. I'll append a rough sketch map—not accurately drawn to scale—suggesting the avenues of approach to #66 from various outside points. ¶ Come to think of it, I guess I'll make *two* charts—a large-scale of the vicinity of #66, & a small-scale of the general approaches. For general interurban guidance, of course, you doubtless have the proper motor road maps—or if not, any Bridgeport filling station will be glad to supply you gratuitously. If you've found your way from good old Zythopolis across the continent to Bridgeport, I guess one needn't worry about your covering of the residual 130 miles!

Now if for any reason you decide to come by motor coach or train instead of by horseless carriage, just let me know what route you're taking, & I'll be on hand at any designated hour at any designated terminal. Coach is much cheaper than train . . . fare from Bridgeport on the 'bus would probably be $2.50 . . . certainly not over three bucks. If you come by coach, be positive to specify what line you're using—New England, Greyhound, Northeastern, &c. &c., since they all have different Providence terminals. Lately I've used the New England more than any other—their Bridgeport terminal is at 693 Water St.—Telephone 4-2122. Or you can enquire at Ritz Candy Shop, 2816 Fairfield Ave.—Tel. 3-9715. This information is gleaned from a time table. I lack data on other lines, but you can doubtless pick up time tables of them all around them. The point is to be sure to let me know just what line you're using, & just what coach you're coming on. Seats, I believe, are reserved in advance on all lines. Incidentally—in case of any situation making it convenient—you'd better have my telephone number. It is *PLantations 2044*—the instrument being in the name of my aunt, Mrs. Gamwell. Of course all this coach information is purely tentative. Probably you'll drive yourself—but it's well to leave nothing to chance.

And so it goes. I'm surely delighted to learn of your advent to these general parts, & hope you'll get to Providence-Plantations soon & repeatedly. Some time you ought to plan to get to Boston & see the historic sights there with the sharpened eye of adulthood. Do you recall much from '23? I'd like to shew you Marblehead again, & reintroduce you to the Coles & the Myerses . . . who would be delighted to renew acquaintance with any progeny of good ol' Mocrates!

Well—I hope all this rambling hasn't tired you out. Trust I shall see you soon. Regards to Pater Mocrates, & tell him a semiannual's about due!

Benedictions—

Grandpa Lo

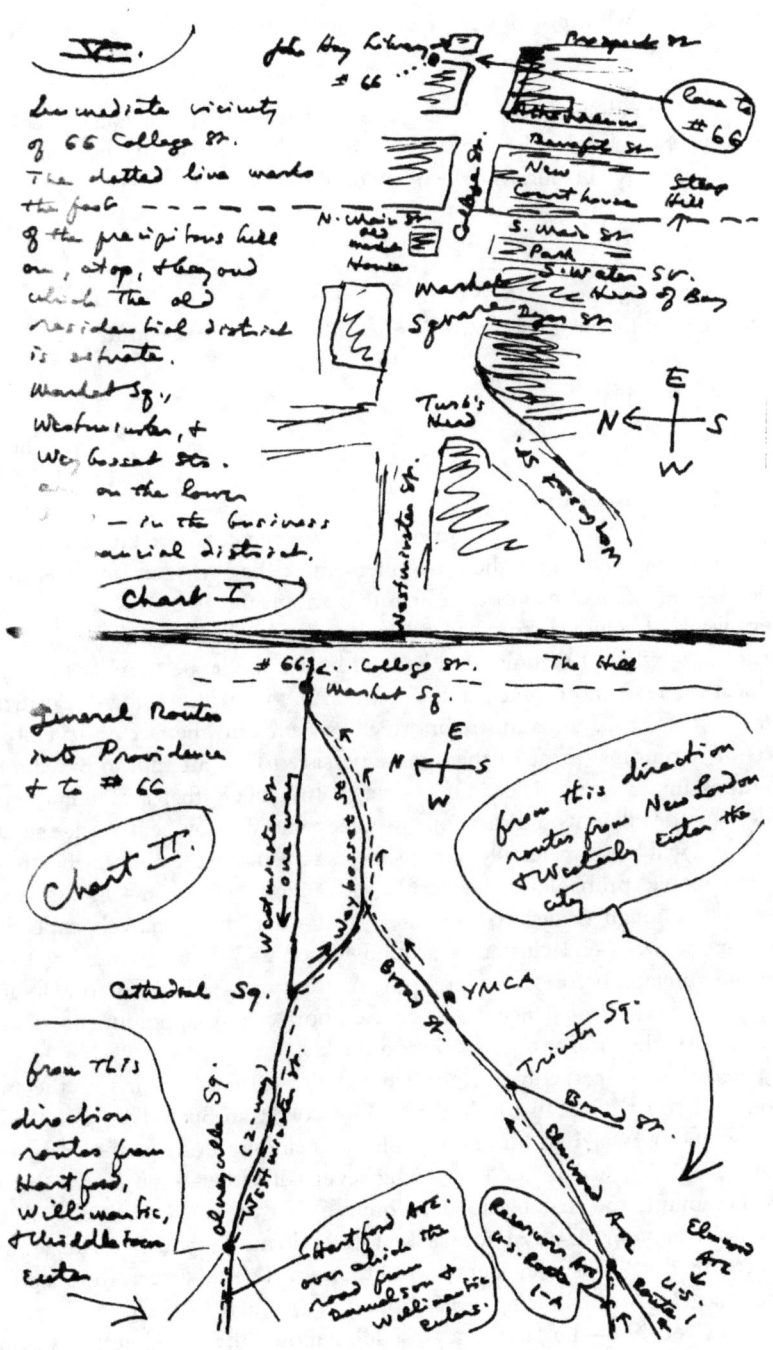

P.S. My aunt (who remembers M W M) sends her regards & says she hopes to see you soon.

[P.]P.S. Is your Bridgeport stationing quasi-permanent? I hope you'll become a fixture in New England! ¶ Tell your father I'll shew you the Journal office where those B K H columns (which you doubtless know about) come from!

Notes

1. See the frontispiece of *SL* 5.
2. HPL appears to refer to his downstairs neighbor, Mrs. Alice Sheppard.

[2]   [ALS, JHL]

Old 66
—Feby. 21[, 1935]

Dear Mocratulus Major:—

Recognising the importance of the current event, I can readily forgive you for the postponement of the Providentian expedition! Indeed—the change may operate to my own advantage in this respect: that every week of removal from the asperities of midwinter makes outdoor excursions (of which I assume we'll have at least a moderate number to points of local interest) more practicable for me. As you may possibly recall from paternal allusions, I am almost abnormally sensitive to the *cold*, & develop all sorts of symptoms (some of them quite persistent) if I attempt to brave temperatures under about +20°. Of course, it isn't likely that any temperature under that deadline would develop this week-end; but by next week-end the likelihood will be so materially diminished as to remove the contingency from all reasonable probability—hence the advantage. However—in any case there'll be enough to discuss indoors! I shall, then, be tentatively expecting you for the week-end clustering around March 2–3—though waiting for a heralding bulletin before considering the matter final. As I said before, I surely hope that Old Providence won't prove a bore & a disappointment—& I'll try not to lay the local antiquities on too thickly!

Bierce's tales certainly are powerful in the extreme. Which of the two books did you read—"In the Midst of Life" or "Can Such Things Be"? Or has somebody issued an 'omnibus' volume including both of them? I have both, & will be glad to lend you whichever—if either—you haven't read. Which reminds me that I also have quite a few other weird books, all of which are at your disposal for as long-term loans as you like. Regarding "Creep, Shadow"—as coincidence would have it, I've just received as a gift a set of the *Argosy* instalments, neatly bound . . . though I haven't had time to read it as yet. No—the tale is not pseudonymous; the genial author having been christened *Abraham Merritt* by his own Pennsylvania Quaker parents. I enclose a brief sketch of him from the old *Science Fiction Digest*.[1] I have been a Merritt fan ever since 1918, when I first saw the original novelette version of his "Moon Pool". Although he has greatly injured his work through "slanting" it toward the popular magazine type, he has a certain subtle magic parallelled by no other writer I can think of. Nobody else is such a master of what I call *geographical* horror & strangeness—the ability to make a whole region seem weird, unearthly, & menacing through the careful selection & handling of details. Also—I don't know of anyone else who has succeeded as well as Merritt in depicting a *non-human* (in fact, *non-animal*) race of beings—beings which differ from mankind not only in aspect, but in *basic psychology*, motivations, activities, & modes of expression. In most cases science-fiction authors are pitifully unable to imagine any kind of *mentality & emotions* (hence, motives & customs) radically removed from those of the mammal primates, hence in their work we find beings of the most bizarre exterior—plant men from Pluto, semi-plastic sentient globules from trans-galactic universes, &c—thinking & feeling & behaving just about as the man around the corner might! This Merritt has escaped to a very marked degree—particularly in "The Metal Monster", which he calls his *best & worst* story[2] on account of the trivial & hackneyed nature of the humans as distinguished from non-human characters. I've read all of Merritt's published work—except the new novel now before me. It is, as a whole, provokingly *uneven*—& many tales begin splendidly, only to peter out amidst the pallid extravagances of stock romance. The *original* "Moon Pool" (merely the first section of the later full-length novel), "The People of the Pit" (short), & "The Woman of the Wood" (novelette) are about the best-rounded of his productions. I met Merritt in N Y a year ago last month—he is a stoutish, sandy, ruddy chap around 50, & exceedingly clever & well-informed. He acts as associate editor of the rather charlantanic & flamboyant "American Weekly"—or magazine supplement to the Hearst Sunday papers, & can be reached at the office of that enterprise . . . 14th floor, Daily Mirror Bldg., 235 E. 45th St., N.Y.C. If you're not familiar with Merritt's work, I can lend you a number of his things—including "The Moon-Pool", "The Face in the Abyss", "The Dwellers in the Mirage", & some of the shorts. Any of them is amply worth reading. My young friend Barlow of Florida could lend you others which I lack.

As I said—there are many issues of the *Fantasy Fan* which I'd be glad to pass on to you. Not many of them have any stories of mine; but they are full of material of general interest connected with weird & science fiction, & several have contributions from Clark Ashton Smith & other top-notchers.

I'm interested to hear of your new camera, & hope you'll find some material worthy of it hereabouts. Several friends of mine have done a good deal with amateur photography—especially young Barlow, & the Wilfred B. Talman whose address I gave you. Talman has two very remarkable cameras sent him by relatives-in-law in Germany (his wife's mother is a first cousin of the rather prominent German financier & statesman, Dr. Hjalmar Schacht[3]), one of which takes pictures of almost microscopic diminutiveness, which will bear enlargement to almost fabulous dimensions without any perceptible loss of sharpness. These instruments have such splendid lenses that they need almost no stopping down, but will function in almost any kind of light—including the ordinary electric lighting of a private home. Last month when our gang assembled at Long's (with 15 present), Talman surreptitiously snapped almost all of us in grotesque poses when we weren't looking—although it was in the evening, with nothing but an ordinary chandelier for illumination. I can shew you some of Talman's shots—landscapes, sunset effects, &c.—when you're here next week.

Being the most ignorant of laymen where any matter of modern electronic physics is concerned, I can't speak with authority about the relative status of the telemegascope & the Zworykin apparatus. No doubt the distinguished & unpronounceable gent has carried the idea somewhat further in a practical, operable way—but you must admit that the *external, superficial* familiarity is really quite striking! Yes—I should be very glad to see a description of the Zworykin invention, even though my comprehension of it might not reach beyond the most rudimentary stages. The whole field of radiant-energy physics opened up during the last generation is almost staggering in its possibilities, & I really regret being so backward concerning it. Every time I see a demonstration of some modern marvel like television—or the "electric eye"—I resolve to brush up, but I never quite get around to it! Electrical energy—with its enormous potentialities in the direction of *automatic* machinery & virtually humanless manufacturing processes—is opening a social & industrial era as sharply differentiated as the preceding age of steam. Whether we like it or not, it will make collectivism in finance, industry, & government as inevitable as the growth of a tree or the cooling of the sun.

The day after I wrote you I had a rather interesting communication from Loring & Mussey of N.Y.—the publishers of my young Wisconsin friend August W. Derleth of Sauk City. (I think Derleth barely missed being in the U. of Wis. at the same time as yourself . . . indeed, you two may have overlapped for a year.) Incited by the said Derleth, they asked to see some of my MSS. with a view to possible book publication. Since this is the *5th* time I have had a similar request (W T 1926, Putnams 1931, Vanguard 1932, Knopf 1933) without any tangible results so far, I am naturally not as naively excited about the matter as I might have been years ago. Nevertheless, I'm shooting some junk along . . . just for the sake of leaving no stone unturned. I'd hate to think, later on, that I *might* have had a published collection *if* I'd heeded the request.

Had a brief but interesting line from Pater Mocrates the other day, & told him in reply how glad I shall be to see you again. I added that I hope you'll settle permanently in New England, & form a goal for visits of his own! I'd like to shew the two of you around ancient Marblehead, & see who'd be the first to plant himself on a stone wall (as in '23) & refuse to be dragged any further!

Well—I shall be on the lookout for a line, & hope to see you early in March. Here are a couple of glimpses of old Providence. The house marked in the Thomas St. view is the one described in my story "The Call of Cthulhu". ¶ Blessings—

Yr obt Grandsire—

Lo

Notes

1. Julius Schwartz, "Titans of Science Fiction: A. Merritt," *Science Fiction Digest* 1, No. 5 (January 1933): 3–4.
2. So stated in F. Lee Baldwin, "Within the Circle," *Fantasy Fan* 2, No. 1 (September 1934): 7.
3. Hjalmar Schacht (1877–1970), German economist and banker who served as president of the Reichsbank (1923–30) and Reich Minister of Economics (1934–37).

[3]   [ALS, JHL]

Tiw's-Daeg
[12 March 1935]

Dear Mocratulus Major:—

Thanks immensely for the snaps, which are truly excellent! You couldn't have picked a better Wickford house—*perfect* 18th century! The blurring in the hill view is really quite inconsequential—some photographers seek even hazier effects just for art's sake! We can get a churchyard view another time. The snap of Grandpa in the ancient doorway is admirably clear—my aunt even noted the unpainted putty around one of the new panes in the cellar door! I'll send you my snaps—if any—just as soon as I take up the remaining two & get the roll developed.

Glad my harangues & article on antiquity proved of some interest.[1] I'll have to ask the return of that hectographed copy some time—but no hurry. I'll let you see the rest (the greater part) of the text when your respected pater gets it duplicated & sends me a copy. No—your generous sire did *not* hold out on you—since this random & really impromptu essay was written on the 10th of last December. I feel flattered by your favourable opinion of my prose. Some day remind me to shew you the surviving instalments of the old *Kleicomolo* of 20 years ago. I don't shew 'em to everybody, since some of my views were flagrantly callow & immature in those days, & many of my pompous arguments sound rather grotesque in the cold light of 1935!

Social-intellectual note—ecce! the weird-science-fiction-fan population of ancient Providence has just been swelled by a very energetic new electron .... as was forcibly impressed on me last Thursday, immediately after the sealing of my epistle to you. I was reading the paper in my study when my aunt entered to announce a caller—a "Mr. Kenneth Sterling". Close on her heels the important visitor appeared . . . . in the person of a little Jew boy about as high as my waist, with unchanged childish treble & swarthy cheeks innocent of the Gillette's harsh strokes. He *did* have long trousers—which somehow looked grotesque upon so tender an infant. It appears that he is one of the numberless kid fans clustering around the weird-science pulps & the fantasy sheets, who had read my stuff & learned my address from the F F. He's a typical New York Yid—but his papa has just been made assistant manager of a local fur shop—so he now takes rank as a Providentian. Goes to Classical High & means to become a research biologist. And oy, vhat ah shild, vhat ah shild! If they all come as precocious as this, I don't wonder that Hitler is afraid they'll juggle the shirts off the German people's backs! Hang me if the little imp didn't talk like a man of 30—correcting all the mistakes in the current science yarns, reeling off facts & figures a mile a minute, & displaying the taste & judgment of a veteran. He has already sold a yarn to *Wonder*,[2] & is bubbling over with further ideas. Wants to organise a branch of the Science Fiction League in Providence, &c. His father is a Harvard graduate, & several in his family seem to have done substantial writing & reviewing. Quite a boy! He says he's coming over again—you may see him some time, & settle the electrical & biological fate of the planet between you!

Glad you enjoyed the Shiel & Chambers material. "The Purple Cloud" is definitely *weird* only at the start, but the ensuing picture of desolation is certainly titanic! The *first half* of the novel is best. In the second half, romantic petering-out becomes apparent. Bierce, as you see, could be a realist as well as a fantaisiste. The Civil War tales (he was a Union major of cavalry) are perhaps his aesthetic high-water mark. Samuel Loveman met Bierce personally years ago, & can talk interestingly to you about him when you look up the N Y gang. "The Yellow Sign" is to me the cream of Chambers. I put it among the 10 greatest weird tales ever written. Don't hurry about any of this stuff.

Hope Skippy will be quite rejuvenated after his impending treatment, & ready to tackle the Providence road again when the boughs overhead burst into a feathery green! My aunt & I had a delightful & unexpected ride Saturday, during which brief stretches of our recent Warren–Providence route were duplicated.

Heard a darned good lecture last night at the college—Prof. W. P. G. Swann of Franklin Institute on cosmic rays[3] . . . assisted by slides & apparatus. You would surely have appreciated it—though it might have seemed to you a bit elementary. I learned several recent points which had not previously been clear to me. ¶ Enclosed is something of possible mild interest—a rotogravure view of the event responsible for the aquatic decorations we saw at the art club. Also a cutting which speaks for itself. ¶ Well—pax vobiscum, & regards to Skippy! ¶ Yr obt Servt—Lo.

Notes

1. "A Living Heritage: Roman Architecture in Today's America."
2. "The Brain-Eaters of Pluto" (*Wonder Stories*, March 1934). Two other stories—"Red Moon" (November–December 1935) and "The Bipeds of Bjulhu" (January–February 1936)—would appear in the magazine.
3. William Francis Gray Swann (1884–1962), British physicist and director of the Franklin Institute (1927–59).

[4]   [ALS, JHL] [fragment?—leaf IV only]

[20 March 1935]

¶ * The Book of Wonder—in the Modern Lib. Ed. which I have, combined with Time & the Gods
¶   The Last Book of Wonder—a little flat & frivolous
¶   Tales of Three Hemispheres (a few good stories)
¶ * Fifty One Tales (brief fables &c)
¶ * Five Plays (including the famous Gods of the Mountain)
¶ * Plays of Gods & Men
¶ * Don Rodriguez—a picaresque novel
¶   The King of Elfland's Daughter (fair)
     The Charwoman's Shadow   ⎫
¶   The Blessing of Pan   ⎬ a bit insipid
     The Curse of the Wise Woman (not really weird—a splendid study of boyhood in Ireland)
     Travel Tales of Mr. Joseph Jorkens ⎫
     Jorkens Remembers Africa   ⎬ flippant & trivial but clever

I can lend you a goodly number of these if you like—without the time-limits imposed by the public library.

Glad you found something passable in "Polaris" & "The Other Gods". Both are old & essentially minor efforts. "The Other Gods" was composed in 1920, during my period of maximum Dunsanian influence, but Polaris—despite its basic similarity—was written in 1918, before I ever read a line of Dunsany .... showing how thoroughly prepared I was to become a Dunsany devotee when (in Oct. 1919) I finally did come across my idol. You'll be interested to note that "Polaris", at the time of writing, was embodied in a Kleicomolo. I used to insert all sorts of separate compositions—verses, tales. &c—in the endless pages of that diversified circulating catch-all. I'll lend you a complete copy of "Sup. Hor. in Lit." when you're ready for it. It was pub-

---

¶ owned by me & at your disposal

lished complete in a super-amateur magazine in 1927, & the current reprint embodies only relatively slight changes.

Glad that Skippy is responding reasonably well to surgery, & hope he'll bear you nobly to the prospective Zythopolitan convention. Before long you ought to get to New York & look up the gang. Koenig (the electrical engineer & weird fiction fan) acknowledged our joint card & asked for your address—saying he wanted to drop you a line in person & expressing a hope that he might soon have a chance to shew you over his really remarkable Electrical Testing Laboratories at 540 East 80th St. You'll find all the crowd very congenial, I feel sure. And don't forget old Prov. in due season!

So you're getting "vaccinated" against hay-fever! I didn't know you were a sufferer. My friend Arthur Leeds (whom you'll probably meet in N Y) is a perennial victim, & all the treatments he has so far received seem to be merely temporary. Hope your course will be "for keeps"!

New *Marvel Tales* is out—I'll send you a copy presently. Improved format, but rather mediocre contents. Derleth has just sent me his new detective novel—"Three Who Died"—& I guessed the solution on p. 145 (out of 252). He kept the mystery longer than in his preceding book "The Man On All Fours"—where I had the key on p. 32! I'll lend you these if you care to glance through them—you probably know Derleth through his W T contributions. As I think I mentioned, his period at the U. of Wis. undoubtedly overlapped yours. The scene of all his books is his own home town of Sauk City (which he calls Sac Prairie), where he still resides. There are many references to Madison, Bascom Hall, &c., which you would recognise.

Some warm weather—up to 71° Saturday! Yesterday I went to see the first cinema I've attended since I was in N.Y. with the gang last January—"Men of Aran", a tremendously artistic presentation shewing the arduous life of the islanders off Ireland's west coast.[1] The Aran Isles have no soil except in deep crevices between the rocks, & the scant potato crops are planted in long mounds of this carefully excavated soil mixed with seaweed & laid along the rock surface. The sea pounds savagely & mountainously at the dizzy cliffs & jagged rocky beaches, & boating is attended by frightful hazards. Yet most of the islanders' living comes from the water—fish, & oil from the giant sharks. One wonders that human beings cling to a site where bare existence involves so terrific a struggle—yet the ancestors of these folk have stuck to the islands for over a thousand years. This is the scene of Synge's famous "Riders to the Sea".

Well—according to the Old Farmer's, ☉ enters ♈ tomorrow at 8:18 a.m.[2]—& I for one can tell the cockeyed world I'm damn'd glad! ¶ Patriarchal blessings—

Grandpa Lo

Notes

1. *Men of Aran* (Gainsborough Pictures, 1934), directed by Robert J. Flaherty; starring Coleman "Tiger" King, Maggie Dirrane, and Michael Dirrane. The film, half documentary and half fictional, treats of the difficult life of people who live on the Aran Islands off the west coast of Ireland.
2. The sun enters Aries; i.e., the first day of spring.

[5]   [ALS, JHL]

Good Friday
[19 April 1935]

Dear Mocratulus Major:—
              Glad to get your line—& thanks tremendously for the views! You were lucky to see Washington in cherry-blossom time—& Mt. Vernon. I must revisit the latter some day—my most recent glimpse being in 1928. You surely caught some interesting & characteristic bits in the metropolis—especially that Florentine nook, & old Trinity at the cañon's mouth. I'll never forget how magnificent Trinity looked one morning at dawn—when all Broadway was in violet shadow, with one prodigious flood of golden radiance pouring up Wall St. & transfiguring the venerable spire, tower, & churchyard.[1] Those brownstone facades certainly form the one unmistakable symbol of Old New York. I lived in one of them—at 169 Clinton St. Bklyn.—from Jany. 1, 1925 to April 17, 1926. Bless my soul, I hadn't realised that day before yesterday was the 9th Anniversary of my Providence homecoming! The old Fishkill Church is intensely interesting. Did you note the very ancient Dutch church (1695) at Sleepy Hollow as you passed north of Tarrytown? On a high bank east of the road. Your pa once slipped a descriptive paragraph of mine about that church & its storied region into a Macmillan reader he was editing . . . . getting my name on the table of contents betwixt Washington Irving & Sir Walter Scott![2] I've never before nor since been in such distinguished company.

Well—you've certainly done some picturesque & enviable travelling during the past few weeks! I'm sure Koenig enjoyed your visit—& hope you'll drop in on Long, Loveman, & others of the gang in course of time. But naturally the Washington trip eclipses all mere Manhattan jaunts! You were lucky to see the cherry blossoms—which is more than I've ever done so far. I always arrive too late. A few were still lingering when I hit the capital last year—but so damn few that I don't consider my record of failure actually broken. Considering your limited time for recuperation, the trip was surely a strenuous one—though my own Charleston jaunts involve quite a bit of wakefulness. Hope you can repeat the journey ere long—& when you do, be sure to see *Annapolis* (Md.) & *Alexandria* (Va.) You must have passed through the latter on your way to Mt. Vernon—but possibly you didn't drink in all its splendid Georgian architecture .... & its impressive old church, of which Gen. Washington was a communicant. Another place worth seeing is ancient Fredericksburg—50 m. from Washington & about half way to Richmond. And some time you ought to visit the great *cavern* region of western Virginia—there are sometimes bargain rail excursions from Washington. I saw the Endless Caverns in 1928—& shall never forget them. I'll let you have a booklet about them if you're interested.

Your Poughkeepsie discussions seem to have been very interesting—& I think your fair confrere is right in giving great credit to old Confucius for clear & realistic thinking. He was refreshingly free from the typical mysticism of the Orient. A friend of mine in Vermont is a great Buddha fan—but after all Prince Gautama became irrationally mystical in his concept of a continuity of life, & of the punishment of "sins" by visitation on oneself in future existences or incarnations. As for the inculcation of a practical ethical code in years to come—it will, of course, have to accompany some strong social movement, as in Russia today. In the interim—& how long an interim we can't predict—there will probably be rather an ethical lapse—with the intelligent experimenting on new codes, & the masses drifting aimlessly while still nominally adhering to the primitive faiths of their fathers.

That promised early spring didn't pan out after all—as you've doubtless noticed! *Snow* here day before yesterday! But every week ought to make a difference. I surely hope you can get around on the 27–8th—let me know the probable hour (or I'll be watching from about 11 a.m. on). Meanwhile be thinking of what sights you'd prefer to take in. How about ancient Newport this time? But let your own tastes form the guide. May 3–4–5 I'm going to the Boston zone to revisit venerable scenes (including Marblehead) with Cole. If you can come the 27th you might drop a postcard bulletin confirming the event—but I'll be on the lookout anyhow. ¶ Grandpaternal blessings—& hope to see you 8 days hence. ¶ Yr obt Servt—Lo

P.S. No hurry at all about the borrowed books. There's no waiting list!

[P.P.S.] May have that roll of film developed shortly. 2 shots of a black kitten completed it.

[P.P.P.S. on envelope:] Some time when you're in Washington (if before June), look up my young friend Robert H. Barlow, 1218 Sixteenth St., N.W.

Notes

1. Trinity Church at 75 Broadway in lower Manhattan, in the Episcopal Diocese of New York, near the intersection of Wall Street and Broadway, is the third and current church, constructed between 1839 and 1846.
2. HPL refers to "Sleep Hollow Today."

[6]   [ANS, JHL][1]

[Postmarked Providence, R.I.,
6 May 1935]

Greetings! Glad to hear that you've been foregathering with Belknap, & hope the meeting of the gang will be staged before long. You'll enjoy meeting Morton (my fellow-champion at Maxfield contests), the Wandreis, Talman (your fellow photographic expert), Loveman (whom Pater Mocrates knows) & all the rest. ¶ Hope the pictures will turn out well—& sincere commiserations on the Agfa embargo! Fall River is surely excusable for its lack of a supply! I am still saving the last two shots of my film for views of little Johnny Perkins (who came to call this morning & consumed a large saucer of salmon), but before long will take it down for developing. Some of the views ought to be pretty fair. ¶ Glad you found a restaurant at once picturesque & dietetically good. Does it beat Ching Ling's (or whatever it was) at Newport? ¶ Hope you had a pleasant drive home. I took a 4-mile walk in the golden summer light—traversing several suburban stretches that I'd never traversed before. The next day cold weather descended upon the town, & I've felt like hades ever since. Had an interesting visit at Cole's—in the Boston zone—this last week end, but the low temperature took all the pleasure out of sightseeing. We went to Marblehead both Friday & Saturday—a splendid feast for the eye, even amid shivers. The Boston amateurs—who know Pater Moe—hope to see you before the summer is over. Cole's Angora kitten—Peter Ivanovitch Romanoff—is getting to be a regal & impressive mountain of tiger fur! ¶ Interested to hear of Bridgeport's architectural antiquities, & hope to see some of them in course of time. ¶ Quite a bit more greenery out in Prov., but Boston's season is more backward. Hope to see you hereabouts when Skippy feels like another spell of road-burning!
Benedictions—
Lo.

Notes

1. *Front:* "Doorway," Old Lafayette House, Marblehead, Mass.

[7]   [ALS, JHL]

Thor's-Daeg
[18 May 1935]

Dear Mocratulus Major:—
I'm certainly glad to hear that I didn't bore you to death! Yesterday I mailed you a copy of that *Texaco Star* with Talman's Providence article[1]—which I had meant to give you in person. Keep it—for I have fully half a dozen more copies. You will recognise some of the pictures—the

alley, of course, is Harding's Alley, which I shewed you. I'll be interested to learn how your photographs turn out—I haven't yet taken up the two remaining pictures on my film.

Don't worry about the accelerated adieux—the fact is, I'd have had to wait endlessly for another 'bus if I hadn't hopped the ochraceous vehicle so conveniently in sight! Delighted to hear that you saw Wickford, & captured a bit of it on the film. On your next trip—which I hope will be at an early date—I'll shew you ancient St. Paul's in Wickford . . . on one of the back lanes. This was built in 1707, five miles south of its present site, to serve the planters of the Narragansett Country, who lived in a rural, patriarchal style much like that of the southern planters. Like the rural churches of Virginia, it lay in the midst of the open fields & woods—being reached by its communicants in coaches or on horseback. The revolution destroyed the old planter civilisation, so that dwellers moved away & the church's congregation dwindled. Then, in 1800, the edifice was taken apart & moved in sections to the village—where it has ever since remained. Glad you caught a schooner. There are a good many of these in Rhode Island waters, though full-rigged ships (which I can remember years ago) have virtually vanished. I can, however, shew you *one* square-rigger—the U.S.S. *Constellation* (1794), now used as a training ship at the Newport Naval Training Station. Sorry that Westerly & New Haven tangled you up a bit. It's curious how scarce signs are in some towns. Providence (if you'll permit some more filial boasting) seems to be very well equipped in this regard—did you notice the frequent "To Boston", "To N.Y.", "To Hartford", "To Cape Cod", "To New Bedford", &c. &c. signs on all the trunk streets & at all the major intersections? Yes—I feel sure you could qualify as a local guide after a few more trips. You were certainly dragged around to most of the historic high spots! The vast West Side, & the picturesque Italian colony on Federal Hill (the site of that distant steeple visible from my west window) are another story . . . all at your ultimate disposal!

Regarding the status of antiquarianism in general (of which, alas, I am certainly *not* a really profound student . . . . you ought to see the genuine article—historians like H. M. Chapin & architects like N. M. Isham![2])—I could ramble on endlessly in a quasi-aesthetic, quasi-philosophical vein. Of course, one's exact degree of enthusiasm for visible reliques of the past depends on accidents of temperament—just as one man likes beef while another likes pork. Some people take naturally to history & its tangible deposits, while others take to lyric poetry, or the sciences, or mechanics, or any other of the endless divisions of human energy & interest. In general, though, the importance of a study of the past lies in the fact *that nothing in the present or future really means anything except in relation to the past* . . . nothing, that is, beyond a narrow radius based on physical comfort & abstract aesthetics & intellection. To relate anything vitally to oneself, *points of reference* are needed—& these the past alone can supply. Any sociologist can tell us that man's criteria of the external world—our standards of what is pleasant or suitable or good—depend almost entirely upon the historic experience of his especial line of cultural ancestry. The experiences of the present & future could have no zest or relish except as fulfilments of certain expectations determined by the past. Take away the past, & the best art of the present & future vanishes as well! In this connexion I can't resist enclosing the introductory section of my recent rambling observations on Roman architecture & its echoes in the present—an introduction in which I endeavour to present the case for traditionalism in aesthetics. As you will probably recognise, the hectographing & typing are of Mocratic source. I wrote the thing in my usual scrawl—in response to a vague hint of the desirability of some such article for one of your father's pupil's MS. magazines—but he thought it worth preserving in duplicated form.... hence the present text. He is doing the copying & duplicating in sections—this being the only part I have. Since it is an only copy, I'll ask you to return it at your leisure—not the slightest hurry, though. Incidentally—don't fancy that my attack on 'modernistic' art implies a belief that everyone should be a red-hot antiquarian! Special consideration of the historic factor in life is no more to be expressly enjoined (or neglected) than special consideration of any other factor. One person may happen to be an antiquarian enthusiast—another may happen to be an astronomical enthusiast—another may happen to be a poetry enthusiast—& so on all along the line. There's room enough for all in a mature civilisation. All that merits our protest is the arbitrary & unjustified *ruling out* of any of these natural factors—as Plato tried to rule out the poet, as the bolsheviks (in theory) try to rule out all non-propagandistic art, & as the modernists try to rule out all the accumulated heritage of the past. Regarding the antiquarian as a type—it seems to me the least bit amusing to think that his special interest is any less justifiable than others because it happens to involve objects which may be either vanished or in decay. What really enthralls him is simply *the drama of time & change*—the vivid pageantry of interacting forces among mankind. It is more or less a matter of chance that he selects, as the chief symbols of this drama, certain tangible objects connected with various anterior points in the time-stream. It is hard to see why this type of symbolism (perhaps the most natural one for a realist, since objects in the past have a *real* existence, while those in the future have a merely *hypothetical* existence) is any less admirable than the cognate type which selects imaginary or tentatively calculated points in the future reaches of the time-stream. Another very sound basis for antiquarianism is its symbolic relationship to man's endless emotional protest against loss & decay. All our lives & aspirations really form one prodigious rebellion against time's ruthless toll & our own pathetic transiency. Change symbolises loss & decay—whereas the contemplation of the ancient & the changeless symbolises whatever of solidity & permanence & good adjustment our whirling atoms may ever know. However—don't fancy that I'm trying to make a yesterday-hound out of everybody else! I'm merely outlining what seems to me to be the *raison d'etre* of a certain type.

I hope I didn't seem too brutal an itinerarial slave-driver last Saturday! You ought to have spoken up if I laid the sightseeing & haranguing on too thick! I'd have been the very last person to interpret the residual effect of earlier strenuous evenings as censurable infirmity or anility! Don't think you must get in training, as for a prize fight, when visiting Grandpa!

Regarding a 'literal translation of my signing-off mark' ..... I didn't know I had any such symbol! You give, in parenthesis, a form of the ordinary mark of *paragraph-separation*, (▫) which I often use in breaking the continuity of text—& therefore now & then in separating the closing words of a crowded & compact letter from the text proper. Is this what you mean? If so, the matter stands self-explained. The symbol, of course, is an old & widely used one. I employ it especially in inditing crowded post-cards—when I don't wish to waste space on marginal indentations. I suppose the device is merely a conventionalised letter P (another form is ¶[3])—standing for "paragraph" & for some obscure reason reversed.

Yesterday was marvellous—as I dare say B'port realised as well as Prov. Mercury up to 65°. I took a long, overcoatless walk through the half-awakening countryside north of the city, covering about 12 miles in all. This, added to our trip of Sunday, surely gives my 1935 travel season an early beginning! Last night my aunt & I attended a very interesting lecture at the School of Design—in that 2-towered ex-church in Benefit st. Thomas Whittemore, the archaeologist who is uncovering the long-hidden 9th & 10th century mosaics in St. Sophia in Constantinople, described his work in the most interesting fashion—illustrated with lantern slides.[4]

Well—so wags the world! I enjoyed your visit immensely, & hope you can arrange to get up again soon. Let me know in advance, & the flags will be waving!

Yrs, &c———Lo

P.S. I've fallen for that 1-volume encyclopaedia at Liggett's.[5] It was inevitable! I brought a copy home last night.

[P.P.S.] Am enclosing the last F F—duplicates just came.

Notes

1. "Texaco at Home: V—Providence." *Texaco Star* 18, No. 5 (May 1931): 23–26.
2. Howard Miller Chapin (1887–1940), librarian of the Rhode Island Historical Society (1912–40) and an authority on colonial American history. Norman Morrison Isham (1864–1943), prominent professor at Brown University and the Rhode Island School of Design, architectural historian, and author. He was a pioneer in the study of early American architecture.

3. I.e., the pilcrow, used in the Middle Ages to mark a new train of thought, before use of the visually discrete paragraphs became commonplace. HPL's conventional version omits the two "legs," but for simplicity the editors use the standard symbol.
4. Thomas Whittemore (1871–1950), American archaeologist and founder of the Byzantine Institute of America.
5. See Bibliography under *The Modern Encyclopedia*.

[8]   [ANS, JHL][1]

[Postmarked Fredericksburg, Va.,
6 June 1935]

All hail from the South! I thought of you as the coach passed through Bridgeport yesterday at 3:30 p.m. Started Wednesday (June 5) & rushed right through N.Y. & Washington. Ancient Fredericksburg is my first pause—a stop of over 6 hours. Have been absorbing decent heat & colonial antiquities—aye, & scenic beauty, too—all at once. Shall take the Richmond coach at 3:15 p.m., connecting at 5 o'clock with the coach for Raleigh & CHARLESTON. Will hit Charleston at 5:25 a.m. Friday. Shall stop 1 night at the Y & do Savannah the next day. Then Jacksonville in the evening, (sleeping there) & De Land around noon Sunday. ¶ Considerable of a tragic mixup about time schedules. Fatuously taking Pater Mocrates' 1923 visit as a sort of criterion, I imagined he'd be coming east some time late in July or early August. Fancy my perturbation on learning—in a letter received just as I hopped off—that the coming pilgrimage will be in **early July**—when I'm virtually pledged to be still in De Land. I shall see what can be done about unscrambling the dates—but it's certainly a tension-filled business! ¶ Hope you are active & flourishing, as usual. Had those films fixed up & will send you your copies before long. ¶ And have noticed *several* Agfa dealers in Prov. ¶ More anon—
Yr obt Grandsire
Lo

[P.S.] Address: % BARLOW, BOX 88, DE LAND, FLORIDA.

Notes

1. *Front:* Rising Sun Tavern, Fredericksburg, Va.

[9]   [ANS, JHL][1]

[Postmarked Charleston, S.C.,
8 June 1935]
June 7

Hit Charleston at 5:25 a.m. & rested at the Y. Now absorbing colonial antiquity & delectable heat, & getting a coat of sunburn on the Battery. What a place! I hate to leave so badly that I may cut out Savannah & spend the bulk of tomorrow here. You ought to see the churchyards—overhung with live oak & Spanish moss. The climate peps me up immensely—feel fifty years younger!

    Regards—Ech-Pi-El

[P.S.] Got some ice cream at the oldest apothecary shop in the U.S.—founded in 1784

Notes

1 *Front:* Pringle House, Charleston, S. C.

[10] [ALS, JHL]

            ℅ Barlow, Box 88,
              De Land, Florida,
                July 24, 1935.

Hail, O Mocratulus Major!

    Delighted to receive yours of the 20th, & to learn what genial temperatures the arctic regions have been enjoying! Even down here we can't equal that 95° . . . 89° being De Land's highest to date. The good thing about Florida is that it doesn't get cold occasionally—or at night—as the north does. Otherwise, the summer here is actually not as hot as that of the north—the presence of the sea on both sides forming an equalising influence. I'm having a great time—revelling in the genial weather & sub-tropical scenery. The enclosed card illustrates quite accurately the sort of a river I rowed along last month in the trip which I described to Pater Mocrates.

  I was interested in hearing of your recent introduction to the massed freaks & sages of amateur journalism, & am hardly surprised that you found them rather a grotesque bunch. However, it is only fair to amateurdom to state that the crowd you met is not quite representative of the hobby as a whole. In the first place, the pseudo-United whose convention you attended is **not** the old U.A.P.A. in which your father & I were active. This is an offshoot which separated in 1912 during a political fight, & which happened to survive despite the decline & disappearance of the original body. It has, of course, some of the old pre-1912 members—but is nothing like the evolved United as it was in its heyday . . . 1914–1920. Most of the persons active in that heyday are now, unfortunately, out of amateur journalism. Secondly: the N.Y. amateurs as a whole do not (aside from Morton, Long, Loveman, & a few others) include the cream of the National membership. You'd form a different estimate if you were to meet (again, as I hope you may) Cole of Boston—or Edkins of Chicago—or some of the other solid standbys. However—it can't be denied that amateurdom has an enormous semi-nut fringe. It amused me when your father wrote of Wheeler Dryden (half-brother of Charlie Chaplin—whose half-baked arguments I recall from old N.Y. days a decade ago), who refused to attend a picnic because—as a "numerologist"—he found that he would bring its personnel to an unlucky number!!!! The Blue Pencil Club are largely unimaginative householders whose interests are social rather than literary, & who don't care very much for amateurdom as a whole. Scattered around the country are members much less philistinic in their purposes—& a few so devoted to amateurdom that a kind of renaissance (after a period of admitted decadence) may result sooner or later from their concerted efforts. On the whole, though, I fear that the institution will have difficulty in regaining its level of a generation or two ago.

You'll like Morton better on closer acquaintance. He's a curious old coot, but delightful when you come to know him & appreciate his varied acquirements. I never met the Mrs. Wood you mention, but believe I recall some of her verse—written under the pen-name (or maiden name) of Chaffee.[1]

My young host Barlow isn't a typical amateur—indeed, his opinion of the body & its personnel is quite ruthless in its analytical realism. He is, though, interested enough to want to participate in the attempted renaissance with a paper of high grade. The especial printing project on which I'm helping him is not an amateur journalistic (in the organised or formal sense) venture at all, but a *book* enterprise[2] about which you will hear more as time passes. I really feel that I owe him a bit of coöperation in recognition of the super-hospitality I am receiving & have received in the past from him & his genial household.

As for energy-squandering in general—I suppose I am a classic example of that careless infirmity—though I fear you are too charitable in believing that conservation & re-direction would prove of brilliant advantage to me. All my efforts are of a peculiarly spontaneous kind which never seem to fit into the scheme of popular demand or practical usefulness; & when I seek to canalise them more consciously & purposefully they tend to expire on my hands or become mediocre [if indeed they are ever more than that] & unacceptable. So far as fame or public acclaim are concerned, I am long past the age at which I could enjoy or derive advantage from such things. What I do hope, however, is that I can some day coördinate my activities in such a way as to gain me a modest & dependable income—say of from $10.00 to $15.00 per week, on which I could manage to live (& *do* live, though the outgo is not balanced by income) through exercise of the economies I have learned in the last decade. It is not impossible that I may do this eventually—in which case I shall not quarrel with a fate whose caprices have cast my few slender talents in other than a commercial or acquisitive mould.

That long-distance wireless set you mention must surely be a glamourous thing. Even frequent repetition could scarcely dull the thrill of being in direct aural contact with the historic areas of the Old World, & hearing with next-room (or this-room) distinctness the accents of voices thousands of miles away. That is something I don't get on the small, weak set over which my aunt receives her Providence & Boston programmes! Down here, though, I've heard quite a few moderately distant things—for my young host's father is quite an experimenter with special short-wave aërials & such-like. He is partial to Spanish programmes from South America.

Glad you find M. R. James reasonably enjoyable. Regarding *motivation*—all tales of this sort must naturally have some weakness in this direction, since they are primarily *portraits of a certain type of mood*—& of a type born of dream & folklore, & therefore necessarily lacking in objective motivation. Some, however, are more successful than others in creating that external *appearance of motivation* which makes fiction aesthetically convincing. With your dominantly *scientific* tastes, you would probably prefer a kind of tale with a greater grounding in physical possibility—which impels me to ask whether you've ever read "The Last & First Men" (1930) by W. Olaf Stapledon . . . . a remarkable novel of the future which I've just read in Barlow's library. This prophetic tour de force follows the human species & its descendants some 5,000,000,000 years into the unknown time-gulfs ahead . . . & through successive migrations to Venus & Neptune. This is the only mature & serious fictional handling of long cosmic aeons that I've ever seen, & I can assure you that it's worth perusal on your part. It catalogues the natural mutations & artificial manipulations of germ-plasm whereby 18 different human genera succeeded one another down the limitless stream of time. Psychological & sociological values, & the general facts of science, are handled with surprising insight, sincerity, & competence. Of course there are occasional improbabilities & extravagances, but the whole thing is so far above the pulp "scientifiction" level that no comparison is even remotely possible. It is, indeed, almost literature. If you can't get this at any Bridgeport library I fancy Barlow would be glad to lend you his copy.

Well—I certainly hope I'll see you before the snow flies! The Barlovii are now urging me to remain down here *all winter*—until next May—but I'm certainly not eager to be away from my books & files & familiar scenes that long! And yet—so hellish is the hyemal climate of the north—I'm more & more convinced that I'll have to live down here some day, as age lessens my resistance to cold.

All good wishes—

    Yr most obt

      Grandpa Lo

P.S. How did the second pack of films (New Bedford—Round Mill—Tiverton) turn out? When some of my prints are returned by borrowers, I'll send you a set of the shots secured by my humble $2.00 1907 Brownie!

Notes

1. Eleanor Alletta Chaffee. She published a few poems in the *Brooklynite* as Eleanor Wood.
2. Barlow published *The Goblin Tower* by FBL under the imprint of the Dragon-Fly Press.

[11] [ANS, JHL]¹

[Postmarked St. Augustine, Fla.,
20 August 1935]

On my way at last! Accompanied the Barlows to Daytona Beach & helped them settle in the flat they are to occupy for a fortnight—then took the coach for ancient St. Augustine. It surely is good to see centuried gables & facades & balconies & garden walls—& hear the sound of tinkling fountains at twilight, & of cathedral chimes cast in 1682—after 2 mo. & 9 d. amidst rural modernity! Am revelling in the atmosphere of a 370-year-old city—a city founded when Shakespeare was a year old, & still containing houses which had 50 years behind them when the Pilgrims landed on Plymouth Rock. ¶ Am staying a week at my usual cheap but cleanly hotel—the Rio Vista, on the bay front—& cutting my food bill down to a minimum. Spend most of my time absorbing ancient vistas & writing atop the venerable fort. Moving north Aug. 25—& will get a few hours in Savannah before striking ancient Charleston. Am so short of cash that my stay in Charleston will be badly cut down—& hopes of stopping anywhere north of there get dimmer & dimmer. However, it has been a magnificent trip, & I'm certainly squeezing the last drop of enjoyment out of it. ¶ Hope all is flourishing in Bridgeport & environs, & that you've had some good motor trips. Don't forget old Prov. next month & later! ¶ I see that Pater Mocrates is well settled in his new dual quarters—an idyllic arrangement! Best wishes—& see you later.
Yr obt Grandsire
Lo

Notes

1. *Front:* Old Curiosity Shop, St. George Street, St. Augustine, Florida.

[12] [ANS, JHL]¹

[Postmarked Charleston, S.C.,
26 August 1935]

Hail, Mocratulus! Hope this isn't the card I sent you before. Got here Monday morning at 8, & am at the Y till Thursday evening at 8. Then northward with only brief stops. It's great to be in the midst of English colonial architecture again after so long an absence. I wander delightedly through ancient

streets & churchyards, & hate the thought of moving along. After Florida, Charleston seems distinctly *northern*—less moss on trees, fewer & smaller palmettos, no jungle effects, no rainy season, &c. I dread the coming chill in the real north!
All good wishes—
H P L

Notes

1. *Front:* Old Post Office, Charleston, S. C.

[13]   [ALS, JHL]

Home Again—
Octr. 2, 1935

Dear Mocratulus Major:—

Hades! I wish you had sent that message to me in Belknap's care! It is my fault that I didn't mention 230 W. 97th as the one sure place for reaching me on all my return journeys . . . . it has become so much a matter of course that I doubtless took universal knowledge for granted! I would have appreciated infinitely your guidance around the Bridgeport region—& still hope I may avail myself of it on some future occasion. My relative ignorance of Connecticut is something I have long desired to remedy.

I surely enjoyed St. Augustine & Charleston, & wish I could have stayed longer in each. I had a day each in Richmond, Washington, & Philadelphia—in the latter place visiting (for the first time since 1924) the suburban estate & ancient stone house of the eminent naturalist Bartram—who in the 1760's made the first scientific survey of Florida plant life. The botanic gardens & house (1731) are preserved by the city in good condition, & form a public park in the midst of a section rapidly going over to factories & cheap villas.

I reached New York Sept. 1, & was a guest of Donald Wandrei (in his flat at 155 W. 10th St., where I occupied the room of his absent brother) for nearly a fortnight. Wish I had dropped you a line! I saw virtually all the gang—Long, Morton, Koenig, Leeds, Kleiner, Loveman, Talman, Kirk, &c—& visited a number of museums.

Home Sept. 14—to confront a devastating array of piled-up tasks of every sort. 3½ months of old papers & magazines to read up, 2 revision jobs, numberless letters that didn't get forwarded—Ædepol, what a mess! My programme won't be back to normal for months!

And yet, in response to an invitation, I briefly renewed my truancies within a week—spending Sept. 20–23 with E. H. Cole in Wollaston, & taking several highly interesting side-trips in his Chevrolet. We visited Nahant & Marblehead, & took a long jaunt into the picturesque, vista-filled hills of the Connecticut Valley—also visiting Cape Cod, where we enjoyed the gentle seaside landscape & loafed on the sands of Chatham with only the Atlantic between us & Spain. This widely representative dose of New England scenery was especially welcome after my long absence amidst palms & live-oaks.

Even further travel possibilities lie ahead. Next Tuesday my aunt & I will probably visit New Haven—right in your direction—in a friend's car, while it is just possible that I shall accompany Cole on a trip over the Mohawk Trail & up into Vermont when the autumn foliage is at its height. I certainly feel the chill of the north most acutely, & haven't half the available energy I had in Florida & Charleston. Still, steam heat reduces discomfort to a minimum .... & I bridged over with the oil stove before the steam was furnished.

Sorry it wasn't practicable for you to attend the gathering at Belknap's. The gang will share my sentiment, since all who met you on a previous occasion expressed a wish to see you again, early & often. However, I fancy you are doing the sensible thing in saving for a Yuletide trip home—which will undoubtedly be worth any number of Manhattan week-ends. You'll find the family in quite a new setting—or settings—both extremely pleasant according to Pater Mocrates. Hope you won't be prevented from making the trip by any rush of work at the Bridgeport end. Your daily programme sounds like an arduous & confining one, but I realise that the *reading* item gives it an infinite imaginative scope. Glad you've come across a really satisfying new book—one which I confess I have not perused. A friend has lent me the Wells–Huxley compendium—"The Science of Life"—which ought (when I get around to reading it) to help in bringing my biological knowledge down to date. Glad your new radio is in good shape. I have yet to hear one which gets European stations really *well*. The Barlow outfit has all sorts of devices—special aërial, &c—yet continues to collect much more static than melody from transatlantic shores.

Meanwhile destruction stalks the land. That row of ancient houses on lower College Hill which you photographed is entirely gone now—just a gaping void with a board fence around it. Don't know when work on the new structure will begin. Another vanished institution is that rugged stevedores' lunch room—"Jake's"—where we had the sausages & griddle cakes. After all these years it has folded up ... & the Providence proletariat is leaner for its passing! Glad you had a chance to sample it!

All good wishes—Yr obt Grandsire—Lo

[14]   [ALS, JHL]

Octr. 22[, 1935]

Dear Mocratulus Major:—
    Thanks endlessly for the generous array of prints enclosed—especially the delightful enlargement of a scene which will, alas, never more meet the eye. You had better luck with Col. Green's windmill than I did [by the way—have I sent you my pictures of our April expedi-

tion?]—& the other views are correspondingly good even if a little darkish. I am especially grateful for the Connecticut glimpses. That archway excites my keenest interest. The building has a sort of 19th century look, so I fancy it is not one of the old colonial inns. Of course isolated specimens of archways under buildings have occurred right along—up to the present time. I was disappointed to find that the "saving" of the old College Hill archway really meant *demolition & reconstruction*. It is gone now, but the massive wooden lintel & adjacent bricks have been saved for re-erection as part of the future School of Design Building. In a certain sense, it will be the same old archway—but in another sense it will scarcely be quite that!

Well—as I prophesied in my earlier note, I've seen a bit more of Connecticut than I had seen before. That New Haven trip of Oct. 8 indeed came to pass—giving me 7½ hours for exploration while my aunt visited a friend. The day was ideally sunny (though I could have wished it warmer), & the ride through autumnal Connecticut delightful. Too bad I couldn't have gone onward to Bridgeport—though it would doubtless have been in your busy hours. New Haven (which I assume you have explored . . . I had never seen it before save from a moving vehicle) is not as rich in colonial antiquities as Providence, but has a peculiar charm of its own. Streets are broad & well-kept, & in the residential sections (some of which involve hills & fine views) there are endless stately mansions a century old, with generous grounds & gardens, & an almost continuous overarching canopy of great elms. I visited ancient Connecticut Hall (1752—the oldest Yale college building, where Nathan Hale of the Class of 1773 roomed), old Centre Church (1812, with an interesting crypt containing the grave of Benedict Arnold's first wife), the Pierpont house (1767—now the Yale Faculty Club), the historical, art, & natural history museums, the Farnham & Marsh botanic gardens, & various other points of interest—crowding as much as possible into the limited time available. Most impressive of all the sights, perhaps, were the great *new* quadrangles of Yale University—each an absolutely faithful reproduction of old-time architecture & atmosphere, & forming a self-contained little world in itself. The Gothic courtyards transport one in fancy to mediaeval Oxford or Cambridge—spires, oriels, pointed arches, mullioned windows, arcades with groined roofs, climbing ivy, sundials, lawns, gardens, vine-clad walls & flag-stoned walks—everything to give the young occupants that massed impression of their accumulated cultural heritage which they might obtain in old England itself. To stroll through these quadrangles in the golden afternoon sunlight; at dusk, when the lights in the diamond-paned casements flicker up one by one; or in the beams of a mellow Hunter's Moon; is to walk bodily into an enchanted region of dream. It is the past—& the ancient Mother Land—brought magically to the present time & place. Nor are the Georgian quadrangles less glamourous—each being a magical summoning-up of the world of 2 centuries ago. Many distinct styles of Georgian architecture are represented, & the buildings & landscaping alike reflect the finest taste which European civilisation has yet evolved or is likely to evolve. Lucky is the youth whose formative years are spent amid such scenes! I wandered for hours through this limitless labyrinth of unexpected elder microcosms, & mourned the lack of further time. Certainly, I must visit New Haven again, since many of its treasures would require weeks for proper inspection & appreciation.

But even this trip did not quit end my 1935 travels. Oct. 16 at 6 a.m. our friend Samuel Loveman blew into Providence on the N.Y. boat, & after a brief session at #66 we both started out for Boston to absorb bookstalls, museums, & general antiquities. Stopped 2 nights at Technology Chambers in Irvington St.—but had no time to look up Cole or any of the local group. We dropped Pater Mocrates a joint card. Back to Providence at noon on the 18th, & did the principal bookstalls here. Then, at 8 p.m., I reluctantly saw the guest off on his steamer for the metropolis.

Cole is still talking about that Mohawk Trail trip, but at this time of year (it wouldn't come till November) I'm a little more hesitant about accepting than I might otherwise be. Still—with a winter overcoat & a heated Chev.... who knows?

You certainly have a strenuous programme, though I fancy the new courses are as enjoyable to you as is the regular work. Hard work & confinement have their compensations with their cause is a congenial one. No hurry about the books—as you can see, they are not reference-volumes which call for frequent consultation. Let me know when you get time for any others. Hope nothing will impede the Christmas trip home—& that weather conditions will prove favourable when the time comes.

Well—again let me thank you for those attractive pictures. I'm tempted to get the College Hill enlargement framed as a memento of days gone by. Eheu fugaces!

Yr most obt & appreciative Grandsire—
Lo

[15] [ANS, JHL]¹

[unaddressed, no postmark or stamp;
August 1936]

Dear Mocratulus Major:—
Thanks immensely for the set of interesting prints, which ably commemorate a highly felicitous occasion. I look back on July 18–19 with the acutest pleasure—& am unendingly grateful for the transportation provided by Skippy. Bulletins from Pater Mocrates indicate that the rest of his trip was extremely pleasant, & I trust he is well braced to fare the coming winter's grind. Hope all is flourishing in Bridgeport. ¶ On July 28 my erstwhile Florida host Barlow blew in, & has been here ever since—stopping at the boarding-house across

the garden. He is quite used to Providence now, & haunts the bookshops unendingly. On Sept. 1 he moves westward—to a possible new residence in Kansas. We've made a few short trips to Newport Aug. 15, & to ancient Salem & Marblehead Aug. 20. A fortnight ago another guest was here—old Adolphe de Castro, one-time friend of Ambrose Bierce & later a revision client of mine. He stayed 5 days—& one afternoon he, Barlow, & I sat in the hidden hillside churchyard & composed rhymed acrostics on the name of Edgar Allan Poe . . . who 90 years ago used to wander & ponder in that self-same necropolis. ¶ Sorry to hear that the warm weather (which actually saved me from a nervous & digestive collapse) has been affecting Pater Mocrates badly. Give him my sympathy & tell him that *I'll* be the laid up one three months from now, when the hellish *cold* arrives! ¶ Hope to see you in Prov. when you come, if you can spend the time from more pressing concernments. Morton is due in a week or two—at which time we shall make a substantial dent in Maxfield's ice-cream supply. Commiserations, by the way, on the poor record of last Sunday. Better luck & less pop-corn next time! ¶ My aunt & I both send regards. ¶ Yr obt Servt—Lo

Notes

1. Betsy Williams Cottage, Roger Williams Park, Providence, R. I.

Nurses' Aid Bernard Austin Dwyer (center) *among other volunteers of the Ulster County Red Cross (Kingston Daily Freeman,* 15 June 1943)

Letters to Bernard Austin Dwyer

[1]   [AHT]

10 Barnes St.,
Providence, R.I.
March 3, 1927

Dear Mr. Dwyer:—
 I enjoyed your letter and enclosures very much, and was especially pleased with the glimpse of Pickman's Model with its frightful companions at its nefandous feast by the black barn in the accursed wood. I duly note all the details of the terrible scene, including the arachnid horror on the sanguineous stone altar. This thing—which I will duly shield from all the sensitive and impressionable eyes of the household—shall repose broodingly in a wallet of skin taken from a wizard's corpse cut down from the gallows in 1692, in a locked secret cabinet in the vaulted crypt beneath my shunned abode. At Roodmas and All-Hallows' shall I view it, and the Objects squatting on nearby coffins or peering monstrously over my shoulder shall shudder as they gaze upon its forbidden revelations. Yet at that I think I'd rather present a visual facade like Pickman's Model than like that of the Horror at Red Hook. Even Richard Upton Pickman, inured to ghastly abominations as he was, could never have stood up against that greater, graver blasphemy whose distorted, misshapen, and leering visage for two years polluted the Arcadian rusticity of the Brooklyn meads and groves. Apropos of your unholy feast by the tarn of black blood—I am reminded of what Baudelaire once asked an aspiring decadent poet who copied—and even exceeded—his colourful Satanism without reflecting to any dangerous extent his genius. A trifle exasperated by the ostentatious 'shockingness' of the young man, Baudelaire 'went him one better' by asking very gravely—"Have you ever tasted young children's brains? They're quite delightful, and taste exactly like walnuts!"[1]

 I am glad to hear that Long's poems[2] are evoking such a favourable recognition from your aesthetic apparatus, and shall let him know of your approval when I write him. Certainly, his work has the authentic breath of youth; and he has a technical facility which will enable his conscious art to keep pace with his genius. Did I send you a copy of *The United Amateur*—organ of an amateur literary association which I was editing a few years ago—with my critique of Long's work in general?[3] If not, let me know and I will do so at once. When I wrote it Long had not done so much verse as he has now—in fact, it was I who urged him to branch into metre when I noted the predominantly poetic quality of his prose. He's a great boy—and I call him my adopted grandson—and bids fair to become a permanent credit to his old

Grandpa Theobald*. I have seen boys *try* to whistle through their fingers, but oddly enough, I never saw one *succeed*. That is probably because my hermit-like tendencies in youth narrowed the range of my opportunities for observation. As to "Little Belknap's" appearance—he is as much the eternal child in face as in poetry, and would be taken anywhere for about sixteen, though he will turn 25 next month.[4] Fortunately I am able to illustrate his aspect quite amply by means of the enclosed snap-shots, (which please return) which although not exceedingly recent, are still quite representative. He inherits this eternal juvenility from his father, who is nearing sixty yet looks about forty. During the war Dr. Long used to be held up by army agents asking to see his draft registration card—as if he were under 31! Belknap's grandfather, Col. Long,[5] was the engineer who put up the Bartholdi Statue of Liberty in New York harbour, and the family still has much of Bartholdi's correspondence, as well as the large flags used at the unveiling, and a model of the statue presented by the workmen at the conclusion of the enterprise. The drawing of Belknap is an attempt of my own. He is dark and almost Mediterranean in appearance, and likes to imagine—in defiance of his genealogical record—that he has the blood of some Italian renaissance nobleman in him.[6] He is 5 feet 8 inches in height, wears a bushy shock of almost black hair, and tries vainly to cultivate a microscopic bit of down on his upper lip—about five hairs on one side and seven on the other, if I remember rightly—which in certain lights is almost visible; giving an appearance of his having been at his mother's jam-pot in the pantry. His health is very delicate, involving both anaemic tendencies and a cardiac weakness which bars him from all exercise—even long walks, or the ascent of long flights of stairs. You must certainly look him up the next time you are in New York, for he will be overjoyed to see you, and his parents are delightfully cordial and hospitable. He is one of the star members of an informal "gang" which meets at the houses of the various components to discuss literature, the arts, and kindred topics, and which comprises Samuel Loveman the poet, James F. Morton, Curator of the Paterson (N.J.) Municipal Museum, Everett McNeil, author of boys' historical novels, George Kirk, bibliophile and dealer in rare editions, Rheinhart Kleiner, an urbane town bard and contributor to the various newspaper 'colyums' of the F.P.A. type,[7] Wilfred B. Talman, a young writer and genealogical expert still in college (postgraduate journalistic work at Columbia) and Vrest Orton, an amateur aesthete connected with the *American Mercury*. Leaving this congenial circle was the only thing I regretted when I came home—but it could not make up for the quiet atmosphere, visible antiquities, and ancestral associations which only Providence can give me. The gang delights to enter-

---

*My principal pseudonym is *Lewis Theobald, Jun.*—after the 18th century pedant, who formed the original butt of Pope's Dunciad. (before he turned the D. against Cibber)

tain visitors who have been in touch with any of its members or former members, and you must not fail to be present at some of their Wednesday evening meetings. You can get in touch with them through Long, whose address—as I think I stated once before—is 823 West End Avenue, New York City. All of us, I guess, are a little freakish in spots; and you'll find the meetings quite a colourful menagerie—but not, thank Heaven, touched with even the faintest tinge of Greenwich-Village bohemianism. We are distinctly an unmodern set, and represent in a feeble way that main stream of conservative letters which we conceive to be the normal expression of the Anglo-Saxon culture. Of us all, I think you will find Morton the most vivid and interesting. He is a fattish chap of about 55, crowned by a shock of tight-curling white hair which once was red, and holding an A.M. from Harvard. By inheritance he is a thorough Yankee, (his material grandfather S. F. Smith wrote the nation hymn "My Country, 'Tis of Thee")[8] but he has a radical streak in his mind which has led him through the most amazing set of intellectual experiences (including philosophic anarchism!) imaginable; experiences which are now taking him back in cyclic rotation to rational conservatism and the settledness of later life. Yes—he has indeed returned to the fold, and if he weren't anchored by his Paterson curatorship I think he'd return to the New England that bred him. As it is, he constantly has me buy and ship him a brand of Boston baked beans which is unobtainable outside New England!

But to return to photographic topics—I also enclose a fairly contemporary picture of Clark Ashton Smith, which will neutralise to some degree the slightly stagey effect of the quasi-Keatsian view attached to the printed copy of "The Lurking Fear". Since that old picture Smith has cut his hair and grown a moustache, although it must be admitted that he retains a certain look of poetic melancholy not inappropriate in a Baudelairian satanist. Smith is in feeble health, and lives a very retired life with his parents in the country near the village of Auburn, Cal. He is inclined to be discontented because of his inadequate public recognition, but I still believe he will come to general notice before he is too old to enjoy it. He is now 33 years of age. I am glad Smith's work is gradually 'getting at' you, and know you will like his drawing and painting as well as his verse. The very next time he circulates a set of his paintings I will see that you are on the circuit, and meanwhile I shall be interested to hear his comment on your work. Looking over such of my files as are not in storage, I find only four small Smith specimens to shew you—all sinister heads—but these I will enclose as samples of his colouring; asking that you return them. The whitish blurs on "The Shoal" are very unfortunate—being due to the sticking of the paper in which it came enclosed. I wish I could get off the adhesive bits without harming the pigment. No—Smith is not, I think, like Harry Clarke,[9] whose work shows a sophistication and mastery of detail which Smith (who never took an art lesson in his life) does not attempt. Colour rather than line is Smith's strong point, and he strives for atmosphere with certain approaches toward the decorative which associate him with S. H. Sime[10] rather than with Clarke. The best collection of Smith material I have seen is that in the possession of Samuel Loveman. I have never seen Smith in person—in fact, of all our gang George Kirk is the only one who has. Smith has never been outside his native state of California.

Take your own time about digesting my junk. There is absolutely no hurry. You surely have the stock formula of the sidereal novelist very glibly, and in your one diagram express the essentials of every popular sky-tale from Garrett P. Serviss's down.[11] Some day I surely must try my luck at this sort of thing—minus the conventionality.[12] I think I shall write about the place where Cthulhu came from. "The White Ship" is the only one of my frankly fantastic things that Weird Tales ever accepted. It appeared in last month's issue, and if the readers favour it I presume Wright will be in the mood to take more—or perhaps reconsider his rejection of some of the old ones. I have just finished my second young novel of the year—"The Case of Charles Dexter Ward", in 147 pages. Now—gawd 'elp me—for the typing of it! Meanwhile I must hasten to type a 60-page history of weird fiction which I wrote last year, and which a friend of mine—W. Paul Cook of Athol, who published Belknap's book—wishes for the first issue of an amateur magazine he is founding. This circle of amateur writers and publishers is quite an interesting one, and if you think you'd care to join in spite of its present state of decadence I'll send you some of its printed matter*. There are two major associations composing it—and although I like the United best, it is so nearly defunct that I think I'll send you an application form for the National first. I am not as active in the administrative affairs of this circle as I used to be, but you can get very full information by writing to the present "live wire" of the institution—Victor E. Bacon, 5932 Julian Ave., St. Louis, Mo. I'll see that you get Cook's magazine when it's out. Meanwhile Cook has a vague and as yet unformed idea of publishing my longish short story "The Shunned House" as a thin book uniform with Long's poems and Loveman's "Hermaphrodite" and coming "Sphinx". If that happens, it will constitute my first book; and will inflate me with a pride of authorship likely to lead to unbelievable heights of arrogance! I'm enclosing some more miscellaneous stuff of mine, about whose return there is no hurry at all. The best, perhaps, of these things is "The Statement of Randolph Carter", which is in essence an actual dream experienced by me in December 1919. The verses are negligible—one of them exhibiting that intense love of *cats* which is one of my outstanding characteristics. In that elegy I mourned the 9-year-old hearthside companion of

---

*One of our editors—a quaint old fellow in Haverhill—is now about to send you his unique little paper. I also send one of my annual birthday poems, written for an aged and lovable poet of Greenwich, N.Y., now 96 years old.

the quaint old publisher of *Tryout*, which will come to you by mail this week.[13]

As to "The White People"—well, I take it that if the girl had not killed herself there would have happened exactly what did happen at the outset of "The Great God Pan". But the great strength of the tale is in the colouring and atmosphere. You have probably gathered that the nurse was a member (or was at least descended from a member) of that persistent secret institution known as the *witch-cult*, whose nocturnal assemblages and celebration of the "witches' sabbath" twice a year were the topics of so much whispered conversation in the old times. When Machen wrote the story the cult was regarded as a popular delusion, but since then the important anthropological work of Prof. Margaret Alice Murray has virtually proved that such a frightful circle did actually exist up to about a century ago. In her work "The Witch Cult in Western Europe" Miss Murray shews that a very ancient cult of nature-worship and fertility-rites, allied to the Dianic cult of the Mediterranean region, certainly existed amongst the Mongoloid peoples (who have left their language in Finland and their race-stock in Lapland) inhabiting Europe just prior to the first wave of Aryan invasion. This cult, driven into secrecy by the hostility of the newcomers but thriving unimpaired and even borrowing from the Druidical, Graeco-Roman, and Christian ceremonies of the religions succeeding it, became a feared and dreaded thing to the majority who were not initiated into its mysteries; and when ascetic Christianity reigned, it was bitterly hated because of the nature of its ritual and practices. It became a furtive, midnight organisation, to whose meetings the few initiated members would steal out silently from their homes, unknown even to the rest of their families. One's own sister or grandmother might be an initiated witch, yet remain undiscovered. Local groups called "covens" were formed, each presided over by a leader called "the devil" or "the black man", who would often attend disguised in the skin of an animal—especially the goat, since the *Pan* notion became engrafted at an early date. Meetings were of two kinds—"estbats", called irregularly for the transaction of business or the laying of spells, (for the deluded devotees firmly believed themselves dowered with Satanic power) and "sabbats" held twice a year at dates once fixed as the breeding-seasons of the flocks and herds—April 30 (Roodmas or May eve) and October 31 (Hallowe'en). This is evidence that the cult reached back to an age of pastoral nomads, antedating the advent of agricultural life, whose natural festal dates are solstitial and equinoctial. (Christmas, Easter, Midsummer's Day, Harvest-home.) The *Sabbat* was what the outside world came to know as the Witches' Sabbath, and was always held in a dark wood or a wild and lonely place. At this great semi-annual convocation a regular programme was followed out, including many rites of the most loathsome and abominable description—"the unnamable", in truth! Initiations to the cult were few, and always followed a rigid study of the prospective witch by the local coven members. The ceremonies were impressive, and included the signing of a book in one's own blood, and the receiving of a tattoo-mark from the presiding "black man". Each neophyte, also, received a new name by which he or she was always subsequently addressed during meetings. The existence of the cult was always vaguely known, and occasionally referred to in whispers of horror. It was altogether rural, (though allied to the diabolist and Black Mass cults of the towns) and comprised mostly the peasantry; though occasionally a person of high birth would become involved. The notorious Gilles de Retz was almost certainly a member, if not the actual "black man" of his local coven.[14] Whether or not Joan of Arc was a member is still disputed, Miss Murray inclining to the view that she was. The plagues of Europe in the Middle Ages, producing a wild despair and "live-while-you-live" attitude reflected in the old Dance of Death woodcuts and the grotesque carvings in late Gothic churches, gave an enormous impetus to the secret cult-orgies; and there is reason to think that the number of actual recruits became very great. Terrible deeds were done o'nights, and more and more people brought in horrified reports of dark things they had stumbled upon in the deep woods. All historic records unite to shew that both clergy and civil authorities were occasioned great concern, so that there is a real basis—and no mere superstition, as the cocksure historians of the 18th and 19th centuries delighted to state—in the famous bull of Pope John XXII against witchcraft. In 1400 the decent-minded noblemen of Southern Germany, despairing of the power of church and state to check the evil, banded together in the secret Holy Vehm, a sort of mediaeval Ku Klux Klan as clandestine as the witch-cult itself, which made captures and held extra-legal trials and executions of suspected cult-members in the woods at night. The Vehm was well and sincerely meant, and probably did much good. No one knew who belonged to it or where it would hold its assizes, or whom it would arrest and condemn. Unlawful though it was, the constituted authorities both civil and ecclesiastical recognised it as a friendly influence, and were correspondingly lenient toward its technical infractions of the nominal code. In 1484 Pope Innocent VIII began a really vigorous anti-witchcraft crusade—during which, of course, the innocent as well as the guilty suffered. In England the campaign against witchcraft began at the accession of James the First, when a band of Scottish cult-members were detected in absurd incantations meant to wreck the ship carrying his bride. James, of course, believed thoroughly in the supernatural; and not only instituted a war on witches, but wrote and published a treatise on daemonology. All through the 17th century witchcraft accusations were common, and hideous injustice was worked through the not unmercenary zeal of the "witch finder" Matthew Hopkins.[15] But in spite of the injustice, the campaign really accomplished its object. The cult as an organised whole was almost certainly stamped out in England—and on the Continent by parallel courses, after the celebrated incident of the "Blockula" (where children were taken by night to an island and initiated in large numbers) in Sweden.[16] The Salem affair of 1692 is the last real case in

America, and was in all probability caused by the formation of an actual coven with the Rev. George Burroughs as "black man". The last witch trial in England occurred in 1712 and did not result in a conviction. The last in Scotland (Scotland was a hotbed of the cult, though Ireland was relatively free from it) was in 1722, when an execution took place. In 1736 British law formally disavowed a belief in witchcraft by penalising supposed witches as common cheats—for we must note that public opinion skipped over the truth when it turned from belief to disbelief. Once men ceased to believe in witchcraft, they fancied that there had never been any witch-cult, and thought that all the trials had been a persecution of innocent people. It remained for the 20th century to establish the cult as an anthropological reality—no supernatural thing, in truth, but a very dismal and disgusting band of furtive degenerates adhering to ancient practices antedating the Aryan occupancy of Europe. Witchcraft belief lingered longest on the Continent, the last execution being at Posen in 1793. Of the older novels dealing with the Witch-cult or Holy Vehm, the best is the realistic quasi-diary of Wilhelm Meinhold called "The Amber Witch" and dealing with the period of the 30 years' war. This is so realistic that the *Weird Tales* contributor Seabury Quinn mistook it for fact and wrote its contents up as a fact article ("culled from old trial records"!!!) for the magazine.[17] The Holy Vehm is best treated in "Faust and the Demon", by George W. M. Reynolds. Of later tales with this element Machen's are notable; and you will find a superb treatment of the general cult-and-sabbath atmosphere in the second tale (called "Ancient Sorceries") of Algernon Blackwood's book—"John Silence—Physician Extraordinary".

Your account of your methods of artistic creation, with the unconscious mind used to the fullest extent of its potentialities, is indeed interesting; and the methods in question seem quite amply sustained by the results you are achieving. In my own humble and careless effusions, one sees the convergence of two separate tendencies—a liking for well-modelled expression in the traditional manner for its own sake, and a wish to get on paper some of the images and impressions constantly running through my mind. I never dealt much in philosophic abstractions; but had the idea that if I hammered away at the perfection of a good technical medium, the ability of that medium to convey what I wished to say would be one of its intrinsic attributes. As a child I was intensely fond of faery lore, and early graduated from Grimm (which formed at the age of 4 my introduction to the art of reading) to the Arabian Nights, which I read at 5 with such effect that I at once assumed the pseudonym of Abdul Alhazred and made my mother fix up an Oriental corner with hangings and incense-vessels in my room. Then in another year I had got hold of the Greek myths in simple form and was discarding Bagdad in favour of Arcadia and Ionia. About that time I started to want to write—in rhyme rather than prose, for I had declaimed doggerel ever since I was 2½, and had always admired the fame of the late poetess Louise Imogen Guiney,[18] whom my parents knew, and at whose home we stayed during the winter of 1892–93, when my father's affairs kept him in Boston. My 6-year-old "verse" was pretty bad, and I had recited enough poetry to know that it was; so I set about to improve matters. I was a nervous half-invalid and could not attend school, but the resources of the family library were at my disposal, and I proceeded to search and browse with an inclusive avidity which not all the tender discouragement of a solicitous family could check. Being highly imaginative, and sensitive to the archaic influences of this old town with its narrow hill streets and glamorous Colonial doorways, I conceived the childish freak of transporting myself altogether into the past; so began to choose only such books as were very old—with the "long ſ"—(which I found mainly in the banished portion of the library in a great dark storeroom upstairs) and to date all my writings 200 years back—1697 instead of 1897 and so on. For my guidance in correct composition I chose a deliciously quaint and compendious volume which my great-grandfather had used at school, and which I still treasure sacredly minus its covers:

THE READER;

Containing the Art of Delivery—Articulation, Accent, Pronunciation, Emphasis, Pauses, Key or Pitch of the Voice, and Tones; Selection of Lessons in the Various Kinds of Prose; Poetick Numbers, Structure of English Verse, Feet and Pauses, Measure and Movement, Melody, Harmony, and Expression, Rules for Reading Verse, Selections of Lessons in the Various Kinds of Verse.

By
Abner Alden, A. M.

Boston
Printed by J. T. Buckingham for Thomas and Andrews,
No. 45, Newbury-Street
1802.[19]

This was so utterly and absolutely the very thing I had been looking for, that I attacked it with almost savage violence. It was in the "long ſ", and reflected in all its completeness the Georgian rhetorical tradition of Addison, Pope, and Johnson, which had survived unimpaired in America even after the Romantic Movement had begun to modify it in England. This, I felt by instinct, was the key to the speech and manners and mental world of that old periwigged, knee-breeched Providence whose ancient lanes still climbed the hill, and whose old brick and wooden buildings (Colony House 1761, College Edifice 1770, Brick Schoolhouse 1769, Market House 1773, 1st Baptist Church with finest classic spire in America 1775, innumerable private houses and mansions from 1750 onward, St. John's and Round-Top Churches circa 1810, Golden Ball Inn 1783, old warehouses along the Great Salt River 1816, etc.

etc. etc.) still survived (and still do survive, thank Heaven!)[20] in such large numbers and in such striking topographical situations. Little by little I hammered every rule and precept and example into my receptive system, till in a month or so I was beginning to write coherent verse in the ancient style—of which the following (from "The Poem of Ulysses, or the New Odyssey") is a verbatim specimen:

> The night was dark, O reader Hark, and see Ulysses' fleet;
> All homeward bound, with Vict'ry crown'd, he hopes his spouse to greet;
> Long hath he fought, put Troy to naught, and levell'd down its walls,
> But Neptune's wrath obstructs his path, while into snares he falls.

At the same time I was reading the 17th and 18th century poetical translations of the classics and the old Queen Anne essayists as fast as I could, so that periwigged Georgianism was absorbing me as utterly as if I had been actually born in its midst. For some time I confined my literary effusions to verses wherein I tried to express the fanciful Grecian beauty which altogether engrossed me. In the mythology of Greece I almost believed, and would actually look for fauns and dryads in certain oaken groves at twilight—for the city was not then built up thickly beyond my home, and the woods and fields were as close and familiar to me as if I had been born in the heart of Arcadia. I am predominantly rural in tastes, and would write pastorals if I wrote any poetry at all. Then I struck **EDGAR ALLAN POE**!! It was my downfall, and at the age of eight I saw the blue firmament of Argos and Sicily darkened by the miasmal exhalations of the tomb! In 1898 I began my prose career, (no—the first was still in 1897, though it was pre-Poe) grinding out such specimens as "The Mysterious Ship" and "The Secret of the Grave" in a Johnsonese that only a pedant of the 1810 period could equal. Candidly, they were *awful*, and I saw that what I had learnt of verse would not serve me in prose. I had a new medium to learn, and must set about it systematically. Then *science* stepped in to sidetrack me. Although I am basically an aesthete with a non-mathematical mind, I became utterly infatuated with the pages of illustrations of "Philosophical and Scientific Instruments" in the back of a Webster's Unabridged of 1864. After that, I would give my mother and grandfather (my father being no more) no peace till they had fitted me up a chemical laboratory in the basement of our home, and there I dabbled in reagents and precipitates from March 1899 onwards, ploughing feverishly through such chemical primers as "The Young Chemist", by Prof. John Howard Appleton, (of Providence)[21] which I still consider the best general introduction to the subject, though it is now virtually forgotten. Literature I spurned altogether unworthy of a "serious scientist", but my prose practice continued through my repeated attempts to write a chemical treatise. At this period I also made abortive stabs at art and music, failing wholly in the first, and dropping the second in boredom and nervous revulsion after two years of quite successful violin lessons. (I'm a little ahead on dates, though. Those lessons were from '97 to '99) Today I vainly regret my ineptitude in art, but have no taste or desire to excel in music. In 1902 geography displaced chemistry in my affections, and the lure of far places was upon me. The *Antarctic* was my favourite region—wonder and the unknown being my ideal. The next year the world had become too small for me, and I took up *astronomy*, using first an old book my grandmother had studied[22] at the seminary in the 1840's and later some new books and a small telescope which I acquired. The sky moved me to verse again, and I wrote copiously and pointlessly on the wonders of infinite space. I had by this time had little snatches of private tutoring and school, and in 1904 was considered able to enter high school. There I was shunted back to literature and begin writing horror-tales again. But Latin now captivated my fancy, and I became a haughty Roman with scant use for the barbaric darkness of the modern world. The impress of this phase is still upon me, and I still thrill at the Roman name and the fasces and the figure of the Wolf of the Capitol. I am heart and soul with Mussolini in his efforts to raise the Imperium to its ancient splendour. S. P. Q. R. Ave, Caesar! Then in the later years of high-school science "came back", and I renewed my devotion to astronomy, chemistry, and physics. In 1906 a new local daily was established, and I got a chance to write its monthly astronomical article, a pursuit which I kept up for twelve years,[23] when a change of management produced a demand for a changed style to which I refused to accede. This astronomical stuff was my debut in print. But after all, high-school was a mistake. I liked it, but the strain was too keen for my health, and I suffered a nervous collapse in 1908 immediately after graduating,[24] which prevented altogether my attending college. Just about then I became impressed with the inferiority of my work and my ignorance of the technique of the short story; so that I destroyed the whole mass of my fiction with two exceptions.

Chemical writing—plus a little historical and antiquarian research—filled my years of feebleness till about 1911, when I had a reaction toward literature. I then gave my prose style the greatest overhauling it has ever had; purging it at once of some vile journalese and some absurd Johnsonism. Little by little I felt that I was forging the instrument I ought to have forged a decade before—a decent style capable of expressing what I wished to say. But I still wrote verse and persisted in the delusion that I was a poet. In 1914 I joined the United Amateur Press Association, and in 1917 W. Paul Cook (who saw one of my two saved tales) urged me to try weird fiction again.[25] I did—"The Tomb" and "Dagon" being my first fresh attempts. Cook spoke so highly of these that I kept on—and I've still been keeping ever since. Meanwhile I put my laboriously gained technique to work in revision on a professional basis—a thing still more lucrative to me than original fiction. As I have aged, my scattered interests have more or less coalesced and coördinated themselves, submitting to the modifications of observation and philosophy. By this time I see pretty well what I'm driving at and how I'm doing it—that I'm a rather one-sided person whose only really burning interests are *the past* and *the unknown* or *the strange*, and whose aestheticism in general is more negative than positive—i.e., a hatred of ugliness rather than an active love of beauty. I see that I am fundamentally a cynic, a sceptic, and an Epicurean—a conservative and quietist without any great breadth of taste or depth of ability, and with a literary ambition confined altogether to the recording of certain images connected with bizarrerie and antiquarianism. With the general atmosphere of books and literature I am bored to death. I had rather visit an ancient and beautiful town or see a marvellous landscape than attend any lecture or bookish discussion in the world. For fame or recognition I have not the smallest wish or expectation, since to my cynical spirit the world is an absolutely negligible and purposeless affair. All intensity or serious purpose rather amuses me, and I regard art not as a fetish or a duty, but as one of many pleasant and elegant diversions proper to a gentleman. I am not satisfied with the stuff I write, but would lose interest in it if I tried to take it seriously enough to improve it. For me it is best to take my prose style as it is—decently correct, at least, through early rhetorical training—and let it tell what I have to say in its own way. I write slowly, correct so extensively that my rough draughts are legible to no one but myself, (and sometimes not to me!) and never hesitate to change the early part of a work when later developments call for different antecedents. Usually, though, I know what is going to happen in a tale—for that is why I write it. I never write except when in the mood, for I have no intrinsic desire to produce written material. Authorship to me is no end in itself, for I respect a gentlemen of leisure and an intelligent pagan in pursuit of rational pleasure far more than any Grub-Street hack. To me authorship is only a mechanical means of getting formulated and preserved certain fugitive images which I wish formulated and preserved. If anyone else has presented an idea exactly as I feel it, I let his work serve me. Indeed, if I could find tales or books or poems expressing everything I wish to say, I would not write at all; and would be highly grateful for the relief from a labour which to my cynical soul holds nothing of glamour or merit. Just now my greatest wish is to capture the beauty and mystery of Old Providence more fully than I have hitherto succeeded in doing. I have tried it in the 147-page novelette finished Tuesday morning, but feel that I have failed. Let us hope that somebody else will do it soon and save me the trouble!

But pardon the autobiography, which I didn't premeditate! What I really set out to say was simply this—that to me the only sensible way to compose seems to be to master one's technical medium thoroughly beforehand—before one thinks about the expressive part at all—and then to forget all about the rules, using the polished instrument as freely and unconsciously as a child lisps its pristine prattle. If this method can't be worked, then one isn't an artist by Nature, for as you truly observe, the essence of aesthetic accomplishment lies in the subconscious. You may wonder how I reconcile this precept with my statement that I correct a MS. repeatedly. Well—for one thing, the revision is about as unconscious as the first writing; being largely an automatic response to something in my head which rebels at something my hand has recorded. Secondly, I don't claim to be much of an artist! I merely recognise a principle which better craftsmen would more spectacularly exemplify. The big thing is to avoid conscious mannerism—to shun calculated literary effects as one shuns the plague. That is why I detest romantic writers with their artificial, geometrical glamour. The Stevenson and Kipling traditions—to say nothing of the Dickens cult—make me nauseatedly weary with their theatrical and mathematical artificiality. Pater and Wilde I can tolerate because the element of music and poetic rhythm enters into their jewelled prose, but as a general thing I balk at any man who writes for the sake of writing or for the ingenious twists he can give our poor old language. The only literary man I respect is one who says a thing straightforwardly for no other reason than that he wants that thing said in the most effective possible way. That is what I call art in the practice of literature, and that is why I am of course wholly out of touch with those modernists who make their disjointed ravings nothing more than pretentious experiments in aesthetic theory.

Your "Old Back Trail" delighted me exceedingly, for it truly captures a mood which is almost constantly mine. I abhor broad prosaic highways with their implications of change, modernity, and decadence, and make for the calm, untainted inner countryside whenever I possibly can. I love great stretches of rolling hills and distant steeples and farmhouse roofs in the sunset, and little winding roads that skirt ancient woods and ramble on between stone walls to some marvellous meeting-place of the fauns or some cryptic gate to another world which lies beyond that crest where pines stand hieratically against a blank, mysterious sky of unknown portent. My ancestry is rural, and last October I visited the western Rhode-Island countryside where my immediate forbears dwelt.[26] So gloriously did I enjoy it, that I wrote it up in a travelogue for young Long and kept a carbon to lend others, and I can't resist enclosing a copy for you, although you'll probably find large sections of it dull. Skip the latter, and merely get the general landscape effects—which form the rustic New England that bred me. I rather wish I had been born and reared rurally myself—although the ancient gables and steep winding ways of Old Providence charm me poignantly in another direction. In reading this travelogue, pardon the occasional intentional quaintnesses and archaisms and whimsicalities to which my old correspondents long ago became hardened. The "daughter" I mention is really my aunt—for I am blessed with no descendants of my own.

[. . .]

Notes

1. Told by Anatole France in the essay "Charles Baudelaire," in *On Life and Letters: Third Series*, tr. D. B. Stewart (London & New York: John Lane, 1922), 20.
2. Dwyer had read FBL's first poetry book, *The Man from Genoa and Other Poems* (1926).
3. "The Work of Frank Belknap Long, Jr."
4. Actually 26.
5. Charles O. Long (1845–1904), superintendent of the Statue of Liberty.
6. FBL referred to himself as "the man from Genoa," also the title of his book of verse.
7. Franklin Pierce Adams (1881–1960), American columnist and wit, known for his syndicated newspaper column "The Conning Tower."
8. "My Country, 'Tis of Thee" (also known as "America") was written by Samuel Francis Smith (1808–1895), a Baptist minister, using the tune of the British national anthem. His daughter, Caroline Edwards Smith (b. 1843), was Morton's mother.
9. Harry Clarke (1889–1931), Irish stained-glass artist and book illustrator.
10. S[idney] H[erbert] Sime (1867–1941), English artist in the late Victorian period and following, known for fantastic and satirical artwork, especially illustrations for Anglo-Irish author Lord Dunsany.
11. Garrett Putnam Serviss (1851–1929), American astronomer and also author of a number of science fiction novels and tales. HPL quotes a passage from one of his astronomy books in "Beyond the Wall of Sleep" (*CF* 1.85).
12. By the end of the month HPL had written "The Colour out of Space."
13. The quaint old fellow HPL refers to is Charles W. Smith, editor and publisher of the *Tryout*. The elegy was "Sir Thomas Tryout," on Smith's cat. The aged poet referred to in HPL's note is Jonathan E. Hoag.
14. Gilles de Montmorency-Laval (1405–1440), Baron de Rais, a knight and lord from Brittany, Anjou and Poitou, leader in the French army, and a companion-in-arms of Joan of Arc. Best known for later conviction as a confessed serial killer of children.
15. Matthew Hopkins (1620?–1647), witch-hunter whose flourished during the English Civil War. He claimed to hold the office of Witchfinder General.
16. Blockula was a legendary meadow where the Devil held court during a witches' Sabbath.
17. "Maria Schweidler" (No. 6 in the "Servants of Satan" series), *WT* 6, No. 2 (August 1925): 223–30.
18. Louise Imogen Guiney (1861–1920), American poet, essayist, and friend of the family.
19. HPL in fact owned the third edition of 1808.
20. The Colony House, i.e., The Old State House (1762), 150 Benefit Street (Rhode Island declared its independence from England in the Colony House two months before the Declaration of Independence); the college edifice, i.e., University Hall—the original, and for fifty years the only, building at Brown University (1770); [brick school house] (1769) [opposite the Sign of Shakespear's Head in Gaol-Lane]; the Market House (1773) is at 1 South Water Street; the First Baptist Meeting House (1775), designed by Joseph Brown, 75 North Main Street; Beneficent Congregational

Church (actually 1809), 300 Weybosset Street; St. John's Episcopal Church (actually 1810), 271 North Main Street; the First Unitarian Church (1816), 301 Benefit Street. Only the Golden Ball Inn Ell (1784 et seq.) stands today at 17–23 South Court Street. In HPL's time, the four-story Golden Ball Inn stood across from the State House (150 Benefit Street) and stable (160 Benefit Street). The main part of the house was demolished in 1941.

21. Appleton had attended Brown University and began teaching there in 1864. He became a professor of chemistry in 1868 and continued to teach at Brown until 1914.

22. By Elijah Hinsdale Burritt. HPL refers to his maternal grandmother, Robie Alzada Phillips (1827–1895). HPL had written that her "copy of Burritt's 'Geography of the Heavens' is today the most prized volume in my library," but his copy was published in 1853, years after her schooling.

23. The paper was the [Providence] *Tribune* (morning, evening and Sunday editions). HPL wrote the column only from 1906 to 1908. He did write articles for the *Pawtuxet Valley Gleaner* (1906–08?), and then the [Providence] *Evening News* (1914–18).

24. HPL did not graduate from high school (unless he eventually completed the necessary course work in evening school).

25. "The Alchemist" appeared in the *United Amateur* for November 1916. Cook published the other of the two tales referred to, "The Beast in the Cave," in his *Vagrant* two years later.

26. In October 1926, HPL visited Foster, R.I., with his aunt Annie Gamwell. The "travelogue" HPL mentions refers to a TLS to FBL (26 October 1926; printed in part in *SL* 2.81–89), carbons of which he circulated to various correspondents.

[2] [AHT]

10 Barnes St.,
Providence, R.I.,
March 26, 1927

My dear Mr. Dwyer:—

Let me thank you exceedingly for the copious account of Red Hook decadence which you so kindly sent, and which interested me so much on account of my close view of the accursed region in 1925. As you will see by the enclosed, some echo of this recent study reached the Providence papers—and I had this brief item all clipped to send you with a somewhat loftily triumphant note . . . . 'Aha, you see the old gentleman was right, and Red Hook *is* an abode of eldritch furtiveness and Satanic horror after all!' I'd like to get a squint at the future articles dealing with individual gangs which your cutting promises—for I am sure that I must have encountered some of these primitive tribal survivals at first hand as they careened from cafeteria to cafeteria in the squalid reaches of Court Street beyond Borough Hall. How well I recall that night in the Tiffany when a party of plain-clothes men entered and searched a party of young roughs for firearms! Every pair of hands shot up as if by instinct—for clearly, these worldly-wise striplings were no strangers to the technique of constabular inquisition. And then that unforgettable overheard conversation in Johnson's Coffee-Pot, when a select group of hackney-coachmen exchanged naive recollections of bygone durance at Blackwell's Island and Sing-Sing; whose inconveniences they vowed were grossly exaggerated, and whose cuisine they extolled to the extreme disadvantage of their host's—a most damnably tactless and indelicate sort of comparison to make out loud in the presence of the sensitive Athenian behind the buffet that gleamed so splendidly with the glory that was Grease. Heigho! I think I shall have to venture into autobiographical reminiscence and write a piquant volume on "My Year in the Slums"! As the anniversary of my deliverance approaches,[1] I am beginning to be amused by the whole incident, and to see around it the glamour of real romance. My knowledge of Red Hook was not one of seriously studied details, but one of impressionistic observation and overheard fragments linked together by the thread of fancy—and yet it was essentially a first-hand one. I saw these gangs with my own eyes as they loafed near Borough Hall, and would have been blind if I had not noted the coarse degeneracy of the physiognomies—a kind of pervasive local decadence and brazen insolence peculiar to the region, and so characteristic that it nearly overrode the marks of race and gave a sinister quality in common to every sort of gang from Nordic to Oriental. Their language and manners were such as I had never encountered before and have never encountered since; and to hear them through open windows in the night, howling afar like wolves at a spectral moon, or piping loathsomely on cracked mouth-organs in melodies whose words and meaning must have been of the pit, was to gain a sort of spiritual insight into gulfs of underlying horror that no mere trip through the district would ever have supplied. My own post of observation, at the corner of State and Clinton Sts., was of course on the mere fringe of the worst parts; but I took several walks of exploration around the waterfront rookeries and acquired a very fair pictorial and aural image of the whole blight, even in its extremest phases. There was an evil hush—a dramatic tension—about the entire sprawling fester; and a hideous element of putrescent homogeneity seemed to spread all over the brooding expanse, wearing down the line of demarcation between the various national colonies and the various architectural areas—which latter differ all the way between the crumbling mansions of vanished aristocracy and the dingy frame tenements of autochthonous slumdom. Clinton Street is of hidden rottenness and masked abomination. It has still its noble skyline of fine old roofs and church-towers which the twilight restores to pristine alluringness, and some of its intersections are truly lovely to the charitable eye in the dusk. It was this quality which deceived me so completely on the winter nights when I was hurriedly seeking a bargain in large rooms. This is not Red Hook proper, but that district itself—beyond Atlantic Avenue and toward the river—has some quaint brick houses that were very modest and lovely in their day. The actual waterfront, of course, is like all other waterfronts; (Providence has a marvellously ancient, squalid, wicked, and fascinating waterfront rich with memories of the old India trade) whilst the Gowanus section near the canal, where the growing town overtook an old Dutch village, has always been a "tough" region of factories, warehouses, and shipping. Gowanus has always had a rough-and-ready, chip-on-shoulder sort of pride and self-respect lacking in other slums; because it has so far resisted the foreigner (who does not take kindly to vigorous physical exertion and adventurous sea-concernments) and preserved its original blue-eyed and tow-headed virility, spiced with husky accents and cauliflower ears. It bred Terry McGovern,[2] b'Jesus, and 'tain't changed such a g. d. helluva lot sence dem g. d. days! De canary-boids sing bass down dere, and de local fauns shave their blue and prognathous jaws wid gasolene blow-torches. It ain' no place fer no g. d. cane-totin' Oswald to be lookin' aroun' unless'n et's de morgue he's lookin' fer—See? On account of the lack of an ambitious building programme in this section, many of the original pre-urban farmhouses remain, including a fine old shingled specimen in Clinton St., now occupied by some charitable enterprise—a kindergarten, day-nursery, or something of the sort. Between Court and Clinton, and in a region where we may consider Brooklyn proper as merging into Gowanus, are some marvellously decaying backwaters where the houses have great iron-railed front yards with mouldy patches of grass and rusted and broken urns. These are numbered places—First Place, Second Place, etc. And across Court st. at about this point is the mangy and depressing expanse of Carroll Park. Ah, me, what colour and mystery it all takes on in retrospect! Surely, its wild squalor was not without a certain wry, Baudelairian sort of beauty; because it represented a natural and strictly local growth, with some of the adaptation of life to landscape which makes for authentic character. It was a study in genre—and some day a real artist may catch its spirit more suavely and effectively then I could do in my brief hymn of hate—written whilst still there, and therefore without the effect of spatial and chronological perspective. I believe I could write of the place better now than I did then.

And I do mean to write of one phase of it—weaving a sort of epic of horror about the mouldering brownstone mansion in which I had my rooms. I was utterly inexperienced in room-seeking, and knew nothing of the precise social geography of Old Brooklyn. All my possible informants were old-Brooklynites living in dreams of a Brooklyn that has gone for ever, and their notion of the recent changes was so vague as to argue a sort of merciful blindness to what is going on. Clinton St. was (in 1880 psychology!) thought good, and several old families were still hanging on there. (My next-door neighbour was the fairly celebrated Dr. Love, State Senator and sponsor of the famous "Clean Books bill" at Albany.[3] He is *still* there—evidently immune or unconscious of the decay, though his block—a sort of "Galen Row"—is full of Syrian doctors) Friends of my aunt still lived in Schermerhorn St., and the friendly Gothic towers of St. Anne's church[4] seemed to promise a restful old-world beauty. Moreover, I had friends in Columbia Heights, and *knew* that was still good. Would that someone had realised clearly enough to tell me what a deadline *Joralemon St.* is. Everything beyond that, as I was soon to learn, is going utterly to hell; whereas north of it the neighbourhood seems holding its own or even rising. In later months I came to love good old Joralemon as a sort of last outpost of civilisation. I hated to leave it behind in going to my quarters, as a desert hermit hates to leave the last oasis behind; and I welcomed the sight of it when I went abroad. But at the start I knew nothing of these things, and took the great room with its two convenient alcoves on a crisp December night when snow and silence veiled the squalor, when the chimes of St. Anne's seemed to sing a welcome, and when a thin young moon trembled over the star-reflecting water glimpsed through quaint sloping side-streets.

Naturally I would have shunned a lodging which seemed to savour of coarseness, but here again unusual conditions conspired to deceive me. I still think that none but a seer and prophet could have escaped error, and that the house *had* until almost that precise time been of the quality I thought I had found. My guess is that its decay had just set in, owing to the spread of the Syrian fringe (all unsuspected by me) beyond Atlantic Avenue. The man having my room before me was a N.Y.U. professor, and there was still in the house a splendid young chap who knew people that I knew in Providence. The landlady was a refined-looking woman with two prepossessing youths as sons, and with a British accent of such absolutely authentic caste that there can have been no mistake about her tale of better days—the usual thing—and her claim of being the daughter of a cultivated Anglican vicar in Ireland, educated in a private school in England. Poor old Mrs. Burns! Only later was I to learn of her shrewish tongue, desperate household negligence, miserly watchfulness of lights and unwatchfulness of repairs, and reckless indifference to the class of lodger she admitted! I think her decadence must have been a gradual one—probably she wanted good lodgers, for she seemed naively impressed with the traditions which my books and furniture and effects seemed to imply, and vowed that they gave her wistful memories of her childhood home at the vicarage in Ireland; but she must have stopped asking references when the sinking of the neighbourhood made the house harder and harder to fill with people of the right sort. I was soon disillusioned—and with what a thud! Voices came from the next room—and *what* voices! Of course poor Mrs. Burns apologised for these particular roomers, of whom she said she was very anxious to get rid—but when I began to see some of the other anthropological types in the hallway my cynicism began to mount. Friends who came to see me—better versed in Brooklyn ways than I, for my metropolitan residence had been confined to the quiet section of Flatbush—were quicker than I to see and tell me what a wretched hole I had crawled into; but by that time I was all settled, and with my desperate finances the idea of a removal was quite impossible. I had only moved twice before in all my life, and was encamped amongst all my effects—for such is my ingrained domesticity that I could not live anywhere without my own household objects around me—the furniture my childhood knew, the books my ancestors read, and the pictures my mother and grandmother and aunt painted. The presence of all these things at the edge of Red Hook was really almost humorous, (although Dr. Love across the street was no doubt equally surrounded by his cherished hereditary things) and visitors not infrequently commented on the virtual transition from one world to another implied in the simple act of stepping within my door. Outside—Red Hook. Inside—Providence, R.I.! For it has always been Providence wherever I have been, and must always remain so. That is the valuable lesson I extracted from my asinine metropolitan experiment—a lesson which will teach me not to separate the spiritual from the geographical Providence again. But at the outset I was deluded. Comically enough, I even persuaded a friend—George Kirk, formerly of Cleveland—to take the room above mine, and for several months we had the mild amusement of telegraphing on the steam-pipes—for one quickly falls into boorish ways in a boorish milieu. Kirk has no sense of neatness, (wait till you see his Chelsea Bookshop in W. 15th St! but perhaps his new wife[5]—acquired on the 5th inst.—will have cleaned up that Augean Stable before you make the gang's acquaintance) so held out uncomplainingly till May; when, having fewer non-portable chattels than I, he betook himself to gay Manhattan. But laden as I was, I stuck; hence came to know that squalid world as few white men have ever known it. The sounds in the hall! The faces glimpsed on the stairs! The mice in the partitions! The fleeting touches of intangible horror from spheres and cycles outside time . . . . once a *Syrian* had the room next to mine and played eldritch and whining monotones on a strange bagpipe which made me dream ghoulish and incredible things of crypts under Bagdad and limitless corridors of Eblis beneath the moon-cursed ruins of Istakhar. I never *saw* this man, and my privilege to imagine him in any shape I chose lent glamour to his weird pneumatic cacophonies. In my vision he always wore a turban and long robe of pale figured silk, and had a right eye plucked out . . . because it had looked upon something in a tomb at night which no eye may look upon and live. In truth, I never saw with actual sight the majority of my fellow-lodgers. I only *heard* them loathsomely—and sometimes glimpsed faces of sinister decadence in the hall. There was an old Turk under me, who used to get letters with outré stamps from the Levant. Alexander D. Messayeh[6]—Messayeh—what a name from the Arabian Nights! I suppose the praenomen implied a Greek strain—those Near-East spawn are hopelessly mongrelised, and belong for the most part to the Orthodox Greek Church. And what scraps of old papers with Arabic lettering did one find about the house! Sometimes, going out at sunset, I would vow to myself that gold minarets glistened against the flaming skyline where the church-towers were! "We take the Golden Road to Samarcand!"[7] My tailor was a Syrian named Habib, and around the corner in Atlantic Ave. were Syrian shops with strange goods and delicacies. Once Kirk and I visited the Cairo Garden, where subtle incense evoked mirages of clustered bulbous domes and city-gates of alabaster, and fat, swarthy minstrels plucked meaninglessly at Eastern lutes whilst tenebrous and unpotable "coffee" (I use the nomenclature of faith, not of analysis or proof) was served in small curious cups without handles. It was a queer enough setting, and one which no person of my acquaintance can yet parallel—though our venerable fellow-gangster McNeil (author of boys' books) was at that time living in the roaring slums of Hell's Kitchen, (W. 49th St. Manhattan—a wild but rather colourless slum without mystery or the memories of fallen grandeur) and Vrest Orton is even now experimenting with life at a Settlement-Workers' headquarters in the Italian (but far from Florentinely resplendent) turmoil of East 105th St. The keynote of the whole setting—house, neighbourhood, and shop, was that of loathsome and insidious decay; masked just enough by the reliques of former splendour and beauty to add terror and mystery and the fascination of crawling motion to a deadness and dinginess otherwise static and prosaic. I conceived the idea that the great brownstone house was a malignly sentient thing—a dead, vampire creature which sucked something out of those within it and implanted in them the seeds of some horrible and immaterial psychic growth. Every closed door seemed to hide some brooding crime—or blasphemy too deep to form a crime in the crude and superficial calendar of earth. I never quite learned the exact topography of that rambling and enormous house. How to get to my room, and to Kirk's room when he was there, and to the landlady's quarters to pay my rent or ask in vain for heat until I bought an oil stove of my own—these things I knew, but there were wings and corridors I never traversed; doors to rear and abutting halls and stairways that I never saw opened. I know there were rooms above ground without windows, and was at liberty to guess what might lie below ground. There lay a pall of darkness and secrecy upon that house—it subtly discouraged from first to last one's inclination to speak aloud, and at times one felt a faint miasmal tangibility in the circumambient air. The great high rooms had something of the mausolean in their crumbling stateliness, and in the halls at night one always had to be sure the great, white flamboyant Corinthian pilasters never moved just the least bit. Something unwholesome—something furtive—something vast lying subterrenely in obnoxious slumber—that was the soul of 169 Clinton St. at the edge of Red Hook, and in my great northwest corner room "The Horror" was written. It is nearly a full year ago that I left it without a pang to come home to my own—to the clean, white, and ancient New England that bred me, and whose hills and woods and steeples are the food and essence of my soul—and as the year has passed the squalid old Brooklyn setting has become less and less of an active outrage and horror and more and more a grotesque and even fascinating legend. The ruffled dignity of thinking I have dwelt in such a place gives ground to a dreamy doubt of my ever having been actually there—the episode becomes a tale told in the third person, and the realities are decked in a glittering mantle of myth. At this distance I am almost glad the mishap occurred—for it gave a touch of colour to a life otherwise tame, conventional, and uneventful, and made me better able to appreciate the slum chapters in many vital works of literature—high among them Machen's autobiographical volumes, wherein are told that dreamer's struggles with squalor and poverty in late-Victorian London. I shall certainly write about 169 Clinton St. some day—and the tale will be one to chill the reader's blood. And if somewhere in the wide world there light upon it the sinful eyes of the two young men who stole my clothing from the alcove, they will so thank Mercurius (who presides over the craft of thieves) for their timely deliverance from such a peril that they may, as a votive offering, make restitution of what they took—in which case I trust they will add a cash balance to compensate for wear and tear on the apparel since May 1925!

And now that we've worked around toward Machen—let me say that I'm glad you are finding his prose such an inspiration, as I felt quite certain you would. I shall send you "The Three Impostors" as soon as I get it back from the man to whom it is now lent—or perhaps I'll send the autobiographical volumes ("Far Off Things" and "Things Near and Far")[8] first—or the wistful cerebral chronicle "The Secret Glory". "The Hill of Dreams" is surely a richly complex synthesis of many undertones, but it's so long since I've read it (spring of 1924) that I can't swear as to the witch-nymph discrepancy you mention. With my predominantly scenic temperament—for like my psychic kindred the cats I care more for places than for persons—I seem to recall the landscape and Roman touches more clearly than the minutiae in Lucian's spiritual orbit, so that I could not make intelligent comments without giving the book the re-reading which I mean to give it some time. It is not like Machen, with his careful methods, to leave a discrepancy or inconsistency in a finished product; and when I see the text again I will tell you what I think of the point you mention. Changing a story before the end—remaining open to thoughts suggested by the writing of the early parts, and even changing the early parts to conform to fresh inspirations evoked by setting down the later parts—is a policy to which all authors ought to remain open for the sake of naturalness, vitality, and spontaneous impression. I practice it frequently myself, at least in details—one particularly vivid case being in the 147-page novelette I finished not long ago. There's no hurry about the return of either Machen or Smith material, and I would urge you to get all you can out of the books before sending them back. Yes—I think you ought to own Machen eventually, and believe you will find the "Hill of Dreams" and "House of Souls" the best ones to start with.

Have I *read* Fitzhugh Ludlow's "Hasheesh-Eater"? Why, Sir, I possess it upon mine own shelves; and wou'd not part with it for any inducement whatever! I first read a reprint in 1922, but was later honour'd by a gift of the original edition (without author's name) of 1857, and have frequently reread those phantasmagoria of exotic colour, which proved more of a stimulant to my own fancy than any vegetable alkaloid ever grown and distilled. I agree with you in conceding its style a greater freshness than De Quincey's, (a sage young friend of mine[9] once summed up De Q. by saying laconically "Poor old boy! he knew too much.") and find a positive delight in its very faults of naivete and early-American floridness. The reeling panoramas out of space and time have an unmistakable tinge of authenticity, and even the metaphysical speculations were far from arid. I seem to know comparatively little of Ludlow's later life, though I have come across scattered references to a short journalistic career terminated by an early death abroad—perhaps due to his collegiate indulgence in the noxious cannabis indica. Thanks exceedingly for your offer of a loan—which I would have accepted with avidity were not the commodity already mine.

I'm glad you found pleasure in "The Hermaphrodite"—which of course must be read wholly for imagery and not for ideas, as must every other work of art. Great Scott—if Loveman and I judged each other by our ideas, we'd have long ago suffered the fate of the Kilkenny cats.[10] According to my social and political theories he ought to be shot or in gaol, whilst according to his, I ought to be guillotined! But since we deal in art and not in ideas, we get along with the utmost cordiality. Didacticism can never be more, in art, than an inconspicuous excuse for displaying a processional wealth of colour and atmospheric splendour. However—as to your point that Christianity is no foe to beauty—I must remark that while you are probably right so far as either the original faith or its present application by intelligent people is concerned, there have been periods when conditions were very different; so that the net historic effect of the religion through all its ups and downs is almost certainly anti-aesthetic. This is particularly true of the two periods touched in "The Hermaphrodite"—the patristic and ascetic era of the declining classical world, when hermits preached against beauty, grace, learning, and even common cleanliness whilst monks destroyed works of liberal culture wherever found; and the feverish age of the Reformation, when Savonarola's disciples cast ornaments, musical instruments, and nude paintings* into a bonfire in a public square at Florence, and the rise of Calvinism gave birth to uncountable ramifications of Puritanic gloom of which our grotesque Fundamentalists and Southern Baptists and Methodists are amusing contemporary survivals. Of course, both of these anti-aesthetic waves of feeling were primarily social rather than religious, and were produced as inevitable reactions against the un-

---

*whereby the world has lost much of the finest early work of that master of composition—Fra Bartolommeo—who was an ardent disciple of Savonarola.[10]

deniably disgusting license of the respective periods in which they were born; but since we are prone to fit all our impulses into our dominant systems of emotional expression, it follows that the rising faith of Theodosius' time and the noontide devotion of the age of Luther became the nuclei and rallying-points of the repressive movements. My own criticism of Christianity is that it does not fit the natural temper of a virile Western civilisation. We are by heritage polytheistic and beauty-loving pagans, bold and warlike, and gloriously dedicated—as you may see by the tone of all spontaneous Celtic and Teutonic myth—to the rule and exultation of the strong. That is our normal biological mood, and our religion and aesthetic ought to be based upon it. Instead, there has been insidiously engrafted upon us through the accidents of Roman politics and diplomacy in the 4th century A.D. a totally alien and exotic faith; bred among whipped and decadent Orientals and nurtured in broken-spirited squalor, hence partaking of characteristics utterly repugnant and unassimilable amongst a proud Aryan people. We have, it is true, superimposed on the original Jewish cult a half-concealing structure of magnificent Gothic splendour; but the primal concepts of humility and meekness remain to furnish countless inconsistencies and place us all more or less in the light of involuntary hypocrites. We know well, after only a moment of scientific reflection, that any attempt at enforcing the actual fantastic and idealistic precepts of Christ would lead at once to utter anarchy, collapse, and cultural extinction. However—I'm as well aware as anyone else of the enormous extent to which the Christian tradition—whatever be its original lack of appropriateness—is now woven into our lives, art, and literature after thirteen-hundred and more years of continuous profession by our main stream of civilisation. Like it or not, the general forms are fixed upon us, so that only a thoughtless radical or cultural parvenu could for a moment think of doing away with its atmosphere and externals as a social and aesthetic force amongst us. No one loves the memory of old moss-covered abbeys and the sweet chimes of Gothic belfries at evening more than I. No one exceeds me in reverence for the quaint and sonorous rituals of antique devotion—the organised symbolisation of our lives and the formulated expression of our emotions—and the pure strain of poetry that runs alike through the exotic Old Testament, the classically dramatic Christ-mythus, and the quaint legends and beautiful traditions of the church. And nothing pleases me more than a lovely old New-England church with tapering Georgian spire and rambling churchyard of archaic slate or sandstone slabs—hieroglyph of the elder time, and anchor of stability in an age of change, sadness, and decadence. Far be it from me to discourage the naive faith of any believer—so that although I am intellectually a complete and absolutely cynical scientific materialist, I leave the futile business of atheistical propaganda (as futile as all other human effort in an eternally cyclic and purposeless cosmos) to such busy and well-meaning friends of mankind as Percy Ward, Clarence Darrow, H. G. Wells, and other didactic emulators of the honest and messianic Mr. Ingersoll.

As to my style—no danger! I shan't give up those occasional flings in the dreamy and poetic vein! In fact, "The Strange High House" is a product of last autumn, long after all my "stick-to-prose" advisers had shot their last bolt in discouragement. When you see my long Randolph Carter novelette[12] you will realise that this fantastic and oneiroscopic mood is a darned hard thing to pry me out of! I am glad, however, to have another specific assurance that the style truly fits me; and shall no doubt grind out a few specimens on the strength of that encouragement the next spare time I get. As it is, I have just finished one new tale which I'll send you in my next. This one has little flashes of the quasi-poetic, but is for the most part realistic; with a homely country setting 'west of Arkham'. Something falls from the sky, and terror broods. The thing is told by an old man forty years after, and the title is "The Colour Out of Space". It is a long-short affair—exactly as long as "Cthulhu". Enclosed are two more of my old ones—just returned by Wandrei which you have not previously seen. "Polaris" is rather interesting in that I wrote it in 1918, **before** I had ever read a word of Lord Dunsany's. Some find it hard to believe this, but I can give not only assurance but absolute proof that it is so. It is simply a case of similar types of vision facing the unknown, and harbouring similar stores of mythic and historical lore. Hence the parallelism in atmosphere, artificial nomenclature, treatment of the dream theme, etc. "In the Vault" was written in 1925, and rather inexplicably rejected by *Weird Tales* as too horrible for the censors!

As I think I have said somewhere before in this interminable scrawl—don't feel the least haste in returning either Machen or Smith. Drain 'em dry—and the more inspirations and ideas you get out of 'em the better. Machen certainly makes one wish like the devil that one could get to Wales, and I should certainly never find myself across the Atlantic without making the ancient Gwent country a part of my itinerary. It's very unfortunate that Caerleon-on-Usk seems to some extent menaced by the abnormal expansion of Newport—three miles farther down stream on the Usk—which has had a sudden growth in shipping and manufacturing since the war and the consequent cityward migration of country-dwellers. Unless great care is taken in safeguarding its antiquities and identity, Caerleon will be hopelessly engulfed and ruthlessly destroyed as a dingy factory-town suburb. I wish somebody would found a Machen Club and see to it that at least some of the antique domed hills and hanging woods and black damp valleys of mystic Gwent are saved from the "realtor" and all other species of modern monster. I am sure that the cryptic reign of Nodens, Lord of the Great Abyss, is much more appropriate; and I shall certainly vote for Silvanus Cocidius over George F. Babbitt at any district election! 'Look for the jar marked Faunus!'[13]

Yes—Belknap's brief quatrain alludes to Walt Whitman.[14] I never could get interested in Whitman myself, for he seems to me so drearily full of didacticism, pose, and turgid affectation. But I begrudge no one else his taste, and have suffered myself to be dragged about unprotestingly to various places in Brooklyn where he lived and worked—especially a dingy nondescript house at the corner of Myrtle Ave. and Pearl or Jay or Lawrence or Bridge St., (I forget which) and a brick block at Fulton and Orange. (or Pineapple—again I forget) By the way—do you know the Poe shrines in N.Y.? There is of course the cottage—but Poe also lived at 111 Carmine St. in Greenwich Village, (house gone) and at the old Planter's Hotel downtown at Greenwich and Albany Sts.—an ancient colonial building recently renovated and used as a business men's restaurant.

I shall look with interest for "Faunus" and "The Hill of Dreams". The latter certainly offers opportunities for more than ordinarily ambitious composition, and of course the trees must be given a certain atmospheric strangeness just short of visible distortion. Faunus will perhaps give you good practice in rendering Lucian if you do him first. Whatever you send me I'll lend to Smith, who certainly appreciates your work. I trust you'll hear in time both from him and from Wandrei. Which reminds me—has Belknap yet forwarded Wandrei's "Hill of Dreams" critique to you as I asked him to when he had sufficiently digested it?

I shall never beat "Nemesis" in metre. It's the only verse of mine that I'm egotistical enough to like myself, but I do like some of those insidious stanzas. If it hadn't been composed in one night it would never have been composed at all—for I can never leave a poem to finish at another sitting. The mood is gone—hence I have to do all that I'm going to do at one time. This does not, however, apply to long narratives like "Psychopompos". But I must cease this rambling! With every good wish, and hoping the enclosed tales won't bore you too badly—
I remain Yr most obt
H P Lovecraft

P.S. You'll see my history of the weird tale before many months. It's reached the proofreading stage now—I've just gone over the first instalment. Proofreading is a damn nuisance, but not so bad as typing!

Notes

1. HPL returned from New York to Providence by train on 17 April 1926.
2. Terry McGovern (1880–1918), American boxer born of Irish parents. For a time he held both the world bantamweight and featherweight titles. He resided chiefly in Brooklyn.
3. William Lathrop Love (1872–?), American physician, New York State Senator for the 8th District (1923–1932), and associate editor of the *North American Journal of Homœopathy*. He may have inspired Dr. Muñoz in "Cool Air."
4. Actually St. Ann Catholic Church (1860), 251 Front Street at Gold Street, Brooklyn. The building was razed in 1992.

5. Lucile Dvorak (1898–1994), whom Kirk married on 5 March 1927. For extensive extracts of Kirk's letters to Lucile, discussing HPL and other members of the Kalem Club, see "The Kalem Letters of George Kirk," in *Lovecraft's New York Circle: The Kalem Club, 1924–1927*, ed. Mara Kirk Hart and S. T. Joshi (New York: Hippocampus Press, 2006), 19–116.

6. Alexander D. Messayeh (1875?–?)

7. A line from James Elroy Flecker's *Hassan* (1922).

8. *The London Adventure: An Essay in Wandering* (1924) is regarded as a third autobiography. HPL also owned this volume (*LL* 619).

9. Probably Alfred Galpin.

10. See MWM 39n10.

11. Fra Bartolomeo or Bartolommeo (1472–1517), an Italian Renaissance painter of religious subjects, and disciple of Girolamo Savonarola (1452–1498), Italian Dominican friar in Renaissance Florence, known for the destruction of secular art and culture and calls for Christian renewal.

12. *The Dream-Quest of Unknown Kadath.*

13. From Machen's *The Hill of Dreams.*

14. The poem is simply titled "W. W." in *A Man from Genoa.*

[3]   [AHT]

[June 1927]

My dear Dwyer:—

..... Yes—my New England is a dream New England—the familiar scene with certain lights and shadows heightened (or meant to be heightened) just enough to merge it with things beyond the world. That, I fancy, is the problem of everyone working in an artistic medium—to take a known setting and restore to it in vivid freshness all the accumulated wonder and beauty which it has produced in its long continuous history. All genuine art, I think, is local and rooted in the soil; for even when one sings of far incredible twilight lands he is merely singing of his homeland in some gorgeous and exotic mantle. It is this point which I seek to emphasise in my 110-page effort "The Dream Quest of Unknown Kadath." Take a man away from the fields and groves which bred him—or which moulded the lives of his forefathers—and you cut off his sources of power altogether. Like Antaeus of old, he needs the touch of his mother earth to preserve his strength. Culture as a whole—sophisticated, critical culture—may be cosmopolitan and international; but creative artistic force is always provincial and nationalistic. That is why I see nothing but unmitigated artistic decadence in modern "civilisation" with its polyglot urban concentration. New York would no more produce art than Carthage or Alexandria. Just as Alexandrian art was affected, superficial, and pedantic, so is that of New York today. The old N.Y. is dead, and this hybrid mass of parvenu and traditionless glitter has no relation whatever to the lives and dreams and aspirations of any one people or stream of culture. Out of this flashy, synthetic spawn of mongrelism nothing but pose and pretence can come. He who would create must return to some scene which is truly his, and which truly possesses roots reaching into the past. But more and more the drift is townward, and more and more the progress of mechanical invention removes life from the natural routine sanctified by the acts and thoughts of uncounted generations of our forbears. Familiar forces and symbols—the hills, the woods, and the seasons—become less and less intertwined with our daily lives as brick and stone horizons and snow-shovelled streets and artificial heating replace them, and the quaintly loveable little ways of small places die of inanition as easy transportation fuses all the surface of a great country into one standardised mould. Craftsmanship and local production are dead—no one man completely makes anything, and no one region subsists to any great extent on its own products either material or intellectual. Quantity and distribution are the watchwords in an age where factories and syndicates reign supreme; and all sectional manners and modes of thought are obliterated in the universal exchange of workers and teachers, luxuries and utilities, books and magazines, which complete industrialism and unimpeded access produce. The result—although an inevitable consequence of the advance of knowledge, which must be lamented impersonally rather than condemned hysterically—is an almost unmitigated loss to artistic life, for beauty comes only when life is closely attuned to its scene, and cannot endure when the spread of standardisation imposes one monotonous set of *mores* upon large and differentiated geographic areas, each of which once fostered and still ought to foster a separate set of manners and institutions as determined by its own especial race and heritage and landscape and climate. The social and political damage of urban industrial life is equally clear. Factory labour and the widespread dissemination of rudimentary knowledge produced an unstable emotional equilibrium wholly destructive of traditional forces of life. The herd becomes unmanageable, and sinks either into the unstimulating and unromantic humdrum of democracy, or into the still deeper slough of socialism and anarchy. Everything gorgeous and golden is dragged in the mud or painted dull grey, and intellectual speculation becomes merely an arena of wild and baseless schemes of life, none of which have any anchors in the past to give them dignity or loveliness. Now in an age like this can art survive? Personally I do not think it can, so far as its original function of the emotional and imaginative expression or its own time is concerned; for the life and thought of this period are wholly without the legacies and overtones which gave artistic possibilities to the life and thought of former periods. They are too ill-founded in tradition, or in the natural conditions and past experiences of the race, to have any deep hold on the vital hereditary memories out of which our sincere aesthetic perceptions and feelings spring. We cannot, then, have a really contemporary art of any appreciable depth so long as we have no materials to build it with save big business, structural steel, universal suffrage, aeroplanes,

The League of Nations, Greenwich Village, the radio, Henry Ford, the Rotary club, McCormick harvesters, soviets, the American Mercury, H. G. Wells, Dadaism, the A. F. of L., Jules Laforgue, Bruce Barton, the pornographic renaissance, Ben Hecht,[1] real estate, Los Angeles, the farm bloc, etc. etc. etc. etc. ad infinitum. But there does still remain the possibility of a *reminiscent* individual art for those who voluntarily remain outside the theatre of change and decay and cling tenaciously to the land and ways of their ancestors. This clinging can be either material and spiritual both, as in the case of one who still lives bodily amidst the ancient hills and woods and farmsteads; or it can be spiritual alone, as in the case of an urban dweller who remains true to the lore and memories of the old, simple, rural things, and saturates himself with their spirit and images even when he cannot spend all his days among them. This individual art will not reflect its own age, but it will sometimes reflect former ages almost as well as the artist of those ages once reflected them—depending on the extent to which the artist is able to merge himself and his soul into the background of bygone life. Or else it will sometimes take on the autumnal, sunset colours of a purely decadent art—the melancholy art of a Hardy or a Housman, or the glitteringly malevolent art of a Baudelaire, a Rops,[2] a Beardsley, or a Eugene O'Neill. And a third branch, of course, will be the fantastic art and literature of escape—which is the descendant of a type which has always existed either isolated or mixed with other types. This has found utterance in Blackwood, Dunsany, Stephens, de la Mare, Machen, Montague Rhodes James, Cabell, Sime, and so on. But this art will, of course, in all its phases depend upon the past; and will grow weaker and weaker as that past and its conditions recede into the background. It will last longest in such regions as cling most tenaciously to old things and old conditions, or somehow keep more than the average share of the old, fresh, unspoiled point of view. Ireland with its renaissance of the last thirty years and its isolation from general European decay is the best example I know, and it remains to be seen whether a revivified Italy under Fascism can prove a rival. Spain would have a chance if it were less played-out—the years will tell whether or not it has the stuff of a revival in it. The Southern part of the United States has many healthy qualities which may blossom out in art if the universal Babbitry of self-conscious "progress" and expansive standardisation does not produce that cultural rottenness-before-ripeness which has ruined the north and will ruin the west. The South, of course, had a frightful blow in the Civil War; when the established civilisation was dethroned by the dominance of a more upstart element; but the parvenus themselves are not by any means bad material, and they cling to a conservatism (amusingly naive and crude at times, as expressed in Baptist revivals, Dayton trials, freak laws, and the like) which ought to protect them mightily in their coming clash with the decadence of the outside world. So, altogether, I think we'll have to admit that the sound art of the future will be either regional or individual, and that it is likely to diminish with the generations unless some unforeseen mental revolution intervenes to check the growth of an artificial and abnormally proportioned life. The universal "art", such as it will be, will consist both of mediocre and meaningless decorative banalities of ultra-sophisticated design and mannered and overemphasised technique, and of morbid and hectic attempts at expressing whatever of nature is left in life—perforce the barest and most primitive instincts in a culture where all the natural overtones of traditional life and memory are swept away. This new hectic art will embrace both extravagant theory—as in cubism and its analogues—and sophisticatedly self-conscious selection and treatment, as in the use of analytical and scientific method, purely physiological or pathological themes, philosophical direction of thought with its attendant confusion, and an attempted directness leading to imitations of savage or primitive art traditions—archaic Minoan and Greek, Polynesian, Congo negro, American Indian, etc. The tone of the people of a mechanical age being intellectual rather than imaginative, we shall see the domain of art invaded by the methods and subject-matter of science and philosophy until virtually nothing of the true art impulse is left. No—universal and cosmopolitan "art" is certainly more definitely an impossibility than the prolongation of individual, provincial, and reminiscent art.

This is a long wandering from the New England background we were discussing, and I hope you can pardon it! To return—I am not really such an opponent of New England sobriety as I may appear, for I see much beauty in regularity of life—a beauty akin to decorative symmetry—and believe that the faith and practice of generations dwelling in the same place and under the same conditions form as valid a standard of life and conduct as can exist in a vast and meaningless cosmos unconscious of the presence of the various suns and worlds, and the inhabitants thereof, which compose it. In other words, I am philosophically a complete materialist unable to concede the existence of any absolute standards of value—good or evil—and recognising no universal principle but the general law of symmetry and harmony manifested to us as beauty. According to that principle, the only test of a thing's value is consistency with itself—so that no possible code of manners or morals is of any significance outside the radius of its sway, or of any absolute superiority or inferiority—as applied to its own group—in comparison with the code which any other group applies to itself. The only valid test of a code is consistency with the nature and history of the group professing it. If laws and natural tendencies coincide, we may call the code a good one. Keeping this in mind, I seem to find the austere manners of New England a fairly good expression of the landscape and the people, and an example of artistic selectiveness worthy of respect as a form of beauty. There is visible in New England life (i.e., the surviving life of the ancient stock) something of that classic restraint which animated New England decorative craftsmanship during its golden age (1720–1820) and gave to our carved doorways and interior panelling and house-proportioning a matchless grace and delicacy whose parallel we seek vainly in other parts of colonial America. The general code, then, I admire and approve as applied to New England people—although of course it would be absurd to apply it to Italians or Spaniards or Frenchmen. What I dislike in it is its occasional extravagance—once very marked, as are the extravagances of other inchoate things, but now happily moderated into a civilised attitude of tolerance. In a word, while I like the unbroken practice of purity and simplicity of life, I do not like the attitude of sanctity which links up morals with the ultimate forces of the universe, and assigns to minute moral values and distinctions such an exaggerated centrality and importance that the natural laws and proportions of the universe are ignored, and the natural scope of artistic expression and enjoyment—wholly impersonal things without any true relation to moral codes—arbitrarily curtailed. What excites my contempt are things involving hypocritical denials of actual scientific facts; unfounded assumptions of values and qualities known not to exist; capricious exaltations or insistences on detailed courses and customs not justified by harmonious relation to the general tradition; and absurd limitations of aesthetic development in contravention of the obvious fact that all beauty ought to be expressed as fully as possible in a cosmos void of any tangible value save beauty. These are the things I hate—not the basic New England tradition as evolved out of Puritanism, but the excrescences and overdevelopments awkwardly and ridiculously surviving from a crudely formative age. The only trouble with New England is that it acquired a premature old age before attaining true maturity. The foundations were magnificent—a lovely land of woods and hills and river valleys and sea coasts, and a population of sturdy yeomen and gentry whose natural and simple life and temperamental stability promised well for continuous growth and permanent achievement. For over two centuries all went well. The age of pioneer crudity and theological obsession was safely outlived, and the 18th century produced an exquisite growth of decorative taste which the Revolution somewhat injured but by no means destroyed. This was the age of the large landowner and prosperous merchant—an age of growing refinement and fastidiousness in life, and of correctness in taste, yet of continued simplicity in personal habits. During the earlier 19th century standards of education gradually rose, until by the Golden Age of Lowell, Holmes, Hawthorne, Emerson, Longfellow, Thoreau, and their fellows, we had a perfectly mature set of literary and artistic forms to match our precocious decorative development of the century before—a development, by the way, which had itself fallen into decay along with the decorative art of all the rest of the world in the 19th century. At that marvellous period—say the age of 1850 to 1880, when its leading figures were in their prime—New England's culture had attained its full stature in conventional intellectual sophistication and technique, so that no Bostonian or Providence man need feel like a clown or a country Æsquire in London, Paris, or Rome; but it had not acquired the philosophic maturity of an old and mellow civilisation. It was on the road to it. Nothing was amiss, any more than anything is amiss in a bright youngster not yet able to think quite like a middle-aged man. What it lacked was the breadth and depth and tolerant disillusion of age—the profound, half-secret realisation that nothing ultimately matters in all the universe save beauty, and that the greatest goal of a human mind is to think beautiful things beautifully, for the sake of that beauty alone. There clung to New England art a trace of the schoolroom, as clings to any young fellow just escaped from his tutor—a trace of naive self-consciousness; of adolescent pride in the new set of good artistic manners it had acquired; of complacency at the even flow of life to which its ordered civilisation had given birth. There were still present the childlike acceptance of religion which kept alive an artificial perspective and justified the retention of some grotesque illusions, disproportions, and limitations in thought; and the intellectual novice's adoration of form for form's sake which led to a growth of aesthetic manner at the expense of matter, and repressed the vigorous exuberance of untrammelled art in fear lest the exquisite balance of classic moderation be destroyed. It was a tame, didactic, handicapped art, as we all admit; but *not unhealthily so*. It was merely trying its wings—trying them in spite of the primitive theology which dictated a moralistic and optimistic philosophy, and the cultural inexperience which dictated a safe-and-sure insipidity of subject-matter and style—and all told, was not trying them ignobly. Its hour for perfect self-realisation and utterance had not yet come, but foundations were being laid which would have made that future hour a mighty one when it did finally arrive. The prospects were bright indeed—scene, people and history all working harmoniously toward a glorious culmination—when suddenly the blight of modernity stepped in and cut short the process.

It was industrialism and modern thought, of course. Factories brought unassimilable population, the old stock concentrated in the towns, and the orderly and continuous growth of the old life was shattered for ever save for isolated regions and individuals. The old stock in the towns, engulfed by different-minded newcomers, were thrown into a posture of resistance and defence, and totally altered in their relation to the entire scene. And what sociological change had not done, intellectual change finished. The old innocent naivete (which of course was a distinctly reckonable reality despite the natural undercurrents of reaction and furtive corruption which so conveniently motivate some of my horror-tales) was not allowed to mellow gradually into a delicate and intelligent recognition of philosophic truths amidst which the old standards of life might survive for reasons of artistic harmony even after the theological compulsion had melted away. Instead, the weary unmorality and fantastic morbidity of a genuinely decadent Europe were veritably forced down our cerebral gullets, whilst the externals of life—costume, housing, manners, art, reading, scholastic curricula, etc.—were imported wholesale to match. Life and thought lost simplicity—"plain living and high thinking"[3] were dead amongst the majority—and gained glitter and cosmopolitanism instead. Everything native was decried, and all New England seemed devoted to the unholy task of concealing its own ancestral features beneath the powder of Paris, the rouge of Rome, the lipstickery of London. To be an honest Yankee was out of fashion—one must have the airs and vices of the Great World about one. Some people began to cultivate the London drawl, and others the San Francisco rrolled rrrr... No poet or painter thought of handling homely local themes any more than of displaying the honest yellow cover of the Old Farmer's Almanack in his chimney-corner. In act, word, and dream New England was trying to get rid of the very foundations which would have made her great—trying to de-provincialise and merge herself into that stream of world-culture which Nietzsche would have considered typical of a 'good European'. Today we can see the grimly bitter humour of that frantic scramble of the 'nineties and the nineteen-hundreds—a scramble which other parts of simple, ancestral America parallelled with equal folly. It makes one think of a man in a staunch small boat leaping desperately to a vast palatial ship which he deems swift and advantageous—but which is already scuttled and close to foundering. This is irony at its keenest! For the local culture of old New England was sound though young, whilst the modern world's general culture is a thing as feverishly decadent as the culture of Aurelian's Rome. Few were immune from the contagion in some form or other, and in a decade or two New England had indeed achieved the position it so blindly sought—that of a small part of a great and crumbling world-fabric. Its sons were and are scattering rapidly, retaining only vestigial traces of their ancestral milieu; and are producing only the most pitiful fragments of authentic and distinctive art, as compared with a time when fully three-quarters of the nation's intellectual activity centered here—when (1891 according to Henry Cabot Lodge) in Massachusetts one man out of every 84 was a person of recognised ability and eminence, and in Rhode Island one out of every 118. New England did indeed become sophisticated and urbane and cosmopolitan—but at what a fearful cost! Like Edinburgh when it began to look toward London, it carried its mania for metropolitan maturity to the extreme of cultural and intellectual suicide.

But the land is still here—and despite much replacement the old blood is still here, entrenched amidst its memories in a dying world. And no matter what disasters come, the old combination of land and race is a hard one to extirpate utterly. Fads come and fads go. Men commit mistakes and recognise them. But the sight of an ancient land by the eyes its soil has bred is a fact—a geographic and biologic circumstance—from which there is no escape. New Englanders still inhabit New England; and in this final period of acknowledged decadence, when post-war ennui and a close reading of Spengler[4] and his school unite to shatter the tinsel hopes and quench the cosmopolitan will-o-the-wisps of 1914, we are beginning to behold the dawn of an era of sober retrospection. Robert Frost, New England's last authentic poet, is gaining a wider audience than he used to have; and New England is certainly in the van of the present craving (in many cases followed to grotesque lengths and by grotesquely inappropriate persons) for "early Americana". Out of this there is bound to arise a new and appreciative survey of the old rock-ribbed hills by the repentant sons of the old rock-ribbed Puritans—and this is the sort of thing which will probably give rise to what I call an "individual and reminiscent" art on the part of many New Englanders, whereby the ancient soil will live and glow again, though with the remoteness and melancholy of acknowledged retrospection. In time—since New England still possesses solid cultural centres like the residential part of Providence and Beacon Hill in Boston, where the old social life flows on among the same ancient families—this individual art may consolidate and unify into a true regional art; thus giving the lovely old realm at least a faint adumbration of the cultural and artistic maturity which it missed. We certainly have the beauty—the exquisite stretches of hill and countryside, and the archaic magic of quaint seaports and mossy gambrel roofs—and there is no doubt about the quantity of creative intellect present, if it will only devote itself to native themes, and not leave such things to second-and-third-raters. I only wish I were sufficiently endowed with the artistic faculty to assist in a real New England renaissance like the Irish renaissance of Yeats and A. E. and Synge and Padraic Colum and James Stephens and Lady Gregory[5] and Dunsany. It will take strong leaders, but I do not altogether despair of their appearance. I myself lean more and more strongly to the past and the old native things as I grow older. I always adored them and regarded them with fascination, being moved almost beyond expression by the ancient hill streets and knockered doorways and Georgian walled gardens of Providence, where all my life has been spent; but in youth I was not wholly unaffected by the same desire for wider horizons which I now deplore so bitterly. I cultivated an universal outlook, and sought the general, the metropolitan, the cosmic in manner and theme; delighting to echo Continental iconoclasm and to experiment in the literary sophistication, ennui, and decadent symbolism which those around me exalted and practiced. This phase, though, was exceedingly brief with me; for the old urge toward antiquarianism was a natural thing which no artificial veneer could long obliterate. And even in its midst my writings constantly betrayed the old New Englandism which I sought to expand into a Baudelairian Continentalism. Then at last the inevitable full reaction came, and I snapped back into my complete and complacent Yankee provincialism with a loud report whose echoes are yet resounding. Today I am a New England antiquarian 'and nothing else but' and my chief interest in life is exploring old towns and hunting out steep archaic lanes and carved colonial doorways. All my spare cash goes into trips to ancient towns like Newport, Concord, Salem, Marblehead, Portsmouth, Plymouth, Bristol, and the like, and whenever I go outside New England it is to some place where the surviving architecture and scenery enables me to revisualise the colourful eighteenth century—Philadelphia and Alexandria, Va. being favourite "foreign" towns of mine. With this archaistic passion joined to a fantastic imagination, you can see how tales like "The Festival" or "The Tomb" come into being. My present abode—although in a Victorian house—is on the crest of Providence's ancient hill, where the steep lanes of the elder town wind picturesquely up to a noble brow from which the westward view of outspread spires and domes and distant countryside is magnificent. Only three doors away is a little white farmhouse two centuries old—long overtaken by the growing city and now inhabited by an artist who still preserves a tiny patch of farmyard—and just around the corner is the old Halsey mansion with its stately Georgian porch and double-bayed facade—built in 1801 and now said to be *haunted*.[6] Could a more fitting milieu be asked for a retrospective and archaistic fantaisiste?

About "The Unnamable"—you are right in assuming that a very darkly fantastic basis indeed underlies it, although the editor of *Weird Tales* would probably have convulsions if he realised the fact! This worthy editor has been amusingly timid about very bizarre tales ever since he had had some trouble with state censors and parent-teacher associations over a story he printed three years ago—a story, as coincidence would have it, by an acquaintance of mine in Providence.[7] The paragraph in Mather's Magnalia (of which I possess an ancestral copy) on which the tale is based is a bona-fide one, and represents the extremes of credulity to which this strange character went in considering vague popular rumors. There was such a fantastic horror in the thing he suggested that I felt it simply demanded a story—hence "The Unnamable", which traced IT to lengths of which the learned divine never dreamed! One thing, though, in your conjecture is wrong. You will see on close reading that *a young man** *was hanged* for having eyes like IT. Well, that young man was the old man's son—and it was *his* grave whose blank slab the giant tree had partly engulfed. (There is actually an ancient slab half engulfed by a giant willow in the middle of the Charter St. Burying Ground in Salem.) The old man was innocent of all evil—but he felt the responsibility of a Biblical patriarch for all persons—and all THINGS, even when *unnamable*—that bore any trace of his blood. He was ITS grandfather, and could not forget it even when the memory of his hapless son had been systematically obliterated from the community. In supplying details I've worked in one or two genuine old New England superstitions—that one about the faces of past generations becoming fixed on windows was told to me *and believed* by a highly intelligent old lady who has a successful novel[8] and other important literary work to her credit. Living things—usually insane or idiotic members of the family—concealed in the garrets or secret rooms of old houses are or at least have

---

*according to my text, "a screaming, drunken wretch".

been literal realities in rural New England—I was told by someone of how he stopped at a lone farmhouse on some errand years ago, and was nearly frightened out of his wits by the opening of a sliding panel in the kitchen wall, and the appearance at the aperture of the most horrible, dirt-caked, and matted-bearded face he had ever conceived possible to exist! Certainly, there is a rich element of stark, grotesque terror in backwoods New England, where the houses are very far apart and people of undeveloped mind and emotions have too many opportunities for brooding alone month in and month out. Mere grotesqueness is very common; sly, malign madness sometimes lurks around the corner; and berserk, revolting murder under peculiarly messy and clumsy conditions is a matter of not infrequent record. It is easy to see how the critic Paul Elmer More[9] traces the horror-element in American literature to the remote New England countryside with its solitude-warped religious fanaticism. The best exponents of New England I can think of are Hawthorne and Mary E. Wilkins. The latter gets the undercurrent of horror remarkably well in "The Shadows on the Wall".

. . . . . .

   Sincerely yours,
    H. P. Lovecraft

Notes

1. Jules Laforgue (1860–1887), a Franco-Uruguayan poet known as a Symbolist poet. Bruce Fairchild Barton (1886–1967), American advertising executive, author, and politician, serving in the U.S. Congress from 1937 to 1940 as a Republican from New York. Ben Hecht (1894–1964), American journalist, novelist, screenwriter, and director.
2. Felicien Rops (1833–1898), Belgian artist and printmaker.
3. From the title of a book by W. H. Davenport Adams.
4. HPL refers to *Der Untergang des Abendlandes* (1918–22) by German historian Oswald Spengler, translated into English as *The Decline of the West*. HPL appears to have read only Vol. 1 of the work.
5. Isabella Augusta, Lady Gregory (née Persse; 1852–1932), Irish dramatist, folklorist, and theatre manager. Co-founder, with William Butler Yeats and Edward Martyn, of the Irish Literary Theatre and the Abbey Theatre.
6. The Jenckes–Pratt House (c. 1775) at 133 North Prospect Street at Barnes Street, only a few doors from HPL's residence at 10 Barnes. HPL made the Thomas Lloyd Halsey mansion (c. 1800) at 100 Prospect Street the residence of the protagonist of *The Case of Charles Dexter Ward* (though he numbered the house 140).
7. C. M. Eddy's "The Loved Dead," co-written with HPL.
8. Edith Miniter, author of *Our Natupski Neighbors*.
9. Paul Elmer More (1864–1937), American journalist, critic, essayist, and Christian apologist. HPL refers to More's essay "The Origins of Hawthorne and Poe," in *Shelburne Essays: First Series* (New York: Putnam's, 1904). See *SHL* 61.

[4]   [AHT]

Friday
[November 1927]

My dear Pickman:—

..... Your dream of the strange and desolate brick depot—and of the sinister slum house where *perspective* went so oddly askew—ought certainly to be elaborated in fiction some day. I can grasp the spirit of such impressions with especial vividness—and can indeed see the scenes of your dream in bold visual outline ..... though my impression, necessarily involving different elements of association and correlation, doubtless differs widely from your own. As for my own Hallowe'en dream—it belonged to a series very prominent in my youth, and involving a whole cycle of *Roman* life which made Machen's "Avallaunius" incident of especial interest and significance to me when I read it. Rome, as I think I have said, has always exercised the most peculiarly potent effect upon my imagination—forming a second fatherland to which all my sense of loyalty, perspective, affection, pride, and personal identity reverts whenever I think myself back into the ancient world. As far back as 450 A.D. my retrospective sense adheres altogether to Britain; but behind that point—when the scene of my memory becomes Roman—the chain abruptly snaps. Instead of following the various elements of Teutonic and Celtic ancestry into their northern forests and druid groves, my sense of personal identity and locale shifts abruptly to the banks of the Tiber—mourning in the downfall of the Empire and of the old gods, and slipping back to the virile, warlike days of the republic, when the conquering eagles of our consuls were carrying the name and dominion of the Roman people to the uttermost confines of the known world. S. P. Q. R.! It is as a Roman that I view and judge all antiquity—as a Roman that I feel toward all the various nations and peoples of the elder world. Thus I *admire* the superior art and intellect of the Greeks—but with the *outside* sense of one who knows Greece only as a conquered province of our republic, whose sculpture is beginning to appear in our temples and villas, and whose crafty, glib natives are beginning to invade our Roman streets with their suave, outlandish jargon. Like De Quincey, I derive a profound and inexplicable thrill from such phrases as *Consul Romanus, non esse consuetudinem populi Romani, senatus populusque Romanus,*[1] etc.—as if from some intimate, unbreakable and personal link, hard to account for in a man without a single drop of blood from any source save the British Isles. Behind the Roman world my sense of personal identity cannot be projected; so that the dimmer, vaster, and more terrible dawn-world of Gnossus and Nineveh, Ur and Babylon, and Persepolis, Memphis and Thebes, Ophir and Meroë, must remain to me for ever a thing existing only on paper as objective historical fact. Whenever my *antique* soul beholds the mysterious East, it is as a centurio, legatus, or tribunus militum of the republic's legions; with the great vallum of the castra Romana[2] close beside me, and the Latin songs and oaths of my fellow-soldiers in a faint chorus that punctuates the thoughts evoked by the decaying palaces and crumbling pylons of the elder, conquered land. But my real dreams are less often filled with the decadent East than with the barbaric West; and it is with the legions in Spain and Gaul and Britain, and on the Rhine and Danube frontiers, that my spirit has most frequently seen service. I am also quite often a private citizen or civil official, either in Rome or some Italian municipium, or in one of the towns of the western provinces. These dreams were most numerous in 1905 and 1906, but have recurred off and on since then. The recent one was undoubtedly the joint product of (a) my re-reading of the Aeneid, with my usual thrill at Anchises' prophecy of future Roman glory, and (b) the Hallowe'en season, as impressed upon me by the echoes of festivities held elsewhere in the neighbourhood.

As for the dream itself[3]—all antecedent visions slowly dissolved into a conversation I was holding with one whom I felt it very necessary to convert to my point of view. The beginning was very definitely an effort to shake off irrelevant thoughts and concentrate my mind on the scene and matter in hand. The sound of the fountain in the atrium where we were sitting distracted me, but instead of having it turned off I led my guest into the library beyond a nearby portiere. It was my own library, and there lay on the table the copy of Lucretius' De Rerum Natura that I had been reading,[4] rolled about three-quarters toward the end to the astronomical part in Book V which I had reached when Cnaeus Balbutius had been announced. I can still see the line where I left off—

LUNAQVE. SIVE. NOTHO. FERTUR. LOCA. LUMINE. LUSTRANS.[5]

Balbutius was legatus of the XIIth Legion, stationed here at Calagurris, on the south bank of the Iberus in Hispania Citerior. He was a stoutish man of about 35, and wore the crested helmet, corselet, and greaves proper to his military capacity. I, on the other hand, was a civil official—a provincial quaestor—and wore only a plain toga with the two purple stripes of the equestrian order. My name appeared to be Lucius Caelius Rufus. Well—Balbutius and I sat down and continued our dispute. It was very grave and determined, for the subject was one of *nameless, hovering horror;* and our respective opinions were very strong and diametrically opposite despite our long and cordial personal friendship.

The whole situation was this. Many miles to the north of us, near the little town of Pompelo at the foot of the Pyrenees, a monstrous doom was brewing in the hills. This territory was inhabited by the restless Vascones, only a part of whom were thoroughly Romanised, but in the hills a still wilder and infinitely more terrible people dwelt—the Strange Dark Folk (in the dream the frequently repeated phrase was *Miri nigri*) who held the monstrous Sabbaths on the Kalends of Maius and November. They had always dwelt somewhere up there, their land unseen by anyone from outside, and twice a year their fires were seen at night on the peaks, and their hellish drums and howlings heard. Just before these semi-annual orgies certain of the townsfolk would queerly vanish—never to return—and it was held probable that these persons had been captured by the Strange Folk for sacrifice to their unknown, unnamable deity. (In the dream, *Magnum innominandum*,[6] a neuter gerundive form of sound Latin etymology, though not found in the classics.) Each summer parties of the *Miri nigri* would appear in the plains and trade with the Vascones and Roman *coloni*. They were hated and feared, and spoke amongst themselves a language that neither Roman, Celtiberian, nor Gaul could understand—no, nor Greek traders, nor Carthaginian sailors nor Etruscan legionaries nor Illyrian and Thracian slaves—whilst most of their transactions were performed by signs. I seemed never to have *seen* one of them, though I had *read* and *heard* much; being indeed a close student of such forbidden mysteries.

Now this year something unusual had occurred. The strange traders—five of them—had indeed come down from the hills, but they had at last precipitated a riot in the streets of Pompelo—because of certain gloating and inhuman cruelties perpetrated upon a dog—and two of them had been slain. The surviving three had gone back to the hills with terrible looks, and now the people of Pompelo were trembling with fear of the doom which they felt about to fall upon their town. They feared this awful thing *because none of their number had vanished as the Kalends of November drew nigh*. It was *not natural* for the Strange Dark Folk to spare them like that. *Something worse* must be brewing. Finally they had persuaded their aedile (Tiberius Annaeus Mela, of half Roman and half Celtiberian blood) to visit Calagurris and ask Balbutius to send a cohort to their aid—a cohort to invade the hills on the momentous night, and to stamp out for ever whatever monstrous worship might be found there . . . a perfectly safe and feasible proceeding if undertaken in the evening, before the evocation of the *Magnum Innominandum* produced those developments about which the natives dared only to whisper. The aedile had made his journey, but Balbutius had refused his request. He thereupon had come to me; and because of what I had read about The Strange Dark Folk I sympathised at once, sending him home with the assurance that I would do all in my power to get the cohort to Pompelo. I had then prepared to visit the camp and talk with Balbutius, when I recollected that he was away on a boar-hunt. Accordingly I sent a slave to leave word at the camp asking him to call on me whenever he might return. Now he was here, and I was trying my best to bring him to my point of view.

His contention was that these local disturbances were never of any seriousness, nor worthy of any special military movement on the part of the authorities. Moreover, he believed that the bulk of the tribal population—far outnumbering the Romanised town-dwellers—were not only in sympathy with the *Miri nigri*, but were actual participants in many phases of their revolting worship. Any suppression on our part, he argued, would, while of course appeasing the oppidani,[7] be equally sure to antagonise the far more numerous wild natives; so that the net result would be to complicate rather than clarify our administrative problems.

To which I made reply, that it was not the custom of the Roman people to fear the displeasure of barbarians, nor to be deterred from doing that which is in consonance with Roman principles of government. That the good-will of the colonists and townsfolk was of far great value in facilitating our administration than the good-will of the tribesmen; since the loyalty of these latter was never certain, while the coöperation of the Romanised element was absolutely essential to the establishment of a sound executive and legislative fabric. Moreover, that the hideous and monstrous nature of the Dark Folk's rites was not unknown to me, and that the sufferance of such malign practices would ill become the descendants of those who, Sp. Postumius Albinus and Q. Marcius Philippus being consuls, had broken up the widespread orgies of Bacchus in Italy, putting to death great numbers of Roman citizens and graving upon a bronze tablet the *Senatus Consultum de Bacchanalibus*.[8]

I now took down from the racks along the walls many books on terrible and forbidden subjects, both in Latin and in Greek; unrolling them to significant passages and shewing the latter to Balbutius. The very sight of some of these books frightened me—especially a Greek text, on Pergamene parchment, titled ἹΕΡΟΝ. ΑΙΓΥΠΤΟΝ[9]—and I would give much for a glimpse of them now! But upon my guest they had no effect. His mind was made up not to send the cohort, and nothing could make him see the need of it. He agreed, however, not to be offended if I put the matter before the proconsul, Publius Scribonius Libo; so as soon as he left I prepared a long and explicit letter to Libo, and had a slave (a sturdy, undersized Greek named Antipater) set off for Tarraco with it. It was now evening, but my dream continued. I bathed and proceeded to the triclinium, where my household (my mother Helvia, advanced in years, and a somewhat younger maternal uncle, Lucius Helvius Cinna) joined me at dinner. During the evening I discussed the matter with them, and was glad to note their agreement—although my mother vainly sought to make me promise not to accompany the cohort if it was sent.[10] I then retired in a room with finely frescoed walls, and awaked (still within the dream) to the singing of birds. A breakfast with the family and a session of reading in the garden ensued. I seemed to reside in a suburban villa on a hill, for below me I could see the red-tiled roofs and pillared forum of Calagurris, and the sparkling bends of the Therus just beyond. Later Balbutius came again, and more futile argument ensued. Then another dinner and conversation with the family—the subject being Lucretius and the Epicurean philosophy. From what was said, we appeared to regard Lucretius as still living though not personally known to us. My uncle, however, spoke of having once known Memmius, to whom De Rerum Natura is dedicated. Then bed again, and another bird-awaking after *a dream within the dream*. This was a nightmare, and involved some stupendous Eastern ruin of which I had read in that frightful Ἱερον Αιγυπτον. During this day I read and wrote in the garden, (for the weather was warm) till just after siesta-time Antipater returned with a letter from the proconsul. I broke the seal and began—P. SCRIBONIUS. L. CAELIO. S. D. SI. TV. VALES. BENE. EST. EGO. QUOQUE. VALEO. AVDIVI. QUAE. SCRIPSISTI. NEQUE. ALIAS. PUTO[11] and so on . . . . To be explicit, Libo agreed with me fully; knowing apparently as much as myself about the rites of the Dark Folk, and seeing a need of instant action at Mela's request. Not only did he enclose an order to Balbutius for the despatch of a cohort to Pompelo before the coming Kalends, but he expressed his intention of going thither himself, in order to investigate a horror of such import not only to the wards of the Roman people, but to the peace of mankind as a whole. Me he authorised to accompany the cohort, and expressed a hope of meeting me in Pompelo two days from the time of his letter's probable receipt. My joy was extreme, and I rushed down the hill and through the town on foot, seeking Balbutius at his camp. The town was fairly sizeable, with one or two streets paved (there were high sidewalks, and stepping stones at crossings) and considerable crowds of soldiers, colonists, Romanised natives of Iberian physiognomy, and wild tribesmen from the plains surging past the whitewashed deadwalls of houses and gardens. The camp was near the river, where there was a landing place for supplies, and I hailed a sentry at the Porta Praetoria. The man took me through the gate (the wall was easily ten feet high and nearly as thick) along the Via Principalis to the Praetorium, (the soldiers dwelt in wooden houses on account of the permanence of the camp) where I found Balbutius reading a shabby copy of Cato's De Re Rustica. He took the sealed packet from the proconsul that I brought, and finally gave in when he saw its indisputable authority. He now pondered as to which cohort he could best spare, deciding finally on the 5th. Sending an orderly for the legatus of that cohort, he soon had before him a young dandy named Sextus Asellius, with foppishly polished equipment, frizzed hair, and a 'sporty' little cloud of beard-growth on his under jaw. Asellius was violently against the sending of the cohort, but did not balk under orders. We saw that it would be hard work getting to Pompelo in two days as Libo had ordered, so resolved to march both day and night with only short naps. I now went home and prepared for travel—ordering a litter with eight Illyrian bearers. In this I went down to the bridge and waited for the cohort, which arrived after a tedious interval. It was infantry—for we had no cavalry at Calagurris—but there were a couple of horses for Asellius and Balbutius—the latter being determined to go along in person and see the thing through. Then came a whole night of dozing and jouncing, and a whole day of the same—through wild, flat country. The meals were frugal and infrequent, and only reading and conversation enlivened the tedium. Balbutius would occasionally ride by the side of my litter and discuss the terrors ahead of us. Night again, and another morning. At last we saw the dim, menacing line of the awful hills ahead. This was the final day of October. At noon we would be in Pompelo, and at night we would go into the horrible hills where witch-fires flamed and drums and howlings echoed.

Pompelo was a small neat village with a paved forum and a wooden amphitheatre east of the compact area. Libo and his train had arrived ahead of us, and greeted us with genuine cordiality. He was slightly known to me—a fine old man with a hawklike Roman face, seamed and tight-lipped, and an almost completely bald head. He wore a toga praetexta befitting his consular dignity. As the afternoon wore on, we all talked earnestly, the aedile Annaeus Mela joining our deliberations. Of the two opposed to Libo, Mela, and me, Balbutius bore his overruling better than Asellius. This talk occurred in the curia just off the forum. Meanwhile the 300 soldiers had been mingling with the townsfolk, and had caught something of the undercurrent of fright. For there was indeed an air of monstrous doom upon that town, and even I felt disposed to tremble as I saw the menacing bulk of the mountains toward the north . . . . brooding and waiting. We could scarcely find a native to guide us toward the usual scene of the orgies, but at length secured a youth—largely of Roman blood though born in Pompelo—named Marcus Accius, who agreed to take us through the foothills and to the head of a certain ravine, but no farther. Only an enormous offer of money moved him, and his lips and fingers twitched nervously as he waited for evening.

Then sunset came with a terrible, apocalyptic weirdness, Asellius gathered and drew up his cohort, and provided horses for Libo, Annaeus Mela, and me—yes, and also for Q. Minucius Laena, the intelligent and well-born secretary accompanying Libo. The villagers flocked around us as we stood in formation west of the town, and we could not help catching the horror of their whispering. At last we set out in the twilight—torches ready to use when necessary, and the guide trembling as he walked beside Libo's horse. And it was worse when the dusk thickened *and the drumming began.* It was an eldritch sound—muffled and monotonous, and hideously deliberate and persistent. It put an idea into my head which frightened me. Surely, I reflected, these alert and furtive Dark Folk must have known of our expedition by this time. Half the tribesmen round about were their secret allies and informers, and gossip had been rife in Pompelo all day. *Why, then, were they going ahead with their rites just the same* . . . . *as if the authority of the Roman people were not moving against them? I did not like what that notion implied.* Then night fell, and one by one the distant peaks blazed with pale flame. Still the drumming pounded damnably on. We were in the foothills now, and with every mile our apprehensions increased. Despite the absence of a moon, Balbutius thought it inadvisable to use torches, fearing lest our course be noticed from afar; so we stumbled on clumsily over black trails which grew constantly steeper as the wooded slopes at our side grew higher and closer. In those wooded depths, now so narrowly pressing on our flanks, we fancied we heard inexplicable sounds and imagined an infinity of loathsome watching presences. And still the drumming and the flames persisted. As the defile narrowed to the proportions of a mere flume or canyon, its steepness became almost precipitous; and the six of us who were mounted were forced to leave our horses. By the aid of shaded torch we tethered them to some spectrally twisted scrub oaks, leaving a squad of ten men to guard them from possible theft—though chance thieves were unlikely enough in such a place on such a night! Then the rest of us scrambled on and on, up and up, toward the peaks where the fires blazed, and the narrow patch of sky where the Milky Way glimmered between the lofty enclosing slopes. It was a frightful climb—fear in the darkness, and the whispers and muffled curses of three hundred frightened legionaries who lurched, slipped, and stumbled; jostling one another constantly, and treading incessantly on one another's toes—or even hands, where the ascent was quite vertical.

Then, amidst that hellish pounding of distant drums, there came a very terrible sound *from behind us*. It was the horses we had left—just the horses, and not the soldiers guarding them. It was not *neighing*, but *screaming*—the frenzied *screaming* of panic-struck beasts face to face with horrors not of this world. We all stopped, half-paralysed with fright. And the screaming continued, and the drums pounded on, and the hilltop flames danced.

Then a brief stir and maddening cry from our vanguard made Balbutius order a torch, voice quavering as he did so. In the faint glimmer we saw the body of the guide Accius weltering in blood and with eyes half started from their sockets with cosmic, ultimate fright. He, who had been born at the foot of these hills and who knew all that men whispered about them, had not been able to face *what he knew had made those horses scream*. He had seized the short sword from the scabbard of the nearest centurion—the primipilus Publius Vibulanus—and had stabbed himself to the heart.

And now, suddenly, the sky itself was snuffed out. Stars and Milky Way vanished in an instant, and only the hilltop flames remained—now silhouetting, for the first time, the blasphemous shapes of the not quite human things that leaped and danced titanically around them. And the drums still sounded, and the horses screamed and screamed in the gulfs below.

Flight was impossible, but a sort of local stampede set in, amidst which many men trampled their comrades to death as all sought vainly to rush away. The screams of the soldiers now rivalled those of the horses, and the single torch which the proconsul had snatched from a fainting bearer and kept alight shewed a sea of faces convulsed with every last extreme of frenzy. Of our immediate party Annaeus Mela was trodden down out of sight, whilst the secretary Laena seemed to have disappeared sometime before. Balbutius went quite mad, and began to grin and sing an old Fescennine verse from his native Italian countryside. Asellius tried to cut his own throat, but could only struggle with a sudden cold wind which coiled down from the heights and wrapped him Laocoön-like in its folds. My own condition was one of absolutely statue-like paralysis and speechlessness. Only the aged Scribonius Libo, veteran of the Jugurthine and Mithridatic Wars, retained to the last a perfect poise and fortitude. I can yet see his calm Roman face in the fading light of the torch he held—see his face and hear the clear, measured words with which he met his doom like a true patrician and consul of the republic. From the slopes and peaks above us a crackling chorus of daemoniac laughter burst, and winds of ice swept down to engulf us all. My spirit could endure the strain no longer, and I awaked—bounding down the centuries to Providence and the present. But still there rings in my ears those last calm words of the old proconsul—*"Malitia vetus—malitia vetus est—venit—tandem venit . . . ."*12

It was the most vivid dream I have had in a decade, and involved subconscious use of odd scraps of boyhood reading long forgotten by my waking mind. Calagurris and Pompelo are real towns of Roman Spain, now known as Calabarra and Pompelona, respectively; as I learned upon consulting the classical dictionary. Pompelo, apparently, escaped its threatened doom, and it would interest me to visit its neighbourhood some time, I would like to dig among the passes in the hills for the crumbling bones and rusted silver eagles of a forgotten cohort!

About a week ago I had another dream of remarkable vividness and coherence, but nothing as compared with this veritable slice of vital and realistic experience in the Roman world. The second dream had an indefinite modern setting.

[. . .]

Yr obt Grandsire—

Theobald

Notes

1. "Roman Consul," "it is not the habit of the Roman people," "the Senate and people of Rome."
2. Roman encampments.
3. HPL sent FBL an account of his dream, which FBL incorporated directly into his short novel *The Horror from the Hills*. Another account, in a letter to Donald Wandrei (3 November 1927), was published as "The Very Old Folk" (*CF* 3.494–500).
4. See Bibliography regarding HPL's own copy.
5. "The moon, too, whether she illumines places with a borrowed light as she moves along." Lucretius, *De Rerum Natura* 5.575 (tr. Cyril Bailey).
6. *The Great Not-to-Be-Named*. Cited without explanation in "The Whisperer in Darkness" (*CF* 2.483).
7. I.e., townspeople.
8. The Decree of the Senate on the Bacchanalia, passed in 186 B.C.E. and prohibiting the celebration of the Bacchanalia throughout Italy.
9. In an English transliteration, *Hieron Aegypton:* "Sacred Egypt."
10. After HPL's mother thwarted his attempts at enlistment for the war in 1917, he said

that any time he left the house, she made him promise not to attempt to enlist again.

11. "P. Scribonius Libo to L. Caelius. If you are well it is good. I also am well. I have heard what you have written and do not think otherwise."

12. "The evil [is] old—the evil is old—it comes—it comes at last . . ."

[5] [AHT]

Saturday
[January 1928]

Sr. Bernardo de Viero
   Oeste Socano,
      Nuevo-York

Muy Señor mío y amigo:—

[. . .]

One of the things Cook did was to buy up a vast supply of Farmer's Almanacks in order to bring his file into competition with mine. I don't know whether or not I've ever mentioned this ancient New England institution to you—but if not, you must realise that this unassuming little annual was established in 1793, and has since then hung beside practically every rustic hearth in the six states of our venerable realm, year in and year out, without a break, and usually saved carefully for storage in the cobwebbed attic. It is such a symbol and summary of the Yankee countryside that Prof. Kittredge of Harvard has written a book about it—"The Old Farmer and His Almanack". Much of its charm arises from the fact that in all its 135 years of publication it has scarcely changed its appearance. The general format of the 1793 issue has known no alteration—a new cover introduced in 1850 and some fresh pictorial embellishments for the calendar pages dating from 1852 being the sole extent of the difference between the opening issue and the 1928 issue now on sale . . . . . save, of course, for the dropping of the long ſ in 1803 and the adoption of a clearer type face in the late 1830's. Well—my family file, complete back to 1877 and scattering back to 1815, always used to be the most delightful of browsing-grounds for me; and this year I resolved to augment it still further by purchase; striving ultimately for a full set back to the very first number. Eddy proved just the right man for the purpose.[1] In his attic were uncounted and unclassified oceans of ancient numbers, and he gave me the free run of the place at a nickel per copy. In this manner I made my personal file complete back to 1839 and scattering back to 1805—not bad as a starter. Cook, catching the enthusiasm, has now begun to add to his somewhat slenderer hereditary supply; and has pushed his unbroken file back to 1842—scattering back to 1828. All this has aroused the genial Eddy to a sense of value of his once despised wares, so that he has just 'boosted' the price of old almanacks up to a dime each! The good old law of supply and demand! Now that I've secured all the variety Eddy has, I'll have to try my luck at the Boston shops if I wish to continue my collecting progress. [. . .]

I rather thought you might find my Roman dream of interest. Sooner or later I may work it up as a story, but there are several points which must be checked up as to accuracy before it sees final formulation. Chief of all is, of course, the matter of the calendar. As you know, the astronomically erroneous Roman year played hell with the months and seasons before the divine Julius called in Sosigenes of Alexandria and set matters straight—so that a Witch-Sabbath, staged by wild tribes who reckoned by Nature and the stars, would (in the later ages of the republic) fall somewhere in the early January of the uncorrected Roman year instead of at the Kalends of November. Roman date and wild Sabbath would coincide only at a very early Republican age, or in the Imperial period after the reform of the calendar. As for the Dark Folk—I *saw* none of them in the dream, but do not think I understood them to be *little* from what I read and from what Annaeus Mela and the Pompelonii told me. They had *strange features*, but could not have conspicuously impressed the villagers as undersized else the aedile would have mentioned it. Nor was their language a *hissing*. It was normal human speech, and Mela even tried to imitate some of it to me. Its nature and affiliations were totally unknown. Its source, as a feature of the dream, must have been my memory of the fact that the *Basques* of the Pyrenees speak a language absolutely unclassifiable by human erudition. It was probably left by the little Mongoloids, although the Basques themselves have none of their blood—just as the Finns speak a Mongoloid language despite an ascendancy of Aryan blood in their actual veins. The dream gave no clue to what was to happen after the point where waking removed me, but as I call it repeatedly to mind and memory I seem to find one more impression which I don't think I wrote you. It is that the steep wooded slopes on either side of the defile were slowly and stealthily creeping together with a morbid vitality and motion—closing in upon the doomed cohort, perhaps to crush and bury it forever in an altered landscape. But the doom could not have reached Pompelo—for the town still lives! How to handle the tale will be quite a problem. I don't think Rufus or anybody else ought to survive—and it ought somehow to be made clear that the sacrifice of the cohort saved the town. Or better still—for of course it would be foolish to follow the dream when it isn't convenient to do so—*the town had better be destroyed;* its identity being of course changed from Pompelo. The best beginning would be an archaeological one. A rusted Roman signum washed down from the Pyrenees in the spring rains and placed in the museum of some surviving town—a sensitive and contemplative traveller inexplicably and continually attracted to it—his fear of the hills, but his visit to them after having been told where the aquila was found. His camp at the base of the foothills and his discovery of ruins. Perfect preservation of the buried town uncovered by the Spanish archaeologists whom he summons. Conclusion that town was overwhelmed instantaneously by an avalanche—households apparently interrupted in the midst of work—*but no human remains found.* Only small heaps of grey dust. *Graffiti* of very puzzling sort on walls—prayers scrawled everywhere, as if in fear of a terrible doom—

NOS.SERVA.IVPPITER.OPPIDUM.SERVA.EX.PERICULO.MAVORS.
NOBISCUM.ESTO.CONTRA.MIROS.NIGROS.PUGNA.FAVNE.
MONTES.TENE.SILVANE.SILVANE.NECA.NECA.MAGNUM.
INNOMINANDUM.NECA.AC.SERVA.MALITIAM.VETEREM.NECA.
APOLLO.NOS.SERVA.²

(The phrase *Magnum Innominandum* must of course excite the keenest awe and speculation.)

Spanish archaeologists tell of fear which natives possess for the Basques of the hills, amongst whom the Evil Sabbath is still said to be celebrated—traveller determines to wait for Sabbath night and go into hills to witness horrors—interests archaeologists and persuades them to accompany him. Makes a preliminary survey of the hills alone, and finds an exceedingly strange altar and circle of monoliths on a distant peak. Meets a strange dark man, who makes an evil sign in the air and flees. Returns to camp and falls ill with fever. Taken to hospital in Pompelona—too ill to go into the hills Hallowe'en night. But the Spanish archaeologists go just the same. That night the dream ensues—exactly as previously related except for identity of town. Horrible waking—but still more horrible news that afternoon. *The party of Spanish archaeologists has disappeared, and the unknown excavated village has been buried again, precisely as it had remained for two thousand years.* The Magnum Innominandum does not forget. By Jove! That doesn't sound half bad! But it'll take a helluva lot of care in handling. This sort of thing has to be damned adroit, or it doesn't convince. Wright has just sent me advance sheets of "Cthulhu" from next month's W.T., and I am horribly disappointed with it upon a re-reading after a year and a quarter. It is *cumbrous*—undeniably *cumbrous*. Well—let's see if I do better this time! By the way—Wright has accepted that tale of Belknap's of which I am "hero".³ Yes—nocturnal *howling* has an element of fearfulness for me. I always associate it with lean, dog-faced beings that walk sometimes on two legs and sometimes on four, and that lope abroad in the night's small hours. Wolves and other animals are of course the ultimate basis of the hereditary folk-fear on which my impression is founded..... Coming back to the possible dream-tale—the irregularities of the calendar would require some explaining rather foreign to the directness and simplicity of good fiction—or at least to the taste of Brother Wright's untutored clientele—so I guess I'll push the date ahead to the early Imperial age, after the calendar's reform. The province will then be called *Hispania Terraconensis,* and the brave old man will be *Legatus propraetore* instead of proconsul. He'd better have a less ancient name. Let's see . . . . . Caius Pomponius Falco; Titus Sosius Caecinus; Marcus Cornelius Balbus . . . . . . any of the middle-grade equestrian houses that weathered the decadence of the late republic and the slaughter of the civil wars and the proscription of the second triumvirate. . . . . . .

Su segura servidor q.s.m.b.

Luis Randolfo Cartero y Teobaldo.

Notes

1. Presumably Arthur A. Eddy, proprietor of Eddy's Book Store at 260 Weybosset St.
2. "Help us, Jupiter, save our town from danger. Mars, be with us against the Strange Dark Folk. Fight, Faunus. Hold the mountains, Silvanus, Silvanus. Kill, kill the Great Not-to-Be Named. Kill and help. Kill the old evil. Help us, Apollo."
3. "The Space-Eaters" (*WT*, July 1928).

[6]   [AHT]

February 14, 1928

Querido Don Bernardo:—

[. . .]

I was greatly interested in the Wandrei material, and will send it on to Belknap very shortly. No doubt Wandrei has told you that he's sold nearly all the "Sonnets of the Midnight Hours" to *Weird Tales*, for gradual publication one by one. Ultimately I fancy he intends to make a book of them, to follow "Ecstasy and Other Poems" at a suitable interval. Enclosed herewith is some more Wandrei verse—received from Belknap to be sent to you and thereafter returned to Wandrei. The kid is getting more and more powerful and proficient in poetry—so much so that I think he will probably drop prose altogether in time. Some of these Midnight sonnets are ineffably powerful—and so provocative of visual images that I feel sure I shall use some of them as mottoes to weave stories around. With these poems I am enclosing an experiment of Klarkash-Ton's—a *literal* translation of some of Baudelaire's poems into English prose.[1] This is virtually the only way to capture all the nuances and overtones of mood in the original—as Baudelaire himself realised when translating the verse of Poe into French prose. I think you would find Baudelaire a poet of extreme and Satanic fascination. Have you read him? If not, I'll be glad to lend you the volume of selections in the Modern Library. As for the Wandrei work you forwarded—it is really excellent, and reveals the growing power of the youthful author as a poet. I think the verse is perhaps better than the prose—for as I grow older, I come to question more and more the art value of those long-drawn, quasi-allegorical, pompously-phrased prose-poems with which the 1890's so profusely abounded. At least, if one is to prepare a thing of that kind he ought to be very sure of his own visual grasp of the theme, and very careful to preserve a certain simplicity of diction amidst the rhythm of his musical paragraphs. A Klarkash-Tonic vocabulary certainly won't do for work of this type—and neither will excessively obtrusive archaisms. [. . .]

I thought you'd find the Railo book of interest, for it really goes into the matter of Gothic fiction far better than any other work extant, including the Birkhead treatise, hitherto the standard. Have you read "The Castle of Otranto" itself? If not, *don't!* Let the summary in Railo continue to give you a "kick", for the original certainly won't! Walpole was too steeped in the classical tradition of the early 18th century to catch the Gothic spirit of the latter half. His choice of words and rhythms is the brisk, cheerful Addisonian one; and his nonchalant and atmosphereless way of describing the most prodigious horrors is enough to empty them of all their potency. Thanks to the second-hand way in which you received it, you have become the first reader to get a genuine shiver from "Otranto" since the days of Sir Walter Scott! I can see how that Walpole dream[2] might affect the imagination powerfully; especially since I myself once had a dream of winding castle stairs, in which all the darkness and mystery of mediaevalism seemed to be concentrated. The vast hand well illustrates those abnormalities of proportion common to fantastic dreams, although I myself think it a rather extreme conception for artistic fiction. Your own castle-staircase dreams sound intensely fascinating— indeed, your description of those under crypts and of the fortress by the nighted sea gave me a very authentic shudder! Mechanical yet animated beings, too, have a charm all their own. Do you recall that tale of Bierce's in "Can Such Things Be?" where the iron chess-player became incensed with its master and creator?[3] I really think, myself, that a genuinely weird artist could even today create a thoroughly fine and potent novel out of the old Gothic paraphernalia—in fact, I rather wish someone *would* try it, if only as a stunt to prove that it can be done! By the way—you'll find your love of the Gothic cathedral poignantly duplicated in Arthur Machen's "Secret Glory". You and he are quite akin in spirit, it seems to me; and I feel sure you'll enjoy reading more of his work. About the terror of *mere size*—that is an undeniable fact, and the artist's only question is how to utilise it without becoming unconsciously comic. Vast *empty* spaces are notoriously terrifying; and unless we are prepared for them, vast solid bulks have a horror all their own. Lafcadio Hearn averred that Gothic cathedrals *frightened* him with their bulk and mystical design. They seemed to him about to rise from the ground. Of this quality of size-terror I fancy Mrs. Radcliffe[4] is, as you say, the chief exponent. Certainly, it recurs throughout her work. [. . .]

Trusting to hear from you when events permit—
con mil besas de mano—
Teobaldo

Notes

1. Clark Ashton Smith published some translations (in verse) of the poetry of Charles Baudelaire, but much of it, including prose translations, remained unpublished in his lifetime. This is now available in *The Complete Poetry and Translations—Volume 3: The Flowers of Evil and Others* (Hippocampus Press 2012).
2. Horace Walpole claimed that *The Castle of Otranto* had been inspired by a dream in which "I had thought myself in an ancient castle (a very natural dream for a head filled like mine with Gothic story) and that on the uppermost bannister of a great staircase I saw a gigantic hand in armour" (letter to William Cole, 9 March 1765).
3. "Moxon's Master."
4. Ann Radcliffe (1764–1823), author of *The Mysteries of Udolpho: A Romance* (1794).

[7]   [AHT]

Dec. 10, 1930

Dear Fra Bernardus:—

[. . .]

By the way—in going downtown tonight I was impressed anew by the mystic beauty of the twilight urban vista from a certain point along the route. Looking westward from the towering precipice on whose brink I dwell, I saw a flaming orange sunset with distant spires & towers, & the marble State House dome looming fantastically against it. And far below me, in the middle distance, the tall buildings of the lower town were bursting into alluring light—thousands of windows rising out of the violet depths like a mystical constellation from outer space. Some sight!

Well—best wishes & all that.

Yr obt Grandpa

Theobald.

[8]   [AHT]

Castle of Udolpho
[1932]

Dear Bernardus:—

[. . .]

Regarding Machen's undercurrents—yes, I fancy there is an element of obscure, twisted eroticism there, along with a great deal of purer and more ethereal imaginativeness. His early work was produced in the '80's and '90's, when suggestions of dark, ill-defined, abnormal instincts were a reigning literary fashion among the younger and more iconoclastic writers; so that this element must have seemed to him ineffably potent as a lurking background and hinted explanation of the horrors forming his chosen province. He needed something tremendously more hideous than anything in ordinarily known life and literature (these psychological byways were virtually unknown to laymen before 1900 or 1910); hence—apparently lacking a sensitiveness toward the conception of cosmic outsideness—seized upon what then formed the subject of the darkest whispers and conjectures. I can't say that I'm highly enthusiastic about such a choice—although of course all subjects are equally authentic as artistic material—but if such stuff was necessary to the working of his fantastic genius, I'll forgive him his choice. I'd a great deal rather have Machen as he is than not have him at all! What Machen probably likes about perverted and forbidden things is their departure from and hostility to the commonplace. To him—whose imagination is not cosmic—they represent what Pegāna and the River Yann represent to Dunsany, whose imagination *is* cosmic. People whose minds are—like Machen's—steeped in the orthodox myths of religion, naturally find a poignant fascination in the conception of things which religion brands with outlawry and horror. Such people take the artificial and obsolete concept of "sin" seriously, and find it full of dark allurement. On the other hand, people like myself, with a realistic and scientific point of view, see no charm or mystery whatever in things banned by religious mythology. We recognise the primitiveness and meaninglessness of the religious attitude, and in consequence find no element of attractive defiance or significant escape in those things which happen to contravene it. The whole idea of "sin", with its overtones of unholy fascination, is in 1932 simply a curiosity of intellectual history. The filth and perversion which to Machen's obsoletely orthodox mind meant profound defiances of the universe's foundations, mean to us only a rather prosaic and unfortunate species of organic maladjustment—no more frightful, and no more interesting, than a headache, a fit of colic, or an ulcer on the big toe. Now that the veil of mystery and the hokum of spiritual significance have been stripped away from such things, they are no longer adequate motivations for phantasy or fear-literature. We are obliged to hunt up other symbols of imaginative escape—hence the vogue of interplanetary, dimensional, and other themes whose element of remoteness and mystery has not yet been destroyed by advancing knowledge. However, it is clear that Machen has a natural affinity for somewhat earthy perspectives which was not common even in the '80's and '90's among purely Nordic artists. In his psychology, without doubt, there is a great deal of the Mediterranean—just as there is a great deal of prehistoric Mediterranean blood in his native Wales, where most of the peasantry are dark and small of stature. As you point out, his heroes generally tend to be of a languishing type rather alien to the natural products of a purely Celtic or Teutonic fancy—while his autobiographical sketches have a certain whine of self-pity not very agreeable to some readers. As for ecclesiastical saints and mystics—a large number undoubtedly were the victims of masochistic and other perversions, since all religious emotion is basically erotic. Others, of course, can be explained as normal persons acting on the grotesque mytho-

logical assumptions which the ignorance of former ages permitted them to take seriously. Close, impartial, and disillusioned historical analysis can do much to distinguish betwixt mystics who suffered from aberrations—like Anthony, Stylites, Theresa, etc.—and those who merely represent a strong ethical zeal operating under the common fallacy of supernaturalism. [. . .]
   Yr most obt hble Servt
      Grandpa

[9] [AHT]

          The Last Days of 10 Barnes St.,
          Providence, R.I.,
          April 23, 1933.

Dear Bernardus:—
   [. . .]
 I thought you'd enjoy Two-Gun's riproaring! As a matter of fact, I didn't disparage his physical interests, but merely pointed out that they do not represent as important and highly evolved a part of him as the imagination which can produce things like "Worms of the Earth"[1] and the myriad rhapsodies on old southwestern days which fill his letters. He is undoubtedly of Herculean strength—his self-disparagements being the products of an exaggerated modesty, or of a wish to represent the physical standards of Texas as altogether superhuman. The quotation from Canevin[2] was indeed vastly interesting. Of course, H S had no such strength during the latter days when we knew him, for his illness had sapped the greater part of his vitality; but in his prime he must have been an absolute marvel. And yet he bore his loss of strength with unbroken cheerfulness. In answering Two-Gun I pointed this out, and suggested that Canevin would not have been so cheerful if the decline had been in his creative ability or imagination. After all, Canevin had a sound sense of *relative* values. He prized the physical, yet knew that it was secondary to the mental—something which (except in certain types bound to manual industry) could be spared if necessary. However—that wasn't my main controversy with Sagebrush Bob. The big issue was civilisation versus barbarism. I claim the barbarian of superior race represents a regrettable *waste of biological capacity;* since his energies are chained to a mere struggle for physical survival, while his intellect and imagination are restricted to a very narrow range of functioning which leaves their richest and most pleasurable potentialities absolutely undeveloped. I fully concede the existence of many admirable qualities in barbarian life, as well as the fact that civilisation brings certain inevitable losses to offset the gains; but must insist that on the whole the boons of civilisation add up to a vastly greater total than do the boons of barbarism. No system of life can be said to be normal or desirable if it leaves unused and undeveloped the very highest qualities which aeon-long evolution has brought to a species. With all the ills

of civilisation, it certainly represents a more effective and rewarding way of life for the Aryan race than does a career of ignorant wandering, plundering, fighting, and butchering. In the later 18th century, of course, there was an extensive school of romantic dreamers who idealised the "noble savage" and affected to decry the artificialities of settled life—people like Rousseau, Lord Monboddo, Chateaubriand, etc.—but it is easy to see the ill-formed and unscientific basis of their position. It almost puzzles me that Two-Gun is able to maintain seriously the position he claims to maintain—yet I suppose the west Texas environment counts for much. With his intense rooting in his native soil, he feels himself called upon to idealise all those tendencies in which the southwest differs from the rest of European civilisation. I never realised, until my correspondence with Longhorn, just how much of the primitive and sanguinary still lingers in Texan life and psychology. It was my idea that all that stuff vanished in the 1890's, and that the "Wild West" of today was a mere convention of cheap fictioneers. Now I see my mistake—a mistake which I think the average Easterner shares. Evidently in Texas mothers send their precious 3-year-olds to kindergarten with six-shooters on their hips, and with instructions to plug the teacher quickly if he draws a gun first! But for all his one-sided theories Bob is a great boy. I don't take his mercenary talk seriously—it appears to me merely a sardonic rhetorical reaction against certain types of the soulful artistic poseur whom he has met and disliked. There is nothing commercial in the way he spreads whole Iliads and Odysseys of the southwest over letters of 15 to 20 closely typed pages, and with a poetic fire and unconscious art which only a finely-developed intellect and imagination could command. Whether he likes it or not, he *is* a genuine creative artist—and of a depth and energy which will carry him far if he doesn't let his perverse external anti-intellectualism frustrate his genius. It is because I have such a high and admiring opinion of his capacities that I am trying to argue him out of his anti-civilised attitude. I have repeatedly urged him to utilise his fine ability and deep erudition in writing a history of Texas—as well as a vivid, coördinated account of the various frontier desperadoes. He could certainly produce something magnificent in this line if he would only buckle down to it. As to the reason he doesn't grind out cheap western stories for the pulp magazines—I've never asked him, but I fancy it is because he knows and loves the West too well to be able to work within the puerile, artificial convention of commercial "western stuff". For all his talk of purely monetary objects, he isn't the sort to sell his birthright for[3] a mess of pottage—and I can imagine how he must feel about the grotesque, absurd caricatures which pass as "western fiction" among easterners. To a chap who knows the west as the everyday life around him, the concoction of stock "westerns" must be the next thing to an impossibility. As well as a real New Englander to write popular tales about the stock Yankees of the midwestern imagination! By the way—I seem to detect a slow, steady improvement in Two-Gun's output. His last W T stories (I'm reading up the recent issues at last) are far ahead of his earlier average. As for Two-Gun's grisly and casual reference to the refined custom of testicle-crushing and pubic epilation—I must admit that I never heard of such a thing before, and have no idea as to where and by whom it is cultivated! My vague guess is that it must be some barbarity of the poor whites of the inner "deep South"—as practiced against transcenders of the moral code. Ku Klux Klan stuff. I know that nigger offenders have sometimes suffered the surgical removal of the membrum virile (often kept as a souvenir by exponents of summary justice!) prior to lynching for crimes in which that member was prominently involved. Which reminds me that your adverse opinion of the South may be justified so far as the upstart lower white element, especially in the *inner* regions (western Georgia, Alabama, Mississippi, etc.) away from the old tidewater civilisation, is concerned. This element really does seem to display a callousness, lawlessness, and residual savagery far removed from our usual concept of civilisation. At the same time, however, it is certainly erroneous to apply such a criticism to the South and its people as a whole. The old tidewater cultures of Virginia and South Carolina are to my mind among the finest flowerings of American civilisation. Crudeness and barbarism were as far eliminated as in any part of the world, and the treatment of nigger slaves averaged better than the treatment of the nominally free industrial and agricultural proletariat anywhere today—with the added point that the negro is undoubtedly an inferior organism whose best capacities are rather primitive. Even to this day relations between the white and black races in the *tidewater* South—Richmond, Charleston, Savannah, etc.—remain extremely friendly; each knowing its place and sticking to it. The crudeness and conflict which lead to lynching and kindred phenomena are very clearly products of the retarded culture of the *inner* South which was built up through pioneering a century and a half or two centuries after the settlement of Virginia. In this inner region the really good families were relatively few, and even they suffered a loss of cultivation through isolation from compact civilisation. When the Civil War removed their feudal influence, there sprang into power an upstart element of pugnacious poor whites who not only hated the negro through different circumstances of contact, but who actually had to adopt an attitude of militant dominance the preserve safety amidst the enormous and engulfing black population of the inner South. I honestly believe that lynching, repulsive though it is, is at times a stern necessity—since absence of a terrorising influence would make the blacks a constant menace. In very recent years, the Boers and British of South Africa are learning this woeful lesson on account of the movement of half-civilised blacks to regions close to the farms and settlements of the white colonists. However—it would be idle to deny that the principle of lynching is often grossly abused. Also—the chain-gang is a distinctly backward institution. But be sure to notice that all this applies only to such parts of the South as represent pioneer offshoots of the original civilisation of Virginia and Carolina. You don't hear of chain-gangs, or of niggers burned alive, in those coastal regions where a continuous culture has been handed down for 250 or 300 years. There are no more civilised cities in the world than Richmond, Charleston, and Savannah; and indeed, the special conditions of Charleston are such that it is perhaps the most mellowly and maturely civilised city in America. Just as an illustration—during the Civil War Charleston had such civilised restraint that (despite the fact that it was the very cradle and focus of secession sentiment) Union sympathisers were treated there with complete consideration and respect. I don't believe there was any northern city where Confederate sympathisers were equally free from the shadow of ostracism or even the threat of mob violence. As for this recent Scottsboro case[4]—there are certainly two sides to it. The fact that a herd of Jew communists from New York City have chosen to exploit it has no bearing whatever on the actual truth of the matter, and all one may ask is whether the evidence against the defendants is good or not. It would be ridiculous to expect niggers to be allowed on a jury in a region where they are so thick—for any such precedent would upset all the equilibrium which makes it possible for whites to live safely in Alabama. Of course, *all* jury trials are tragic jokes—for no chance bunch of untrained laymen is *ever* able to pass competently and unprejudicedly on highly controversial issues involving complex evidence—but if one has juries at all, they must be all-white. This particular case is a tough one, but there seems to be much evidence against the blacks. The bad character of the victims is not legally relevant except so far as their credibility as witnesses is concerned. One must ask what motivation these women could have in falsely accusing the blacks—and one must also take into account the obvious element of bribery by the defence (with alien bolshevik money behind it) in the changed story of one complainant. On the other hand, however, one must not let an instinctive dislike of the negro race—or an abhorrence of the communistic foreigners who are exploiting the case—sway one's intrinsic opinion as to whether or not the crime actually occurred. Scientific impersonalism must govern any rational decision. I (without any special study of the case) am inclined to think the niggers were really guilty, but in view of the limited evidence I think it would be a good idea if the death sentences were changed to life terms in prison—some distant prison far outside the area of mob attack. About the custom of duelling—I am strongly inclined to question the complete wisdom of its total abolition. Most certainly the duels over trivial matters which abounded in past times—especially in New Orleans—represented a barbaric waste of life; and yet there *are* grave affronts and injuries in life which can hardly be tastefully and honourably met except by sanguinary expiation. If there be no legitimate outlet, these matters will rankle and fester destructively—creating a very bad psychological state, and often giving rise to actual murders, or to other savage revenges of a calculated, scheming sort. Certainly, if any man of responsible standing attacked my honour as a gentleman—or visited any grave wrong on a sister, wife, or daughter of mine—I would not feel rightly adjusted to the world till I had either killed him or caused him to grovel in some especially ignominious way; in short, till I had publicly registered my superiority to the affront in some aesthetically adequate and socially recognised manner. Having no fondness for murder, I would feel greatly at a loss if no open and honourable mode of redress lay open to me. The serious duel over some really adequate issue is not in any way to be compared with the callous and irresponsible slashings of mobs and barbarians. It is a responsibly organised, clear-cut thing which visits no violence except on those who have consciously undertaken the risk. Of course, there are barbaric duels with unsuitable weapons—sabres, shotguns, bowie-knives, etc.—but one does not need to condone these. The weapons of gentlemen—rapiers, or pistols of decent calibre—are not such as to cause the messy body-outraging deaths in which barbarians and callous folk in general seem to revel. However—I dare say it will take more than my opinion to reestablish the custom. The last known duel in Rhode Island (fought by two New Yorkers) occurred in 1835. In 1838 the state legislature forbade duelling, and there is no record of an encounter subsequent to that date. The only duel I know of in my own family was fought by my great-grandfather William Allgood (a native of Northumberland, England) in 1829, in the country near Rochester, N.Y., over animosities bequeathed by the War of 1812. Slight bullet-wounds to both participants formed the only results.

I thought you'd enjoy Comte d'Erlette's "Evening in Spring". It is certainly a piece of genuine art, with a singular power of evoking its readers' early memories—however much those memories may differ from those which the author records. Little Augie certainly leads the gang in aesthetic progress to date. I'll send you his more objective tale "Five Alone" (three-starred by O'Brien) when the Peacock Sultan returns it. As for M. le Comte's opinion of "The Weir"[5]—surely all such opinions are purely matters of individual taste. Usually, though, the best poetry inclines toward the general and the universal (or what is capable of illustrating the general and the universal) rather than the narrowly personal. At that, I doubt very much whether the youthful John Daly failed to be pleased by "The Weir". If, as you mention, he is an habitually indifferent correspondent, it is more than likely that sheer negligence lies behind his lack of acknowledgment. [. . .]

With regards and blessings—
      Grandpa

Notes

1. *WT,* November 1932.
2. HPL's nickname for his colleague Henry S. Whitehead, based on a recurring character, Gerald Canevin, cited in many of his stories.

3. AHT reads "of."
4. In 1931, nine African American boys were accused of raping two white women in Scottsboro, Alabama. After several trials, the boys were found guilty, even though one of the women later recanted her testimony. Charges against four of the boys were dropped; the other five were sentenced to death or long terms of imprisonment.
5. Presumably a story or poem by Dwyer (nonextant).

[10]   [AHT]

The Antient Hill
[January 1934][1]

Dear Bernardus:—

[...]

Well—I've read Weigall's "Wanderings in Roman Britain" at last, and parts of it were a real eye-opener. He has done a tremendous lot of original research—both historical and archaeological—and has shed any amount of light on that melancholy period so fascinating to me . . . . . . the end of the Roman civilisation in the Imperial province of Britannia. To anyone who conventionally assumed (as I did—in my recent letter on the Arthur problem) that the Saxon conquest was virtually complete by 500 A.D., and that Arthur was a Cymric-speaking tribal chieftain, this new body of information (well-authenticated, and scarcely subject to dispute) is a knock-out punch—something necessitating a complete revaluation of previously acquired ideas. So many of my earlier conceptions—on which my recent letter to you was based—are shewn to be outmoded, that I was on the point of writing you to cancel much that I said before. For one thing, get this: *Arthur was a Britanno-Roman who spoke Latin, wore the Roman helmet and armour, and fought the Saxons in order to save Britain for the Roman Empire, whose authority was never repudiated despite the withdrawal of the legions and the collapse of the Western Emperor in 476.* Our idea of Arthur as a shaggy Welsh tribal chief was just as cockeyed as the conventional idea of him as a silken-tabarded Norman gallant. He was a Celtic-Roman whose name was Artorius, and whose idea of a fatherland was not that of a Brythonic-speaking wilderness of camps and thatched villages, but that of an orderly Roman countryside of villas and estates, and of settled towns and great cities with baths, amphitheatres, crowded streets, sewer-systems, central heating, works of art, and a Latin-speaking population. It was for a Roman world that Arthur fought—his role being like that of Syagrius, last of the Roman governors in Gaul, of whom I wrote some weeks ago.

As a preliminary, Weigall makes two points clear. First—that in spite of all our notions to the contrary, *Britain was thoroughly Roman.* The only Celtic-speaking tribes were in northern Scotland and western Wales. The bulk of the two provinces of Britannia Prima and Britannia Secunda were as Latin as Gaul or Spain—or Italy itself. All the natives spoke Latin and bore Roman names, and the great bulk of the Roman legionaries never left the island but settled down and married British wives. Thus the people under Arthur were a solidly Roman people—with names like Flavius Pudens, Valerius Amandus, L. Julius Juvenis, Aurelius Cocceius, Tib. Claudius Paullinus, etc.—whose blood was about half Celtic (including the Welsh Mediterranean strain) and half that of the Roman legionaries. Of course this "Roman" blood was only fragmentarily of the ancient hawk-nosed Italic strain, since the legions were recruited from all over the Empire. There were cohorts from Spain, Greece, Thrace, Illyricum, North Africa, Syria, and even *Mesopotamia*—though the numerical majority were from Gaul and Germany. This gave the people a marked blood mixture—with even Semitic elements—although the preponderance of Gallic and German troops preserved a general Nordic ascendancy. The Britanno-Roman of Arthur's time was distinctly Celtic-Teutonic in blood, though with strong alien elements. The Second Augustan Legion at our good old Caerleon was Germanic—from the Romanised Rhine region.

The second point made by Weigall is what gives Point I a double significance in modern times—namely, that the Britanno-Romans were *not* extirpated by the Saxons, and that their blood is as plentifully represented in modern British veins as is that of the Saxons and Normans. No wholesale massacres, and very few limited ones (as of the Roman garrison at Pevensey on the South Coast) occurred, and the migration to Brittany was of wild Welsh tribes rather than of the Britanno-Roman population. The provincials were not killed but enslaved or bound to the soil, and in two or three generations their fusion with the Saxons was complete. Long before the Norman conquest they had become thoroughly amalgamated and indistinguishable, since their dominant race-stock was so similar. Their *language and culture* were extirpated in a generation, but their *blood* has survived to the present as one of the three main streams in the English people. In other words, there is no question but that something like a third of my own personal blood ancestors bore Roman names, wore togas, spoke Latin, fought in the 2nd, 9th, 6th, and other Legions of the Imperial Roman Army, worshipped Apollo, Pan, Mithra, and Silvanus Cocidius at altars with Latin inscriptions, lived in Roman villas or towns with baths, temples, and amphitheatres of classic design, and were proud to bear the designation "Civis Romanus".[2] Of course, the visible and cultural connexion was effaced, so that our present heritage of Roman culture comes wholly through Gaul from the Normans. But the plain fact remains, that the forgotten blood link is there. Lineal ancestors of mine have had names like P. Sanfeius, T. Aurelius, M. Valerius, L. Claudius, and so on .... and amidst the legionary mixture there must have been at least a *thin* strain of the *real* old Roman blood—the Oscan-Umbrian-Sabine-Samnite-Latian-Etruscan blend from Central Italy which produced the familiar Roman face with its broad brow and hawk nose. Also—less pleasing thought—there must be traces of Carthaginian, Syrian, Slav, Egyptian, Persian, Arab, and whatever other Oriental and Sarmatian stocks formed part of the army in Britain. And Greek, of course, though one doesn't object to that. Tablets indicating the presence of all these races at the British army posts have been discovered—although, as previously stated, the Gallic and Germanic troops, plus native Cymric ones, were in the vast majority. The real blood heritage of the Britanno-Romans is Celtic-Teutonic. One effect of Weigall's researches and expositions is to make Roman Britain seem vastly less remote to us than formerly. Heretofore we have looked on it almost as on pre-colonial America, as a land of *other* people which *our* ancestors conquered. Now we see that this picture is all wrong. It represents only *half* of us; and for the other half Roman Britain is *our own* ancestral land which the invading enemy conquered. It is no longer possible—despite the fact that the Saxon's language and institutions triumphed—to identify oneself with the Saxons and regard the Britanno-Romans as *'other'* people'. These neo-Romans are as much "us" to an Englishman as the Saxons—at least, in a biological sense. We are *both* conquered and the conquerors—hybrids, though not visibly or ethnologically so because the two stocks were so much alike in dominant composition. The Celts (except the Welsh Mediterranean element) were very close to the Teutons to start with, and the legions brought in loads of Teutonic blood ahead of the Saxons.

Well—now to get at the real facts concerning the fall of Roman Britain. The province, as a compact part of the Empire, may be said to date from the reign of Claudius—A.D. 43, when Plautius brought in the 2nd, 9th, 14th, and 20th Legions, subdued Caratacus (King of the powerful Cotuvellani), and left permanent colonies both at various camp sites and in some of the Celtic towns. Even before that date, however, there had been a great deal of Romanisation in Britain, for ever since Caesar's expeditions of B.C. 55 and 54 Roman merchants had been gradually penetrating the coast towns. At places like Lindum (Lincoln) even the native Britons had begun to speak Latin and adopt Roman names and ways. Many prominent Britons, moreover, had visited Rome. And here again Weigall explodes a common conventional myth. *The pre-Roman Celts were not savages or even real barbarians.* They used bronze and iron, and made weapons, costumes, razors, jewellery, etc. with the most exquisite craftsmanship. They dressed with great taste and elegance, lived in towns, read and wrote in the Greek alphabet, mined gold, iron, tin, and lead, and traded with all the other nations of antiquity—Carthage, Tyre, Egypt, Greece, Etruria, and later Rome. They appreciated art, and imported Greek and Etruscan vases. Egyptian beads of the 18th Dynasty (the age of Akhneton and Tutankhamen) have been dug up at Stonehenge. Their connexion with Gaul on the continent was very close—some tribes being distributed partly on the island and partly in Gaul. All this explains why Britain was so quickly Romanised. The people were virtually civilised to begin with—fully ready for the orderly and enlightened way of life which the legions brought. The last great revolt was that of the Iceni under Boadicea in A.D. 61, which C. Suetonius Paullinus (fresh from his suppression of the Druids in Anglesey) put down after the 9th Legion was almost wiped out. In this revolt many towns such as Camulodunum (Colchester), Verulamium (St. Albans), and Londinium (London) were burnt down, and afterward each of these was rebuilt from the ground up by the legions in a thoroughly Roman manner. Thus the province quickly assumed a perfectly Italian aspect—the cities and houses retaining no trace of pre-Roman architecture. Also, many of the Roman camps—established where no Celtic villages had ever been—grew into thoroughly Roman towns. Take our old friend "Caermaen"—Caerleon—Isca Silurum.[3] This was established as a camp in A.D. 78 by C. Julius Frontinus (a real Roman from Italy) and the Second Augustan Legion (of Romanised Rhineland Germans). Before long a town grew up around the camp walls, and the Romanised Silures of the region made a market centre of it. Baths, temples, and an amphitheatre were built—the latter surviving in almost perfect condition after over a thousand years of complete burial beneath drifted earth and grassy turf. It has been excavated only within the last decade. The people of Caerleon—Welsh and German in blood—were cultural Romans in every sense, and we see names like Julius Julianus and Caius Valerius Victor on the local funerary steles. And this Roman life was no brief moment's incident, either. *It lasted over 500 years*—longer than America has now been discovered. When it fell, it could look back on a continuous existence longer than the span separating Richard III and the Wars of the Roses from ourselves. Roman Britain lasted longer than the time between the death of Chaucer and this moment.

And now—after all this rambling—for the sad story itself. *Forget all that I told you in my earlier letter*—that was obsolete dope, and I'm ashamed to have hung on to it so long. Here are the facts:

The Saxon menace began as early as A.D. 300. In 364 and for the next 5 years there was a period of great peril precipitated by attacks by Scots on the northern frontier and by Irish tribes on the Welsh coast. The Saxons took advantage of these attacks to raid the eastern and Southern coasts with redoubled vigour, and the whole existence of the province was imperilled until the Emperor Valentinianus sent an army under the extremely able Spanish general Theodosius—father of the emperor of that name. In 369, with a reorganised fleet, Theodosius dispersed all the raiders and gave the Province a new lease of life. Meanwhile the east and south coasts—open to Saxon pirate raids—were recognised as the chief danger spot of the Province, and were organised into a special naval and military district called the Litus Saxonicum, or Saxon Shore. This district, whose governor was known as Comes Litoris Saxonici, was defended by a vast chain of naval fortresses, many of whose great masonry walls survive to this day. These fortresses were Branodunum (Brancester), Gariannonum (Burgh Castle near Yarmouth), Walton Castle near Felixstowe, Othona (Bradwell), Ythanceaster in Essex, Ragulbium (Reculver), Rutupiae (Richborough—the chief naval base), Dubrae (Dover), Portus Lemanis (Lympne), Anderida (Pevensey), and Portus Adurni (Porchester).

The real crumbling began about 383 A.D., when the principal commander in Britain—the Spaniard Magnus Clemens Maximus—withdrew a large body of troops to bolster up his vain claims to the Imperial throne. Scots, Irish, Picts, and Saxons took advantage of the weakening to raise general hell, and only the famous general Stilicho (a Vandal by birth—great defender of Rome against the Visigoths) was able to restore order. In 401 Stilicho withdrew the 6th and 20th Legions to the Continent to fight the Visigoths, while the Britanno-Roman general Cunedda repelled the western attacks of the Irish raider called Niall of the Nine Hostages. Another dispute about the Imperial throne soon afterward took more troops out of Britain, and in 410 the Emperor Honorius issued his famous message saying that no more Imperial troops could be supplied to the Province. Note that this was not a "withdrawal of the legions" as we used to be taught. Honorius simply said he could send no more. The Empire *did not give up the Province*, nor did the Britanno-Romans consider themselves as severed from the Empire. It was simply that the Empire expected the Province to use its own "auxiliary troops"—militia or national guard—for its own defence. In 411 some outside troops were sent back, though these were withdrawn again in 423. From this time onward, Saxon raids were virtually continuous. But a few Imperial troops were still in Britain despite all the edicts and withdrawals. It was not till the decade 430–440 that the Province was *entirely* stripped of outside men and left altogether to the local militia. In 442 the first Saxon hold of permanent nature on the east and south coasts was obtained, but even then the bulk of the Province was peaceful, uninvaded, and wholly Roman. There was no thought of any severance from the Empire. Around 450 A.D. the provincial government had begun to split up; the east and south being ruled by Aurelius Ambrosius (a Roman from Rome), and the west by the Welshman Vortigern. We all know how Vortigern (after a feud with Aurelius in which the latter was killed) foolishly enlisted the services of the Saxon brothers Hengist and Horsa against wild Celtic raiders, and how the Saxons used this pretext to swarm in themselves. It was then that the great crumbling began; so that by 475 all the fortresses of the Saxon Shore had fallen into Teutonic hands, whilst Wessex and the coast as far north as Yorkshire were largely occupied by the invaders. *But Roman Britain kept right on functioning in the same old way*—only a small fraction of the whole being invaded. When Vortigern died the chief power fell to Ambrosius Aurelianus, son of his old rival Aurelius; and when Aurelianus died in 490 the succession fell upon *the Roman-British general Artorius, known to posterity and to legend as "King Arthur".* Artorius defeated the Saxons twelve times, his final victory in 500, at Mons Badonis, being so overwhelming that Roman Britain was saved for three quarters of a century more. Arthur is not overrated. What he did, considering his disorganised forces and the savage enemy he fought, was prodigious and heroic in every sense. But it must not be forgotten that he was a Latin-speaking Roman who fought to save Britain for the Roman world. As a Celt by blood, he is justly a Celtic national hero—but the Roman background is important to remember. He represents, in our national history, *the last stand of the orderly ancient world against the barbarism and disorder of the dark Middle Ages*. He was a man who lived in furnace-heated houses with running water, bathed twice a day, behaved civilisedly at dinner, and read and wrote Latin; fighting against men who lived in rough huts, dressed in dirty furs and wool, gnawed half-raw meat from bones, and had no idea of reading or writing save as a despicable accomplishment of special underlings. And what he did was so lasting, that many infants born on the day of his culminating triumph lived to be old men and died natural deaths in a Britannia still wholly Roman. After Artorius another descendant of the Aurelian line—Aurelianus Caninus—was the leader of the Britanno-Romans. Still later this man's son—Aurelius Candidanus—appears as *the final defender of Roman Britain*. The Germans were now coming over in tremendous numbers—especially the Angli, whose nation was migrating in a body and preparing to give the region and the future composite race its name. The frontier of Roman Britain slowly shrank inward from the eastern and southern coast, till finally—in 582—the invaders were faced by the Britanno-Romans in a supremely desperate last stand at Disham—10 miles east of Bristol and the same distance north of Bath. The earthworks of the Roman camp are still visible. The battle was a terrible disaster—Aurelius Candidanus and two other Roman generals being killed, and the Saxons sweeping onward unchecked. The last Roman cities—Aquae Sulis (Bath), Corinium (Cirencester), and Glevum (Gloucester)—fell at once, and the enemy ravaged and encamped all over the fallen province. The Romans were largely enslaved, and their towns left to fall to ruin while the Saxons built new villages nearby in their own crude manner—sometimes ripping stones from Roman masonry to construct barbarous shelters. Latin died out as the conquerors imposed their own folkways, and as the conquered population rose from serfdom or became absorbed in later years it forgot that it had any origin save Saxon.

Roman Britain lasted 539 years—as great a space as that betwixt the sack of primitive Rome by the Gauls (390 B.C.) and the full flowering of the Age of the Antonines (circa 150 A.D.) .... or, as before mentioned, as great as that betwixt Chaucer's period and our own. It is only 1352 years at this moment since Britain last was Roman. The age of the Magna Charta is almost as close to the Roman period as it is to ours. Weigall points out that only 45 generations separate us from the Britanno-Romans—so that without doubt more than one great-grandfather of mine had such a name as Lucius Valerius Celsus or Publius Aufidius Proculinus, spoke Latin, and wore a toga on ceremonial occasions. And at least one of those multiply great-grandparents *may* have been a Cornelius, Claudius, Ostorius, Suetonius, Pomponius, Plautius, or Didius from the old Roman *race* itself. The reliques of Roman days, as Weigall enumerates them, are decidedly more numerous than I had ever suspected. Mosaic pavements of town houses and villas are constantly being dug up all over England, and the amount of Roman masonry still standing (usually mistaken for mediaeval material) is impressive.Ædepol! but what wouldn't I give for about six months of leisurely rambling around the old country from Dubrae to Pons Aelii, Bremetennacum to Deva, Uriconium to ISCA. SILURUM, and Isca Dumnoviorum to Lindum Coloniae! S. P. Q. R. ROMA! I don't wonder at the way Machen is fascinated by this period. If I ever write again, I vow to God I'll use it myself—despite my lack of any first-hand glimpse of the territory in question.

And this reminds me—have you heard of the *new Machen book?* It is called "The Green Round", and Comte d'Erlette assured me that it is in Machen's typical fantastic vein. This despite the author's resolution of some years ago to write no more weird material. M. le Comte adds that the book is undoubtedly *new*—no reprint stuff. I must see it somehow. Klarkash-Ton is ordering it, and if he reports favourably I shall try to do likewise myself. It is $1.50, obtainable at the Argus Bookshop of Chicago. Oh, yes—and let me add—if you wish to borrow the Weigall book, pray consider it at your disposal. I don't know how it would appeal to another, for of course a good part is devoted to a description of specific reliques at various sites; but I certainly found it fascinating. And it does give a tremendously significant sidelight on "King Arthur". My aunt has nearly finished "Anthony Adverse"[4] and enjoys it tremendously. I hope to get at it before long despite a wretchedly congested programme. Trust we're not holding it from other prospective borrowers! [. . .]

Grandpa L. Caelius Rufus

Notes

1. AHT misdates as November 1933.
2. "Roman citizen."
3. Caermaen is the name that, for reasons unknown, Machen applied to the Welsh town of Caerleon-on-Usk, founded in Roman times as Isca Silurum.
4. A bestselling historical novel by Hervey Allen.

[11] [AHT]

YMCA
Charleston, S.C.,
April 29, 1934

Hail, O BnādvaēAā!
[. . .]
A $1.75 per week eating programme is easy if you know how to manage it. It means merely keeping down to a quarter a day, & I can do that without

half trying. When restaurants are high, I fall back on canned & package goods—knife, fork, spoon, & can opener being with me. A 5¢ package of ginger wafers is a more than sufficient breakfast, while a 10¢ can of spaghetti or beans will do for dinner—with the residue of the cookies for dessert. That's only 15¢—leaving a margin for luxury on other days. Coffee can be cut out—it isn't much for *nourishment* anyhow—or at 5¢ a cup it isn't a great item at worst. In Charleston the cheap lunch rooms are so incredibly reasonable that I don't have to resort to "home cooking". I follow either one of two plans. Sometimes I get a dime's worth of ice-cream for breakfast, & a 10¢ bowl of Mexican chili con carne (with lots of crackers) & coffee for dinner. Total for the day, 25¢. Or else I cut out breakfast altogether & stuff up at night on the incredible *25¢ bargain dinner* provided at the Mexican Chili Place in Marion Sq. Boy, what a gorge for a quarter! It couldn't be approached in the north—Jake or no Jake![1] Not only is it a full feast, but a choice of three meats is offered. Last night I had the following Lucullan trough-fest . . . . & all for one solitary quarter: Pork sausage (generous allotment), fried potato, huge mountain of hominy, load of beets, two corn biscuits & butter, coffee, & bread pudding. Can you beat it? I fear it will set back my reducing—although I've knocked off 4 lbs. since last Sunday, when I bade farewell to the dangerous luxury of the Long board. (By the way, my Y room is only $3.75 per week.)
[. . .]
   Yrs. for the Elder Sign—
    Grandpa E'ch-Pi-El.

Notes

1. Jake's was a diner in a depressed section of Providence that provided ample portions for a low price.

[12] [AHT]

                 The Antient Hill
                 May 29, 1936

Dear Bernardus:—
   [. . .]
  Your visit to the seeress must have been picturesque. Those people are shrewd guessers, and some of them are so clever that it seems a pity their energies are wasted on charlatanry. They are practical psychologists in their own informal way. As for malfunctioning nerves—a real doctor could tell you more than any chiropractor about such things. Actually, I doubt whether the basis is physical. What we *call* a "case of nerves" is usually a purely psychological matter—a matter of maladjusted emotions or attention rather than any organic defect in the nervous tissue. Thus in my own case in youth—when a neurotic (i.e., psychologically maladjusted) temperament gave me all the

symptoms of various organic disturbances which I didn't really have. It wasn't that the nervous tissue itself was diseased (except, perhaps, by being hypersensitive to pain-stimuli), but that the messages sent through it were not well coördinated. You surely don't need to worry, since by all accounts your pulling around finely. One can't expect to revolutionise an entire temperament in a day—hell! it took about 20 years to pull me out of the weak, excitable, easily-fatigued, violent-tempered state which characterised my middle teens, & produce the plodding, easy-going, mild-mannered old gentleman of the last decade! The great secret of victory over emotions—whether exaggerated & ill-proportioned normal emotions or actually abnormal emotions—is a *transference of the basis of life to the plane of logic & analysis*, & a consequent ability to view all emotion objectively as something relatively trivial & irrelevant. Thus my early rages faded into nothingness when I became impressed by the principle of cosmic determinism—the utter automatism of all human events, & the meaningless, almost impersonal nature (organic reflexes determined by accidents of heredity & environment) of those hostile acts of others which had formerly provoked me to sputtering, fighting extremes of anger. And so with yourself. The more clearly and habitually you recognise your unwelcome emotions as mere accidental, meaningless phenomena, the less hold over you they will have. Psychologists are right in predicting a successful reorientation—and you have surely made enough progress already to remove all doubt of ultimate triumph. It's simply a question of time, and of keeping at it . . . . and of keeping so well occupied with objective interests that subjective emotional life will come to hold a less and less important place in your consciousness.

[. . .]

        Benedictions—Grandpa

Samuel Loveman

Letters to Samuel Loveman

[1]   [ALS]

                                                  The Old Dump 11/17 [1922]

Cherish'd St. Sam:—
            Thunderclap? I'll say it was! The MS. arrived safely, & I've been working madly at the job ever since. Editing the damn book is no joke, I'll say! I've bunched all the unfinished revision & sent it to Morton, & have myself collected all the revised pieces for the final copy. Some job? I'll whistle it to aethereal vortices!! I had to paw over all my old MSS., drag out all my forgotten amachoor papers, hunt up all my moth-eaten clippings, copy everything that wasn't in form for sending Morton—Oh, boy, but life is one happy song! Bah. But at last I've done it—collected every blessed thing Hoag ever wrote, revised & unrevised, & put the whole aggregation—67 pieces—in Morton's hands in classified form. The book will have nine sections—"Songs of Home", "Songs of Childhood", "Songs of Nature"—&c. &c. I'll write a critical & biographical preface, & have already provided an appendix of tributes to the venerable bard. The entire book will bear the modest but comprehensive title: "Collected Poems of Jonathan E. Hoag."[1]

Your new revision comes to 120 lines, which at the established rate earns you *$5.00*. I have told Hoag to send you a cheque—notify me if he is tardy, & I'll rectify things.

And now let me ask whether or not I sent you Hoag's photograph for the frontispiece of the book. DAMN MY AGED MEMORY! I *thought* I had—but from the absence of its mention in your note I now fear I *didn't*![2] And if I didn't, gawd alone knows what I did do with it . . . . I can't find it around this bally joint, though I've turned everything inside out! Coises! If, by any streak of rare good fortune, you have it after all; you might shoot it to Morton . . . . If I should find it anywhere hereabouts, I'll drop you a card, so that you won't feel any worry at your end. . . . . . I can't say how damn sorry I am to bother you about these trivialities! I mean well, even if my commercial deals are apt to get clumsy!

I can sympathise in full with your diurnal labours—man, yuh'd otta see the jobs amidst which I am ingulph'd! Bush—a perennial nuisance & more than usually insistent. Houtain—clamouring like hell for his new four-part story which I haven't written yet![3] He has paid up his past debts & advanced ten sestertii[4] on the yarn to come—shewing how damn bad he must want it. He's after Clark Ashton Smith to furnish 8 horrible illustrations—two for each instalment.

S H G[5] was in town Sunday, Wednesday, & Thursday, & acted as hostess to my aunts & myself—or both—at dinner at the Biltmore* several times. She is looking forward to her stay in Cleveland as the chief event—if not the very raison d'etre—of her western tour; & I trust you will find it equally enjoyable.

In spare moments—i.e., moments when I'm too damn tired to do anything else—I've been going over my bookshelves; placing obsolete material on the retired list upstairs, & gradually assimilating my N.Y. purchases on the main shelves. The immediate corner where I sit has taken on quite a new atmosphere & colouring—shelves groaning with Balzac, de Maupassant, the Lock & Key Library, &c. &c. I'm deucedly glad to have Bierce represented, if only by one book![6]

I trust the Saltus venture is progressing well,[7] & that the second Bierce edition will sell out as rapidly as the first.[8] Don't fail to send little Belknap both books—he idolises you & cherishes every scrap you write. And of course put Grandpa Theobald down for the Saltus—I'll have it if it costs a fortune! I must write Kirk—tell him I'm going to patronise him when he gets the new Clarkashton book, "Ebony & Crystal" in stock![9] Likewise give him my best regards. Spoof along Lawrence, be kind to old Sommer, slap Hatfield & Sloane on the wrist, forget Crane, & remember me to all the fauns in Wade & Rockefeller Parks![10]

Atta boy!

Θεοβαλδος

Notes

1. *The Poetical Works of Jonathan E. Hoag*, edited by HPL and funded by Allen C. Balch, a wealthy entrepreneur and apparent friend of Hoag. HPL's own contributions to the book are listed in the bibliography.
2. Hoag's photo is not in the book (see SL 2 below). See *Lovecraft Annual* No. 10 (2016): 121, for a portrait of Hoag.
3. "The Lurking Fear" for Houtain's magazine *Home Brew*. The story was completed no later than 2 December 1922.
4. HPL was to have been paid $5 per installment for both "Herbert West—Reanimator" (6 parts) and "The Lurking Fear" (4 parts).
5. Sonia Haft Greene. Her visit to Providence evidently occurred on 11, 15, and 16 November.
6. HPL refers to Julian Hawthorne, ed., *The Lock and Key Library: Classic Mystery and Detective Stories* and Ambrose Bierce, *Can Such Things Be?* His holdings of Balzac are unknown.
7. See MWM 19n7.
8. I.e., *Twenty-one Letters of Ambrose Bierce*. So far as is known, there was no second edition in HPL's day.
9. By Clark Ashton Smith.

---

*whose architectural & decorative scheme is 18th CENTURY!

10. The artist William (Bill) Sommer (1867–1949), the composer Gordon Hatfield (1896–1971), and Wesley Wellington Sloane (1857–?) were friends of SL and the poet Hart Crane (1899–1932) in Cleveland. HPL made derogatory comments about Hatfield's and Sloane's dress and effeminate manners, but either ignored or was not aware of SL's and Crane's sexual orientation, presumably because they were not as overtly demonstrative. For Carroll Lawrence, a young man who strove to write weird tales, see SL 2n27.

[2]   [ALS]

Old 598

March 24[, 1923]

Ave, Samuele!

Good work—that recovery stuff! May aegritude[1] long shun your honour'd door, & health triumphant reign for evermore! But what a siege we've been having in this humble dump! I think I told you how completely my nerves gave out early this month—but that was only the beginning. Thursday, March 8, seemed quite propitious—we made an 18th century day of it, seeing Mr. Sheridan's new comedy, "The School for Scandal", eating in a restaurant in a building standing during George III's reign, & winding up by seeing the cinema of "Java Head"—which I wanted my aunt to see because it shew'd Old Salem so well.[2] So far, so good. But the next day my aunt came down with grippe—to whose devastating rigours you can so well testify!—and yesterday was the first day she could be up & about. Naturally, I was obliged to sink my haughty dignity in the vicissitudes of domestick labour—ugh!—& perform the dual functions of nurse & housekeeper; aided only by the matutinal visitations of my younger & non-resident aunt.[3] The latter, however, stayed here Saturday & Sunday—the 10–11th—so that I took in the Hub banquet,[4] stayed over night at Cole's, & spent the next day exchanging "wise-cracks" & barroom repartee with my tough little friend Al Sandusky,[5] who came over to horn in on the highbrow bunch. But the whole strain of the situation got on my nerves, so that I've been good for nothing for two weeks. My correspondence—migawd! I now owe the trivial number of **34** letters . . . . but nay, with yesterday's mail coming in the number hath went up to *37!* Pegāna only knows when I'll answer 'em— probably I shall get the reputation of being a damn haughty & unresponsive cuss. Hell, but I shall be glad to get this damned presidency off me shoulders[6]—that's what brings the most voluminous & least interesting part of the postal mountain range whose inaccessible pinnacles tower skyward before me. The only thing I could do during my aunt's illness was to *read*, & I went through two endless Gothick novels (apparently of the 1820–1830 period) which Alfredus had lent me—"Faust & the Demon" & "Wagner the Wehr-Wolf", both by one George W. M. Reynolds. They are quite childish in plot & incident—unworthy children even of so grotesque a sire as "The Castle of Otranto"—yet withal they have a certain quaint charm. The bombast of the language is priceless . . . . one half suspects a burlesque intent sometimes, tho' 'tis not so. And by the way—who in Pete's name is this bimbo Reynolds? Nobody I knew ever heard of him, yet he seems to have slung quite a mean pen a hundred or so years ago.[7] Slip me a line, kid, ef ya got a line on 'im.

G—— d—— x!?%$£# hades! Pardon the lapse, but the conditions under which I am writing are conducive to unworthy eloquence. My Welsbach gas light gave out an hour ago, & I'm trying to use a beastly oil lamp whose radius of refulgence is damned microcosmic. Yah! And it won't be much better when the damned sun comes up, (for these are the small hours) since it's gonna be a nasty rainy day. I like "The spring of the year", but dunno about "the silver rain"![8]

De re Clevelandica—I wish to hell I could be more certain about the cash question! It looks like a damn gloomy season, for nerves & household illness have reduced my Bushic capacity to a minimum, & I gotta helluva lotta expenses ahead. Imprimis—I simply can't appear in publick till I get a new summer suit. You saw what my present one was in August,[9] & can imagine what the remainder of the season—with hiking & palisade-climbing—did to it. Shantih! And nothing respectable comes for less than XXX shiners nowadays . . . . . . nor is a suit even of that price anything to brag about. Secondly—there is the *Conservative*,[10] without which my grand farewell to the amateur world becomes a flivver. I simply gotta pull off a big issue, for I've boasted so long about the MSS. on hand that I gotta make good. The issue, as it now stands in MS., is really a knockout—it ought to break all qualitative records save that of the *Saturnian*[11]—& it owes most of its future celebrity to your "Satan".[12] So as I say, when I think of finance, my naturally long face tends to acquire an exaggeration of its original proportions! But still—if I can get me noives together enough to punish a record pile of Bush junk, there's no telling what I can do by July . . . provided my conservative aunt doesn't make too big a kick against my barbaric extravagance. Well—it's up to the gawds!

If I make it, though, it'll be a purely Lovemanic affair; for I don't share the fears of yourself & Martin[13] about the convention. Next year is a safe bet—Mrs. Adams[14] will be elected president almost if not quite unanimously, for all the clubs*—even Houtain's—are behind her. And as to *presiding*[15]— gawd help me! I don't know enough of parliamentary law to conduct a boys' club meeting, & am sure I haven't the time to read up for the occasion. All I knew of it has been forgotten these XX y'ars—for I hate technicalities & red tape. Glad your club is coming along—& that "Hypnos"[16] didn't disgust 'em permanently with amateurdom.

Alfredus says that you & he are made up—good stuff! Two such leaders can't afford to be divided. One has to be patient with the kid, & enter into his varying moods sympathetically. He doesn't mean half he says, for his psycholo-

---

*assuming that Cleveland and Akron have no objections

gy is of that complex & curious sort which comes from a philosophical consciousness of the futility of life & meaninglessness of human emotion, plus those natural gland-functionings which in a less objective & analytical personality would create strong emotions. His situation is really a very painful one. With a mind too restless & inclusive to let him settle down to a fixation of his impulses on any one art, his impulses are yet too strong to allow him to become a placid, kindly, & tolerant philosopher. He is neither bird nor beast, as it were; but a spirit uneasily fluttering betwixt two domains. Critical scholarship, I believe, is his natural field; for it furnishes food for both sets of his tendencies better than anything else. He will appreciate the arts, but will not create. And in view of the really titanic magnitude of his steel-cold intellect, I believe we are justified in expecting magnificent things of him. There is no limit to what he can achieve in philosophy & criticism. He will, I believe, become a definitely great man; but he will never be *liked* except by a discriminating few who have carefully studied his warring tendencies & have sympathetically resolved to judge him not by what he says but by what he means to say. I believe that, in a rather humble way, I understand the kid—for I have watched him with a grandpaternal eye since before his sixteenth birthday. His mind is of the same *type* as mine: objective, analytical, cynical, & ironic; but it is so much more vigorous & finely organised, that few could trace the resemblance. He is what a son of mine might have been—a son inheriting my general tendencies, but with immeasurably greater mental power & nervous energy. I understand his savage attitude toward the world—for I share his contempt for humanity. With me, that contempt becomes a sort of ironic pity because I realise how the poor devils suffer & have not enough emotional energy of my own to be irritated by the stupidities, pomposities, & affectations of the race. But Galpin has the energy—despite the fact that his perspective prevents its localisation into definite emotions. Thus he can never escape a certain mood of defiant scorn when he beholds the spectacle of mankind with its jumble of self-devised values, aspirations, beliefs, prejudices, standards, & idols; not one of which has any genuine significance whatever. He knows—just as I know—with the certainty of scientific conviction, that it does not matter a whit what becomes of mankind, what mankind does, or whether mankind exist or be blotted from the planet. He knows that all the emotions, illusions, ideals, standards, & convictions of humanity are so much meaningless rubbish; solely the result of cosmic chance & depending wholly on blind physiological processes. But whilst I am content to know this, & to see the poor self-important creatures called men strut about with their illusions in quest of unattainable phantoms—content because I am so detached & emotionless—Galpin becomes disgusted & defiant at such an intelligence-affronting farce; & bursts out occasionally in rebellion against it, since it seems an insult to him as a human being. The fact that other men have such absurd things as ideals in this futile cosmos, seems to him an implication that he might have them also—& that he cannot bear. With me it is different—it never occurs to me to classify myself as a human being; I am simply a bland external eye which sees, & is either amused or bored, according to the particular passing phase of the terrestrial puppet-show. I am so much more of an analyst than an emotionalist, that the futility of life is to me the central fact of existence. Comprehending the valuelessness of everything, I have not that fund of sensation & potential emotion which makes Galpin attach factitious & evanescent values to various things—first this, then that. That is, whilst he is led by impulse into various temporary *ambitions & aspirations,* (which his intellect of course knows to be purely subjective & illusory, & which are therefore always taken *cum grano salis* & soon abandoned) I am absolutely without ambition or aspiration except to be comfortable & amused. My perception of cosmic futility is so unalloyed with blind emotion, that I frankly admit that my object in life is merely to keep fed, warm, & amused till death comes to end the boredom. I admit brutally that death is better than life, and would commit suicide tomorrow with **genuine** cheerfulness & an **unforced** jest on my lips if I had any perfectly easy, painless, & certain means at my disposal. The only reason I haven't long ago, is that I am too lazy to look up a good way, & have never had sufficient discomfort to make life really unbearable. I am, in fact, fairly happy in my sluggish way despite occasional fits of boredom which I call "melancholy" for dramatic effect. I shan't shuffle off till my cash gives out—or till I have to work hard for it. The only two things which could ruin life for me are hard work & the necessity of living in an unaesthetic neighbourhood. I must have leisure & an harmonious environment. Now with this starkly realistic conception of life as a sort of boredom to be dragged through, you can see why human effort does not disgust me as it does Alfredus. He rebels that man should attach importance to meaningless things—but I hold that, since all things are equally meaningless, it is the logical & proper thing for each man to follow whatever activity he finds necessary for the dispelling of the world-ennui. I don't despise the golf-player—he is doing what he needs to do in order to forget boredom till he can die. I appreciate the artist, for his intense devotion to beauty is the natural means of gratifying a craving natural to all highly organised mankind—you will recall how forcibly I was struck by the universality of this craving when we explored the Metropolitan Museum & beheld the equally sincere artistic strivings of the most widely separated civilisations. Whereas some philosophers affect to despise art, because they think it inferior to their mocking phantom "truth"; I respect it highly, since I view it simply as the necessary escape of the highly organised mind from boredom. It is to some minds what golf is to others, or candy to still others. It is, indeed, to the artist, what truth is to the philosopher. Both mean equally much—or equally little. Taking nothing seriously, I dabble in pseudo-artistic perception & expression only as much as I am naturally impelled by whatever impulse for it I have. If I can get amusement from real art, I gladly take it; but if I don't, I never bother to cultivate a taste. Pleasure is only a balance betwixt desire & fulfilment—it never hurts us not to have what we don't want. I openly admit that the lot of the house cat, with his simple needs, is much happier than that of the human being. I wish I were a house cat, or a monkey in some tropical jungle, or something of the sort. It is mildly interesting to wish things when one doesn't care much one way or the other. I do not agree with the hedonist that keen or active pleasure is worth the trouble of securing. The αταραξια or ατιμια of Epicurus is good enough for me.¹⁷

But Galpin is a horse of another colour. He has fire & energy, & the loss of the common illusions gives him more pain than he realises. It is of persons like him that Anatole France is thinking when he says that illusions are necessary to the world—that we should perish without them. I had the same idea when writing my "Aletheia Phrikodes" in 1916—that blank verse thing which Cook published in his July 1918 *Vagrant*.¹⁸ I must get him to send you a copy if he didn't at the time—& if he has an extra one left. So all in all, as to Galpin, I'd fain conclude with the loftily philanthropic injunction—be kind to the kid! No matter what he may say at times, he is in truth an acute intellectual sufferer; & from countless utterances it is clear to me that he values your friendship more than any other human tie—values it in undiminished degree despite the divergence of mental processes which maturity brings out; the divergence which is but natural betwixt an analytical scholar & an inspired artist, & which ought not to diminish congeniality & regard on either side. When you think he speaks brutally, just reflect on the slings & arrows he has hurled at Belknap & me—missiles which sometimes sting, yet which we bear with admiring & amicable equanimity because we believe we understand the complex little divvle behind 'em.

Oh, by the way—speaking of life, & all that sort of rot—I've been having rather a bit of fun with the *Haldeman-Julius Weekly*, which is the poor old socialistic *Appeal to Reason* turned partly sane under a new name. They had a symposium, suggested by a correspondent, on the topic "What is the paramount end, aim, & object of life?", & I pulled the following wise saw—which, incidentally, Haldeman-Julius printed in addition to an 8-page letter of mine, not meant for the vulgar eye. Ho, hum . . . . not that it matters. But now to see the saw, as it were:

> The paramount end, aim, & object of life is contentment or tranquil pleasure; such as can be gained only by the worship & creation of beauty, & by the adoption of an imaginative & detached life which may enable us to appreciate the world as a beautiful object (as Schopenhauer tells us it is) without feeling too keenly the pain which inevitably results from reflecting on its relation to ourselves.¹⁹

Sage stuff, Oswald—sage stuff! Now let's have a drink.

It certainly is too bad that S H G should be having such a siege of suffering, & I am sure that it is far too genuine an affliction to profit by the spoofing-along of a Con, or Notre Dame de Lourdes, or anything of that sort. When things get to the surgical stage, they are generally the real article! But she seems to be vastly better now, & will—according to latest advices—be on the road again in May; honouring the classic fane of Saturn & Moses Cleaveland[20] with her presence & devotion toward the middle of that month . . . . which possibly signifies that the dreaded nasal operation was averted after all.[21] Perhaps teeth and tonsils—now subtracted—were the sources of the neuritis.

Yes—for Pegāna's sake write to 'Ittle-Sonny Belknap, who mourns your silence with truly filial devotion. A great child, that—you should see his preface for the Loveman Issue of the U.A.[22] And by the way—don't fancy that Cole's attack on his anti-White critique[23] contained any reflection on your work! Cole says that you expressed to him such a fear, but assures me that it was wholly groundless. Cole has a touch of New-England narrowness, but is not in any way a barbarian like that ass White. He really appreciates your poetry, & fully understands the absurd limitations of his dense fellow-townsman. What Cole disliked was the first half of Belknap's article, & that alone. I don't agree with him in his censure, & shall defend my grandchild if necessary; but at any rate, you were not attacked. I haven't seen the article in question, but take Cole's word. He confesses to a little savagery in dealing with the B.P.C.,[24] Mortonius, & a few others—& I wonder just what effect the critique will have. He wrote it in extreme pain—while suffering from an abscess following a tonsil operation—how manifold & widespread is misery!

When can you let me have the Herm? I'm still holding Fritter off, & have as you know a splendid & intelligent preface from Little Belknap.[25] When you send it you can let me know how to go about the *copyrighting* business—which I believe you desire. I'm totally inexperienced in that field, tho' not yet too old to learn.

And more—could you shoot me back that Lurking Fear MS.? Not that it's any good—but I like to have it around. And more yet besides—is there any human or inhuman way to pry my Dunsany book from the artistic clutches of that admirable jester, Will Somers? I might be able to live without it, 'tis true; yet on the other hand, so might Aestivus Artifex. And (whilst I'm about the cataloguing business) I wonder if that duplicate of the Keatsian early Lovemanic portrait was ever made. Yes—the monster Theobald is insatiate in his acquisitive suggestions! All due to a temperament naturally savage & cynical.

The Hoag book is done! Alleleuia, Kyrie Eleison, & all that sort of thing! Mortonius has it in the printer's hands, & you'll see a copy in a month or so. Hoag wants to present you with one. Incidentally, I finally got up the nerve to tell him I'd lost his picture. And he didn't kill or maim me therefor! But Bush is ever with us. Eheu! Would you like me to throw some of his work in the direction of the new bureau which you & Kirk announce in the Nat. Am.?[26] Command, & the work is yourn!

I wrote to Kid Lawrence[27] t'other day—hope he hasn't forgotten the old

gentleman. And I sent his ghoulish sketch—"That Laugh"—to Henricus Martinus for publication. Here's hoping the kid makes a good amateur. ¶ Well, that's that! Shoot us a line when you can . . . . & let's hope I can get to Cleveland to tear down that Soldiers' Monument in the publick square & put up an A-1 Temple of Apollo Musagetes—1537E93.²⁸ // Yr aff Grandfather
   Θεοβαλδος

Notes

1. I.e., illness.
2. *Java Head* (Famous Players/Paramount, 1923; silent), directed by George Melford; starring Leatrice Joy, Jacqueline Logan, and Frederick Strong. Based on the novel by Joseph Hergesheimer. HPL refers to his elder aunt, Lillian D. Clark.
3. Annie E. P. Gamwell.
4. The Hub Club was an amateur journalism group in Boston. See Lovecraft's poem "The Feast (Hub Journalist Club, March 10, 1923)," *Hub Club Quill* 15, No. 2 (May 1923): [13–15].
5. Cf. "The Feast," dedicated "To WISECRACK SANDUSKY, Esq., B.I., M.B.O. (Bachelor of Intelligence, Massachusetts Brotherhood of Owls)" (*AT* 370).
6. HPL was president of the NAPA from November 1922 to July 1923.
7. George W[illiam] M[acArthur] Reynolds (1814–1879) was a prolific British author and journalist. During his lifetime he was more read than Dickens or Thackeray, but he is virtually forgotten today.
8. See HPL's "Waste Paper," l. 18: "In the spring of the year, in the silver rain".
9. See *SL* 1.192–93 re HPL's attire during his Cleveland visit of August 1922.
10. No. 13 (July 1923), at 28 pages the largest issue, was also the last.
11. SL's irregular amateur journal.
12. I.e., SL's poem, "To Satan," *Conservative* No. 13 (July 1923): 1–2, dedicated to HPL.
13. Harry E. Martin (1887–1972), official editor of the NAPA during HPL's presidency.
14. Hazel Pratt Adams (1888–1927) was elected president of the NAPA for 1923–24. HPL wrote the elegy "The Absent Leader" following her death.
15. HPL refers to presiding over the NAPA convention, held in Cleveland on July 2–5, 1923. He did not do so. The *National Amateur* 46, No. 1 (Sept. 1923): 1 reports on a resolution passed at the convention: "The delegates to the N.A.P.A. Convention here assembled regret the absence of President Howard P. Lovecraft and move that a night letter be sent him expressing our regret and giving him our unanimous thanks for the efficient services which he has rendered as President during the past seven months." HPL's "The President's Annual Report" was read at the convention by Maurice W. Moe and published in the September 1923 issue of the *National Amateur* (1–3).
16. A typescript of "Hypnos" shows that HPL dedicated the story to SL. See Ted Robinson, "The Philosopher of Folly," *Cleveland Plain Dealer* (13 March 1923): 10, which reported that at a meeting of the Colophon Club, "Hypnos" was regarded by members as one of eight of the greatest short stories ever written. (The group was aiming for the six greatest, and in the end "Hypnos" did not make the cut.)

17. "Tranquility" and "lack of fear," respectively.
18. "Aletheia Phrikodes" [The Frightful Truth] is the central section of the poem "The Poe-et's Nightmare," *Vagrant* No. 8 (July 1918): [13–23].
19. *Haldeman-Julius Weekly* No. 1424 (17 March 1923).
20. Moses Cleaveland (1754–1806), soldier and land speculator who founded Cleveland, Ohio. "Saturn" alludes to SL's amateur journal.
21. See HPL's discussion of Sonia's continued medical complaint after their marriage (MWM 28).
22. This special issue was never published.
23. FBL "An Amateur Humorist," *Conservative* No. 12 (March 1923): 2–5, a defense of SL's poetry against the attack made upon it by Michael White. Edward H. Cole criticized FBL in the "Bureau of Critics" column of the *National Amateur* for March 1923. HPL discusses the controversy in "In the Editor's Study," *Conservative* No. 13 (July 1923): 21–24.
24. The Blue Pencil Club, an amateur journalist organization in Brooklyn.
25. The preface to SL's *The Hermaphrodite: A Poem* is by Benjamin De Casseres.
26. Kirk and SL evidently established a "literary" column "where it is planned to publish as much choice matter from members as space allows" (*National Amateur* 45, No. 4 [March 1923]: 6). HPL's "What the Moon Brings" appeared in the column in the issue for May 1923.
27. Carroll E. Lawrence, a friend of SL in Cleveland. HPL recruited him into the NAPA in the fall of 1923.
28. The Cuyahoga County Soldiers' and Sailors' Monument (1894) to Civil War soldiers and sailors from Cuyahoga County, Ohio. SL's address in Cleveland was 1537 E. 93rd Street, Suite 2.

[3]   [ALS]

[Hotels Statler . . . Detroit]

Old 598
29 April [1923]

Shantih! Shantih! Shantih![1]

Hell, but this has been some month! The trip tired me out like the devil, & on top of that has come a kind of near-grippe which takes every ounce of my energy. I'm snuffling, wheezing, coughing, and—just for novelty—nearly *stone deaf!* My left ear couldn't hear a cannon—or George Julian Houtain—at the present writing, & the right isn't any too prosperous. My work—which piles up shockingly—is beyond all adequate performance, & I haven't had a bally second to devote to reading or unofficial letter-writing. This epistle is being penned at a time when I ought to be shooting our friend Henricus Martinus a presidential message[2]—but gawdamighty, I think I ought to have at least a bit of a vacation! If Mortonius doesn't thank me all the rest of his life for taking this theokateramene[3] presidency, I'll denounce him as a fat ingrate! Bah!

Jhesu! But I'd like to get to Cleveland for that convention! I wouldn't let you risk any finance helping me—for Pegāna knows that bimbo Eglinus[4] doesn't loosen up enough to put you in the opulent division—but you can bet your last stanza I'm grateful for the suggestion! If I hit the ties west, it's gotta be Bush stuff that supplies the motive power—Bush stuff & *diplomacy,* for my family are dead set against any wholesale expenditures at this melancholy season of monetary sterility. I laid in the suit last Tuesday—a sedate grey affair that set me back 42 plunks.[5] It ought to be ready for a fitting now, but I've been too beastly laid up to get down town about it. More of my financial future is mortgaged in a half-paid-for 28-page *Conservative* which Charles A. A. Parker is doing for me; (boy, ya'd orta see your "Satan" looming up on the first page as the leading contribution!) but if I can work Bushly miracles, I may be able to dispose of even that burthen & come out ahead by the Kalends of Quintilis.[6] It rests with the dim immortal ones atop Pegāna.

Shoot along the H. as soon as you can without absolutely forcing the composition. And say—what do you think about some illustrations by Clericus Ashtonius?[7] I was just on the point of asking him point blank, when I noticed how in certain cases he failed to follow the text in H.B.[8]—& of course I'd hate to have him prepare anything which on critical analysis I'd find unsuitable. The H. has gotta be put across in absolutely *1st. class* shape, with nothing in the least amateurish tacked on, because I'm gonna shoot copies to a hades of a lot of editorial big bugs—Burt Rascoe, Hank Canby, the octaroon Bill Braithwaite[9]—& any of the rest of the gang whom you or other literati may recommend as deserving. Glad Saltus is up & coming, & that Ambrosius is trotting along comfortably. I knew that latter would be O.K. once 'twas got goin'. And here's hoping the Debs lines win in *Pearson's*[10]— which they sure ought to if the judges haven't allowed their bolshevism to extend from politics to aesthetics! Congratulate Georgius Circus[11] for me on persuading you to wade into the contest, & tell him I'll be anxious to go rowing with him when I hit the lake country—if he'll only remember to pull in the anchor when he gives me two bells!

Dunsany blew in all right, & looks fine in the shelf space I saved for him when I rearranged my books last November. I read his novel "Don Rodriguez"[12] last month, & advise you to do the same. Some day I'll convince you what a genius he is—& that goes for Alfredus too—but until then I'll merely ask you to be patient with what you consider an old man's false taste!

Glad E. Hyde[13] is on the right side of the Mike White controversy—she's his next critical victim, though perhaps she doesn't know it yet. By the way— I haven't any feud with her, as you seem to have gathered. Whatever strafing there is, is all on her side—she cherishes a subtle dislike based on antipathetical temperament. I ceased hostilities when political expediency forced her to apologise for the nasty digs in *Giddy Gazette* & *Inspiration.* Her verse is, as you say, very good—though it isn't the sort that interests me. The only ridiculous thing is to try to compare it with material of your own grade—that joint laureateship made me tired! Speaking of White—there's no limit to the density of that dumbbell. At the April meeting he expressed *pleasure* at the fairness of that critique of mine—which I tried as hard as possible to make subtly venomous! My gawd—ya gotta bean 'im with a sledge-hammer or he thinks you're petting him! Some day I'm gonna get after him without gloves, & expose his crudities. The bozo spells *Carlyle* as *Carlisle*,[14] & accents *Andromeda* on the penult. Yah!

Glad you liked my preceding epistle—but holy hell! The junk isn't worth preserving! How will all my undignified language look a century hence?

And speaking of centuries—Mortonius has got the Hoag book done at last! An unbound copy lies before me, (*lies* is right, for there are a helluva lotta Tryoutisms[15] which I could kick J. Ferd for not removing in proofs!) & duly elates me with its mention of me on the title page as writer of the biographical & critical preface. And for refined bull-throwing, I'll say it's some preface! The bound books will be done in about a month—gilt top 'n' everything—& you will be among the first supplied. I'm striking Jonathan E. for XX copies.

Glad you're writing letters again. When next you write S H G, pray assure her that you're not enmeshed in the toils of matrimony, as she gathered from the *National Amateur's* news note of a meeting attended by "Samuel Loveman & Mrs. Loveman". That was as bad as your—& Alfredus'—premature fears of similar nature regarding Little Belknap last year! And speaking of this latter infant—enclosed is my metrical tribute to his XXIst birthday last Friday.[16] Of age at last—Grandpa's little man! I hope to induce the child to visit the Old Gentleman for a few days in late May or early June—he wants me to come to N.Y., but my pocketbook favours the reverse plan. I'd like to show him to my elder aunt, who hasn't seen him. I hope Sonny-Boy isn't hurt at Cole's dig at the early part of his White article—I haven't heard from him since the appearance of the last N.A. And so the delectable Crane is now wallowing in the underworld of N.Y.? Good idea, your going there, but don't get in his Bohemian, near-Oscar-Wilde sort of circles! Gawd, how I hate that swinish Heliogabalan type! I like N.Y. prodigiously—but prefer the wholesome realms of northern Manhattan where Belknap lives, or Brooklyn with its Museum & Japanese garden, (which you MUST see) or the quaint crooked streets of lower Manhattan around Fraunce's [*sic*] Tavern & Hanover Square, to the bizarre dens & insane garrets which leer behind the once lovely Colonial facades of the so-called Greenwich-Village district. You must get Belknap & Mortonius to pilot you over the routes we traversed last autumn—the old mansions, the museums, the quaint rural spots, & such like. Or better still, I hope I can some time raise the cash to make the trip & pilot you myself!

Oh, by the way! I'm enclosing a letter which Campbell[17] wrote Belknap, & which may interest you because of the reference to the White incident. P. J. C. is all right—& this compliment is especially disinterested because he hasn't the least idea you'd ever see it. Please return the epistle to Little Sonny when you write him.

My late Massachusetts trip was quite a jaunt. I lit out Thursday the 12th, lapped up the Hub meeting, & camped out at the Parker–Miniter joint,[18] where there is a 1½ months old kitten whose antics diverted my entire sojourn there. I was glad to see me fren Sandusky at the get-together . . . he was there wit' bells on—you tell 'em, kid!—& ladled out enough spoonfulls of 190-proof syncopated socony to cop the fleece-lined electric fan for bulging brows. Sizzling sausage! but that bimbo sure did knock the other goofs west for a row of Æthiopian aeroplane hangars! We have no bananas today![19]

The next day I went to Salem on the electrics; & after looking the burg over, finally embarked for Danvers—called "Salem-Village" in the 17th century, & forming the seat of most of the 1692 witchcraft cases. I had quite an itinerary mapped out, but added to it when I saw a likely looking old mansion from the car window—a mansion of brick with such venerable ivy & such a fine doorway that I hailed the driver, disembarked, & proceeded to explore. The place was the Samuel Fowler mansion, built in 1809 by a dashing sea-captain & soldier. It is now owned by the Society for the Preservation of New-England Antiquities, & accessible for 15¢. Pathetically enough, the caretakers are two hideous ancient sisters who live in a squalid lean-to behind the house without money for sufficient food, fuel, & clothing; yet who were born in the mansion, & are the granddaughters of dashing Capt. Fowler himself! Such is the end of too many great New-England lines—to think of these indescribable creatures; ragged, guttural-voiced, unkempt, sinister-featured, impiously aged, & almost witch-like in their eery expression; and of their fastidiously elegant grandfather who demanded the best French wall paper, the finest brass latches, the choicest carved mantels, cornices, & wainscoting, & the most delicate silver, china, & ornaments that Europe & America could afford. In the veins of these terrible living corpses flows the mingled blood of all that was proudest in the Salem region—Endecotts, Pickmans, Fowlers, Pages—their own great-grandmother was that sprightly Mrs. Page who, at the time of the Colonial tea agitation, served her guests with the beverage *on the roof* after her husband had forbidden her to serve it *under his roof*. The Fowler house is finely preserved & restored, & filled with Colonial objects of art. Many architects & designers visit it for ideas—one had been there the day before my visit. The decorations are of unrivalled beauty; & the artistic furniture, ornaments, china, & silver are beyond description. Fine ancestral portraits, old garments of the greatest richness, priceless laces & other Colonial remnants of domesticity—all these recall uncannily a bygone prosperity which the present mocks. I was allowed to don a beaver hat & cream-coloured swallow-tail coat belonging to Capt. Fowler about 1810—they fitted me moderately well!

After leaving this place, I walked to Danvers Square & visited the old Page house, (1754) where the great-grandmother of the pitiful Fowlers had once served tea on the roof, & where now the Danvers Historical Society holds forth. The architecture interested me extremely, & I climbed to the gambrel roof where the tea-party was held.

Thereafter I put the age of Colonial refinement behind me, & harked back to that age of darker & weirder appeal—the age of the dreaded witchcraft. Leaving the village, I struck out along the roads & across the fields toward the lone farmhouse built by Townsend Bishop in 1636, & in 1692 occupied by poor old Rebekah Nurse—who was accused of witchcraft by a West-India slave woman & some children, tried in Salem, & on July 19 hanged on Gallows Hill at the age of 70. She lies buried some distance from her home, the grave being marked by a monument erected in 1885 & having an epitaph by Whittier. As I approached the spot to which I had been directed, after passing through the village of Tapleyville, the afternoon sun was very low. Soon the houses thinned out; so that on my right were only the hilly fields of stubble, & occasional crooked trees clawing at the sky. Beyond a low crest a thick group of spectral boughs bespoke some kind of grove or orchard—& in the midst of this group I suddenly descried the rising outline of a massive & ancient chimney. Presently, as I advanced, I saw the top of a grey, drear sloping roof—sinister in its distant setting of bleak hillside & leafless grove, & unmistakably belonging to the haunted edifice I sought. Another turn—a gradual ascent—& I beheld in full view the sprawling, tree-shadowed house which had for nearly 300 years brooded over those hills & held such secrets as men may only guess. Like all old farmhouses of the region, the Nurse cottage faces the warm south & slopes low behind toward the north. It fronts on an ancient garden, where in their season gay blossoms flaunt themselves against the grim nail-studded door & the vertical sundial above it. Everything about the place is ancient—even to the tiny-paned lattice windows which open outward on hinges. The atmosphere of the witchcraft days broods heavily upon that low, lone hilltop.

Admitted by the nondescript caretaker, I found myself amidst large, low rooms & passages whose massive beams almost touched my head. All was sombre & barren—panelled apartments with colossal fireplaces in the vast central chimney, & with occasional pieces of the plain, heavy furniture & primitive farm & domestic utensils of the ancient yeomanry. In these wide, low-pitched rooms a spectral menace broods—for to my imagination the 17th century is as full of macabre mystery, repression, & ghoulish adumbrations as the 18th is full of taste, gayety, grace, & beauty. This was a typical Puritan abode; where amidst the bare, ugly necessities of life, & without learning, culture, beauty, freedom, or ornament terrible stern-faced people in conical hats or poke-bonnets dwelt 250 & more years ago—close to the soil & all its hideous whisperings; warped in mentality by isolation & unnatural thoughts, & shivering in fear of the devil on autumn nights when the wind howled through the twisted orchard trees or rustled the hideous corpse-nourished pines in the graveyard at the foot of the hill. There is eldritch fascination—

horrible buried evil—in these archaic farmhouses. After seeing them, & smelling the odour of centuries in their walls, one hesitates to read certain passages in Cotton Mather's strange old "Magnalia". You must some time visit New-England & see them—they exist nowhere else. After exploring the ground floor I crept up the black crooked stairs & examined the bleak chambers above. The furniture was as ugly as that below, & included a small trundle-bed in which infant Puritans were lulled to sleep with meaningless prayers & morbid hints of daemons riding the night-wind outside the small-paned lattice windows. I saw old Rebekah's favourite chair, where she used to sit & spin before the Salem magistrates dragged her to the gallows. And the sunset wind whistled in the colossal chimney, & ghouls rattled ghastly skeletons from unseen rafters overhead. I now persuaded the caretaker to let me ascend to that hideous garret of centuried secrets. Thick dust covered everything, & unnatural shapes loomed on every hand as the evening twilight oozed through the little bleared panes of the ancient windows. I saw something hanging from the wormy ridge-pole—something that swayed as if in unison with the vesper breeze outside, though that breeze had no access to this funereal & forgotten place—shadows..... shadows..... shadows...... And I descended from that accursed garret of palaeogean arcana, & left that portentous abode of antiquity; left it & went down the hill to the graveyard under the shocking pines, where twilight shewed sinister slabs & rusty bits of fallen iron fence, & where something squatted in shadow on a monument—something that made me climb the hill again, hurry shudderingly past the venerable house, & descend the opposite slope to Tapleyville as night came.

Returning to Maplewood, I was again a Parker–Miniter guest; delighting in the company of the small kitten. This gentleman, after he got tired of chewing his grandpa's fingers & watch-charm, climbed up to his favourite place behind the Old Gentleman's neck, & there slumbered till removed to his nocturnal quarters. Blest atom of happy life! Would that all the world might be as thou! And yet are not thy brothers the subtle sphinx & the insatiable lion of Libya & Numidia?

Saturday I went via Haverhill to Merrimac, where I was the guest of that 15-year-old near-Galpin, Edgar Jacobs Davis. Edgar is a great kid—he came out highest in an intelligence test covering all the pupils in the Merrimac High School. I wish he were better appreciated at home—for though he has a studious & sympathetic mother & sister, his father is a practical, semi-rustic Yankee who despises culture & considers his scintillant child rather a ne'er-do-well.

On the afternoon of my arrival, Edgar & I visited old graveyards & houses in Amesbury, where Whittier lived & died. We saw the poet's home & grave, the famed "captain's well", & other typical reliquiae. Toward evening we returned to the Davis mansion, where I argued with the prodigy's father, held William the aged cat, & generally bored the household till bedtime intervened. Sunday I was up betimes for the big event—the trip with Edgar to ancient Newburyport, which I had never seen. We had wished to take honest *Tryout* along with us, but he wrote that he was nervously ill & could not bear even so much as a caller at his Plaistow retreat. Poor, amiable, old faun!

Embarked for Newburyport, the car took us through some of the choicest scenery of New-England, for in this northerly region the hills are gentle & graceful, & unexpected vistas of village roofs & spires are frequent. Commerce & manufactures have not destroyed the quiet simplicity of the inhabitants, & they still dream the years away amidst scenes but little altered by the passing centuries. Crossing Chain Bridge—the oldest suspension bridge in America—we approached the suburbs of Newburyport & began to get whiffs & glimpses of the neighbouring sea, & to descry the ancient houses & chimney-pots of the famous town which, though said a century and a quarter ago to possess a social life more cultivated & brilliant than that of Washington, is today locally known as the "City of the Living Dead".

Up the narrow street we rattled—deciding to stick to the one-man car for a preliminary panorama, & to defer the pedestrian exploring till later. Ineffably quaint & archaic are the Georgian streets which we saw from the windows—fascinating hills lined with venerable dwellings of every description, from 200-year-old hovels huddled together in nondescript groups with rambling extensions & lean-to's, to stately Colonial mansions with proud gables & magnificent doorways. One feature possessed in common by nearly all the houses, great & humble alike, was the curious old-world abundance of *chimney-pots*, here more prevalent even than in magic Marblehead! All at once the car reached a spacious square, lined on every side with the quaint brick mercantile buildings of the Revolutionary period. It was a sight such as we had never seen before—a city business section of the 18th century, preserved in every detail. As the car passed on, entering again a delicious maze of ancient streets & turning almost every corner in sight, we wondered when we should reach the modern business section; but after a time the houses thinned out & we found ourselves speeding past the shanties ... of fishermen toward the salt marshes of the open country to the south, with the sand-choked harbour on our left, & the long stretch of Plum Island in the distance beyond. Then we questioned the driver, & discovered the truth of a suspicion which had crossed our minds but fleetingly before. It was really so—that Georgian business section was in truth the business section of today as well! You saw it, I think, on the joint card Davis & I sent you—can you imagine the reality? The commercial Newburyport of 1780 still stands .... truly, a City of the Living Dead!

Upon alighting from the car, at the end of the route, we strolled back through the maze of picturesque streets; ecstatically drinking in the antique houses of wood, brick, & stone, with peaked, gambrel, or flat roofs, massive or graceful chimneys, quaint chimney-pots, & artistic Colonial doorways. It was the past brought to life—flashes of 18th century bye-streets, silhouettes of Christopher Wren steeples, kaleidoscopic etchings of old-time skylines, snatches of glistening harbour beyond delectably rambling & alluringly antediluvian alleys that wind lazily down hill—a true paradise of the born antiquarian! Once we walked the whole length of a ramshackle alley without losing for a second the illusion of the Colonial age of sea-power. Through a cross-alley we saw the splendid facade & columns of a stone mansion in the distance—engaging vista! Thoughts of the past welled up—here were the lodgings of adventurous sailors who knew the far Indies & the perfumed East, & there dwelt a solid, periwigged captain whose skill had led many a sturdy barque around the Horn, or through Magellan's tortuous strait, or past the Cape of Good Hope. Then we went down to the rotting wharves & dreamed of old days, & in fancy saw the heaps of cordage & bales of strange Asian wares, & the forest of masts that reached half across to Plum Island. Ah, me—the days that were! After this we returned to the business section, bought some cards, & set out for famous & opulent High St., where stands the old mansion of the celebrated eccentric Timothy Dexter.[20]

You must have heard of Dexter & his lucky speculations, attempts to enter society, freakish extravagance, grotesque house & grounds, ridiculous escapades, hilarious pretensions to titled aristocracy, liveried poet-laureate, (an ex-fishmonger, the D. V. Bush of his day) outdoor museum of wooden statues, (including one of himself, labelled "I am first in the East, first in the West, & the greatest philosopher of the Western World") & absurd book called "A Pickle for the Knowing Ones". That book was misspelled & unpunctuated; & when people objected to the latter feature, "Lord" Dexter published a second edition, (1796) still unpunctuated, but with a page of assorted punctuation marks at the end, plus the note:

"mister printer the Nowing Ones complane of my book the fust edition had no stops I put in A Nuf here & thay may peper & solt it as thay plese."[21]

In our family there is an old print of Dexter's house, made in 1810, four years after his death, & shewing the ludicrous ornaments & the statues of celebrities atop the fence-posts. Today, however, all the extravagances are decorously removed; & all that one sees of Dexter's follies are the oddly turned columns by the doorway, & the gilt eagle atop the cupola.

Strolling south from Dexter's mansion, Edgar & I noted the ancient churchyard & the new church going up within it. That edifice will mark Newburyport's awakening to the great aesthetic truth which Salem has always realised—namely, that every old town has its architectural atmosphere, to which all new buildings must conform. In the hideous Victorian age of tastelessness, nearly every own [sic] town but Salem was ruined by the construction of ugly nondescript buildings like New York's post-office, &c. Salem alone knew the need for harmonious congruity, & stuck to classical & Colonial models. But just now Newburyport is waking up, & is trying to reclaim its heritage. In this old churchyard, where once a Colonial belfry saluted the sky, an ugly neo-

Gothic church was built some time in the 19th century when the original structure decayed or burned. It was horribly out of place in Newburyport—but what could you expect of Victorian times? Now—Pegāna be prais'd—taste has reappeared; & the Gothick monstrosity hath been torn down to make way for a beautiful new stone edifice on the simple & classical lines of the original Georgian structure. Gloria in excelsis! Once more the ancient slabs will look up to noble walls in harmony with their atmosphere, & the quiet corner—where a venerable bye-street slopes shadily & beckoningly down from the travell'd way—will assume again that immemorial tranquillity which comes only to such old regions as grow in organic fashion, building cell by cell from the vital impulses of elder aeons.

Still further south we went, admiring the stately mansions of old captains of the sea, with the tall cupolas where they used to scan the distant waves with spyglasses. Good old days! Providence has some of those cupola'd houses—on the old hill overlooking the bay, which you must see some time. Salem has many, but Newburyport probably has most of all. On a side street we found an old house whose lower floor was being converted into a shop. The new shop window, with its glassless frame & broad seat, invited us; & we sate down for a long rest, gazing at ancient houses—one fully 250 years old—& stately, gigantic elm trees.

But time was flying, & it was getting damn cold. We had now reached a point which involved a retracing of those quaint, narrow streets & alleys we had first explored; & delightedly we went about it, pausing now & then to admire some particularly picturesque scenic effect—whether of quaintness, magnificence, or antique decay. Reaching once more the central square, we partook of a meal at the *one* decent restaurant in the "city", (the cafe of the more-than-a-century-old Adams House) where for 65¢ apiece we were served with more than I could eat. (Clark's Lunches & Mills' & Chapin's Cafeterias please take notice!) Finally filled, we took the car back to Merrimac; where after an evening of discussion we dispersed—to meet but briefly the next morning before Edgar hustled off to high school.

Monday I spent the morning arguing with the Senior Davises, rode into Haverhill with Davis Sr. in the family Ford, & spent the afternoon at the Haverhill Public Library looking up antique data. Haverhill is a very live city for its size—54,000—having extensive boot & shoe manufactures which about 50 years ago transformed the original Colonial village (1640) to a modern town. Naturally it has fewer Colonial houses than the towns whose development came earlier, yet it is quite pretty withal. It is the natural mart of such Newburyporters as do not shop in Boston, & has a busy life of its own.

In the evening I turned homeward, passing through Boston & reaching my hermitage about midnight. 'Twas a great trip, yet it fatigued me greatly; & I have been more or less laid up & grippe-harassed since. How the past fascinates me! Next month I expect to see Concord & Lexington with Edward H.

Cole, & later in the summer I must "do" the South-of-Boston region—Plymouth, Duxbury, Hingham, &c.—where I have never yet been. Nothing stimulates my imagination like the relics of the past—ancient roofs, chimneys, streets, & skylines—& when that damned presidency is off my hands I expect I shall get some fictional echoes of this globe-trotting business!

Before I close—will you rejoin the United, sending one bean for reinstatement to the Secretary, Miss Alma B. Sanger, 667 Lilley Ave., Columbus, Ohio? Fritter's chief objection to my Loveman Issue has been your lack of continued active United membership.

Well—I hope these XVI pp haven't knocked you flat! CHEER UP, laugh at the trivial farce of life, & drop your old Grandpa Theobald a line when you feel like it.

    Attaboy!

        H P

P.S. Say—do you ever see Kid Lawrence nowadays? If so, tell him to get active amateurically! Martin hasn't heard a word from him, & he's dubious about printing that ghoulish yarn I sent him. I hope Lawrence isn't provoked over my delay in answering his letter—'twas bad enough, but an inevitable result of my frenetically crowded contemporary calendar.

Notes

1. See MWM 27n1.
2. "President's Message," *National Amateur* 45, No. 5 (May 1923): 5–6.
3. HPL's coined neologism, meaning roughly "god-damned."
4. HPL refers to SL's employment at Eglin's bookstore in Cleveland.
5. This was one of the suits stolen from HPL's Brooklyn apartment in May 1925 (see *SL* 2.12).
6. I.e., the first of July.
7. HPL refers to Clark Ashton Smith's illustrations for SL's *Hermaphrodite*, which evidently do not survive.
8. I.e., Smith's illustrations for "The Lurking Fear" in *Home Brew*.
9. Henry Seidel Canby (1878–1961), critic and book reviewer. For Rascoe, see MWM 17n23. For Braithwaite, see MWM 19n4.
10. SL's "Debs in Prison" was unpublished in his lifetime.
11. I.e., George Kirk.
12. See S. T. Joshi, "Lovecraft and Dunsany's *Chronicles of Rodriguez*," in Joshi's *Lovecraft and a World in Transition* (New York: Hippocampus Press, 2014), 383–87, for the possible influence of this novel on "He" and "The Strange High House in the Mist."
13. Edna von der Heide (later Edna Hyde), secretary of the NAPA for 1923–24.
14. See "In the Editor's Study," *Conservative* No. 13 (July 1923): 22: "Should we after all denounce our Eminent Victorians merely because of their support of the critic who

classified Macaulay, Carlisle, [*sic*] Emerson, and Shaw as 'great poets' . . . ?"

15. I.e., typographical misprints, as frequently found in Charles W. Smith's amateur magazine, the *Tryout*.

16. "To Endymion: (Frank Belknap Long, Jr.): Upon His Coming of Age, April 27, 1923," *Tryout* 8, No. 10 (September 1923): [15–16] (as by "L. Theobald, Jun."). FBL was in fact born in 1902; therefore, he was twenty-two in 1923.

17. Paul J. Campbell, a longtime amateur.

18. See MWM 20n2.

19. A line from "Yes! We Have No Bananas," a novelty song by Frank Silver and Irving Cohn from the Broadway revue *Make It Snappy* (1922). It became a major hit in 1923 (number 1 for five weeks).

20. See MWM 34n5.

21. A similar anecdote is attributed to Mark Twain regarding his submittal of *A Connecticut Yankee in King Arthur's Court* to his publisher.

[4]   [TLS, Wisconsin Historical Society][1]

Happy New-Year!
[c. 5 January 1924]

Agathon,[2] my Son!

Both the lyricks duly came—and marvellous lyricks they are! One of them shall surely head the first *United Amateur* to appear under my auspices[3]—both of 'em would, if the page were broad enough! Your gift with the lyre is something I can only envy mutely, but you know how keenly and sincerely I appreciate it! There must be something hereditary in it—note the enclosed review from the *Boston Transcript* about your late cousin Robert Loveman.[4] He, you know, is one whom Mencken so greatly admires. I am sending this for your permanent retention in case you do not have it already, for surely you wish a family tribute of this sort for your scrap book.

And how are the Providential plans? The old town is still here, and beckoning alluringly. Mortonius came and went, and I am sure he will attest to a pretty good time exploring local antiquities according to my latest modes in personally conducted tours. After a festive session in Boston and vicinity he blew in Thursday, Dec. 27, at 11:04 a.m., and Eddy[5] and I were on hand to meet him. I was only fifteen minutes late—a degree of promptness which will through all my after life give me the sensation of being as punctual as a tradesman.

The first objective of our trip was that supreme landmark of Providence, the First Baptist Church, finish'd in 1775. This is my maternal ancestral church, but I had not been in the main auditorium since 1895, or in the building at all since 1907, when I gave an illustrated astronomical lecture in the vestry to the Boys' Club.[6] We found this fane as pleasing within as without, the panelling and the carving above the doors being especially notable as specimens of Georgian workmanship. We ascended to the organ loft, and I endeavour'd to play "Yes, We Have no Bananas", but was balk'd by lack of power, since the machine is not a self-starter. Later we explor'd the pulpit, and the interesting baptismal font or celestial bathtub behind it, but I had had a cold tub at home, so did not sample the sacred pool. Besides, I didn't know how to turn the water on.

Then we began to climb flight after flight of hand-hewn Georgian steps into the steeple, till finally we were beside the massive bell—cast in 1775 in London, weighing 2500 pounds, and having the following inscription:

> "For freedom of conscience the town was first planted.
> Persuasion, not force, was us'd by the people:
> This church is the eldest, and has not recanted,
> Enjoying and granting bell, temple, and steeple."

A lockt door obstructed our further progress, so we settled ourselves to enjoy the view to be had from that moderate level. It was, I assure you, very beautiful; for we spy'd an amazing number of antient colonial roofs and belfries contemporary with the steeple in which we stood, including the Golden Ball Inn where Gen. Washington stopt, and which now bask'd reminiscently in the midday sun, its row of dormer windows giving forth little twinkles from the small panes.[7] Southward the antique harbour brooded—the blue harbour where the India packets ride at anchor, and the rum, slave, and molasses brigs come from Africa, Charleston, and New-Orleans—the placid harbour with the hoary brick warehouses still as they were in the days of periwigg'd merchants. Suddenly a great iron clapper we had not seen descended on the bell from the outside in twelve measur'd strokes, shaking the air with swelling reverberations. It was the striking of the great clock, by which all the antient men of the village set their bulbous watches. But no sooner had this clapper ceas'd its beats, than the great bell itself began to heave; so that in a moment the whole scene was a riot of extatick clangour. The bell-ringer was at his post, for ever since the church was built it hath rung forth its message each day at sunrise, noon, and nine o'clock curfew. And as I stood there in that Georgian steeple, looking out over the quaint Colonial town and vibrating with the peals of that bell rung from elder custom, I swell'd with a new consciousness of the past, and a pride in the traditions nourish'd here unbroken since our rightful Sovereign sate on the throne, and the Union Jack of our fathers flew over that white Colony-House belfry which even now rose to my sight thro' the tangle of bare December branches. GOD SAVE THE KING! And that spire itself, with noble arch and classick pilaster! What a monument to Gibbs, its designer, to Wren, and to ENGLAND is that noble architecture which, rejecting the distorted baroque of Italy and the lands around, and the Italo-Vitruvian specimens to which all men lookt as prime exemplars of the classick, went straight to the reliques of Greece and Rome, and reviv'd in unsully'd purity an art whose perfection had not been known since the days of Septimius Severus! WREN, I salute thee! Titanick soul! It was not for thee to tread Italia's vales and Graecia's templed crags, and thus to learn in aw'd proximity the secrets of the elder art. Thine but to scan the painted canvas and the graven page, and like me to dream of what thou might'st not behold. But out of thy dreaming rare beauty came, and to the memory'd spire thou didst with wizard art wed arch and column, capital and frieze, till without one hybrid stigma there sprang compleat the loveliness that will never die—the loveliness that is of Old ENGLAND, and destin'd only for the sacred soil of her Empire, past and present. If you have read Arthur Machen's "Three Impostors", you must have noticed the tribute to the spire of St. Mary le Strand.[8] That is by Gibbs, who design'd our Providence spire. There is now afoot a design to transport the Wren churches (i.e. of Wren and his pupils) of London to the several dominions, their sites being now ingulph'd by trade. This I hope may never be, for the old ground is holy. Lovers of London shou'd rise up to save the beauty and the mystery that are theirs—but I thank the gods our Providence church is on safe territory, which can never fall to the evil uses of trade. It is on a grassy hillside that holds the dew of old days whilst yet facing the busy town, and on one side winds antient Thomas-Street with its swinging signs and colonial doorways. Old Providence dead? Pouf! It is immortal!

But at last we climb'd down thro' the beam'd and cobwebb'd mysteries of the lower steeple, sign'd our names in a book, and went out on the antient hillside. We stroll'd on past Georgian facades with iron-rail'd steps and brass knockers, mounted the old-world steps that form a part of Gaol-Lane, linger'd about the quaint vistas of "Tippy Corner", where none but colonial houses are in sight, slid down the unpav'd expanse of Bowen-Street,[9] ferreted out the hidden hillside churchyard of St. John's,[10] where ghouls stalk at evening and where the stones go back to 1730, and finally struck north in quest of the oldest brick house in Providence, (1750)[11] which I had never seen, and which lies in a region that my foot had never trod. And such a region! Antient .... unbelievably antient cottages and sheds and houses, some of them urban, and some of them farmhouses overtaken in 1740 or 1745 by the growing town. Networks of dusty unpav'd byways darting narrowly and nervously hither and thither off the main streets, and leading down from the crest of old Constitution Hill to the brow of the vertiginous slope that frowns over the river .... the antient Moshassuck, at the falls where Goodman Smith's mill and the foot-bridge were put up in 1642. There were all the symbols of the antient town—Olney's Lane, with the gambrel-roof'd tavern where the Boston coach us'd to leave every Thursday with passengers and His Majesty's mail—and the first brick house itself, freshly painted and admirably preserv'd, tho' in the worst sort of mongrel slums. Then we turn'd into the maze of colonial alleys toward the river, and suddenly saw a sight of incredible picturesqueness. From one of these lanes an abrupt declivity fell, descending at a steepness almost prohibitive to human feet, and provided with an iron handrail. Intersecting at intervals several hidden Georgian lanes on the hillside, it reach'd a group of early stone mill buildings—1815 or 1820—and slid betwixt two of them whose second stories were connected above it with a passage like the Bridge of Sighs, finally crossing the river by a wooden bridge and coming out near Randall-Square, a hideous polyglot slum district. This declivity we travers'd without disaster, thence turning southwest toward the centre of the town, skirting the marmoreal majesty of the state-house, and passing under the Union Station to the mall and business district. Crossing the latter, we imbib'd the antiquity of Pine and Orange Streets, where little antient buildings cower timorously, and old men shyly ply delicate, forgotten trades and crafts. After this James Ferdinand suggested a Li Ho Chan repast, wherefore we left Anglo-Saxon colonialism to seek the marble steps and golden carvings of King Fong's, the nearest place of its kind to where we were.

An hour later we enter'd another colonial district—the Market Parade with its great bridge, 1773 market house,[12] and Georgian warehouses—and crossing through to where the Providence Bank's sign swings from a 1774 building in South-Main Street,[13] we ascended the hill past the 18th-century cottages of Planet-Street and reach'd our appointed destination—the museum of Col. Shepley,[14] as describ'd in my last travelogue—where my aunt Mrs. Gamwell promptly met us. Of this museum I have already told you, and I only need add that I was pleasantly surpriz'd by having handed to me as a gift the etching of 1762 Providence which was promis'd me last month. So long a time had elaps'd, that I had thought it unobtainable. I made my aunt carry it with care, lest it be creas'd before we cou'd get it to a framer's. Subsequently we all struck south along Benefit-Street to still another colonial part of the town in which I had never before set foot. (The 3d to be unearth'd by me within a month) It was sunset now, and the mellow gold transfigur'd with magick a scene magical enough without it—a vivid realm of undulating street and precipitous cross lanes running upward to the left and downward toward the river to the right. Antient ... antient ... antient ... Ornate Georgian doorways, queer little cupola'd cottages of sea-captains perch'd on hillsides whence the masters us'd to watch the blue harbour and the spreading bay, and the oddest conceivable stone church with conical spire, that us'd to hold St. Stephen's congregation,[15] tho' now the seat of nigger worship. Dusk fell as we rounded Wickenden into South-Main, and observ'd the painful squalor lurking beneath the unbroken colonial silhouette on both sides. Now and then a light wou'd appear in a small-pan'd window, and sometimes a fanlight wou'd mellowly gleam forth. At such times I was certain that the spirit of the slums had fled away for a moment, and that old hands had put flint and steel to tallow dips. At one place we search'd out a court whose etch'd likeness we had seen at the museum, Harding's Alley—dream of colonial yesterdays with its cobbled pavement, one dim lanthorn, fanlighted doorways with knockers and double flights of iron-rail'd steps, and in the distance—on the steep hillside above and beyond—a white Georgian belfry to crown the witching scene. GOD SAVE THE KING!

At this point Eddy had to leave, and the trio of Mortonius, my aunt, and I kept on through colonial vistas till we reach'd the twinkling fanlights of antient Rosemary-Lane or College Hill. There, in a building where Lafayette once slept, we visited the little shop of an old picture-framer, and left the old Providence etching for him to prepare for my study wall. This was half way up the hill, in the heart of colonialism. But turning round and looking down past the old market house, we saw the night starred with the mounting witch-fires of skyscraper windows. I had never seen that vista at night before, and I found it very lovely.

But not long did we tarry, for I was set on shewing Mortonius the region of southwestern colonial horror and decay that Eddy introduc'd to me last month.[16] Across the busy lanes of surging traffick we went, till coming to the venerable Round Top Church (1808)[17] we turn'd into the gruesome court which is the outer vestibule of unnamable elder labyrinths. Dim flickering lights . . . . crawling, shapeless mists and shadows . . . . blear'd windows . . . crumbling colonial doorways . . . dank pools, jagged stones, sharp turns, unbelievable convolutions and constructions . . . . all was as I had found it last month, tho' I cou'd not get either of my companions to own the macabre charm of it. Ghouls' Court[18] was terrible . . . . one shou'd flee away from places where century'd secrets titter inaudibly . . . . . .

So at length we regain'd the business district, trudg'd to the station and got Jacobus Ferdinandus' valise, eat some sodas and sundaes (tho' they didn't have the fresh fruit salad kind you can get at 105th and Euclid) at Gibson's, bade adieu to my aunt, and set out to walk to the New-York packet along the frightful deserted length of horrible South Water-Street, where murther lurks in the alleys, and one stumbles over corpses in the gutters. Reaching the ship without stumbling, but carrying a confus'd blur of pallid lamps and Hogarth vistas in our eyes, we dispos'd of Mortonius' valise and set out to kill the few moments before sailing time.

We edg'd thro' ghastly channels between black silent freight cars on the India wharf at the southern tip of Providence's eastern peninsula, a region I had never penetrated, tho' I had for twenty years and more wonder'd about it. It was an eldritch wriggle, like that of Alciphron in the tortuous crypts of Egypt,[19] and at last we came out where pale phosphorescence effus'd from century'd rotting piles, and the distant harbour lights bobb'd and twinkled away to the south, the far south, the south of dreams and templed isles, and curious ports, and pagodas of gold with savour of spice and incense around them. Then we edg'd back to the *Concord* frigate, said farewell, and ended the travelogue. Mortonius sail'd into the starry sea . . . . . I went to a cinema.

Yr obt Servt:

HPL

Notes

1. On the TLS (or carbon), HPL has written "Original to Saml Loveman, Esq." with "please return" on top left corner.
2. Agathon (448?–400? B.C.E.) was an Athenian tragic poet whose works have been lost.
3. HPL was re-elected official editor of the UAPA for the 1923–24 term. SL's "Bacchanale," dedicated to HPL, appeared on the first page of the *United Amateur* 23, No. 1 (May 1924).
4. Robert Loveman (1864–1923), a minor poet. He died on 10 July.
5. C. M. Eddy, Jr.
6. Cf. *The Rhode Island Journal of Astronomy* 4, No. 9 (April 1907): 2: "On Fri., Jan. 25, 1907, H. P. Lovecraft, Edtr. of the *R. I. Journal* delivered a lecture on Astronomy before the Boys' Club of the 1st. Baptist Church, in Providence."
7. Only the Golden Ball Inn Ell (1784 et seq.) stands today at 17–23 South Court Street. In HPL's time, the four-story Golden Ball Inn stood across from the Court House (150 Benefit Street) and stable (160 Benefit Street). The main part of the house was demolished in 1941.
8. See Arthur Machen, *The Three Impostors* (London: John Lane, 1895): "As for St. Mary le Strand, its preservation is a miracle, nothing more or less. A thing of exquisite beauty" (164f.). HPL owned the Knopf (1930) ed. (*LL* 623).
9. *Commonplace Book* entry 98 (c. 1922): "Hideous old house on steep city hillside—Bowen St.—beckons in the night—black windows—horror unnam'd—cold touch & voice—the welcome of the dead." "Tippy Corner" appears to refer the very steep intersection of Congdon, Meeting, and South Court Streets, where a horse-drawn carriage would be prone to tipping in trying to negotiate the corner.
10. St. John's Episcopal Church (1810), 275 North Main Street. The churchyard is mentioned in "The Shunned House" (1924) and "The Messenger" (1929). It was there HPL wrote his Poe acrostic, "In a Sequester'd Providence Churchyard Where Once Poe Walk'd" (1936).
11. Cf. HPL to August W. Derleth, 2 September 1931: "Behind me is the old gambrel-roofed Richard Brown house—erected 1750 & the second brick house (the very first is also standing in good shape down town) to be built within the corporate limits of Providence" (*Essential Solitude* 271). (HPL was writing in an open field, about one mile from his residence at 10 Barnes St.) The Richard Brown house stands on the Butler Hospital grounds. The house was actually erected in 1731.
12. On Market Square.
13. The Joseph Brown House (1774, Joseph Brown architect), 50 South Main Street. John and Moses Brown founded the Providence Bank at this location in 1791, which remained the bank's headquarters until construction of a new bank at 100 Westminster Street (1929).
14. See MWM 25n1.
15. St. Stephen's Church (1840) at 400 Benefit Street.
16. See MWM 25.

17. The Beneficent Church on Weybosset Street.
18. I.e., Gould's Court. See MWM 25.
19. Referring both to the unfinished poem *Alciphron* and the novel *The Epicurean* (1827), based upon it, by Thomas Moore (1779–1852). HPL owned the novel (LL 674); he quotes Moore's poem in "The Nameless City" (1921).

[5]   [ANS][1]

[Postmarked Somerville, N.J.,
10 November 1924]

All hail! Here's the healthy village 4 miles from which I'm parking the wiff.[2] Lots of colonial houses, panoramas of meadow & farmland dotted with autumnal sheaves, distant purple hills, &c. I stayed over till the next day to size up the terrain—& now I'm on the way to Philly. If I stay over till Wednesday, I may miss the meeting—or be later than usual to it—but there are plenty more coming. More anon.
Yr obt Servt
HPL

Notes

1. *Front:* Main Street, Somerville, N.J.
2. Sonia was staying at a rest home in Somerville.

[6]   [ANS][1]

[Postmarked Philadelphia, Pa.,
11 November 1924]

Took a look at the Centaur but didn't go in[2]—I have nothing in common with moderns. But boy! Why haven't you gone delirious about their locality? Georgianism!!!!!!!!! I was incoherent for the better part of an hour, till I came on something still better elsewhere. Oh, what a burg is Philly! After getting next to all the inside antiquities, I'm prepared to agree that N.Y. isn't so much.
Thine in Quakerism—
Grandpa

Notes

1. *Front:* Betsy Ross Grave, Philadelphia, Pa.
2. I.e., The Centaur Book Shop, 1224 Chancellor Street, Philadelphia; later the Centaur Press, proprietor Harold Trump Mason (1893-1983). The press was to publish SL's book on Edgar Saltus.

[7] [ALS]
                                                    Wednesday
                                            [29 September 1926]

Ave!
   Have dropped Cook another line, but can't say how effective it will prove. There wasn't anything from him awaiting me when I returned.
   It certainly is good to be in Old Providence again, & I had an absolutely glorious stagecoach ride home through rural Connecticut—leagues of rock-ribb'd rolling pasture, vistas of wood & valley, & hills beyond hills, & white ancient villages dreaming under their elms. The coach stopt 40 minutes in New London for lunch, but I passed up the gross feeding & devoted the time to sightseeing & card-buying. Here's the 1784 courthouse that stands on a hill at the head of one of the principal streets—I must certainly visit the town again when I have time to explore it. Hope Mac gets a good attendance tonight—& sorry I can't be present.
   As to a pome for G D's week-end book[1]—for Gawd's sake, what ever gave you all the delusion that I can write verse? My metrical flounderings are not to be taken seriously. As I recall my past performances I can't think of anything passable except "Nemesis"—& that's too long—& it's too damn much bother anyway looking through all my scattered files to find my sundry Aonian *corpora delictorum*. So I might as well grind off one more mechanical bit—based on a dream I had last night—& here it is. If you think it's *too* rotten, just tear it up & let me know in time to do another; otherwise, pass it on to the Sage of Chelsea with my sincerest compliments. Incidentally—tell him that I can't send a copy of "Cool Air" (the tale about dear old 14th St.) until I get back one of the two copies now out. Henneberger has one,[2] & *Ghost Stories* the other—though the last named will undoubtedly be back soon.[3] This magazine has just rejected "In the Vault." Oh, yes—one thing more. We were talking about the *hate poems* in that week-end book, & Georgius said he'd never seen my touching little ballad to Medusa—dear Mrs. Haughton of Woodbee fame.[4] Accordingly I enclose a copy for him—which he can keep if he wants it, since I have plenty of duplicates.
   Have naturally been swamped with accumulated correspondence & work, but hope to get in some local antiquarian trips before long. Trust you're planning plenty of relaxation—try to join some of Mortonius' Paterson hikes—I think you'd enjoy 'em. Hope the radio is still working well—& that they're giving you some sort of music better than op'rys which just go "da-da-dee-da", with words you can't understand!!!
   Well—such is which. Behave yourself!
      Yr obt Servt
         Theobaldus

Notes

1. "G D" (i.e., "God damn") is George Kirk. It is not known what Kirk's "week-end book" is, nor what poem HPL wrote for it, nor whether the book or the poem was ever published.
2. J. C. Henneberger (1890–1969), former owner of *WT*, was attempting to interest book publishers in a collection of HPL's stories (see *SL* 2.53).
3. *Ghost Stories* rejected the tale, as *WT* had earlier; it appeared in *Tales of Magic and Mystery* (March 1928).
4. "Medusa: A Portrait" was about Ida C. Haughton, editor of the *Woodbee*. See MWM 28n3.

[8]   [ALS]

Woden's-Day
[17 September 1930]

Aonian Endymion:—¹
        Damn your postman! Shall Novanglian thrift capitulate to the standardized demands of metropolitan bureaucracy? What complaint has the rascal to make if addresses be clear & legible? Does he want headline-type the size of a barn-door? Why, sir, I make the addresses on all my cards just as plain & as large as the printed address-slips stuck on newspapers & magazines . . . . . but this curst impertinent dog has to cavil because my particular specimens don't come off a printing-press! Pox on such presumption! 'Zounds, Sir, I shall write to the papers about it! Upstart publick servants—we'll see, by God, Sir, we'll see! However, if it comes to a question of your own visual comfort, that's another matter. Why, Sir, I'll have the next one embossed in Braille!

And now permit me to felicitate you upon the wisest move you have made since your rash step of 1927! Back to the old stand—where Grandpa advised you to stay in the first place! Make it permanent this time, Sir! The Dauber & Pine firm is clearly an institution of great and increasing importance, & they are now sensible of how great an asset they have in your presence as expert & cataloguer. Grow up with them—& you will find that for an aesthete, such a salaried post offers a future much more tolerable than could any independent commercial venture. I envy you—& sincerely wish I had the bibliophilic erudition to land one of those similar posts whose numerousness you remark . . . . especially if any of them permitted a Providence locale. I don't know just what extent of specialisation they demand—one could easily learn the stock terms & characteristick fashions of cataloguing, but no doubt these positions require a genuine knowledge of books & bibliophily from the merchant's & collector's standpoint.

I trust you are duly refresh'd & reinvigorated by your Antaeus-like contact with Cleveland soil. If you have any vocational openings in the ensuing weeks, don't forget that eastward routes are equally open to traffick! Providence in the autumn is a mystick & glamorous place—& side trips to ancient Newport & the Boston region are perennially pleasing supplements.

Quebec . . . . (o gawd, give me a vocabulary!) Que . . . . Que . . . . yes, I must see Old England before I totter irrevocably into the sunset. But how could I ever come back, once I saw ancient London, & the rural lanes of Kent, & the thatched-roof'd villages of Lincolnshire, & the sombre stretches of Dartmoor leading down to those Devonian shores whence full half my ancestral lines sprang! I would have to take along some Providence views & crank up a case of homesickness to break away from Britannia once I sat foot upon the beloved, never-beheld sod—

> This royal throne of kings, this sceptred isle,
> This earth of majesty, this seat of Mars,
> This other Eden, demi-paradise . . . .
> This precious stone set in the silver sea . . . .
> This blefsed plot, this Earth, this realm, this ENGLAND![2]

Glad to hear that RK's[3] return to the fold is proving stable. Tell him to make another Providence trip, & I'll try to hook up some crumb-cake to match the easily obtainable coffee of the region! And little ol' Arturo![4] What a damn shame you missed him! I'd like to see the old boy myself, & certainly hope he'll look me up if his itinerant outfit traverses this part of the world. Hope his prosperity is permanent—he deserves some ease and freedom from anxiety after the long gruelling years of the past. But what a beastly shame his Old Cap Colliers[5] were not waiting for him!

Heard from the Alfredus-child last week. He's back in Chicago from his summer at the old Appleton homestead, & has secured a better & more expensive flat. The new address (note for reference) is 1406½ Elmwood Ave., Evanston, Ill. Next summer he hopes to go to Europe, spending much time at Antibes (the ancient Antipolis) on the Riviera. He reports the death of the old-time Wisconsin amateur Alfred L. Hutchinson of Weyauwega. Do you recall this somewhat crude and eccentric old fellow? Speaking of amateurs—Paul J. Campbell is alas a Chicagoan now. Still in the oil-drilling business, & wants me to make a fortune by putting 200 bucks into some new project. What a pity I haven't the spare cash. I would so enjoy sudden affluence!

And so it goes. Once again, congratulations on the return to Smear 'em & Weep![6] And get around to these parts when you can. Yes for politer postmen & larger postcards,
    Theobaldus Senex

Notes

1. Endymion was variously a handsome Aeolian shepherd, hunter, or king said to rule and live at Olympia in Elis. Also the the "brain-sick shepherd-prince" of Mt. Latmos, and subject of Keats's *Endymion* (1818).
2. Shakespeare, *Richard II* 2.1.46–50.
3. I.e., Rheinhart Kleiner.
4. I.e., Arthur Leeds.
5. *Old Cap. Collier Library,* a dime novel series published from 9 April 1883 to 9 September 1899.
6. I.e., Dauber & Pine, the bookseller where SL worked. HPL used the parodic name in "The Battle That Ended the Century" (1934). SL is referred to there as "Samuelus Philanthropus, Esq."

[9]   [ANS, not seen][1]

[Postmarked Boston, Mass.,
2 January 1932]

[Signed: HPL and W. Paul Cook.]

Notes

1. *Front*: [Head of a Greek athlete, The Fogg Art Museum, Harvard University.]

[10]   [TLS]   [*Nonconformst*][1]

The Antient Hillside Citadel
Feby. 12, 1936.

Hail, Endymion!
    Yuggoth, what a turmoil I fell into upon my return to these plantations! Found every imaginable kind of business in the mails—including the most intricate kind of constitutional junk to straighten out as N.A.P.A. exec judge[2]—and finally got laid up with a sort of damn grippe attack of the sort I had just a decade ago when I was helping out the noble house of Dauber and Pine with superscriptory activities. Couldn't eat anything but ice cream, and couldn't sit up more than an hour or so continuously. Less than a week saw me emerge from that, but my energies are still very limited—my eyes tending to set up vortex-like effects after much continuous application. So my correspondence has all gone to hell, and I've had to pass up on the job of writing a critical report for the March N.A.[3]
    However, I'm gradually trying to whip up my programme into shape, hence am getting around to various matters one by one. It now occurs to me that I haven't yet sent you that "rare first edition" of Ulthar which I shew'd you up at Sonny's—hence am herewith repairing the deficiency .... my eight dupli-

cates having arriv'd some time ago. If it doesn't fit into your private collection, you might catalogue it at 9000 bucks or so as an early Dragon-Fly Press item.[4]

Also, I'm taking you up on that promise to rejoin N.A.P.A., and am enclosing a properly corrected application blank for your use. Now do your duty! Ernie Edkins has rejoined on my blank . . . . Grandpa fishes 'em up out of the very best tombs in the cemetery! When you see Edkins' new paper—*Causerie*—you'll think the dear old 1880's are back for sure! I'm likewise sending sample papers and blank, as promised last month, to your bright young poetic colleague Pryor[5]—hope he'll join and give a new vitality to the languishing herbage on Parnassus' slopes.

Meanwhile I trust the Bodley prospers,[6] and that you're duly planning your next raid on New England. In the Feb. Astounding you'll find the first instalment of my Mts. of Madness—with illustrations not half bad. Some misprints (like palaeocene for palaeogean), but you can get a fair idea of what I'm trying to say. Also a tale by the Child in the same issue.[7] A sort of hillbilly printer down in Everett, Pa., is planning to publish my "Shadow Over Innsmouth" as a book, and has sent the first batch of proofs for revision. Hope it make better progress than the Shunned House![8]

Speaking of books—I've sent a circular of the new Herm to every separate correspondent to whom I've written since getting my supply, and believe this flood (75 or more before I'm through) ought to net you a few orders, several state positively that they are purchasing copies—Ernie Edkins, young Morse, and others I can't recall at the moment. Hope the edition goes over big and proves a factor in encouraging you to start a new set of lyrics.

N.Y. visit ended up pleasantly.[9] Went to the planetarium[10] again Sunday with Sonny and Wandrei, and the evening we got together with Arturo—seeing a cinema show. Monday Little Belknap and I went to Paterson to beard James Ferdinand in his lair, and had a very animated evening—arguing and tanking up on food and ice cream. That midnight I hopped the coach for antient Providentium and ran into a snowstorm—held up an hour at dawn in the exquisite colonial village of Hampton, Conn.—with houses dating back to 1712 on every hand, and an ethereal white Georgian steeple peeping over the freshly white-deck'd boughs. The delay was for the sanding of a long, sinuous hill—and I was sorry when we got in motion again. Since getting home, the arctick visitation has descended upon me—and I haven't been out of the damn house since Jan. 13. But Mr. Perkins, the onyx Bast-effigy,[11] comes often to see the old Gentleman!

                    Yr obt Servt
                        H P L

[*Marginal note:*] I wrote Dana Rice[12] promptly, cancelling your order.

Notes

1. Text from *Nonconformist* 1, No. 3 (April 2009): 8–9.
2. Cf. "Report of the Executive Judges," *National Amateur* 58, No. 4 (June 1936): 2–3 (with Vincent B. Haggerty and Jennie K. Plaisier); rpt. *CE* 1.396–98.
3. I.e., *National Amateur* (March 1936).
4. This special copy of *The Cats of Ulthar* (one of only two), bound on Red Lion text paper and inscribed "To Samuel E. Loveman, Eſq., / A 'Rare Firſt Edition' with yᵉ / Perpetrator's Compliments— / H. P. Lovecraft / —MDCCCCXXXVI," was offered by L. W. Currey for $27,500.
5. Probably Anthony Pryor, a poet and amateur journalist.
6. SL was proprietor of Bodley Book Shop in New York City.
7. FBL, "Cones" (*Astounding Stories*, February 1936).
8. W. Paul Cook had printed HPL's "The Shunned House" as a booklet in 1928, but except for only a few copies (bound by R. H. Barlow in 1935), the edition was not bound and distributed. Arkham House ultimately bound and sold the book in 1961. HPL claimed it had no errors, unlike *The Shadow over Innsmouth*, published by William L. Crawford's Visionary Publishing Co. HPL inscribed his presentation copy of *Innsmouth* to SL thus: "To Samˡ. E: Loveman, Eſq., with yᵉ ſincere Eſteem & unaffected Compliments of H. P. Lovecraft—who, tho' reſponſible for yᵉ bad Writing, can ſcarce be held accountable for yᵉ wretched Printing & Binding. Jany. 1937." There also exists a TMS of *Fungi from Yuggoth* with HPL's inscription: "To Samˡ E. Loveman and Patrick McGrath, Eſqs. with the Compliments & Appreciation of the author—H. P. Lovecraft May 22, 1930."
9. HPL had visited New York from 29 December 1935 to 7 January 1936.
10. The Hayden Planetarium in New York.
11. John Perkins, a black cat so named by HPL, and brother of Sam Perkins eulogized in HPL's poem of 1934. John himself would perish early the following June.
12. See HPL to R. H. Barlow (21 October 1935): "One of these—the Dana Rice Galleries, run by a man whose sisters my aunt knows—contained such alluring bargains that Loveman may revisit it within a month" (*O Fortunate Floridian* 302).

Vincent Starrett

Letters to Vincent Starrett

[1]   [ALS]
10 Barnes St.,
Providence, R.I.,
April 11, 1927

My dear Mr. Starrett:—

I feel very highly complimented by your request to see some of my tales, for work of yours which I have read gives me a very respectful opinion of your judgment in such matters. I only hope that Mr. Loveman, with that friendly enthusiasm so characteristic of his generous & spontaneous nature, has not given you such a notion of my products that the actual goods will prove an anticlimax & disillusion.

I am sending under separate cover a dozen of these horrific articles, whose dates are scattered somewhat evenly over the last ten years. If the consignment be too ample, I might suggest that the perusal of any one of the narratives will give a fair idea of the tone of them all—so that there need be no wholesale wading through repellent dulness in quest of a hidden gem. If, on the other hand, you find the things really worth reading, you may like to have an array in which some variety of theme & setting, if not of style & mood, can be found. In reality I suppose the pieces are sadly uneven, though I am not able to give a truly unbiased view as to just which ones are conspicuously worse than the rest.

I regret very much to say that I have absolutely no remaining copy of "The Shunned House"—either rough draught or typed version. Mr. Loveman—under the amiable delusion that the reliquiae of nonentities possess value—annexed my original MS. & best typed copy three years ago, & has them stowed away inaccessibly in Cleveland; whilst the only other copy—a tattered carbon—is held by a gentleman in Athol, Mass. who intends to print it as a thin brochure. When, however, that brochure appears, I shall be delighted to send you a copy for permanent retention—provided you are not by that time thoroughly bored by the amateurish crudity of my effusions.

I certainly agree that the lack of a market for spectral material above the penny-dreadful grade is a very unfortunate circumstance; yet fear it is an irremediable one, since the actual number of persons to whom such things appeal is apparently small indeed. I have had a fair assortment of stories published in the crowd-cultivating *Weird Tales,* but believe this market is gradually closing to me on account of the editor's deference to a clientele demanding simple, understandable ghostliness with plenty of 'human interest' & a brisk, concrete, cheerful, & non-atmospheric style.[1] I have never had a volume published, & am not at all sure that the merit of my nightmares & fantasies warrants one. When I compare my results with Dunsany, De la Mare, Machen, Bierce, Blackwood, (at his best, as in "The Willows") M. R. James, or any other recognised master of the macabre, I lose at once whatever tendency toward egotism or complacency I might otherwise acquire.

Thanking you again for the flattering interest implied in your request, & assuring you that there need be no haste in reading the accompanying yarns, I am
Most cordially & appreciatively yours,
H. P. Lovecraft

Notes

1. At the time, HPL had had about nineteen stories, three poems, and six other stories revised for clients published in *WT*. HPL had greater success placing stories in *WT* under the editorship of Edwin Baird (1923–24) than under that of Farnsworth Wright (1924–40).

[2]   [ALS]

10 Barnes St.,
Providence, R.I.,
June 24, 1927

Dear Mr. Starrett:—

No haste at all is needed in looking over the tales—& no need of careful reading if they don't look promising! Glad those you've read have repaid the effort. Was pleased to learn the other day that *Amazing Stories* (a flashy affair whose only merit lies in its voluminous standard *reprints*) has accepted a rather longish short story of mine called "The Colour out of Space". It will probably appear soon.

I have carefully recorded the new address. You have my deepest condolences on the moving process—which I have endured four times in my prosaic career.

Hoping you won't find the residue of the stories boresome, I am
Your most obt
H. P. Lovecraft

[3]   [ALS]

10 Barnes St.,
Providence, R.I.,
August 23, 1927

Dear Mr. Starrett:—

I am tardy in acknowledging the safe receipt of the returned tales, but like you have been engulfed in a bewildering vortex of hard labour—including the hurried editing of as volume of posthumous poems by a man who didn't leave enough first-rate material to make a real volume![1] I am penning these lines whilst on a visit to the man who is going to publish my "Shunned House" some day—& am in the midst of a most delightful country of hills & vales & vistas, whose influence is tremendously pleasant if not literally inspiring.

I am indeed glad that you found some enjoyment—as well as some merit—in my macabre efforts, & especially that you share my own predilection for "Arthur Jermyn" & "The Cats of Ulthar". It is always comforting to have one's own undisciplined likes upheld by a recognised authority. I will surely let you have "The Shunned House" when it appears—though I must candidly warn you that its quality is not by any means as distinctive as Mr. Loveman's generous enthusiasm may have caused you to believe.

I have never tried my luck with the British market, but believe I will later take advantage of your much-appreciated suggestion. No—I have patronised no agents in England, although I am told that *Weird Tales*'s London representative systematically endeavours to re-market all the contents of that dubious congeries of mediocrity on the other side. As a result of this arrangement, they tell me that one of my poorest printed effusions—"The Horror at Red Hook"—is about to be reprinted in the latest number of the Selwyn & Blount "Not At Night" anthology—an institution which has already used two stories by Frank Belknap Long.[2] I have recently compiled a sketchy article on the history of weird literature, which Mr. Cook is to use in his coming non-professional magazine, *The Recluse*, & of which I shall see that you receive a copy.[3] It may not be of any value or much interest, but it at least gave me a proper excuse to read many things I ought to have read, but had theretofore neglected. Incidentally—my latest tale appears in the current issue of *Amazing Stories*;[4] it being the first piece I have ever placed outside *Weird Tales*.

Again expressing my flattered pleasure that you found my lucubrations worth perusing, I remain
    Most cordially & sincerely yrs—
    H. P. Lovecraft

Notes

1. John Ravenor Bullen, *White Fire*.
2. Christine Campbell Thomson, ed., *You'll Need a Night Light*. FBL's "Death-Waters" appeared in *Not at Night* (1925), "The Sea-Thing" in *More Not at Night* (1926).
3. "Supernatural Horror in Literature."
4. "The Colour out of Space"

[4]   [ALS]

                                  10 Barnes St.,
                                  Providence, R.I.,
                                      Decr. 6, 1927

My dear Mr. Starrett:—

        I am glad that you found my article in *The Recluse* not devoid of interest. Recalling the interest you had expressed in the subject of fantastic fiction, I asked Mr. Cook to include your name in his mailing list some time ago. The rest of the contents, of perhaps superior interest creatively & scholastically, makes the magazine a rather unusual thing for a purely non-professional enterprise. I am persuading ye Editor to keep all of Mr. Coates's Vermont material in type for a future book, since it covers such little known & unexploited territory in the annals of minor American letters.[1]

        I fear, however, that the columns of my own contribution have long since been dissociated to their primal "pi"; for Cook is fond of clean sweeps & has but little storage space in his limited small-town plant. Had he suspected any ampler demand, he would undoubtedly have been glad to meet it—but one never divines the right thing in advance! As it is, I imagine that he might be able to furnish a few duplicate *Recluses* on request—indeed, I could supply two or three myself if there were any persons with an especial interest in the weird who would be likely to enjoy my rambling observations. I'll ask Cook how matters stand at his typographical headquarters. Yes—I noted with regret the Housman misprint,[2] which came in an eleventh-hour appendix sent in too late for proofreading. In such copies as I have personally distributed, I have made a pen-&-ink correction.

        The article itself attempted only an exceedingly cursory touching of high spots—being based on a criminally desultory reading programme & containing some woefully regrettable omissions—& inclusions. It is really meant to be only a general introduction to a series of articles by various hands, in the course of which nearly all aspects of weird literature & near-literature will be mentioned in one way or another. The next in the series[3] will be a very informal paper on *popular* fantastic tales (of the *All-Story, Argosy,* or *Weird Tales* grade) by H. Warner Munn, who has had the patience to search out endless & arid reams of that sort of thing; & subsequently the less-known corners of the more standard field will be explored & recorded by Donald Wandrei—a remarkable youth of nineteen, himself gifted with much bizarre genius, now a senior at the Univ. of Minnesota. The concluding item will be an encyclopaedic bibliography of all sorts of weird writing, good & bad, on which this same Wandrei has been working since infancy, & which he expects to carry to a phenomenal degree of completeness. A certain taint of amateurishness & heterogeneity will naturally hover over the whole enterprise, yet when it is all done & assembled it will certainly be fairly unique—& perhaps even worthy of book form if there were enough devotees of the subject to warrant its publication. So far there is no general account of weird literature which I know of. The early Gothic novel has been adequately treated by Railo, Birkhead, & Killen, but the later fortunes of fictional fantasy remain without a chronicler unless the treatise of Dorothy Scarborough (which I haven't seen)[4] is better than it is reported to be by those who have seen it.

I am exceedingly grateful for the additional weird material which you mention—in fact, I always solicit such suggestions from everyone, being acutely conscious of the narrow & capricious one-sidedness of my own fictional explorations. I have heard of the Jacobs weird tales aside from "The Monkey's Paw", but have never been able to place my hands on them. Indeed, I only found the tale in question in a queer sort of anthology of parallel English & Italian texts in the N. Y. Public Library, evidently designed for the aesthetic edification & linguistic improvement of the Mediterranean stranger in our midst.[5] A collected volume of Jacobean horror would meet with no more appreciative reader than I! H. G. Wells is a ticklish question on my literary scales. I *can't* derive a really *supernatural* thrill from matter which keeps my *mental* wheels turning so briskly; & yet when I think of some of his things *in retrospect,* supplying my own filter of imaginative colour, I am reduced to doubt again. W. C. Morrow fell flat with me, though I've seen only one volume of his tales. (The Ape, the Idiot, &c.)[6] All through his work I could feel nothing but ingenious mechanics, and the fatally artificial cleverness of the 1900 era—though of course my opinion represents no real critical authority whatsoever. The Norris, Dawson, & Quiller-Couch[7] material will be new to me when I find it—as I shall certainly try to do. I wish that I might have an opportunity of seeing your own work in macabre vein,[8] concerning which a survey of your published critical appreciations leads me to entertain high expectations. If you ever have a MS. or old magazine copy of some typical tale in loanable form I would be infinitely grateful for a glimpse of it—prompt & safe return being of course solemnly guaranteed.

I read neither Stevenson's "Body Snatcher" nor Crawford's "Upper Berth"[9] till ludicrously late in life, but received a very profound & authentic "kick" from both. "The Upper Berth," in particular, belongs in the very highest circle of weird triumphs. Poe I knew from incredibly early times—from my tenth year, at the latest—& I believe he has affected me more than any other writer. "Amontillado" moved me strongly, but not so much perhaps as those in which the *implications* were more deliciously vague & terrifyingly monstrous. "Usher", "Metzengerstein", "Arthur Gordon Pym", "MS. Found in A Bottle", some of the *poems,* were the things which "got" me & opened up for my impressionable mind the most awesomely adventurous vistas it has ever enjoyed. Aside from Poe, I think Algernon Blackwood touches me most closely—& this in spite of the oceans of unrelieved puerility which he so frequently pours forth. I am dogmatic enough to call "The Willows" the finest weird story I have ever read, & I find in the "Incredible Adventure" & "John

Silence" material a serious & sympathetic understanding of the human illusion-weaving process which makes Blackwood rate far higher as a creative artist than many another craftsman of mountainously superior word-mastery & general technical ability.

I have just read "The Weird O' It", by Clive Pemberton, (very average) & am about to delve into a reputedly weird writer now wholly unknown to me—Vernon Knowles.[10] Here's wishing myself a pleasant session! ¶ Appreciating very keenly your kind opinion of my article, & thanking you again for the suggestions, I remain

        Most sincerely yrs—
            H. P. Lovecraft

Notes

1. Walter J. Coates had a lengthy article, "Early Vermont Minstrelsy," in *Recluse* No. 1 (1927): 3–14, prefaced by a "Study List: Vermont Poets and Poetry" (1–2).
2. In the *Recluse* appearance of the essay the first name of Clemence Housman, author of "The Werewolf," was rendered as "Clarence" (49).
3. No other issue of the *Recluse* was published.
4. HPL did not read this book until late March 1932, when it was lent to him by J. Vernon Shea (see *Letters to J. Vernon Shea* 95).
5. Unidentified.
6. HPL first read Morrow's collection in the fall of 1925 at the suggestion of SL (HPL to Lillian D. Clark, 27 September 1925; *Letters to Family and Family Friends*, 415). Entry 152 in HPL's *Commonplace Book* ends with the late appended note: "Avoid copying tale by W. C. Morrow," the tale in question being "The Monster Maker."
7. Possibly Mary Harriott Norris (1848–1919), *The Veil: A Fantasy* (1907), a novel about reincarnation, but more likely Frank Norris (1870–1902), author of *Vandover and the Brute* (1914), which includes a character who hallucinates that he turns into a wolflike monster, and *A Deal in Wheat and Other Stories of the New and Old West* (1903), which has some weird tales; Emma Frances Dawson (1851–1926), *An Itinerant House and Other Stories* (1897); Sir Arthur Quiller-Couch (1863–1944). The work referred to here is unknown, but HPL's library contained *Noughts and Crosses: Stories, Studies, and Sketches* (London: Cassell, 1893; *LL* 784); *Old Fires and Profitable Ghosts: A Book of Stories* (New York: Charles Scribner's Sons, 1900; *LL* 785); and *Wandering Heath: Stories, Studies, and Sketches* (New York: Charles Scribner's Sons, 1896; *LL* 786), each of which contains a few weird tales.
8. Some of Starrett's macabre fiction was collected in *The Quick and the Dead* (1965).
9. Robert Louis Stevenson (1850–1894), "The Body Snatcher" (see *SHL* 48); F. Marion Crawford (1854–1909), "The Upper Berth" (see *SHL* 27, 69).
10. Vernon Knowles, *Here and Otherwhere* (1926) and *The Street of Queer Houses and Other Stories* (1924). HPL had borrowed both books from W. Paul Cook.

[5] [ALS]
                                    10 Barnes St.,
                                    Providence, R.I.,
                                    Jany. 10, 1928

Dear Mr. Starrett:—
            I am glad to be able to furnish at least a slight idea of who John Martin was—a thing I could not have done prior to 1922, when our mutual friend Mr. Loveman took very kindly pains to introduce him to me. Under Lovemanic guidance I looked up engravings of his work in the N.Y. Public Library, & was enthralled by the darkly thunderous, apocalyptically majestic, & cataclysmically unearthly power of one who, to me, seemed to hold the essence of cosmic mystery; notwithstanding the blandly low estimate placed upon his work by the tamely & urbanely correct artists & critics of his own period. The library engravings—of relatively small size & not from his own pencil—really failed to do him full justice, impressive though they were; & I was very much gratified by a chance, three years later, to see some really good & original plates of the best subjects in the stock of a bookselling acquaintance. I have mentioned him several times in stories,[1] for he is almost a stock fixture in my fantastic imagination, though I have never engaged in any real research concerning him. The little I know of him comes from the sketch of him in my old (9th Edition) Encyclopaedia Britannica[2]—which is indeed worth looking up in the absence of fuller sources.
    John Martin (1789–1854) was of humble Northumberland origin, & was apprenticed by his father to a coachmaker—to learn heraldic painting—in view of his boyish artistic talent. Later he was placed under an Italian artist named Bonifacio Musso, & with him went to London in 1806. He studied, especially, perspective & architecture, which were to prove of significant importance to him later on. He seems to have been a person of Calvinistic intensity, like many rural yeomen; & was certainly influenced enormously by the spirit of Hebraic grandioseness in the Old Testament. He was, in a sense, a Milton among painters. I have somewhere heard that he was an opium-eater, though I am always sceptical of a stock rumour so frequently raised by the vulgar against an artist of fantastic attainments. In 1812 he appeared as a painter, his subject being "Sadak in Search of the Waters of Oblivion". The picture was hung in the Royal Academy & sold for 50 guineas. It was (as I can judge from having seen an engraving of it) very fairly typical of what he was to paint & draw all the rest of his life—Biblical & other archaic conceptions in a spirit of awful & tenebrous sublimity; with wild & rugged scenery, objects of solemn & decaying grandeur, & strange nocturnal lighting-effects predominating in nearly every case. Basically Martin was not at all inclined to the fantastic or grotesque. He had none of the subjective primitiveness & spiritual symbolism of Blake, or of the weird decorative grotesquerie of the living artist Sime. It is more fitting to compare him with Gustave Doré, since

his scenes were always conceived in the external spirit of classic naturalism; the element of terror, mystery, or sublimity being infused by a process much subtler than mere distortion. His greatest weakness was the rendering of the human figure, but this was no major defect because with him figures were only slight & subsidiary parts of great landscape & architectural conceptions. Night; great desolate pillared halls; unholy abysses & blasphemous torrents; terraced titan cities in far, half-celestial backgrounds whereon shines the light of no familiar sky of men's knowing; shrieking mortal hordes borne doomward over vast wastes & adown cyclopean gulfs where Phlegethon & Acheron flow; these are the dominant impressions one [i.e., myself, at least!] carries away from the study of a set of Martin engravings. Of the paintings as paintings, of course, I can say nothing—except to quote the encyclopaedist's smug Victorian judgment—"his colouring is hot & unpleasant." As a summary, I would say that Martin's characteristic qualities were the use of vast space-suggestions, colossal effects of ancient architecture, & a daemon-dowered mastery of subtle & unearthly lighting effects amidst an all-engulfing gloom—the ravenous gloom of the outer void, whose *fluctus decumanus* beats so perilously on the frail dykes of our little world of light. The most typical Martin effect is that of a distant Babylon-like city or vision of a city bathed in some terrible supernal light—a form of aesthetic appeal so especially potent to my individual imagination that I may be inclined to give the artist too high a proportionate rating. To me, assuredly, he is one of the few preëminent giants of pictorial fantasy. In addition, I find in him great elements of pure landscape beauty; some of his milder conceptions giving me sensations not remote from those supplied by Constable or Claude Lorrain. My ignorance of art & its principles, however, makes my judgment of little value in this particular. Martin's real fame must rest on his febrile & oneiroscopic glimpses of other worlds—or atmospheric emanations of other worlds. In his day he was an idol of the Radcliffe-revering & Lewis-loving herd, but a doubtful question to the sedate & well-bred academicians. Today his favour amongst a microscopic minority of fantaisistes, & his absolute disappearance from the general view, (for he has in truth found what his Sadak sought!) constitutes a reversal of the most ironic sort. After his first picture came "The Expulsion from Paradise", (1813) Paradise, (1813) [*sic*] Clytie, (1814) & Joshua (1815). In 1821 (I cull dates from the Britannica) appeared the very famous "Belshazzar's Feast", which precipitated acute controversy. This took a £200 prize at the British Institution, "Joshua" having taken one of £100. In 1822 came "The Destruction of Herculaneum", in 1824 "The Creation", & thereafter a vast number of paintings well-known in their day, of which "The Fall of Nineveh" (1828) & "The Eve of the Deluge" (1841) perhaps excited the greatest notice. They were widely circulated as engravings, some of which were wrought by Martin's own hand. In 1832–33 Martin illustrated Milton[3]—much better than did Doré later on, in my opinion—& somewhat later he collaborated with the celebrated Westall in producing a set of Bible illustrations.[4] During the last four years of his life he completed some large & highly impressive canvasses—"The Last Judgment," "The Day of Wrath," & "The Plains of Heaven." He was finally seized with paralysis whilst at work, & died on the Isle of Man on Feby. 17, 1854, at the age of sixty-four. I do not know where, apart from the N.Y. Public Library, one might find an easily accessible set of Martin engravings; though the art departments of other libraries would be logical foci of inquiry. Chicago, if anywhere, ought to have some specimens; & I would certainly advise your conducting a search there. Loveman once owned some fine Martin engravings, but I do not think he has them now. They would, indeed, be packed away in Cleveland if he had. It is my impression that he gave them to a bookselling friend, & that the ones I saw were these selfsame copies. This friend has probably sold them long ago, but you might at least ask him—his name & habitat being George W. Kirk, Chelsea Book Shop, 58 West 8th St., New York, N.Y. It is certainly atrocious that Martin's work is nowhere popularly accessible, but that is the fate of many another strange & beautiful creation. If ever a selection of plates were made up for sale at a rational price, I would be among the first to indulge. As to published references—like you I have come across the name elusively, yet like you I have never found any connected comment, critique, or biography. There is much work for a gifted & energetic archaeologist here—& I wish indeed that you might ultimately add this splendid specimen to your already notable catalogue of Caesarean exhumations![5]

It remains only to add—as postscriptive afterthoughts—

(a) That Martin had an odd streak of civic-mindedness running parallel with his art interests, so that he published many plans & pamphlets dealing with the improvement of London through water, sewer, dock, & railway facilities, and

(b) That bad copies or adaptations of some of his work may now & then be found in 19th century family Bibles—that which my own parents procured when setting up their own household in '89 having a clumsily "elegant" imitative engraving of "Belshazzar's Feast", which I recognised upon seeing a proper plate of the subject for the first time.

And now permit me to thank you for the poem which you so kindly enclosed, & which impresses me as marvellously poignant & authentic in its fantastic visual value & its cumulative & climactic horror-appeal. It has the music of true poetry, & at the same time the stealthy atmospheric convincingness of first-rate Gothic horror; a combination not often found in such felicitous completeness. I must look up your volume "Ebony Flame"[6]—& I am glad of such an interesting excuse to dispel a little more of my criminally abysmal ignorance of contemporary letters. With my characteristic lack of energy & initiative, I never read anything till supplied with some such external impulsion! Incidentally, this verse comes very opportunely, considering the fact that it is scarce two weeks since I read, *for the first time*, that delightfully sombre adaptation of Ambrose Bierce's from the German—"The Monk & the Hangman's Daughter." I had been told it was not weird—that being my reason for postponing its reading so long after my discovery of Bierce (which I owe to Loveman, by the way, as completely as I owe my discovery of Martin!) in 1919—but in truth it has a pervasive air of the imminence of spectral horrors, which is none the less keen because the supernatural does not actually appear. I shall not soon forget the general picture afforded of the wild Bavarian mountains, the sombre, ancient life of the salt mines, & the whispered, fearsome lore of the crag-fringed tarns & black hanging woods.

In conclusion, I am exceedingly glad that chance has enabled me to supply some rudimentary Martin data; & hope very much that you will, at your later leisure, not only succeed in seeing some of the engravings in question, but feel moved to do something toward spreading the fame of one who so well deserves to be known.

Thanking you again for the poem—whose melody & imagery continue to haunt me as I write, I remain

Most cordially & sincerely yours,
H. P. Lovecraft

Notes

1. There is no reference to John Martin in HPL stories, although other weird artists—Goya, Sime, Doré, Angarola, Beardsley—are mentioned.

2. The citation in the *Encyclopaedia Britannica* reads as follows:

MARTIN, John (1789–1854), a popular English painter, was born at Haydon Bridge, near Hexham, on the 19th of July, 1789. On account of his early interest in art he was apprenticed by his father to a coachbuilder to learn heraldic painting, but owing to a quarrel the indentures were cancelled, and he was placed under Bonifacio Musso, an Italian artist, father of the well-known enamel painter Charles Musso. With his master Martin removed to London in 1806, where he married at the age of nineteen, and led a struggling life, supporting himself by giving drawing lessons, and by painting in water colors, and on china and glass. His leisure was occupied in the study of perspective and architecture. His first picture, Sadak in Search of the Waters of Oblivion, was executed in a month. It was exhibited in the Royal Academy of 1812, and sold for fifty guineas. It was followed by the Expulsion (1813), Paradise (1813), Clytie (1814), and Joshua (1815). In 1821 appeared the famous Belshazzar's Feast, which excited much favorable and hostile comment, and was awarded a prize of £200 at the British Institution, where the Joshua had previously carried off a premium of £100. Then came the Destruction of Herculaneum (1822), the Creation (1824), the Eve of the Deluge (1841), and a long series of other Biblical and imaginative subjects, many of which are widely known through engravings. In 1832–33 Martin received £2000 for drawing and engraving a fine series of designs to Milton, and along with Westall he produced a set of Bible illustrations. He was also much occupied with schemes for the improvement of London, and published various pamphlets and plans dealing with the metropolitan water supply, sewage, dock, and railway systems. During the last four years of his life he was engaged upon large subjects of the Judgment, the Day of Wrath, and the Plains of Heaven. He was attacked with paralysis while painting, and died in the Isle of Man on the 17th of February, 1854.

The bold originality of Martin's productions startled and attracted the public, but they are without the qualities of solid execution and truth to nature upon which a lasting fame in the arts must be built. His figures are badly drawn, his coloring is hot and unpleasant. To most of his professional brethren his works seemed theatrical and tricky; and the best lay critics of his time, like Charles Lamb, were disposed to deny that they evinced true imaginative power. His popularity may be said to have culminated in 1828, the year of his Fall of Nineveh; since then it has been gradually declining.

3. *The Paradise Lost of Milton,* with illustrations by John Martin (London: Septimius Prowett, 1826). The illustrations appeared separately as *Illustrations to Milton's Paradise Lost* (London: Septimius Prowett, 1825–27).

4. *Illustrations of the Bible* (London: C. Tilt, 1838).

5. HPL refers to Starrett's *Buried Caesars: Essays in Literary Appreciation* (1923), containing essays on Machen, Bierce, W. C. Morrow, and other obscure or forgotten writers.

6. *Ebony Flame* is a collection of poems. The poem Starrett sent HPL apparently was "The Changeling," contained in *Ebony Flame.* Starrett's *Fifteen More Poems* appeared in 1927.

Appendix

Maurice W. Moe

Why I Am Not a Freethinker

Those who received the *Villa De Laura Times* recently were treated to a recital of the reasons why one of our best known amateurs is a freethinker. Mr. Morton wields such a facile pen and puts his arguments with such for that one trembles for fear that he may inject a astray bacillus of doubt into the mind of some reader. True, he says that "the reader who would be convinced by a single article would not be worth convincing." But he has taken occasional flings at the Christian religion for some years past, and it is time to say something on the other side.

Lincoln always began a case in court by admitting everything that he could, sometimes going so far that he seemed to be giving away his case at the start. In arguing with a critic of Christianity, it is likewise necessary to admit the truth of his accusations. I have no doubt that in doing so I shall go so far as to convince some of my orthodox friends that I have given away my case at home. But Orthodoxy gains nothing by assuming itself to be infallible. If we ever wish to meet and cope on even terms with the destructive criticism of today, we must first clear away some of the debris that is hampering the progress of the Church.

Here are a few of the counts in Mr. Morton's indictment that may be admitted at once:

"The bible is out of harmony with many historic and scientific facts."

"It is full of noble thought, but is evidently the work of many different writers each of whom mingled his lofty spiritual aspirations with the limited knowledge of his time."

"Its story of the creation is obviously a childish myth, wholly contradicted by the scientific knowledge of the present day."

"The Deluge and Tower of Babel stories are no less convincingly overthrown."

I admit these counts, altho I should like to stop to qualify them if I had the space. But even so, what have we lost? Not a single element that is essential to the Christian faith.

But what Mr. Morton continues: "It is too full of demonstrable error to be taken as the inspired word of an omniscient being, and if less than that, it has no more authority than any other book," we come to blows. It is apparent that he would hold us to the old, worn-out conception of inspiration as a sort of spiritual fountain pen which God occasionally hands down to a mortal to write out a record of eternal truth. The modern idea of inspiration, however, is something far different from this. To understand it we must first understand what is meant by revelation.

No one but a naïve thinker of the old orthodox school any longer believes that God revealed himself in bodily form to the Israelites. The day of wonders is past, simply for the reason that we are able to explain wonderful things without resorting to the supernatural.

But for all that, we still believe that God actually revealed Himself. To understand what this revelation was, we must look at the Bible as a *record* of revelation rather than the original revelation itself. Study the Old Testament with this end in view, and you will come to see with increasing clearness that the original revelation lies in *God's actual historical dealing with the children of Israel.* In no other way than by divide agency can we adequately explain the facts of Jewish history.

Israel started as a local Semite tribe in no way differing from the other tribes round about. Her God, Jahweh, was at first a tribal deity, unknown to the outside world except as a god who ruled over a few Palestinian hills. The Assyrian invasion laid Israel as low as her neighbors. One by on the Semitic tribes fell before the repeated assaults of Tiglath-Pileser, Sargon, Sennacherib and Nebuchadnezzar, and their tribal deities fell with them.

But Israel proved an exception. Jahweh remained a unique conception among the gods of the ancients, in that the late of the Jewish nation had little or no effect on the faith of the people in their own peculiar destiny. What was the *secret of this faith?* The answer is written on every page of the Old Testament for those who can read it. A verse of the 111th Psalm gives us the key-note:

"And his righteousness endureth forever." In a word, the prophets saw *Jehovah exalted in righteousness.*

This was the sublime conception of Israel from the most ancient times. Professor George Adam smith elaborates this point:

"In what are confessedly ancient documents, Jehovah is the cause of Israel's being, of the union of their tribes, of their coming to Palestine, of their instinct to keep separate from other peoples, even when they do not seem to be consciousness of the reason why. But from the first, the influence upon them was ethical. It sifted the great body of custom and law which was their common heritage with all the other Semitic tribes; it added to this both justice and mercy, mitigating the cruelty of some laws, where innocent life was in danger, but strenuously enforcing others, where carelessness had crept in with regard to the most sacred interests of life. It is past all doubt that the ethical agent at work in these laws was at work in Israel from the beginning and was the character, the justice, the holiness of Jehovah.

"But at first it was not in law so much as in the events of the people's history that this character impressed them. They knew all along that he had found them, chosen them, brought them to the land, borne with them, forgiven them, and redeemed them. If no law had come to them from him, therefore, the memory of all that he had been to them, the influence of himself in their history, would have remained their distinction among the peoples."

What more of a revelation of the living God could we ask than this record of his work? If we judge the Bible in this light, it becomes unique among books. In the words of Dr. King of Oberlin college:

"If we judge the Bible by the facts—he actual results, the effects in the life of individuals and nations, it becomes unique. As a matter of fact, there is no book of antiquity we can put beside the Old Testament, no modern book that we can put beside either the Old or the New Testaments for permanent universal moral and spiritual appeal, for inspiring qualities, for making real to us the spiritual world, for making God real, for giving us assurance of Him, and drawing us to Him."

If this be revelation, may we not say, then, that the men who wrote down these records were really inspired of God? For inspiration, as I said before, is no longer thought of as a miraculous ability to take dictation from the Almighty. It is simply the power given to man, in whatever way it may be, of *pertaining human affairs in their true relation to the divine.*

We are now prepared to take up Mr. Morton's argument, that as the Bible is full of demonstrable error, it cannot be taken as inspired, and so can have no more authority than any other book. Mangasarian glosses over the fallacy concealed in this argument even more subtly when he says that "poison mixed with honey is still poison."

This brilliant epigram shows how very shallow and inconclusive it is to hinge an argument on a figure of speech. To be sure, poison mixed with honey is still poison; but it is just as true that you may sprinkle any amount of poison on the outside of a bee hive without in the least tainting the honey within. The honey in the exalted ethical ideals of the Bible is in no way tainted by the Oriental myths, traditions, and metaphors with which those ideals are expressed.

But what is the nature of the "demonstrable errors" of which Mr. Morton speaks? And how do they affect our faith?

In considering these questions, we must beat in mind that our new view of revelation involves nothing of the purely miraculous, but rather the fullest use of the human element God began with the Israelites just where he found them. Their customs and forms of worship were not set aside under the revelation, but were retained, purified, given new motives, and so put on a different religious basis. It is to be expected, therefore, that in the earlier stages of Israel's training, under what men took to be God's revelation, we should find very imperfect conceptions of the will of god, crude morals sentiments of revenge, hatred of enemies, wars of extermination.

That the ethical tone of these conceptions was gradually elevated, a careful study of the Old Testament conclusively shows, God's revelation of himself, indeed, was essentially a progressively revelation thruout the whole course of Jewish history. Step by step the ethical ideas of the people were exalted, until at last they were ready for the final supreme step to which God had been leading up; the coming of Jesus Christ and *the full consciousness of divine sonship*, which is the essence of Christianity.

It hardly seems possible that Mr. Morton would have referred to the Bible as "the inspired word of an omniscient being" had he conceived of inspiration and revelation as here presented. In a like manner, the extremely logical essay of G. Lowes Dickinson on "Revelation" collapses like a house of cards upon merely supplying the true conception of these two terms.

It is strange that rationalism should set up these intellectual scarecrows merely for the pleasure of bowling them over. The best Christian thought of this and other ages has always tried to take away the emphasis from the supernatural in Christian theology and place it on the ethical, where it belongs. Even so early a Christian as Clement of Alexandria, one of the three greatest father of the Greek church, declared that he knew no distinction "between what man discovers and what God reveals," and he went so far as to explain Christianity as a natural development from the earlier religious thought of mankind.

"But hold!" the rationalist will probably cry. "in all this reasoning you have begged the question by assuming the existence of the very God whose revelation you defend. What right have you to make such an assumption? If God is one explanation of the universe, so is 'force' or 'eternal law' or 'the eternally incomprehensible Absolute'(this from Mr. Morton's autobiography) or even Matthew Arnold's 'Eternal Not-ourselves that makes for righteousness.' All of these substitutes for God have been urged at one time or another. Why isn't one of them just as worthy of belief as another, seeing that none of them is amendable to scientific proof?"

Let me ask first, on what does the Christian base his belief in God? the great majority of us, it must be confessed, have little time or ability to think deeply about the matter, and we naturally take the traditional conception as our own. Obviously, we cannot look for scientific demonstration in a problem that contains so many factors lying outside the realm of direct experience. We can, however, discover inferences thruout the realm of nature that are well nigh irresistible.

John Fiske has pointed out the inferences of this sort which may be found in the process of evolution. From the freshwater alga in its tiny pond up to civilized man, every stage of enlargement which evolution has brought about has been with reference to actual external conditions which demanded that enlargement. We have learned, for instance, that the senses of sight and hearing were evolved from the sense of touch in certain parts of the head which happened to be exceptionally sensitive to light and sound. In the same way, mother-love was developed in response to the infant's needs, and fidelity and honor were slowly developed as the social life began to have need of them to hold it together. In every case the internal adjustment has been brought about so as to harmonize with *some actually existing external fact.*

Finally, in the earliest dawn of civilization, we know that the newly born soul of man began reaching vaguely forth toward something akin to itself which it felt was out in the spiritual Beyond. Here again there was an internal adjustment of ideas in correspondence with the Unseen World. Now, triumphantly declares Mr. Fiske, if the relation thus established in the earliest stage of man's existence between the Human Soul and the spiritual world is a relation between a real condition within and an unreal condition outside, *then*, he says, it is something utterly without precedent it the whole history of creation!

He clinches the argument by saying: "The lesson of evolution is that all through these weary ages the human soul has not been cherishing in religion a delusive phantom, but in spite of seemingly endless groping and stumbling, it has been rising to a recognition of its essential kinship with the ever-living God. Of all the implications of the doctrine of evolution with regard to man, I believe the very deepest and strongest to be that which asserts the everlasting reality of religion."

When Darwin's theory first appeared, it was severely criticized by Agassiz because it did away with the creative action of Deity. And yet we have fond in this very theory a wonderful assurance of the central fact of religion.

Having seen the evidence of God, I should like to speak of the real need of God in our lives, but this and other aspects of the great question of religion must be left to future articles.

In conclusion, I would say, as Mr. Morton said, I give you these thoughts primarily to show you why I am *not* a free-thinker. That any thoro-going agnostic should be turned back to the faith of his fathers by anything in this article is hardly thinkable. As Dickinson says, an agnostic is one who says not merely, "I do not know," but "I will not consider." Or better still, in the words of Dr. Martineau:

"To one who dishonors himself by sloth and excess, God becomes invisible and incredible. Sorrowfully the awful form of Deity retires and lets him believe that life is given him to play his own game and not to serve another's will. From such men the very power of perception itself is absent; they look through no transparent medium, but through a glass clouded with earthly steams: so that, demonstrate as you will the realities beyond, they *cannot* see."

But should this chance to be read by one who has merely been led to doubt whether the religion which has proved such a help to him may after all be nothing more than a state of mind, let him remember that the heavens declare the glory of God, and every discovery of science sheweth his handiwork.

The Church and the World

What is it—inquired the Churchman—that you have against the church? Don't you think that it has any place in the life of the world?

Let me answer each of your questions separately—replied the Agnostic. In the first place, I have this against the church: From time immemorial she has acted as a mill-stone around the neck of civilization, holding her back and impeding her progress in every forward movement. Can you name a single revolutionary discovery of science or a single pronouncement of philosophy which is new accepted as a matter of course which was not fought tooth and nail by the church? Copernicus and Galileo were considered heretics because their theories obliged the church to revise its old rock-bound ideas of the universe. Darwin's theory of evolution was for years an anathema to the church because it seemed to take away from your man-made god the power you had always attributed to him. It has always been the same and always will be; for the church, as a body, always thinks more slowly and timidly than the unimpeded portion of society; and it is only the presence of radical elements in it, pulling, hauling, and tugging at it, urging it to catch up to the progressing world, that keeps you even within shouting distance of us. If it wasn't for those radical elements you would have died of stagnation long ago, but even with them you have always been a heavy drag on us who would move forward.

Now, as to your second question,—Just one minute—broke in the Churchman—before you get too far from that point, I would like to say a word on it. Your metaphor of the mill-stone is a striking one, but if we are going to deal in metaphors, you must allow me to change the form of it an call it a brake on the fly-wheel or, better still, a governor on the engine of progress, holding it back, it is true, but only for its own good. History shows that civilization needs just such a brake as this to keep it from flying off at every tangent or developing such an overwhelming velocity in some one direction that it is upon the rocks before it can stop itself. Take any of the ancient and vanished civilizations for an example. Do you think that if the Roman—the old Roman[—]civilization had become permeated with the leaven of Christian charity and altruism, it would have fallen a prey to insidious vice and corruption as it did? These same influences are at work today just as they were in ancient Rome, but there is also at work the saving spirit of the Man of Galilee: the consciousness of an intimate relationship with a Supreme being, and coupled with it the *aspiration*, at least, to love our neighbor as ourself. If we can keep that leaven active, we need not fear that we shall go the way of Rome. It is that that has made us what we are today. It is just that that has made the world a good place to live in. Why, isn't it self-evident to you that every good and wholesome principle of action which you approve of is taken out of the Sermon on the Mount?

I am amused—smiled the Agnostic—to hear you talk about Christianity and the Sermon on the Mount when the subject we are discussing is the Church. Christianity is about as much like the Church as the piles of bricks and stones that the Church meets in. Your ministers preach Christianity and talk about the Sermon on the Mount, but there is not a single principle of that Sermon that you incorporate into your own lives. I grant you that those principles are the foundation of everything that is good and worthy today; but their efficiency is due rather to their general acceptance as moral principles by the world and their gradual permeation of the world's institution, rather than to the exemplification by the Church.

Yes, my friend—replied the Churchman—but even granting that what you say is entirely true—and I do not—it is the Church, not the world, that has held to these ideals through all the centuries even though she has not always exemplified them in her acts. The Church and the world are two fundamentally hostile camps, one under the standard of the law of love, the other under that of "Every man for himself and the devil take the hindmost." And if you find evidences of Christian principles throughout the secular world today it is merely an encouraging omen of the Church's final triumph. You say that the Church has always been slow to follow the lead of evolution and progress toward higher things. I turn the tables on you by declaring that it is the *world* that is laggard. It is slow to adopt the standard of Christian benevolence; it doesn't do so in any case, in fact, until it find through long experience that that standard pays in the long run. Aren't you rather ashamed, then, to appropriate the principles of the Church after that institution has proved their eternal fitness through long ages of trial and experience, and then calmly turn around and deny that she has any excuse for existence? No, my friend, I stick right to the contention I made at first, and that is, that the Church and the principles she stands for is that to which we are indebted for a large part of the blessings of civilization today.

The point—said the Agnostic—is about as capable of final and definite solution as the old debating-society question, Resolved, That the pen is mightier than the sword. To me, altruism, or benevolence, as you call it, is just as much a product of the countless selections and rejections of evolution as society itself. I don't need your deity to tell me that honesty is the best policy; and that it is going to pay me the biggest character-dividends in the long run if I love my neighbor as myself. Those motives of human action have weeded themselves out from the mass of motives of dishonesty, revenge, anger, treachery, and the like, just as the ideal combination of brain and muscle we call the modern man has weeded himself out from the millions that have gone before him, and the resulting product is what it is regardless of whether God exists or not. That is my position in the matter. But we could each of us quote history on our side till we were black in the face, and we would get nowhere. I simply demur to your assertion, therefore, and let it go at that. It brings me, however, to the second part of your original question:

do I think the Church has any place in the life of the world? Yes, I think that it has, but it is merely a temporary, not a permanent place. The primitive man evolved his religion as naturally as he breathed the air about him, and in primitive and adolescent society religion played a more or less beneficial part, depending largely on its connection with morality. When it stood for high ideals and morality, its place was surely an important one, for it supplied the goad of fear and terror of spirits which the abstract morality could never have carried with it to his mind. But the ideal man is not a creature of emotion but of intellect; and it is to this ideal that the race is steadily progressing. People like you and me don't do right because we are afraid an angry God is going to hand us over to the devil to toast over hot coals forever—at least I should hope we don't. Our motive for right action is the absolute, cold-blooded knowledge that it pays. The Church, therefore, must play an ever-diminishing part in society. She chooses her own old-fashioned way to make you moral members of society; but once you have come to the realization that morality is *intrinsically* the best, your dependence on the Church must inevitably grow less. And when finally the whole world emerges into the full white light of reason, the Church's part will have been played, and she will atrophy and disappear—if, indeed, she has not succeeded in committing suicide before that time; for no institution outlives its usefulness.

You have touched—said the Churchman—upon the much-discussed question of religion versus ethics, and I must admit that you have stated your side of it very well. But you overlook two very essential points: one is, that you are not dealing with a world of static conditions; and the other, that you are not dealing with a world of ideal men and women. Granting that we bring our world to an approximate state of rightness and reason: do you think she is going to "stay put?" Do you think that the great struggle of good and evil is forthwith going to cease and that men are going to be ruled henceforth by their reasons alone? It is just that erroneous assumption that is the weak spot in the socialistic program. The world is and always will be a collection of human beings like passions as our own, and for such a society pure reason is insufficient. That there are people for whom it is sufficient, I think may be admitted; although it is impossible to say whether such people, with a warm faith to kindle their cold, reasoning natures into a glow, would not be even more noble than they are. These are the "tough-minded" of whom William James speaks, then people who argue from the facts they can see, touch, taste, and hear. But he admits that the "tender-minded" also exist and must be taken into account. And this is the type, I hold, that represents the world at large, educated or uneducated. *Here is the final crux of the whole problem:* You hold that man should be ruled altogether by his reason; while I say that he is so constituted that without the resource of appeal to the emotions he is as a house build upon sand which the flood may some time wash away.

"And there ye ar-re," as Mr. Dooley says.

Life for God's Sake

This is an age of revolution. Art is attacked by futurism and cubism, poetry by verse libre and imagism; government by Bolshevism and kindred breeds of radicalism. It is not strange, then, that it should become a popular sport to demolish the claims of religion, pick up the scraps to subject them to scornful examination, and finally fling them contemptuously to the four winds.

Our new thot devotees proudly cast off the shackles of religion—to quote their own words—and step forth with a delicious sense of freedom. "Life for Life's Sake!" What a free, simple, glorious, irresponsible creed! Life for God's sake, we are told, is the unseemly, tiresome burden of a weak-charactered idealism. Life for Life's sake is healthy, strong, and selfish. Thus the exuberant life-for-life's-saker.

This creed possesses one merit at any rate: it is perfectly comprehensible. It involves no esoteric obscurities, no difficult points of casuistry where the right course of action is hard to divine. It follows the line of the least resistance, the promptings of instinct and animal spirits. We find no difficulty in tracing out the plain implications of such a creed.

It is no task to be selfish. The natural struggle has made each of us egocentric and the first impulse is inevitably toward self-preservation and self-satisfaction. If we are living only for life's sake, that primal impulse is the logical one; the unwelcome task can appeal only to sentimental idealism. What place has sacrifice in a philosophy of this sort? None whatever; that is for the sentimental idealist. Shall we "scorn delights to live in laborious days"? Bah! Leave that to the sentimental idealist!

Shall we strive for any element of nobility? Not for life's sake. The narrow scope of one short life—the one we are now living—has no room for any consistent principle except that of selfishness. With a conception of life as a brief flash of light between the utter darkness of two eternities, a man tends inevitably toward pessimism, misanthropy, and the complete stagnation of all within him that nominally aspires and reaches up toward the higher righteousness.

True, we may find here and there a notable exception in some materialist whose denial of the claims of religion has not bereft him of high ideals. This is nothing but the afterglow of Christianity. What a wonderful tribute it is to the faith that it can so deeply impress itself on the habits of thot and action of a race that where an eccentric individual here and there succeeds in casting off, as he conceives it, the shackles of his religious belief, he cannot shake himself free from the very ideals whose source he repudiates! In general, however, those ideals do not flourish in atheistic and agnostic soil. It is unthinkable that a nation that loses its religious faith should continue for any considerable time to hold up ideals of national and civic righteousness. In place of these will grow up the single brutal standard of expediency, as exemplified in that insolent Prussian definition of its *kultur*: The subordination of every faculty, every hope, every aspiration, to the attainment of a certain end.

These are the plain implications of life for life's sake. Frankly it does not appeal to me. Selfish it certainly is, but there is nothing really healthy or strong about it. Believing in life for God's sake, I am accused of being good in life for the sake of the sugar at the end. This is one of those statements which would be very telling if it were true. Christ said, "The kingdom of heaven is within you." The Christian does not force himself into goodness for the sake of the sugar at the end of this life, for he does not have to wait until the end for the sugar; he has it as soon as the wonderful thaumaturgy of spiritual rebirth readjusts him to his environment. As for the end, for him there is no end nor any fear of any end, for every instinct—unless smothered by the miasma of materialistic philosophy—tells him that individuality persists in some form beyond this life; that his common sense adds that whatever the form of this future existence, a life of growing character is a better, safer preparation for it than a life of selfish, degrading indulgence.

Live for life's sake is life for self's sake, and aimless drifting down stream; life for God's sake is a fine, courageous battle upstream, with all the tang and zest of accomplishment, toward the high, beautiful uplands of noble character. Self and God: Choose ye this day whom ye will serve.

Looking Backward

My introduction to amateur journalism dates to the fall of 1906, when I walked into the room of a college class-mate one evening and spied an attractive little booklet entitled "The Eternal Question." I turned the pages and was quite won by the lively style of the contents and the curiosity-provoking signatures, "Miss Incognito" and "Miss Anonymous."

"For Heaven's sake," I exclaimed to my friend, "Al, tell me what would make two girls get out a pamphlet like this, and who are they?"

"I think you'd be interested in that sort of work, Moe," was the reply. "That's a sample of what is called amateur journalism. I can't tell you so very much about it except that there's a band of writers scattered all around the country who publish and contribute to little magazines like that one just for the love of it. A girl in my home town by the name of Litta Volchert is interested in the work, and I'm pretty sure that Miss Anonymous is Litta. If you wish, I'll give you her address so that you can write to her and find out all about it."

Since then I have learned from a multitude of experiences that getting recruits for amateur journalism is not like going out and picking roses; but once you find that rare bird known as the "born amateur," almost before you have finished explaining the manifold attractions of the hobby and producing an application blank, he asks, "Where do I sign?" He has swallowed the bait, hook, sinker, bobber, and line, and is an amateur for life. That is exactly what happened to me. In less than one month I had sent my application with a written credential, received a copy of the UNITED AMATEUR and some of the recent publications, written to some of the editors, and had replies from several. In a short time I had the satisfaction of seeing some of my work appear in amateur print—copy which had gone the round of the professional editors and had been retired to my files after my postage and patience had been exhausted—and before the year was out I was a member of the Bureau of Criticism of the UNITED AMATEUR and preparing to get out a paper.

That first APPRENTICE, all mine from the cover design of daisies even to an inserted song supplement, gave me more of the thrills of literary creation than anything else I have since produced. I was looking over my sole remaining copy the other day, and it occurred to me how lucky I was to have made my debut in those distant days of unbelievably low prices. As I recall, the total bill for printing, etching, and engraving was something like $37, a sum which nearly bankrupted the editor at the time. Today this issue, I am sure, could not be duplicated for $125.

And what a joyful time we had in assembling and mailing it! I was now home from the university, and had met Milwaukee's Grand Old Man of amateur journalism, Edward F. Daas, and had helped him to organize the local amateurs into the Sesame Literary Club. I had the Sesames over to the house for the assembling bee, and in one noisy, happy evening we got the work all done, even to the mailing of outgoing copies. The kind letters of appreciation that came piling in from all over the country in the next few weeks are still among my treasured possessions.

Nothing was lacking to complete my captivation by the hobby except a national convention, and that came in good measure the next summer, when the two amateur press associations, the United and the National, both held their conventions in Milwaukee, and I had an opportunity of meeting such celebrated amateurs as James F. Morton, Jr., Tim Thrift, Charles Heins, Pop Mellinger, "Sunny Jim" Irene Maloney, and I don't know how many other from the East and the middle West.

A convention is quite necessary for the complete rounding out of a recruit's experience. I have often, in the conventionless years since then, looked back on those two gatherings, when the wild scramble for mere existence has elbowed me away from amateur highways for months or even a year at a time, and have sighed at Wisconsin's dwindling amateur list, which prevents us from bringing another convention to Milwaukee. Only tonight I was talking with Eddie Daas, which has just returned from a globe-trotting trip, and if we can get him to settle down in our well known midst long enough and not break away for C-U-B-A again, maybe we shall be able to gather about us another devoted group that will put Milwaukee on the amateur map again and in line for another convention.

"Once an Amateur, Always an Amateur"

The old proverb so familiar to United members, "Once an Amateur, Always an Amateur," is about as true as most generalizations—it simply isn't. If it were, the various amateur press associations would soon become as congested and unwieldy as civilization would be if nobody died for fifty years. Probably there isn't any such a creature as an average amateur, any more than there is an average human being; but if there is, I venture to fix the span of his amateur life at four years. The first year he usually spends in finding himself, getting acquainted with amateurs at large, and discovering the varied sources of enjoyment in the Hobby. The next two years he joins clubs, attends conventions, forms correspondence friendships, and relieves himself of most of his stored-up literary impulses by contributing to amateur journals and publishing one of his own. Toward the end of the third year, this "average" amateur has used up most of his literary inspirations, the novelty of the new life opened up to him has largely worn off, and life is calling insistently for him to come and do his allotted task. He pays his dues for another term, but by the end of the fourth year the Hobby has lost him.

Some there be, however, who live up to the proverb, and of such I am one. I remember the words of my first proud editorial, ten years ago: "It was a case of love at first sight with me, and from all indications it is going to be 'till death do us part'." Amateurs have come, and amateurs have gone, but in those ten years my affection for amateur journalism has dimmed not a bit. In the last few years the daily moil of bread-winning has claimed me more and more, but not a year has passed without some bit of amateur activity. Everybody has dreamed of what he will do when his ship comes in. My dream includes an attic or basement printshop where my boys and I can stick type and kick the press to turn out some exclusive little *Apprentices* that will recall the palmy days of *Torpedoes, Lucky Dogs, Dilettantes*, et al.

Meanwhile, it must suffice me to pen an occasional contribution and to sit back to watch my amateurs try their wings, advising them here and there against Icarian flights. May this little scribble serve as a greeting to the select few who with me have remained faithful for a decade to the Prince of Hobbies, and as a wish that we may be able to multiply the ten by two, three, even four or five.

First Steps in the Appreciation of Poetry

The two procedures to be described cover from four to six class periods. Procedure No. 1 uses the well-known *Exercises in Judging Poetry*, by Abbott and Trabue, not to test, but to compare good and bad examples of poetic form, imagery, and feeling. Buy a set of Form Y from Columbia Teachers College Publication Bureau and analyze thoroughly the three methods of mutilating the poetic original on each page; read, if necessary, the explanatory article in the supplementary bulletin, *A Measure of Ability To Judge Poetry.* Place on the board the symbols "O" (original), "M" (mechanically mutilated version), "P" (prosaic), and "S" (sentimentalized version) and explain the construction of the test. Have the class print "A," "B," "C," "D," to indicate the four versions on each page; then tell them to turn to Set 2, "Going to the Tournament," find the version containing false rhyme and roughened meter, and record "M" after the proper letter. Next seek the version lacking all imagery and label that "P." From the two remaining, select the one which is over-ornamented, insincere, or otherwise sentimentalized, and call it "S." Now read the correct order "MSOP" and ask how many had it right. After each exercise take one or two of the worst mutilations, compare them with corresponding lines in the original, and show the definite principle of poetic artistry violated. At the end of the booklet summarize the principles of good poetic form, imagery, and sentiment thus evolved.

Procedure No. 2 applies these principles to actual poems. Type eight pieces of magazine verse on separate sheets with a brief suggestion under each as to what principle is chiefly exemplified.* On the back of each sheet type what you consider an adequate response to these suggestions.

Distribute Sheet I. Give time to read the poem and the suggestion and to write down a single definite poetic quality observed. Read a number of these and discuss them for the degree of appreciation they show or fail to show. A few typical comments on a poem "Midnight," from the Bookman, will show what help is needed to orient average third-year high-school students to real poetry:

> RALPH: I think this poem is excellent. It has perfect rhyme. It has the proper name. It never leaves the subject, it is always referring to midnight. I believe anyone of any age could understand this simple poem.

Ralph needs to be shown that such vacuous comment leaves entirely untouched the real artistry of the poem.

> HORACE: The poem after saying a strange black beast, then says it is a dog. I think this is unnecessary. A nun don't fold its hands when she prays. And there is no such thing as a village being drugged with moon unless they were all drunk.

Horace is a two-fisted, matter-of-fact modern youth; but even this type can be brought, in a surprisingly short time, to realize that imagery must not be taken literally but visualized through the same eye of fancy that the poet used.

> HAROLD: Even if you didn't know what time it was, by the sentence, "The old clock, stern yet patient, folds its hands to heaven like a nun," you could see it was twelve o'clock.

---

*Copy of the set actually used in this project will be sent for five cents to cover materials and postage.—M. W. Moe, West Division High School, Milwaukee, Wisconsin.

Harold is to be commended for taking at least one step toward appreciation in that he saw a reality not right on the surface of the poem, but he is to be warned that a keener appreciation lies in seeing clearly the primary image of the praying nun than in merely grasping the fact that it is twelve.

After a few more comments have been read and discussed, the class should be given time to read the comment on the back:

The poet sees the common objects we all see, but to him they take on forms of fancy and tap fields of emotion somewhat outside our ordinary prosaic range. Here in three sharp, incisive strokes, we have a homely village scene: a dog shifting restlessly on a hearth and an old hall clock ticking away, while outside the moon shines down on the quiet houses. But the poetic touch converts the dog into a nameless black beast, the village into a sleeper drugged into insensibility, and the clock into a nun praying with clasped hands and upturned face, stopping only to click an occasional rosary bead. The poetess has nothing to teach; she merely senses life keenly and through imagery and sense appeals tries to lead the reader to similar appreciation.

After eight poems, selected for the opportunities they afford to sharpen a student's awareness of the various pleasures poetry has to offer, make a short summary emphasizing five principles an appreciative reader of poetry must have constantly at his command: (1) the function of poetic form and its powerlessness to make cheap commonplaces poetic; (2) the need for seeing imagery through the poet's own eyes and letting it enhance the reality; (3) the lively response to suggestion; (4) sensitivity to legitimate emotional appeals and ability to discriminate between these and shallow sentimentality; and (5) the sure knowledge that the central concern of poetic expression is with the senses and emotions and not with lessons. Inculcation of these five principles by means of the two procedures just described will mean for most high-school students a new approach to poetry and a revolutionary change in attitude toward poetic beauty.

Maurice W. Moe on Amateur Criticism

Again, speaking of criticism: I am through! It has been forced upon me this year in an unmistakable manner, however, that the whole activity of **public** amateur criticism is a false and useless creation which serves no wide purpose and merely apes an institution which from its very nature it can never hope to duplicate. Just stop and consider a moment and see whether this is not true. What is the function of the book review in the professional magazine? Is it to assist the struggling author to correct his mistakes? The very statement of that supposition reveals how ridiculous it is. There is only one other possible function: to inform the general public of the subject matter and quality of the book in order that it may choose its reading matter with the least waste of effort. The private review, from its very nature, cannot perform this latter function and in fact is not intended to perform it. No argument is needed to clinch this fact; it is self-evident. The only question that remains is: does or can amateur criticism in any considerable degree teach the beginner his mistakes and help him to avoid them? From eleven years of experience in amateur journalism I can deliver to this question an emphatic negative. No matter how loudly the amateur cries for candid criticism, nine times out of ten he comes before the amateur public with the pretty firm conviction that he has done something pretty clever which will need little or no correction, and if the review is anything but adulation, his feelings are apt to be ruffled. Time and again he comes back with a specific argument to show himself right and the critic most woefully wrong, or with a tirade against the whole tribe of critics in general; but as for accepting the criticism in good spirit and mending his ways, well it simply isn't done. Therefore I repeat that amateur public criticism serves no useful purpose but merely apes professional criticism, whose real function, that of informing the reading public what to buy, it can never from its very nature hope to perform.

I do not include in this category the private criticism. Where amateurs of sufficient training and intelligence can be found who have the time to handle this work, it can undoubtedly be made of value to those who take advantage of it. Those who send work for private criticism are usually more in earnest; and as the criticisms can be made more in detail and right in the margins of the original manuscripts, they are of real informative value and can be made the basis of considerable improvement.—Maurice W. Moe, under date of April 26, 1918.

Through the Eyes of the Poet

What I am about to say seems much like a confession of the obvious, but like the Ancient Mariner I cannot rest until the tale is told. For some years I have been trying to teach the appreciation of poetry, and I have rested fairly content under the apprehension that I was turning out my pupils with at least a bit more of an idea as to why some famous poems are great and beautiful. It is only in the last year or so that I have come slowly to a realization that any reading of a poem without a clear vision of the poet's primary pictures can hardly be dignified by the name of reading. To read is to look at words on a page and transmute them, through the alchemy of the brain, into images, the coinage of thought. Training in reading, therefore, must devote itself to perfecting the process of image formation.

Like any other act requiring the least skill, this image-forming process is something which the natural man performs poorly or hardly at all. The fact that he usually reads to "see what happens" or to "see how it turns out" demonstrates this clearly enough. It is sufficient for him if the author introduces a number of vague figures, barely distinguished by particular names, ages, sexes, and maybe an outstanding scrap or two of costume, and proceeds to put them through an interesting set of paces. What they *do* he is interested enough to visualize quite clearly; what they are, however, he hardly sees, and usually he doesn't care enough to make the effort.

It is evident that the instructor must do some breaking of ground to fertilize and cultivate such fallow imaginations. He must develop the pupil's ability to imagine people and things as well as motions, and, at the author's suggestion, to endow those persons and things with form, shape, color, and individual characteristics. How can this be done? As in learning to swim, principally by doing it.

In my classes the question "What do you see?" has been repeated so often that I am quite expecting to behold it some time in the high school monthly under "Favorite Remarks of Our Faculty." But that repetition is beginning to bear fruit. Where at first it was greeted with blankness or an attempt to explain or interpret the figure in place of describing, it is now almost sure to bring forth a clear-visioned "I see" with plenty of trimmings not in the original picture—a very good sign.

Thorough appreciation of poetry has little to do with anything except the sensations, chiefly those of sight and sound. A knowledge of the foot, the line, and the stanza-form should of course be well in hand, but one may be an expert technician and still fail miserably to sense the beauty of a poem. If he can be given the poet's glasses, however, and made to feel, ever so remotely, the rapture which inspired the poem, his appreciation has begun.

Let me illustrate with a few lines from some of the great English poems commonly studied in high school. I will begin with a very simple but vivid picture from the "Deserted Village":

> To husband out life's taper at the close.

To interpret these words in literal terms is one thing, a very important part of the reading process; but fully as important is the clear vision of a guttering little candle-end with a hand protectively curved around it to shield the feeble flame from the eddying currents of this drafty existence. Do you think the picture in that line is already too distinct to need such additional outlining? Just try it on a group of ordinary young people and see how many "will catch the picture" at the first reading. You will be amazed at the percentage of times it either fails to register altogether or else leaves only a cloudy image.

But if that was too easy to bother with, try another couple from the same poem:

> Princes or lords may flourish or may fade;
> A breath can make them as a breath has made.

Never have I tried that on a class and received a clear image from the first reading. Disregarding the probably unconscious imagery of the first line, endeavor to reconstruct the scene Goldsmith must have had in his mind as he penned the second line—for be assured that no image flows from the pen of a poet until it has been limned upon his mental canvas with a wealth of color and detail he cannot hope to crowd into the narrow limits of his figure. There can be no doubt that we have here a scene at court during the conferring of knighthood, the accolade of the royal blade on the bowed shoulder, accompanied by the "I dub thee knight" of the king. In this case the real value of this image exercise becomes apparent, for if the line was obscure upon first reading, its interpretation is a very simple matter once the primary picture is made distinct.

Sometimes the picture is so vast and startling that one's cramped imagination refuses to register it in its original form. A good example of this is found in the "Ancient Mariner:"

> Still as a slave before his lord,
>   The ocean hath no blast;
> His great bright eye most silently
>   Up to the moon is cast.

Here again there can be no doubt that Coleridge visioned a gigantic master with a slave lying prostrate before him—but flat on his back instead of on his face, for his eye is directed upward. The size of that stupendous blue eye, the whole visible surface of the ocean from horizon to horizon, implies such a still more stupendous size in the whole figure of the slave and his master that imagination falters and must be coaxed to do its work.

Again, in Byron's famous apostrophe to the ocean:

> Thou glorious mirror, where the Almighty's form
> Glasses itself in tempests. . . .

the poet's sublimated imagination conjures up an image so vast and so majestic that our poor mundane minds can only grope at the outlines of it. It is a figure, however, to make one realize, once it is outlined, how rarely modern art—whether verbal or pictorial—has presumed to visualize Deity. A study of poetry from this particular angle brings many interesting facts to light. It reveals, for instance, that Shelley's poems are the most nearly continuous cinema of images in the whole realm of English poetry. Any adequate proof of this assertion would string this article out to unreasonable lengths. One has only to read such wonderful poems as his "Ode to the West Wind," "To a Skylark," "The Cloud," or "Adonais," with imagination's lens sharply in focus to realize in what rare profusion the images tumble out of the poet's mind. The leaves become

> Yellow and black and pale and hectic red
> Pestilence-stricken multitudes.

Thunder-clouds are to him

> The Locks of the approaching storm
> Like the bright hair uplifted from the head
> Of some fierce maenad.

Surely no poet has ever built a more beautiful picture of

> Life, like a dome of many-colored glass,
> Staining the white radiance of eternity,
> Until Death tramples it to fragments.

In a few cases the close succession of metaphors applied to the same subject carries Shelley very nearly over the border-line of poetic taste in a mixed metaphor. It is one virtue of our moving-picture process of study that it infallibly plays the spotlight upon such lapses. Take, for instance, the lines

> Make me thy lyre, even as the forest is:
> What if my leaves are falling as thine own.

The first line contains a picture of a gigantic lyre. Such an instrument the poet wishes to be; and yet in the very next clause he assumes himself to be a tree with falling leaves ("growing bald," quoth one of my youthful appreciators). This comes about as near as possible to being a mixed metaphor without actually being one.

Often class discussion will wage furiously as to just why the poet chose the picture he did. Shelley, for example, says to the skylark,

> Like a cloud of fire
> The blue deep thou wingest.

On the face of it this simile pictures the little bird as a mass of flame moving along in the sky. Why should a little speck away up so high as to be almost if not quite invisible suggest to the poet a mass of flame? Is it not an inept comparison? At first a class gropes blindly for the solution of this riddle, and then almost infallibly it will dawn on one or two that the little lark, as it wings its way through the deep, pours forth a flood of melody which to the rarefied vision of the poet envelops it in a perfect nimbus of fire. The blending of the visual and the auditory image into one is a daring device, but Shelley shows himself partial to this very thing several times in this poem, as in the moonbeam and the glow-worm similes. Nothing finer can be found to sharpen the appreciative powers of the amateur reader than the exercise in leaping the gap between one sense and another, as one must in such similes.

I have spoken of this method as if it were solely for the benefit of the beginner; but there can be little doubt that the mental gymnastics it affords will have their value even to the veteran reader. Let me repeat that the best of us are all too apt to glide over the mere surface of figurative language "to see what happens," often throwing away the opportunity of reveling in some beautiful little vignette the painstaking word-artist has etched for us. What, for instance, are you going to do with these lines from William Vaughan Moody's "Gloucester Moore"?

> And the racing winds that wheel and flee
> On the flying heels of June.

Are you going to think merely of wind blowing across flowery meadows, or are you going to be so alive to the poet's words that those heels of June cannot fly unless they have a body to propel them? And in personifying June are you going to make her a beautiful, light-footed maiden, or what? And when you have gone so far with your picture, are you going to be satisfied with those wheeling, fleeing winds merely as invisible currents of air, or will they take tangible forms and become the only things that naturally wheel and flee about human beings in an excess of animal enjoyment, namely dogs? If you don't like my picture, construct one of your own, but in any case don't leave the words unimaged.

After some systematic exercise of the kind I have just described you will be almost sure to find that you are developing a more or less dormant photographic faculty in your mind, and the reading of poetry, and even of prose, where the latter abounds in figure, will become a delightful excursion through the endless picture-galleries of the world's great minds.

Imagism

The essence of imagism, aside from the deliberate casting away of all restraint as to form and taste, is an intense concentration on the percept of every sensation. The imagist concentrates his attention on any object or phenomenon he happens to select for description and then, turning his mind in upon itself, strives to capture the exact image of every sensation at the very instant it registers on his brain. After it has been assimilated and classified as a concept, it no longer interests him.

Now I must confess that this is not the easiest thing in the world to do, for the economy of our mental life has through long years taught us to combine into concept groups the multitudes of perceptions that are constantly impinging on the consciousness. Life is too short to deal with each of these precepts lightly. If we did, we should have no time for the larger units of thought that constitute real intellection; we should be living on a plane just one degree removed from that of the unthinking animal. But it can be done. There is a trick about it, and the novelty of the effort, childish as it is, at first proves rather fascinating, just as it proves exhilarating for grown-ups occasionally to cut loose in the antics of boyhood days and play leap-frog and prisoner's base. One "poem" I discovered recently describes the imagist as a child sitting in a sunny corner and letting the brightly-coloured pebbles of life trickle through his fingers. And that's it exactly: he is playing with his sensations, watching them sparkle and glance in the sun, but not using them for any real purpose in the business of existence.

This—even if we forgive the imagist his anarchy of form, which I do not—lays bare the fundamental weakness of the whole cult: there is absolutely no attempt at interpretation. Amy Lowell herself takes pride in admitting this. We take the exact picture and present it to the reader without comment, she says; it is for him to put his own interpretation upon it. But images are in quality—not in content—all alike; stark, bare, and lacking any touch of personality. It is the interpreting touch of the artist that gives to a word-picture the subtle touch of his personality. In the volume of imagistic poems entitled "Others," almost any one of the poems might have been turned out by any one of the "Others," so lacking are these formless attempts in style and personality. That such otherwise sane critics as William Stanley Braithwaite and such otherwise sane publications as the **New Republic** bow down at the new fane, is utterly beyond me.

If this be poetry, then anyone, even I, can be a poet. To prove this I wrote one of these things myself. I never thought I should be guilty of such a thing, but I did it in the interests of good literature. One morning as I was "coming to the surface," my first thought was that it would be a good experiment to scrutinise my waking sensations one by one. So I took about five minutes to wake up, noted carefully every sight and sound that trickled in upon me, then rose and hastened to record the whole hodge-podge. "Seven O'Clock" is the result. Maybe is isn't real imagism, but if it isn't, the distinction is beyond a poor ordinary reader like me. If this is the new poetry, Lord help literature!

Literary Appreciation

I. Appreciation of form includes sensitiveness to
  A. poetic feet, not only to recognize each, but to realize that
    1. the iambus marches, and is therefore good for
      a. lofty, exalted epic poetry,
      b. steady narration, and ordinary verse;
    2. the trochee trips lightly along, and is best for
      a. gay, cheerful expression, and
      b. poems of sprightly action;
    3. the anapest gallops, and is best for
      a. poems of flight and pursuit, and
      b. narration with a stirring sweep;
    4. the dactyl waltzes or swings along, and is good for
      a. tales a bit more swinging than anapestic, and
      b. poems with a modified suggestion of a gallop;
  B. the various meters, with ability to
    1. detect faults in regular meter, and
    2. realize the esthetic effect of long and short meters;
  C. rime, with ability to
    1. detect imperfect rimes, and
    2. realize the contribution of rime to word-music;
  D. stanza-form, with ability to recognize such standard forms as
    1. the heroic couplet and its artistic and esthetic qualities

        2. the two well-known sonnet-patterns:
            a. Elizabethan sonnet, with quatrains and final epigram, and
            b. Italian sonnet, with rime-scheme, octave and sextet; also
        3. various French forms, with their artistic intricacy; and lastly
    E. prose rhythms good, bad, and indifferent.
II. Appreciation of a writer's appeal to the imagination includes
    A. increased sensitivity to the five sense appeals in the printed word;
    B. ability to recall myriad impressions stored up in words;
    C. sensitivity to imagery, such as that of
        1. the simile, with its
            a. primary image, and its
            b. qualities that make it effective or cheap;
        2. the metaphor, with its
            a. various forms, including personification, allegory, etc.,
            b. its less obvious primary image, and
            c. qualities that make it effective or cheap;
    D. sensitivity to the poet's power of suggestion by means of
        1. mimetic effects and general word-music;
        2. connotation and the use of suggestive key-words, and
        3. allusions to myths, the Bible, and history and literature.
III. Appreciation of emotional appeal in the printed word includes
    A. increased sensitivity to the whole gamut of emotional appeals; and
    B. the ability to distinguish sincere, spontaneous emotion from
        1. distortion of reality for cheap emotional effect;
        2. sentimentality, which shows itself in such forms as
            a. spurious, overdone emotion (loud-pedal stuff)
            b. emotional short circuits, and
            c. rehashing trite situations merely for effect;
        3. cliches—all trite, hackneyed banalities;
        4. cheap use of archaisms merely for effect; and lastly
        5. padding, with cheap, forced rimes and hollow phrases.

From *Poem Comments*

The Wind Is a Woman
By A. M. Sullivan

The Wind is a woman who scrubs the sky;
Above, her billowing soapsuds fly.

She grumbles, and lo, it starts to rain—
Her mop is swishing against the pane.

She washes the dirt from Heaven's stairs,
Trafficked by men and their selfish prayers.

She cleans the tracking of angel and saint
And brightens the floor with her azure paint.

She rinses the porch of Heaven and spills
Her foaming bucket upon the hills,

Then hangs her wash-rags out to dry—
They're flapping in the Eastern sky.

And when her menial task is done,
She plucks her mantle from the sun.

The Wind is a woman who loves to fuss
And tidy up the sky for us.

From LADIES' HOME JOURNAL*

Suggestions

    Which is more vivid here, the reality or the poet's images? Are the two appropriately related throughout? Which image is the most apt? Why?

    Is there a moral present? Is it obtrusive? Does it seem to any extent to have been the reason for the writing of the poem?

Comment on "The Wind Is a Woman"

    There is something humorous in this picture of the wind as an industrious but rather shrewish housewife. Her various tasks of scrubbing, mopping, rinsing, hanging out wash-rags and tidying up all bear such clever and appropriate relation to literal functions of the wind, that the mind is fascinated by their aptness.

    If there is a faint trace of moralizing in the reference to men's selfish prayers, bear in mind that the poet's central purpose at this point is evidently not to teach but to present a whimsical fancy. It is indeed a lovely whimsy—this picture of selfish men as trudging up Heaven's stairs with their unworthy petitions and defiling the steps with the mud of this earth.

---

*In his teaching aids, MWM printed a poem with his thought-provoking questions on one sheet, and his detailed "comment" on a separate sheet, so as not to show his hand prematurely.

From *Imagery Aids*

Imagery

The chief difference between prose and poetry lies in the various sense-appeals (form, color, sound, etc.) with which the poet enriches the common things of life. These common things constitute REALITY. Let us think of the poet's enriching sense-appeal as his PRIMARY IMAGE. The REALITY blends with the PRIMARY IMAGE to produce IMAGERY. The true appreciation of IMAGERY—and so of poetry in general—depends largely upon the vividness with which the mind is able to split the image into these two component parts and blend it together again.

Direction for Using Imagery

Read verse No. 1 and say to yourself, "The primary image is ....; the reality is ....,["] making each as vivid as possible. Now turn the page over to check your accuracy. If necessary, repeat the process to get the two pictures just right. Work slowly through figures in numbered order—as they are numbered in approximate order of difficulty—and note the gradual improvement in your ability to see, hear, feel, smell, and taste in response to the suggestion of the printed word. This is the essence of poetic appreciation.

Recognizing Various Kinds of Imagery

While it is not nearly so important to know the technical name given any image as it is to feel the sense impression intended by the poet, some students will want the ability to label figures of speech as similes (S), metaphors (M), personifications (P), or allegories (A). As an aid to self-checking the identifying initial will be found on the back of each verse. Occasionally two types will be found merged in one figure of speech, in one case three.

[...]

22 THE ENGAGED COUPLE

Like a beauteous barge was she,
Still at rest on the sandy beach,
Just beyond the billow's reach;
But he
Was the restless, seething, stormy sea!
    From *The Building of the Ship*
    By *Henry W. Longfellow*

The primary image

A beautiful barge, fully equipped and ready for launching, on a sandy beach. The foaming breakers dash up nearly to it.

The reality

A young man very much in love gazes at the beautiful girl he is soon to marry, and he fairly quivers with impatience as he thinks of the time that must pass before the wedding.

S

Introduction to Poetry

Poetry would be much more popular if the general reader knew its real nature. When an average group is faced with the question, "What is poetry?" the majority will say it rimes, and the rest will talk about rhythm, cadence, or the length of the lines. Now a definition of poetry which stops with these things fails dismally to capture its very essence, and that failure is the clue to the reader's distaste. He has never been able to see why some people waste their time with jingly rimes like Swinburne's:

> A baby's hands, like rosebuds furled
>   Whence yet no leaf expands
> Ope if you touch, though close upcurled,
>   A baby's hands.

Or roundabout, obscure expression encasing a simple familiar idea, like Mrs. Browning's

> Experience, like a pale musician, holds
> A dulcimer of patience in his hand
> Whence harmonies we cannot understand,
> Of God's will in His worlds, the strain unfolds
> In sad, perplexed minors.

He is impatient with figures of speech because they call upon his imagination to paint a thought in terms of something else remote when he could get it much more quickly if it wore its literal label.

Many definitions of poetry have been framed, most of them long and cumbrous, but for a short working definition I know no better one than this: "Poetry is beauty in a pattern." "Beauty" and "pattern" are the two elements without which real poetry cannot exist. The pattern sets it aside from the irregular disordered stress and accent as they occur in the prose I am now using; but if there is nothing *except* pattern, the result is mere doggerel, like

> Hi diddle diddle, the cat and the fiddle

or

> Old Mother Hubbard went to the cupboard.

The "beauty" which must be added to this patter to make it satisfying to poetry-lovers will include appeals to any or all the five senses and to the emotions. Remember this definition, then, as a foundation for poetic appreciation: "Poetry is beauty in a pattern."

This definition sets up no new and narrow standard. If the best poetry of all time were collected and analyzed, its qualities would fit into this simple definition, and no great poetry lacks those qualities. Sometimes the pattern is the vague one of free verse rhythms as in "Fog"

> The fog comes in
> on little cat feet
> it sits for a minute
> on silent haunches
> looking over the city
> and then moves on

or the beautifully balanced structure of the Psalms of David, as in

> The heavens declare the glory of God;
> and the firmament showeth his handywork.
> Day unto day uttereth speech,
> and night unto knight showeth knowledge.

But either of these forms is a long step from the hit-and-miss stresses of casual prose toward that orderly arrangement of stress-intervals which begins to please the ear. As we leave the rougher forms and approach the domains of ordered stanzas, we find symmetry and regularity playing a larger and larger part, until it reaches very nearly its apex of perfection in the Italian sonnet of fourteen lines. Here the first eight lines must have a certain foot and meter and rime-scheme, and it must set forth the thought of the sonnet in a picture, a situation, or an idea. The sestet, or final six lines of the sonnet, varies the rime of the octave, but only in a fashion strictly regulated by rule, and it takes the thought propounded and draws a conclusion or caps it with a startling turn. This is generally conceded to be the noblest pattern the poetry of our language has produced—of the language of Italy either, for that matter, as it was translated originally from the form invented by the Italian Petrarch. It has been tried by nearly every poet of note, but few have reached the success of Milton and Wordsworth in adapting a sublime poetic thought to this strict pattern without cramping its sublimity.

So much for the pattern of poetry; now for its beauty. Sometimes this beauty is found in a profusion of sense appeals, as in the opening stanza of the poem entitled "Flight," written by the American poet Percy Mackaye,* where every one of the five senses is appealed to in eight lines:

> Jock bit his mittens off and blew his thumbs;
> He scraped the fresh sleet from the frozen sign:
> MEN WANTED—VOLUNTEERS. Like gusts of brine
>   He whiffed deliriums.
> Of sound—the droning roar of rolling, rolling drums
> And shrilling fifes, like needles in his spine,
> And drank, blood-bright from sunrise and wild shore,
>   The wine of war.

Sometimes it resides in imagery which bewitches the imagination, as in

> Today dawned not upon the earth as other days have done:
> A throng of little virgin clouds stood waiting for the sun.
> Till the herald-winds aligned them, and they blushed and stood aside,
> As the marshals of the morning flung the eastern portals wide.†

Again, this beauty will be found in a simple little picture like that in the poem entitled "Winter Field,"‡ taken from the *New Republic*.

Winter Field

> Snow on the acres,
>   Wind in the thorn,
> And an old man ploughing
>   Through the frosty morn.
>
> A flock of dark birds,
>   Rooks and their wives,
> Follow the plough team
>   The old man drives.
>
> And troops of starlings
>   A-tittle-tat and prim,
> Follow the rooks
>   That follow him.

A poem like that yields its enchantment only to the reader who has every faculty alert and tuned. This by no means exhausts the multitude of forms

---

*Percy Mackaye (1875–1956), "Fight: The Tale of a Gunner at Plattsburgh, 1814." *Outlook* No. 108 (7 October 1914): 330, ll. 1–8.—ED.
†Guy Wetmore Carryl (1873–1904) "The Débutante, ll. 1–4.—ED.
‡A. E. Coppard (1878–1957), "Winter Field." *New Republic* (24 February 1926): 20.—ED.

which beauty may assume in poetry; but always, in one form or another, poetry will be found to be a combination of these two elements of beauty and pattern.

This poem is entitled "Icicles and Snow[.]" [It] was written by a high-school student of Columbus, Ohio.

Icicles and Snow

This morning polished daggers hang
Beneath the bristling eaves,
    And all the trees
    Are armories
Of pointed crystal leaves.

The moon, a golden grinding stone,
Was whirling all the night.
    It burnished them
    And furnished them
Their chilled and dazzling light.

And as it ground them, sparkling chips
To glistening slopes were streaming.
    This morn the sea
    Of gemmed debris
Like powdered pearls lay gleaming.

Here, coming from a fresh young imagination, is a perfect flash-picture of an ice-clad landscape, but poetic vision has added to an almost photographic reproduction of a winter scene the magic touch of a heavenly artisan busy all night grinding on a huge golden stone the crystal, pointed bayonets for his armory, while the debris fell around in heaps of crystal gems. Anyone can wake up on a winter morning and see the icicles and the trees in their casing of ice, but it takes the rarefied imagination of the poet to clothe that scene in a mystic light which enhances our pleasure ten to a hundredfold. This is the supreme—and indeed the only—function of true poetry: to attune us to the beauties and the grandeur of the universe.

In a Sequestered Churchyard Where Once Poe Walked

Explanatory Note: In 1847 and 1848 Edgar Allan Poe was frequently in the city of Providence, R. I., either on lecture tours or in the course of his ultimately unsuccessful courtship of the local poetess Sarah Helen Whitman. Mrs. Whitman's home abutted on the ancient and picturesque churchyard of St. John's—a bit of rural England imprisoned in the midst of the New World and completely hidden from public view by adjacent buildings and by the steep slope of the hill upon which it is situated. In this churchyard—the same today as in the 1840's—Poe is said to have walked frequently in silent meditation.

On August 7, 1936, H. P. Lovecraft (a resident of Providence whose home is on the ancient hill not far south of the churchyard) and his guests R. H. Barlow and Adolphe de Castro (the latter a friend of Ambrose Bierce and a scholar of reputation) sat on a tomb in the hidden churchyard and composed at Barlow's suggestion, a rhymed acrostic apiece on the name of EDGAR ALLAN POE. Despite the presence of only thirteen letters in the name, a pseudo-sonnet form was chosen. Lovecraft's specimen follows—full, of course, of the defects incidental to forced and hurried composition under the limitations of the acrostic scheme, but nevertheless giving one an excellent idea of the extreme versatility of this brilliant and talented man.

Edwin and the Red Knight

To Camelot, when countless blossoms filled
With scent the dim, rich city's winding streets,
There rode one morn a youth of knightly mien
Edwin by name, son of a distant earl,
Who, hearing oft of deeds by Arthur's knights
Performed in righting wrong throughout the land,
Had won his noble father's hard consent
To join, if Arthur willed, the Table Round.

The wondrous gate shone splendid in the sun,
Which Edwin, wide-eyed, stopped to marvel at,
And as he gazed and tried to trace the wars
Of Arthur carved upon the living stone,
Came Dagonet, the jester of the court,
Tripping a merry measure as he went
To gather daisies for Queen Guinevere
Who cried with mock salute as he passed out,
"All hail, Sir Stripling! welcome to the court!
Art come to drive our Lancelot from the lists?"
And Edwin, flushing, answered not, but spurred
On through the gate and up to Arthur's hall.

Within the dim-lit, many-raftered hall,
Upon a dragon-throne in purple drape,
The King, the great Pendragon of the West,
Held audience, surrounded by his knights;
And as the youthful Edwin forced his way
Through jostling knights in armor to the throne,
He felt beset with doubts that he should stand

Some day an equal in this goodly throng.
But boldly pressing to the royal throne,
He knelt in meek submission to the King,
Who, raising the youth, inquired of him his quest.

   "A boon, oh King: to show by valiant deeds
My right to join the order of thy knights."

But Arthur, hardly liking these proud words,
Bent down his blue, soul-searching eyes to probe
The heart of Edwin, nor was reassured
By what he found there. "Nay," he said, "'tis not
Alone by valiant deeds my knighthood prove
Their right to sit about the Table Round,
But also by such vows of purity,
Humility and love as strain the soul
Of man to keep."

   "Yea, lord," replied the youth,
"The vows I know, and long to take them all
And then to go upon the first brave quest."

   "A boon, Sir King!" cried one who now pressed up,
A man in garments frayed and torn by briers
Of many a woodland path. "A godless rogue
Infests. our county Kent and harries us,
Who bids defiance to thy Christian court,
And there would found its baneful opposite,
Enthroning vice and liberty in Kent.
We pray thee, send and stamp him from the earth
That we may dwell in peace and amity."

   "Thou seest," spake Arthur, turning to the youth,
"How all the petty troubles of the realm
Fly here for succour. Wouldst thou have this quest?
Art versed with sword and weapons of the list?"

   "Yea, sire, oft in joust I've held my own
Against the best retainers of the earl,
My father. Make me now, I pray thee, knight,
That I may go to seek this pagan rogue."

Whereon the King, misdoubting in his heart,
Dubbed the youth knight and laid on him the vows

Of utter hardihood and chastity.
Then Edwin, rising up, his face transformed
To momentary likeness of the King,
Passed out the doorway counter to the hearth.
Got him to horse, and bid the Kentish churl
Lead on; and ever as they spurred along
Through the green-glooming twilight of the woods,
Sir Edwin, pricked at once by the twin spurs
Of high resolve and zeal for selfish fame,
Leapt on ahead, in fancy, to the fight
And saw himself the victor with the spoils
Return to acclamations of the knights,
But ever in his mind the thought of self
Bulked larger, overshadowing zeal for right.

They camped that night within a ferny dell,
And, rising when the languorous, scented dawn
And silver-throated thrushes made a heaven
Of sound and scent the little sylvan crypt,
Passed on and came at noon to Kent.
There stood an ancient, ivy-covered keep .
Whose empty moat and drawbridge half upraised
Proclaimed no recent occupants save birds.

  "There," spake the churl, "this caitiff knight
With his foul crew hath made his nest, and thence
He sallies forth upon the country round.
God shield that he should catch you unaware,
For treacherous is he and devoid of ruth."

  "What ho!" cried Edwin at the castle walls;
"Come out, thou varlet, and submit thyself
To Arthur's doom, through me, his chosen knight."

Then, as upon a day in mid-July
When heat-oppressed silence yields at length
To ominous mutterings from the rising West,
Which grow and overwhelm the world with sound,
There rose within the keep a murmurous noise,
And down the rusty bridge protesting shrieked,
And out upon it trooped a rabble throng
Led by a burly knight in armor red
Who seemed a dull, red coal i' the noonday sun.

As a whipped cur slinks off with dropping tail,
The peasant scuttled through a leafy hedge,
Leaving the maiden knight a prey to fears,
For here was not a formal test of strength
In joust or tourney, guarded by strict rules,
But moral battle 'gainst unnumbered odds
Wherein the loser had no meed but death!
Fine vows were these to swear men to and then
Send them to death as 'twere a little thing!
With rage and desperation burned his heart,
And, clicking his visor down with angry snap,
He laid his lance in rest and spurred to the charge.

     "Have at thee, dog!" he bellowed and the two shocked
On the central bridge that both their lances brake;
And as a little boat is carried to sea
Despite the rower straining at the oars,
So Edwin, borne by the onrush of his charge,
Clove out an easy path through craven knaves
And ere he knew it found himself within
The castle walls; then, wheeling 'round his steed,
Returned to the charge with flashing brand upraised.

As a wounded deer, beset by timber-wolves,
Keeps back its foes by savage rushes, till,
At last, weakened by loss of blood, it sinks
And lets the fatal circle narrow in,
So Edwin, compassed about by slinking knaves,
Too cowardly to meet him face to face,
Beheld with sickening dread the circle close
And rushed again upon his crimson foe.
His sword descended, met the hostile steel,
And glancing, shore the red plume from the crest.
But meanwhile all the rest had stolen up,
And now a dozen windy buffets beat
Upon the doomed young lad's unguarded helm,
And like the massive crag that's undermined
By waves and thunders down to the sea,
He crashed down, dying with curses in his heart.

Within the raftered hall at Camelot,
A wild-eyed peasant told the tragic tale,
And in the heart of Arthur pain was lord.

Seven O'Clock

I heave one hugely weighted eyelid—
The other refuses to budge.
Through the pillow come big, vague ticks
Of my Ingersoll.
At the edge of the curtain
Shows a narrow slice of greenish yellow.
I turn my head slowly toward the door—
A tall slit of yellowish blue.
Spokes of black shadow
Swing leisurely across the ceiling
With the door-slit as an axis:
The wire-workers hurrying by.
Crisp, brittle sounds on the icy sidewalk
Plusk-plusk-plusk-plusk . . . . . .
Swelling, chaotic, diminishing words,
One nasal female louder than the rest:
"Well he seen me; why didn't—"
Others:
"No—I said—If she—all around—"
Plusk-plusk-plusk-plusk . . . . . .
Between groups
Silence wedges in:
But into the silence
Pours a low cataract of sound,
Microscopic,
Insistent;
The far-off roar of the dam decreeing forever
That perfect silence
Shall not be in Appleton.
More plusk-plusking
Breaking into a run
As a distant whistle,
Shrilling and needle-like,
Stabs into the silence.
A nearby bassoon now takes up the tune,
And the chorus is swelled
By three or four more.
Shouldering in between blasts
Come the four double-bells:

Clang-clangg! Clang-clangg! Clang-clanggg!
Then a lower note; mellow, deliberate:
Bong-bong-bong-bong-bong-bong-bongg ! !
Time to get up!

Bernard Austin Dwyer

Ol' Black Sarah

Ol' Black Sara come up outen de groun'—
    Go 'way, Black Sarah! go 'way!
Don' you' heah de yelp o' dat ol' black houn'?
    Ooh! go 'way! Black Sarah, go 'way!

Fetch in de chilluns—shet de do'—
    Go 'way, Black Sarah! go 'way!
Snack up de shutters—Ah heah her fo' sho'—
    Ooh! go 'way! Black Sarah, go 'way!

De screech-owl screech—de moon am dim—
    Go 'way, Black Sarah! go 'way!
De bat fly ovah de hick'ryu limb—
    Ooh! go 'way! Black Sarah, go 'way!

Her teef am sharp—her lips blood-red—
    Go 'way, Black Sarah! go 'way!
Her eyes am white, turn back in her head!
    Ooh! go 'way! Black Sarah, go 'way!

Ol' Shara was a voodoo—long ago!—
    Go 'way, Black Sarah! go 'way!
De pickaninny's bone an' de mistletoe—
    Ooh! go 'way! Black Sarah, go 'way!

When de ol' houn' bark—de moon jus gleams—
    Go 'way, Black Sarah! go 'way!
Ol' Sara's face fill de darkies' dreams—
    Ooh! go 'way! Black Sarah, go 'way!

Beautiful Night

Beautiful Night, when day is done,
Follows on the set of sun;
Who does not love the fading light,
That brings to the world the Beautiful Night?
Beautiful Night! The Owls awake!
With their great voice the mountains shake;
Out hangs the moon, our lantern bright,
While the Owls give praise to the Beautiful Night.
Beautiful Night! the World of Dreams
In its pale moonshine spectral gleams—
There are all sorrows solved aright,
In the Dreams that come with the Beautiful Night.
Beautiful Night! when dawning grey
Brings us back the dust of day—
Then must the Owls—the Dreams—take flight—
To wait for the coming of Beautiful Night!

Fairies

Come sit here, little laddie,
Beside an old man's knee;
We'll make a song of the moonbeams
That come flitting through the tree;
Early dew is sparkling—
Shadows fall and fade—
Sure they say the elves of Ireland
Once landed in this glade.

Their ship was all o' silver,
With silver-silken sail;
There were a hundred men-at-arms,
And knights along the rail;
The King and Queen sat together,
(Themselves with crowns of gold!)
Then the ship spread broad its silken wings
As the argosies unfold.

Where the sedgy grasses
Ripple down the lane,

They floated it under a scotchcap leaf,
To shield it from the rain
Spread their pale pavilions—
Airy as a dream—
Hung their little firefly lamps
Above the gentle stream.

They say the Little People
Go forth such nights as these,
To slide upon the grasses,
And go floating on the breeze;
And they love a little laddie,
Who loves to sit and dream.
And watch the fairy firefly lamps
Go floating down the stream!

The Snake-God

I do not remember how or when we first came upon the temple of the hideous Snake-God, Dora and I—but there it stood, deep in the heart of the obscene and festering deep green jungle. Vines and creepers were draped all around it, giving it the aspect of a snake-clad ruin. Red in the sunset, white in the moonlight, with the hideous effigies of the Snake-God sculptured over all.

Then there were the natives, small, nut-brown Indians, vastly inferior to the mighty race which had reared the ruins. They were a handsome people, save for a peculiar gliding furtiveness that characterized their every movement. But they were called the [people] of the snake, and [accordingly] they worshipped the Serpent-God with [s]trange devotions when the moon was full.

Then there was Ajuna, daughter of the chief, priest and medicine man. Slender was Ajuna, lithely supple as a willow wand, with a rippling, gliding grace in all her movements. Black as Hadean Styx at midnight was her hair, reflecting deep blue elf-lights, her eyes large, lucent and compelling, with something vaguely disturbing if one gazed too far down into those deep wells of darkness. But she was beautiful, even as beauty is measured by us here of the North; so that there grew up an attraction between us, subtle as the seas' tides, irresistible as the pull of Earth's gravity. For the silences were dark and deep—the green glades ached with loneliness—I was man, and she was woman, as it hath been since the ordination of the world. Then—I met Dora.

Tall, blonde, exquisitely white and golden was Dora, the fair daughter of the conquering Northern race. Flowing of pale gold was her hair—the blue of Northern skies in her eyes. Cream-white of purest milk was her skin—and her figure was the figure of a goddess. And when I saw her, I realized that all my dreams of happiness were come true.

Dora had come in on the steamer with her father, the old Professor, who was making a study of the ruins in the neighborhood. And I became his assistant, for such my studies had fitted me at college. From the old Professor I learned—much. And from Dora I learned—to love.

The winding pathway through the jungle them became our path, ours the ramble beside the vine-hung ruins of the temple. I had not seen Ajuna since I first met Dora—and deeply I now realize my wrong to her. But then carried away by the ardent attractions of love, I forgot the hot passions of awhile before. I lived only—I breathed only—I existed but for Dora.

Then, as we whispered our confidences in the darkling forest shades, she said—ah, frequently—that she felt eyes—unfriendly eyes—upon her from the seeking quiet of the deep-green jungle. But I saw nothing, and could only attribute it to her imagination—an imagination rendered sensitive by her awe of the to[w]erring strangeness, the vital breathing presence of the jungle.

On the night-of-the-full-moon, the Serpent-God was worshipped with special devotions. Then the deep throb of drums boomed from the jungle, with the high thin reedy wailing of a flute and beneath a waning moon suitable sacrifice was offered to the Snake-God. Of the nature of that sacrifice I did not venture to inquire—and the natives were reticent.

Then there was to be the grand night of his coming, when the Serpent-God, summoned by the incantations of his faithful, would appear, and would choose a bride from among the daughters of men. Then, with her, would he reign over the whole world, from his throne deep in the heart of hell. And after that should Snake-God no more be summoned by the beating of drums, and the wailing of flutes. It was the greatest honor that could befall an earthly maiden, they said—and a maiden she must be—but woe to her, woe! should she prove unwilling or unheeding to the call of the Serpent. Strangely enough, the ancient myths had it that the chosen should not be one of his own dark-skinned worshippers but the fair daughter of a stranger race. I had no belief in old legends—why, then should the mere wording of this one strike a terror in my heart?

Upon the day of the Full-Moon, we walked together in the forest, Dora and I. Lovely were the filigrees of the green and gold shadow that fell among the trees—and lovely was the white and gold maiden who walked by my side. We strolled down the pathway to the ancient temple—and there, leaning by the vine-clad ruins, Dora confessed to me of the fears that had so lately oppressed her. Every day, she said, since she had met me, and now more and more of late, had she felt the resistless closing in of evil forces—forces that flowed relentlessly toward her from all sides—forces that flowed relentlessly from all sides—forces from which there was no hope of escaping—she felt that deadly basilisk eyes watched her every movement—that she was held helpless in her place, like a prisoner in a cage, for some frightful, unguessable fate. Waking, she dared not picture what—though nightly it was whispered to her in her dreams. And on a sudden, bursting into a flood of tears, she was sobbing on my breast, and clinging to me, as a child clings for protection against the terrors of the night.

"But you do love me, Frank?" she quavered, "even if anything should happen to me—if we should be separated far apart, you would not forget me?"

"Never, my own!" I whispered, holding her close and kissing her tenderly—"never will I forget you, never cease to love you" and here I thought incontinently of a few lines of a poem by the immortal John Milton, in his blindness—"never can I forget you, while the old serpent is held in shackles underground!" Was there, at that moment, a derisively hissing laugh from the green ring of trees surrounding the temple? I do not know—but the day turned cold, for both of us—I felt Dora's body strain suddenly against mine—a shadow fell athwart the sunlight, and, shuddering, I hurried her away from the accursed place.

The sun had gone down and the swift darkness of the tropics was falling.

I saw her safely to her father's door, then went to my own room and to bed, for I was grown suddenly very tired. It was terrifically hot, and the odors of the tropical night flowers were wafted in upon the breeze. The bright moonlight lay upon the pillows of my bed. And my last thoughts, sinking down the steeps of sleep, were of Dora.

Then I was wandering somewhere, and it was not in this bright, sunlit world of ours—not in our God's universe at all—it was on a far, dark star", outlawed from our solar system, exiled from space and time—and there were endless miles of horrible underground caverns—there were terrible sights—and a hoarse voice grunted in my ear—"You are in Hell" Then there was weeping and wailing and gnashing of teeth—and someone I loved dearer than life itself was in uttermost horror of danger—and I could not rise, I could not go to her assistance, because of the serpent-bonds, that bound me fast to the rock. In endless darkness, a shriek—and all Hell laughed! Then I made a final titanic effort—I burst my bonds—sat up in my bed.

I was streaming with cold perspiration, and my sheets, tightly twisted into a rope, were wound around me, like the coils of a gigantic serpent. And I knew what had sounded all through my dreams—the throb of drums, and the thin, high, reedy wailing of a flute.

I slipped into my clothes; I buckled on the broad belt of my holstered Colt .45; I sped down the path. And ever I prayed that I might not be too late.

White the temple rose before me, in the broad baleful light of a tropic moon. I saw the drummers on the hideous black damballah drums—I saw the players upon the mystic reed pipes—and I saw more.

I saw the shape, slenderly, Lilithly lovely, that swayed in the glow of the tropic moon—swayed in the mystic mazes of a dance—and at once I recognized it for the dance of invocation to the Snake-God. And in her high clear voice she was singing the Song-That-Summons-The-Serpent. Nude she was, as the day she was born, save for the flashing gold jewelry, that shot back amazingly the glances of the moon. Anklets—armlets—a slender, golden girdle—all in the form of slim, twisting serpents, coiling around and around—the tiara, a snake coiled twice around her head, with its head uplifted—little, flashing green stones for the eyes—and the sinuously linked necklace of gold that, rippling from her throat suspended the sacred serpent emblem between her breasts. She raised her arms —and she sang. Velvet, clear brown skin—hair like Styx at midnight—eyes, dark and luminously lustrous—it was Ajuna, daughter of a thousand priests, and priestess of the snake.

Now there swam into the moonlight, from out of the darker recesses of the shadows of the temple, another form—all of clear white and gold. *She* wore no jewels, no amulets—nothing save her own unadorned beauty but that was enough. Like a tropical white night flower, radiant with the moonlight and with the dew. No words of mine can describe how beautiful she was. Such beauty had Odin All-Father given to the entranced daughters of the Rheingold; it was for such beauty that sailors wrecked their ships on the high rocky cliffs of the Lorelei. It was Dora, the pure, pale daughter of the conquering Nordic race.

As she emerged more clearly into the moonlight, I perceived that her eyes were closed; that she was as one sleep-walking or in a trance; that though she followed perfectly the movements of the dance, it was obvious that she did so at the bidding of a volition not her own. And I saw the Indian girl watching her with those hypnotic eyes, as compelling as the basilisk stare of the serpent. I noticed the stretching forth of her hands, tense with hypnotic power; it was as if blue, electric sparks flew from her fingers—I felt the quivering force of a will, powerful enough to drag forth Satan himself from the very heart of Hell.

Sadder throbbed the drums; more despairingly shrieked the flutes; and swifter swirled those glamorous young bodies in the mystic mazes of the dance. Swifter the supple brown figure, more swiftly the dazzling white one, almost too fast for the eye to follow—yet ever the eyes commanded, the [other] obeyed. They wove a pattern of color exc[ellent]ly-hued as a Persian carpet, alluringly beautiful as the odalisques of Bagdad. And I could feel unchained the full forces of that will—blue bolts of lightning in the moonlight. And something was forming—taking unto itself solidity—coalescing, as it were, out of the very jungle mists of the moonlight—now it was——HERE!!!

A huge, scaly Horror reared and coiled high, weaving above the temple, swaying to the reedy notes of the flute. Frightful basilisk eyes regarded us from on high—there was the darting and flickering forth of a fiery, forked tongue—a hissing—as if steam was escaping . . . I thought of the Serpent of Eden, of the Midgard Serpent, but this was not either . . . And I saw Dora, shuddering to the very depths of her being yet, obeying a gesture of command from the priestess, kneel forward, to prostrate herself in obeisance before that midnight horror. And I saw the apparition bend its neck, arch itself into a curving loop over her—I fired.

Led by some instinct I shot, not at that horror out of Hell, but at the breast of the weaving brown girl. The shot shattered the sacred serpent-emblem between her breasts; and the blood gushed forth. Ajuna shrieked once, despairingly—she turned a reproachful glance on me—the[n] fell forward on her face in the dust and died. And I? I had wrought her a great wrong, for she had loved me—but what else could I have done? And that horror from elder hells—long before this universe of ours was created—was gone, melted into the moonlight mists that encompassed the jungle. I heard a sigh, as of a breeze going afar off, in the treetops. And I felt a great sorrow, for all the loneliness, all the weariness of the universe.

Dora opened wide her blue eyes. Fully awake she was now, and conscious. With a blush she glanced down at her beautiful, unclad body—and fainted in my arms.

Letters to *Weird Tales*

"I note with interest and some amusement," writes Bernard Austin Dwyer, of Kingston, New York, "the frequently expressed opinions as to who *Weird Tales'* best writer—as if there could be any question! Lovecraft is of course so far above the others that there can be no comparison. I make exception in favor of Wandrei: he possesses real artistic feeling; and a sense of color and audacity of imagination seldom equaled. Clark Ashton Smith is a genius, as impossible to duplicate as are the faery fantastical forests traced by the frosts on winter mornings. I wish I could see much more of Smith's work. But excepting these two there is nobody who deserves mention in the same breath with Lovecraft. Lovecraft never descends to anticlimax—never starts 'in a wild weird clime' and ends in one's own back yard—no; with every word the reader feels the horror more engulfing—the terror of abysmal outer spaces; and unguessed chasms of infinity. I regard him the greatest weird writer living today. "The Outsider"—"The Picture in House"—"The Rats in the Walls"—"The White Ship"—and last, but by no means least, "The Dunwich Horror"! I can not find words sufficiently to declare my admiration of his virginity of conception—the weird, outré, unhackneyed, fully satisfying depth of colorful imagery and fantasy—as strange, as terrible, and as alien to the land of our everyday experiences as a fever-dream. Lovecraft, I am sure, will in after days be noticed as one of the very greatest writers of the weird and the grotesque that ever lived. Indeed I consider him as equal to Bierce and Blackwood, and at times equal to Poe—"The Outsider," for instance. Of Seabury Quinn's "The Phantom Farmhouse" in your last issue, I can not speak too highly. That is a thing of poignant, pathetic beauty, full of moon-filled and tender sylvan atmosphere through which flit shapes of Horror—the Undead."

* * *

A letter from Bernard Austin Dwyer, of Kingston, New York, is so interesting that we quote it in full: "Having yesterday purchased—as soon as it was out—and last night read the most of *Weird Tales*, I feel impelled to offer a few random ideas and criticisms.

"*Weird Tales* is to me the "magazine irresistible," never being on the stalls more than a day before I have it. The well-known—and well-loved—red cover is something that I can not pass by. The magazine offers an excellent evening's entertainment. Nearly all of the stories are good—not Lovecraft, of course, but one can not expect to equal this giant of literary fantasy. Lovecraft, apart from the unguessed, startling originality of his climaxes, has a quality of tone, a sheer eery atmosphere of his own, that is at once inimitable and unapproachable. When one reads Lovecraft, one enters into a dream-world in all verity—one tiptoes timidly amid a million shadowy horrors—beastly phantoms of an unguessed midnight potency. There the evil charms and machinations of the Other Gods in the Elder World surround me, and one shudders at the mystic horrors hidden behind the snowy peaks of unknown Kadath in the cold waste, or peering filmy-eyed from beneath the aged and rotting gambrel roofs of archaic Arkham or Kingsport cottages. No—they can't all equal Lovecraft!—but because the sun shines supreme one doesn't deny light to the lesser luminaries.

"For instance, Henry S. Whitehead is a real artist—though I didn't care so much for his last story, "The Shut Room"—he isn't so convincing outside of the West Indies. But I have greatly enjoyed his stories of those islands—they have truly artistic handling and color, and real atmosphere—beautiful jeweled effects.

"Clark Ashton Smith is a genius, as great in his way as Lovecraft, a real fantaisiste, and it is a very encouraging sign that you are beginning to print his work regularly. I feel sure that many readers of the magazine are capable of appreciating his work.

"E. Hoffmann Price is also an artist—his story about the Oriental rug is fine as the weavings of such a rug itself—a rare web of exotic color.

"Edmond Hamilton is a good pseudo-scientific thriller, always guaranteeing a half-hour's entertainment. He has vastly improved since writing "The Monster[-]God of Mamurth."

"Robert E. Howard is not bad. "The Dream Snake" was a wonderful piece of sinister moonlight painting, and "Wolfshead" was about as good. He has written many fine tales since these two, but they are my favorites.

"Seabury Quinn is always good for an hour's pastime. I can't see where so many get their ideas from who declare him supreme. If he wrote such stories as "The Phantom Farmhouse," I would agree, but not with the present stuff he gets out. Much of the praise of him is undoubtedly mere parrot-talk—people repeating what they hear others say, without knowledge or discrimination. He is, to me, just a good thrill-concocter, neither more nor less, and a good craftsman, handling well his effects. His yarns are always interesting, and usually more or less unpredictable. Think they get better as time goes on. One thing, however, I miss—de Grandin's one-time Gallicisms—his French bulls, so to speak. These used to be really laughable, startling; such as a Frenchman might make when struggling with English. Now, his mistakes—when he remembers to make them—are mechanical, artificial, labored and unconvincing. But that does not do away with the fact that the stories themselves are most fascinating, and I read every one that comes out.

"Now, a word about the illustrations. Harold Markham, writing in the current Eyrie, is right about the cover designs. The work is technically good—but the weird is conspicuous by its absence, and the covers remind one of *Paris Nights*, or an advertisement for *Ziegfeld's Follies*. Raw and rank sex-appeal, trite and obvious; always the inevitable naked woman, and the human, or half-human, beast gloating over her. That has been the motif for over a year. It may be necessary in order to sell the magazine—probably the mind of the general Public runs mostly along such lines. This applies to the illustrations, too, which are seldom weird, and usually embody the same obviously flaunted nudity. Not that I have the least objection to the nude, in its place. I have handled it a great deal myself in my own pictorial work and know that it may be made—as for example in Beardsley—a very effective part of a weird and sinister unit. But that is not the case in the drawings I have referred to. Rankin is a good—an excellent—anatomist, and I have seen some fine work of his. His charcoal originals may be splendid, but they lose too much in reproduction on the rough paper of the magazine. I have seen such good work, and such poor work, by Rankin, that they didn't seem to come from the same man. His present cover has some good points—the green color, the figure of the crouching evil priest, and the outstretched, dressing-gowned arm of de Grandin, holding the sacred ikon. This last is very effective and dramatic—in fact, the arm, and its symbolism, are the best part of the picture.

"Doak is sometimes terrible—sometimes very good. He rightly uses pen and ink technique; charcoal and half-tone work are not adapted to the paper of the magazine—and at times he gets peculiar, weird effects; in the heading to "Suzanne," for instance, and "The Shut Room," both in this issue. The highwayman's pistol should be longer and heavier—horse-pistols, such as he would be likely to carry, were usually of good size—but the swampy woods are fine. He also did well with Robert E. Howard's "Battle of Bones," and I have seen several things of his striking the true weird note. He has possibilities.

"C. C. Senf is a perfect technician. His pictures have usually been as well-drawn, and as totally lacking in every element of eery effect, as an illustration in the *Cosmopolitan Magazine*. But his heading to Frank Belknap Long's "On Icy Kinarth" is absolutely different. If this isn't imaginative and weird, I have never seen a picture that was. The primitive man staring upward, and the swarming cloud of flying phantom dragons, are surely monstrously effective.

It seems to me the best picture you have ever printed, and I wish the whole magazine could be so illustrated. The poem is worthy of the picture.

"In conclusion, I hope you have not been offended by my, at times, unfavorable comments. The Magazine is, truly, as I have said, 'irresistible' to me, and I never miss a copy. But all things earthly can be improved, and these are my honest opinions, not intended as slams or brickbats. I hope you like to hear your readers' true opinions, favorable and otherwise, for it is only so that you can estimate their reactions.

"By the way—whatever you do, don't discard the red-bordered, white-lettered cover!"

Quinn's Masterpiece

Bernard Austin Dwyer writes from West Shokan, New York: "My first choice of stories in the January issue is "Roads" by Seabury Quinn. This is truly Quinn's masterpiece; I have never seen anything even remotely so good by him. In my opinion, it far overtops even "The Phantom Farmhouse." Apart from the story itself, which is delightful and wonderful—the fetching together of such ordinarily widely separated elements as Christ's crucifixion, a blond heroic warrior from the North, a harlot from the house of Magdalene, the Eastern and Western dynasties, and the Middle Ages, the little carved sleighs, the dwarf faery, smiths of the mountains and the legend of Santa Claus—the style itself is very beautiful. I love especially the last few paragraphs with their flavor of the iron and heroic North, the Valhalla-like feast; how Klaus laid aside his arms, and the final piercing and beautiful paragraph. But I love everything—the story and the style, from beginning to end. . . . This story will go down as one of the very best, by *any* author, ever to be published in *Weird Tales*. It is a masterpiece fit to rank with Howard's "Kings of the Night" or Lovecraft's "Whisperer in Darkness." I feel impelled to thank Mr. Quinn heartily for giving me the opportunity to read so satisfactory, wonderfully imaginative and beautiful a story. That style is something to dream about. Next, I will mention a very short poem—"Lost Dream," dedicated to our departed master Lovecraft, by Emil Petaja. May I express my appreciation of how that little poem coincides with one's impressions of the works of Lovecraft? "One fumbles in his scarlet cloak; I see his slender fingers move—he turns a key . . ." a silver key of course. Congratulations to Mr. Petaja for his splendid little poem. May we hope for more? My next favorite story is "Toean Matjan" by Vennette Herron—a very good story, well tied together, and beautiful style. It is exquisitely written. I don't know when I have read a more entertaining story, written in better style. In fact, I like the style quite as well as that of "Roads" only that it is of course shorter. I am quite sure that I should not care to court that lady. I like "The Witch's Mark," and "The Hairy Ones Shall Dance." In the latter, it is already rather obvious that the wolfish materialization came from Doctor Zoberg—*vide* his thick, sinewy wrists! It is right entertaining. Let me, too, commend most warmly "The Inn," in a recent issue. Splendid atmosphere."

A de Grandin Movie

Bernard Austin Dwyer writes from West Shokan, New York: "I always enjoy Quinn, and of course like his Jules de Grandin tales; have often wondered why a de Grandin movie cannot be produced, with Adolph Menjou (blonded, of course) in the title role. Vic MacLaglen would do for Costello, while Lewis Stone, if a little younger, would be admirable as Friend Trowbridge. Of course, the best thing by Quinn that I have yet seen is "Roads." One thing I wish you'd do: commission Quinn to write an equally long story of "the iron and heroic North,' as I naïvely enough expressed it in my letter to the Eyrie. The essence of those last few paragraphs of his; of Robert E. Howard's description of the Aryan's subconscious memories of Nordheim Valhalla; meadhorns and ale-halls; feasting and roaring warriors; the rude comfort and majesty of the North, its wild spirit, its indomitable rudeness: the song of the Valkyrie; the last great battle in the west, and the gathering home to Wotan. All the mighty roaring wassail and weird battle glory of the wild yellow-haired clans. Quinn could do it perfectly. So could Howard, if he were alive; Howard now feasts in Valhalla but perhaps the black Irishman wouldn't thank me for sending him off with a bunch of Squareheads; why not let Quinn? I have left the best till last. In the present issue, I consider "Slave of the Flames" by Robert Bloch (apart from the Lovecraft story) the finest and most powerful thing in the magazine, and beyond comparison Bloch's best. Living and wonderful description; the character of Nero perfectly summed as we know it, and all seen through the glow of a fearful, fiery dream. I tell you, I don't know when I have seen words used more effectively. I honestly believe this is one of the best stories you have ever published. Nothing by Howard ever had more living force. The descriptions of the blazing buildings and of the reactions of the gloating idiot are absolute masterpieces of weird imagery. Then the cleverness of combining those elements; the modern degenerate; the ancient lyre with its implications of Nero, who sang poetically while Rome burned—these surpass my present mastery of adjectives. Cheers for Mr. Bloch, on producing such a work! Finlay's illustration of the same is marvelous."

Who Is This Gal?

Bernard Austin Dyer writes from Wawayanda, New York: "Please, who is Caroline Ferber? Is she Trudy Hemken operating incognito or under a *nom de plume?* Or is she some base, envious female, trying to steal our Trudy's thunder? Please explain this deep and dark mystery, which has me tearing my hair (what there is left of it), weeping and wailing, and walking the floor o' nights, to the no small annoyance of tenants on the floor beneath. Let me, right here, give my vote for first place to the shortest story in the magazine—Manly Wade Wellman's "Up Under the Roof." (I am not taking into the account the Lovecraft reprint. There is only one Lovecraft. Here was a Caesar! When comes such another?) However, very short stories seldom receive warm enough commendation to grant them first place. I unhesitatingly give Mr. Wellman's brief opus first place in my regard, and prefer it to anything (except the Lovecraft) in the book. Lovecraft himself would pronounce that tale good. It strikes me as very highly original, and as a masterpiece of atmosphere and of brooding terror. . . . The description of that weird old house; the little boy all alone with his nightly terrors; the dreary rainy day, and the faint brown light of the lumber room—the kid's search in the utter darkness and the splendidly strong simplicity of the ending: 'Nor did I ever know fear again, not even in the war.' These are superb. The thing is so plainly, simply, and naturally written, has such exquisite atmosphere, and carries such utter conviction. I can fairly feel and see that old house, and the kid in bed, up under the roof, listening to the stirring trees outside, the terrible noises overhead, and shuddering. This is the best thing of Mr. Wellman's that I have ever read."

Letter to Strange Tales

"Oy! Oy! Oy!"

Dear Editor:

I have read the two issues of Strange Tales so far published, and think that you have the beginning of a fine magazine. In these issues, three tales stand way out above the rest, and it is of them that I would speak a couple of words.

In the present issue, "Cassius," by Henry S. Whitehead, is remarkable. It is good, even for Whitehead, and that's saying a great deal. Dr. Whitehead is a past master at depicting the joys and sorrows and strange macabre terrors of the West Indian negro. The abnormal little evil entity, the "twin brother" cheated out of his birthright, is a grotesque, yet very pathetic conception. Certain scenes in this story stand out as vivid, unforgettable pictures. The grotesque little black abnormality scuttering across the floor, black against the white moonlight; the sinister suggestive swinging of the liana vine; the monstrosity pursuing the madly fleeing pickaninny lying crushed, bleeding and helpless, beneath the mangling and tearing claws of the cat. In the depicting of the Western Indian negro, Whitehead bas no equal, and' all his pictures of them have all the color and subtle shading of an exquisite oil painting. Whitehead is not merely a supreme story-teller, he has the feeling of a true artist, and I hope in the future to see a great many of his stories in S. T.

"The Place of the Pythons" by Arthur J. Burks, in the last issue, is a masterpiece. No other word will adequately describe it. I consider it worthy of

Poe or Bierce. I shall take very good care that my copy of this story is not lost. Its originality of conception is unique, astounding. The man's being the python and the python the man, is exceedingly powerful, the more so as it is not postulated or explained; it is simply taken for granted. The steaming jungle night, the warm slash of the rain, the dread of the swamp, the sinuous and sinister shapes that glide, heads upraised among the vine-clad depths and the lyrical, exquisite poetical style in which these things are narrated; all these make up a story, the reading of which is one of the events of a lifetime. I congratulate the author most warmly on having produced such a wonderful piece of work, and am certain that it will go down in history as one of the finest masterpieces of weird tales. I cannot sufficiently express my admiration for it.

"The Return of the Sorcerer,' by Clark Ashton Smith, is a deliciously gruesome tale. Oy! oy! oy! if those moving parts, separated or conjoined should to-night make an entry into our bedroom—*Quick Henry, the Flit! Oy! oy! oy!* What a story to read when one is all alone on a sharp autumn night when the wind rattles the shutters, the bare boughs beat on the side of the house and the wildly weeping autumn raindrops tap insistently at the pane!

All success to Strange Tales, its enterprising editor, and its gifted authors.—Bernard Austin Dwyer, West Shokan, N. Y.

Samuel Loveman

Collecting Curious Books

We assure you that the title isn't at all what you may be led to believe. By the collecting of curious books—curious in the actual sense of the word—we mean books on odd subjects, out-of-the-way poetry, low- or high-cast novels written in such a state of actual unsophistication that the years have made them subjects for hilarious laughter rather than that of the deep and thorough profundity inculcated or intended by their author. Literature of this sort arose early. Elizabethan England, with its wholesale slaughter of pamphlets of prose and poetry, began the steady and varying stream that was to trickle with such persistence through to the 18th century, when the renaissance started anew. We have now no parallel in the number of books and pamphlets, all curious, that smothered, or (as Rabelais would have phrased it) "larded" the open literary market.

Shining examples of the 18th century English curiosa may be stipulated by such works as Amory's "John Buncle" (beloved by Lamb), Paltock's "Adventures of Peter Wilkins and the Flying Women," Ned Ward's "The London Spy"—while from the printed shambles of the shameless Edmund Curll, Pope's vociferous adversary, came a verbal inundation that flooded the sinks and sewers of London's Grub Street, and finally precipitated their publisher into the stocks for a timely, penitential whipping.

American has been consistently a home and harboring of the curious book. Beginning with 1820, the literature of roguery and confession flourished at its height like the proverbial green bay tree. Every unprotected female who had ever been the victim of deliberate seduction, flew to her reputation's rescue in the solidarity of print. From the criminal end came wholesale, early reports of trials for murder—veritable fests of rapine and revenge in a civilization that was to all other intents decent and violently sweet-smelling. Dainty, leather-bound tomes entitled "Gift Books" and "Tokens," with borders of illuminated amaranths centered by young women provided with extensive posteriors, who leaned against gilt funerary urns—made life just the vale of tears or hell on earth that it has always been suspected to be. The virgin of fifty sat herself down to read with all the abject, outer humility of one for whom hope had departed, "the Weeping Willow," a miniature volume of poetry published by Lydia H. Sigourney at Hartford, Connecticut, in 1847. A female of the same unblemished status but duly more kittenish, would have perused "The Floral Gift from Nature and the Heart," by Miss Mary Chauncey, a darling bijou printed in Worcester, Massachusetts, 1846. Its frontispiece depicts a red, red rose, with thorns, buds and emerald foliage—a rose that must have risen and fallen on the alabaster bosom of many a meek maiden of the Poe period. From Philadelphia, in the 1848, stems a tiny volume bound in full sheep, entitled "The American Joe Miller." Among its titles that must have set them hee-hawing, may be noted the following: Colonel Crockett's Quandary; Vocals in Rhode Island; Negro Jockeys; Dialogue in a New Jersey Tavern; a Kentuckian among Ladies; Maryland Wit; Scene in Nashville; A Kentucky Steamboat, etc., etc. In it, masculine virility may have sought refuge by combatting, in a sort of savage and belligerent rough-neckery, the influence that threatened to smother its valor in sentiment spread thick with drivel and honey. The seventies and eighties beheld a still more advanced phase—the utterly elegant and divinely trivial. Presses groaned, moaned and protested, but nevertheless tossed them off—books on etiquette, dancing, courtship, fortune-telling, sex, Mormonism, New York lowlife, Henry Ward Beecher, Tennessee Claflin, Lola Montez, Adah Isaacs Mencken, *ad nauseam* and *in perpetuum*—without rest, without hope, without even a future. And then—miracle of miracles!—

Along came Nietzsche!

A Conversation with Ambrose Bierce

Now that dear George Sterling is dead and books about Ambrose Bierce already number a proverbial baker's dozen, posterity assumes proportions that make the latter a permanent literary legend. I visited Ambrose Bierce in the summer of 1913, only a few weeks before his disappearance from Washington, D. C. "Massive" and "leonine" were the two adjectives that best describe him, in perfecting a portrait that he has clearly remained before me to this day. Beneath an exterior of fierce irony, there was something definitely soft and alarmingly gentle. He was kindly, he was condescending, he was surprisingly human. He appeared not a day over sixty, although printed records had placed him at seventy-four. "Come in and have some beer," he promptly accosted me with, at the elevator on the floor of his apartment. I declared my instant version to beer, but the temptation to include "skittles" also, was overwhelming. "Come in anyway," was his smiling response, and so I entered. "You look like a poet," he remarked. "Can't be very old, either," he continued, after introducing me to the guests—his publisher, his friend and secretary, Carrie Christianson," [*sic*] and a Miss White. I nodded with due modesty. Conversation sprang into being like an incorrigible firefly dance of the far-flung atoms. So far as Bierce was concerned, it ran the gamut from an egoistic forcefulness usually associated with the omniscient period of Johnson or Pope, to an Ariel-like manipulation of subjects that must always characterize the born conversationalist.

The actual topic was, of course, George Sterling. Bierce fired his first salvo. "George is very ugly," he began, "something like Dante—they call him Dante, Ha! Ha! . . . . Sterling, unlike so many other poets, has never known a time when his published work was other than mature. Curious, isn't it, that a poet who has failed to reach the highest peak, is, in the eyes of his public the most despicable of human creatures. It is hard to understand. Men like Lord Tennyson are lauded to high Olympus, while the minor poet is relegated to the degradation of an insect. The truth is, that great poets are rarely, if ever, understood by their wives. Look at Heine, married to a woman so stupid she couldn't conceive what the world meant by calling her dead husband a man of genius. The average man is a fool—and so is the average woman, too, for that matter.

Talk veered to Shaw. "An imposter!" vociferated Bierce bringing down his fist, "all that is good in him I have written myself. It is difficult to say who is really the great light at present. Hardy is a decidedly vague name. Kipling, I believe to be the greatest living influence. I don't exactly see a necessity for the silly laureateship, but a man like Tennyson gave it an upward boost that will never be quite forgotten. The rest were batterheads!" Whitman and Masefield being next discussed, he declared tacitly and with finality: "Whitman was no poet. In Masefield I can see no good whatever. A correspondent has written me," he added, "that sterling by way of comparison with Masefield, has signed himself in a letter as 'The Worm.' Imagine," he chuckled uproariously, "a great poet such as Sterling indubitably is, ever doing a thing as incredible as that!"

"Does this 'Collected Edition' mean that your work is completed?" was asked in parting. "Yes," he replied. "I have a half-humorous idea that the proceeds will support me—if not in luxury—at least in comfort, for the remainder of my life. But such things are for futurity. Journalism has been my work for the past thirty years. Of course, I had the cream and could pick exactly what I wanted."

A Holiday Post-Card

Offhand, we should say that by far the worst place to be in, during the year's holidays, must be a large city. Retrospection brings an endless chain of winding country byways, indefinably buried in snow; roadside trees and hedges, heavy with clinging rime; field and pasturage, covered with a spaceless carpet so white and unsullied that beside it, certain lines in Whittier's classic "Snowbound," are endowed with permeating warmth or undeviating heat. Heaven conspires with the season in a perfect color-scheme, an endless mockery of blue. Not the blue as we know it on the fringe of a garment by Titian, a sonnet of Keats, or in the flashing and glittering skies above the Mediterranean—but a flawless resurrection of something that burns as well as freezes—an ode that might well have been written to a piece of Attic sculpture set in a temperature of minus zero.

Yet in our parasitic moments we prefer the city. Here you have us—seven or eight million souls tossed on one gigantic location, each as certain of its indomitable identify as the tiniest contributory figure in the cosmic calculation of a thundering theorem by Dr. Einstein. Here, is the one place in the world to forget everything—or to remember nothing. Charles Lamb loved it; George Gissing wrote about it; Walt Whitman prophesied for it. In the face of creation as Nature presents herself to us, men must ever remain the remote but invincibly sturdy and nihilistic figures represented as dancing motes by Thomas Hardy in his "Dynasts." Dwellers and inmates of a huge city, the spirit of their stalwart bravado persists, even as a sense of their just irony remains.

Love the city we do, much as those who have gone before us—lights, types, throngs, theatres, buildings, music, bookshops—bitter, sordid, witty, brilliant and gay at all times, but especially so at Christmas and the close of the old year. In it, are compounded to an infinitesimal fraction of correctness, the mysterious components of that profound chemical prescription commonly known as the "Joy of Life."

The Coast of Bohemia

The backwoods of literature are filled with books about the never-never lands—elusive marginalia on the desire of human beings to escape the dead-rot of civilization, the boundaries that provide for the jumping-off place in many a man's materialistic life. To it, some of the majors have largely contributed—notably De Foe, for whom the unreal was as actual as a bubble of dew solidified in crystal, and in our own day, W. H. Hudson.

It is rather for the minors of this particular aspect of literature that we choose to make our plea—a field that is seemingly as limitless in number as are its outrageously obsolete or forgotten specimens. Who, for instance, has ever heard of "Revi-Lona" by Frank Cowan of Greensburg, Pa? Originally sold for as low as five cents a copy, prices eventually gained an ascendancy to five dollars. We haven't seen a copy in three years, but this is one of the best of its sort. The hero is described as a brave man, with all of the vices and a few of the virtues of his sex, who becomes sick to death of the routine of everyday life. He embarks on an oldtime whaler which sets sail for the South Seas, where a shipwreck (and what a shipwreck it is!) casts him on an unknown island inhabited only by Amazonian women. We defy even De Foe to produce anything so similarly brilliant and unconsciously witty as the hero's espousal with nine or ten Amazonian woman, each on a successive nuptial night. Beautifully written and horribly printed, here is one book that cries for a modern edition. It deserves clear type, good paper and a sympathetic editor.

Better known, but more fastidious in its conscious, fantastic phases, and more deliberate in its conformable appeal to the reader's element of realism will be found John Uri Lloyd's "Etidorpha." This is a far-better book than anything ever written by Mr. H. G. Wells in his much-touted, earlier, pseudo-scientific vein. A breathless but tragic pathos hangs over the mysterious narrator: "I admit anything, everything. I do not know that I am here or that you are there. I do not know that I have ever been . . . perhaps vacuity alone is tangible."

The 18th century gave us two novels that were to win the immortal laudation of Lamb and Coleridge—Paltock's "Peter Wilkins and the Flying Women" and "The Live and Adventures of John Buncle" by Thomas Amory. The first contains some of the most sheerly beautiful, imaginative writing of any period since "The Tempest" of Shakespeare. The curious wedding night of "Peter" and "Youwarkee" has been praised by no less a person than Hazlitt, for its rich, romantic flavor. It deserves that, and more. Meredith's "Richard Feverel" alone holds up beside it, for oddly-heightened ecstasy. In "John Buncle," the realistic type of the fantastic novel reaches its apogee. Mistakenly, this book has been compared to Rabelais, but George Borrow would be far more to the point. Such romping bluster, self-sufficiency and virile bravado, belong—not to the 18th—but to the 20th century. Somewhat with more dignity, but certainly with no less exaggeration, an 18th century novelist lands cheek-by-jowl with the virulent virtuosity of Mr. James Joyce.

A Whittier Discovery

In the days when our American literary torch flared with specious glitter, Poe's attack on Longfellow, accusing him in no mild or moderate terms of plagiarism and piratical theft, was designated as the last word in sensational word-baiting. True enough, the illustrious victim, from whom Poe had previously solicited and received a loan of money, remonstrated only in a private letter against the unjustifiable rudeness of his opponent's charge. Open or anonymous, defence of Longfellow became numerous and warmly partisan. But the born dreamer and gentleman-poet, seated like one of his own legends in the book-lined study at Cambridge, kept his own counsel and (in justice to his memory) his entirely equable temper. Only then, had Poe's foaming anger slowly subsided.

The literature of verbal analogy and plagiarism knows no greater and more delicately-refined work than "The Road to Xanadu," where a mind so beautifully unbalanced and nebulously-colored as that of Coleridge, is finally tracked from traces that are blindly intermingled and waste, into a single, clairvoyant source of inspiration. Mr. Lowes proves to such of us who need proof, that the brain, like the "loop'd and window'd raggedness" of Lear, is open to the persuasive habitation of all elements, even as its vigilances are accessible to every phase of emotional truth.

We have before us a copy of a bygone London annual edited by Allan Cunningham—"The Anniversary," for 1829. In its table of contents may be found a surprising number of first-hand contributions by George Darley, John Clare, James Hogg, J. G. Lockhart, Miss Mitford, Caroline Bowles and Robert Southey. Many of the additional contributions are unsigned or merely initialed and it is one of the latter that excites our instant attention. This is a poem of sixty lines in the metre of Whittier's "The Barefoot Boy," entitled "The Blackberry Boy," identified, at the end, with the initial "C," and accompanied by an illustrative plate. So startling is the similarity between this poem printed in 1829, and Whittier's famous lines, published many years later, that one is moved to believe Whittier's actual reading of this poem and its eventual use for his composition.

Incredible as it may seem, practically every mood and color of phrasing in the American poet's one hundred odd lines, find their equivalent in this earlier poem. Here is an instance:

> "For gladness as the bees which sup
> On honey when the sun is up,
> Was I; and pure as rose in June,
> Or star which rises next the moon,
> And restless as the running stream,
> And joyous as the morning beam,
> And light of heart and bright of face
> I started on life's oft-run race."

And in the allusions to nature:

> "Ah! Different when, sweet Child, like thee,
> I hunted wild the murmuring bee;
> Or loitering o'er my school-boy task.
> In sunshine stretched me out to bask;
> Chased speckled trout from stone to bank,
> Made whistles, swords of rushes rank;

> To trees and streams as brethren spake,
> And dyed my lips with berries black;
> **The wild fruit, in the wildest tree,**
> **Might 'scape from birds, but not from me."**

Had Whittier read this poem, and if so, did it seep into his consciousness? Or again, is it simply another instance of those curious but undefinable transmigrations that occur in literature as well as in life? One hesitates to hazard an answer. Yet those haunting, wizard lines:

> "The wild fruit, in the wildest tree,
> Might 'scape from birds, but not from me—"

Whose poetry could it be, but that of Samuel Taylor Coleridge!

[Untitled]

"**365 Ghost Stories.** The Collected Ghost Stories of M. R. James. Sq. 8vo. N.Y. and London, 1931. $2.50

"Nearly 650 pages of enchanted and haunting fiction by the one man living, who can—with a single exception—retrace the footsteps of loneliness on the wizard beach once trodden by Edgar Allan Poe, Ambrose Bierce, and Mary E. Wilkins-Freeman. THAT SINGLE EXCEPTION IS HOWARD PHILLIPS LOVECRAFT, OF 66 COLLEGE STREET, PROVIDENCE, RHODE ISLAND—THE GREATEST MASTER OF WEIRD STORY-TELLING SINCE POE."

Vincent Starrett

[TLS]

940 Buena Park Terrace
Chicago
24 May 1928

Dear Sam:

Answering your inquiry at the close of item No. 263 in your amusing Catalogue No. 4: I was hard up. That's why I sold a lot of my books. And I still miss them.

Did you receive the packet of Bruce Roger's, etc., sent you some time ago? How much do you owe me? I mean in trade? I should like to pick here and there in your good lists, but can't run the risk of overshooting my credit. I am still reasonably hard up, and perhaps *shall* be until I have a royalty check. I hope you are helping out in that connection by urging *Seaports in the Moon* upon all your customers. And have you read it, yourself?

If it is still available, I should like your copy of *Jezebel Pettyfer*, item 425, priced at $15.00. There are others I should like, too, including the Bierce presentation copies and the Aries Press "Ghost Ship," etc.; but I can not commit myself until I know where we stand. Anyway, they will probably all be gone when you get this letter.

I hope you are doing well, and I hope you like your new shop. Are you somewhere [near] the Park Book Shop?

Kindest regards and all good wishes

        Sincerely
        Vincent Starrett

My interests are still Stephen Crane, Bierce, and the *ana* of "Edwin Drood." Let me hear when you have anything in my line.

Glossary of Frequently Mentioned Names

Adams, John D., amateur journalist from Oklahoma, editor of the *Literati*, and member of the Coryciani round-robin letter group.

Babcock, Ralph W., Jr. (1914–2003), a lifelong writer and printer (since the age of seven). He was active in amateur journalism (President of the NAPA 1934–35 and Official Editor 1939–40), and publisher of the *Scarlet Cockerel* and other papers.

Bacon, Victor E. (1905–1997), amateur journalist and editor of *Bacon's Essays*, which published work by HPL and Clark Ashton Smith, and Official Editor of the UAPA (1925–26).

Barlow, R[obert] H[ayward] (1918–1951), author and collector. As a teenager he corresponded with HPL and acted as his host during two long visits in the summers of 1934 and 1935. In the 1930s he wrote several works of weird and fantasy fiction, some in collaboration with HPL. HPL appointed him his literary executor. He assisted August Derleth and Donald Wandrei in preparing the early HPL volumes for Arkham House. In the 1940s he went to Mexico and became a distinguished anthropologist.

Basinet, Victor L. (1889–1956), designer, longtime nurse, and artist; first president of the Providence Amateur Press Club.

Blackwood, Algernon (1869–1951), prolific British author of weird and fantasy tales whose work HPL greatly admired when he read it in 1924.

Bloch, Robert (1917–1994), author of weird and suspense fiction who came into correspondence with HPL in 1933. HPL tutored him in the craft of writing during their four-year association.

Bradley, Chester P. (1917–1983), Official Editor of the NAPA (1934–35) and editor of the *Perspective Review*.

Bradofsky, Hyman (1906–2002), correspondent of HPL (1934–37). He was president of the NAPA (1935–36) and edited the *Californian* (1933f.), one of the most distinguished and voluminous amateur journals of the period.

Brobst, Harry K[ern] (1909–2010), late associate of HPL who moved to Providence in 1932 and saw HPL regularly thereafter.

Bush, David Van (1882–1959), prolific author of inspirational verse and popular psychology manuals, many of them revised by Lovecraft.

Clark, Franklin C. (1847–1915), husband of HPL's aunt Lillian, a physician and writer on medicine and local and natural history. He translated Homer, Virgil, Lucretius, and Statius into English verse. HPL possessed Clark's translations of the Georgics and Aeneid of Virgil and mentioned on several occasions his desire to see the work published.

Clark, Lillian D[elora] (1856–1932), HPL's maternal aunt. She married Dr. Franklin Chase Clark in 1902. From 1926 to her death she shared quarters with HPL at 10 Barnes Street.

Coates, Walter J[ohn] (1880–1941), amateur journalist, printer, editor of *Driftwind*, and staunch advocate of the literature of Vermont.

Cole, Edward H[arold] (1892–1966), longtime amateur associate of HPL, living in the Boston area; editor of the *Olympian*.

Cole, Ira A. (1883–1973) of Bazine, Kansas. Historian of the UAPA and member of the Kleicomolo.

Cook, W. Paul (1880–1948), publisher of the *Monadnock Monthly*, the *Vagrant*, and other amateur journals; a longtime amateur journalist, printer, and lifelong friend of HPL. He first visited HPL in 1917, and it was he who urged HPL to resume writing fiction after a hiatus of nine years. In 1927 Cook published the *Recluse*, containing HPL's "Supernatural Horror in Literature."

Daas, Edward F. (1879–1962), amateur journalist who joined the UAPA within a year of its founding in 1895. He was elected President and in 1907 and served as Official Editor in 1913–14 and 1915–16. Recruited HPL to the UAPA in 1914. At the time of his death, he was serving as UAPA Secretary.

Davis, Edgar J[acobs] (1908–1949), young amateur journalist with whom HPL explored Newburyport and other locales in New England.

de Castro, Adolphe [Danziger] (1859–1959), author, co-translator with Ambrose Bierce of Richard Voss's *The Monk and the Hangman's Daughter*, and correspondent of HPL. HPL revised his "The Last Test" and "The Electric Executioner."

Derleth, August W[illiam] (1909–1962), author of weird tales and also a long series of regional and historical works set in his native Wisconsin. After HPL's death, he and Donald Wandrei founded the publishing firm of Arkham House to preserve HPL's work in book form.

Duffee, May M., amateur journalist and poet. Author of *Poems That Are Real, That Appeal, That You Feel* (1917) and other books.

Dunn, John T[homas] (1889–1983), Irish-American living in Providence who met HPL in late 1914 in the Providence Amateur Press Club. He assisted HPL in editing two issues of the *Providence Amateur* (June 1915, February 1916). Dunn was briefly imprisoned for refusing to register for the draft. After the war became a Catholic priest. He was interviewed late in life by L. Sprague de Camp (see "Young Man Lovecraft," *Xenophile*, October 1975; rpt. *LR*).

Dunsany, Lord (Edward John Moreton Drax Plunkett, 18th baron Dun-

sany) (1878–1957), Irish writer of fantasy tales whose work notably influenced HPL after HPL read it in 1919.

Eddy, C[lifford] M[artin] (1896–1967), pulp fiction writer for whom HPL revised several stories in 1923–24 and who also worked with HPL on ghostwriting work for Harry Houdini in 1926.

Edkins, Ernest A[rthur] (1867–1946), longtime amateur journalist with whom HPL began corresponding in 1932. HPL persuaded him to rejoin the amateur journalism movement, and Edkins subsequently edited several issues of the journal *Causerie*.

Fritter, Leo (1878–1948), lawyer, amateur journalist, and member of the Woodbee Press Club. HPL supported Fritter's campaign to be President of the UAPA (1915–16), which Fritter won.

Galpin, Alfred (1901–1983), amateur journalist, French scholar, composer, and protégé, then longtime friend, of HPL. When he lived in Appleton, WI, he was MWM's high school student.

Gamwell, Annie E[meline] P[hillips] (1866–1941), HPL's younger aunt, living with him at 66 College Street (1933–37). She had been married (1897–1936) to Edward F[rancis] Gamwell (1869–1936).

Goodenough, Arthur H[enry] (1871–1936), amateur poet who resided in Brattleboro, VT. HPL visited him there on several occasions.

Greene, Sonia Haft (1883–1972), HPL's wife (1924–29). Born Sonia Haft Shafirkin in Ichnya (near Kiev), in the Ukraine. Settling in the United States, she eventually joined the amateur journalism movement, publishing two lavish issues of the *Rainbow* and becoming president of the UAPA (1924–25). After her divorce from HPL, she moved to California and married Dr. Nathaniel Davis. *The Private Life of H. P. Lovecraft* (1985; rev. 1992) is her memoir of HPL.

Guiney, Louise Imogen (1861–1920), a once noted Massachusetts poet and essayist. HPL claims that his family stayed with her at her home in Auburndale during the winter of 1892–93, but this has not been confirmed.

Haggerty, Vincent B[artholemew] (1888–1943) amateur journalist associated with the NAPA in the 1920s and 1930s.

Hasemann, John H., Jr. (1894–1974), ed. of *Flatbush Amateur Press*, of Flatbush, NY. He produced at least six issues from January 1918 to April 1920.

Haughton, Ida C. (1868–1935?) amateur journalist and foe of HPL, about whom HPL wrote the satiric poem "Medusa: A Portrait" (1921).

Heins, Charles W. (1877–1967), editor of the *National Critic* and forty-first president of the NAPA.

Hoag, Jonathan E. (1831–1927), the amateur poet, came to HPL's notice around 1916. Beginning in 1918, HPL wrote annual birthday tributes that appeared in the *Troy [New York] Times* and various amateur journals, and also edited (with James F. Morton) Hoag's *Poetical Works* (1923).

Houtain, George Julian (1884–1945) amateur journalist who with his wife, E. Dorothy (MacLaughlin) Houtain (1889–1980), established the semi-professional humor magazine *Home Brew*, for which he commissioned HPL to write "Herbert West—Reanimator" (1921–22) and "The Lurking Fear" (1922).

Howard, Robert E[rvin] (1906–1936), prolific Texas author of weird and adventure tales for Weird Tales and other pulp magazines; creator of the adventure hero Conan of Cimmeria. He and HPL corresponded voluminously from 1930 to 1936. He committed suicide when he heard of his mother's impending death.

Hutchinson, Alfred L. (1859–1930), amateur journalist from Weyauwega, WI, and editor of *The Trail*.

Kirk, George W[illard] (1899–1962) member of the Kalem Club. He published *Twenty-one Letters of Ambrose Bierce* (1922) and ran the Chelsea Bookshop in New York.

Kleiner, Rheinhart (1892–1949), amateur poet and longtime friend of HPL. He visited HPL in Providence in 1918, 1919, and 1920, and met him frequently during the heyday of the Kalem Club (1924–26). He was the editor of the amateur journal, the *Piper*.

Koenig, H[erman] C[harles] (1893–1959), late associate of HPL who spearheaded the rediscovery of the work of William Hope Hodgson.

Kuntz, Eugene B. (1865–1944), Prussian-born poet, Presbyterian minister, and amateur journalist. HPL edited Kuntz's slim collection of poems, *Thoughts and Pictures* (Haverhill, MA: "Cooperatively published by H. P. Loveracft [sic] and C. W. Smith," 1932), probably revising the poems in the process.

Leeds, Arthur (1882–1952?), an associate of HPL in New York and member of the Kalem Club. He was the author (with J. Berg Esenwein) of *Writing the Photoplay* (Springfield, MA: The Home Correspondence School, 1913; rev. ed. 1919).

Long, Frank Belknap (1901–1994), fiction writer, poet, member of the Kalem Club, and one of HPL's closest friends and correspondents.

Lynch, Joseph Bernard (1879–1952), amateur journalist and member of the Hub Club.

Machen, Arthur (1863–1947), Welsh author of weird fiction whose work influenced HPL significantly after he read it in 1923.

McNeil, [Henry] Everett (1862–1929), author of historical and adventure novels for boys; member of the Kalem Club.

Miniter, Edith (1867–1934), amateur author who also professionally published a novel, *Our Natupski Neighbors* (1916) and many short stories. HPL was guest at her home in Wilbraham, Massachusetts, in the summer of 1928.

Morse, Richard Ely (1909–1986), poet, librarian at Princeton University, and correspondent of HPL.

Morton, James Ferdinand (1870–1941), amateur journalist, author of many tracts on race prejudice, free thought, and taxation; longtime friend of HPL and member of the Kalem Club.

Munn, H[arold] Warner (1903–1981), contributor to the pulp magazines, living near W. Paul Cook in Athol, MA.

Munroe, Addison Pierce (1861–1955), father of Chester, member of the R.I. Senate (1911–1914).

Munroe, Chester Pierce (1889–1943), boyhood friend of HPL. When he took a job in Asheville, NC, in 1913, brokered a writing opportunity for HPL with the *Asheville Gazette-News*, where HPL published at least 14 astronomy articles between February and May 1915.

Munroe, Harold Bateman (1891–1966), boyhood friend of HPL.

Murphy, William R., fortieth president of the NAPA (1906). He won all the NAPA laureateships: poetry, essay, story, history, and editorial (twice). Editor of the *Pioneer*. Member of the editorial staff of the Philadelphia *Evening Ledger*, specializing in dramatic and musical criticism.

Myers, Denys P. (1884–1972) and **Ethel May Johnston Myers** (1882?–1971?), described by HPL as "old-time amateurs," living in Cambridge, MA.

Orton, Vrest (1897–1986), a late member of the Kalem Club. He was for a time an editor at the Saturday Review and later the founder of the Vermont Country Store. He compiled an early bibliography of Theodore Dreiser, *Dreiserana* (1929).

Parker, Charles A. A. (1880–1965), amateur journalist and editor of the little magazine *L'Alouette*, chiefly devoted to poetry.

Price, E[dgar] Hoffmann (1898–1988), prolific pulp writer of weird and adventure tales. HPL met him in New Orleans in 1932 and corresponded extensively with him thereafter.

Renshaw, Anne Tillery (1890?–1953?), prolific amateur journalist and professor. She met HPL during his visit to Washington, DC, in April 1925. In 1936 she commissioned HPL to revise *Well-Bred Speech*, a textbook of English usage, although much of the work HPL did for it was excised.

Sandusky, Albert A[ugust] (1896–1934), amateur journalist whose use of slang amused HPL. HPL met him frequently during trips to the Boston area, member of the Hub Club.

Sechrist, Edward Lloyd (1873–1953), amateur journalist and beekeeper. HPL met him on several occasions, especially during visits to Washington, DC.

Shea, J[oseph] Vernon (1912–1981), writer and weird fiction fan in Pittsburgh who corresponded with HPL in the 1930s. He later went on to edit two non-weird anthologies and write some Lovecraftian fiction.

Smith, Charles W. ("Tryout") (1852–1948), longtime amateur journalist, editor of the *Tryout,* and friend and correspondent of HPL.

Smith, Clark Ashton (1893–1961), prolific California poet and writer of fantasy tales. He received a "fan" letter from HPL in 1922 and corresponded with him until HPL's death.

Smith, Edwin Hadley (1869–1944), a leading amateur journalist of the period, chiefly associated with the NAPA. The Library of Amateur Journalism (also known as The Edwin Hadley Smith Collection The Fossil Collection), initially housed at the Franklin Institute in Philadelphia, is now at the University of Wisconsin–Madison. HPL directed that, upon his death, his amateur journals be turned over to Smith.

Spink, Helm C. (1909–1970), printer and Official Editor of the NAPA in 1930–31 and again in 1935–36 (with O. W. Hinrichs). He printed HPL's *Further Criticism of Poetry.*

Strauch, Carl Ferdinand (1908–1989), friend of Harry Brobst and correspondent of HPL. He later became a distinguished professor and critic.

Talman, Wilfred Blanch (1904–1986), correspondent of HPL and late member of the Kalem Club. HPL assisted Talman on his story "Two Black Bottles" (1926) and wrote "Some Dutch Footprints in New England" for Talman to publish in *De Halve Maen,* the journal of the Holland Society of New York. Late in life he wrote the memoir *The Normal Lovecraft* (1973).

Wandrei, Donald (1908–1987), poet and author of weird fiction, science fiction, and detective tales. He corresponded with HPL from 1926 to 1937, visited HPL in Providence in 1927 and 1932, and met HPL occasionally in New York during the 1930s. He helped HPL get "The Shadow out of Time" published in *Astounding Stories.* After HPL's death he and AWD founded the publishing firm Arkham House to preserve HPL's work. For their joint correspondence, see *Mysteries of Time and Spirit* (Night Shade Books, 2002).

Wandrei, Howard (1909–1956), younger brother of Donald Wandrei, premier weird artist and prolific author of weird fiction, science fiction, and detective stories; correspondent of HPL.

Whitaker, Noah F. (1870?–1953), amateur journalist and editor of *Pegasus.*

Whitehead, Henry S[t. Clair] (1882–1932), author of weird and adventure tales, many of them set in the Virgin Islands. HPL once described him as "Musician, artist, athlete, traveller, cleric, liturgiologist, author, boys' camp leader, psychologist, civic leader, anthropologist" as well as an alienist and psychiatrist." HPL corresponded with him and visited him in Florida in 1931. HPL wrote a brief eulogy of Whitehead for *WT.*

Bibliography

A. Works by H. P. Lovecraft

Books
The Ancient Track: Complete Poetical Works. Ed. S. T. Joshi. 2nd ed. New York: Hippocampus Press, 2013.
The Annotated Supernatural Horror in Literature. Ed. S. T. Joshi. 2nd ed. New York: Hippocampus Press, 2012.
Collected Essays. Ed. S. T. Joshi. New York: Hippocampus Press, 2004–06. 5 vols.
Collected Fiction: A Variorum Edition. Ed. S. T. Joshi. New York: Hippocampus Press, 2015 (Volumes 1–3), 2016 (Volume 4).
An Epistle to the Rt. Hon[ble] Maurice Winter Moe, Esq. of Zythopolis, in the Northwest Territory of His Majesty's American Dominion by L. Theobald, Jun.: An Epic Poem. Annotated by R. Alain Everts. [Madison, WI]: Strange Co., 1987. Text in *AT*.
Essential Solitude: The Letters of H. P. Lovecraft and August Derleth. Ed. David E. Schultz and S. T. Joshi. New York: Hippocampus Press, 2008. 2 vols.
Fungi from Yuggoth: An Annotated Edition. Ed. David E. Schultz. New York: Hippocampus Press, 2017.
Letters to Alfred Galpin. Ed. S. T. Joshi and David E. Schultz. New York: Hippocampus Press, 2003.
Letters to Elizabeth Toldridge and Anne Tillery Renshaw. Ed. David E. Schultz and S. T. Joshi. New York: Hippocampus Press, 2014.
Letters to F. Lee Baldwin, Duane W. Rimel, and Nils Frome. Ed. David E. Schultz and S. T. Joshi. New York: Hippocampus Press, 2016.
Letters to Family and Family Friends ed. S. T. Joshi and David E. Schultz, New York: Hippocampus Press, forthcoming.
Letters to J. Vernon Shea, Carl F. Strauch, and Lee McBride White. Ed. S. T. Joshi and David E. Schultz. New York: Hippocampus Press, 2016.
Letters to Rheinhart Kleiner. Ed. S. T. Joshi and David E. Schultz. New York: Hippocampus Press, 2005.
Letters to Samuel Loveman and Vincent Starrett. West Warwick, RI: Necronomicon Press, 1994.
Mysteries of Time and Spirit: The Letters of H. P. Lovecraft and Donald Wandrei. Ed. S. T. Joshi and David E. Schultz. San Francisco: Night Shade Books, 2002.
O Fortunate Floridian: H. P. Lovecraft's Letters to R. H. Barlow. Ed. S. T. Joshi and David E. Schultz. Tampa, FL: University of Tampa Press, 2007.

Selected Letters. Edited by August Derleth, Donald Wandrei, and James Turner. Sauk City, WI: Arkham House, 1965–76. 5 vols.

The Shadow over Innsmouth. Everett, PA: Visionary Publishing Co., 1936.

The Shunned House. Athol, MA: Recluse Press, 1928 (printed but not bound or distributed until 1959–61).

Fiction

"The Alchemist." *United Amateur* 16, No. 4 (November 1916): 53–57. In *CF* 1.

"The Beast in the Cave." *Vagrant* No. 7 (June 1918): 113–20. In *CF* 1.

"Arthur Jermyn." See "Facts concerning the Late Arthur Jermyn and His Family."

"The Call of Cthulhu." *WT* 11, No. 2 (February 1928): 159–78, 287. In *Beware After Dark! The World's Most Stupendous Tales of Mystery, Horror, Thrills and Terror,* ed. T. Everett Harré. New York: Macaulay, 1929. 223–59. In *CF* 2.

The Case of Charles Dexter Ward. In *CF* 2.

"The Colour out of Space." *Amazing Stories* 2, No. 6 (September 1927): 557–67. In *CF* 2.

"Dagon." *Vagrant* No. 11 (November 1919): 23–29. *WT* 2, No. 3 (October 1923): 23–25. In *CF* 1.

The Dream Quest of Unknown Kadath. In *CF* 2.

"The Evil Clergyman." *WT* 33, No. 4 (April 1939): 135–37 (as "The Wicked Clergyman"). In *CF* 3.

"Facts concerning the Late Arthur Jermyn and His Family." *Wolverine* No. 9 (March 1921): 3–11. *WT* 3, No. 4 (April 1924): 15–18 (as "The White Ape"). *WT* 25, No. 5 (May 1935): 642–48 (as "Arthur Jermyn"). In *CF* 1.

"The Festival." *WT* 5, No. 1 (January 1925): 169–74. *WT* 22, No. 4 (October 1933): 519–20, 522–28. In *CF* 1.

"Gone—But Whither?" Nonextant.

"The Haunter of the Dark." *WT* 28, No. 5 (December 1936): 538–53. In *CF* 3.

"The Horror at Red Hook." *WT* 9, No. 1 (January 1927): 59–73. In *You'll Need a Night Light,* ed. Christine Campbell Thomson. London: Selwyn & Blount, 1927. 228–54. In *Not at Night!,* ed. Herbert Asbury. New York: Macy-Masius (The Vanguard Press), November 1928. 27–52. In *CF* 1.

"The Hound." *WT* 3, No. 2 (February 1924): 50–52, 78. *WT* 14, No. 3 (September 1929): 421–25, 432. In *CF* 1.

"Hypnos." *National Amateur* 45, No. 5 (May 1923): 1–3; *WT* 4, No. 2 (May–June–July 1924): 33–35. *WT* 30, No. 5 (November 1937): 626–31. In *CF* 1.

"Ibid." *O-Wash-Ta-Nong* 3, No. 1 (January 1938): 11–13. *Phantagraph* 8, No. 2 (June 1940): 2–7. In *CF* 2.

"In the Vault." *Tryout* 10, No. 6 (November 1925): [3–17]. *WT* 19, No. 4 (April 1932): 459–65. In *CF* 1.

"The Loved Dead" (by C. M. Eddy, revised by HPL). *WT* 4, No. 2 (May–June–July 1924): 54–57.

"The Lurking Fear." *Home Brew* 2, No. 6 (January 1923): 4–10; 3, No. 1 (February 1923): 18–23; 3, No. 2 (March 1923): 31–37, 44, 48; 3, No. 3 (April 1923): 35–42. *WT* 11, No. 6 (June 1928): 791–804. In *CF* 1.

"The Mysterious Ship." In *CF* 3.

"The Mystery of the Grave-Yard." In *CF* 3.

"Pickman's Model." *WT* 10, No. 4 (October 1927): 505–14. In *By Daylight Only*, ed. Christine Campbell Thomson. London: Selwyn & Blount, 1929. 37–52. *WT* 28, No. 4 (November 1936): 495–505. In *The "Not at Night" Omnibus*, ed. Christine Campbell Thomson. London: Selwyn & Blount, [1937]. 279–307. In *CF* 2.

"The Picture in the House." *National Amateur* 41, No. 6 (July 1919 [*sic*]): 246–49. *WT* 3, No. 1 (January 1924): 40–42. *WT* 29, No. 3 (March 1937): 370–73. In *CF* 1.

"Polaris." *Philosopher* 1, No. 1 (December 1920): 3–5. *National Amateur* 48, No. 5 (May 1926): 48–49. *FF* 1, No. 6 (February 1934): 83–85. In *CF* 1.

"The Quest of Iranon." *Galleon* 1, No. 5 (July–August 1935): 12–20. In *CF* 1.

"The Shunned House." In *CF* 1.

"The Statement of Randolph Carter." *Vagrant* No. 13 (May 1920): 41–48. *WT* 5, No. 2 (February 1925): 149–53. In *CF* 1.

"Strange High House in the Mist." *WT* 18, No. 3 (October 1931): 394–400. In *CF* 2.

"The Tomb." *Vagrant* No. 14 (March 1922): 50–64. *WT* 7, No. 1 (January 1926): 117–23. In *CF* 1.

"The Unnamable." *WT* 6, No. 1 (July 1925): 78–82. In *CF* 1.

"The Very Old Folk." *Scienti-Snaps* 3, No. 3 (Summer 1940): 4–8. In *CF* 3.

"The White Ship." *United Amateur* 19, No. 2 (November 1919): 30–33. *WT* 9, No. 3 (March 1927): 386–89. In *CF* 1.

Poetry [all poems are in *AT*]

"Alfredo; a Tragedy." Moe is represented as the character "Mauricio."

"An American to Mother England." *Poesy* 1, No. 7 (January 1916): 62. *Dowdell's Bearcat* No. 16 (November 1916): [12–14].

"[Christmas Greetings.]": 7. "A Brumalian Wish"; 56. Untitled; 110. Untitled. Sent to Moe.

"Edith Miniter: Born on Wilbraham Mountain, Massachusetts, May 5, 1869. Died at North Wilbraham, Massachusetts, June 8, 1934." *Tryout* 16, No. 8 (August 1934): [5–6].

"An Epistle to the Rt. Honble Maurice Winter Moe, Esq. of Zythopolis, in the Northwest Territory of HIS MAJESTY'S American Dominions."

"Gems from 'In a Minor Key.'" *Conservative* 1, No. 3 (October 1915): 8.

"In a Sequester'd Providence Churchyard Where Once Poe Walk'd." *Science-Fantasy Correspondent* 1, No. 3 (March–April 1937): 16–17. "Winged Summer" [Part 2]. *WT* 31, No. 5 (May 1938): 578 (as "Where Poe Once

Walked: An Acrostic Sonnet"). In *Four Acrostic Sonnets on Poe* (1936), ed. Maurice W. Moe.

"The Introduction." Dedicated to Moe.

"The Isaacsonio-Mortoniad." 1915. Unpublished in HPL's lifetime.

"Lines on Gen. Robert Edward Lee: Born Jan. 19, 1807." *Coyote* 3, No. 1 (January 1917): 1–2.

"Medusa: A Portrait." *Tryout*, 7, No. 9 (December 1922): 32–34 (as by "Jeremy Bishop").

"My Lost Love." Dedicated to Moe.

"Nemesis." *Vagrant* No. 7 (June 1918): 41–43. *WT* 3, No. 4 (April 1924): 78.

"New-England Fallen." 1912. Unpublished in HPL's lifetime.

"The Odes of Horace: Book III, ix." 1936. Unpublished in HPL's lifetime.

"[On Cheating the Post Office.]" In *Marginalia* by H. P. Lovecraft and Divers Hands. Sauk City, WI: Arkham House, 1944. Facing p. 278.

"On the Return of Maurice Winter Moe, Esq., to the. Pedagogical Profession."

"The Poem of Ulysses, or The Odyssey." 1897. Unpublished in HPL's lifetime.

Poemata Minora, Volume II. 1902. Unpublished in HPL's lifetime. [Includes "Ode to Selene or Diana," "To the Old Pagan Religion," "On the Ruin of Rome," "To Pan," and "On the Vanity of Human Ambition."]

"The Power of Wine: A Satire." [Providence] *Evening News* 46, No. 46 (13 January 1915): 8. *Tryout* 2, No. 5 (April 1916): [5–7]. *National Enquirer* 5, No. 26 (28 March 1918): 3.

"Providence in 2000 A.D." [Providence] *Evening Bulletin* 50, No. 55 (4 March 1912): Sec. 2, p. 6.

"Psychopompos: A Tale in Rhyme." *Vagrant* No. 10 (October 1919): 13–22. *WT* 30, No. 3 (September 1937): 341–48 (without subtitle).

"Quinsnicket Park." *Badger* No. 2 (June 1915): 7–10. [Providence] *Evening News* 48, No. 58 (February 1916): 8.

"Regner Lodbrog's Epicedium." *Acolyte* 2, No. 3 (Summer 1944): 11–15 (as "Regnar Lodbrug's Epicedium").

"The Simple Speller's Tale (Translated into English)." *Conservative* 1, No. 1 (April 1915): [1].

"Sir Thomas Tryout." *Tryout* 7, No. 9 (December 1921): [31–32] (as by "Ward Phillips"). *Tryout* 21, No. 1 (March 1941): [3–4].

"The Smile." *Symphony* No. 12 (July 1916): [3–4]. *Little Budget of Knowledge and Nonsense* 1, Nos. 5–6 (August–September 1917): 68.

"The Teuton's Battle-Song." *United Amateur* 15, No. 7 (February 1916): 85 (with author's note, 85–86).

"To Charlie of the Comics: (With Profuse Apologies to Rheinhart Kleiner, Esq., Poet-Laureate and Author of 'To Mary of the Movies')." *Providence Amateur* 1, No. 2 (February 1916): 13–14 (unsigned).

"To Samuel Loveman, Esquire, on His Poetry and Drama, Writ in the Elizabethan Style." *Dowdell's Bearcat* 4, No. 5 (December 1915): [7].
"To the Members of the United Amateur Press Association from the Providence Amateur Press Club." *Providence Amateur* 1, No. 1 (June 1915): [1–3].
"To the Old Pagan Religion." *Tryout* 5, No. 4 (as "The Last Pagan Speaks"; as by "Ames Dorrance Rowley"). See also *Poemata Minora, Volume II.*
"Unda; or, The Bride of the Sea: A Dull, Dark, Drear, Dactylic Delirium in Sixteen Silly, Senseless, Sickly Stanzas." *Providence Amateur* 1, No. 2 (February 1916): 14–16 (as "The Bride of the Sea"; as by "Lewis Theobald, Jr."). *O-Wash-Ta-Nong* 2, No. 3 (December 1937): [10–11] (as part of "Perverted Poesie or Modern Metre"). Dedicated to Moe.

The Poetical Works of Jonathan E. Hoag. Contains HPL's "Introduction," iii–vii; "Prologue" to "Amid Inspiring Scenes (Near Greenwich, N.Y.)" by Hoag, 41; "Jonathan E. Hoag, Esq.: On His Eighty-seventh Birthday, February 10, 1918," 61–63; "To Jonathan Hoag, Esq.: On His 88th Birthday, February 10, 1919," 63–64; "Ad Scribam: Jonathan E. Hoag, Esq., Aetat LXXXIX: February 10, 1920," 64–65; "To Mr. Hoag: On His Ninetieth Birthday, February 10, 1921," 65–66; "On a Poet's Ninety-first Birthday: (To Jonathan Hoag, Esq., February 10, 1922)," 66; "To Mr. Hoag; Upon His Ninety-second Birthday, February 10, 1923," 67.

Nonfiction
"An Account of a Trip to the Antient Fairbanks House, in Dedham, and to the Red Horse Tavern in Sudbury, in the Province of the Massachusetts-Bay." In *CE* 4.
"The Allowable Rhyme." *Conservative* 1, No. 3 (October 1915): 3–6. In *CE* 2.
"Astrology and the Future." [Providence] *Evening News.* 45, No. 123 (13 October 1914): 8 (as "Astrlogh and the Future"; as by "Isaac Bickerstaffe, Jr."). In *CE* 3.
"Delavan's Comet and Astrology." [Providence] *Evening News.* 45, No. 134 (26 October 1914): 8 (as by "Isaac Bickerstaffe, Jr."). In *CE* 3.
"Department of Public Criticism." *United Amateur* 15, No. 9 (April 1916): 111–17. In *CE* 1.
"The Falsity of Astrology." [Providence] *Evening News.* 45, No. 122 (10 October 1914): 8. In *CE* 3.
"In a Major Key." *Conservative* 1, No. 2 (July 1915): 9–11. In *CE* 1.
"Is There Life in the Moon?" *Pawtuxet Valley Gleaner* 31, No. 37 (14 September 1906): 1. In *CE* 3.
"[Letter to Bernard Austin Dwyer, November 1927.]" In *Dreams and Fancies* (Arkham House, 1962), 14–26.
"[Letter to Maurice W. Moe , 15 May 1918.]" In *Dreams and Fancies* (Arkham House, 1962), [3]–4.

"Letters to the Coryciani." *Lovecraft Annual* No. 11 (2017): 118–52.
"Letters to Vincent Starrett." *Crypt of Cthulhu* No. 46 (Eastertide 1987): 31–37.
"List of Certain Basic Underlying Horrors Effectively Used in Weird Fiction." In *CE* 5.
"A Living Heritage: Roman Architecture in Today's America." *Californian* 3, No. 1 (Summer 1935): 23–28 (abridged; as "Heritage or Modernism: Common Sense in Art Forms"). In *CE* 5.
"Lovecraft's Letters to Vincent Starrett." *Crypt of Cthulhu* No. 46 (Eastertide 1987): 31–36.
"News Notes." *United Amateur* 16, No. 9 (July 1917): 128, 131, 134, 137 [unsigned]. In *CE* 1.
"No Transit of Mars." *Providence Sunday Journal* (3 June 1906): Sec. 2, p. 5. In *CE* 3.
"The Poetry of John Ravenor Bullen." *United Amateur* 25, No. 1 (September 1925): 1–3, 6. In *CE* 2.
"Science versus Charlatanry." [Providence] *Evening News* 45, No. 95 (9 September 1914): 8. In *CE* 3.
"Sleepy Hollow Today." An extract from "Observations on Several Parts of America." In Sterling Leonard and Harold Y. Moffett, ed. *Junior Literature: Book Two*. New York: Macmillan, 1930, 1935. 545–46. In *CE* 4.
"Supernatural Horror in Literature." *Recluse* No. 1 (1927): 23–59. In *CE* 2.
"Vermont—A First Impression." *Driftwind* 2, No. 3 (March 1928): [5–9]. In *CE* 4.
"The Work of Frank Belknap Long, Jr." *United Amateur* 23, No. 1 (May 1924): 1–4 (unsigned). In *CE* 2.

B. Works by Maurice W. Moe

Books
Comma Mastery. Wauwatosa, WI: Kenyon Press Pub. Co., 1927.
"Doorways to Poetry." Unpublished ms., 1929?
First Steps in the Appreciation of Poetry. Milwaukee, WI: West Division High School, 1935.
Four Acrostic Sonnets on Edgar Allan Poe. Milwaukee, WI: Maurice W. Moe, 1936. All poems (including Moe's) rpt. in David E. Schultz, "In a Sequester'd Churchyard." *Crypt of Cthulhu* No. 57 (St. John's Eve 1988): 26–29. Moe's poem only rpt. in *Poetry out of Wisconsin*, ed. August Derleth and Raymond Larsson. New York: Harrison, 1937.
Imagery Aids. Wauwatosa, WI: Kenyon Press Pub. Co., 1931.
Junior Literature: Book Three. Ed. Sterling A. Leonard, Harold Y. Moffett, and Maurice W. Moe. New York: Macmillan, 1930.
The Moe Book Tests: One Hundred Selections on High School Reading. Wauwatosa, WI: Kenyon Press Pub. Co., 1927, 1931, 1940. [Set No. 3: 100 numb., in box (1927); Set No. 5: cards in box (1931); Set No. 6 (1940).]
Poem Comments. Milwaukee, WI: West Division High School, 1934.

The Apprentice: An Amateur Journal. Ed. Maurice W. Moe. 1, No. 1 (June 1907)–No. 5 (June 1913).
The Pippin. Journal of the Appleton High School Press Club.

Nonfiction
"After Prohibition." *Silver Clarion* 3, No. 6 (September 1919): 2–3.
"Amateur Journalism." ("An Address delivered July 19, 1922 before the English teacheers at the summer session of the University of Wisconsin.") *Apprentice* n.d. [1922]: 1–8.
"Amateur Journalism and the English Teacher." *English Journal* 4, No. 2 (February 1915): 113–15. ("Address delivered at a meeting of the National Council of Teachers of English, at Chicago, November 27, 1914.")
"Amateur Journalism as Training School." *Weaker Moments* No. 35 ([1950?]): [1]–[?].
"Appreciation of Poetry." *United Amateur* 22 No. 3 (January 1923) 33–35. Second in a series.
"Before We Part." *Apprentice* "Informal Number" (August 1921): [12].
"The Calisthenics of Literary Appreciation." *English Journal,* 19, No. 5 (May 1930): 363–74.
"Checking Up on Outside Reading" (with A. Stevenson). *English Journal* 15, No. 6 (June 1926): 464–68.
"The Church and the World." *Vagrant* No. 7 (June 1918): 17–22.
"Chiefly Regarding Prose." *United Amateur* 12, No. 2 (November 1912): 20–22.
"Comma Usage." *United Amateur* 19, No. 6 (May 1920): 135–36.
"Comment." *Southern Amateur Journalist.* New series No. 2 (December 1910): [3].
"Connecticut Byways—A Chapter of a Milwaukee Teacher's Vacation Narrative." *Californian* 3, No. 3 (Winter 1935): 104–05.
"A Correspondence Course." *United Amateur* 12, No. 2 (November 1912): 2.
"Correspondence Criticism." *United Amatuer* 12, No. 3 (January 1913): 36.
"Dictionary Drill." *Word Study* 5, No. 4 (December 1929): 4.
"Do You Like Good Poetry." *United Amateur* 22 No. 4 (March, 1923): 60–62. Third in a series.
"The Elimination of the Commencement Oration." *English Journal,* 5, No. 6 (June 1916): 401–3.
"Editorial." *Apprentice* 1, No. 3 (December 1911): 1, No. 4 (March 1913): 8; 1, No. 5 (June 1913): 8.
"Editorials." *Apprentice* 1, No. 2 (April 1911): 5–8.
"The End of the Year." *United Amatuer* 12, No. 6 (July 1913): 87–92.
"The Ethics of Stimulation." *Prometheus* [No. 1] (September–November 1914): 12–14.
"The Fall Journals." *United Amateur* 12, No. 2 (November 1912): [17]–20.
"The Fall Styles." *United Amatuer* 13, No. 1 (September 1913): 12–14.

"First Steps in the Appreciation of Poetry." *English Journal,* 24, No. 3 (March 1935): 218–20.
"Foreword." *Winged Summer* (1936): [1].
"A Four-Part Oral Project." *English Journal* 25, No. 1 (January 1936): 41–49.
"Golden Girls." *Apprentice* 1, No. 2 (April 1919): 5.
"The Graceful ART." *Apprentice* "Informal Number" (August 1921): [5]–11.
"A Honeymoon Vacation." *Continent* 44, No. 24 (12 June 1913): 824–25.
"How to Use the Primary Image Drills." *English Journal* 18, No. 6 (June 1929): 490–94.
"Howard Phillips Lovecraft: The Sage of Providence." *O-Wash-Ta-Nong* 2, No. 2 (Fall 1937): [3]. In *Caverns Measureless to Man: 18 Memoirs of H.P. Lovecraft,* ed. S. T. Joshi. West Warwick, RI: Necronomicon Press, 1996. 16–17. In *LR* 90–91.
"The Humor of Kipling." *Olympian* 5, No. 2 (November 1912): 24–28.
"Imagism." *Conservative* 5, No. 1 (July 1919): 6–7.
"In Explanation." *O-Wash-Ta-Nong* 4, No. 1 (February 1939) [Winter 1939]: 1.
"Individual Student Magazines." *English Journal* 15, No. 10 (December 1926): 776–78.
"'John Barleycorn.'" *National Official* (June 1913): [6–10].
"Jumbo." *Pippin* 1, No. 1 (December 1913): [4–5].
"Keep off the Track." *Apprentice* 1, No. 5 (June 1913): 5–7.
"Life for God's Sake." *Wolverine* No. 6 (February 1920): [1]–5.
"Literary Appreciation." *Californian* 3, No. 3 (Winter 1935): 24–26.
"Literary Appreciation through Experience." Unpublished? TMS carbon copy in HPL Papers at JHL.
"The Literary School: The Use of Words." *Cynosure* 6, No. 6 (July 1909): 165–67.
"The Literary School: Word Curiosities." *Cynosure* 6, No. 3 (January 1909): 141–42.
"Looking Backward." *Apprentice* "Informal Number" (August 1921): 1–4.
"Magazine Poetry in the Classroom." *English Journal,* 4, No. 8 (October 1915): 523–25.
"Maurice W. Moe on Amateur Criticism." *Vagrant* No. 11 (November 1919): 36-37.
"Memory-Building." *Trail* No. 1 (Spring 1915): [10–12].
"Moe's Letter." *Spark Plug* 2, No. 3 (June 1913): 5.
"News and Notes" (with Lulu M. Dysart). *English Journal* 21, No. 1 (January 1932): 70–76.
"Not Entirely Critical." *United Amatuer* 12, No. 3 (January 1913): [33]–36.
"'Once an Amateur, Always an Amateur.'" *Pippin* 1, No. 6 (May 1917): [9–10].
"An Open Letter." *Lake Breeze* 3, No. 16 (March 1913): 117.
"The Perspective Review's Department of Literary Criticism: Introduction to Poetry." *Perspective Review* (Summer 1934): 10–12.
"Poetry from a New Angle." *Californian* 3, No. 3 (Winter 1935): 27–29.
"Polishing a Poem." *Amateur Journalist* 1, No. 3 (May 1913): [53]–57.

"Quantity and Quality in English." *English Journal,* 21, No. 6 (June 1932): 475–82.

"A Quotation Game." *English Journal* 15, No. 8 (October 1926): 623–26.

"Report of a Private Critic." *United Amateur* 4, No. 3 (January 1915): 42–43.

"The Servant in the House." *Cynosure* 6, No. 4 (March 1909): 154–55.

"A Simplified Essentials Test." *Elementary English Review,* 3, No. 10 (1 December 1926): 315–20.

"Some Noted Amateurs and Their Magazines." *Lake Breeze* 3, No. 16 (March 1913): 111–13.

"Something New in Stageland." *O-Wash-Ta-Nong* 4, No. 1 (February 1939) [Winter 1939]: 8–9.

"Spontaneous Righteousness." *Silver Clarion* 3, No. 4 (July 1919): 2–3.

"The Spring Journals." *United Amatuer* 12, No. 4 (March 1913): [49]–51; 12, No. 5 (May 1913): [65]–67.

"Teaching the Comma."·*English Journal* 16, No. 2 (February 1927): 139–42.

"Teaching the Use of the Comma." *English Journal* 2, No 2 (February 1913): 104–8.

"Tentative Trip Schedule." *Winged Summer* (1936): [2].

"Through the Eyes of the Poet." *Rainbow* No. 2 (May 1922): 16-17[?].

"Truing up the Sentence.' *United Amateur* 19, No. 4 (May 1920): 78–79.

"United Convention Echoes." *O-Wash-Ta-Nong* 4, No. 1 (February 1939) [Winter 1939]: 10.

[Untitled diary entries.] *Winged Summer* [Part 1] (1936): 3–9. A mimeographed booklet.

"Winged Summer" [Part 2]. *O-Wash-Ta-Nong* 2, No. 1 (January 1937): 12–19.

"Vision." *Apprentice* 1, No. 5 (June 1913): [1]–5.

"Vitalizing and Visualizing a Sermon." *Continent* 43, No. 33 (15 August 1912): 1145–46.

"Why I Am Not a Free Thinker." *Argus* 1, No. 3 (December 1910): 1–12.

"William de Morgan." *Missourian* No. 7 (January 1911): [1].

Poetry

"Christmas Wish." *The Man Says* No. 28 (December 1949): [1]. ("Written 12-25-1939.")

"Class Poem." *Apprentice* 1, No. 2 (April 1919): [1]–4.

"A Clean Page." *United Official Quarterly* (April 1923): 8; rpt. *Pegasus* (October 1924): 31.

"Edwin and the Red Knight." *Apprentice* 1, No. 4 (March 1913): [1]–5.

"Evening Calm." *Apprentice* 1, No. 5 (June 1913): [1].

"In a Providence Churchyard." *O-Wash-Ta-Nong* 2, No. 1 (January 1937): 19. In August Derleth and Raymond E. F. Larsson, ed. *Poetry Out of Wisconsin* (New York: Henry Harrison, 1937): 191. *Crypt of Cthulhu* No. 57 (St. John's Eve 1988): 28.

"Invocation." In August Derleth and Raymond E. F. Larsson, ed. *Poetry Out of Wisconsin* (New York: Henry Harrison, 1937): 190–91.

"The Laborer and His Hire." *Wisconsin Presbyterian* 4, No. 11 (November 1915): [18].

"Night." *Wisconsin Literary Magazine* 1, No. 1 (December 1903): 10.

"A Poet Died Today." *Winged Summer* (1936): 9–10.

"A Psalm of Trust." In August Derleth and Raymond E. F. Larsson, ed. *Poetry Out of Wisconsin* (New York: Henry Harrison, 1937): 191.

"Seven O'Clock." *Conservative* 5, No. 1 (July 1919): 7.

"The Roamer's Wife." *O-Wash-ta-Nong* 1, No. 2 (April 1936): 1.

"Those Melancholy Days." *Apprentice* 1, No. 5 (June 1913): 8.

"To a New Born Babe (From the French of Daudet)." *Wisconsin Literary Magazine* 1, No. 2 (January 1904): 59.

"Ups and Downs of Phaeton." *O-Wash-Ta-Nong* 4, No. 1 (February 1939) [Winter 1939]: [1].

"Walt Whitman." *O-Wash-Ta-Nong* 4, No. 1 (February 1939) [Winter 1939]: 11.

C. Works by Bernard Austin Dwyer

Fiction

"The Black Elephant." Submitted to *WT* c. Jan. 1929.

"Brooklyn Nights." HPL to Robert E. Howard, 8 June 1932: "Dwyer's 'Brooklyn Nights' is real poetry of a sort. It is the only thing that ever made me able to see Brooklyn in a favourable light!" *A Means to Freedom: the Letters of H. P. Lovecraft and Robert E. Howard*, New York: Hippocampus Press, 2009, 313.

"The Castle of Golden Dreams." HPL to J. Vernon Shea, 31 October 1931: "**Of course** many of the passages are 'sheer slush', for isn't the whole damn thing the pathetic mental maundering of an illiterate, cheaply sentimental, frustrated old maid? This isn't a weird tale—it's a study of a pathetic & simple type in the spirit of Derleth's 'People' though in a widely different manner. Still, I dare say it hasn't the professional finish some could give it. It is a study from life—from an actual old maid in the Shokan hills, who (unlike the heroine at the end) is still living & in good health. Dwyer has a sensitiveness to atmospheric nuances beyond that I have seen in any other person, & if he only buckled down to the art of technical form he could knock the rest of the W.T. gang off the map." *H. P. Lovecraft: Letters to J. Vernon Shea, Carl F. Strauch, and Lee McBride White*, 76–77.

"Flash." Circulated to Lovecraft circle c. Feb. 1933. HPL to August Derleth, c. 27 February 1933: "Dwyer's 'Flash' is a bit sentimental & immature, but I think it shews distinct promise—considering the author's late start & limited reading opportunities." CAS: "It is quite good—would be vastly better if the sentiment at the end were left to the reader's inference rather than expressed." *Essential Solitude*, 547. Apparently only a cover sheet for the story survives at JHL.

"The Night Call" (verse?). Apparently unpublished and nonextant.

"Old Black Trail." Apparently unpublished and nonextant.

"The Old Dark House." *Blue Mountain Survey.* [C.C.C paper; Company 256, Peekskill, NY. Cf. Alfred Emile Cornebise, *The CCC Chronicles: Camp Newspapers of the Civilian Conservation Corps 1933–1942* (Jefferson, NC: McFarland & Co., 2004), 56.]

"The Snake God." *Fantasmagoria* 1, No. 5 (Winter 1939–40): 4–10[?].

Poetry
"Beautiful Night." *O-Wash-Ta-Nong* 3, No. 2 (Spring 1938): 5.
"Fairies." *O-Wash-Ta-Nong* 4, No. 1 (February 1939) [Winter 1939]: 4.
"A Song of Gordon's Men." *Inklings* (September 1939). In Haden, 32–35.
"Ol' Black Sarah." *WT* 12, No. 4 (October 1928): 540.
"The Road to Samarkand." *Inklings*. In Haden, 30–32.
"The Weir." Nonextant.

Letters
[Letter to the Editor.] *WT* 13, No. 6 (June 1929): 852, 854. *WW* 69–70.
[Letter to the Editor.] *WT* 15, No. 6 June 1930): 724, 726, 729, 731, 732. *WW* 72.
[Letter to the Editor.] *Strange Tales of Mystery and Terror* No. 6 (October 1932): 426–27.
[Letter to HPL.] In HPL to R. H. Barlow (20 April 1935). *O Fortunate Floridian* 236.
[Letter to the Editor.] *WT* 31, No. 3 (March 1938): 380–81. *WW* 94.
[Letter to the Editor.] *WT* 32, No. 3 (September 1938): 379–80.
[Letter to the Editor.] *WT* 32, No. 6 (December 1938): 760.

HPL mentions Dwyer's "Old Back Trail," but it is not known if the work is fiction or verse, or if it is extant.

D. Works by Samuel Loveman

The Hermaphrodite: A Poem. Athol, MA: W. Paul Cook, 1926. (*LL* 593)
The Hermaphrodite and Other Poems. Caldwell, ID: Caxton Printers, 1936. (*LL* 594)
Out of the Immortal Night: Selected Works by Samuel Loveman. Ed. S. T. Joshi and David E. Schultz. New York: Hippocampus Press, 2004. This title contains a lengthy bibliography of Loveman's work.
The Sphinx: A Conversation. [North Montpelier, VT: W. Paul Cook, 1944.]

"The Coast of Bohemia." Catalogue 125 *General Literature with an Addenda* [*sic*] *of Americana, Sport and Naturla History*. New York: Dauber and Pine Bookshops, n.d.: n.p.

"Collecting Curious Books." *Catalogue 107*. New York: Dauber and Pine, n.d.: 25.

"A Conversation with Ambrose Bierce." *Catalogue 121*. New York: Dauber and Pine, n.d.: n.p.

"A Holiday Post-Card." *Catalogue 124*. New York: Dauber and Pine, n.d.: 124.

"Howard Phillips Lovecraft." *Arkham Sampler* 1, No. 3 (Summer 1948): 32–36. In Lovecraft's *Something about Cats and Other Pieces*, ed. August Derleth (Sauk City, WI: Arkham House, 1949), pp. 229–33. In *Lovecraft Remembered*, ed. Peter Cannon. Sauk City, WI: Arkham House, 1998: 204–8. In *Out of the Immortal Night* 219–23.

"Lovecraft as a Converstionalist." *Fresco* 8, No. 3 (Spring 1958): 34–36. In *Caverns Measureless to Man: 18 Memoirs of H. P. Lovecraft*, ed. S. T. Joshi. West Warwick, RI: Necronomicon Press, 1996: 45–46. In *Lovecraft Remembered*, ed. Peter Cannon. Sauk City, WI: Arkham House, 1998: 209–11. In *Out of the Immortal Night* 223–24.

"Of Gold and Sawdust." In *The Occult Lovecraft*. Ed. Anthony Raven. Saddle River, NJ: Gerry de la Ree, 1975. 21–22.

"To Satan." *Conservative* No. 13 (July 1923): 1–2.

[Untitled, description of book by M. R. James, mentioning H. P. Lovecraft.] *Catalogue 135*. New York: Dauber and Pine, [1933]: 30.

"A Whittier Discovery." *Catalogue 127*. New York: Dauber and Pine. N.d.: n.p.

E. Works by Vincent Starrett

Arthur Machen: A Novelist of Ecstasy and Sin. Chicago: Walter M. Hill, 1918.

Books and Bipeds. New York: Argus Books, 1947.

Buried Caesars: Essays in Literary Appreciation. Chicago: Covici-McGee, 1923.

Ebony Flame. Chicago: Covici-McGee, 1922.

Fifteen More Poems. Ysleta, TX: Edwin B. Hill, 1927.

The Quick and the Dead. Sauk City, WI: Arkham House, 1965. Contains: The Fugitive; The Man in the Cask; The Quick and the Dead; The Sinless Village; The Head of Cromwell; Penelope; The Elixir of Death; Coffins for Two; The Tattooed Man; Footsteps of Fear.

Seaports in the Moon: A Fantasia on Romantic Themes. Garden City, NY: Doubleday, Doran, & Company, Inc., Garden City, NY: Country Life Press, 1928.

Editor of Arthur Machen, *The Shining Pyramid*. Chicago: Covici-McGee, 1923.

———. *The Glorious Mystery*. Chicago: Covici-McGee, 1924.

"Books Alive." A review of *Beyond the Wall of Sleep*. *Chicago Sunday Tribune* 103, No. 1 (2 January 1944): Sec. 6, p. 12. In *Books and Bipeds* 119–22 (as "H. P. Lovecraft"). In *Lovecraft Remembered* (as "H. P. Lovecraft") 426–28.

"Books Alive." A review of *Marginalia. Chicago Sunday Tribune* 104, No. 9 (4 March 1945): Sec. 6, p. 8. *Vigilantes* 3, No. 1 (July 1945): 31–32. In *Books and Bipeds* 203–4 (as "The Lovecraft Legend"). In *Lovecraft Remembered* (as "The Lovecraft Legend") 429–30.

"Books Alive." A review of *Something about Cats and Other Pieces. Chicago Sunday Tribune* (18 December 1949): Magazine of Books, p. 2.

"Books Alive." A review of *The Shuttered Room and Other Pieces. Chicago Sunday Tribune* 119, No. 2 (10 January 1960): Sec. 4, p. 5.

"Changeling" [verse]. In *Dark of the Moon,* ed. August Derleth. Sauk City, WI: Arkham House, 1947.

"The Death of Santa Claus" [verse]. In *Fire and Sleet and Candlelight,* ed. August Derleth. Sauk City, WI: Arkham House, 1961.

"The Evil Eye." *Short Stories.* (25 January 1922): 154–64.

"Extraordinary Visit" [verse]. In *Dark of the Moon,* ed. August Derleth. Sauk City, WI: Arkham House, 1947.

"Femme Fatale" [verse]. *Fire and Sleet and Candlelight,* ed. August Derleth. Sauk City, WI: Arkham House, 1961.

"Fragment" [verse]. *Arkham Sampler* 2, No. 2 (Spring 1949): 16.

"The Fugitive Statue." *Short Stories* (10 April 1924): 161–73.

"Full Circle" [verse]. *Arkham Sampler* 2, No. 2 (Spring 1949): 69.

"Gooseflesh" [verse]. In *Dark of the Moon,* ed. August Derleth. Sauk City, WI: Arkham House, 1947.

"H. P. L." [verse]. In H. P. Lovecraft et al, *Something about Cats and Other Pieces.* Ed. August Derleth. Sauk City, WI: Arkham House, 1949.

"Hieroglyphics" [verse]. *Arkham Sampler* 2, No. 3 (Summer 1949): 23.

"In Which an Author and His Character Are Well Met." (1928)

"Legend" [verse]. In *Dark of the Moon,* ed. August Derleth. Sauk City, WI: Arkham House, 1947.

"The Mid-Watch Tragedy." *Short Stories* (10 June 1924).

"The Money Lender." *WT* 2, No. 2 (September 1923): 75–76.

"The Quick and the Dead." *WT* 20, No. 6 (December 1932): 785–92.

"Riders in the Dark." *WT* 2, No. 1 (July–August 1923): 63–65.

"Penelope." *WT* 1, No. 3 (May 1923): 57–59. In *The Moon Terror* by A. G. Birch et al. Indianapolis: Popular Fiction Publishing Co., 1927. (*LL* 104)

"The Quick and the Dead." (1932)

"Romantic Episode" [verse]. In *Fire and Sleet and Candlelight,* ed. August Derleth. Sauk City, WI: Arkham House, 1961.

"Sea Story" [verse]. In *Dark of the Moon,* ed. August Derleth. Sauk City, WI: Arkham House, 1947.

"Travel Talk" [verse]. *Arkham Sampler* 2, No. 1 (Winter 1949): 74.

"Two Horsemen" [verse]. *Arkham Sampler* 2, No. 3 (Summer 1949): 81.

"221B" [verse]. In *Dark of the Moon,* ed. August Derleth. Sauk City, WI: Arkham House, 1947.

"Visitation" [verse]. In *Dark of the Moon,* ed. August Derleth. Sauk City, WI: Arkham House, 1947.

F. Works by Others

Adams, W. H. Davenport (1828–1891). *Plain Living and High Thinking; or, Practical Self-Culture: Moral, Mental, and Physical.* London: John Hogg, 1880.

Ahlhauser, William C. (1879–1941). *Ex-Presidents of the National Amateur Press Association: Sketches.* Athol, MA: W. Paul Cook, 1919. (*LL* 16)

Alden, Abner (1758?–1820). *The Reader: Containing the Art of Delivery, Articulation, Accent, Pronunciation,* [etc.]. <1802> 3rd ed. Boston: Printed by J. T. Buckingham for Thomas & Andrews, 1808. (*LL* 25)

Allen, Hervey (1889–1949). *Anthony Adverse.* New York: Farrar & Rinehart, 1933.

Appleton, John Howard (1844–1930). *The Young Chemist: A Book of Laboratory Work for Beginners.* Providence, RI: J. A. & R. A. Reid, 1876. (*LL* 47)

Asbury, Herbert (1891–1963), ed. *Not at Night!* New York: Macy-Masius (The Vanguard Press), 1928. (*LL* 54)

Atherton, Gertrude (1857–1948). *The Conqueror: Being the True and Romantic Story of Alexander Hamilton.* New York: Macmillan, 1902.

Baldwin, Charles Sears (1867–1935). *Ancient Rhetoric and Poetic, Interpreted from Representative Works.* New York: Macmillan, 1924.

[Barnitz, Park] (1878–1901). *The Book of Jade.* New York: Doxey's, n.d. [1901]. In *The Book of Jade: A New Critical Edition.* Ed. David E. Schultz and Michael J. Abolafia. New York: Hippocampus Press, 2015.

Baudelaire, Charles Pierre (1821–1867). *Baudelaire: His Prose and Poetry.* Ed. T. R. Smith. New York: Boni & Liveright (Modern Library), [1919]. (*LL* 78)

Benson, A. C. (1862–1925). *From a College Window.* London: Smith, Elder, & Co. 1906.

Bierce, Ambrose (1842–1914?). *Can Such Things Be?* <1893> New York: Boni & Liveright (Modern Library), 1918. (*LL* 98)

———. *In the Midst of Life: Tales of Soldiers and Civilians.* <1891> Introduction by George Sterling. New York: Modern Library, 1927. (*LL* 99)

———. *Twenty one Letters of Ambrose Bierce.* Cleveland: George Kirk, 1922. (*LL* 101)

Bierce, Ambrose, and Adolphe Danziger [de Castro], (1858–1959). *The Monk and the Hangman's Daughter; Fantastic Fables; [etc.].* New York: Albert & Charles Boni, 1925. (*LL* 100)

Birkhead, Edith (1889–1951). *The Tale of Terror: A Study of the Gothic Romance.* New York: E. P. Dutton, 1921. (*LL* 105)

Blair, Hugh (1718–1800) *A Critical Dissertation on the Poems of Ossian, the Son of Fingal.* London: Printed for T. Becket and P. A. De Hondt, 1763.

Blackwood, Algernon (1869–1951). *John Silence—Physician Extraordinary*. London: Eveleigh Nash, 1908. Boston: John W. Luce, 1909. London: Macmillan, 1912. New York: Vaughan & Gomme, 1914. New York: Knopf, 1917. New York, E. P. Dutton, [1920]. [Contains "Ancient Sorceries."] (*LL* 107, 108)

Bloomfield, Robert (1766–1823). *The Farmer's Boy: A Rural Poem*. Ornamented with Elegant Wood Engravings by A. Anderson. The 5th American, from the 6th London ed. New York: Printed by Hopkins & Seymour, and Sold by G. F. Hopkins, 1803. (*LL* 117)

Boguet, Henri (1550?–1619). *An Examen of Witches*. Tr. E. Allen Ashwin. Ed. Montague Summers. Bungay, UK: John Rodker, 1929.

Braithwaite, William Stanley (1878–1962), ed. The *Anthology of Magazine Verse for 1921 and Year Book of American Poetry*. Boston: Small, Maynard and Company, 1921.

Bulfinch, Thomas (1796–1867). *The Age of Fable; or, Beauties of Mythology*. <1855> Edited by J. Loughran Scott. Rev. ed. Philadelphia: David McKay, [1898].

Bullen, John Ravenor (1886–1927). *White Fire*. Athol, MA: Recluse Press, 1927 [actually January 1928]. (*LL* 143)

Burritt, Elijah Hinsdale (1794–1838). *The Geography of the Heavens, and Classbook of Astronomy: Accompanied by a Celestial Atlas*. A New Edition, Revised and Illustrated by Hiram Mattison. New York: F. J. Huntington, 1853. (*LL* 150)

Butler, Samuel (1835–1902). *Erewhon*. London: Trübner & Co., 1872.

Cabell, James Branch (1879–1958). *Jurgen: A Comedy of Justice*. New York: Robert M. McBride, 1919.

Campbell, Thomas (1777–1844). *The Poetical Works of Thomas Campbell: Including Several Pieces from the Original Manuscript, Never Before Published in This Country*. 2nd ed. Baltimore: Philip K. Nicklin, 1811.

Cannon, Peter, ed. *Lovecraft Remembered*. Sauk City, WI: Arkham House, 1998.

Casey, Silas (1807–1882). *Infantry Tactics: For the Instruction, Exercise, and Manœuvres of the Soldier, a Company, Line of Skirmishers, Battalion, Brigade, or Corps d'Armée*. New York: D. Van Nostrand, 1862.

Cattell, James McKeen (1860–1944), and Jaques Cattell (1904–1960). *American Men of Science—A Biographical Directory*. New York: Science Press, 1933.

Chambers, Robert W. (1865–1933). *The King in Yellow*. New York: F. Tennyson Neely, 1895. (*LL* 184) [Includes "The Yellow Sign."]

Churchill, Winston (1871–1947). *Richard Carvel*. New York, London: Macmillan, 1899.

Cline, Leonard (1893–1929). *The Dark Chamber*. New York: Viking Press, 1927. (*LL* 198)

De Castro, Adolphe (1859–1959). *Portrait of Ambrose Bierce*. New York: Century Co., 1929.

Derleth, August (1909–1971). *Evening in Spring.* New York: Charles Scribner's Sons, 1941.

———. "Five Alone." *Pagany* 3, No. 3 (Summer 1932): 14–44. In *Place of Hawks.* New York: Loring & Mussey, 1935. (*LL* 250)

———. *The Man on All Fours.* New York: Loring & Mussey, 1934. (*LL* 249)

———. *Three Who Died.* New York: Loring & Mussey, 1935. (*LL* 253)

Dewey, John (1859–1952). *Studies in Logical Theory.* Chicago: University of Chicago Press, 1903.

Dreiser, Theodore (1871–1945). *Sister Carrie.* New York: Doubleday, Page & Co., 1900.

Dunsany, Edward John Moreton Drax Plunkett, 18th baron (1878–1957). *The Blessing of Pan.* London: G. P. Putnam's Sons, 1927. (*LL* 287)

———. *The Book of Wonder* (1912) [with *Time and the Gods* (1906)]. New York: Boni & Liveright (Modern Library), [1918]. [Contains: "How One Came, as Was Foretold, to the City of Never."] (*LL* 288)

———. *The Charwoman's Shadow.* New York: G. P. Putnam's Sons, 1926.

———. *The Curse of the Wise Woman.* London: William Heinemann, 1933. New York: Longmans, Green, 1933.

———. *Don Rodriguez: Chronicles of Shadow Valley.* New York: G. P. Putnam's Sons, 1922. (*LL* 289)

———. *A Dreamer's Tales and Other Stories.* New York: Boni & Liveright (Modern Library), [1917], [1919], or [1921]. [Contains "Idle Days on the Yann."] (*LL* 290)

———. *Fifty-one Tales.* <1915> (*LL* 291)

———. *Five Plays.* London: Grant Richards, 1914. Boston: Little, Brown, 1923. (*LL* 292)

———. *The King of Elfland's Daughter.* London: G. P. Putnam's Sons, 1924. (*LL* 294)

———. *The Last Book of Wonder.* Boston: John W. Luce, 1916. (*LL* 295)

———. *Mr. Jorkens Remembers Africa.* London: William Heinemann, 1934. New York: Longmans, Green, 1934 (as *Jorkens Remembers Africa*).

———. *Plays of Gods and Men.* Boston: John W. Luce, [1917]. (*LL* 296)

———. *The Sword of Welleran and Other Stories.* London: George Allen & Sons, 1908.

———. *Tales of Three Hemispheres.* <1919> (*LL* 298)

———. *Time and the Gods.* London: Heinemann, 1906. See *The Book of Wonder.*

———. *The Travel Tales of Mr. Joseph Jorkens.* London: G. P. Putnam's Sons, 1931. (*LL* 299)

The Encyclopaedia Britannica: A Dictionary of Arts, Sciences, and General Literature . . . With . . . Revisions and Additions by W. H. De Puy. 9th Ed. Chicago: Werner Co., 1896. (*LL* 318)

Farnham, Joseph E. C. (1849–1933). *Brief Historical Data and Memories of My Boyhood Days in Nantucket.* [Providence, RI:] Snow & Farnham Co., 1915.

Flaubert, Gustave (1821–1880). *Salammbô: A Romance of Ancient Carthage.* <1862>
———. *The Temptation of St. Anthony.* <1874> Translated by Lafcadio Hearn <1910>. New York: Boni & Liveright (Modern Library), [1920].
Gautier, Théophile (1811–1872). *Mademoiselle de Maupin.* <1835> New York: Boni & Liveright (Modern Library), [1918]; *or* New York: Modern Library, 1925.
The Gentleman's Magazine. London, 1731–1907. (LL 371)
Goodenough, Arthur H. (1871–1936). *Songs of Four Decades.* Athol, MA: W. Paul Cook, 1927.
Grimm, Jakob Ludwig Karl (1785–1863), and W. K. Grimm (1786–1859). *Fairy Tales.* <1812–15> (LL 405)
Gummere, Francis Barton (1855–1919). *A Handbook of Poetics, for Students of English Verse.* Boston: Ginn & Co., 1885.
Haden, David. "'A Mighty Woodcutter': Bernard Austin Dwyer and His Possible Influence on Lovecraft." In *Lovecraft in Historical Context: The Fifth Collection.* n.p.: David Haden, 2014. 8–29.
Haeckel, Ernst (1834–1919). *Die Welträthsel.* <1899> Tr. Joseph McCabe as *The Riddle of the Universe.* New York: Harper & Brothers, 1900.
Hakluyt, Richard (1552–1616). *Voyagers' Tales: From the Collections of Richard Hakluyt.* New York: Cassell, [1886?]. (LL 412)
Hammett, Dashiell (1894–1961), ed. *Creeps by Night: Chills and Thrills.* New York: John Day Co., 1931. (LL 421)
Harkness, Albert (1822–1907). *A Latin Grammar for Schools and Colleges.* <1867> Revised Standard Edition of 1881. New York: Appleton & Co., 1889. (LL 424)
Harré, T. Everett (1884–1948), ed. *Beware After Dark! The World's Most Stupendous Tales of Mystery, Horror, Thrills and Terror.* New York: Macaulay, 1929. (LL 425)
Hawthorne, Julian (1846–1934), ed., *The Lock and Key Library: Classic Mystery and Detective Stories* New York: Review of Reviews Co., 1909. 10 vols. (LL 428)
Hawthorne, Nathaniel (1804–1864). *Tanglewood Tales for Girls and Boys: Being a Second Wonder-Book.* <1853> New York: A. L. Burt, [189-?] or [1907]. (LL 435)
———. *A Wonder Book for Boys and Girls, Comprising Stories of Classical Fables.* <1852> New York: A. L. Burt, n.d. (LL 437)
Hearn, Lafcadio (1850–1904). *Kwaidan: Stories and Studies of Strange Things.* <1904> Boston: Houghton Mifflin, 1930. (LL 440)
Hesiod (fl. 700 B.C.E.?). *The Works of Hesiod.* Translated from the Greek by Mr. [Thomas] Cooke. London: Printed by J. Wilson for J. Wood and C. Woodward, 1740. (LL 449)
Hoag, Jonathan E[than] (1831–1927). *The Poetical Works of Jonathan E. Hoag.* [Edited by H. P. Lovecraft.] New York: [Privately printed], 1923. (LL 453)

Holmes, Oliver Wendell 1809–1894). *The Autocrat of the Breakfast-Table: Every Man His Own Boswell.* <1858> Boston: Houghton Mifflin, 1887.

———. *The Poetical Works of Oliver Wendell Holmes.* Boston: Houghton Mifflin, 1887.

Homer (fl. 750 B.C.E.?). *The Iliad of Homer.* Translated by Alexander Pope <1715–20>. With Notes and Introduction by Theodore Alois Buckley. New York: A. L. Burt, [1902]. (LL 462)

Huxley, Aldous (1894–1963). *Proper Studies.* London: Chatto & Windus, 1927.

Huxley, Thomas Henry (1825–1895). *Man's Place in Nature and Other Anthropological Essays.* New York: D. Appleton & Co., 1894.

Huysmans, J.-K. (1848–1907). *Against the Grain [A Rebours].* <1884> Tr. John Howard. Introduction by Havelock Ellis. New York: Albert & Charles Boni, 1930. (LL 483)

———. *Down There [Là-Bas].* <1891> Tr. Keene Wallis. New York: Albert & Charles Boni, 1924. (LL 484)

Hylton, J. Dunbar (1837–1893). *The Bride of Gettysburg: An Episode of 1863. In Three Parts.* Palmyra, NJ, 1878.

Ingram, John H. (1842–1916). *Edgar Allan Poe: His Life, Letters, and Opinions.* London: James Hogg, 1880. 2 vols. (LL 488)

Joshi, S. T., ed. *A Weird Writer in Our Midst: Early Criticism of H. P. Lovecraft.* New York: Hippocampus Press, 2010.

Killen, Alice M. *Le Roman "terrifiant"; ou, Roman "noir" de Walpole à Ann Radcliffe et son influence sur la littérature française jusqu'en 1840.* Paris: G. Crès, 1915. Rev. ed. Paris: E. Champion, 1923.

Kittredge, George Lyman (1860–1941). *The Old Farmer and His Almanack.* Boston: W. Ware & Co., 1904. (LL 539)

Kremer, Heinrich (1430–1505), and Jakob Sprenger (1436?–1495). *Malleus Maleficarum.* Tr. Montague Summers. London: J. Rodker, 1928.

Leith, W. Compton (pseud. of O. M. Dalton, 1866–1945). *Sirenica.* <1913> With an Introduction by William Marion Reedy. Portland, ME: Thomas Bird Mosher, 1927. (LL 560)

Locker-Lampson, Frederick (1821–1895). *London Lyrics.* New York: Macmillan, 1904.

Long, Frank Belknap (1901–1994). "At the Home of Poe: A Poem in Prose." *United Amateur* 21, No. 5 (May 1922): 53–54.

———. "Felis: A Prose Poem." *Conservative* No. 13 (July 1923): 3–4.

———. *The Horror from the Hills. Weird Tales* 7, No. 1 (January 1931); 7, No. 2 (February–March 1931). Sauk City, WI: Arkham House, 1963.

———. *The Goblin Tower.* Cassia, FL: Dragon-Fly Press, 1935. (LL 580)

———. *The Man from Genoa and Other Poems.* Athol, MA: W. Paul Cook, 1926. (LL 581)

Lowell, James Russell (1819–1891). *The Poetical Works of James Russell Lowell.* Boston: James R. Osgood, 1876. (LL 597)

Lucretius (T[itus] Lucretius Carus) (98?–50 B.C.E.?). *De Rerum Natura Libri Sex*. Recognovit Iacobus Bernaysius [i.e., Jakob Bernays]. Lipsiae [i.e., Leipzig]: Sumptibus et Typis B. G. Teubneri, 1879. (LL 600)

———. *Lucretius on the Nature of Things*. Tr. Cyril Bailey (1871–1857). <1910> Oxford: Oxford University Press, 1921.

[Ludlow, Fitz Hugh (1836–1870).] *The Hasheesh Eater: Being Passages from the Life of a Pythagorean*. New York: Harper & Brothers, 1857. (LL 601)

Machen, Arthur (1863–1947). *Far Off Things*. <1922> New York: Alfred A. Knopf, 1923. (LL 615)

———. *The Green Round*. London: Ernest Benn, 1933. Sauk City, WI: Arkham House, 1968.

———. *Hieroglyphics: A Note upon Ecstasy in Literature*. London: Grant Richards, 1902. (LL 616)

———. *The Hill of Dreams*. London: Grant Richards, 1907. New York: Alfred A. Knopf, 1923. (LL 617)

———. *The House of Souls*. London: Grant Richards, 1906. New York: Alfred A. Knopf, 1923. [Contains "The White People" and "The Great God Pan."] (LL 618)

———. *The Secret Glory*. London: Martin Secker, 1922. New York: Knopf, 1922. (LL 620)

———. *Things Near and Far*. New York: Alfred A. Knopf, 1923. (LL 622)

———. *The Three Impostors*. <1895> New York: Alfred A. Knopf, 1930. (LL 623)

MacLeish, Archibald (1892–1982). *Conquistador*. Boston: Houghton Mifflin, 1932.

McNeil, Everett (1862–1929). *The Lost Nation*. New York: E. P. Dutton, 1918.

———. *Tonty of the Iron Hand*. New York : E. P. Dutton, 1925.

———. *The Totem of Black Hawk: A Tale of Pioneer Days in Northwestern Illinois and the Black Hawk War*. Chicago: A. C. McClurg & Co., 1914.

———. *The Lost Treasure Cave; or, Adventures with the Cowboys of Colorado*. New York : E. P. Dutton, 1905.

———. *With Kit Carson in the Rockies: A Tale of the Beaver Country*. New York: E. P. Dutton, 1909.

Macy, William Francis (1867–?), ed. *The Nantucket Scrap Basket: Being a Collection of Characteristic Stories and Sayings of the People of the Town and Island of Nantucket, Massachusetts*. Nantucket: The Inquirer & Mirror, 1916. (LL 630)

Mandeville, Sir John (14th c.). *The Voyages and Travels of Sir John Maundeville, Kt*. New York: Cassell, 1886. (LL 637)

Mariconda, Steven J. *H. P. Lovecraft: Art, Artifact, and Reality*. New York: Hippocampuspress, 2013.

Mather, Cotton (1663–1728). *Magnalia Christi Americana; or, The Ecclesiastical History of New-England, from Its First Planting in the Year 1620, unto the Year of Our Lord, 1698*. London: Printed for T. Parkhurst, 1702. (LL 645)

Matthews, Brander (1852–1929). *A Study of Versification.* Boston: Houghton Mifflin, 1911.

Maupassant, Guy de (1850–1893). *A Selection from the Writings of Guy de Maupassant.* With a Critical Preface by Paul Bourget . . . and an Introduction by Robert Arnot. New York: D. A. McKinlay & Co., 1903. 6 vols. (*LL* 648)

Meinhold, Johannes Wilhelm (1797–1851). *Mary Schweidler: The Amber Witch.* Tr. Lady Duff Gordon (1821–1869). London: John Murray, 1844.

Merritt, A. (1884–1943). *Creep, Shadow! Argosy* (8 September–20 October 1934). Garden City, NY: Doubleday, 1934. (*LL* 51)

———. *The Dwellers in the Mirage. Argosy* (23 January–27 February 1932). New York: Liveright, 1932.

———. *The Face in the Abyss. Argosy* (8 September 1923). New York: Liveright, 1931 (combined with *The Snake Mother*). (*LL* 654)

———. *The Metal Monster. Argosy* (7 August–25 September 1920). New York: Hippocampus Press, 2002.

———. "The Moon Pool." *All-Story Weekly* (22 June 1918) (*LL* 26). Expanded as *The Moon Pool.* New York: G. P. Putnam's Sons, 1919. *Amazing Stories* (May–July 1927).

———. "The People of the Pit." *All-Story Weekly* (5 January 1918). *Amazing Stories Annual* (1927).

———. "The Woman of the Wood." *WT* (August 1926). *Science Fiction Digest* (February–March 1933). *WT* (January 1934).

Miller, Alice Duer (1874–1942). *Instruments of Darkness and Other Stories.* New York: Dodd Mead & Co., 1926.

The Modern Encyclopedia: A New Library of World Knowledge. Edited by A. H. McDannald. New York: Grosset & Dunlap, 1935. (*LL* 668)

Morrow, W. C. (1854–1923). *The Ape, the Idiot and Other People.* Philadelphia: J. B. Lippincott Co., 1897.

Morton, James F. "Culture in Capsules." *Villa de Laura Times* (June 1910): [20]–24.

Murray, Margaret A. (1863–1963). *The Witch-Cult in Western Europe.* Oxford: Clarendon Press, 1921.

Norris, Frank (1870–1902). *McTeague: A Story of San Francisco.* New York: Boni & Liveright, 1899.

O'Neill, Eugene (1888–1953). *Strange Interlude.* New York: Boni & Liveright, 1927.

Ovid (P. Ovidius Naso) (43 B.C.E.–17 C.E.). *The Heroycall Epistles of the Learned Poet Publius Ouidius Naso, in English Verse.* Set Out and Translated by George Tuberuile [i.e., Tuberville]. London: Henry Denham, 1567. (*LL* 725)

———. *Ovid.* Translated by Dryden, Pope, Congreve, Addison, and Others ["Garth's Ovid"]. New-York: Harper & Brothers, 1837. 2 vols. (*LL* 727)

Parker, Richard Green (1798–1869). *Aids to English Composition: Prepared for Students of All Grades.* Boston: R. S. Davis; New York: Robinson, Pratt & Co., 1844. (*LL* 738)

Pater, Walter (1839–1894). *Marius the Epicurean: His Sensations and Ideas.* <1885> New York: Boni & Liveright (Modern Library), [1921]. (*LL* 742)

Pemberton, Clive (1881–1854). *The Weird o' It.* London: Henry J. Drane, 1906.

Pendergast, Patrick James (1850–?). *Selected Gems.* [Jamaica Plain, MA: Angel Guardian Press, 1917.]

Pepys, Samuel (1633–1703). *The Diary of Samuel Pepys, from 1659 to 1669, with Memoir.* Edited by Lord Braybrooke. London: Frederick Warne, 1825. (*LL* 751)

Pidgin, Charles Felton (1844–1923). *Blennerhassett; or, The Irony of Fate: A Dramatic Romance in a Prologue and Four Acts.* Boston: C. M. Clark, 1900.

———. *Quincy Adams Sawyer and Mason's Corner Folks: A Story of New England Home Life.* Boston: C. M. Clark, 1900.

Poe, Edgar Allan (1809–1849). *The Works of Edgar Allan Poe.* The Cameo Edition. With an Introduction by Edwin Markham. New York: Funk & Wagnall's, 1904. [Vol. 9 contains *Eureka*.] (*LL* 769)

Proust, Marcel (1871–1922). *Swann's Way.* Tr. C. K. Scott-Moncrieff. New York: Holt, 1923.

Railo, Eino (1884–1948). *The Haunted Castle: A Study of the Elements of English Romanticism.* New York: E. P. Dutton, 1927.

Reeve, Clara (1729–1807). *The Old English Baron.* <1777/1778> (*LL* 793)

Reynolds, George W. M. (1814–1879). *Faust: A Romance of the Secret Tribunals.* London: Vickers, 1847. New York: Hurst, n.d. (as *Faust and the Demon*).

———. *Wagner, the Wehr-Wolf.* London: J. Dicks, 1848, 1857, 1872.

Sacher-Masoch, Leopold von (1835–1895). *Venus im Pelz.* <1870> First Eng. tr. as *Venus in Furs.* Paris: C. Carrington, 1902.

Saintsbury, George (1843–1933), ed. *Tales of Mystery.* New York: Macmillan Co., 1891. (*LL* 824)

Santayana, George (1863–1952). *Interpretations of Poetry and Religion.* New York: Charles Scribner's Sons, 1900.

Saunders, Margaret Marshall (1861–1947). *Beautiful Joe: An Autobiography.* Toronto: Standard Pub. Co., 1893.

Scarborough, Dorothy (1878–1935). *The Supernatural in Modern English Fiction.* New York: G. P. Putnam's Sons, 1917.

Schmidt, J. H. Heinrich (1834–?). *An Introduction to the Rhythmic and Metric of the Classical Languages: To Which Are Added the Lyric Parts of the Medea of Euripedes and the Antigone of Sophocles, with Rhythmical Schemes and Commentary.* Boston: Ginn & Heath, 1878.

Sheridan, Richard Brinsley (1751–1816). *The Works of Richard Brinsley Sheridan: Dramas, Poems, Translations, Speeches, and Unfinished Sketches.* Edited by F. Stainforth. London: Chatto & Windus, 1874. (*LL* 867)

Shiel, M. P. (1865–1947). *The Purple Cloud.* <1901> New York: Vanguard Press, [1930]. (*LL* 871). Rpt. in *The House of Sounds and Others.* Ed. S. T. Joshi. New York: Hippocampus Press, 2005.

Smith, Clark Ashton (1893–1961). *Ebony and Crystal: Poems in Verse and Prose.* Preface by George Sterling. Auburn, CA: [Auburn Journal,] 1922. (LL 881)

Spengler, Oswald (1880–1936). *The Decline of the West.* Tr. Charles Francis Atkinson. New York: Knopf, 1926–28. 2 vols.

Spenser, Edmund (1552?–1599). *The Shepherd's Calendar.* <1579> (LL 900)

Sienkiewicz, Henryk (1846–1916). *Quo Vadis: A Narrative of the Time of Nero.* Tr. Jeremiah Curtin. Boston: Little, Brown, 1896.

Stapledon, Olaf (1886–1950). *Last and First Men.* London: Methuen, 1930.

Stormonth, James (1824–1882). *A Dictionary of the English Language.* <1871> New York: Harper & Brothers, 1885. (LL 928)

Summers, Montague (1880–1948). *The Geography of Witchcraft.* London: Kegan Paul, Trench, Trübner; New York: Alfred A. Knopf, 1927.

———. *The Vampire in Europe.* London: Kegan Paul, Trench, Trübner, 1929.

———. *The Vampire: His Kith and Kin.* London: Kegan Paul, Trench, Trübner, 1928.

Synge, John Millington (1871–1909). *Riders to the Sea.* London: Elkin Mathews, 1905. [Premiered 25 February 1904.]

Teter, George E. (1877–1940) *An Introduction to Some Elements of Poetry.* Wauwatosa, WI: Kenyon Press, 1927. (LL 951)

Thomson, Christine Campbell (1897–1985), ed. *You'll Need a Night Light.* London: Selwyn & Blount, 1927. (LL 966)

Tyndall, John (1820–1893). *Fragments of Science for Unscientific People: A Series of Detached Essays, Lectures, and Reviews.* 3rd ed. London: Longmans, Green, 1871.

[Unsigned.] "Maurice Winter Moe: 188?–1940." TMs., JHL (photocopy; possibly by Alfred Galpin).

Van Dusen, Washington (1857–?). *Sonnets on Great Men and Women and Other Poems.* Philadelphia, 1929. (LL 991)

Walker, John (1732–1807). *A Critical Pronouncing Dictionary and Expositor of the English Language.* <1804> 3rd American ed. New-York: S. Stansbury, 1807. (LL 1005)

———. *A Rhetorical Grammar; or, Course of Lessons in Elocution.* <1785> 1st American ed. Boston: J. T. Buckingham, 1814. (LL 1006)

Walpole, Horace (1717–1797). *The Castle of Otranto.* London: Thomas Lowndes, 1765 [i.e. 1764]. (LL 1007)

Wandrei, Donald (1908–1987). "Arthur Machen and *The Hill of Dreams.*" *Minnesota Quarterly* 3, No. 3 (Spring 1926): 19–24. *Studies in Weird Fiction* No. 15 (Summer 1994): 27–30.

———. *Ecstasy and Other Poems.* Athol, MA: Recluse Press, 1928. (LL 1010)

Ward, Mary Augusta (Mrs. Humphry) (1851–1920). *Robert Elsmere.* Chicago: J. S. Ogilvie, 1888.

Webster, Noah (1758–1834). *An American Dictionary of the English Language.* Rev. & enl. by Chauncey A. Goodrich and Noah Porter. Springfield, MA: G. & C. Merriam, 1864. (*LL* 1021)

Weigall, Arthur (1880–1934). *Wanderings in Roman Britain.* London: T. Butterworth, 1926. (*LL* 1025)

Wells, H. G. (1866–1946); Huxley, Julian (1887–1975); and Wells, G. P. *The Science of Life: A Summary of Contemporary Knowledge about Life and Its Possibilities.* London: Amalgamated Press, 1930 (2 vols.). Garden City, NY: Doubleday, Doran, 1931 (4 vols.).

Whitaker, Noah F. (1870?–1953). "Crude Criticism." *Pegasus* (October 1924): 35–36.

———. "Moe-ing Time." *Pegasus* (October 1924): 17–33.

———. "The Moe–Whitaker Case." *Plain Speaker.* [n.d., c. September 1925]: 7, 9–11.

———. "Our Final Review of the Case." *Plain Speaker.* [October 1924]: 3.

———. "A Word to Our Friends." *Pegasus* (October 1924): 34.

———. [untitled, unsigned editorial. *Plain Speaker.* [c. August 1925]: [3–8].

———. [untitled, unsigned editorial. *Plain Speaker.* [c. September 1925]: [1–7].

———. [untitled, unsigned editorial. *Plain Speaker.* [c. October 1925]: [1–12].

White, Gilbert (1720–1793). *The Natural History of Selborne.* <1789> New York: Harper & Brothers, 1842. (*LL* 1038)

White, Trumbull (1868–1941) *Our New Possessions: A Graphic Account, Descriptive and Historical, of the Tropic Islands of the Sea Which Have Fallen under Our Sway.* Rock Island, IL: L. E. West, 1898.

Wilde, Oscar (1854–1900). *Poems.* New York: Modern Library, [19—]. (*LL* 1052)

Williamson, Charles Norris (1859–1920), and Alice Muriel Williamson (1869–1933). *The Lightning Conductor: The Strange Adventures of a Motor-Car.* New York: Henry Holt & Co., 1903.

Wood, Clement (1888–1950). *Hints on Writing Poetry.* Girard, KS: Haldeman-Julius, [1924].

Index

À Rebours (Huysmans) 265
Abbott-Trabue tests 287, 312, 384
Adam Bede (Eliot) 175
Adams, Franklin Pierce 424
Adams, Hazel Pratt 490
Adams, W. H. Davenport 456n3
Adams, John D. 357, 364–65, 374
Addison, Joseph 45, 115, 161, 166–67, 469
Aeneid (Virgil) 458
Age of Fable, The (Bulfinch) 45
Agrippa, M. Vipsanius 86
Ah, Wilderness! (film) 391
Ahlhauser, William C. 9
Aids to English Composition (Parker) 171
"Alchemist, The" (Lovecraft) 436n25
Alden, Abner 228n2, 243, 430
"Aletheia Phrikodes" (Lovecraft). *See* "Poe-et's Nightmare, The"
Alfredo (Lovecraft) 9
Alhazred, Abdul 429
Allgood, Helen. *See* Lovecraft, Helen (Allgood)
Allgood, Sir Lancelot 43, 293
Allgood, William 476
almanacs 242, 244, 453, 465
Alouette, L' 357
Amazing Stories 169, 522
Ambrosius, Aurelius 481
American Book Co. 19
American Men of Science (Cattell) 368
American Mercury 424
American Museum of Natural History (New York) 99
"American to Mother England, An" (Lovecraft) 59
American Weekly 401
Amesbury, MA 501
Amundsen, John 282–84
Ancient Rhetoric and Poetic (Baldwin) 189
"Ancient Sorceries" (Blackwood) 429
Anglicans 51, 327
"Annabel Lee" (Poe) 98
Anne (Queen of England) 37, 38, 45, 431
"Antarctic Atlas" (Lovecraft) 226, 334

Anthony Adverse (Allen) 483
Ape, the Idiot and Other People, The (Morrow) 525
Appeal to Reason 493
Appleton, John Howard 431
Appleton High School Press Club 9, 49n5
Apprentice 9
Arabian Nights 299, 429, 440
Argosy 8
Aristaenetus 131
Aristotle 180
Arkham House transcripts 18, 21, 24, 33
Arkham Sampler 33
Arnold, Benedict 146
Ars Amatoria (Ovid) 278
Arthur, King 477–78, 481–82, 483
"Arthur Jermyn" (Lovecraft). *See* "Facts concerning the Late Arthur Jermyn and His Family"
Aryans 53, 54, 429, 466, 473
Astounding Stories 517
"Astrology and the Future" (Lovecraft) 38
"At Her Window" (Locker-Lampson) 233
"At the Home of Poe" (Long) 100
At the Mountains of Madness (Lovecraft) 517
Athol, MA 183, 185
Atterbury, Francis 387
Augustus (Emperor of Rome) 86
Aurelianus, Ambrosius 481
"Autumn" (Crowley) 78–80
Avery, Stephen 134, 136

Babcock, Ralph E. 363, 374
Bacon, Victor E. 141–42, 269, 426
Badger 48n2, 49n6
Badham, Charles 387
Baird, Edwin 31
Baldwin, Charles Sears 189
Baldwin, F. Lee 403n2
Baldwin, John Osman 88, 169
Balieff, Nikita F. 99
Baptists 51

Barlow, R. H. 20, 21, 374–75, 408, 413, 414, 415, 416, 417, 421–22
Barnitz, Park 340
Bartholdi, Frédéric Auguste 424
Bartram, John 145–46, 418
Basinet, Victor L. 42
Basques 466
"Battle That Ended the Century, The" (Lovecraft-Barlow) 24
Baudelaire, Charles 107, 266, 423, 425, 438, 468
Beattie, James 38
Beautiful Joe (Saunders) 317
"Belshazzar's Feast" (Martin) 528, 529
Benson, A. C. 234, 242
Berkeley, George 154, 345
Berkeley Square (film) 361
Bernadine, Sister 317–19
Bernon, Gabriel 298
Best Short Stories of 1928, The (O'Brien) 195
Betterton, Thomas 57
Beyer, Dr. 148
"Beyond the Wall of Sleep" (Lovecraft) 26
Bible 192, 278, 527, 529
Biblical Alliance 10, 67–68, 77–78
Bickerstaffe, Isaac 38, 40
Bierce, Ambrose 24–25, 31, 364, 400, 404, 422, 469, 488, 497, 530
Biglow Papers, The (Lowell) 61
"Bird, A. J." 47–48
Bishop, Zealia 28, 363–64
Bixbee, Mrs. 115
Black, R. Coursin 142
Blackwood, Algernon 429, 525
Blair, Hugh 39
Blake, Mrs. 42
Blake, William 527
Blue Mountain Survey 24
Blue Pencil Club 90, 94, 119, 258, 415, 494
Boccaccio, Giovanni 274, 276
Bodley Book Shop 517
"Body Snatcher, The" (Stevenson) 525
Boguet, Henri 367
Bookman 48
Books and Bipeds (Starrett) 33
Boston, MA 114, 115, 154, 186, 194, 363, 366, 393, 421, 516
Boston Budget and Beacon 43–44
Boston Globe 114
Boston Transcript 19, 195, 506
Bradley, Chelster P. 20, 363
Bradofsky, Hyman 22, 390–91
Braithwaite, William Stanley 19, 106, 220
Brâncuși, Constantin 178
Brattleboro, VT 184
Bride of Gettysburg, The (Hylton) 169
"Bride of the Sea, The" (Lovecraft). *See* "Unda; or, The Bride of the Sea"
Bridge, The (Crane) 27
Brideport, CT 21, 23, 367, 380, 383, 398, 400, 409, 418, 420
Bridges, Robert 352, 354
"Brief Course in Astronomy, A" (Lovecraft) 381
Brinkley, John Romulus 282n4
Bristol, RI 378–79
Brobst, Harry K. 330, 345
Bromley, Grace M. 142
Brooke, Rupert 295
Brooklyn, NY 142–44, 146–48, 257–58, 436–42, 446
Broome, William 323
Brown, John 170n15
Brown University 46, 80, 126, 241, 331, 436n21
Brownell, Mary 299
Browning, Robert 165
Bryan, William Jennings 10, 77
Buddhism 408
Bulfinch, Thomas 45, 336
Bullen, John Ravenor 141, 169, 223, 523n1
Burgomaster, The (Pixley-Luders) 180, 224
Burns, Mrs. 439
Burritt, Elijah Hinsdale 45, 436n22
Burroughs, George 429
Bush, David Van 88, 89, 234, 317, 487, 490, 494, 497, 503
Butler, Samuel 275
Byland, Frederick Aloysius 48
Byron, George Gordon, Lord 166, 168
Cabell, James Branch 253
Caesar, Julius 479
Californian 28, 390
"Call of Cthulhu, The" (Lovecraft) 196, 445, 467
Campbell, Paul J. 14, 19, 25, 64, 207, 358, 498, 515

Campbell, Mrs. Paul J. 273
Campbell, Thomas 233
Can Such Things Be? (Bierce) 400, 469
"Can the Moon Be Reached by Man?" (Lovecraft) 49n8
Canby, Henry Seidel 258
Candidanus, Aurelius 482
Candide (Voltaire) 252, 278
Caninus, Aurelianus 482
Canok, Miss 387, 388
Caratacus 479
Carroll, Lewis 12n11
Carter, Nick 42
Carter, Thomas 347
Caruso, Enrico 67
Case of Charles Dexter Ward, The (Lovecraft) 426, 433
Casey, Edward Pearce 298
Casey, Samuel, Jr. 298–99, 346
Casey, Silas 298
Casey, Thomas 298
"Cask of Amontillado, The" (Poe) 525
Castle of Otranto, The (Walpole) 469, 489
"Cats of Ulthar, The" (Lovecraft) 523
Cats of Ulthar, The (Lovecraft) 516–17
Cattell, James McKeen 368, 369
Catullus (C. Valerius Catullus) 162
Causerie 517
Cavalcade (film) 361
Centaur Book Shop 512
Chaffee, Eleanor Alletta 417
Chambers, Robert W. 404
Chapin, Howard Miller 410
Chaplin, Charlie 415
Charlemagne 293
Charleston, SC 262–65, 385, 413–14, 417–18, 475, 484
"Charleston" (Lovecraft) 16
Chaucer, Geoffrey 354
Chauve-Souris, La 99
"Chemistry" (Lovecraft) 334
Chicago, IL 233
Chicago Tribune 12n11, 32, 33, 85, 98, 113n8, 175
Chipiez, Charles 86
Christianity 52, 53, 66–75, 78, 300, 305, 427, 443–44
"Church and the World, The" (Moe) 75n2
Cibber, Colley 92

Cicero, M. Tullius 57, 250, 288
"City of Spiders, The" (Munn) 196
Clark, Franklin Chase 43, 46, 303
Clark, Lillian D. 43–44, 133, 326–27
Clarke, Harry 425–26
Claudius (Emperor of Rome) 479
"Clean Page, A" (Moe) 14
Cline, Leonard 224
Clinton, Sir Henry 264
Clough, Arthur Hugh 170n3
Clough, Benjamin C. 189
Coates, Walter J. 29, 185, 196, 524
Coffin, Sir Isaac 359
Cole, Edward H. 13, 60, 114, 115, 116, 195, 269, 359, 363, 366, 376, 393, 408, 409, 414, 418–19, 421, 489, 494, 498, 504–5
Cole, Ira A. 12, 52, 61, 70, 80, 171, 271, 321
Coleridge, Samuel Taylor 162
Collins, Louise H. 55, 60
"Colour out of Space, The" (Lovecraft) 169, 234, 435n12, 445, 522, 523n4
Comet 328
Commonplace Book (Lovecraft) 511n9, 526n6
Concord, MA 114, 328
Congdon, H. W. 226
Conover, Howard R. 142
Conquistador (MacLeish) 375
Conservative 8, 27, 96, 180, 272, 490, 497
Constantine (Emperor of Rome) 51
Cook, W. Paul 25, 28, 29, 30, 85, 155–56, 159, 169, 183, 184, 223, 265, 280, 320, 331, 359, 363, 426, 432, 465, 493, 513, 521, 523, 524
Cooke, Thomas 83
"Cool Air" (Lovecraft) 513
Coolidge, Calvin 185
"Corners and Characters of Providence" (Laswell) 137
Coryciani 21
Cosmopolitan 24–25
Craig, Mrs. R. A. 144
Crane, Dr. 144
Crane, Hart 26, 27–28, 30, 498
Cranmer, Thomas 373
Crawford, F. Marion 525
Credential 9
Creep, Shadow! (Merritt) 400

Creeps by Night (Hammett) 311
Critical Dissertation on the Poems of Ossian, A (Blair) 39
Crowley, James Laurence 78–80
Cthulhu 426
Cunedda 481
Curley, James Michael 115
Curry System 288
Cynosure 9

Daas, Edward F. 7, 22, 37, 41, 141
"Dagon" (Lovecraft) 31, 139, 432
Dailey, Peter F. 180
Danvers, MA 499–501
Dark Chamber, The (Cline) 224
Darrow, Clarence 307, 309
Dauber & Pine (bookshop) 28, 395, 514, 516n6
Davis, Alexander Voigt 358n8
Davis, Edgar J. 141–42, 501–4
Davis, Graeme 62, 358
Davis, Sonia H. 28–29. *See also* Greene, Sonia H.
de Castro, Adolphe 21, 28, 230, 364, 422
De Quincey, Thomas 443, 457
De Rerum Natura (Lucretius) 161, 458
Dean, Judge 74
Decameron (Boccaccio) 278
Dedham, MA 124
Deerfield, MA 183
"Delavan's Comet and Astrology" (Lovecraft) 38
Dell, Floyd 266
Dempsey, Jack 155
Dench, Ernest A. 256
Derleth, August 20, 21–22, 24, 29, 33, 195, 196, 247, 269, 284, 289, 325, 340, 402, 406, 476, 483
Description of the Town of Quebeck . . ., A (Lovecraft) 15–16, 279–80, 282
"Destruction of Herculaneum, The" (Martin) 528
Dexter, Timothy 186, 503–4
Diamond Dick 42
Dickens, Charles 434
Don Juan (Byron) 166
Don Rodriguez (Dunsany) 497
Dooley, Mr. 70
Doorways to Poetry (Moe) 16–20, 170n1, 189, 198, 210, 229, 230, 231–32, 243, 244, 260, 291, 310, 312, 352, 356, 362, 373, 385

Doorways to Poetry (Untermeyer) 20
Doré, Gustave 527, 528
Dowie, John Alexander 314n2
Drayton, Michael 170n6
Dream-Quest of Unknown Kadath, The (Lovecraft) 445, 447
Dreiser, Theodore 266
Driftwind 185, 196
Dryden, John 45, 115, 166, 170n11, 327
Dryden, Wheeler 257, 415
Duffey, May M. 317
Dunciad, The (Pope) 61
Dunn, John T. 42
Dunne, Peter Finley 75n4
Dunsany, Lord 26, 84, 92, 132, 235, 405, 445, 471, 494, 497
"Dunwich Horror, The" (Lovecraft) 196
Dwyer, Bernard Austin 23–24, 169, 265
Dyckman cottage (New York) 105–6
Dyer, Mary 292
Dyer, Mercy 346

East Greenwich, RI 380
Ebony and Crystal (Smith) 488
Ebony Flame (Starrett) 529
Eclectic 192
Eddy, Arthur A. 465–66
Eddy, C. M., Jr. 31, 135–36, 139, 154, 456n7, 510
Edkins, Ernest A. 414, 517
Edward VIII (King of England) 391
Eglin's (bookstore) 497
Electrical Testing Laboratories 367, 375, 383, 406
Elegy Written in a Country Churchyard (Gray) 38
Eliot, Charles William 126
Eliot, George 175
Eliot, T. S. 139n1, 287
Ellis, Laura 9
Encyclopaedia Britannica 32, 56, 527, 530n2
English Journal 9, 373, 390
"Epistle to Francis, Ld. Belknap . . ., An" (Lovecraft) 198–200
"Epistle to the Rt. Honble Maurice Winter, Moe. Esq., . . ., An" (Lovecraft) 18, 210–15

"Epitaph on yᵉ Letterr Rrr . . ." (Lovecraft) 62
Erewhon (Butler) 275
Ericson, E. E. 102n18, 106
Esperanto Society 9
Essay on Criticism, An (Pope) 165
Euripides 174, 233
Evans, Justus J. 63
Evans, Mary Ann. *See* Eliot, George
Evening in Spring (Derleth) 476
"Evil Clergyman, The" (Lovecraft) 24
Examen of Witches, An (Boguet) 367
Facts concerning the Late Arthur Jermyn and His Family" (Lovecraft) 139, 523
Faig, Kenneth W., Jr. 304n1
"Fair Harvard" (Gilman) 263
Fairy Tales (Grimm) 45
"Fall of the House of Usher, The" (Poe) 208
"Falsity of Astrology, The" (Lovecraft) 38
Fantasy Fan 366n7, 395, 401, 404, 412
Far Off Things (Machen) 442
Farnham, Joseph 359
Faust and the Demon (Reynolds) 429, 489
"Feast, The" (Lovecraft) 495n5
Felis (cat) 96
"Festival, The" (Lovecraft) 455
Festus, Porcius 75
First Steps in the Appreciation of Poetry (Moe) 17, 384
"Five Alone" (Derleth) 476
"Flash" (Dwyer) 24
Flecker, James Elroy 447n7
Fosdick, Harry Emerson 309
Four Acrostic Sonnets on Edgar Allan Poe (Moe) 21
Fowler, Samuel 499
Fragments of Science for Unscientific People (Tyndall) 290
France, Anatole 435n1, 493
Francis, Philip 387
Frank, Glenn 343–44
Franklin, Benjamin 130, 145, 359
Fredericksburg, VA 413
Freeman, Mary E. Wilkins 120
French, Eunice 23
Fritter, Leo G. 505
From a College Window (Benson) 235

Frontinus, C. Julius 480
Frost, Robert 453–54
Fulford, Francis 292
Fungi from Yuggoth (Lovecraft) 16, 27, 365
Gallomo 13
Galpin, Alfred 9, 13, 26, 27, 69, 77, 81n5, 93, 99, 103–4, 107–8, 123, 153, 265, 283, 305, 312, 324, 364, 447n9, 489, 490–93, 515
Galpin, Alfred, Sr. 77, 364
Galsworthy, John 365
Gamwell, Annie E. P. 24, 43–44, 102, 103, 115, 143, 311, 351, 398, 400, 436n26, 495n3, 497, 509
Gamwell, Edward F. 43, 46
Gamwell, Phillips 47, 83, 234–35, 303
Garrick, David 57
Garth, Sir Samuel 45, 170nn12–13
Gautier, Théophile 322
Gazette Française de Newport 133
Gentleman's Magazine 83
Geography of the Heavens (Burritt) 45
George II (King of England) 106, 145, 378
George III (King of England) 97, 262, 293, 489
George V (King of England) 391
Ghost Stories 513
Gibbons, Grinling 124–25, 130, 131
Gibbs, James 122, 125, 508
Gilder, Richard Watson 311
Gilles de Rais 428
Gilman, Samuel 263
Gish, Grace I. 59
Gloucester, MA 187, 263
"Gods of Our Fathers, The" (Cole) 52
"Gold Bug, The" (Poe) 263
Goldsmith, Oliver 48, 130
"Gone—But Whither?" (Lovecraft) 381
"Goodbye, Dolly Gray" (song) 180
Goodenough, Arthur 156, 183–84
Gotham Weekly Gazette 41
Gourmont, Remy de 177
"Grapes of Eschol, The" (Miller) 364
Gray, Thomas 38, 161
"Great God Pan, The" (Machen) 427
"Greatest Law, The" (Lovecraft) 109–13
Green, E. H. 419
Green Round, The (Machen) 483

Greene, Florence 93–94
Greene, John Holden 125
Greene, Sonia H. 26, 84–86, 87–89, 90, 93–94, 95, 97, 98, 99–100, 102–4, 142, 143–48, 149, 209n1, 487–88, 493–94, 498, 512
Grimm, Brothers 45, 299
Guest, Edgar A. 217, 273, 276, 277, 310
Guiney, Louise Imogen 44, 299, 429–30
Gummere, Francis Barton 353
Gwynnedd, Owen 300

Haldeman-Julius Weekly 493
Hammett, Dashiell 311
Handbook of Poetics (Gummere) 353
Harding, Warren G. 91
Hardy, Thomas 75
Harkness, Albert 173
Harper's 368, 372
Harré, T. Everett 196
Harris, Frank 227
Harris, William 357
Harrison, Benjamin 310
Hart, Bertrand K. 247, 266, 314n7, 328, 343n56, 352, 374, 384, 400
Hartmann, J. F. 38
Hasheesh Eater, The (Ludlow) 105, 442–43
Haughton, Ida C. 150n3, 513
"Haunter of the Dark, The" (Lovecraft) 392n8
Haverhill, MA 186, 331, 504
Hawthorne, Nathaniel 45
Hazard, Robert 345
Hazard, Thomas 299
Hearn, Lafcadio 469
Hecht, Ben 266
Heins, Charles W. 273
Hemingway, Ernest 267, 285, 286, 323
Henneberger, J. C. 31, 513
Henry, William 236, 241
Henry VI (Shakespeare) 92
Herakles 337–38, 339–40
"Herbert West—Reanimator" (Lovecraft) 102n17, 488n4
Herdman, Edward F. 59
"Heritage or Modernism: Common Sense in Art Forms" (Lovecraft) 21
Hermaphrodite, The (Loveman) 28, 29, 85, 86, 107, 426, 443, 494, 497

Hermaphrodite and Other Poems, The (Loveman) 28, 517
Hermit, The (Beattie) 38
Herodotus 389
Hesiod 83, 87
Hieroglyphics (Machen) 175
Hill, Emma Jane 43
Hill, Isaac 43
Hill of Dreams, The (Machen) 442, 446
Hitler, Adolf 404
Hoag, Jonathan E. 435n13, 487, 494, 498
Holmes, Oliver Wendell 44, 65, 103
Holy Vehm 428, 429
Home Brew 91, 497
Homer 50, 87, 160, 337
Honorius (Emperor of Rome) 481
Hopkins, Matthew 428
Horace (Q. Horatius Flaccus) 163, 174, 191, 240, 304n4, 386–90
"Horror at Red Hook, The" (Lovecraft) 196, 423, 436, 441, 523
Horror from the Hills, The (Long) 464n3
"Hound, The" (Lovecraft) 139, 234
House of Souls, The (Machen) 442
Housman, Clemence 524
Houtain, George Julian 87–88, 91, 92, 93, 487, 490, 496
Howard, Daniel 238
Howard, Robert E. 24, 49n8, 472–74
Howard, Whipple 238
"Howard Phillips Lovecraft: The Sage of Providence" (Moe) 21
Hub Club 89, 141, 269, 489
Hubbard, Elbert 273, 310, 322
Hudibras (Butler) 166
Hugo, Victor 135
Hutchinson, Alfred L. 61, 81n5, 515
Huxley, Aldous 321, 322
Huxley, Thomas Henry 50, 290
Huysmans, J.-K. 265–66
Hyde, Edna 497
Hylton, J. Dunbar 170n21
"Hypnos" (Lovecraft) 27, 32, 85, 490
"Ibid" (Lovecraft) 15, 22, 192, 280–82
Idylls of the King (Tennyson) 289
Iliad (Homer) 39
Imagery Aids (Moe) 16–17
"In Pierrot's Garden" (Loveman) 24–25
In the Midst of Life (Bierce) 400

"In the Vault" (Lovecraft) 445, 513
Incredible Adventures (Blackwood) 525–26
Innocent VIII, Pope 428
Instruments of Darkness (Miller) 385
"Introduction to Poetry" (Moe) 20
Introduction to the Rhythmic and Metric of the Classical Languages, An (Schmidt) 198
Ireson, Capt. 116
Irving, Washington 120
"Is There Life on the Moon?" (Lovecraft) 42
Isaacson, Charles D. 94
"Isaacsonio-Mortoniad, The" (Lovecraft) 101n9, 140
Isham, Norman M. 410
Isocrates 288

Jackson, Winifred Virginia 106
Jacobs, W. W. 525
James I (King of England) 428
James, M. R. 416
Janvier, Meredith 195
Java Head (film) 489
Jerrold, Walter 49n19
Jesus Christ 74, 339
Jews 53–54, 73, 92, 94, 444, 475
John XXII, Pope 428
John Hay Library (Brown University) 22, 27, 33, 331, 374
John Silence—Physician Extraordinary (Blackwood) 429, 525–26
Johnson, Samuel 57, 431, 432
Joyce, James 266, 287
Jurgen (Cabell) 253

Kalem Club 28, 30, 31
Keats, John 65, 167, 425, 494
Keil, Paul Livingston 94, 96, 100, 142
Keila, Louis 90–91
Kendall, Frank A. 358n5
Kenyon Press 16, 310, 386
Kingman, Dr. 144
Kingston, RI 349
Kipling, Rudyard 289, 434
Kirk, George W. 28, 142, 143, 148, 350, 424, 440, 441, 488, 494, 497, 513, 529
Kittery, ME 129
Kittredge, George Lyman 465
Kleicomolo 12, 61n1, 62, 63, 67, 68, 75, 192, 248, 260, 267, 271–72, 282–83, 364, 374, 395, 403

Kleiner, Rheinhart 12, 61, 84, 86, 90, 91, 93, 96–97, 98, 100, 103, 143, 220, 257, 271, 283, 386, 395, 424, 515
Knopf, Alfred A. (publisher) 28
Knowles, Vernon 526
Knowlton, H. L. 19
Koenig, H. C. 367, 375, 380, 383, 395, 407
Ku Klux Klan 428, 474
Kuntz, Eugene B. 142, 171, 220, 362

Là-Bas (Huysmans) 265
La Farge, John 137
Laing, Gordon Jennings 386
"Landor's Cottage" (Poe) 96
Lashinsky, Mr. 94
Last and First Men (Stapledon) 416
Laswell, George D. 138n6
Lawrence, Carroll E. 494–95, 505
Lawrence, D. H. 266
Lawton, Louis 234
Lazare, Edward 143
Leaves 20
Lecky, W. E. H. 250
Lee, Nathaniel 170n11
Lee, Robert E. 59
Leeds, Arthur 151n9, 257, 406, 515
Lehmkuhl, Harry N. 150n4
Leiser, Adeline E. 88
Leith, W. Compton 234, 235, 260
Leonard, Sterling A. 19, 189–90, 304–5, 310
Leonard, William Ellery 307
Leuba, James H. 368–72
Lewis, Matthew Gregory 90, 528
Lincoln, Abraham 238
Lindbergh, Charles 365
"Lines on Gen. Robert Edward Lee" (Lovecraft) 59n7
"Lines upon the Magnates of the Pulp" (Lovecraft) 246–47
Literary Digest 196
Little, Richard Henry 385n9
"Living Heritage: Roman Architecture in Today's America, A" (Lovecraft) 366n6, 405n1
Lock and Key Library, The (Hawthorne) 120
Locker-Lampson, Frederick 233
Lodge, Henry Cabot 453
Lodbrog, Regner 39–40

Long, Charles O. 424
Long, Frank Belknap 23, 27, 29, 32, 93, 95–96, 99, 100, 105, 107–8, 120, 142, 143, 149, 154–55, 156, 180, 198, 247, 255, 256, 257, 260, 265, 282, 289, 291, 310–11, 312, 322, 325, 349, 350, 364, 367, 374, 395, 402, 409, 418, 419, 423–24, 425, 426, 445, 446, 464n3, 467, 468, 488, 494, 498, 516, 517, 523
Long, Frank Belknap, Sr. 95, 154–55
Long, Mrs. Frank Belknap 95–96, 144, 149, 155
Longfellow, Henry Wadsworth 185, 186, 324
Longhurst, Sarah 108
Loring & Mussey (publisher) 402
Love, William Lathrop 438, 440
Love and Lunacy and Other Poems (Whitaker) 14
Lovecraft, George 43, 294
Lovecraft, H. P.: on aesthetics, 286–91, 315–20, 325–26, 327–28, 329–30; and amateur journalism, 7–8, 41–43, 141–42, 356–58, 363, 494, 517; ancestry of, 43, 235–45, 292–99, 434; on antiquarianism, 410–12; on architecture, 120–23, 124–27, 192–95; on astronomy, 38, 40, 191; autobiography of, 43–47, 299–304, 429–33, 484–85; on beauty, 176–80; on cameras, 401–?; on civilization, 447–50, 472–76; diet of, 483–84; on eroticism in art, 248–54, 265–68, 273–78; on introverts and extraverts, 320–22; on marriage, 64, 205–9; on mythology, 336–40; on New England, 114–18, 124–27, 328–29, 359–60, 447, 450–56; on 1900–1904, 152–53, 210–15, 224–27, 230, 332–36; on poetry, 16–20, 37–38, 39–40, 57–59, 78–80, 81–83, 106–13, 159–68, 170–75, 209–11, 217–23, 227, 232–33, 243–44, 270–71, 309–14, 322–24, 352–56, 468–69; on politics, 200–204; on pronunciation, 55–57, 60–62, 65; on prose, 234–35, 258–60, 272–73, 284–86, 445; on religion, 51–52, 53–54, 66–75, 76, 304–9, 367–72, 443–45; on Roman civilization, 77–78, 86–87, 365, 457–58, 477–83; Roman dream of, 458–64, 466–68; on science fiction, 416; on translation, 386–90; travels of, 15–16, 26, 83–100, 104–6, 114–18, 129–30, 131–32, 183–87, 233–34, 235–42, 244–45, 262–65, 278–80, 326, 331–32, 344–49, 350–51, 360–61, 366–67, 374–75, 377–80, 393, 409, 413–14, 417–19, 420–21, 499–505, 512, 515, 517; on weird art, 425–26, 527–29; on weird fiction, 119–20, 196, 400–401, 404, 405, 442–43, 469, 470–72, 521–22, 523, 524–26, 529–30; on witchcraft, 427–29; and word games, 12, 175–76, 361–62
Lovecraft, Helen (Allgood) 43, 294
Lovecraft, John 293
Lovecraft, Joseph 294
Lovecraft, Mary 43
Lovecraft, Sarah Susan (Phillips) 43, 44, 55, 191, 295, 302
Lovecraft, Sonia H. *See* Greene, Sonia H.
Lovecraft, Thomas 44, 293–94
Lovecraft, Winfield Scott 43, 44, 294, 295
"Loved Dead, The" (Lovecraft–Eddy) 456n7
Loveman, Robert 506
Loveman, Samuel 15, 24–31, 32, 84–90, 91, 93–94, 95, 96, 97, 98, 99, 100, 105, 106–7, 123, 143, 145, 260, 322, 326, 350, 395, 404, 421, 426, 443, 521, 523, 527, 529, 530
Lowell, James Russell 61–62
Lucky Dog 322
Lucretius (T. Lucretius Carus) 161, 458
Lucullus, L. Licinius 131
Ludlow, Fitz Hugh 105, 442–43
"Lumbermen, The" (Whittier) 168
"Lurking Fear, The" (Lovecraft) 425, 488nn3–4, 494, 505n8
Lynch, Joseph Bernard 115, 269, 363
Lysias 389

Macauley, George W. 22
McClure's Magazine 230
McCormack, John 67
McGovern, Terry 438
Machen, Arthur 31, 78, 175, 427, 429, 442, 445, 469, 470–71, 483, 508
McIntire, Samuel 126
MacLeish, Archibald 375

Macmillan (publisher) 19
McNeil, Everett 189, 255–58, 424, 441, 513
Macpherson, James 39, 348
MacSparran, James 346
Macy, Richard 360
Maecenas, C. Cilnius 191
Magazine World 357
Magnalia Christi Americana (Mather) 245, 455, 501
Magnolia, MA 102–3
Magnum Innominandum 459, 467
Malleus Maleficarum (Kremer-Sprenger) 367
Man from Genoa and Other Poems, The (Long) 435n2
Man on All Fours, The (Derleth) 406
Man's Place in Nature (Huxley) 290
Marblehead, MA 114–18, 124, 129, 154, 187, 195, 265, 332, 359, 383, 393, 408, 409, 502
Martin, Harry E. 490, 495, 496
Martin, John 32, 527–30
Marvel Tales 406
"Master, The" (Wilde) 89
Mather, Cotton 245, 455, 501
Matthews, Brander 180, 229, 270, 271
Maturin, Charles Robert 119
Maxfield, Julia A. 155, 379, 422
Maximus, Magnus Clemens 481
May, Arthur P. 225
Medea (Euripides) 233
"Medusa: A Portrait" (Lovecraft) 140, 513
Melmoth the Wanderer (Maturin) 119
Men of Aran (film) 406
Mencken, H. L. 138, 176–80, 200, 506
Merrimac, NH 501
Merritt, A. 400–401
Messayeh, Alexander D. 440
Metal Monster, The (Merritt) 401
Metamorphoses (Ovid) 161, 336
Metropolitan Museum of Art (New York) 86, 194, 298, 346
Middleton, Lilian (pseud. of S. Lilian McMullen) 83, 106
Midland 325
Millard, Esther. *See* Whipple, Esther (Millard)
Miller, Emily Huntingon 366

Milton, John 160, 165, 239, 527
Miniter, Edith 89, 114, 115, 116, 363, 499, 501
Mitchell, Maria 360
Mitchell, Susanna Valentine 375
Mitchell, William 360
Moe, Donald James 9, 22, 83, 119, 191, 233, 269, 383
Moe, James G. 8
Moe, Maurice W. 8–23, 393, 396, 397, 402, 409, 413, 417, 421, 422
Moe, Robert Ellis 9, 21, 23, 83, 119, 191, 196, 269, 343, 366–68, 375, 376–80, 383
Mohammad 54
Monk and the Hangman's Daughter (Voss [tr. Bierce-Danziger]) 530
"Monkey's Paw, The" (Jacobs) 525
Montreal, Canada 332
"Moon, The" (Lovecraft) 226
"Moon Pool, The" (Merritt) 401
Moon Terror, The (Birch et al.) 31
Moore, Thomas 512n19
Moosup Valley, RI 235–42, 244–45
More, Paul Elmer 456
Morris, Sir John 293
Morris, Rachel 300
Morrow, W. C. 525
Morton, James F. 52, 53, 84, 88–90, 91, 92–93, 94–95, 96, 97, 98, 105, 154, 155, 169, 230, 234, 256, 269, 280, 288, 321, 322, 336, 358, 379, 415, 424, 425, 487, 494, 496, 498, 506–10, 513, 517
"Moxon's Master" (Bierce) 470n3
Munn, H. Warner 155–56, 169, 196, 524
Munroe, Addison P. 48
Munroe, Chester P. 48
Murphy, W. R. 115
Murray, Margaret A. 427–28
Museum of Fine Arts (Boston) 194, 298, 346
"Music of Erich Zann, The" (Lovecraft) 311
Musso, Bonifacio 527
Myers family 366, 393
"Mysterious Ship, The" (Lovecraft) 225, 334, 431
"Mythology for the Young" (Lovecraft) 334

Nantucket, MA 359–61, 384

National Amateur 27, 363, 494, 495n15, 498, 516
National Amateur Press Association 15, 25, 26, 345, 357, 363, 374, 516, 517
Neilan, Francis H. 226
"Nemesis" (Lovecraft) 446, 513
New Bedford, MA 416
New Haven, CT 419, 420–21
New London, CT 513
"New Odyssey, The "(Lovecraft). *See* "Poem of Ulysses, The"
New York, NY 84–100, 104–6, 130, 143, 255–58, 374–75, 395, 407, 418, 447–48, 498, 517
New York Public Library 525, 527
New York Tribune 41, 68, 98, 357
Newburyport, MA 186–87, 331, 502–4
Newport, RI 154, 348, 379, 408
"News Notes" (Lovecraft) 10
Niall of the Nine Hostages 481
Nietzsche, Friedrich 88, 453
Nigger-Man (cat) 301
North American Review 8–9, 68
Not at Night (Asbury) 196
Not at Night (Thomson) 196, 523
Nurse, Rebekah 500, 501
"Nyarlathotep" (Lovecraft) 27

O-Wash-Ta-Nong 22
O'Brien, Edward J. 195, 340, 476
"Observations on Several Parts of America" (Lovecraft) 15
Odd One 356
"Of Gold and Sawdust" (Loveman) 29
"Old Black Trail, The" (Dwyer) 434
"Old Dark House, The" (Dwyer) 24
Old Farmer and His Almanack, The (Kittredge) 465
"On an Unchang'd Rural Prospect" (Lovecraft) 313
"On the Return of Maurice Winter Moe, Esq., to the Pedagogical Profession" (Lovecraft) 10
O'Neill, Eugene 278, 391
Orton, Vrest 196, 268, 320, 424, 441
Osgood, Frances Sargent 65
"Other Gods, The" (Lovecraft) 405
Out of the Immortal Night (Loveman) 27
Outlook 73
Ovid (P. Ovidius Naso) 45, 104–5, 161, 166–67, 278, 336

Owen, D. C. 9
Pan 336–37
Paradise Lost (Milton) 165
Paradise Regain'd (Milton) 160
Parker, Charles A. A. 114, 115, 116, 357, 363, 497, 499, 501
Parker, Richard Green 171–73
Partridge, John 38
"Passer-By, A" (Bridges) 354–56
Pater, Walter 434
Paullinus, C. Suetonius 479–80
Pawtuxet Valley Gleaner 42, 46, 436n23
Payne, Charles M. 48n3
Pearson's Magazine 497
Peck, Henry J. 193
Pegasus 14
Pemberton, Clive 526
Pendergast, P. J. 169
Pendleton, Charles Leonard 128
"Penelope" (Starrett) 31
"People of the Pit, The" (Merritt) 401
Perspective Review 20
"Perverted Poesie or Modern Metre" (Lovecraft) 22
Philadelphia, PA 144–46, 350, 512
Philadelphia Public Ledger 115
Phillips, Anna 238
Phillips, Asaph 234, 235, 236, 237, 238, 240
Phillips, Christopher 245
Phillips, Edwin E. 43, 301
Phillips, Frank 244
Phillips, George 245, 270, 296
Phillips, James 235, 238, 241–42, 244
Phillips, Jeremiah 43, 236, 237, 238, 240, 242, 244, 297
Phillips, Michael 245, 296–97z
Phillips, Robie (Place) 43, 44–45, 299
Phillips, Samuel 296
Phillips, Seth Whipple 237
Phillips, Susan Esther 237
Phillips, Ward (pseud. of HPL) 110
Phillips, Whipple 234
Phillips, Whipple Van Buren 43, 44, 46, 236, 297, 298, 299, 301, 302
Phillips, Zilpha Ann 238
Pickle for the Knowing Ones, A (Dexter) 503
"Pickman's Model" (Lovecraft) 196, 423
"Picture in the House, The" (Lovecraft) 139

Pilgrims 296
Pindar 161, 337
Pippin 9, 42, 64, 356, 364
Place, Raymond 235
Place, Stephen, Jr. 44, 242, 243, 244, 299
Place, Stephen, Sr. 242–43
Plain Speaker 14
Plato 411
Poe, Edgar Allan 21, 65, 90, 93, 95, 96, 98–99, 107–8, 120, 155, 167, 208, 235, 263, 301, 322, 350, 422, 431, 446, 468, 525
"Poe-et's Nightmare, The" (Lovecraft) 493
Poem Comments (Moe) 17, 384
"Poem of Ulysses, The" (Lovecraft) 45, 431
Poemata Minora (Lovecraft) 224, 225, 334
Poems (Loveman) 25
Poesy 59
Poet and the Philosopher 169
Poetical Works of Jonathan E. Hoag, The (Hoag) 27, 487
Poetics (Aristotle) 180
Poetry out of Wisconsin (Derleth) 21
"Polaris" (Lovecraft) 22, 75n3, 405, 445
Pope, Alexander 39, 61n2, 165, 167, 170n8, 323, 352–53
Portland, ME 185–86
Portsmouth, NH 129–30, 131, 186
"Power of Wine: A Satire, The" (Lovecraft) 38
Price, E. Hoffmann 345, 349, 476
Priscian (Priscianus Caesariensis) 204
Progress of Poesy, The (Gray) 161
Prokosch, Frederic 329
Proper Studies (Huxley) 321
Proust, Marcel 198, 224, 269, 286, 289, 325
Providence, RI 125–28, 133–37, 193–94, 376–78, 396–97, 400, 419, 420, 422, 430–31, 433, 506–10
Providence Amateur Press Club 42
[Providence] *Evening Bulletin* 137, 351
[Providence] *Evening News* 7, 38, 46, 55, 63, 436n23
Providence Journal 46, 80, 197n3, 226, 247, 357, 400
[Providence] *Tribune* 7, 46, 436n23
Pryor, Anthony 517

"Psychopompos" (Lovecraft) 446
Puritans 66, 76, 250, 292, 296–97, 346, 451, 454, 500
Purple Cloud, The (Shiel) 404
Pyke, James T. 46
Pythagoras 177

Quebec, Canada 332, 515
"Quest of Iranon, The" (Lovecraft) 139n2
"Quinsnicket Park" (Lovecraft) 39

Rabelais, François 252, 274, 276
Radcliffe, Ann 469, 528
Railo, Eino 469
Rascoe, Burton 98
Rathbone, John 299
Rathbone, Rhoby 237, 299
Rathbone, Sarah 299
Rawdon, Lord 264
Raymond, Clifford S. 109, 200–201, 203
Reader, The (Alden) 228n2, 243, 430
Recluse 156, 523, 524
"Red Brain, The" (Wandrei) 153
Red Cross 73
Reilly, Mr. 48
"Religious Beliefs of American Scientists" (Leuba) 368–72
Remarque, Erich Maria 276, 277
Renshaw, Anne Tillery 55, 288
Revere, Paul 124, 125
Reynolds, George W. M. 429, 489–90
Rhetorical Grammar, A (Walker) 56, 61
Rhode Island Journal of Astronomy 7, 46, 225, 511n6
Rhode Island National Guard 63
Rhode Island School of Design 128–29
Rice, Dana 517
Rice, Mr. 204
Richard III (King of England) 480
Richard III (Shakespeare-Cibber) 92
Richmond, VA 350
Robinson, Hannah 347–48
Robinson, Rowland 347, 348
Robinson, William 347
Rogers, Will 319
"Royal Atlas of the World, The" (Lovecraft) 226
Russell, John 7
Ryder, Melvin 357

Sacher-Masoch, Leopold von 253
"Sadak in Search of the Waters of Oblivion" (Martin) 527
St. Augustine, FL 350, 417
Salem, MA 187, 455, 499, 500
Saltus, Edgar 107, 145, 488, 497
Samples, John Milton 76
Sandusky, Albert A. 13, 114, 115, 195, 288, 393, 489
Sanger, Alma B. 505
Saturday Review 258
Saturnian 26, 490
Saunders, Margaret Marshall 320
Sayle, William 264
Scarborough, Dorothy 525
Schacht, Hjalmar 402
Schilling, George S. 41n1, 42
Schmidt, J. H. Heinrich 198
School for Scandal, The (Sheridan) 127, 489
Schwartz, Julius 403n1
Schwartz, William B. 48n4
Science Fiction Digest 401
Science Fiction League 404
Science of Life, The (Wells–Huxley–Wells) 419
"Science versus Charlatanry" (Lovecraft) 38, 40
Scientific Gazette 7
Scott, Arthur E. 32
Scott, Sir Walter 271, 169
Scottsboro case 475
Sechrist, Edward Lloyd 208–9
Secret Glory, The (Machen) 442, 469
"Secret of the Grave, The" (Lovecraft) 334, 431
Selected Gems (Pendergast) 169
Selected Letters (Lovecraft) 7, 12
Serviss, Garrett P. 426
Shadow over Innsmouth, The (Lovecraft) 517
"Shadows on the Wall, The" (Freeman) 120, 456
Shakespeare, William 92, 170n4, 209n2, 353, 417
Sharkey, Jack 155
Shea, J. Vernon 312
Shelley, Percy Bysshe 166, 167
Shepley, George L. 133, 509
Sheridan, Richard Brinsley 489
Sherman, Philip Darrell 85
Shining Pyramid, The (Machen) 31

Shirley, William 122
"Shunned House, The" (Lovecraft) 27, 32, 517, 521, 523
"Sideshow, The" (Hart) 247
Sime, S. H. 426
"Simple Speller's Tale, The" (Lovecraft) 180
"Simplicity; a Poem" (Lovecraft) 81–83
"Sir Thomas Tryout" (Smith) 366n5, 435n13
Sirenica (Leith) 230, 234, 260
"Sleepy Hollow To-day" (Lovecraft) 15, 314n5
"S'Matter, Pop?" (Payne) 41
Smith, Charles W. ("Tryout") 114, 186–87, 331–32, 356–57, 363, 365, 435n13, 506n15
Smith, Clark Ashton 25, 26, 107, 151, 375, 425–26, 446, 468–69, 483, 487, 488, 497
Smith, Edwin Hadley 363
Smith, John 193
Smith, Samuel Francis 88, 425
Snappy Stories 253
Solon 321
"Some Causes of Self-Immolation" (Lovecraft) 15
Somerville, NJ 512
Sommer, William 194
Sonnets of the Midnight Hours (Wandrei) 17, 468
"Space-Eaters, The" (Long) 468n3
Spectator 161
Spengler, Oswald 453
Spenser, Edmund 163–64, 173, 174
Sphinx, The (Loveman) 28, 85, 107, 426
Spink, Helm C. 15, 269, 363
Stapledon, Olaf 416
Starrett, Vincent 31–33
"Statement of Randolph Carter, The" (Lovecraft) 22, 27, 263, 426
Steinmetz, Charles Proteus 375
Sterling, George 25
Sterling, Kenneth 30, 403–4
Stevenson, Robert Louis 434, 525
Stilicho 481
Stormonth, James 60, 204
"Story of Bob and Orry, The" 74
"Strange High House in the Mist, The" (Lovecraft) 445

Strange Interlude (O'Neill) 278
Strange Tales 24
Stratam, Evelyn von 364
Strauch, Carl Ferdinand 330
Stuart, Gilbert 346–47
Study of Versification, A (Matthews) 180, 229, 270
Sudbury, MA 230
Summers, Montague 367
Sunday, Billy 63
"Supernatural Horror in Literature" (Lovecraft) 25, 32, 405–6, 426, 523n3
Swann, W. P. G. 404
Swann's Way (Proust) 198
Swift, Jonathan 38, 254
Swinburne, Algernon Charles 162, 275
"Tales of the Marvellous and the Ridiculous" (Wilson) 33
Talman, Wilfred B. 292, 379, 401–2, 409, 424
Tanglewood Tales (Hawthorne) 45
Taylor, Bert Leston 12n11, 85, 181n10
Tennyson, Alfred, Lord 161, 162, 277, 289, 324
Teter, George E. 20, 210
"Teuton's Battle-Song, The" (Lovecraft) 39
Teutons 50–51, 53, 54
Texaco Star 409
"That Laugh" (Lawrence) 495
Theobald, Lewis 61
Theobald, Lewis (pseud. of HPL) 61, 81, 424n
Theobald, Ludwig von (pseud. of HPL) 109
Theodosius I (Emperor of Rome) 480
Things Near and Far (Machen) 442
Three Impostors, The (Machen) 442, 508
Three Who Died (Derleth) 406
Thrift, Timothy Burr 322
Tilden, Leonard E. 83
Time 356–57
"To Charlie of the Comics" (Lovecraft) 59
"To Mr. Theobald" (Loveman) 28
"To Samuel Loveman, Esq." (Lovecraft) 30
"To Samuel Loveman, Esq., on His Poetry and Drama . . ." (Lovecraft) 25, 101n3

"To Samuel Loveman, Esq., upon Adorning His Room for His Birthday" (Lovecraft) 30
"To Satan" (Loveman) 27, 490, 497
"To the Members of the U.A.P.A. from the Providence Amateur Press Club" (Lovecraft) 48
"To the Old Pagan Religion" (Lovecraft) 52
"To Zara" (Lovecraft) 108–9
Toldridge, Elizabeth 18
"Tomb, The" (Lovecraft) 432, 455
Torrey, Silvia 346
Trail, Armitage 31–32
Trail 61
"Translations from the American" (Orton) 196
Traveller, The (Goldsmith) 130
"Travels in the Provinces of America" (Lovecraft) 15
Treasure Island (Stevenson) 361
Truth Seeker 72
Tryout 113, 357, 427
Tuckerman, Frederick 340
Twenty-one Letters of Ambrose Bierce (Bierce; ed. Loveman) 25
Tyndall, John 290
Ullman, Allan 28
"Unda; or, The Bride of the Sea" (Lovecraft) 61
United Amateur 8, 28, 107, 141, 357, 423, 494, 506
United Amateur Press Association 8, 12, 25, 26, 39, 42, 48, 62, 94, 99, 140, 141–42, 414, 426, 432, 505
United Official Quarterly 9–10, 52, 59
"Unnamable, The" (Lovecraft) 14, 455
Untermeyer, Louis 20
"Upper Berth, The" (Crawford) 525
Upton, Winslow 225
Vagrant 69, 72, 493
Valentinianus (Emperor of Rome) 480
Van Dusen, Washington 146, 230
Vaughan, Sarah Place 242
Venus in Furs (Sacher-Masoch) 253
Vermont 183–85
"Vermont—A First Impression" (Lovecraft) 188n2
"Very Old Folk, The" (Lovecraft) 464n3

Virgil (P. Vergilius Maro) 57, 66, 87, 161, 191, 296
Vision of Judgment, The (Byron) 168
"Visitor from Egypt, A" (Long) 311
Voelchert, Miss 94
Voltaire (François-Marie Arouet) 93, 276
Vortigern 481
"Voyages of Capt. Ross, R.N." (Lovecraft) 334

Wagner the Wehr-Wolf (Reynolds) 489
Walker, John 45, 56, 57, 61
Walpole, Horace 263, 469
Wanderings in Roman Britain (Weigall) 477
Wandrei, Donald 17, 21, 23, 151, 153–56, 169, 330–31, 340, 375, 395, 418, 446, 464n3, 468, 517, 524
Wandrei, Howard 375, 395, 418
Ward, John 124
Ward, Samuel 133
Warren, Sir Peter 378
Warren, RI 155, 378, 379
Warwick, Thomas, earl of 293
Washington, George 105, 408
Washington, D.C. 150, 350, 407–8
"Waste Paper" (Lovecraft) 139n1, 495n8
Watch and Ward Society 253, 277
Weakly Squawk 41
Weaver, John V. A. 285
Webster, Noah 14, 204, 431
Weigall, Arthur 477–79, 483
"Weir, The" (Dwyer) 476
Weird o' It, The (Pemberton) 526
Weird Tales 7, 8, 23, 24, 31, 33, 139, 151, 153, 195, 196, 289, 331, 345, 390, 406, 426, 445, 455, 468, 473–74, 521, 523
Wells, H. G. 525
Wentworth, Benning 186
Westbrook, Dr. 144
"What Amateurdom and I Have Done for Each Other" (Lovecraft) 8
"What Are the Apple-Trees Whispering" (Gish) 59
Whipple, Abraham 299
Whipple, Benjamin 298
Whipple, Esther (Millard) 237, 298
Whipple, John 298
"Whisperer in Darkness, The" (Lovecraft) 23–24, 464n6
Whitaker, Noah F. 14–15, 140, 169
White, Michael Oscar 27, 494, 497–98

"White People, The" (Machen) 427
"White Ship, The" (Lovecraft) 426
Whitehead, Henry S. 281, 305, 309, 472
Whitman, Sarah Helen 377, 383
Whitman, Walt 445
Whittemore, Thomas 412
Whittier, John Greenleaf 168, 501
"Why I Am Not a Freethinker" (Moe) 52, 53
Wickford, RI 346, 380, 383, 403, 410
Wilde, Oscar 89, 127, 275, 434
Wilder, Thornton 286, 290
"Wilkes's Explorations" (Lovecraft) 226, 334
Willett, Allan Herbert 225
William I (the Conqueror) (King of England) 293
Williams, Roger 133, 377, 379
"Willows, The" (Blackwood) 522, 525
Wilson, Edmund 33
Wilson, Woodrow 77
Witch-Cult in Western Europe, The (Murray) 427
"Wolfert Webber" (Irving) 120
"Woman of the Wood, The" (Merritt) 401
Wonder Book, A (Hawthorne) 45
Wonder Stories 404
Wood, Clement 223
Wood, Mrs. 415
"Word Curiosities" (Moe) 40
Wordsworth, William 311
"Work of Frank Belknap Long, Jr., The" (Lovecraft) 435n3
Wormius, Olaus 39
"Worms of the Earth" (Howard) 472
Wren, Sir Christopher 122, 124–25, 144, 502, 508
Wright, Farnsworth 31, 390–91, 426, 467
Wright, Harold Bell 276

Y.M.C.A. 10, 13, 73, 185, 186, 262, 263, 265, 367, 397
Yale University 420–21
"Yellow Sign, The" (Chambers) 404
"Yes, We Have No Bananas" (song) 506n19, 507
Yesley, Mr. 151n9
Young Chemist, The (Appleton) 431

Zworykin, V. K. 367, 395–96, 402

www.ingramcontent.com/pod-product-compliance
Lightning Source LLC
Chambersburg PA
CBHW060358230426
43663CB00008B/1308